# Moral Development: An Introduction

**William M. Kurtines** and **Jacob L. Gewirtz, Editors**
*Florida International University*

**Allyn and Bacon**
*Boston • London • Toronto • Sydney • Tokyo • Singapore*

*Executive Editor:* Laura Pearson
*Vice President, Publisher:* Susan Badger
*Marketing Manager:* Joyce Nilsen
*Production Administrator:* Marjorie Payne
*Cover Administrator:* Linda Knowles
*Editorial Assistant:* Jennifer Normandin
*Composition/Prepress Buyer:* Linda Cox
*Manufacturing Buyer:* Megan Cochran
*Editorial-Production Service:* Chestnut Hill Enterprises, Inc.

Copyright © 1995 by Allyn & Bacon
A Simon & Schuster Company
Needham Heights, Mass. 02194

**Library of Congress Cataloging-in-Publication Data**

Moral development : an introduction / William M. Kurtines and Jacob L.
    Gewirtz, editors.
        p.   cm.
    Includes bibliographical references and index.
    ISBN 0-205-15519-7
    1. Moral development.   I. Kurtines, William M.   II. Gewirtz,
Jacob L., 1924–  .
BF723.M54M665   1995
155.2'5--dc20                                                        94-32899
                                                                        CIP

Printed in the United States of America

10   9   8   7   6   5   4   3   2   1        99   98   97   96   95

# Table of Contents

# Preface

## Why an Introduction to Moral Development?

In the last two decades the psychology of moral development has emerged as a distinct field of study. As the size and scope of the moral development literature grew over the past several years, signs that the literature was beginning to mature into a distinct field became evident. Publications began to appear that captured the richness and diversity of the newly emerging field. In 1976, Lickona edited a volume (Lickona, 1976) that captured this growing diversity. The appearance of the Lickona book helped to shape the direction of the field. It provided a broad overview of the diverse perspectives and variety of issues that characterized the literature and aided the consolidation of the field. Eight years later, Lickona's pioneering work was followed by the publication of an overview edited by Kurtines and Gewirtz (1984). This volume documented the subsequent growth that had taken place in the psychology of moral behavior and development. The appearance of more current works such as the recently published three-volume *Handbook of Moral Behavior and Development* (Kurtines & Gewirtz, 1991) reflect the extensive range and diversity of perspectives that exist in the contemporary literature and make it clear that the field has emerged as an area of scholarly activity in its own right. The field has thus come of age and has become broad and diverse enough to require its own introductory textbook. This *Introduction* is designed to provide a systematic, broad-based "state of the art" introduction to the large and growing field of moral development.

In organizing this book, as with our past volumes, we have adopted a particular orientation, one that might best be described as eclectic. We adopt such an orientation because it appears to be the most appropriate for organizing a book about a field that has been historically characterized by a broad range of diversity. The existence of robust diversity and variety is, in our view, part of what makes the study of moral behavior and development a vigorous and growing field. The existence of a healthy degree of controversy and skepticism, a variation in perspectives, topics, issues, and themes, and a hearty tolerance for diversity have contributed to the growth of the field.

We have sought to capture the excitement of working in a rapidly developing area by inviting professionals active in the field, representing diverse perspectives, to convey, in their own words, the themes, topics, and issues that define the current "state of the art" in moral development.

## Organization of the Book

Work in the field of moral behavior and development has thus emerged as a distinct field of study in its own right and has progressed to the point where the need exists for a clear, readable introduction to current core topics and issues in the field, for both students and professionals. This book is designed to meet the need for a readily accessible, integrated, and up-to-date source of information. The book provides the student, beginning researcher, and interested professional from outside the field with a basic introduction to the richness and diversity of theoretical orientations, research methods, styles, strategies, and applied interests that have characterized this literature, as well as the most recent developments that have taken place.

The book has a number of features that make it suitable for use as an introductory textbook or a general introduction to the field.

First, the book includes original chapters prepared by a distinguished group of contributors in a format intended to provide the reader (both student and professional) with an integrated introduction to the literature. The chapters of the book are written at a scholarly level but without the extensive use of specialized and technical language.

Second, to facilitate the reader's introduction to the field and enhance its integration, theoretical perspectives are used as the organizing principle for the book. This organizing principle is consistent with the main trends that have helped to define the literature, and thus such organization offers the reader an accurate and representative portrayal of the field. This format is also designed to be consistent with the type of organization that is frequently used in upper-level undergraduate and graduate-level courses in the field.

Third, the format for each chapter includes a Recommended Readings section as well as a standard Reference section. This section is designed to assist the reader in pursuing a deeper understanding of the theoretical perspectives represented by the chapters. The Recommended Readings section for each chapter contains a short, selected list of core readings related to that theoretical perspective as recommended by the contributor. This feature of the book is designed to make the central corpus of work in the field more accessible to interested professionals and students.

Fourth, the editors of the volume provide a general introduction to the book that outlines basic themes and issues and notes core topics and questions. In addition, the editors also provide a brief prologue/introduction to each major part of the book, tying it in to previous and forthcoming chapters and to basic themes and topics in the book.

By bringing together in one place a representative set of scholarly but non-technical writings by prominent theorists, researchers, and professionals currently active in the area, this book provides the student with an introduction to the field and to the most recent developments that have been taking place. The book is unique in that it provides a variety of perspectives on core issues written in clear, informative language. The book brings together the most recent work in diverse areas and provides a broad introduction to new developments in theory, research and application.

## *Key Features of the Book*

- Original chapters by widely recognized scholars, researchers and professionals.
- Scholarly writing without the extensive use of specialized and technical language.
- A Recommended Readings section for each chapter.
- An introduction to basic themes and overview of core topics by the editors.

This book would not have been possible without the collaboration and cooperation of the contributors. We also wish to thank friends and colleagues who provided support and encouragement, the editorial staff at Allyn and Bacon, and others whose contributions at various stages were instrumental in its successful completion.

# Contributors' Biographies

Steven Berman is a doctoral student in life-span developmental psychology at Florida International University. He received his M.A. in educational psychology from McGill University and an M.S. in clinical psychology from Nova University. His interests are social and personality development in general, and moral and identity development in particular.

Augusto Blasi is a professor of psychology at the University of Massachusetts, Boston. He received his doctorate in clinical psychology from Washington University. He has done extensive work in the area of moral judgment, moral action, and moral identity.

Lyn Mikel Brown is an assistant professor at Colby College. Formerly a lecturer in education, human development and psychology and research associate at the Project for the Psychology of Women and the Development of Girls at Harvard University, her research focuses on female social and personality development and on feminist methodology. Her recent publications include: "Reading for self and moral voice: A method for interpreting narratives with real-life moral conflict and choice" (with M. Tappan, C. Gilligan, B. Miller, and D. Argyris) in *Entering the circle: Hermeneutic investigation in psychology.*

Roger Burton is a professor of psychology at the State University of New York at Buffalo. He received his doctorate in psychology from Harvard University. He is the author of studies on resistance to temptation and guilt, the socialization of self-control, child rearing practices associated with the trait of honesty, development of the concepts of "lie" and "truth" related to children's giving legal testimony, and sex-identity development.

Philip Davidson is an assistant professor in psychology and a member of the Life Cycle Institute at the Catholic University of America. He received his doctorate in psychology from the University of California, Berkeley. His research interests include moral, social, cognitive, and family development.

Nancy Eisenberg is a professor of psychology in the Department of Psychology at Arizona State University. She received her doctorate in developmental psychology from the University of California at Berkeley. Her interests are in the area of social development, moral reasoning, and sympathy. She is a recipient of a Career Developmental Award from the National Institute of Child Health and Development. Dr. Eisenberg's books on the topic of altruism and moral development include *The roots of prosocial behavior in children* (1989; co-authored with Paul Mussen), *Altruistic emotion, cognition, and behavior* (1986), and editor of both *The development of prosocial behavior* and *Empathy and its development* (1987; edited with Janet Strayer); and *Social and moral values: Individual and societal perspectives* (1989; edited with Janusz Reykowski and Ervin Staub).

Nicholas Emler is a professor of social psychology at the University of Dundee. He received his doctorate in social psychology from the London School of Economics. His interests are in crime and delinquency, the relation between morality and politics, the psychology of reputation, and the development of social knowledge. He is currently chief editor of the European Journal of Social Psychology.

Jacob L. Gewirtz is a professor of psychology at Florida International University and professor of pediatrics at the University of Miami Medical School. He received his doctorate in developmental and experimental psychology from the University of Iowa. Dr. Gewirtz's theoretical and research contributions have been on the topics of social learning and development including attachment acquisition and loss, imitation/identification, parent-child interaction and directions of influence, and the behavioral effects of shifts in maintaining environments. He co-edited a number of volumes in the area of moral development, including the *Handbook of moral behavior and development: Theory, research, and application (Vols. 1-3)*, *Morality, moral behavior and moral development*, and *Moral development through social interaction*.

John C. Gibbs is professor of psychology at the Ohio State University. He received his doctorate in social psychology from Harvard University. His recent work has included assessment methods, theory and interventions with conduct-disordered adolescents. He is the author of *Social intelligence: Measuring the development of sociomoral reflection*.

Carol Gilligan is a professor of education at Harvard University. She is author of *In a different voice: Psychology theory and women's development* and co-editor (with J. V. Ward and J. M. Taylor) of *Mapping the moral domain: A contribution of women's thinking to psychological theory and education* and (with N. Lyons and T. Hanmer) of *Making connections: The relational world of adolescent girls at Emma Willard school*.

Ann Higgins is an assistant professor of psychology at Fordham University. Formerly a lecturer in education and research associate at Harvard University, she received her doctorate in developmental psychology from the Pennsylvania

State University. Dr. Higgins' interests are in the area of moral assessment and the educational implications of moral development theory and research. Dr. Higgins is the author of *Moral education: Justice and community*.

Robert Hogan is the McFarlin professor of psychology at the University of Tulsa, Chairperson of the department of psychology, and Director of Research at the Tulsa Psychiatric Center. The author of over 60 articles, chapters, and books, he has been a lifelong student of how the development of character impacts personality and society.

Angela Ittel is a doctoral student in developmental psychology at the University of California, Santa Cruz. Her interests include social and cognitive development in general, and moral development in particular.

Linda Kunce is a graduate student in the child clinical program at the State University of New York at Buffalo. She was a teacher in public schools before entering the graduate program.

William M. Kurtines is a Professor of psychology and Director of Graduate Studies in the Department of Psychology at Florida International University. He is also Research Professor of Psychiatry in the School of Medicine at the University of Miami. He received his doctorate in psychology from The Johns Hopkins University. His current areas of interest include social, personality, moral, and family development. He has co-edited and/or co-authored a number of books, including *Intersections with attachment*, *Breakthroughs in family therapy with drug abusing and problem youth*, and *The role of values in psychology and human development*.

Sharon Lamb is an assistant professor at Bryn Mawr College. She received her doctorate from Harvard University. She was an NIMH clinical research fellow at Children's Hospital in Boston. Her research interests include moral development in early childhood, the physiological correlates of early empathy, play therapy, self-blame and psychosocial health in sexually abused children, and normal childhood play and games.

Marta Laupa is at the University of Nevada at Las Vegas. She received her doctorate from the University of California at Berkeley. Her interests are in the development of moral and social reasoning, with particular emphasis on concepts about authorities in varying social contexts.

Darcia Narváez is a research associate in the Center for the Study of Ethical Development at the University of Minnesota and is a doctoral student in educational psychology.

Mordecai Nisan is a professor of educational psychology and head of the Department of Education at the Hebrew University of Jerusalem. He received his M.A. from the Hebrew University and his doctorate in Human Development from the University of Chicago. His current interest is in the development of a desirable and personal identity.

Martha Peláez-Nogueras received her doctorate from Florida International University. Her interests are the experimental analysis of behavior in general and the development of attachment behaviors in particular.

James Rest is a professor of educational psychology at the University of Minnesota and research director for the Center for the Study of Ethical Development. His doctorate is from the University of Chicago. He originated the Defining Issues Test of moral judgment (DIT), an objective test of moral judgment derived from Kohlberg' approach. He is first author of *Development in judgment moral issues*, 1979 and *Moral development: Advances in research and theory*, 1986.

John Snarey is an associate professor of ethics and human development at Emory University. He received his doctorate in human development from Harvard University. His applied interests include the use of developmental theory to improve the quality of care provided by helping specialists, including parents, educators, and clergy. His research interests include the development of moral reasoning about the social and natural environments, family studies and human development, and the interrelations of social equality and human development. He is co-editor of *Conflict and continuity: A history of ideas on social equality and human development* and *Remembrances of Lawrence Kohlberg*.

Ervin Staub is a professor of psychology at the University of Massachusetts, Amherst, Massachusetts. He received his doctorate in psychology from Stanford University. He has conducted research and published articles on the social, personality, and developmental origins and correlates of helping and altruism and wrote a two-volume book on the subject, *Positive social behavior and morality*. Violence is an additional, more recent focus of his work. His book, *The roots of evil: The origins of genocide and other group violence* (1989) also explores the origins of war and torture, and ways to create caring and nonaggressive persons and societies. He also edited *Personality: Basic issues and current research*, and co-edited *Development and maintenance of prosocial behavior: International perspectives on positive morality* and *Social and moral values: Individual and societal perspectives*.

Mark B. Tappan is an assistant professor at Colby College. Formerly a lecturer in education, human development and psychology at Harvard University, he is interested in late adolescent development, female social and personality development, and interpretative research methods. His recent publications include "Stories lived and stories told: The narrative structure of late adolescent moral development," in *Human Development*.

Theresa A. Thorkildsen is an assistant professor of educational psychology at the University of Illinois at Chicago. She received her doctorate from Purdue University. Her current research is in moral development and achievement motivation in educational contexts. She has published in journals such as *Child Development, American Educational Research Journal*, and *Contemporary Educational Psychology*.

Elliot Turiel is a professor of education at the University of California at Berkeley. He received his doctorate in psychology from Yale University. His interests are in the development of social judgments, their relations to social actions, and, most recently, ways of conceptualizing cultural categories with regard to social development. He is the author of *The development of social knowledge: Morality and convention*.

Lawrence J. Walker is an associate professor of psychology at the University of British Columbia, Vancouver. He received his doctorate in developmental psychology from the University of Toronto. Dr. Walker's research interests include factors in the development of moral reasoning, sex and cultural differences, and family interactions.

Alan Waterman is a professor of psychology at Trenton State College. He received his doctorate in psychology from the State University of New York at Buffalo. He is author of *The psychology of individualism* and numerous articles in the areas of personality development and philosophical psychology. His research interests include identity formation during the span from adolescence to adulthood and the nature of optimal psychological functioning.

Susan Williamson received her M.A. in psychology from Florida International University. She received her bachelor's degree from the University of Miami. Her research has focused on the development and validation of measures of critical thinking in sociomoral dilemmas.

James Youniss is a Professor of Psychology and Director of the Life Cycle Institute at the Catholic University of America. He has published recent articles on the social-cultural roots of the discipline of developmental psychology. He is also the author of two books on the role of particular relationships in psychological development: *Parents and peers in social development* and *Adolescent relations with mothers, fathers, and friends*, with Jacqueline Smollar as co-author.

# Chapter 1

# Moral Development: An Introduction and Overview

WILLIAM M. KURTINES
*Florida International University*

JACOB L. GEWIRTZ
*Florida International University*

Morality and psychology have never been easy to separate. Psychologists have been long fascinated by moral questions and moralists have been equally intrigued by psychology. In fact, a good case can be made that morality and psychology are inseparable. In *Beyond good and evil*, Nietzsche, who was first and foremost a moralist, goes so far as to claim that psychology lies at the heart of all basic moral issues. In Nietzsche's words,

> All psychology so far has got stuck in moral prejudices and fears; it has not dared to descend into the depths . . . and there are in fact a hundred good reasons why everyone should keep away from it who—*can*. . . . we crush, we destroy perhaps the remains of our own morality, but what matter are *we*! . . . and the psychologist who [takes this risk] will at least be entitled to demand in return that psychology shall be recognized again as the queen of the sciences. . . . For psychology is now again the path to the fundamental problems. (Nietzsche, 1866/1966, pp. 31-32)

And few problems are more fundamental than those having to do with morality, moral behavior, and moral development. Moral and ethical issues have been at the core of Western intellectual history from its beginnings in classical antiquity to the modern age. Moreover, recent historical events and developments indicate that interest in moral and ethical issues shows no signs of diminishing. On the contrary, the radical social upheavals that have taken place in the United States and elsewhere over the last four decades, the growth in violent crimes, delinquency, drug abuse, and the increasingly greater burdens on judicial, penal, and similar institutions have focused attention on basic research in the area of morality, moral behavior, and moral development. Consistent with these trends, theory and research in these areas has increased enormously over the last several decades, and the psychological study of moral phenomena has emerged as a distinct field of study.

In addition to the enormous increase in size, the literature on moral development has also undergone striking transformation that reflects the broader changes taking place in developmental psychology. Traditional theoretical orientations have undergone dramatic change and new perspectives have begun to emerge.

Change is stimulating and invigorating, and this book seeks to capture some of the excitement of the developments taking place in the field of moral development. Our aim in organizing the book, however, was to do more than to convey to the reader the excitement of the field. We also sought to convey the richness of perspectives and the diversity of issues encompassed within it. To this end, we have assembled a diverse array of contributors representing a variety of perspectives. Who better to convey the richness and excitement of the field than the people who have helped to shape and influence it? The chapters included in this book were written by scholars and researchers whose work has contributed to the changes in moral development. More importantly, the chapters themselves will also help to shape the future directions of the field because they were written by professionals whose work represents the forward edge of progress. This book, then, is intended to provide an introduction to some of the richness and excitement of the work being done in the field of moral development.

## Organizational Framework for the Chapter

In this chapter we provide you with background material helpful in getting started in the moral development field. We seek to provide you with a broader framework from which to view the field. We will begin by outlining some of the features that make the scientific study of moral phenomena unique as a form of scientific inquiry. We will also provide you with some historical background on the emergence of moral development. The theoretical orientations, themes, topics, and issues that define the moral development field have their roots in the broader themes that have been historically influential in developmental psychology. In this respect, the field of moral development is no different from any other field within developmental psychology (indeed, psychology in general). Finally, we will conclude the chapter by outlining the organizational structure that we have used for the book. We will begin with a discussion of what makes the field of moral development unique and challenging.

## *The Scientific Study of Moral Phenomena*

We can begin with the issue of what we mean by *morality*. Morality involves substantive assumptions with respect to the good and the right. The question of the nature of the good and the right is at the core of the nature of morality (Frankena, 1963). This question has historically been a topic of persistent as well as passionate debate and subject to a variety of interpretations. Debate over the nature of morality usually centers around the issue of the nature of the rules, norms, standards, principles, or values by which right or wrong and good or bad can (or should) be determined. Debate over the nature of morality takes many forms. Sometimes debate over the nature of morality is open and explicit; sometimes it is an implicit (or underlying) theme or issue. Sometimes it is very abstract, as when philosophers discuss the nature of morality.[1] Sometimes it is very concrete, as in ordinary discussion of everyday moral dilemmas. In the moral development field, debate over the nature of morality extends the full range—concrete to abstract to *extremely* abstract—and it is sometimes explicit and sometimes implicit.

To understand the unique role that debate over moral issues plays in the scientific study of moral phenomena, it is necessary to understand the broader issue of the role that moral issues play in science in general. This issue, which is typically described as the question of the role of "values" in science, has long been a matter of debate (Howard, 1985). Here the word *values* is used as a generic term for the normative assumptions[2] that underlie morality. At the beginning of the 20th century, under the influence of a tradition in the philosophy of science that is usually termed *positivism* or *logical positivism,* science was generally considered to be *value free* or *value neutral.* According to this view, science requires a strict distinction between *values* and *fact* and a separation of *is* and *ought.* Moreover, this view holds that questions regarding values are sub- jective matters of opinion and hence incapable of being empirically (i.e., scien- tifically) demonstrated as objectively true or false. Questions regarding facts, on the other hand, can be empirically and therefore objectively demonstrated to be true or false. According to this view, values should have no influence on science (and science should have no influence on values). The widespread influence of positivism during the first half of the 20th century had a powerful influence on shaping the view[3] of science as value neutral. The pervasiveness of this view accounts, in part, for the relatively recent emergence of moral devel- opment as a distinct field. For a large part of the early 20th century, it was generally held that moral phenomena could not be studied scientifically. In- deed, the question of whether moral phenomena can be studied scientifically is still subject to debate (Haan, 1982; Waterman, 1988). However, as we will discuss next, views concerning the role of values in science have undergone substantial transition.

Developments in the philosophy of science over the past several decades have challenged the assumption of the value neutrality of science. The result has been a growing consensus that science is not and cannot be value free

(Bhaskar, 1975, 1979; Fiske & Shweder, 1986; Hanson, 1958; Habermas, 1973; Howard, 1985; Kuhn, 1962/ 1970; Manicas & Secord, 1983; Toulmin, 1953, 1961). As a consequence, debate has moved beyond the issue of *whether* values influence science to focus on the issue of *how* values influence science. Taking this issue as a starting point, it has been proposed (Kurtines, Alvarez, & Azmitia, 1990) that although values play a role in *all* scientific discourse, values play a more explicit role in the scientific study of moral phenomena. More specifically, it has been proposed (Kurtines, et al., 1990) that debate over values plays a more explicit role in all fields within the human sciences (e.g., anthropology, psychology, sociology, etc.) that touch on human morality. Thus, although ordinary scientific discourse is complex and multi-faceted due to the complex nature of the type of phenomena scientists study, theoretical discourse in scientific study of moral phenomena is further complicated by the fact that it frequently includes explicit debate over normative issues (i.e., value assumptions) as well as debate over theoretical, factual, and methodological issues. What this means, as we will discuss next, is that in your introduction to the study of moral development you have to be prepared to deal with issues concerning the nature of normative assumptions that are usually considered "philosophical" as well as the theoretical, factual, and methodological issues that make up ordinary scientific discourse. This section will therefore serve to introduce you to the role that debate over normative assumptions plays in the scientific study of moral phenomena. We will begin by outlining what is involved in ordinary scientific discourse.

When scientists study phenomena they develop theories to explain the type of phenomena they study. Different scientists can (and do) have different theories about how to explain the same phenomena. Much of ordinary scientific discourse is concerned with debate over competing theories. Theoretical debate[4] is concerned with resolving conflict between rival or competing theories. Scientists frequently use data ("facts") in order to resolve debate over theoretical issues. In the process, scientists devise methods for collecting and evaluating facts. Ordinary scientific discourse, consequently, usually involves debate over theoretical, methodological, and factual issues. As you begin reading the chapters in this book you will find that debate over theoretical, methodological, and factual issues plays as an important role in the scientific study of moral phenomena as it does in the scientific study of other types of phenomena.

The picture of scientific discourse that we have painted thus far presents a somewhat simplified but essential accurate portrait of what is involved in ordinary scientific discourse. The picture, however, is incomplete in one very important respect. We have thus far left out one very important type of debate. This is a type of scientific debate that goes beyond theoretical, methodological, and factual issues. What kind of debate goes beyond ordinary scientific discourse? What type of debate goes beyond theory, method, and facts? The answer is a type of debate that is usually called *metatheoretical* debate or discourse. To understand what we mean by metatheoretical discourse, it will be useful to complete our portrait of the nature of scientific discourse.

We described how scientists develop theories about the type of phenomena they are studying. Each scientist, however, does not develop a theory independent of every other scientist. On the contrary, it is a tradition in science that every scientist draws on the work of other scientists. Many scientists share in the construction of scientific theories. Thus, although there are many scientific theories, they are not all completely independent of each other. On the contrary, many scientific theories share certain assumptions with other similar theories. Scientific theories, in other words, do not ordinarily stand alone. Key assumptions shared by many theories often define clusters or "families" of theories. These clusters of theories not only share common assumptions, they frequently address similar issues and seek to explain similar phenomena. Within clusters or families of theories these assumptions are not usually included as part of ordinary scientific discourse involving theoretical, factual, and methodological issues. Indeed, these shared presuppositions are assumptions precisely because they are assumed rather than tested. These shared assumptions make up part of the background activity that makes possible the debate over theoretical, methodological, and factual issues that define ordinary scientific discourse.

The types of background assumptions that make ordinary scientific discourse possible usually involve issues that are sometimes seen as "philosophical" issues. As Reese and Overton (1970) have pointed out, scientific theories and models are never free of philosophic presuppositions. Even the most circumscribed and concrete model is dependent upon the availability of more general models, and these upon more general models yet, in an ever-widening series terminated only by the most general and hence the most basic models—metaphysical models. Scientific theories thus involve background assumptions that are "meta" theoretical. Metatheoretical assumptions are substantive presuppositions (e.g., logical, epistemological, ontological, normative, etc.) that are part of the shared background that makes ordinary scientific discourse possible. They are assumptions that are ordinarily "meta" theoretical with respect to the factual, methodological and theoretical issues that make up the immediate content of scientific debate.

Theoretical discourse in science is thus oriented toward the resolution of conflicting factual and methodological issues that arise in the ordinary conduct of scientific activity while metatheoretical discourse is debate concerning the shared background assumptions or presuppositions that make scientific discourse possible. Metatheoretical discourse thus makes up an extremely important part of scientific discourse. Metatheoretical discourse is scientific discourse that moves beyond the level of theory, method, and fact. As Habermas (cited in McCarthy, 1981, p. 308) has pointed out, in scientific discourse there must be freedom to move from a given level of discourse to increasingly more reflected levels. Metatheoretical discourse is discourse that moves beyond the validity of particular theoretical claims to the level of the metatheoretical frameworks that provide the context for the particular theoretical claims. As the history of science illustrates, it is at this level that the most profound developments in cognitive understanding have occurred. What Kuhn (1962/1970) has called "ordinary science" involves critical discussion of problematic theoretical claims carried out within the context of implicitly shared metatheoretical frameworks; "scientific revolutions," on the other hand, involve critical discussion that challenges the metatheoretical frameworks themselves.

Metatheoretical discourse is an important part of scientific discourse and metatheoretical debate necessarily entails the full range of metatheoretical assumptions, including assumptions that are normative. In this frame, normative assumptions (i.e., values) can be viewed as having the same conceptual status as any other metatheoretical assumptions (e.g., logical, epistemological, or ontological) that do not ordinarily enter into scientific debate as factual, theoretical, or methodological issues. They may not play a central role in ordinary scientific discourse, but they do play an important role in metatheoretical discourse. Thus, although the belief that science is (should be) value free has been viewed as justifying the view that scientific discourse does not (should not) include value assumptions, there is no more justification for excluding from scientific debate assumptions that are "normative" than there is for excluding any other assumptions. Indeed, on what grounds could *any* assumptions be excluded, as a matter of principle, from scientific discourse? Shared value assumptions are part of the background or framework that makes scientific activity possible, and as such cannot be excluded from scientific debate. Thus, values play an important role in scientific discourse, particularly at the metatheoretical level.

The view that debate over normative assumptions ordinarily enters scientific discussion at the metatheoretical level, however, does not necessarily mean that is the *only* level at which such debate enters into scientific discourse. We have argued elsewhere (Kurtines, Alvarez, Azmitia, 1990) that one of the unique characteristics of the scientific study of moral phenomena is the nature of the debate that takes place over normative assumptions (i.e., rules, norms, standards, principles, or values). We have argued that debate over normative assumptions plays a more explicit role in all fields within the human sciences that touch on morality. Such debate plays a more explicit role in the scientific study of moral phenomena because of the particular focal phenomena of the field, viz., normative assumptions themselves. That is, because the scientific study of moral phenomena includes human morality as an object of study, normative assumptions necessarily enter into scientific debate at the theoretical level as well as the metatheoretical level. This is not to say that there is no debate in such fields over factual, methodological, and theoretical issues. As you will discover, the moral development field, like other fields of psychology, is characterized by extensive debate over factual, methodological, and theoretical differences. Nothing, however, has aroused more impassioned debate in the moral development field than metatheoretical differences, particularly with respect to the normative assumptions that underlie the meaning and significance of theory, method, and the interpretation of facts. Thus, what is unique about the moral development field is that theoretical discourse in this field includes extensive debate over normative assumptions and that this debate takes place as part of ordinary theoretical discourse. Consequently, in your introduction to the field of moral development you will find that "philosophical" issues dealing with the nature of morality play a particularly central role in the scientific study of moral phenomena.

The moral development field, however, is also defined by extensive debate over theoretical, methodological, and factual issues. In the next section we will begin to introduce you to the origins of many of the theoretical, methodological, and factual issues that you will encounter throughout the book. You may already be familiar with some or many of these issues because they are the same issues that have defined the broader field of developmental psychology. Moral development may not have always been a distinct field, but the themes, topics, and issues that have been central to its theoretical discourse have also played a central role in developmental psychology in general and theories of human development in particular. In fact, many of the changes within the moral development literature have occurred as part of the broader changes within developmental psychology and psychology in general as well. Consequently, the next section will briefly outline the historical context out of which the moral development field emerged.

## Historical Background

The history of developmental psychology in the United States over the last century can be with reasonable accuracy called revolutionary. By revolutionary we mean a period of change involving dramatic transformations in theoretical orientation or perspective. At the beginning of the 20th century, Sigmund Freud and the psychoanalytic school of thought had an early and powerful influence on U.S. psychiatry and clinical psychology—an influence that continues even today. However, the psychoanalytic movement had far less of an impact on the beginnings of developmental psychology in the United States. Rather, its earliest origins can be traced to other sources such as "baby biographies" and the "genetic" psychology movement that also appeared at the turn of the century (Charles, 1970). These early influences marked the beginning of developmental psychology.

### The Behavioral Revolution

These early influences on the formation of developmental psychology, however, were soon replaced by the growing behavioral movement that came to dominate U.S. academic psychology until mid-century. Like academic psychology in general, developmental psychology during this period came under the influence of behaviorism. Beginning with the work of J. B. Watson (1913), the next several decades (the 30s, 40s, and 50s) were a period in which U.S. developmental psychology was predominately defined by a behavioral orientation or perspective. During this period, the theoretical focus was on environmental influences on behavior change with an emphasis on learning/conditioning processes (e.g., reinforcement, imitation, modeling, etc.).

## The Cognitive Revolution

Beginning in the early 60s and continuing into the 70s and 80s, the predominately behavioral orientation in developmental psychology was replaced by a cognitive orientation in what has been termed the "cognitive revolution" (Maccoby, 1980). Among other things, a growing awareness on the part of U.S. psychologists of Piaget's work (e.g., Flavel, 1965) was instrumental in facilitating a shift in theoretical emphasis to cognition and the role of maturational type processes such as stage and sequence in cognitive change. The cognitive revolution of the 60s, 70s, and 80s with its emphasis on cognition and maturational type processes such as stage and sequence, has been oftentimes viewed as correcting the behavioristic and environmentalistic excesses of the previous decades.

## Developmental Psychology Today

Developmental psychology today is once again undergoing a transformation. The cognitive revolution had an important impact on the field, but stage theories themselves have subsequently undergone a period of re-evaluation. In the case of Piaget's stage theory, for example, evidence of asynchrony in the emergence of Piaget's stages, the heterogeneous skills that contribute to stage performance, and the susceptibility of performance to environmental influences accumulated. The accumulation of this evidence contributed to an increasing disenchantment with Piaget's stage theory during the decade of the 70s and 80s (Kuhn, 1984). As stage theory became more a topic of debate and discussion (Brainerd, 1978; Flavel, 1982), developmental psychology underwent another transition, resulting in the current state of the discipline.

Without the benefit of historical hindsight, any assessment of the current state of the discipline must be considered at best provisional. The precise direction that the discipline will take in the future is at this point unclear. However, there appear to be some global trends that have emerged over the past few years. For example, developmental psychology no longer appears to be predominately defined by any one theoretical orientation. Although the influence of the cognitive developmental tradition remains robust, the psychoanalytic and behavioral traditions have maintained a central role in the discipline. Indeed, if there has been any consistent trend, it has been that developmental psychology appears to have become increasingly more pluralistic. Like the moral development literature, developmental psychology is currently defined by a diversity of themes, topics, and issues. The long-range implication of this pluralism, however, is open to debate and it is not clear what the future will bring. It is not clear, for example, whether the current period of pluralism is an end state or the transition to another period of directional growth. Consequently, in this, the last decade of the 20th century, the most reasonable conclusion about the outlook for developmental psychology is that it is not clear what the future holds. The future will be what we make it. This is one of the reasons why working on the forward edge of a growing field is stimulating and exciting—it presents the opportunity to help create the future.

## Organizational Framework for the Book

Although the future direction of developmental psychology is unknown, we can draw some conclusions about the themes, topics, and issues that define the discipline today. These conclusions will be helpful in providing a perspective from which to understand the changes and transitions that have taken place in the moral development field. They will also serve to provide an organizational framework for the book.

Developmental psychology, we noted, no longer appears to be predominately defined by any one theoretical orientation. Following Dixon and Lerner (1988), we will suggest that contemporary developmental theory tends to be pluralistic, defined by a multiplicity of reasonable theoretical alternatives. According to this view, developmental psychology is defined by diverse but identifiable clusters of theories, methods, and ideas. These clusters of theories share certain identifiable foci, themes, and historical roots. For example, in their work, Reese and Overton (1970; Overton & Reese, 1973) have identified two major philosophical models, which they termed "organicism" and "mechanism," that provide the basis for many assumptions about human development. These models provide a set of assumptions, or metatheoretical ideas, about human nature and so influence lower order, theoretical and methodological claims. Drawing on the work of Reese and Overton (1970; Overton & Reese, 1973) as well as Wohlwill (1973), Dixon and Lerner (1988) have identified *five* different theoretical models or systems that currently have an influence on developmental psychology. The five theoretical models are: organismic, psychoanalytic, mechanistic, contextualistic, and dialectic. These models or systems, which we will briefly outline next, will serve as a foundation for the organizational structure of this book.

### Organicism

Organicism developed out of the early work of G. Stanley Hall and James Mark Baldwin, through Pierre Janet to Jean Piaget and Heinz Werner. Organicism (as described by Dixon & Lerner, 1988; Lerner, 1976; Overton & Reese, 1973; Reese and Overton, 1970) was patterned after the view of biological growth that prevailed in the preceding century. The basic metaphor employed for the organismic model is the organism, the living, organized system presented to experience in multiple forms. In this model, the *whole* is organic rather than mechanical in nature. The nature of the whole, rather than being the sum of its parts, is presupposed by the parts. The whole has qualities that are not explicable in terms of the parts that make up the whole, but rather the parts gain their meaning, their function, from the whole in which they are embedded. The organismic model is, consequently, non-reductive in that the explanation of phenomena is viewed as related to the level of the analysis involved. Whole and parts generate different explanatory concepts.

In the organismic model, human development is thought to be goal-directed and teleological in character, involving movement toward a predefined end state. Developmental change is characterized as qualitative rather than quantitative, unidirectional and irreversible. Following the emphasis on qualitative changes, a stage pattern is often employed, resulting in a conception of development that is discontinuous and universal in sequence and pattern. The organism is seen as relatively active, constructing a relatively passive environment.

## The Psychoanalytic Tradition

The psychoanalytic tradition grew out of the works of Sigmund Freud. The psychoanalytic model had an influence on developmental psychology, in part, through the work of Freud's former student and long-standing critic, Carl Jung. The main influence of Freud's views in contemporary developmental psychology, however, is through the work of Erik Erikson. Erikson proposed a life-span theory of personality development that has had an impact on developmental theory and research.

The psychoanalytic tradition is organismic in orientation, differing from the mainly cognitive orientation of other theories in the organismic tradition in its emphasis on personality processes in general, and affective or emotional processes in particular. The psychoanalytic tradition, according to Dixon and Lerner (1988), shares with other organismic theories a view of developmental change as qualitative rather than quantitative. Freud, Jung, and Erikson's theories all postulated stages of development with predefined end states. Indeed, Jung and Erikson were early advocates for the type of life-span orientation to developmental theory that has an important impact on contemporary developmental theory and research. And, as with other organismic approaches, theories in the psychoanalytic tradition tend to have a view of the organism as relatively active, constructing a relatively passive environment, although in Erikson's work the relation between the organism and the social environment is seen as more clearly interactive.

## Mechanism

Mechanism has its origins in the work of Wilhelm Preyer and Sir Francis Galton and the later work of G. Stanley Hall. John B. Watson, however, had the most prominent and direct role in shaping the early emergence of a mechanistic orientation in developmental psychology. The work of B. F. Skinner and modern behavior analysts Bijou and Baer (1976) represent the mechanistic tradition in contemporary developmental psychology.

The mechanistic model represents the organism as analogous to a machine (see Dixon & Lerner, 1984; Overton & Reese, 1973; Pepper, 1973; Reese & Overton, 1970). The parts of the machine and their relations form the basic reality to which all other more complex phenomena are ultimately reducible. The mechanistic model is, consequently, reductive in that complex phenomena are viewed as ultimately explicable (reducible) in terms of simpler elements or constituents. At the psychological level, reductionism dictates that any complex behavior is in reality comprised of a constellation of very simple behaviors. It holds that to understand complex behavior it is necessary to isolate and investigate individually the smallest possible behavioral units that make up the complex behavior. Once the process governing each of individual units is understood, explanations of the more complex forms of behavior will follow.

In the operation of the machine, forces are applied and these result in discrete chain-like sequences of events. These forces are the only efficient or immediate causes; purpose is seen as a mediate or derived cause. From the perspective of the machine metaphor, phenomena are eminently susceptible to quantification. Functional analysis yields descriptions of the relationship between the operation and parts. According to this model, development depends on the level of stimulation, the kind of stimulation, and the history of the organism. The organism is seen as relatively passive (or reactive), whereas its environment is considered relatively active. Developmental change is viewed as a continuous process of quantitative change.

## Contextualism

Contextualism can be traced to the work of the American pragmatic philosophers William James, Charles Sanders Peirce, and John Dewey. The emergence of the pragmatic movement in philosophy was perhaps the most significant contribution of U.S. philosophy to modern thought. Pragmatism, as a philosophic movement, had a strong influence on a number of social action theories in the social sciences such as open systems theory (Allport, 1967; Katz and Kahn, 1978) and critical social action theory (Habermas, 1971). Pragmatism and the contextualist tradition also had an influence on symbolic interactionism and the "role theoretical" tradition in U.S. social science, a heuristic whose earliest formulations can be found in the work of Charles Cooley (1920) and George Herbert Mead (1934) and more recently has been influential in the work of such diverse theorists as Goffman (1959), Parsons (1951), Sarbin (1976), and Sarbin and Allen (1968). In developmental psychology contextualism has had an influence on the works of a number of scholars and researchers (Dixon & Nesselroade, 1983; Hultsch & Pentz, 1980; Lerner, Hultsch, & Dixon, 1983).

The basic metaphor for the contextual model is change or the historical event. The contextualist model, like the mechanistic model, stresses the quantitative nature of developmental change. However, the contextualist model shares the organicist's view of the organism as an active organism, but the contextualist model also views the environment as active. Individual developmental change is viewed as interacting with socio-historical change, and the reciprocal effects as inseparable. According to this view, the organism's behavior must be interpreted in the context of a multiplicity of influences that include both developmental and socio-historical processes. The meaning and significance of human behavior and developmental change, therefore, cannot be interpreted independent of the context in which it occurs. The focus of the contextualist's model is thus on the interaction between the organism and the environment. The individual and the social environment are viewed as mutually influential, acting upon one another in dynamic interaction.

## *Dialecticism*

Dialecticism has its principal roots in the philosophy of G. W. F. Hegel and Karl Marx and the biology of Charles Darwin. Although neither Hegel nor Marx proposed a specific program of individual development, their views of both ideational and social change have been adapted for the individual psychological level. Hegel's work had a direct influence on Marx, although Marx replaced Hegel's idealism with materialism. Darwin's work, on the other hand, had an indirect influence on the dialectical model through his influence on Marx, although Marx's evolutionism more closely resembled Spencer's or Lamarck's rather than Darwin's. Nevertheless, both Darwin and Marx shared a concern, emerging on multiple fronts in the nineteenth century, with historicity and with development. The dialectical model was developed more fully at the psychological level by Lev. S. Vygotsky (1978) and, more recently in the United States, by Klaus F. Riegel (1976; 1979).

The basic metaphor of the dialectical model is contradiction or conflict. As with the contextual model, the activities of the individual are viewed as being in dynamic interaction with the activities of the environment. In the dialectical model, however, conflict or contradiction drives the forces of individual and historical change. The individual, like society, develops through a continuous process of thesis, antithesis, and synthesis (Wozniak, 1975). Developmental psychology is viewed dialectically as the study of the changing individual in a changing world (Meacham, 1984). The dialectical models stress developmental change as teleological-historical, social-cultural, and active-organismic.

## *The Organization of the Book*

To help introduce you to the field, the chapters that follow will be organized into six major parts. *Part I*, Cognitive Developmental Perspectives, *Part II*, Behavioral/Learning Perspectives, *Part III*, Personality Perspectives, *Part IV*, Social Constructivist/Interpretative Perspectives, *Part V*, Integrative Perspectives, and *Part VI*, New Directions in Research on Moral Development. Each of the parts contains several chapters illustrating the types of themes and issues characteristic of the perspective represented in that part. These perspectives, in turn, illustrate the theoretical systems that we described in the previous section (e.g., organicism, mechanism, contextualism, etc). These theoretical systems, we noted, are comprised of clusters of theories that share common assumptions about themes, topics, and issues as well as common historical roots.

We recognize that our organizational framework (like any other abstract representation) is only intended to *represent* the basic themes that have defined the field—it is not intended to be exhaustive. It does, however, provide a helpful framework for organizing the book and for your introduction to the moral development field because the perspectives represented by each part of the book share many of the features of these theoretical systems we have described and have historical roots in one or more of these models.

## Endnotes

1. The branch of philosophy that is concerned with the nature of morality is termed *Ethics*.

2. That is, assumptions about the rules, norms, standards, principles, or values by which the nature of the good or right is determined.

3. By both scientists and the public alike.

4. We would note that we use the term debate to denote *both* oral and written debate. Sometimes scientists engage in actual oral public debate such as, for example, at scientific conventions and meetings. Sometimes this type of debate receives widespread publicity, and appears to play an important role in science. However, although it does have a role to play in science, this type of debate is actually far less important than it appears. The most important form of scientific debate, in terms of both amount and impact, is written and this type of "debate" takes place in the books and journals that help to shape a particular scientific field.

## References

Allport, F. H. (1967). A theory of enestruence (event structure theory): Report of progress. *American Psychologist, 22*, 1-24.

Bhaskar, R. (1975). *A realist theory of science.* Leeds, England: Leeds Books.

Bhaskar, R. (1979). *The possibility of naturalism.* Brighton, Great Britain: Harvester Press.

Bijou, S. W. & Baer, D. M. (1976). *Child development: The basic stages of early childhood.* Englewood Cliffs, NJ: Prentice Hall.

Brainerd, C. (1978). The stage question in cognitive-developmental theory. *Behavioral and Brain Sciences, 1*, 173-213.

Charles, D. C. (1970). Historical antecedents of life-span developmental psychology. In L. R. Goulet and P. B. Baltes (Eds.). *Life-span developmental psychology: Research and theory* (pp. 24-38). New York: Academic Press.

Cooley, C. H. (1920). *Human nature and the social order.* New York: Scribner.

Dixon, R. A. & Lerner, R. M. (1988). A history of systems in developmental psychology. In M. H. Bornstein and M. E. Lamb (Eds.), *Developmental psychology: An advanced textbook* (pp. 3-39). Hillsdale, NJ: Lawrence

Erlbaum Associates.

Dixon, R. A., & Nesselroade, J. R. (1983). Pluralism and correlational analysis in developmental psychology: Historical commonalities. In R. M. Lerner (Ed.), *Developmental psychology: Historical and philosophical perspectives.* Hillsdale, NJ: Lawrence Erlbaum Associates.

Falvell, J. (1982). On cognitive development. *Child Development, 53*, 1-10.

Fiske, D. W. & Shweder, R. A. (1986). *Metatheory in Social Science.* Chicago: University of Chicago Press.

Flavel, J. H. (1965). *The developmental psychology of Jean Piaget.* New York: Oxford University Press.

Frankena, W. (1963). *Ethics.* Englewood Cliffs, NJ: Prentice-Hall.

Goffman, E. (1959). *The presentation of self in everyday life.* New York: Doubleday.

Haan, N. (1982). Can research about morality be "scientific?" *American Psychologist, 37*, 1096-1104.

Habermas, J. (1971). *Knowledge and human interest.* Boston: Beacon Press.

Habermas, J. (1973). *Theory and practice.* Boston: Beacon Press

Hanson, N. R. (1958). *Patterns of discovery.* Cambridge, England: Cambridge University Press.

Howard, G. S. (1985). The role of values in the science of psychology. *American Psychologist, 40*, 255-265.

Hultsch, D. F. & Pentz, C. A. (1980). Encoding, storage, and retrieval in adult memory: The role of model assumptions. In L. W. Poon, J. L. Fozard, L. S. Cermak, D. Arenberg, & L. W. Thompson (Eds.), *New directions in memory and aging: Proceedings of the George A. Talland Memorial Conference.* Hillsdale, NJ: Lawrence Erlbaum Associates.

Katz, D. & Kahn, R. L. (1978). *The social psychology of organizations.* (2nd Ed.). New York: John Wiley & Sons.

Kuhn, D. (1984). Cognitive development. In M. H. Bornstein and M. E. Lamb (Eds.), *Developmental psychology: An advanced textbook* (pp. 205-256). Hillsdale, NJ: Lawrence

Erlbaum Associates.

Kuhn, T. (1962/1970). *The structure of scientific revolutions.* (2nd ed.). Chicago: University of Chicago Press. (1st ed., 1962)

Kurtines, W., Alvarez, M., & Azmitia, M. (1990). Science and morality: The role of theoretical and meta-theoretical discourse in the psychological study of moral phenomena. *Psychological Bulletin, 107*, 283-295.

Kurtines, W. & Gewirtz, J. L. (1984). (Eds.) *Morality, moral behavior, and moral development.* New York: John Wiley & Sons.

Kurtines, W. & Gewirtz, J. L. (1987). (Eds.) *Moral development through social interaction.* New York: John Wiley & Sons.

Kurtines, W. & Gewirtz, J. L. (1991). (Eds.) *The handbook of moral behavior and development: Theory, research and application (Vols. 1-3).* Hillsdale, NJ: Lawrence Erlbaum Associates.

Lerner, R. (1976). *Concepts and theories of human development.* Reading, MA: Addison-Wesley.

Lerner, R. M., Hultsch, D. F., & Dixon, R. A. (1983). Contextualism and the character of developmental psychology in the 1970s. *Annals of the New York Academy of Sciences.*

Lickona, T. (1976). *Moral development and behavior.* (Ed.) New York: Holt, Rinehart, & Winston.

Maccoby, E. E. (1980). *Social development: Psychological growth and the parent-child relationship.* New York: Harcourt, Brace & Jovanovich.

Manicas, P. T. & Secord, P. F. (1983). Implications for psychology of the new philosophy of science. *American Psychologist, 38*, 399-413.

McCarthy, T. (1981). *The critical theory of Jurgen Habermas.* Cambridge, MA: The MIT Press.

Mead, G. H. (1934). *Mind, self, and society.* Chicago: University of Chicago Press.

Meacham, J. A. (1984). The individual as consumer and producer of historical change. In K. A. McClusky & H. W. Reese (Eds.), *Life-span developmental psychology: Historical and generational effect.* (pp. 47-72). New York: Academic Press.

Nietzsche, F. (1886/1966). *Beyond good and evil.* (W. Kaufmann, Trans.). New York: Vintage Books.

Overton, W. W. & Reese, H. W. (1973). Models of development: Methodological implications. In J. R. Nesselroade, H. W. Reese (Eds.), *Life-span developmental psychology: Methodological issues.* New York: Academic Press, 65-86.

Parsons, T. (1951). *The social system.* New York: Free Press.

Pepper, S. C. (1973). *World hypotheses: A study of evidence.* Berkeley: University of California Press.

Reese, H. W. & Overton, W. F. (1970). Models of development and theories of development. In L. R. Goulet and P. B. Baltes (Eds.), *Life-span developmental psychology.* New York: Academic Press, 115-145.

Riegel, K. F. (1976). The dialectics of human development. *American Psychologist,* 689-700.

Riegel, K. F. (1979). *Foundations of dialectical psychology.* New York: Academic Press.

Rosnow, R. L. & Georgoudi, M. (Eds.) (1986). *Contextualism and understanding in behavioral science.* New York: Praeger.

Sarbin, T. R. (1976). Contextualism: A world view for modern psychology. In A.

Landfield (Ed.), *Nebraska symposium on motivation.* Lincoln, Nebraska: University of Nebraska Press.

Sarbin, T. R., & Allen, V. L. (1968). Role theory. In G. Lindzey & E. Aronson (Eds.), *Handbook of social psychology.* Vol. 1 (2nd Ed.), Reading, MA: Addison-Wesley, 488-567.

Toulmin, S. (1953). *The philosophy of science.* New York: Harper & Row.

Toulmin, S. (1961). *Foresight and understanding.* New York: Harper & Row.

Vygotsky, L. S. (1978). *Mind and society.* Cambridge, MA: Harvard University Press.

Waterman, A. S. (1988). On the use of psychological theory and research in the process of psychological inquiry. *Psychological Bulletin, 103,* 283-298.

Watson, J. B. (1913). Psychology as the behaviorist views it. *Psychological Review, 20,* 158-177.

Wohlwill, J. F. (1973). *The study of behavioral development.* New York: Academic Press.

Wozniak, R. H. (1975). A dialectical paradigm for psychological research: Implications drawn from the history of psychology in the Soviet Union. *Human Development, 18,* 18-34.

Part *I*

# Cognitive Developmental Perspectives

## *Prologue*

We will begin with a look at the cognitive developmental perspective. We begin with this tradition because of the pivotal role that it has played in the moral development field. For the past four decades the cognitive developmental approach in general and the work of Lawrence Kohlberg (1958; 1964; 1976; 1981; 1984) in particular has been at the center of the emergence of moral development as a distinctive field of study. Indeed, more than any other single individual, Kohlberg can be justly said to have pioneered the field of moral development, and his cognitive developmental approach has been responsible for shaping the field as it evolved. As a consequence, over the past several decades an extraordinary quantity and diversity of work in the area of moral development has come out of the cognitive developmental tradition. In the process, the cognitive developmental perspective has been instrumental in defining many of the fundamental themes, topics, and issues that have come to delineate the field.

To understand the importance of the impact that Kohlberg and the cognitive developmental tradition had on the field of moral development, it is useful to consider this work in the context of the broader, revolutionary changes that were taking place during the decades of the 60s and 70s. One important change that was taking place at the time the field was beginning to emerge involved the transformations that took place with respect to the nature of science itself. For the first half of the 20th century, we noted, the philosophy of science was under the influence of the positivist tradition. As we pointed out, the positivists considered science and morality to be distinct and essentially irreconcilable. Science, according to this view, is (and should be) value free or value neutral. In 1962, however, Thomas Kuhn (1962/1970), published a book, a history of

17

science entitled *The Structure of Scientific Revolutions*, that challenged the positivist tradition and eventually revolutionized the philosophy of science. Following the publication of Kuhn's book, many of the most important assumptions of the positivist tradition were successfully challenged, including the assumption that science is value free. The result was a decline in the influence of the positivist tradition. The waning of the influence of the positivist tradition had a wide-ranging impact on the natural and social sciences. For our purposes, however, the most important impact concerned the changes that occurred with respect to the role of values (i.e., normative assumptions) in science. More specifically, with the fading of the positivist's influence it became increasingly more difficult to justify the exclusion of values from the domain of scientific investigation. As the general philosophical climate underwent change and the impact of these changes extended to the social sciences, it became increasingly more possible to pursue scholarly and research activity involving moral issues, although not without arousing skepticism and resistance, particularly in the early years of transition. It was in these early years of transition that Kohlberg's first works appeared.

The changes in the general intellectual milieu that were taking place helped to set the stage for the emergence of the moral development field. The transformations that were taking place in developmental psychology, however, had an even more direct influence on Kohlberg's work and the emergence of the moral development field. Beginning in the early 60s and continuing into the 70s, we noted, the predominately behavioral orientation in developmental psychology was replaced by a cognitive orientation. Among other things, a growing awareness on the part of U.S. psychologists of Piaget's work was instrumental in bringing about the cognitive revolution. Piaget's became best known for his seminal work in the area of cognitive development. According to Piaget, during the course of cognitive development the individual's thinking undergoes a series of transformations. Piaget's well known four stages of cognitive development (sensorimotor, preoperational, concrete operational, and formal operational stage) defined developmental transformations in the child's ability to use logical operations in problem solving tasks.

Although Piaget is best known for his work on cognitive development, early in his career, in 1932, Piaget (1932/1965) published a book that had an enormous influence on the moral development field. The book, entitled *The Moral Judgment of the Child*, outlined work that Piaget had done on moral reasoning in children. In this work, Piaget described three phases of moral reasoning (nonmoral, heteronomous, autonomous) that he identified in his interviews with children. This book proved to be the stimulus for a vast array of work in the area of moral development, both directly and indirectly. Indeed, it has proved to be one of the most frequently cited books in the entire moral development literature, oftentimes with diverse and sometimes conflicting interpretations. More important for the present discussion, Piaget's work served as a direct inspiration for Kohlberg's work, which in turn was instrumental in defining the moral development field.

Kohlberg was almost single-handedly responsible for a "cognitive" revolution in the moral development literature that paralleled the cognitive revolution that was taking place in developmental psychology during the decades of the 60s and 70s.[r] Building on Piaget's work, in 1958, Kohlberg began his work in the area of moral development by studying the moral reasoning of children and adolescents. Kohlberg's 1958 study represented a radical break with both the behaviorist and positivist traditions that defined the scientific climate in psychology at the time. Kohlberg's research was ground breaking in a number of ways. To begin with, it was ground breaking at the time because it involved cognition (reasoning) rather than behavior. However, his work did more than break with the behavioral tradition. It was also ground breaking in its break with the positivist tradition. His study was not simply concerned with reasoning; it was concerned with "moral" reasoning—themes and issues that were not considered appropriate topics for scientific research at the time.

Over the next several decades Kohlberg expanded and refined his work. In the area of theory, he proposed a more elaborated developmental sequence that involved three levels of development (preconventional, conventional, and postconventional) with two developmental stages within each level. His theory thus came to be known for its claim that the development of moral reasoning proceeds through six stages. In contrast to Piaget's theory, Kohlberg proposed that the stages were "true" stages that form an invariant sequence, i.e., that individuals proceed through the stages in a fixed order, without stage skipping or reversals. Kohlberg also extensively refined Piaget's method for measuring moral reasoning. Piaget had used a relatively open-ended "clinical" method for interviewing the children in his study. In extending Piaget's method, Kohlberg developed a highly refined interview procedure that has been used for assessing moral judgment development across the life span in hundreds of studies. Finally, Kohlberg pioneered the application of moral development theory to practical problems such as moral education. Kohlberg and his colleagues have developed innovative methods of moral education that involve facilitating moral reasoning through participation in moral discussions and democratic rule-making.

The cognitive developmental tradition has thus played a pivotal role in the emergence of the moral development field. Like all of the theories that we will cover in this book, the cognitive developmental perspective has its roots in the broader metatheoretical frameworks that have defined the major traditions in developmental theory. The cognitive developmental perspective is representative of that tradition that we defined as the organismic model. Piaget, we noted, was a seminal thinker in the organismic tradition. As is characteristic of theories in the organismic tradition, theories of moral development such as Piaget's and Kohlberg's tend to be goal-directed and teleological in character, involving movement toward a predefined end state. Piaget considered his phases of moral reasoning to define developmental trends and Kohlberg considered his stages of moral development to define an invariant sequence. This has been true in a more general way of theorists and researchers working within the cognitive developmental tradition. They tend to view change as qualitative rather than quantitative, and discontinuous, unidirectional, and irreversible, involving a universal sequence and pattern. Finally, consistent with the organismic tradition, the cognitive developmental tradition views the individual as relatively active, constructing a relatively passive environment.

## Overview of Chapters in Part I

The chapters in this part provide a more detailed introduction to the cognitive developmental perspective in general and Lawrence Kohlberg's cognitive developmental theory in particular. Chapter 2 provides an overview of the historical origins of Kohlberg's theory of moral development and an introduction to basic concepts. Chapter 3 continues the introduction to Kohlberg's theory by describing the characteristics of moral development stages and how they can be applied to moral education.

Chapters 4 and 5 touch on some of the research issues that grew out of Kohlberg's theory. The existence of robust diversity and variety is part of what makes the study of moral behavior and development a vigorous and growing field. The existence of a healthy degree of controversy and skepticism, a variation in perspectives, topics, issues, and themes, and a hearty tolerance for diversity have contributed to the growth of the field. Chapters 4 and 5 illustrate some (but by no means all) of the more controversial issues that grew out of Kohlberg's theory, namely, the issue of gender, social class, and cultural bias in his stages of moral development. These chapters also illustrate the type of research that has been carried out in an effort to resolve these issues.

Chapter 2, by *John Gibbs*, provides an overview of Kohlberg's theory. The chapter begins with the historical roots of his theory. Kohlberg's theory, we noted, draws on work of Jean Piaget and the chapter begins with an overview of Piaget's theory of moral development. In introducing us to Piaget's theory, the chapter describes Piaget's view that morality is linked to justice, and tracks the development of the concept of justice in the young child. Piaget's interviews with young children about the concept of justice provided the basis for his observation that in their construction of justice, children move from a relatively simple and concrete "tit-for-tat" or "eye-for-eye" conception of justice to a more contextual and ideal sense of justice that recognizes the situational and psychological contexts that moderate justice and fairness. The young child's sense of morality, Piaget also found, was more "external" than the older child. When asked about the consequences of children's actions, young children tend to give more weight to the external, tangible consequences of the actions rather than the intentions of the children. This external sense of morality, Piaget noted, gives way to a more internal sense of morality, one that takes into account intentions and psychological context. Piaget's term for these developmental phases was a transition from heteronomous (external) morality to autonomous (internal) morality.

Using Piaget's work as a starting point, Lawrence Kohlberg extended it in a number of directions. First, he extended Piaget's view that moral judgment development was defined by a definite direction of overlapping phases to include the view that the developmental differences were pervasive and consistent enough to be considered stages. He also extended and refined Piaget's three phrases to encompass six stages, classified within three levels. Drawing upon certain early twentieth-century writings, Kohlberg subsumed stages 1 and 2 under a "preconventional" level defined as a "concrete individual perspective." At this stage, right and wrong are defined relative to the individual. Stages 3 and 4 were subsumed under a "conventional" level defined as a "member-of-society perspective." At this stage, right and wrong are defined relative to society. Stages 5 and 6 were subsumed under a "postconventional" level defined as a "prior-to-society perspective" featuring morally principled reasoning. According to Kohlberg, the postconventional person has differentiated his or her self from the rules and expectations of others and defines his or her values in terms of self-chosen principles. Stage 5 features principles of social contract, whereas stage 6 focuses on universal principles of justice.

In the process of testing his stages, Kohlberg developed and refined an elaborate and widely used methodology for assessing stage development. This measure provided the basis for much of the research that will be discussed in this part of the book. Finally, he extended Piaget's emphasis on the importance of peer interaction as the cause of developmental change to include a more enlarged conception of the social processes that mediate moral judgment development. Chapter 2 provides an extensive discussion of the contribution that Kohlberg has made in each of these areas.

The chapter also discusses moral development in the context of cognitive development. One of the most important contributions of the cognitive developmental perspective has been its championing of a non-relativistic conception of moral judgment maturity, achieved largely by basing moral development in cognitive development. Chapter 2 notes that the superficial-to-mature progression in moral development is strikingly similar to age trends in other areas of social cognitive development. Just as more advanced forms of logical thought represent an advance beyond less advanced forms, so ideal justice is seen as an advance beyond superficial moral judgment, irrespective of cultural or historical context. The chapter also discusses the limitations of the cognitive developmental perspective in terms of providing an account of the motivation for moral behavior. Chapter 2 outlines a framework for understanding the role of empathy as well as justice as a motivator of moral behavior. Finally, the chapter discusses the role of cognitive distortion in accounting for instances in which persons with mature moral judgment competence nevertheless engage in antisocial behavior.

Chapter 3, by *Ann Higgins*, describes the history and development of the moral educational interventions pioneered by Lawrence Kohlberg. The chapter begins with a review of Kohlberg's six stages of moral development, and the fundamental assumptions of the theory of individual moral judgment development. These include the assumptions that the six stages form an invariant sequence with each stage in the sequence more advanced than the previous one. The hypothesized invariant sequence means that the stages occur in the same order in each person's development. Cultural factors may speed up, slow down, or even stop development, but not change the order. There can be no regression or moving backward in moral reasoning according to this assumption.

In introducing us to Kohlberg's educational interventions, the chapter puts Kohlberg's theory of individual development in the context of the three major approaches that have defined moral education in the United States: the character education approach, the values clarification approach, and the cognitive developmental approach advocated by Kohlberg. The cognitive developmental approach of Kohlberg is rooted in John Dewey's view of development as the aim of education. The idea of education as development was elaborated by Kohlberg and his colleagues as the just community approach to moral education. The just community programs have three basic aims: (1) enhancing student's moral reasoning through participation in moral discussion, (2) creating a moral culture of norms and values through democratic rule-making and building group solidarity or community, and (3) providing a context in which students and teachers can act on their moral intuitions.

The just community approach represents the effort to balance justice with community to introduce the powerful appeal of the collective while both protecting the rights of individual students and promoting their moral growth. In an ideal just community program, the students and teachers evolve through moral discussion their own value positions and translate those positions into rules and norms for group behavior through democratic decision-making. The teachers not only facilitate discussion among students, but they also lead the way towards decision-making by advocating certain value positions which they see as being in the best interest of the group. However, they are conscious of the difference between advocating and indoctrinating; that is, they present positions that can be criticized, they encourage students to formulate their own perspectives on issues, and they accept as binding the democratic vote of the majority of the community. The justice side of the just community is thus embodied in the democratic process and institutions of the program and in the focus on moral discussions, consideration of fairness, rights, and duties. The community side is an attempt to create a more ideal form of school society in which the pragmatic aspects of schooling, such as attendance, classroom, and school order, and the formation of cliques and groups, are transformed by a "sense of community" shared by the members who relate towards these issues not simply as school routines, but as aspects of communal life to be shared. "Community" is a call for students and teachers to participate in school in such a way that the rules and the concerns of the program become the personally-felt and community-shared responsibilities of all the members. This sense of community becomes, along with justice, the main moral content that is advocated within the just community approach. The participation of the students and teachers in such a complex, democratic, rule-governed organization is the appropriate means to enhance the social and moral development of individuals as well as the appropriate means for making the school itself a more fair and just place in which to learn, to work, and to act morally.

The just community approach to moral education has been implemented in a number of different high schools reflecting a range of academic and sociodemographic characteristics. Chapter 3 provides extensive examples of the process by which the approach is implemented in high schools and the results of using the just community approach.

Chapter 4, by *Lawrence Walker*, addresses the issue of sexism in moral psychology in general and as it has been raised in the case of Kohlberg's theory in particular. Gender differences and gender bias are issues that are significant and controversial in any domain of theory, research, or application. Gender bias, however, is particularly significant and controversial in an area so central to our self-definition as morality.

The issue of gender differences in moral functioning is not a new one. Historically, women and men have often been accorded and claimed to have different moral qualities and, not infrequently, differential moral worth. The most prominent current controversy regarding gender bias has emerged with respect to gender differences in Kohlberg's stages of moral reasoning. More specifically, early research on Kohlberg's stage theory suggested that males and females proceed through his stages at different rates and that adult males and females tend to be characterized by different stages of moral reasoning. In particular, the evidence appeared to suggest that adult females tend to be characterized by stage 3 reasoning and adult males by stage 4 reasoning.

In response to these findings and other developments, a body of research emerged that focused on gender differences in the development and use of moral reasoning. Stimulated by the work of Carol Gilligan, this research focused on two claims. The first is that there are gender-related orientations for moral decision-making, with male moral reasoning defined by what Gilligan termed an ethic of justice and female moral reasoning by an ethic of care. The second is that influential theories of human development (e.g., Erikson, Freud, Kohlberg, Levinson, McClelland, and Piaget) have been insensitive to females' "different voice" on morality and have caricatured females as morally deficient and aberrant. Gilligan, for example, has maintained that what Kohlberg termed stage 3 moral reasoning (care/response orientation) is rooted in an ethic of care that is as philosophically defensible as the ethic of justice that provides the basis for what Kohlberg termed stage 4 moral reasoning (justice/rights orientation). Chapter 4 provides a detailed overview of the theoretical claims made by both Gilligan and Kohlberg and an extensive review of the growing research literature addressing these issues. The results of the research reviewed in Chapter 4 appear to provide little support for the view that the care/response and justice/ rights orientation are gender-related or for the view that the care/response orientation is down-scored by Kohlberg's theory.

Chapter 5, by *John Snary*, addresses the issue of social class and cultural bias in Kohlberg's theory. Like gender bias, social class and cultural bias is an issue that is significant and controversial in any domain of theory, research, or application. Social class and cultural bias, however, is also particularly significant and controversial in an area so central to our self-definition as morality.

The issue of social class and cultural differences in moral functioning is not a new one. Historically, the nature of morality has been understood differently by members of working class and folk (village) communities and members of the middle and upper classes. Working class and folk people tend to emphasize communitarian ideas of society and morality with an emphasis on such values as happiness, tradition, understanding, reciprocity, role relationships and solidarity, and the unity of life. Middle-class people, in contrast, tend to emphasize "universalistic" ideas of society and morality with a value on self-chosen universal rights and principles. These differences have been accorded, not infrequently, different moral worth. In the case of moral reasoning, early research on Kohlberg's stage theory suggested that there were social class and cultural differences in the rate at which the stages develop and that adult members of working class and folk communities tend to be characterized by different stages of moral reasoning than members of middle class urban communities. More specifically, in Kohlberg's stage theory, moral reasoning that values happiness, tradition, understanding, reciprocity, role relationships and solidarity, and the unity of life is scored at what he has termed stage 2, 3, and 4 moral reasoning. Not surprisingly, the moral development literature has been characterized by considerable controversy and debate about the meaning and significance of these findings.

Reminiscent of Gilligan's feminist critique suggesting that Kohlberg's "universal" model left out the voices of women, Chapter 5 provides examples of how using the privileged classes and elite cultural groups' moral values as universal moral criteria leaves out the voices of the working class and of folk subculture. Chapter 5, for example, maintains that misinterpreting the moral reasoning of the working class and folk subcultures promotes a misunderstanding of their ethical values and a silencing of their claims against the status quo of inequality. Chapter 5 provides a detailed overview of the theoretical background for both the communitarian voice and the universalist voice and an extensive review of the large research literature addressing the issue of social class and cultural differences in moral reasoning. The results of the research reviewed in Chapter 5 appear to provide extensive support for the universality of stages 1 to 4, but very little support for the universality of stages 5 and 6 (postconventional) moral reasoning. Moreover, in nearly all samples, adults from urban cultural groups or middle-class populations exhibited some postconventional reasoning, but all samples of adults from folk subcultures failed to exhibit any postconventional reasoning and all samples of working class populations evidenced lower levels of postconventional reasoning as defined by Kohlberg's theory. Chapter 5 thus concludes that Gilligan insightfully identified a missing voice in Kohlberg's theory, but inappropriately primarily linked it to gender rather than class and culture.

## *Endnote*

1.  In making this claim we do not mean to imply that Kohlberg was the only person responsible for the changes that took place. Many other scholars and researchers have contributed to the changes that have taken place over the past several decades. It is therefore not our intention to either ignore, overlook, or neglect the contribution of others to this "cognitive" revolution. Nevertheless, we think it only fair to recognize the unique role that Kohlberg played in the emergence of the field. As you will discover reading this book, Kohlberg's work has had extensive influence, either directly or indirectly, on a great deal of the work that is currently being carried out in the area of moral development.

## *References*

Kohlberg, L. (1958). *Development of modes of moral thinking and choice in the years ten to sixteen.* Unpublished doctoral dissertation, University of Chicago.

Kohlberg, L. (1964). Development of moral character and moral ideology. In M. L. Hoffman & L. W. Hoffman (Eds.), *Review of child development research. (Vol. 1).* New York: Russell Sage Foundation.

Kohlberg, L. (1976). Moral stage and moralization: The cognitive developmental approach. In T. Lickona (Ed.), *Moral development and behavior: Theory, research, and social issues.* New York: Holt, Rinehart & Winston, pp. 31-53.

Kohlberg, L. (1981). *Essays in moral development: The philosophy of moral development., Vol. 1.* New York: Harper & Row.

Kohlberg, L. (1984). *Essays in moral development: The psychology of moral development., Vol. 2.* New York: Harper & Row.

Kuhn, T. (1962/1970). *The structure of scientific revolutions.* (2nd ed.) Chicago: University of Chicago Press. (1st ed., 1962)

Piaget, J. (1932/1965). *The moral judgment of the child.* (M. Gabain, Trans.). New York: Free Press. (Originally published 1932).

# The Cognitive Developmental Perspective

*JOHN C. GIBBS*
*The Ohio State University*

### Abstract

This chapter broadly describes the cognitive developmental perspective on morality and moral development, and introduces supplementary considerations important for an adequate understanding of moral maturity, motivation, and behavior. Whereas Piaget accounted for the child's developing conceptions of justice in terms of processes of peer interaction, Kohlberg attributed a more extensive moral developmental sequence to diverse opportunities for social role-taking. The core sequence, from superficial to more mature levels of moral judgment, can be related to the processes and products of cognitive development. In general, moral development and maturity are seen as based in cognitive development and maturity. Although the cognitive developmental perspective can partially account for moral motivation, the co-motivating role of empathy and the deleterious effect of cognitive distortions should be included in a more comprehensive understanding of moral behavior.

The cognitive developmental perspective as propounded in the theories of Jean Piaget and Lawrence Kohlberg challenges traditional notions concerning moral maturity, motivation, and behavior. In contrast to traditional views of morality as relative to different cultures, the cognitive developmental perspective seeks to identify cross-culturally general age trends in moral development culminating in an end-state of moral adequacy or maturity. Also, in contrast to traditional views of moral behavior as owing its motive power to affect, cognition is emphasized as the source of moral motivation. Essentially, the cognitive developmental perspective bases morality in cognition and cognitive development. This chapter describes in broad terms the cognitive developmental perspective on morality and moral development, and concludes with a consideration of processes which—although not readily assimilable to the cognitive developmental perspective—may be crucial for an adequate understanding of situational moral behavior.

## Piaget's Contribution

In his classic study of children's developing moral judgment, Piaget (1932/1965) challenged Emile Durkheim's (1925/1961) view of morality as simply the direct internalization of the norms and values of a particular culture. In Piaget's view, the essence of mature morality is fairness or justice, which Piaget defined as "an ideal equilibrium . . . born of the actions and reactions of individuals upon each other" (p. 318). In other words, children naturally construct ideals of equality and reciprocity as they engage in the interaction (cooperating, sharing, competing) normal to growing up in any society. Mature justice, Piaget wrote, is the "equilibrial limit . . . toward which reason cannot help but tend as it is gradually refined" (pp. 317, 395) through exchanges of viewpoints in peer interaction.

Although Piaget championed justice as the essence of morality, he acknowledged that justice in its initial appearance is less than mature. The first notion of fairness children develop through peer interaction is that of a concrete and simple "you scratch my back I'll scratch yours" or "eye for eye" morality. Lickona (1983) in several anecdotes quoted a 5-year-old who told his father: "I do something nice for you, then you do something nice for me!" A 6-year-old suggested that "It's not nice to lie . . . because people might lie back to you" (p. 148). Similarly, "If somebody punches you in the arm three times, you should punch them back three times—no more, no less" (p. 139). Piaget called this "crude equality" (p. 323) or in the case of eye-for-eye pay-back, "sheer equality in all its brutality" (p. 217).

Normally by late childhood, tit-for-tat justice begins to give way to a more contextual and ideal justice in which "the circumstances of the individual are taken into account" (Piaget, 1932/1965, p. 272). In one story, 95 percent of 13- to 14-year-olds but only 17 percent of 6- to 9-year-olds made allowance for the natural ineptness of a young child in a distributive justice story (whether a family's youngest child who dropped his allotment of bread should be given another piece). Older children and adolescents, then, "attempt to understand the psychological context" (p. 267). Furthermore, their construction of justice becomes more idealistic, as they conceptually reverse roles and achieve a "do as you would be done by" morality. The older "child sets forgiveness above revenge, not out of weakness, but because 'there is no end' to revenge (a boy of 10)" (p. 323).

Piaget termed these two conceptions of justice "reciprocity as a fact" and "reciprocity as an ideal" (p. 323). In the "fact" or pragmatic version of reciprocity, the child calculates whether his or her prospective action has been or will be matched by a reciprocal action; that is, one's action and its effects on another person are considered in terms of a tit-for-tat exchange of rewards or punishments. In the "ideal" version of reciprocity, one evaluates one's prospective action as if it *were* the reciprocal action; that is, one's action and its effects on another person are hypothetically inverted ("if you were to treat me that way, how would I feel?") and used as a guide to conduct.

Ideal justice, then, takes into account psychological contexts and inverted psychological effects. Even pragmatic justice considers individuals' motives to reciprocate rewards or punishments. Piaget also detected among his youngest subjects, however, an external morality marked by a failure to consider either psychological context or motive. Presenting pairs of stories of transgression, Piaget asked children which story entailed a "naughtier" transgression and why. Perhaps the most widely noted story pair contrasts a child who accidentally breaks 15 cups as he comes to dinner with a child who breaks one cup as he tries to sneak jam out of the cupboard. The 6- and 7-year-old children, impressed by the "external, tangible" (p. 166) event of so many broken cups, often judged the former child to be the naughtier. In contrast, older children generally paid more attention to the underlying intentions involved, and on that basis judged the latter child to be naughtier. This age trend in childhood from superficial (e.g., physical) considerations to underlying psychological considerations such as intentions as the basis for moral judgment has been replicated in more recent studies (Grueneich, 1982; Keasey, 1977).

Piaget found a similar age trend in terms of children's conceptions of lying (pp. 139-174). Following Piaget's original study, Peterson, Peterson, and Seeto (1983) generally found that external physical considerations decline—and intangible considerations ascend—in children's ideas about lying. In response to the question, "What happens when lies are told?," 92 percent of 5-year-olds mentioned punishment by an external authority or agency (e.g., "You get sick/belted/into trouble," p. 1533), whereas only 28 percent of 11-year-olds did so. Just how entrenched this physical-consequence orientation can be is suggested by the following interview (concerning authority versus justice) with a 5-year-old:

(If Michelle's mother tells her that she has to stay in even after she's cleaned up her room, is that fair?) Yes. (How come?) Whatever mothers tell their little kids to do, they have to do. (Why is that?) If you don't you'll get in trouble. (What if you don't get in trouble, you don't get caught?) It's still not right. (Why not?) Because she'll find out. (How will she find out?) She'll ask her friends to tell her, or she would find out any way she could find out. (Well, let's pretend she just never does find out, what then?) You don't get in trouble. (Is it O.K. then not to do what your mommy says?) No. (Why not?) 'Cause you're not supposed to. (Why aren't you supposed to?) Because your father would punish you even if your mommy didn't. (Damon, 1977, p. 189)

In contrast, it is rare for young children to appeal to the underlying intangible effects of lying. In the Peterson et al. study, guilty conscience and the loss of trust were mentioned, respectively, by 0 and 10 percent of the 5-year-olds; in contrast, 28 and 48 percent of the 11-year-olds mentioned guilty conscience and loss of trust. That the older children were more likely to take intentions and psychological contexts into account was indirectly suggested by their general unwillingness to define inaccurate guesses as lies (8 percent versus 55 percent of the 5-year-olds), or to state that lying is "always wrong" (28 percent versus 92 percent of the 5-year-olds).

It is ironic how often a young child who declares that lying or cheating is "always wrong" will without compunction engage in precisely those behaviors. Piaget accounted for this disparity by noting that consistent conduct and conscience cannot be expected until the child understands the underlying reasons for *why* lying, cheating, etc. are wrong. The absolute but superficial or "stuck on" (p. 166) quality of young children's morality Piaget termed "heteronomous," meaning literally "rules from others"—especially highly salient others such as powerful adults. Because heteronomous children's absolute declarations are without mature roots, their declarations may be readily abandoned in actual situations away from adults, where egocentric impulses or desires are more salient than adult constraints.

In contrast, the child who has constructed through peer interaction an understanding of the intangible reasons for morality may be less likely to lie or cheat insofar as he "feel[s] *from within* the desire to treat others as he himself would wish to be treated" (p. 191; emphasis added); in this sense, Piaget characterized mature morality as "autonomous," meaning literally, "rules from self." Mature moral judgment provides, then, a motivational basis for consistent conduct and conscience.

Piaget (1932/1965) noted the presence of considerable overlap in the age trend from superficial to more mature moral judgment; even within a single child's interview, both less and more advanced levels of reasoning could be discerned:

[Const., age 7] (Let's pretend that you are the mummy. You have two little girls. One of them breaks fifteen cups as she is coming into the dining room, the other breaks one cup as she is trying to get some jam while you are not there. Which of them would you punish more severely?) The one who broke the fifteen cups. . . . (Have you ever broken anything?) A cup. (How?) I wanted to wipe it, and I let it drop. (What else have you broken?) Another time, a plate. (How?) I took it to play with. (Which was the naughtier thing to do?) The plate, because I oughtn't to have taken it. (And how about the cup?) That was less naughty because I wanted to wipe it. (Which were you punished most for, the cup or the plate?) For the plate. (Listen, I am going to tell you two more stories. A little girl was wiping the cups. She was putting them away, wiping them with the cloth, and she broke five cups. Another little girl is playing with some plates. She breaks a plate. Which of them is the naughtiest?) The girl who broke the five cups. (pp. 125-126)

Because of such variability, Piaget refrained from referring to his modes of moral judgment (heteronomous, tit-for-tat, ideal-autonomous) as "stages," because the term "stage" for him implied considerable uniformity in the level of a given subject's stage usage. Instead, he used the term "phases" (p. 317). With age, the mixture in children's moral judgment increasingly favors the more mature phases. Piaget concluded that there is in general a "definite direction" (p. 386) in moral development from "primitive" to "more evolved" (p. 335) phases of moral judgment: in summary, from an external morality of physical appearance and consequences, to a pragmatic morality of tit-for-tat reciprocity, and finally to a more internal or autonomous morality entailing consideration of psychological contexts and ideal reciprocity.

## Kohlberg's Contribution

Piaget's work provided the stimulus for Lawrence Kohlberg's major contribution to the field of moral development. Interestingly, Kohlberg's seminal 1955 dissertation on moral judgment was intended to be scarcely more than a replication study of Piaget's findings, utilizing a somewhat different methodology (moral dilemmas instead of story pairs) and including adolescents in the sample "to allow for the laggards" (Kohlberg & Kramer, 1968, p. 93) in moral judgment development. Instead, Kohlberg's work came to entail a much more elaborate sequence of moral judgment stages (for a review of pertinent research, see Walker, 1988). Whereas Piaget described a "definite direction" of three overlapping "phases" (nonmoral, heternomous, autonomous), Kohlberg made more assertive claims. He replaced the term "phase" with "stage," arguing that a given subject's use of a particular phase was pervasive and consistent enough to justify use of the term stage and replaced the three phases with the six stages shown in Table 2-1. Furthermore, with reference to the "definite direction" discerned by Piaget, Kohlberg claimed that the stages progress in an invariant sequence, i.e., that subjects over the course of moral development should evidence the six stages in consecutive order, without stage skipping or stage reversal (see Colby, Kohlberg, Gibbs, & Lieberman, 1983). Finally, Kohlberg extended beyond Piaget's emphasis on peer interaction to argue for an "enlarged" (p. 428) conception of the social interaction processes mediating moral judgment development (see discussion below).

**TABLE 2-1   The Six Stages of Moral Judgment**

| Level and Stage | Content of Stage | | Social perspective of stage |
| --- | --- | --- | --- |
| | *What is right* | *Reasons for doing right* | |
| LEVEL I. Pre-conventional<br><br>Stage 1: heteronomous morality | Avoiding breaking rules backed by punishment; obedience for its own sake; to avoid physical damage to persons and property. | Avoidance of punishment, and the superior power of authorities. | *Egocentric point of view.* Doesn't consider the interests of others or recognize that they differ from the actor's; doesn't relate two points of view. Actions are considered physically rather than in terms of psychological interests of others. Confusion of authority's perspective with one's own. |
| Stage 2: Individualism, instrumental purpose, and exchange | Following rules only when it is to someone's immediate interest; acting to meet your own interests and needs and letting others do the same. Right is also what's fair, an equal exchange, a deal, an agreement. | To serve your own needs or interests in a world where you have to recognize that other people have their interests too. | *Concrete individualistic perspective.* Aware that everybody has his own interest to pursue and these conflict, so that right is relative (in the concrete individualistic sense). |
| LEVEL II. Conventional<br><br>Stage 3: Mutual interpersonal expectations, relationships, and interpersonal conformity | Living up to what is expected by people close to you or what people generally expect of people in your role as son, brother, friend, etc. "Being good" is important and means having good motives, showing concern about others. It also means keeping mutual relationships, such as trust, loyalty, respect, and gratitude. | The need to be a good person in your own eyes and those of others. Your caring for others. Belief in the Golden Rule. Desire to maintain rules and authority which support stereotypically good behavior. | *Perspective of the individual in relationships with other individuals.* Aware of shared feelings, agreements, and expectations which take primacy over individual interests. Relates points of view through the concrete Golden Rule, putting yourself in the other guy's shoes. Does not yet consider generalized system perspective. |

|  | | | |
|---|---|---|---|
| Stage 4: Social system and conscience | Fulfilling the actual duties to which you have agreed. Laws are to be upheld except in extreme cases where they conflict with other fixed social duties. Right is also contributing to society, the group, or institution. | To keep the institution going as a whole, to avoid the breakdown in the system "if everyone did it," or the imperative of conscience to meet your defined obligations (easily confused with stage 3 belief in rules and authority). | *Differentiation of societal points of view from interpersonal agreement or motives.* Takes the point of view of the system that defines roles and rules. Considers individual relations in terms of place in the system. |
| LEVEL III. Post-conventional or principled | | | |
| Stage 5: Social contract or utility and individual rights | Being aware that people hold a variety of values and opinions, that most values and rules are relative to your group. These relative rules should usually be upheld, however, in the interest of impartiality and because they are the social contract. Some nonrelative values and rights like *life* and *liberty*, however, must be upheld in any society and regardless of majority opinion. | A sense of obligation to law because of your social contract to make and abide by laws for the welfare of all and for the protection of all people's rights. A feeling of contractual commitment, freely entered upon, to family, friendship, trust, and work obligation. Concern that laws and duties be based on rational calculation of overall utility, "the greatest good for the greatest number." | *Prior-to-society perspective.* Perspective of a rational individual aware of values and rights prior to social attachments and contracts. Integrates perspectives by formal mechanisms of agreement, contract, objective impartiality, and due process. Considers moral and legal points of view; recognizes that they sometimes conflict and finds it difficult to integrate them. |
| Stage 6: Universal ethical principles | Following self-chosen ethical principles. Particular laws or social agreements are usually valid because they rest on such principles. When laws violate these principles, one acts in accordance with the principle. Principles are universal principles of justice: the equality of human rights and respect for the dignity of human beings as individual persons. | The belief as a rational person in the validity of universal moral principles, and a sense of personal commitment to them. | *Perspective of a moral point of view* from which social arrangements derive. Perspective is that of any rational individual recognizing the nature of morality or the fact that persons are ends in themselves and must be treated as such. |

*Source:* Kohlberg 1984: 174-176.

## Kohlberg's Stages of Moral Judgment

Piaget's three moralities are discernible in Kohlberg's first three stages of moral judgment. Like Piaget's external morality, Kohlberg's stage 1 reflects "the natural tendency of young children to embody . . . moral notions in concrete places or events" (Damon, 1988, p. 15). Stage 1 morality entails a physicalistic understanding of moral authority (e.g., "the father is the boss because he's bigger"; Kohlberg, 1984, p. 624), or the moral worth of human life (one of Kohlberg's longitudinal subjects suggested that saving the life of more than one person is especially moral since "one man has just one house, maybe a lot of furniture, but a whole bunch of people have an awful lot of furniture," p. 182). Similarly, keeping a promise might be justified by an appeal to physical consequences (otherwise the person "will beat you up"). Salient features of a situation (e.g., size, objects, or physical consequences), then, tend to capture the young child's attention or imagination and dominate the child's moral judgment.

Like Piaget's external morality, Kohlberg's stage 1 is increasingly supplanted with increasing age by more advanced moral judgment. Piaget's tit-for-tat morality corresponds to Kohlberg's stage 2.

> The perspective at [Kohlberg's] stage 2 is pragmatic—to maximize satisfaction of one's needs and desires while minimizing negative consequences to the self. The assumption that the other is also operating from this premise leads to an emphasis on instrumental exchange. . . . For example, it is seen as important to keep promises to insure that others will keep their promises to you and do nice things for you, or it is important in order to keep them from getting mad at you. (Kohlberg, 1984, pp. 626-628)

Finally, corresponding to the advance from tit-for-tat to ideal morality described by Piaget, Kohlberg noted that

> At stage 3 the separate perspectives of individuals are coordinated into a third perspective, that of mutually trusting relationships. . . . Stage 3 reciprocity . . . allows one to understand reciprocity as going beyond concrete notions of equal exchange to maintaining relationships, mutuality or expectations, and sentiments of gratitude and obligation. (Kohlberg, 1984, pp. 628-629)

Kohlberg noted that not all aspects of his adolescent subjects' moral reasoning were adequately captured by Piaget's levels. For example, the older adolescents raised considerations regarding not only the need for trust or mutual caring in relationships but also the need to commonly accept standard and interdependent expectations in society. One of the subjects in Kohlberg's 20-year longitudinal study (Colby et al., 1983) reasoned: "You've got to have certain understandings in things that everyone is going to abide by or else you could never get anywhere in society, never do anything" (Colby, Kohlberg,

Speicher, Hewer, Candee, Gibbs, & Power, 1987, p. 375). In the absence of such commonly accepted "understandings" such as the responsibility to respect one another's rights and to contribute to society, not only will society "never get anywhere," but (in the words of another of Kohlberg's longitudinal subjects) "chaos will ensue, since each person will be following his or her own set of laws" (p. 375; cf. Adelson, Green, & O'Neil, 1969). On the basis of data such as these, Kohlberg concluded that with his adolescent subjects he had not only "allowed for the laggards" but had also discovered yet more advanced levels of moral judgment. He proposed an extension of Piaget's original three-level sequence to include at least a fourth, societal-level stage of moral judgment.

As reviewed thus far, the general age trend in moral judgment identified in Piaget's and Kohlberg's research is from a superficial level (external morality or stage 1; pragmatic morality or stage 2) to a more profound or mature level in which the underlying rationale for moral values is understood. Mature moral understanding applies first to interpersonal relationships (stage 3, mutual trust or caring underlying interpersonal relationships), and then to the institutions and social networks of society (stage 4, commonly accepted standards and "understandings" as the basis for society). This age trend is the focus of a new moral judgment assessment measure, the Sociomoral Reflection Measure—Short-Form (Gibbs, Basinger, & Fuller, 1992; Basinger, Gibbs, & Fuller, in press).

The superficial-profound moral judgment age trend has been evidenced in longitudinal studies (e.g., Colby et al., 1983; Page, 1981; Walker, 1989), as well as in cross-cultural research. In a review of moral judgment studies in 27 countries, Snarey (1985) concluded that Kohlberg's stages 1 through 4 are "represented in a wide range of cultural groups" (p. 218). At least stages 1 through 3 are discernible in Damon's (1977) study of children's reasoning concerning fair distribution and legitimate authority, Youniss's (1980) study of friendship conceptions, Selman's (1980) broader investigation of interpersonal understanding (stage 4 is also found among adolescents), and Eisenberg's (1982) study of prosocial reasoning.

Kohlberg's original stage sequence included not four but six stages, classified within three levels. Drawing upon certain early twentieth-century writings (Dewey & Tufts, 1908; McDougall, 1908), Kohlberg (1984) subsumed stages 1 and 2 under a "preconventional" level defined as a "concrete individual perspective;" stages 3 and 4 under a "conventional" level defined as a "member-of-society perspective"; and certain further stages featuring morally principled reasoning under a "postconventional" level defined as a "prior-to-society perspective" (Kohlberg, 1984, p. 33). Kohlberg wrote that the "postconventional person . . . has differentiated his or her self from the rules and expectations of others and defines his or her values in terms of self-chosen principles" (p. 173). Stage 5 features principles of social contract, whereas stage 6 focuses on universal principles of justice.

Stages 5 and 6 would seem to be poor candidates for the exclusive representation of moral judgment maturity. Included among Piagetian expectations for mature stages are that they be "commonly in evidence through humanity" (Gibbs, 1977, p. 50), and relatively spontaneous or unconfounded with cultural ideology (Gibbs, 1979). Yet Kohlberg (1984; cf. Colby et al., 1983) found that only 13 percent of his longitudinal subjects reached stage 5 (even counting subjects who only showed stage 5 as a minor stage), and all of these subjects "had some graduate education" (p. 458). Similarly, Snarey (1985) in his cross-cultural review noted that stage 5's "frequency within any particular sample is seldom high," and that it was not found at all in "traditional tribal or village folk societies" (p. 218). Furthermore, *none* of Kohlberg's longitudinal subjects clearly reached stage 6 (at least as defined in the 1987 Colby et al. scoring manual).

Research results such as these led Kohlberg (1984) "to suspend" (p. 273) his empirical claims for stage 6, although he continued to defend stage 5 as an empirically based concept. Kohlberg acknowledged that his definition of stage 6 "came from the writings of a small elite sample, elite in the sense of its *formal philosophical training* and in the sense of its ability for and commitment to moral leadership" (p. 270; emphasis added). Snarey concluded that even stage 5 is based on the individualistic philosophies of "Kant, Rawls, and other Western philosophers" and hence is "incomplete" (p. 228). Snarey suggested that the characterization of stage 5 be supplemented with more "collective" (p. 226) postconventional principles from non-Western societies (cf. Vasudev & Hummel, 1987).

In my view, even stage 5 is an inappropriate definer of moral judgment maturity, not because it is cross-culturally incomplete, but more basically because *any* ethical philosophical level, even in broadened form, misrepresents moral judgment maturity as restricted to those who are philosophically articulate. I regard "stage 5" not as a standard developmental stage (relative to which other stages are immature), but rather as a reflective philosophy indicative of an "existential" phase of human development in which life itself becomes an object of contemplation (see Gibbs, 1977, 1979, 1991b; Gibbs, Basinger, & Fuller, 1992).

## Social Role-Taking Opportunities

As noted, Piaget emphasized peer interaction as critical to the development of mature conceptions of justice. In contrast to the uneven power relations between children and their parents, children are on more or less equal footing with other same-aged children. Piaget saw egalitarian social conditions as optimal for the open exchanges of viewpoints by which self-centered or "egocentric" assertions are tempered and conceptions of fairness or justice develop. Although acknowledging the value of such peer exchanges, Hoffman (1988) pointed out that even same-aged children often develop dominance hierarchies that negate egalitarian conditions. Furthermore, Hoffman argued that even when children do consider one another to be equal their interactions may not be beneficial unless adults encourage the children to consider one another's viewpoints.

Kohlberg (1984) argued that peer interaction should be conceptualized as but one mode of social role-taking opportunity. He acknowledged that peer interaction "appears to stimulate moral development" (p. 77; cf. Keasey, 1971; Sedikides, 1989). Nonetheless, Kohlberg argued that peer interaction "seems better conceptualized in terms of providing general role-taking opportunities than as having very specific and unique forms of influence" (p. 77).

> If moral development is fundamentally a process of the restructuring of modes of role-taking, then the fundamental social inputs stimulating moral development may be termed "role-taking opportunities." ... Participation in various groups ... [stimulates] development. ... The child lives in a total social world in which perceptions of the law, of the peer group, and of parental teaching all influence one another. ... Various people and groups ... [stimulate] *general moral development*. ... The more the social stimulation, the faster the rate of moral development. (pp. 74, 78)

Studies of social experiences and moral judgment have generally been consistent with the thesis that social participation and perspective-taking play an important role in moral judgment development. Keasey (1971) found that moral judgment stage in childhood is positively related to peer popularity as well as number of social club memberships and leader roles. Similarly, Sedikides (1989), using a measure of childhood role-taking opportunities constructed by Schnell (1986), found that for a sample of preadolescents social role-taking opportunities are in fact related to movement through the first three stages of moral judgment. In support of Piaget, however, by far the most important category of role-taking opportunity for Sedikides's sample was represented by a peer interaction factor (more important than home and school factors). Comprising the peer interaction factor were items such as: "I have many friends and talk with them very often," and "My friends and I talk about our opinions when they differ."

In the context of moral judgment development beyond stage 3, Kohlberg (1984) emphasized the importance of "enlarged" (p. 428) or expanded role-taking opportunities in college and occupational settings. As adolescents or adults move beyond small, local communities to universities or complex work settings, they increasingly deal with many more individuals and heterogeneous values. Kohlberg claimed that such experiences were important for development beyond stage 3. To investigate this claim, Gibbs and Mason (1989) devised a measure of post-childhood role-taking opportunities in which subjects respond (along a three-point scale from "not true or rarely true" to "somewhat true or sometimes true" to "very true or often true") to items such as: "I have encountered and become friends with other students or co-workers of different ethnic or cultural backgrounds (for example, a student from another country)"; "I have found that professors generally encourage me to consider other points of view"; "I have been involved in a group or organization where it was necessary for me to deal with various points of view"; and "I have learned just how culturally varied the world is since coming to college." Mason and Gibbs (1993b) administered both the Schnell childhood role-taking opportunities measure and the Gibbs and Mason post-childhood measure focusing on work and college role-taking experiences to a college sample evidencing mixtures of stage 3 and stage 4 moral judgment. The post-childhood measure, but not the childhood measure, was highly correlated with moral judgment level in this advanced sample. Hence, Kohlberg was right to stress the importance of socially expanded perspective-taking experiences for moral judgment development beyond childhood.

## Moral Development in the Context of Cognitive Development

The superficial-to-mature progression in morality seems strikingly similar to age trends in other areas of social cognitive development. A transition from physicalistic or egoistic responses to more mutualistic or system-level responses is evident in studies of ego development (Loevinger & Wessler, 1970) and development of the self-concept (e.g., Harter, 1983; Montemayor & Eisen, 1977). Similarly, a progression from judgment based on superficial, immediate appearances or actions to judgment based on underlying, inferred meaning is evident in children's developing social explanations (J. Miller, 1986), person descriptions (Livesley & Bromley, 1973), comprehension of narratives (e.g., Paris & Upton, 1976), and understanding of gender constancy (e.g., Kohlberg, 1966; Marcus & Overton, 1978; Smetana & LeTourneau, 1984; Wehren & Delisi, 1983; but cf. Bem, 1989).

The superficial-mature progression is also discernible in physical-cognitive development, especially in terms of Piaget's widely studied "conservation" phenomenon ("conservation" refers to knowledge that basic attributes of an object remain the same even though the superficial appearance changed). Flavell, Miller, & Miller (1993) have illustrated the child's development from judgment based on "perceived appearances" to conservation judgment based on "inferred reality" in these terms:

> Piaget's test for conservation of liquid quantity illustrates the meaning of this and other . . . [progressions]: (1) the child first agrees that two identical glasses contain identical amounts of water; (2) the experimenter pours the water from one glass into a third, taller and thinner glass, with the child watching; (3) the experimenter then asks the child whether the two amounts of water are still identical, or whether one glass now contains more water than the other. The typical preschool

nonconserver is apt to conclude, after the liquid has been poured, that the taller and thinner glass now has more water. . . . [She] is more given than the older child to make judgments on the basis of the immediate, perceived *appearances* of things. . . . The middle-childhood conserver, on the other hand, may also think that the tall glass *looks* like it contains more water because the liquid column is higher, but she goes beyond mere appearances to *infer* from the available evidence that the two quantities *are really* still the same. That is, she makes an *inference* about *underlying* reality. (p. 134; last two emphases added)

Consistent with Flavell's analysis, Ricco (1989) found that conservers (relative to nonconservers) more often inferred conceptual classes despite figurative dissimilarities in an object classification task.

## *Role of Decentration*

According to the cognitive developmental perspective, the child actively "constructs" moral meaning. One can discern in the very description of the moral stages (provided earlier) the notion that they are resultants from a progressive coordinating or interrelating of perspectives (for example, from pragmatic exchanges to mutuality). In physical-cognitive development, Flavell (1985; cf. Case, 1985; Piaget, 1975/1977) attributes the progression from superficial appearances to underlying meanings to the child's increasing tendency to attend to and interrelate multiple features of a situation.

> Preschoolers are more prone to concentrate or *center* (hence *centration*) their attention exclusively on some single feature or limited portion of the stimulus array that is particularly salient and interesting to them, thereby neglecting other task-relevant features. In the present [conservation] example, the difference in the heights of the two liquid columns is what captures most of the child's attention. . . . In contrast, the older child is likelier to achieve a more balanced, "decentered" (hence, *decentration*) perceptual analysis of the entire display. While, of course, attending to the conspicuous height differences, just as younger children do, older children also carefully note the correlative differences in container width. (p. 134)

Flavell characterized decentration, then, as a shift from judgment "captured" by attention to the most "salient" or "interesting" aspects of a situation, to judgment based on a more extensive, equally distributed, and "balanced" situational attention. Extending from Flavell's analysis, I suggest that decentration naturally generates logical and moral prescriptions of equality and reciprocity.

In the social realm, peer interaction may be important precisely insofar as it fosters a more extensive, equal, and balanced distribution of the child's attention. By confronting and reacting to one another's viewpoints, peers facilitate social decentration and the cognitive construction of justice (cf. Doise & Mugny, 1984; Walker, 1983; Youniss, 1980). Interestingly, the constructive process entailed in peer-stimulated social decentration may be best illustrated in the physical-cognitive realm. For example, Ames and Murray (1982) found conservation knowledge to result from the confrontation of one preconservational child by another, e.g., the confrontation of a child who believes that there is more lemonade when the lemonade is poured into a taller, narrower glass by a peer who (centering instead upon the narrowness of the glass) argues that there is now *less* lemonade.

Such studies find that as a result of such conflictual social interaction between children with opposing types of centration, the children "construct" conservation judgments. Presumably, the conflict brings home to each child the alternative feature ("narrower" or "taller"), and the need to resolve the contradiction (the glass cannot hold both "more" and "less" liquid; Feffer, 1970).

The active character of cognitive construction is especially clear in such studies. The children cannot be said to have simply acquired conservation knowledge from an external source, since the information from their peers was also incorrect; hence the clever title of the Ames and Murray study: "When Two Wrongs Make a Right." Nonetheless, it is important to point out that

> The constructive process, whatever its precise nature, does not take place in a vacuum. In the course of their everyday experience, children encounter all sorts of implicit or explicit examples of the higher level concepts which they themselves will acquire. That does not imply that they internalize the examples to which they are exposed in any direct or automatic way. But it is equally unlikely that they systematically ignore them. . . . The objective . . . must be to understand the specific ways in which the individual's constructive activity utilizes these external data. (Kuhn, 1988, p. 229)

Constructive processes in the context of social decentration are functionally linked to the decline of the self-centered bias referred to as egocentrism. Consider that the "feature" or aspect of a *social* situation that is often "particularly salient and interesting" to the child may be the child's own claims, needs, or desires (or those of someone similar and familiar to the child). Hence, unless a highly salient authority figure is present, the child's own viewpoint is likely to "capture most of [the child's] attention." Other persons' viewpoints or needs are either ignored altogether or assumed (appropriately or inappropriately) to be the same as the child's. Such an egocentric bias, allied with egoistic motives, probably accounts for the young child's unfair yet unabashed, self-serving allocations in distributive justice tasks (Damon, 1977).

Although the egocentric bias tends to decline with decentration and the development of justice conceptions, it is probably never entirely eliminated. Even with cognitive maturity, it remains true that "we experience our own points of view more or less directly, whereas we must always attain the other person's in more indirect ways. . . . Furthermore, we are usually unable to turn our own viewpoints off completely, when trying to infer another's viewpoints" (Flavell, et al., 1993, p. 181).

### Decentration as a Cognitive Source of Moral Motivation

Decentration can motivate behavior. Conservation and other decentration-based cognitive constructions are experienced "as necessary, as something that *must* be true," rather than "as merely one of many facts that happen to be true about the world" (Miller, 1986, p. 3; cf. Nicholls & Thornkildsen, 1988; Piaget, 1971a, 1971b). In so-called "counter-suggestion" studies, children who make conservational or other largely logic-based judgments are confronted with (false) evidence of non-conservation (for example, the experimenter may surreptitiously add or remove material). Although interpretations of the counter-suggestion research are controversial (S. Miller, 1976), studies involving "basic . . . Piagetian concepts" (S. Miller, 1986, p. 17) generally find that children using logic-based judgment are surprised and upset when the experimenter confronts them with an apparent violation of "necessary" reality as they have inferred it. They seek some explanation, some logical means of accounting for or correcting, for example, an apparent non-conservation (Smedslund, 1961; but cf. Winer, Hemphill, & Craig, 1988). In general, they act as if illogical imbalances or violations of reciprocity and equality "shouldn't be." The pertinent cognitive structuring of the situation as incorrect or wrong generates a motivation to restore the "necessary" reciprocity or equality.

The parallel with the motivating quality of prescriptive *moral* feelings would seem to be straightforward. Injustice, likewise, "shouldn't be." The cognitive structuring of a situation as *unfair* generates a motivation to restore the "necessary" reciprocity or equality (cf. Hammond, Rosen, Richardson, & Bernstein, 1989). As Kohlberg (1984) put the point, "violation of logic and violation of justice . . . arouse . . . strong affects" (p. 63). The motivation to account for or correct a "reciprocity imbalance" (Gouldner, 1961, p. 167) in the social context may be no less cognitively based than is the corresponding motivation in the physical context. The intimate relationship of morality with logic is intriguingly expressed in Piaget's (1932/1965) assertion that "logic is the morality of thought just as morality is the logic of action" (p. 398). Similarly, Rest (1983) suggested that the sentiment of justice may have "a counterpart in people's sense of logical necessity" (p. 616).

Although morality and logic may be intimately related, Kohlberg (1984, pp. 389-391) argued that the conditions for facilitating moral-cognitive development are more complex than are those for physical-cognitive development, and hence that there is a necessary-but-not-sufficient relation between physical-cognitive and sociomoral-cognitive stages. Kohlberg emphasized the importance of social role-taking opportunities in making possible the attainment, in the sociomoral domain, of the developmental "ceiling" set by the physical-cognitive domain (see Walker, 1988, pp. 48-52; but cf. Damon, 1975; Helkama, 1988).

## Moral Judgment, Empathy, and the Motivation of Moral Behavior

In the cognitive developmental perspective, cognition is primary. The construction of moral meaning through decentration generates motivating feelings such as logical necessity or sentiments of justice—but such affect is secondary in the sense that it owes its motivational properties and indeed its existence to cognitive constructive processes. Not only justice, however, but also empathy (as well as related emotions such as empathy-based guilt) contribute to the motivation of moral behavior. In other words, the "construction" of the meaning of a social situation as unjust may generate moral motivation in not only cognitive terms (correction of the reciprocity imbalance) but also affective terms (empathic distress in response to the victim's suffering). If cognition is motivationally primary for cognitive developmentalists, affect is motivationally primary for moral socialization theorists such as Martin Hoffman (1981, 1983), who argue that empathy is a biologically rooted predisposition discernible even in infancy.

Granted, the two sources of moral motivation may be in conflict: Justice and empathy may tend to impel opposite behaviors in situations where one individual is more deserving, while another is more needy (cf. Hoffman, 1987). In the philosophy of normative ethics, Frankena (1973) proposed that justice must be tempered with beneficence where a just decision will result in grievous suffering, just as beneficence must be tempered with justice where a beneficent act will result in moral inequality. Frankena concluded that justice and beneficence are equally basic and mutually irreducible principles in normative ethics. Similarly, I argue that justice and empathy are equally primary and mutually irreducible sources of moral motivation (Gibbs, 1991b).

Although sometimes conflicting, the two sources of moral motivation are intimately intertwined and often compatible. Although cognition plays an important role in the motivation to correct an injustice, empathy for the distressed victim of the injustice may play a critical role in the intensity and persistence of the moral behavior in behalf of the victim. Hoffman (1987) provides a fascinating and moving example of an effort to remedy (what I would interpret as) a reciprocity imbalance, in this case, between the respect someone accords others and the lack of respect—to say the least—that person receives in return. Hoffman described Coles' (1986) interview with a "14-year-old Southern male 'redneck.' . . . After several weeks of joining his friends in harassing black children trying to integrate his school, this boy, a popular athlete,

> . . . began to see a kid, not a nigger—a guy who knew how to smile when it was rough going, and who walked straight and tall, and was

polite. I told my parents, "It's a real shame that someone like him has to pay for the trouble caused by all those federal judges."

Then it happened. I saw a few people cuss at him. "The dirty nigger," they kept on calling him and soon they were pushing him in a corner, and it looked like trouble, bad trouble. I went over and broke it up. . . . They all looked at me as if I was crazy. . . . Before [everyone] left I spoke to the nigger . . . I didn't mean to. . . . It just came out of my mouth. I was surprised to hear the words myself: "I'm sorry." (Coles, 1986, pp. 27-28, cited in Hoffman, 1987, p. 56)

"After this incident, he began talking to the black youth, championing him personally, while still decrying integration. Finally, he became the black youth's friend and began advocating 'an end to the whole lousy business of segregation.' When pressed by Coles to explain his shift, he attributed it to . . . seeing 'that kid behave himself, no matter what we called him, and seeing him insulted so bad, so real bad. Something in me just drew the line, and something in me began to change, I think' (Coles, 1986, p. 28)" (Hoffman, 1987, pp. 56-57).

Hoffman posited empathy to be the primary source of moral motivation in this episode. In my view, however, both cognitive and affective sources are involved from the outset. The cognitive construction of the injustice to the black youth ("It's a real shame that someone like him has to pay"; "someone like him" being someone mature enough to refrain from a tit-for-tat reciprocation of insults and harassment) itself generates some motivation for the shift in behavior toward the youth. This cognitive motivation is no doubt bolstered considerably by empathy for the youth's plight and by the sudden promptings of empathy-based guilt ("I was surprised to hear the words myself: 'I'm sorry'"). Interestingly, construction of the injustice and/or empathy for the victim apparently dissipated a defensive out-group classification, as the boy "began to see a kid, not a nigger."

In general, it seems clear that "both cognitive and affective sources of motivation are usually required for the accomplishment of good and fair behavior in the face of narrowly egoistic impulses" (Gibbs & Schnell, 1985, p. 1078). The cognitive developmental perspective has made an important contribution to the field of moral development in championing the role of cognition in moral motivation. A comprehensive understanding of moral behavior requires, however, consideration not only of cognitive but also of affective sources of moral motivation.

## Cognitive Distortions and Antisocial Behavior

A neglected consideration in discussions of the relationship between moral judgment and moral behavior is the role of cognitive distortions (see Gibbs, 1991a, 1993). Cognitive distortions are non-veridical attitudes or beliefs pertaining to self and the self's social behavior. Egocentric bias in effect constitutes a cognitive distortion natural to early childhood. Damon (1977) found that young children's reasoning on distributive justice tasks confuses fairness with "the child's own desires," e.g., the child may assert "I should get it because I want to have it" (p. 75). In effect, the child mistakenly believes that entitlement to an object automatically follows from his desire for it. Persistence of this egocentric distortion into adolescence renders the individual high-risk for serious antisocial behavior, given the size, strength, independence, sex impulses, and ego capabilities of adolescents.

As noted earlier, egocentric bias does not totally disappear even with advances in moral judgment maturity. It is entirely possible to achieve stage 3 moral judgment competence and still engage in immoral or antisocial behavior, if one's egocentric bias preempts consideration for the legitimate expectations and feelings of others in actual social situations. Even in cases where harm to others is obvious and difficult to ignore, egocentric bias may eventuate into antisocial behavior if certain rationalizing cognitive distortions come into play. Consider the recollection of a 17-year-old delinquent concerning his recent burglaries: "If I started feeling bad, I'd say to myself, 'tough rocks for him. He should have had his house locked better and the alarm on'" (Samenow, 1984, p. 115). I would interpret the delinquent as saying in effect: "Upon experiencing empathy-based guilt for causing innocent people to suffer, I would neutralize my guilt by blaming the suffering on the victim." Similarly, experimental research (e.g., Dodge, 1980) has found that aggressive boys make "distorted" (p. 167) or gratuitous attributions of hostile intent to non-aggressive peers. Moral judgment interventions which include improvement in conduct among their objectives should aim not only to facilitate moral judgment but also to correct cognitive distortions (Gibbs, 1993; Gibbs, Potter, & Goldstein, in press).

## Conclusion

The primary contribution of the cognitive developmental perspective on morality has been its championing of a non-relativistic conception of moral judgment maturity, achieved largely by basing moral development in cognitive development. Just as conservation represents an advance beyond superficial impressions, so ideal justice is seen as an advance beyond superficial moral judgment, irrespective of cultural or historical context (see Gibbs, 1991b). Moreover, constructed cognition such as conservation or justice can be motivating, as when the child seeks to account for a non-conservation or to remedy an injustice.

The limitations of the cognitive developmental perspective on morality are most apparent with respect to the question of moral behavior. Not only cognition but also affect, most notably empathy, are important in the motivation of moral behavior. In my view, justice and empathy both represent primary sources of moral motivation. Finally, the cognitive developmental perspective should attend to the role of cognitive distortion in accounting for instances in which persons with mature moral judgment competence nonetheless engage in antisocial behavior.

Cognitive developmental theory has achieved an established place among perspectives on morality and moral behavior. Prior to that achievement, it was perhaps necessary for cognitive developmentalists to emphasize the distinctiveness of their perspective through pejorative critiques of other perspectives (e.g., Piaget's critique of Durkheimian theory, Kohlberg's critiques of social learning or psychoanalytic theory). Now that cognitive developmental theory has become a recognizably distinct perspective, cognitive developmentalists should feel more secure in acknowledging theoretical limitations and in seeking integrative relationships with other perspectives capable of remedying those limitations.

## Recommended Readings

*Moral Judgment of the Child*, by Jean Piaget. Although originally published in 1932, this classic is still well worth reading. Piaget interweaves research and theory masterfully as he uses a diversity of methods to explore the development of children's moral judgment.

*Essays on Moral Development, I: The Philosophy of Moral Development: Moral Stages and the Idea of Justice*, by Lawrence Kohlberg. San Francisco: Harper & Row, 1981. In these classic writings, Kohlberg addresses the problem of value relativity. He successfully argues for a non-relativistic conception of moral adequacy focused on the principle of justice or the Golden Rule as "at the heart of ethics." Kohlberg's writings in this volume show extraordinary breadth, as he extends his perspective to political science, literature, and theology.

*Essays on Moral Development, II: The Psychology of Moral Development*, by Lawrence Kohlberg. San Francisco: Harper & Row, 1984. This important volume includes both classic and recent writings. The opening essays, taken together, provide an excellent statement of the cognitive-developmental approach. More abstruse but still worth scrutiny is the presentation in later chapters of recent theoretical revisions, responses to critics, and recent research.

*The Moral Child: Nurturing Children's Natural Moral Growth*, by William Damon. New York: Free Press, 1988. Damon draws upon cognitive-developmental and other research to make the case that the aim of moral socialization and education should be the cultivation of the child's natural moral emotions (such as empathy) and naturally developing ideals (such as fairness). Damon's combination of solid, up-to-date scholarship with a highly readable style makes this a very attractive supplemental reading.

## References

Adelson, J., Green, B., & O'Neil, R. (1969). Growth of the idea of law in adolescence. *Developmental Psychology, 1*, 327-332.

Ames, G., & Murray, F. (1982). When two wrongs make a right: Promoting cognitive changes by social conflict. *Developmental Psychology*, 1982, *18*, 892-895.

Basinger, K. S., Gibbs, J. C., & Fuller, D. (in press). Context and the measurement of moral judgment. *International Journal of Be-*

*havioral Development.*

Bem, S. L. (1989). Gender knowledge and gender constancy in preschool children. *Child Development, 60,* 649-662.

Case, R. (1985). *Intellectual development: Birth to adulthood.* New York: Academic.

Colby, A., Kohlberg, L., Gibbs, J. C., & Lieberman, M. (1983). *A longitudinal study of moral judgment.* Monographs of the Society for Research in Child Development, *48*(1-2, Serial N. 200).

Colby, A., Kohlberg, L., Speicher, B., Hewer, A., Candee, D., Gibbs, J. C., & Power, C. (1987). *The measurement of moral judgment* (vol. 2). Cambridge, England: Cambridge University Press.

Coles, R. (1986). *The moral life of children.* Boston: Atlantic Monthly Press.

Damon, W. (1975). Early conceptions of positive justice as related to the development of logical operations. *Child Development, 46,* 301-312.

Damon, W. (1977). *The social world of the child.* San Francisco: Jossey-Bass.

Dewey, J., & Tufts, J. H. (1908). *Ethics.* New York: Holt.

Dodge, K. A. (1980). Social cognition and children's aggressive behavior. *Child Development, 51,* 162-170.

Doise, W., & Mugny, G. (1984). *The social development of the intellect* (A. St. James-Emler & N. Emler, Trans.). Oxford: Pergamon Press.

Durkheim, E. (1961). *Moral education: A study in the theory and application of the sociology of moral education.* (E. K. Wilson & H. Schnurer, Trans.). New York: Free Press. (Original work published 1925)

Eisenberg, N. (1982). The development of reasoning regarding prosocial behavior. In N. Eisenberg (Ed.), *The development of prosocial behavior* (pp. 219-249). New York: Academic Press.

Feffer, M. (1970). Developmental analysis of interpersonal behavior. *Psychological Review, 77,* 197-214.

Flavell, J. H., Miller, P. H., & Miller, S. A. (1993). *Cognitive development* (3rd ed.). Englewood Cliffs, NJ: Prentice-Hall.

Frankena, W. K. (1973). *Ethics* (2nd ed.).

Englewood Cliffs, NJ.

Gibbs, J. C. (1977). Kohlberg's stages of moral judgment: A constructive critique. *Harvard Educational Review, 47,* 43-61

Gibbs, J. C. (1979). Kohlberg's moral stage theory: A Piagetian revision. *Human Development, 22,* 89-112.

Gibbs, J. C. (1991a). Sociomoral developmental delay and cognitive distortion: Implications for the treatment of antisocial youth. In W. M. Kurtines & J. L. Gewirtz (Eds.), *Handbook of moral behavior and development* (vol. 3). Hillsdale, NJ: Lawrence Erlbaum Associates.

Gibbs, J. C. (1991b). Toward an integration of Kohlberg's and Hoffman's theories of morality. In W. M. Kurtines & J. L. Gewirtz (Eds.), *Handbook of moral behavior and development* (vol. 1). Hillsdale, NJ: Lawrence Erlbaum Associates.

Gibbs, J. C. (1993). Moral-cognitive interventions. In A. P. Goldstein & C. R. Huff (Eds.), *The gang intervention handbook* (pp. 159-185). Champaign, IL: Research Press.

Gibbs, J. C., Basinger, K. S., & Fuller, R. L. (1992). *Moral maturity: Measuring the development of sociomoral reflection.* Hillsdale, NJ: Lawrence Erlbaum Associates.

Gibbs, J. C., & Mason, M. G. (1989). *The Post-Childhood Opportunities for Role-Taking Measure.* Unpublished work, The Ohio State University, Columbus.

Gibbs, J. C., Potter, G., & Goldstein, A. P. (in press). *EQUIP: Motivating and equipping youth to help one another.* Champaign, IL: Research Press.

Gibbs, J. C., & Schnell, S. V. (1985). Moral development "versus" socialization: A critique. *American Psychologist, 40,* 1071-1080.

Gouldner, A. W. (1960). The norm of reciprocity: A preliminary statement. *American Sociological Review, 25,* 161-178.

Grueneich, R. (1982). The development of children's integration rules of making moral judgments. *Child Development, 53,* 887-894.

Hammond, G. S., Rosen, S., Richardson, D. R., & Bernstein, S. (1989). Aggression as equity restoration. *Journal of Research in Per-*

*sonality*, *23*, 398-409.

Harter, S. (1983). Developmental perspectives on the self-system. In J. H. Flavell & E. M. Markman (Eds.), *Handbook of child psychology* (4th ed., Vol. 3, pp. 275-386). New York: Wiley.

Helkama, K. (1988). Two studies of Piaget's theories of moral judgment. *European Journal of Social Psychology*, *18*, 17-37.

Hoffman, M. L. (1981). Is altruism part of human nature? *Journal of Personality and Social Psychology*, *40*, 121-137.

Hoffman, M. L. (1983). Affective and cognitive processes in moral internalization. In E. T. Higgins, D. N. Ruble, & W. W. Hartup (Eds.), *Social cognition and social development: A sociocultural perspective* (pp. 236-274). Cambridge, England: Cambridge University Press.

Hoffman, M. L. (1987). The contribution of empathy to justice and moral judgment. In N. Eisenberg and Janet Strayer (Eds.), *Empathy and its development*. Cambridge, England: Cambridge University Press.

Hoffman, M. L. (1988). Moral development. In M. H. Bornstein & M. E. Lamb (Eds.), *Developmental psychology: An advanced textbook* (2nd ed., pp. 497-548). Hillsdale, NJ: Lawrence Erlbaum Associates.

Keasey, C. B. (1971). Social participation as a factor in the moral development of preadolescents. *Developmental Psychology*, *5*, 216-220.

Keasey, C. B. (1977). Children's developing awareness and usage of intentionality and motives. In C. B. Keasey (Ed.), *Nebraska symposium on motivation* (pp. 219-258), *25*. Lincoln: University of Nebraska Press.

Kohlberg, L. (1966). A cognitive-developmental analysis of children's sex-role concepts and attitudes. In E. Maccoby (Ed.), *The development of sex differences*. Stanford, CA: Stanford University Press.

Kohlberg, L. (1984). *The psychology of moral development: Essays on moral development* (Vol. 2). San Francisco: Harper & Row.

Kohlberg, L., & Kramer, R. (1968). Continuities and discontinuities in childhood and adult moral development. *Human Development*,

*12*, 93-120.

Kuhn, D. (1988). Cognitive Development. In M. H. Bornstein & M. L. Lamb (Eds.), *Developmental Psychology: An advanced textbook* (2nd ed., pp. 205-260). Hillsdale, NJ: Lawrence Erlbaum Associates.

Lickona, T. (1983). *Raising good children*. Toronto: Bantam Books.

Livesley, W. J., & Bromley, D. B. (1973). *Person perception in childhood and adolescence*. London: Wiley.

Loevinger, J., & Wessler, R. (1970). *Measuring ego development 1. Construction and use of a sentence completion test*. San Francisco, Jossey-Bass.

Marcus, D. E., & Overton, W. F. (1978). The development of cognitive gender constancy and sex role preference. *Child Development*, *49*, 434-444.

Mason, M. G., & Gibbs, J. C. (1993a). Role-taking opportunities and the transition to advanced moral judgment. *Moral Education Forum*, *18*, 1-12.

Mason, M. G., & Gibbs, J. C. (1993b). Social perspective-taking and moral judgment among college students. *Journal of Adolescent Research*, *8*, 109-123.

McDougall, W. (1908). *An introduction to social psychology*. London: Methuen.

Miller, J. G. (1986). Early cross-cultural commonalities in social explanation. *Developmental Psychology*, *22*, 514-520.

Miller, S. A. (1976). Extinction of Piagetian concepts: An updating. *Merrill Palmer Quarterly*, *22*, 257-281.

Miller, S. A. (1986). Certainty and necessity in the understanding of Piagetian concepts. *Developmental Psychology*, *22*, 3-18.

Montemayor, R., & Eisen, M. (1977). The development of self-conceptions from childhood to adolescence. *Developmental Psychology*, *13*, 314-319.

Nicholls, J. G., & Thornkildsen, T. A. (1988). Children's distinctions among matters of intellectual convention, logic, fact, and personal preference. *Child Development*, *59*, 939-949.

Page, R. A. (1981). Longitudinal evidence for the sequentiality of Kohlberg's stages of moral judgment in adolescent males. *Journal of Genetic Psychology, 139,* 3-9.

Paris, S., & Upton, L. (1976). Children's memory for inferential relationships in prose. *Child Development, 47,* 660-668.

Peterson, C. C., Peterson, J. L., & Seeto, D. (1983). Developmental changes in ideas about lying. *Child Development, 54,* 1529-1535.

Piaget, J. (1965). *Moral judgment of the child* (M. Gabain, Trans.). New York: Free Press. (Original work published 1932)

Piaget, J. (1971a). *Biology and knowledge.* Chicago: University of Chicago Press.

Piaget, J. (1971b). The theory of stages in cognitive development. In D. R. Green, M. P. Ford, & G. B. Flamer (Eds.), *Measurement and Piaget* (pp. 1-11). New York: McGraw-Hill.

Piaget, J. (1977; A. Rosin, Trans.). *The development of thought: Equilibration of cognitive structure.* New York: Viking Press. (Originally published, 1975)

Rest, J. R. (1983). Morality. In J. H. Flavell & E. M. Markman (Eds.), *Handbook of child psychology* (4th ed., Vol. 3, pp. 556-629). New York: Wiley.

Ricco, R. B. (1989). Operational thought and the acquisition of taxonomic relations involving figurative dissimilarity. *Developmental Psychology, 25,* 996-1003.

Samenow, S. (1984). *Inside the criminal mind.* New York: Times Books.

Schnell, S. V. (1986). *Delinquents with mature moral reasoning: A comparison with delayed delinquents and mature non-delinquents.* Unpublished doctoral dissertation. Columbus: The Ohio State University.

Sedikides, A. (1989). *Relations between role-taking opportunities and moral judgment development.* Unpublished doctoral dissertation, The Ohio State University.

Selman, R. L. (1980). *The growth of interpersonal understanding: Developmental and clinical analyses.* New York: Academic Press.

Smedslund, J. (1961) The acquisition of conservation of substance and weight in children. III. Extinction of conservation of weight acquired normally and by means of empirical controls on a balance scale. *Scandinavian Journal of Psychology, 2,* 85-87.

Smetana, J. G., & LeTourneau, K. J. (1984). Development of gender constancy and children's sex-typed free play behavior. *Developmental Psychology, 20,* 691-696.

Snarey, J. (1985). The cross-cultural universality of social-moral development: A critical review of Kohlbergian research. *Psychological Bulletin, 97,* 202-232.

Thompson, R. A., & Hoffman, M. L. (1980). Empathy and the development of guilt in children. *Developmental Psychology, 26,* 155-156.

Vasudev, J., & Hummel, R. C. (1987). Moral stage sequence and principled reasoning in an Indian sample. *Human Development, 30,* 105-118.

Walker, L. J. (1983). Sources of cognitive conflict for stage transition in moral development. *Developmental Psychology, 19,* 103-110.

Walker, L. J. (1988). The development of moral reasoning. In R. Vasta (Ed.), *Annals of child development* (Vol. 5, pp. 33-78). Greenwich, CT: JAI Press.

Walker, L. J. (1989). A longitudinal study of moral reasoning. *Child Development, 60,* 157-166.

Wehren, A., & DeLisi, R. (1983). The development of gender understanding: Judgments and explanations. *Child Development, 54,* 1568-1578.

Winer, G. A., Hemphill, J. & Craig, R. K. (1988). The effect of misleading questions in promoting nonconservation responses in children and adults. *Developmental Psychology, 24,* 197-202.

Youniss, J. (1980). *Parents and peers in social development: A Sullivan-Piaget perspective.* Chicago: University of Chicago Press.

# Chapter 3

# Educating for Justice and Community: Lawrence Kohlberg's Vision of Moral Education[1]

*ANN HIGGINS*
*Fordham University*

## Abstract

This chapter introduces the just community approach to moral education and sets it in the contexts of both Lawrence Kohlberg's theory and research on individual moral judgment development and the three streams of moral education popular in the United States. It then recounts the history of educational interventions begun by Lawrence Kohlberg and his colleagues and the development of the just community ideas over the last 20 years. The first "Kohlbergian" moral educational program was the introduction of hypothetical moral dilemmas into classroom discussion, an intervention based on Kohlberg's theory and research of individual moral development, with the goal of enhancing student moral reasoning. Kohlberg's broader concern with education for justice and community led to the development of the just community approach, a way of creating "moral" schools as contexts for individual moral development. Just community interventions have spread among several high schools and spawned research which has defined school moral culture and described its impact upon adolescents and their peer groups. Descriptions of incidents in several just communities illustrate this educational approach and introduce some primary issues in moral education, especially indoctrination, value relativity, and teacher advocacy.

This chapter recounts the history and development of moral educational interventions begun by Lawrence Kohlberg and his colleagues. In order to tell the story of just communities,[2] it is important to situate them in two contexts: (1) Lawrence Kohlberg's theory of individual moral judgment development and (2) within the different streams of moral education in the United States at the time the just community idea was born.

## An Overview of Lawrence Kohlberg's Theory and Research of Moral Judgment Development

Kohlberg's empirical work into the moral reasoning of children and adolescents began in 1958 with his dissertation study of 72 Chicago-area boys ages 10, 13, and 16. It ended in 1987, thirty years later, with the publication of a scoring manual (Colby, Kohlberg, Speicher, Hewer, et al., 1987) for assessing moral judgment development across the lifespan and after literally hundreds of studies had been done by Kohlberg and many others evaluating the validity, usefulness, and generalizability of his theory of moral reasoning development.

Assessing the moral reasoning of people of all different ages, of both sexes, of various ethnic and racial backgrounds, of all walks of life from criminals to the well-educated, from poor to rich, and from over 50 different cultures has produced several consistent and strong results (cf. Kohlberg, 1984; Snarey, 1985; Walker, 1983; Walker, DeVries, and Bichard, 1984; etc.).

As all children grow, their moral reasoning changes in a systematic way that is captured by Kohlberg's theory and method of assessment, the *Moral Judgment Interview* and *The Standard Form Scoring Manual Vols. 1 & 2* (Colby and Kohlberg, 1987). All children reason using Stage 1 and then Stage 2 until early adolescence when most proceed to use Stage 3 and many move into Stage 4 reasoning in early adulthood. A minority of adults later move into Stage 5 reasoning. Kohlberg illustrated Stage 6, the final stage, with moral exemplars such as Marcus Arelius, Martin Luther King, Jr., Ghandi, and a few contemporary examples that appear in his writings.

The research studies referred to above also show important ways in which people differ in their moral reasoning. For instance, in our society, people who have completed a college education are more likely to continue developing, reasoning fully at Stage 4 and eventually Stage 5. In contrast, people who have spent some part of their lives in juvenile delinquency homes or prisons tend to reason at the early childhood Stages 1 and 2, even when they are adults. Thus, normal stage development seems to be hindered by institutions that isolate people from society and it seems to be enhanced by institutions, especially higher education in our society, that engage and involve people in society. The research from many different cultures indicates that very few people worldwide reason at Stage 5; however, the proportion of adults reasoning at Stage 4 seems to be similar from one industrialized culture to another. In cultures in which most of the business of the society can be carried out in face-to-face groups many adults tend to solve moral problems reasoning at Stage 3, a good fit since Stage 3 reasoning often invokes and relies on shared group norms as a moral basis for decision-making.

Differences in levels of reasoning between men and women and among racial and ethnic groups in the United States are not commonly found, but when they are, such differences are better explained by the educational differences that exist between the groups in each sample than by gender or ethnicity (see Walker, this vol.).

Between the mid 1970s and the early 1980s, Kohlberg and some others found that in U.S. research studies women, on the average, were making Stage 3 judgments and men, on the average, were making Stage 4 judgments. About the same time, Kohlberg also found that some college students in his longitudinal Chicago study seemed to be regressing, reasoning at Stage 2 instead of their prior high stage reasoning (Stages 4 and 5). Kohlberg looked carefully at these data and found that the scoring system was not focused sufficiently on the structure or the logic of how people made moral judgments.

This problem sent Kohlberg and his colleagues into a "bootstrapping" round of analyzing data, revising the scoring system used to assess each stage, and finally making some theoretical revisions. Just as the expression, "pull yourself up by your own bootstraps," means that one should use what she has to help herself, so Kohlberg used what he had to help improve his theory and assessment system. How he did it is a fascinating story of how science proceeds and how social scientists work, but for now I will only point to some highlights as a way to illustrate the basic ideas of his theory of individual moral judgment development.

Kohlberg's initial interest in morality had led him to Piaget. He took from Piaget the method of interviewing people with stories or dilemmas and, important for the story of this chapter, he took the definitions and main assumptions of cognitive structural developmental theory. These definitions and main assumptions were the "bootstraps" that Kohlberg used to pull up his own theory. By cognitive, I mean a view of thinking as an activity—an active constructing, transforming, and creating of relations and inferences by a person based on his or her own perceptions and experiences with the world and the meanings they have for him or her. Therefore, interviewing a person with moral dilemmas is an opportunity to find out how a person is thinking and becomes a dialogue or genuine communication between two people.

A cognitive-developmental theory claims that mature thinking emerges through a process of reorganization of psychological structures or stages and that development is dependent upon experience; moral development is dependent upon interpersonal and social experiences including role-taking. Kohlberg said, "It (cognitive development) is a 'dialogue' between the structures of the human mind and the structures of the environment." (Kohlberg, 1984, p.57.)

The four main assumptions of cognitive developmental theories postulate or describe characteristics of the structures or stages.

1. Each stage is a distinctive or qualitatively different mode or way of think-ing that still serves the same function, like solving moral problems, or has the same focus, like justice, at various times in development.
2. The stages form an invariant sequence, that is, they occur in the same order in each person's development. Cultural factors may speed up, slow down, or even stop development, but not change the order. There can be no regression or moving backward in reasoning according to this assumption.
3. Each stage or way of thinking forms a "structured whole." Each way of thinking is a coherent and organized "worldview" or perspective, and is used to solve various kinds of problems in a whole domain, such as the moral domain.
4. Stages fit together in a hierarchy of increasing complexity and organization. One stage is integrated into the next one, and each stage is more advanced than the previous one. This assumption means that reasoning at higher stages is better in the sense that they solve problems more adequately and more fairly than does reasoning at the lower stages.

When Kohlberg confronted problems like regressions and not understand-ing why one group of adults reasoned at a different stage than another group of adults, he used the four structuralist assumptions as standards to criticize his own theory and his method of assessing moral judgment stage and the scoring manual. As a result, Kohlberg's theory of moral stage development is probably the finest example of a truly structural theory, a theory that says moral thinking and problem solving are organized in the human mind and experience.

From this vantage point then, the stages are not moral ideas, rather each stage is a perspective that is used to solve moral problems. Each perspective is broader, takes into account more variables or aspects of a moral problem, and is more truly or intrinsically moral. Thus, at Stages 5 and 6, the post-conventional stages, moral problems are solved by taking into account all particular facts and all actual perspectives by imagining them in full reciprocal relations to each other using a moral principle or ideal. At the conventional stages, Stages 3 and 4, the moral view that organizes the facts and perspectives involved are moral norms, rules, and laws—those informal and formal ideas that people use to create social harmony and order. At the pre-conventional level, Stages 1 and 2, the person sees the facts and perspectives of others from his or her own point of view, and makes a moral decision based on what is right in his or her own best interest, whether getting a reward, avoiding punishment, remaining uninvolved, or taking over.

## Kohlberg's Work in Relation to Some Other Developmental Views

Having said quite a bit about Kohlberg's theory of moral judgment develop-ment, I must also say what it is not. It focuses on making moral judgments, not on moral action. It is a theory of thinking and most clearly fits into James Rest's Component #2 from Chapter 14 by Narvaez and Rest. However, one should note that there are cognitive aspects to all of Rest's components, and Kohlberg's idea of a stage as a structured whole or a world view cuts across Rest's componential model. Since Kohlberg's theory is not one of behavior or action, moral or otherwise, Rest's model is helpful to us in our educational work. As Narvaez and Rest point out, there are important situational and personal aspects that arise when a person must decide whether to act on her moral judgment or not. How we have tried to identify these aspects in our educational work is at the heart of this chapter.

Kohlberg began his work looking at the reasons children give for why a character in a dilemma should "do the right thing," as morally muddy as that often is—witness Spike Lee's film by that name. But he did not try to find out whether the children were sensitive enough to see the moral problem; nor did he make ratings of their empathy or sympathy with the characters. Being sensitive enough to "see" a dilemma and having feelings of empathy and sympathy as a source of motivation for action and perserverence are important aspects of being a moral person. This is Rest's Component #1 and also is discussed by John Gibbs in Chapter 2 in which he maintains that empathy and justice are equally necessary and primary sources of moral motivation. Kohlberg did not ignore emotions but thought that feelings or sentiments were known and expressed through thoughts.

Kohlberg said:

> . . . the cognitive-developmental view holds that 'cognition' and 'affect' are different aspects, or perspectives, on the same mental events, . . . Moral judgments are largely about sentiments and intuitions of persons, and to a large extent they express and are justified by reference to the judger's sentiments. . . . The development of sentiment (or emotion), as it enters into moral judgment is, however, a development of structures with a heavy cognitive component. . . . In general, then, the quality (as opposed to the quantity) of affect involved in moral judgment is determined by its cognitive-structural development and is part and parcel of the general development of the child's conception of a moral order. (Kohlberg, 1982, pp. 139-141)

Chapter 17, by Laupa and Turiel, describes research studies showing the ability of even young children to differentiate the moral domain from either the conventional or the personal domains. This relates in two ways to Kohlberg's view. First, it points to a universal human capacity to think in moral terms and use moral categories. Certainly Kohlberg agreed with this and his stages represent the increasing ability to use this very human capacity. Both views point to the non-reducible nature of morality; it cannot be reduced to, nor understood, only in biological, psychological, sociological, anthropological, or ethological terms. Second, Kohlberg would both agree and disagree with the tripartite division of the social world. He would agree that the social world be divided into the moral, the personal, and the conventional and that people often agree on such divisions. However, he would disagree on how much agreement can be reached about where the divisions should be made. Based on Kohlberg's theory, I would suggest that these boundaries may change in relation to the developing moral thinking of the individual. Furthermore, even though we may agree that there is a universal moral core of issues, that core may not define the whole moral domain. In addition, the boundaries between the personal and conventional seem especially problematic and dependent upon situation and culture.

What comprises the moral domain is an issue that is dealt with throughout this book. It is an area in which philosophers in every era have disagreed. It is a controversial area for any society undergoing changes in values and policies and an especially controversial area for a pluralistic and democratic society such as ours. More narrowly, psychologists have argued over Kohlberg's definition of morality and moral reasoning. Not that this will settle the debate, but one of the strengths of the structural approach of Kohlberg's theory of moral stages is that the stages are defined by the relations or operations of moral ideas with each other, the different perspectives used to solve moral problems, not by any moral ideas themselves.

Kohlberg defined the scope of his moral theory as follows:

> In my view, the basic referent of the term moral is a type of judgment or a type of decision-making process, not a type of behavior, emotion or social institution. . . . I make no direct claims about the ultimate aims of people, about the good life, . . . These are problems beyond the scope of the sphere of morality or moral principles, which I define as principles of choice for resolving conflicts of obligation. (Kohlberg, 1982, p. 169)

Those of us interested and invested in moral education agree that "becoming a moral person" and "doing the right thing" are enormously complicated and entail more than making moral judgments, therefore we welcome the differentiations made by these and other authors in this book.

## *A Broad View of Moral Education in the United States*

In the United States historically there have been three major approaches to moral education, the character education approach, the values clarification approach, and the cognitive-developmental approach. In the 1920s and 1930s, the approach of character education was widely prevalent in public schools. The educators and psychologists who developed these interventions defined character as the sum total of a set of "those traits of personality which are subject to the moral sanctions of society." (Havighurst and Taba, 1949). For

Hartshorne and May (1928) these traits included honesty, service and self-control. For Havighurst and Taba (1949) they included honesty, loyalty, responsibility, moral courage and friendliness. These traits are similar to those noted by Aristotle which included temperance, liberality, pride, good temper, truthfulness, and justice, and those encouraged by the Boy Scouts—honesty, loyalty, reverence, cleanliness, and bravery.

One difficulty with this approach to moral character is that the composition of the list of virtues and the priorities given different virtues varies from one theory or practice to another. However, the problem runs deeper than the particular list of virtues and vices. Although it may be true that the notion of teaching virtues, such as honesty and integrity, seems agreeable to many people, it is also true that a vague consensus on the value of these terms conceals real disagreement over their meanings. What someone may call "integrity," another will call "stubbornness." "Expressing your true feelings" may also be considered as being "insensitive to others' feelings" in some situations. For instance, in times of war in the United States, protestors against war in some circles are "upholders of a moral ideal of peace," and in other circles are seen as acting "irresponsibly" and violating "law and order." They exemplify virtue or vice depending upon one's viewpoint.

Although as adults we recognize the problem of people having different values, we don't always see that it exists from the time children enter school. We may think that teachers of young children can and should make judgments in terms of a list of virtues that are fairly objective and accepted, moral ideas that we think all children should come to understand. However, a parent will not agree that a child's specific failure to obey an "unreasonable" request by the teacher was wrong, even if the teacher calls the child's act "uncooperative." Such disagreements are hardly rare.

Character education programs have had an upsurge of popularity in the 1980s in the United States. They seem to be a response to, and often a reaction against, the long, difficult, and unfinished self-examination of our society's values which arose out of the Civil Rights Movement, the Feminist Movement, and the Viet Nam War. Insofar as character education programs are part of this searching for "traditional American values" and are based on the belief that we as a society ever really had one set of shared values seems to be a search for an illusion. On the other hand, the legitimate power of many current character education programs is their emphases on behavior and the use of "moral heroes" in several of the curricula (cf. Character Education Network).

There is a response to the relativity-of-values problem of character education approaches that is embodied in the values clarification approach, a second method of moral education. This view says that we should acknowledge that people have different values and encourage students to explore their own values, creating a society in which there are many values and values positions, none better than any other.

As summarized by Engel, this position says that

. . . in consideration of values, there is no single correct answer, but value clarification is extremely important. One must contrast value clarification and value inculcation. Inculcation suggests that the learner has limited control and hence limited responsibility in the development of his own values. He needs to be told what values are or what he should value. This is not to suggest, however, that nothing is ever inculcated. As a matter of fact, in order to clarify values, at least one principle needs to be adopted by all concerned. Perhaps the only way the principle can be adopted is through some procedure which might best be termed inculcation. That principle might be stated as follows: in the consideration of values there is no single correct answer. More specifically it might be said that the adequate posture both for students and teachers in clarifying values is openness. (In Simon, 1971, p. 202.)

Although the basic premise of the value clarification approach is that "everyone has his own values," it is further advocated that children can and should learn: (1) to be more aware of their own values and how they relate to hierarchies of decisions; (2) to make their values consistent with each other and to order them into hierarchies for decision-making; (3) to be more aware of the differences between their value hierarchies and those of others; and (4) to learn to be tolerant of those differences. In other words, although values are regarded as somehow private and relative, values clarification says that there may be logical strategies for making hierarchies of values and for making decisions to maximize one's own values. Part of these strategies is to recognize that all values are relative. Therefore, within this view, it is quite reasonable to teach children that values are relative as part of an overall educational program.

Moreover, accepting this idea that all values are relative leads to the conclusion that a teacher should not attempt to teach any particular moral values. Problems arise from this approach as well. A teacher who values being honest and not cheating has no moral basis for imposing her view on her students from this relativistic vantage point. The students of a teacher who has been successful in teaching moral relativism will believe, like the teacher, that "everyone has his own bag." If one of these students has learned this lesson well, when he is caught cheating he will argue that he did nothing wrong. The basis of his argument will be that his own hierarchy of values, which certainly seems to be different from the teacher's, made it right for him to cheat. The student can recognize that the teacher and others believe that cheating is wrong, but still hold the "value" that one should cheat when the opportunity arises. If the teacher wants to be consistent and retain her own relativistic ideas, she will have to concede.

The values clarification approach was widely used in the 1960s and 1970s and is still used today. It can be a valuable component of a moral education program if clarifying values is recognized as only one aspect. If it is done alone, however, it may leave students feeling unsure about how to understand their own values and viewpoints in relation to those of others.

The third approach and the focus of this chapter is the cognitive-developmental approach to moral education, which was first fully stated by John Dewey (1944, orig. 1916).

According to Dewey, "The aim of education is growth or development, both intellectual and moral. Ethical and psychological principles can aid the school in the greatest of all constructions, the building of a free and powerful character. Only knowledge of the order and connection of the stages in psychological development can insure this. Education is the work of supplying the conditions which will enable the psychological functions to mature in the freest and fullest manner." (Dewey, 1944, p. 10)

These ideas about a cognitive-developmental approach to moral education were elaborated by Kohlberg and his colleagues as the just community approach. Just community programs are Kohlberg's fullest expression of the third method of moral education. They have three basic aims: (1) enhancing students' moral reasoning through participation in moral discussions; (2) creating a moral culture of norms and values through democratic rule-making and building group solidarity or community; and (3) providing a context in which students, and teachers as well, can act on their moral intuitions and decisions.

Since just communities are democratic, they encourage egalitarian relationships between teachers and students and among students themselves. These programs tend to be small (about 80 to 100 students and 4 or 5 teachers), informal, and not bureaucratic. Problems in the program are settled by open discussion in meetings with students and teachers together rather than by teachers alone. Finally, there is explicit attention given to informal sociability or building community among all members rather than teachers trying to ignore or control student peer groups. These programs exist as a part of each school day within regular public high schools. Thus, a just community program should provide an environment in which issues of fairness, justice, and community can be debated and rules established and enforced through active participation of all members, teachers, and students, with each member having one vote. The participation of the students and teachers in such a complex, democratic, rule-governed organization is the appropriate means to enhance the social and moral development of individuals as well as the appropriate means for making the school itself a more fair and just place in which to learn, to work, and to act morally.

## Theoretical Rationale of the Just Community Approach

Before describing what the just community approach looks like in practice, it is important to give some explanation of a theoretical rationale. A complete discussion of this theory is given in *Lawrence Kohlberg's Approach to Moral Education* by Power, P. C., Higgins, A., and Kohlberg, L. (1989) from which much of this section is drawn.

The just community approach represents the effort to balance justice with community to introduce the powerful appeal of the collective while both protecting the rights of individual students and promoting their moral growth. In an ideal just community program, the students and teachers evolve through moral discussion their own value positions and translate those positions into rules and norms for group behavior through democratic decision-making. The teachers not only facilitate discussion among students, but they also lead the way towards decision-making by advocating certain value positions which they see as being in the best interest of the group. However, they are conscious of the difference between advocating and indoctrinating; that is, they present positions that can be criticized, they encourage students to formulate their own perspectives on issues, and they accept as binding the democratic vote of the majority of the community. The teachers obviously have special authority by virtue of their position, but they try to operate as formally equal members of a democratic group and exercise authority by virtue of their wisdom and expertise and by means of consent rather than by virtue of their position of authority and by means of coercion or dictate. Teachers must walk the fine line between excessive advocacy—approaching indoctrination—and excessive permissiveness. To create a just community the moral advocacy of the teachers must be strictly bound by the safeguards of democratic process in order to avoid becoming indoctrinative; and the democratic process must be structured, embodied in institutions, in order to avoid becoming ruled by the crowd, the strong, or the highly verbal.

The justice side is embodied in the democratic process and institutions of the program and in the focus on moral discussions, consideration of fairness, rights, and duties. The community side is an attempt to create a more ideal form of school society in which the pragmatic aspects of schooling, such as attendance, classroom and school order, and the formation of cliques and groups, are transformed by a "sense of community" shared by the members who relate towards these issues not simply as school routines, but as aspects of communal life to be shared. "Community" is a call for students and teachers to participate in school in such a way that the rules and the concerns of the program become the personally-felt and community-shared responsibilities of all the members. It becomes, along with justice, the main moral content that is advocated within the just community approach.

## Discussion of Hypothetical Moral Dilemmas as Moral Education

The just community is not the end of my story, however; Kohlberg's interest in moral education began in 1968 in Chicago when one of his graduate students, Moshe Blatt, tried to convince Kohlberg that students could "learn" to reason at higher stages through group discussions of standard hypothetical moral dilemmas used in his research on moral development. Blatt believed that the cognitive stimulation of moral discussion, that is of children hearing themselves and others argue at different stages of moral reasoning, ought to create movement to the next stage up for the children involved. Kohlberg thought that development occurred slowly over years and resulted from the natural interaction between the child and the social environment, parents and peers. He did not believe that development could be stimulated through interventions. It turned out that Kohlberg was wrong. Blatt's twelve- to fourteen-year-old children moved up one-third of a stage in their moral reasoning on average, or in other words, one-third of the children reasoned one stage higher at the end of the twelve-week intervention of moral dilemma discussion than when it began.

After Kohlberg insisted and got several replications (Blatt & Kohlberg, 1975) of this finding, he, Edwin Fenton, Anne Colby, Betsy Speicher, and others began a large-scale study funded by the Stone Foundation. Kohlberg also began writing in educational philosophy. His often reprinted and cited paper, "Development as the Aim of Education" (Kohlberg & Mayer, 1972), spells out his arguments about the connection of psychological facts of stages of moral reasoning and their development with the goals of education. Basically Kohlberg argued that development of the child is and ought to be the aim of education. Secondly he argued that children are natural philosophers, that they are engaged by dilemmas that raise fundamental philosophic questions about right and wrong and good and bad. Thirdly, he concluded that the discussion of such dilemmas promotes the development of children's moral reasoning.

Working in educational philosophy also led Kohlberg to revise his thinking about moral education as a practice. He felt that moral dilemma discussion could be a dimension of any course but it had to be truly integrated into the subject of the curriculum. The last result had even greater implications for practice—teachers and students wanted to discuss real moral issues, not only hypothetical ones.

## *Lessons Learned*

At that point we had learned several things: (1) that upward stage change was possible and lasting when students and teachers engaged in moral dilemma discussions that challenged them; (2) that a mixture of viewpoints and different stages of reasoning are necessary for moral reasoning development; and (3) that teachers want a hand in using moral dilemmas in ways they felt would enhance their curricula and their teaching as well as create a good classroom atmosphere or easier classroom management. We also learned that several concerns of teachers and administrators were unmet by this approach. Specifically, (1) they wanted to influence students' behavior not only their reasoning; (2) they wanted to decrease problem behaviors that beset most U.S. high schools—vandalism, stealing, cheating, cliquishness, fighting, etc.; (3) they were frustrated by, but respectful of, the idea that they should not impose their values on students but wished dearly that somehow students would adopt their values; and lastly, (4) they became convinced of the powerful truth of the idea that moral education goes on in every class and school regardless of whether there is an explicit program, it is embodied in the *hidden curriculum.* This term, introduced by Philip Jackson (1968), means the norms and values invoked by the administrators and teachers to maintain order and discipline.

The influence of the hidden curriculum upon students' thinking and behavior as something teachers should respond to is discussed by the director, Tony, of the Scarsdale Alternative School, a just community all-day program. While describing why he prefers democracy as moral education he acknowledges the reality of the hidden curriculum.

He said, "Moral education happens by default in any case. So it is haphazard or it's not. When you think about it, you have to be on the side of thinking about something, rather than having it haphazard. We are making something happen that is meant to happen. It's not an imposition. It is simply creating the proper environment in which a natural growth is nudged along. The students think more about their actions in this program. It is built into the structures of this program, that they are called upon to think about what they do more so than in the traditional school. The whole thing becomes clearly conscious. Students' consciousnesses are raised and hopefully they are much less likely to be passive people later on in life."

To make the hidden curriculum explicit or to do moral education in schools meant two ideas should be realized according to Kohlberg. If values were to be publically taught teachers needed to be able to be advocates for certain moral positions or values. However, if teachers were to be advocates, their power needed to be grounded in the context of participatory democracy so as to provide a system of checks and balances against abuse of their authority and to protect against indoctrinative teaching. Historically, Kohlberg was first concerned that moral education should not be indoctrinative (1971) and that teachers' authority be limited (1978). It was later, in 1980, that he began to write about the idea that teachers also needed the freedom to advocate. In practice he had been encouraging teachers and correctional officers to be advocates for ideas and values of justice that would further the welfare and development of the community since 1971 when the first just community participatory democracy was launched in a women's prison in Niantic, Connecticut.

Following his adaptation of Durkheim (1925/1973), Kohlberg thought teachers should speak not only for themselves but also speak so as to represent the spirit, traditions, and future of the community. With this idea, he said, teachers could advocate making a rule or developing a collective norm important to the school and attempt to tie that norm to the welfare and spirit of community or group solidarity.

In 1980, Kohlberg forcefully stated his view of the teacher as advocate, grounding it in Durkheim and contrasting it with the model of teacher as process-facilitator, a popular position taken to guard against indoctrination. He wrote, "Cluster teachers advocate. They advocate for the same reason that they hope the students will advocate. They advocate in the name of making the Cluster School more just or fair and more of a community. They hope, and have found, that if they advocate in this manner, so will many students." (Mosher, 1980, p.42). Kohlberg compared his preferred stance of the Cluster teachers to the positions taken by Durkheim's priest of society or the Israeli Kibbutz group leader, the madrich. He wanted the teachers to advocate for collective responsibility by the entire community believing that the group acting as a whole in creating and carrying out moral decisions is one necessary and strong impetus for the moral growth of individuals within the group. Advocacy with the goal of creating more positive moral group norms is free of indoctrination which rests upon the personal authority of the teacher or group leader.

For instance, in arguing against the use of marijuana, the Cluster teachers did not say that they felt its use was wrong or immoral. They rightly saw that this was a weak argument psychologically since the students could and did easily think of escapist habits indulged by teachers and their parents. Arguing on personal authority is also objectionable philosophically since it does not appeal to reason or use the means of democratic discussion and decision-making. Therefore, the teachers rested their arguments against the use of marijuana on the group value of building community, advocating against any behaviors that rationally and demonstrably harm the community as wrong actions.

By 1985, Kohlberg spelled out his position that advocacy had to be just in order not to be indoctrinative. He wrote:

> Following, for instance, Downey and Kelley's (1978) review of the indoctrination issue in moral education, we may consider indoctrination in terms of (a) the content of what is taught, (b) the method of teaching and (c) the intent of the teacher. In terms of content teaching, Darwinian evolution is not indoctrination because its content is within limits verifiable; teaching Creationism is a content which is not verifiable. Within broad limits I believe principles of justice represent content on which it is possible to reach some rational consensus, a consensus in America expressed by the Declaration of Independence's enumeration of equal rights to life, liberty and opportunity in the pursuit of happiness. (1985, p. 35)

Kohlberg distinguished both the method of teaching justice and the intent of the teacher in advocating for justice from indoctrination. He argued that the moral advocacy of justice, when done by teachers appealing to reasons they themselves accept and not by appealing to their personal or role authority and when done with the conscious intent to respect each student as an automonous moral agent, i.e., with justice, is in no danger of becoming indoctrination.

Philosophically, he said, advocacy, even by teachers as the first among equals, is not indoctrination in a participatory democracy; rather the context of a participatory democracy encourages just advocacy in its means and intent as well as its content.

## The Quick Move from Hypothetical
## Moral Dilemmas to Just Community

Historically, Kohlberg never really fostered or evaluated classroom discussions of real moral dilemmas. Instead, his first attempt at conducting discussions of real-life moral dilemmas occurred in a prison setting but moved very quickly to concerns of institutional or bureaucratic justice—apparent in the breach. In 1971, Kohlberg with Joe Hickey and Peter Scharf (1980) began a hypothetical moral dilemma discussion intervention in the Cheshire Men's Reformatory in Connecticut. Hickey and Scharf in their book, *Toward a Just Correctional System* (1980), describe these interventions and their results in detail, and they recount that discussions turned to real-life problems early in the program, although the discussions began by their posing hypothetical dilemmas to the group. Furthermore, they report that in only a few weeks the inmates began showing more supportive behavior to each other, seeking out the group leaders to relate real-life dilemmas from both prison and street life for discussion, and trusting each other and the guards with knowledge of their personal lives.

Hickey and Scharf reported meaningful but, presumably, not statistically significant change in moral reasoning for the participants of their experimental program. Six of the nineteen inmates in the program moved up one-third of a stage on average, or achieved the Blatt effect, most moving from pre-conventional Stage 2 to conventional Stage 3 reasoning. Some other inmates also changed in terms of their dominant stage of reasoning. No change was found in the reasoning of the comparison group inmates. Although they reported being pleased with the inmates' response to the program, Hickey, Scharf, and Kohlberg were troubled by the still numerous failures and recidivism of paroled inmates. The inmates' bitter stories of failure seemed to be related to both the subjective and objective injustice of the prison as an institution and societal system. Hickey and Scharf tested this assumption by comparing inmates' moral reasoning on the standard moral judgment interview hypothetical dilemmas with their reasoning on more realistic hypothetical dilemmas in the prison context. They found that many inmates reasoned at a lower stage when solving the prison dilemmas than when solving the standard dilemmas. This "situational regression" they felt grew out of a common inmate view of the prison as a place of "war of all against all." These observations led to the decision that "instead of trying to reform the prisoners, we would seek to change the prison. Only then could we hope to affect the inmate's moral reasoning." (1980, p. 58).

## The Ideas of the Just Community Approach

In 1974, when Kohlberg was asked to consult with the Cambridge school system about creating a second "alternative school," he quickly accepted but made one, and only one, clear demand: The program should be a self-governing participatory democracy, with each person, teacher or student, having one vote. His unpaid consultancy would not hinge on acceptance of his theory of moral development or even on the implementing of moral dilemma discussions in the curriculum, so convinced was Kohlberg in the power of open and public discussion of day-to-day dilemmas and their resolution in the form of rules agreed to by all, not only as the means of individual moral development, but more importantly, as the way to change the school as an institution—into a fair community of people who respected and cared for each other. The focus on changing institutions and their social and moral environments, normative structures, and values is the earliest as well as a very clear demonstration of Kohlberg's deep interest in moral action and of his desire to help people act consistently with their best ideas and from their deeply held ideals. Although Kohlberg was not satisfied that he theoretically understood the relation of moral judgment to moral behavior (however, see Kohlberg & Candee, 1984) nor the critical role of the self's definition of herself as a "moral self" as a motivator and support for creating consistency between judgment and action, all of Kohlberg's own motivation and perseverance as a consultant and as an evaluator of the just community approach were toward these ends. He thrilled to a student proudly reporting that she had broken up a fight outside the high school, to his own observations of students using the democratic process to put forth what they believed in, and to reading interviews in which students used the moral terms of justice and responsibility, and good and bad when struggling to articulate their felt self-definitions. In the same volume edited by Gewirtz and Kurtines (1984) in which Kohlberg and Candee articulated a theoretical bridge of a judgment of responsibility between moral judgment and action, we (Higgins, Power, and Kohlberg, 1984) offered examples of such judgments of responsibility from interviews with just community students. Judgments, from our interpretation, that arose from and were supported by the positive moral culture created by the democratic process of building community and prosocial norms. Later in this chapter, my idea of a school moral culture will be presented in some depth.

Kohlberg's idea, then, in creating just community programs was to create conditions that he thought would influence both student reasoning and behavior. These conditions are:

1. Open discussion focussing on fairness, community, and morality.
2. Cognitive conflict stimulated by exposure to different points of view and higher stage reasoning.

3. Participation in rule making and rule enforcement and the public exercise of power and responsibility.
4. The development of community or group solidarity at a high stage.

## Institutional Components of a Just Community

The primary structural components of a just community that are necessary to create a rule-governed participatory democracy are: orientation, core or advisor group, community meeting, agenda committee, and discipline or fairness committee. I will describe these components as they exist in the Scarsdale Alternative School in Scarsdale, New York. This alternative school has been using the just community approach for 20 years.

The two-week *orientation* introduces students to the idea of the school, provides opportunities for them to practice the skills necessary for participation—careful listening, effective speaking, and critically considering and solving issues, and making rules. This is also a time of building mutual trust, creating a basis for allowing students to raise sensitive issues, confront each other, and make difficult decisions in the future.

The major activity during the orientation period is participating in meetings to establish the basic rules of the program. This time ends with meetings to discuss and make rules against the use of drugs and alcohol, especially focused upon creating expectations for behavior at the three-day retreat that marks the end of the orientation period. The openness of these discussions and the public expressions of strong expectations by old students and teachers are often shocking to new members. In contrast, in traditional schools, one aspect of the hidden curriculum is usually an unspoken understanding that feelings and behavior that may lead to confrontations are simply not mentioned; in just community programs, the expression of conflicting views is encouraged with the goal of building new and strong norms held by all community members.

The primary institution of any just community is the *community meeting.* Throughout the academic year they are held weekly lasting about one and one-half to two hours. All members are required to attend. The meetings are chaired by one or two students with a teacher usually serving as friend of the chair. After announcements, the chairperson gives the agenda, which is the outgrowth of discussion and decisions made by the *agenda committee.* This committee meets to gather together issues that have arisen in the community, to clarify and then rank order them for discussion in the community meeting. The agenda committee is made up of 8 to 12 students and one teacher.

During the community meeting, the discussion of each issue is a moral discussion and it's purpose is manyfold—to resolve the issues at hand in a fair and community-building way, to create cognitive conflict in members, to generate empathic role-taking among members, and to consolidate the underlying norms of justice and community that pertain to the issue being discussed.

In preparation for the community meeting, the students meet each week in a smaller meeting called a *core or advisory group*, each of which is made up of 20 to 25 students and one teacher/advisor. These small groups explicitly create an informal atmosphere in which personal issues as well as issues of the school are discussed. The close relationships which develop between the teacher/advisor and the advisory group students provide a basis for the students to gain an understanding of the issues, practice presenting their points of view, and generate proposals for consideration by the whole community at the community meeting.

Since the just community school establishes its rules, it must also provide a structure to enable the community to determine fair consequences for those members who break the rules. This is the major purpose of the *discipline or fairness committee.* When individuals fail to maintain the rules, the question of fair consequences and fair punishments are not theoretical, but involve making decisions about real consequences for one's friends and other community members. Most adolescents are hesitant to accept responsibility for enforcing rules among their personal friends, even those rules that they believe should be enforced and that they have committed themselves to uphold. In these circumstances students oftentimes want the teachers to decide upon and administer the punishment. The conflict for many students begins when they have a choice between ignoring or following up on their knowledge of rule infractions. Observing someone breaking a rule or being told about it raises further conflicts for students.

The existence of the discipline committee in the daily life of the program depersonalizes and demystifies the relation between the processes of rule-making and rule enforcement. Discussing and deciding upon appropriate sanctions for their peers helps the student members of the discipline committee realize the balance between maintaining loyalty to a friend or peer and fulfilling one's responsibility to one's community or group.

In each just community program, the discipline committee's roles and duties develop over time. Because this committee acts for the entire program, it becomes clear that the individuals who comprise it are fulfilling a program-wide responsibility. In this sense, membership becomes viewed as a duty, not just something to be volunteered for out of interest, and over the course of one year all students have a turn on this committee.

Also since the discipline committee represents the whole community, decisions it makes can be appealed to the community for review and reconsideration. In each just community program it has been the case that the duties expand by the second or third year to include hearing cases of interpersonal problems or "personality conflicts" as well as rule infractions. In such cases the committee acts more as a mediation board or group of sympathetic listeners who help the people involved to solve their problems by taking each other's point of view and coming to a genuine understanding of each other's positions.

The last institutional component was historically the first, moral dilemma discussions in the academic curricula. English, social studies, history, biology,

**TABLE 3-1   The Organizational Structure of a Just Community Program**

| Institution | Members | Tasks |
|---|---|---|
| Agenda committee | 10 to 12 students<br>1 teacher | Prioritizes issues for discussion.<br>Puts together the agenda for community meeting. |
| Advisory group | 20 to 25 students<br>1 teacher/advisor | Creates trusting atmosphere for discussing personal issues.<br>Has moral discussion of issues facing the community to generate proposals/solutions. |
| Community meeting | All students and all teachers, as equal members, one person/one vote. | Moral discussion.<br>Resolution of issues through democracy.<br>Rule-making.<br>Appeals of committee decisions. |
| Discipline or fairness committee | 10 to 12 students<br>1 teacher | Hears cases of rule violations, interpersonal conflicts.<br>Gives sanctions.<br>Focuses on role-taking by all in making decisions. |

and even mathematics curricula have been created to present some of the central ideas in these fields as moral dilemmas for use with Socratic questioning and discussion. Whatever academic classes are associated with the just community program use moral dilemma discussion and function within the democratically-made rules of the community. Table 3-1 summarizes the organizational structure of a just community program.

## Developing the Norm of Trust and the Sense of Community: Illustrations of Stealing Incidents in the Cluster School and in the Roosevelt Community School

The Cluster School in Cambridge Rindge and Latin High School met for half of each day as an alternative program with 60 to 80 students in the tenth through twelfth grades, four teachers and a guidance counselor, Elsa Wasserman, who has written on the development of the just community idea and its implementation (Wasserman 1975, 1979). Throughout the life of the Cluster School, 1974 to 1980, Kohlberg and several other consultant/researchers augmented the staff and were members of the Cluster community, including Clark Power and myself.

In the first year of Cluster School there were repetitive episodes of theft. The issue was raised in a community meeting by the staff. Students agreed it should be made a disciplinary offense though they voiced the Stage 2 opinion that if someone was stupid enough to leave something around it was their own fault if it was ripped off. Not happy with leaving the matter there, Kohlberg said, "Maybe somebody can explain why the stealing is going on? Don't people think its wrong and a violation of the community?"

Students were nonresponsive to this appeal. One student said, "I don't think you should worry about that. The fact is that it happened. To worry about why it happened isn't worth it."

Yet Kohlberg persisted, "I think ripping off is not an individual business; it is a community business. It is not a discipline issue as much as some feeling by the community that people have to have some level of trust which is inconsistent with anybody ripping off from anybody else in the community."

Only one student saw his point. The others believed making a rule against stealing was the best that could be done. They voted for the rule and with that the meeting ended. But the problem of stealing persisted. Discussions about the necessity for building trust and mutual care continued throughout the first year.

Cluster members began the second year optimistically. However, in October there was another stealing incident. Nine dollars was taken during a class from someone's purse, and no one would admit to taking the money. A community meeting was convened to discuss the theft. One group of students came to the meeting with a proposal that each member of the school should chip in fifteen cents to make up for the nine dollars stolen from the girl's purse. Phyllis, a girl from this group, offered an elaborate rationale for reimbursing the stolen money. "It's everyone's fault that she don't have no money. It was stolen because people just don't care about the community. (They think) they are all individuals and don't have to be included in the community. Everybody should care that she got her money stolen, (and therefore) we decided to give her money back to her."

Not everyone agreed with the proposal. Bob was worried that if they adopted the proposal, "then anyone can say I lost ten dollars."

Jill asked, "How do you know whether to believe someone who says her money has been stolen?"

Bob and Jill both thought the fault lay not with the community but with the girl for having left her pocketbook unattended. "She gives you a chance to steal it; if you had it in your arms (length), wouldn't you be thinking about stealing it?"

In response, Phyllis reiterated her point. She began with the assumption that Cluster ought to be a community and its members ought to trust one another. If people could not be trusted, it was the group's failure, and they would have to pay for the fault. Some staff members and students both pointed out that the community should put pressure on the guilty party to return the money. The community adopted a compromise. "If the money is not returned anonymously by a certain date, everyone will be assessed fifteen cents." This combined proposal was voted in and in fact proved effective. The person who stole the money eventually admitted it and was given a schedule of repayment. Even though the girl who stole the money only repaid a portion, this incident ended stealing in the Cluster School. A certain level of group trust had been established based on a sense of the group as a true community. There were no thefts in the school in the three years after that meeting. For a discussion of the history of stealing incidents in the Cluster School see Power and Reimer (1978) and Power, Higgins, and Kohlberg (1989).

In 1984, ten years later, Kohlberg and I were in Theodore Roosevelt High School in the Bronx, New York, working with teachers and students to begin another just community program, Roosevelt Community School or RCS. The parent high school is made up primarily of working class African-American and Hispanic-American students and other minorities and middle-class and middle-aged white teachers. Certainly, like other schools it is working to increase its number of minority faculty. At that time it was reported by the *New York Times* as being one of the worst New York City schools in terms of violence, theft, and dropping out. Almost one-third of the students are absent or truant on any given day.

The RCS program meets for only two periods each day, one of the periods is lunch. Such limited time together in a school environment in which classrooms are often locked, instruction is most often by lecturing, and security and discipline are handled by security officers and deans of discipline, the new found freedom to discuss and participate in decision-making was necessarily at first chaotic. The community meetings were full of disruptions and inattention to the issues, with only a few students bent on participating in a democratic process. In the meetings, teachers preaching of the need for order and mutual respect and for the goals of building a community and making fair decisions were scarcely heard and little understood. Building trust, respect, and a process of dialogue had to emerge in small advisory group meetings, "getting to know you" exercises, and an Outward Bound type day excursion involving "trust falls" and cooperative team solutions to outdoor challenges. Accordingly, a day-long trip was planned for the first fall of the program's existence. The students readily accepted the teachers' proposals that no drugs or alcohol should be allowed on the trip and proposed no knives or guns should be allowed either. The discussion of whether to allow radios and walkmans was more heated but the binding group vote was to leave them behind.

The excursion was a great success with no violations of these rules and a good time and a sense of sharing was experienced by all. The next day, however, a teacher told us that twenty dollars had been stolen from her purse by one of the students, and she didn't know who. She was apprehensive about casting gloom on a happy event and confronting students with the problem. Let the discipline or fairness committee investigate the facts of the theft, we suggested; your obligation is to confront the community with this violation of trust and of fairness.

The teacher, Dorothy, announced the problem at the next community meeting and it was agreed that the thief should be given the opportunity to anonymously restitute before the next community meeting. A few students and staff suggested that if it was not returned the whole community should contribute 25 cents to make up the twenty dollars to the teacher. The money was not returned and the next week a discussion about collective restitution was held. Many students said that the teacher had been with them and they should help her out. Some students said it was not their responsibility since they had not attended the trip.

While the students who saw some responsibility by the entire community for restitution believed it should be voluntary, the basic debate between the students was between those who felt there was no responsibility to the victim by those not involved with the theft versus those who felt that all members of the community should care enough to restitute. Some students disagreed with community restitution and saw it as only a concern of the teachers. Other students, like Diane, saw it in the context of student-teacher equality and community solidarity.

The key issue was raised by two students, Michelle and Diana. Michelle said, "I think it would be more fair for the ones on the trip to pay for her, not the ones who didn't go for what they didn't do."

Diana countered, "I don't think that is the point that we are talking. We are talking about showing Dorothy that we care for her; and it is not only the people who went, it is the whole community."

For Diana responsibility comes not from being at fault but as responsibility to express concern on behalf of the entire community. However, she argued for voluntary restitution as the best way since she felt it to be the most genuine expression of caring. She said, "I think it should be voluntary because I don't want nobody to feel that they have to do it, that they are forced into it. I just want everybody if they want to; they should out of their heart. So I think it should be voluntary."

The teacher who was chairing the meeting (students began to chair in the second semester) responded, "Ok, Diana gave us a very good point about the voluntary part. Does anybody want to speak as to why it should be compulsory?"

Another articulate student leader like Diana, Nelson, supported her point. He said, "You are forcing everyone to pay. You shouldn't force them. You see the reason we pay her back is because we feel sorry. And not probably everybody feels sorry for her. You know, I am not saying no, but probably not everybody feels sorry. Right? So the people who do feel sorry for her are the ones who want to pay, pay. You can't make a person pay."

Diana took an idealistic view that everyone should voluntarily care and contribute, Nelson took the view that it is totally up to the individual whether they care or want to contribute, and would violate their rights to make them contribute. Harriett, a third student, was both pragmatic and concerned about fairness. She raised the point that if everyone contributed, the teacher, Dorothy, would get too much money. She stated, "I think it should be voluntary because if it is compulsory then everyone has to give and she is going to get too much money. No, she is going to get much more and then it is going to end up that half of us is going to pay her twenty dollars and then we are going to have a whole other discussion saying this is not fair because all of us had to pay (were supposed to pay, and only half will have paid)."

A vote was taken that payment should be voluntary. However, then Harriett and Nelson expressed skepticism that those who raised their hands for voluntary restitution would not in fact contribute money, creating yet another unfair situation. Harriett said, "The people who voted voluntary, all those people who raised their hands are not going to pay. Maybe she won't get back all of her money, but maybe she can get back some of it."

Nelson added, "The people who voted, should pay. But they are going to have garbage (because) the other people who voted that we should have voluntary, they are not going to back up what they talk. What are you going to do? No, that is not right."

Diana tried to clarify her point, even though it is voluntary everyone should use the golden rule, see it from Dorothy's position, and contribute. She said, "Put yourself in Dorothy's position. Do you think that everybody who votes should see how it feels if you were the person that they took the money away from. If it was you who were stolen from, how would you feel?"

Harriett then spoke for the opposition to collective restitution of any sort and questioned Diana's logic. If Harriett put herself in Dorothy's place, she wouldn't be for collective restitution because it was Dorothy's individual responsibility for letting her money be stolen. Harriett argued, "Diana is kind of right and kind of wrong. But if I had twenty dollars stolen from me, I wouldn't feel that you as a community have to give my money back because I lost it. It was my responsibility. Something happens to me, and I would come in and say I want my money back? I think everyone has blown this out of proportion."

Harriett then raised yet another issue of trust and suggested that this was the teachers' special concern for another teacher. She challenged, "If it were a student it happened to they wouldn't be making such a big fuss about."

This challenge about concern for students being equal to the concern shown for teachers by teachers was reiterated by a few other students. Teachers gave assurances that their concern for students would be greater due to the proportionally greater loss suffered by a student. Whether this argument was convincing was not apparent, but what was convincing about the layers of argument and eventual agreement to collectively voluntarily restitute was that real mistrust among community members existed even though the discussion revealed that the ideals of trust and caring for one another were felt by some of the students.

The meeting ended with a paper bag being passed around the circle and people putting in money. The good-natured teasing about people putting their hands in to take out money as well as put it in turned to real anxiety when a teacher, Al, put the bag full of money in the middle of the circle and left it unattended. As he raised a new topic for discussion, more and more students became agitated, whispering to each other and giggling. After a few minutes, one student leaped from his chair, grabbed the bag and gave it to the teacher, Al, saying that he shouldn't tempt people and he shouldn't trust them either. Al then took the floor and delivered the punchline of the day. He pointed to the students sitting on their books and notebooks with their coats on, and to girls clutching their purses. He said, "Look at all of you, you're hot and uncomfortable. Wouldn't it be nice if we all trusted each other enough that we could relax when we are together here and trust each other not to steal our stuff. What would it take for us to really begin to trust people here? I wonder if we can ever get it that way? I would certainly feel better and I think we would all feel better about ourselves as well as about each other, too."

A short time later one student brought another to the discipline or fairness committee on the suspicion of stealing from her. Discussion in the committee did not lead to any clear conclusion regarding guilt and, therefore, no restitution plan.

By the spring accusations of stealing within the community were absent and both teachers and students left their belongings freely about the community and classroom during the RCS periods. Teacher support and democratic discussion about community ideals of trust and collective responsibility helped to build a shared norm of respect for individual property rights and a moral climate in which stealing became an unacceptable behavior.

It seems clear from these examples that the practice of democratic governance in a community setting creates the first three conditions outlined above— open discussion focused on moral issues, cognitive conflict, and active participation in making decisions that affect each person and the group. The last condition, development of a high-stage community, is less obvious and more controversial. The elaboration of this claim has been our research on the development of a moral culture or moral atmosphere in a program or school. Sharing the teachers' concerns about students' behavior and the content of the rules and decisions that are made, we have hypothesized that the norms or expectations held by group members have a strong influence on behavior and that democratic open discussion was a means to create more positive and higher stage norms than exist in schools where moral education is only the hidden curriculum.

In the stealing incidents from both schools we assessed whether a norm of trust had been established and whether the group was valued as a community, for its own sake, as a community "sui generis." In the case of the Cluster School, we viewed the change as due to the development of the community rather than to the moral reasoning development of individual students. In both meetings some students reasoned at Stage 2 and others primarily at Stage 3. The important difference that ended stealing in the Cluster School was the student Phyllis' argument. She spoke for the ideals of the community as a community member, rather than only giving her own opinions. She assumed that the Cluster School as a whole desired to be a community in which caring and trust were felt and where students felt obligated as community members to live up to those expectations. She used these expectations to argue against stealing and for collective restitution. Basing her argument on the clearly shared ideas that the students wanted Cluster to be a community gave force to her exhortation that in order to be a community the students had to trust and be responsible to each other and to the community.

Analyzing these meetings, we saw that in the first year, the students did not value the Cluster School as a community for its own sake (low valuing of the sense of community) and that they had no shared expectations to guide their behavior or to give real meaning to the rule against stealing (no collective norms of trust or respect for individual property rights). In the second year, the sense of group solidarity had become a shared ideal and felt desire, mostly understood in Stage 3/4 terms. This, combined with the realization that the rule against stealing was ineffective, created the beginning of genuinely shared expectations to trust and be responsible for each other, norms understood also as Stage 3/4 ideas. These norms formed the basis for a change in behavior and eliminated stealing as a problem for the Cluster School and its members.

Although we have not done a formal analysis as yet of the development of the sense of community and collective norms in RCS over its three-year history, I think it is evident that in its first year it looked somewhat similar to the Cluster School in its first year.

When Diana made her eloquent argument for voluntary collective restitution and her plea that everyone should take the teacher's perspective, she was speaking as a community member for the ideal of community that she, as an individual, had and that she thought others should have. She sounded very much like Kohlberg in year one of the Cluster School. Her pleas, like his, however, seemed to be understood by only a few.

Although Nelson supported voluntary restitution, after the vote was taken he raised a point of self-consistency and justice. He thought that those who voted for restitution ought to act on their vote. His concern for consistency between one's judgment and behavior is ours as well. Moreover, we believe that such public discussions which encourage students like Nelson to articulate their ideas of fairness and self-consistency also, then, support acting in ways consistent with their judgment of what is fair and caring.

Harriett's assumption that all the people who voted for restitution would not pay shows she didn't believe there was a real sense of community nor any shared expectations to guide behavior. When Diana responded urging Golden Rule role-taking by Harriett and others of the teachers' position, Harriett saw her point but countered with a strong statement of individual responsibility. Thus, she revealed that she, and many others, did not share Diana's ideal that RCS should be or could be a caring community.

The teacher, Al, ended the meeting dramatically confronting the students with the effect that not being able to trust had on their daily lives. He offered the seemingly utopian notion that if they all could trust, they would feel better about themselves and each other. Al's clear advocacy for the community to develop a collective norm of trust and to work to create a relaxed atmosphere is an example of teacher advocacy at its best. He advocated for a just community through reasoning and Socratic questioning, respectful of the students' rights and needs to think through the issue themselves. Al's and Diana's advocacy, combined with similar efforts by other teachers and students, bore fruit. I can report that there have been no incidents of stealing within the RCS program since that time.

An analysis of this meeting would show that most students were reasoning between Stages 2 and 3, with the notable exception of Diana's Stage 3/4 use of the Golden Rule to argue that the whole community should care for one of its members. Her voice carried some moral weight because she spoke for the group urging them to become a high-stage community with shared expectations or norms. We would say that in this meeting most students still valued the group instrumentally, as a place to get an education, and felt little sense of obligation or responsibility to it or the other members. Diana valued it intrinsically, as a community "sui generis," and expected others to feel obligated to restitute to the teacher as a member, both for her personal well-being and for the well-being of the community.

We think that actually resolving a moral problem like this one through discussion, voting, and acting is a powerful way of doing moral education, of changing schools, and of fostering the full development of students.

## *The Idea of Moral Culture*

Reflecting on the illustrations just given, explanations can be given of moral culture, norms or normative expectations, and sense of community. Ethnographers experience culture as a shared, supraindividual phenomenon representing a consensus on a variety of meanings among members of an interacting community. Generally the concept of culture is used to refer to large social system, such as societies or ethnic groups. In our work (see Power, Higgins, & Kohlberg, 1989) we use the idea of culture to refer to a specific social institution, the school. We acknowledge the observation of several critics (Enright, Lapsley, & Levy, 1983; Minuchin & Shapiro, 1981) that our attempts to create and study a moral culture shared by a specific group of students and teachers are influenced and limited by larger cultures representing ethnic groups, the neighborhood, and U.S. society. Even so, we see schools as having cultures which can often be determining influences upon students' thinking and behavior. Our research hypotheses rest on this observation.

In defining the culture of a school or group within a school, we first distinguish between moral and non-moral aspects, highlighting moral aspects as found in the formalist tradition of moral philosophy from Kant to Rawls. Within that tradition the moral is defined in terms of categorical principles that regulate social interactions. These principles are universalizable prescriptions, supported by reasoned argument.

In the definition and study of school climate, a focus upon the specifically moral has not been done (see Anderson, 1982; Epstein, 1981). Our focus upon the moral culture allows us to distinguish the different aspects of a school climate or culture; for instance, from prudential concerns such as preparing for a job or college which are other important aspects of any school culture. Social conventions are other non-moral aspects of a school culture which regulate social interactions but are not moral since they are not understood to be prescriptive nor universally applicable even within a specific school culture.

We looked to Durkheim's (1925/1973) three goals of education as the basis of the major units in our analysis of the moral culture of a high school. The collective moral norm and moral element of institutional valuing of community are linked to two of Durkheim's goals: the development of discipline and a feeling of attachment to the group. For Durkheim moral education involves practices designed to foster respect for group norms and to build a strong sense of belonging to the group. Kohlberg named his approach to moral education the just community approach because he, like Durkheim, wanted to combine a concern for "the right" with an equally strong concern for "the good." Both attempted to design educational programs in which the ideal of the collective or group life was one in which members autonomously accepted limits upon their behavior to moral demands and choices understood as necessary for a desirable social existence. Durkheim's third goal of moral education, autonomy, corresponds most closely to our analysis of the stage of norms and values. The willingness to do one's moral duty or meet the moral demands of one's social group is autonomous if encouraged by reason rather than any external force or authority. A moral education program that promotes this element of rational autonomy in children must explain the reasons behind group rules and social obligations. Although the just community approach uses democracy as the means for moral education, it also stresses group solidarity leaving it vulnerable to the forces of conformity and heteronomy. Therefore, we use Kohlberg's moral stages as indices of adequacy in judging the extent to which a moral education program meets Durkheim's third goal of moral education, developing autonomy. We evaluate the justifications given by students and teachers when they propose or defend collective norms or the valuing of the school as a community according to Kohlberg's moral stage scheme. Numerous cases of the immoral use of the collectivist model by various sects and totalitarian governments make the inclusion of an index which assesses group norms and values according to explicit criteria for moral rationality necessary.

## Highlights from the Moral Culture Analyses of Three Schools in Cambridge, Brookline, and Scarsdale

These results are from a four-year study of three democratically run alternative programs and their comparison groups of students in the larger parent high schools in Cambridge and Brookline, Massachusetts and Scarsdale, New York.

The Cambridge Cluster School and the Scarsdale Alternative School followed Kohlberg's just community ideas while the Brookline School-Within-A-School stressed procedural democracy and spontaneous feelings of community. The students in the three comparison groups represented the diversity of students in the mainstream of each high school.

One of the most striking results is that the moral cultures of the three parent high schools were the same even though the schools differ dramatically in terms of the demographic characteristics of the students, their social and geographical locations, their academic reputations, and the number of students who aspire to and go on to higher education. The other measures of school climate reviewed by Anderson (1982) and briefly mentioned earlier would measure these differences and report the climate of the three high schools as being quite different from each other. Why do we consider it a strength that our measures of moral culture and its norms do not discriminate among these parent schools? We think, that despite real differences, these three parent schools share common characteristics that press on students and teachers and create the same hidden curriculum of authoritarian, individualistic, self-protectionist, and instrumental norms with little valuing of a sense of community or group relations. In other words, that what is moral about them is left to the haphazard interplay of a bureaucratic structure with isolated and often anomic students and teachers, and that what is created is not a moral culture, and that what we assessed was the real lack of any explicitly shared or positive moral culture at all.

The second finding that follows from the first is the effect of the moral culture or lack of it on the development of students' moral reasoning and behavior. In this study we looked at the development over one to three years of the moral reasoning of students and only anecdotally can report on changes in student behavior. Although overall the students in the democratic programs showed significantly more moral reasoning growth than the comparison students, for the students in the two just community programs the moral culture seemed to function as the leading edge in the development of their moral reasoning. Some of these students showed signs of higher stage thinking first when solving school-related dilemmas and later on the hypothetical dilemmas of the moral judgment interview. In contrast, the comparison students showed growth on neither measure over the course of the study. Since normal moral reasoning development seems to advance about one-half stage every three years (Colby & Kohlberg, 1987), the lack of a moral culture in the large high schools actually seemed to be a drag on the development of their students, locking them into preconventional or early conventional thinking throughout their high school tenure.

The third important finding from this research which looks at the difference between the moral culture of the group and the moral reasoning of the individuals that are members of the group invoked for us the idea of pluralistic ignorance. Pluralistic ignorance, that is, ignorance of what others in the same group think and feel, occurs when moral education is only the hidden curriculum. We found that the comparison students, as individuals, reasoned at the same stages as their peers in the just community programs on the standard moral judgment interview. They also reported more prosocial intentions and behavior when describing themselves than when describing their peers or their ideas of the operative norms governing their peers' behavior. They characterized the student life of the school and the authority of the teachers as governed by low-stage, primarily preconventional, considerations rife with self-protection, selfishness, and rigidity. That they each characterized themselves so differently means that the potential for the group to manifest higher stage considerations, norms and values is inherent but latent in these schools. The democratic school students, on the other hand, used more consistent moral reasoning when describing their own and their peers' intentions and beliefs. They also showed greater agreement in describing the content of the valued norms and ideas of community as well as in ascribing higher stage rationales for their norms and sense of group solidarity.

The fourth and last critical finding is that the idea of responsibility for others and a shared sense of being tied together in a common group seem to promote not only individual moral reasoning development but also a strong and high-stage moral culture. These results indicate that students expect themselves and others to behave in ways consistent with their best ideas about what is moral when they are in groups they value which have publically shared prosocial norms. We see a positive moral culture as being a boost to moral behavior and as being a context in which students are challenged to think about their own identity in moral terms.

## Comments of the Bronx Students about the Effects of the Just Community

The initial results from the Bronx study seem to substantiate the findings reported above. When the Bronx just community students were asked what they got from the RCS program, they reported that the just community program helped them to take the role of others, and to feel more effective and empowered.

In the first year in Theodore Roosevelt High School, the Roosevelt Community School (RCS) students who emerged as leaders were those who most quickly developed and used the abilities to understand the perspective of others in the group and to integrate those perspectives into their own positions and discussions of the issues at hand. An extended discussion of just community and role-taking can be found in Higgins, 1989. In this section I will use some of the same examples of both leaders and followers to demonstrate the importance of their learning to take the perspectives of others—the importance for the growth of the community as well as for themselves as individuals. Nelson, a Hispanic young man born in Honduras, began the program saying what he wanted from it was "Credit and a couple of girlfriends; to get 'popular.'" Nelson became popular within the RCS and the larger high school. He also learned to take the perspective of others and to listen to others, outcomes he did not anticipate and tasks he found difficult for a time. When interviewed in the spring of the first year, he described a situation in which he became aware of this new way of relating to people.

He said, "I felt that Ruble was trying to upstage me, calling me out of order and taking me to the Discipline Committee. But what was I complaining about? I wanted this to happen, to have other people come out of their shells. I think I understand now that he is not trying to upstage me, he just cares and is trying to make RCS work. But I've been a little jealous and now I know RCS doesn't revolve around me."

For Nelson, the just community program was an experience that promoted both moral growth and self-understanding. When he was asked why he chose to run for the presidency of the high school student organization, he first spoke of his political ambitions and then of the role the RCS program had played in his decision to run for office. He began by saying he wanted the practice:

> In order to run for politics. Some of my teachers called me a used car salesman. . . . I'm always talking ever since I can remember. I used to be talking out in the classes. I used to get in trouble and all that. The teachers said I didn't have anything to say and probably I didn't have then, but now I have something to say. . . . In RCS I would make my mind work and stop talking. Six months ago some of my views changed, I changed my mind in the RCS. Now I listen to other people's thoughts. I take some of this and believe some of that and put it together. It's changed my thoughts. I'm listening more to people now.

Nelson is describing the process of change that occurs through democratic discussion: stating an idea, listening to others agree or disagree with it, taking others' perspectives and considering their ideas, modifying one's own, restating it, and listening again. In discussions of issues of fairness and community, strategies of double-talk, asking off-target questions, and not thinking and tuning out drop off dramatically with the students' growing sense that they, with the teachers, must build a positive normative community in order to grow as a group. For Nelson and others building a school community meant that they had to begin to seriously consider the views of others. This is a critical component of moral education. Active perspective-taking and active consideration of others' views is moral role-taking. These actions are the essence of respect, of acting out of a concern for fairness and care which enables one to make connections with the thoughts, beliefs, and feelings of others in the community.

However, the process of moral education is not the same for all students. Even though they share common experiences and sit in the same democratic community meetings, whether and how they become active participants differ. Here we want to illustrate two kinds of students who describe themselves as quiet. Our observations and the work of other researchers (e.g., Eakins &

Eakins, 1978; Tittle, 1986) suggest these quiet students are more apt to be girls than boys. For these students the process of moral education is almost the reverse of what I have illustrated with Nelson's responses. These girls articulate movement from feeling like outsiders, to becoming interested, and then deciding that they have some responsibility to the community for speaking up at meetings and offering their opinions, and finally they begin to participate actively.

Maria, also a Hispanic student, said her essential quality is her shyness. She offered a behavioral analysis of changes that can be attributed to membership in the RCS program. When asked if she is different in RCS than the way she is in the regular high school, she said:

> I am very quiet (in RCS). I won't say anything. I listen. I listen to what everyone is saying, but I don't give my opinion. The reason I am not saying anything is I won't. I like to hear what other people are saying. And I want to think about that. I like to hear the different views, you know, why you think we should do something that way. I like to hear them out. . . . You should pay attention to what is going on so you won't be a total blank. And you have your own feelings, like if afterwards, if someone asks you what is your opinion on the subject, you know, you have an opinion. You don't lay there like a lump on a log. . . . I don't talk in the big meetings but I talk in the advisory group.

Not only is Maria genuinely interested in listening to others, she also considers that to be a responsibility of a good member of the RCS. However, the rowdy enthusiasm of the large community meetings kept her from actively contributing throughout the entire first year of the program. In the next fall, Maria volunteered to speak before a new just community program with 80 ninth-grade potential drop outs in her own high school. Maria chose to speak on overcoming shyness.

She said, "When I joined RCS we talked about many subjects I knew a lot about. I wish I had the courage then that I have now to raise my hand and express myself, but I sat and watched. I began to realize that if you chair the core group meetings it becomes easier to express your opinion in a large community meeting, such as yours. Don't be afraid to speak or express your opinion; what you say no one else may have thought of, you never know; your opinion may be just what the community is looking for."

Maria's sense of responsibility to the RCS community, supplemented by opportunities to practice in a small group in which she knew everyone, convinced her that being responsible meant adding her unique viewpoint to the discussion, and in fact, that this may be to the benefit of the community. Active participation fostered the transformation from fear of being in a spotlight to a desire to be a contributing member of an ongoing discussion.

Doris, an African-American young woman, described herself as moody. She felt, and was, somewhat alienated from other students and from the school. She said, "I'm just unpersonable, I don't like to communicate with people."

The basis for Doris' view of herself as private and closed is related to her desire to be respected and her perception that she was not. In her interview she defined morality as respect; she said, "I seldom give respect because I don't ever get respect. It all depends on the person I'm talking to. If I'm talking to a person that I get the distinct impression that he doesn't respect females, then I'm not going to respect him. But if I'm talking to a person who respects me, then, hey."

At an early meeting of a new just community program in Theodore Roosevelt High School, some RCS students spoke describing the ideas behind a just community, the organizational structures and committees, and their own personal feelings about the program. The new students paid attention to the clearly experienced and knowledgeable RCS members. However, when a young woman new to the RCS program began speaking, the community meeting erupted in laughter and private conversations among the students, primarily commenting on her speaking too softly and not having anything to say. Diana, an articulate and very strong RCS leader, took over the floor and chastised the new group using Golden Rule role-taking of the most forceful sort.

Diana addressed the community: "Ok, we have somebody who is new to the RCS, who wanted to express herself to you because she is new like you. If you have any respect for anybody you should have respect for her because she is new like you. Every old member got good respect but the new one, like you, didn't get anything. I can see you are a good group, really, I can see it. We were wild when we started. We used to have side conversations. But we got together, we're strong now, we won now. Now everybody defends everybody else. When we disagree with someone there are no fights. And if you don't agree with someone, you don't beat them up, you don't say, 'well, you're stupid.' You only say, 'I don't agree with you at all,' and that's it. You know."

Our understanding of how people develop a sense of themselves as moral and how that moral identity guides and determines their behavior is just beginning. This work was Lawrence Kohlberg's last interest and challenge. It remains our challenge today.

## *Endnotes*

1.  Although Kohlberg's colleagues were many over the course of his life, some centrally involved in education have been Ralph Mosher, Edwin Fenton, Clark Power, Elsa Wasserman, Joseph Reimer, Bill Jennings, Marvin Berkowitz, Judith Codding, Robert Kenny, Robert Howard, Andrew Garrod, and myself, as well as scores of teachers, administrators, and students.

2.  The development of the idea of the just community approach to moral education and the research to better understand the moral climate of schools has been generously supported by the W. T. Grant Foundation with a multi-year grant to the late Professor Lawrence Kohlberg and to this author to evaluate the effects of the just community programs in the Bronx, New York. Earlier projects discussed in this chapter were supported by grants from the Danforth Foundation, the Ford Foundation, the Stone Foundation, and the Kennedy Foundation.

# References

Anderson, C. S. (1982). The search for school climate: A review of the literature. *Review of Educational Research, 52,* 368-420.

Blatt, M. (1969). The effects of classroom moral discussion upon children's levels of moral thought. Unpublished doctoral dissertation, University of Chicago.

Blatt, M. and Kohlberg, L. (1975). The effects of classroom moral discussion upon children's moral judgment. *Journal of Moral Education, 4,* 129-161.

Codding, J. and Arenella, A. (1981). Supporting moral development with a curriculum of ethical decision making. *Moral Education Forum, 6,* 14-23.

Colby, A., Kohlberg, L., Speicher, B., Hewer, A., Candee, D., Gibbs, J., and Power, C. (1987). *The Measurement of Moral Judgment, Volumes I and II.* New York: Cambridge University Press.

Dewey, J. (1944). *Democracy and education.* New York: Macmillan, Free Press. (Originally published 1916.)

Diessner, R. (1988). A preliminary inquiry regarding the reliability and validity of an evaluation of the adolescent moral self. Unpublished Ed.D. dissertation, Harvard University.

Durkheim, E. (1925/1973). *Moral Education: A Study in the Theory and Application of the Sociology of Education.* New York: Free Press.

Eakins, B. and Eakins, R. (1978). *Sex Differences in Human Communication.* Boston: Houghton Mifflin.

Enright, R., Lapsley, D. and Levy, V. (1983). Moral Education Strategies. In M. Pressley and J. Levin (Eds.) *Cognitive Strategy Research: Educational Applications.* New York: Springer-Verlag.

Epstein, J. (1981). Secondary school environments and student outcomes: A review and annotated bibliography. *Center for Social Organization of Schools,* 315.

Erikson, E. (1968). *Identity: Youth and Crisis.* New York: W. W. Norton.

Gewirtz, J. and Kurtines, W. (Eds.) (1984). *Morality, moral development, and moral behavior: Basic issues in theory and research.* New York: Wiley-Interscience.

Hartshorne, H. and May, M. A. (1928-30). *Studies in the nature of character. Vol. 1: Studies in deceit. Vol. 2: Studies in self-control. Vol. 3: Studies in the organization of character.* New York: Macmillan.

Havighurst, R. J. and Taba, H. (1949). *Adolescent character and personality.* New York: Wiley.

Hickey, J. and Scharf, P. (1980). *Toward a Just Correctional System.* San Francisco: Jossey-Bass.

Higgins, A. (1980). Research and measurement issues in moral education interventions. In R. Mosher (Ed.) *Moral Education: A First Generation of Research and Development.* New York: Praeger.

Higgins, A. (1987). A feminist perspective on moral education. *Journal of Moral Education, 16,* 3, 240-248.

Higgins, A. (1989). The just community educational program: The development of moral role-taking as the expression of justice and care. In M. M. Brabeck (Ed.). *Who cares: Theory, research, and educational implications of the ethic of care.* New York: Praeger.

Higgins, A. and Kohlberg, L. (1986). Year I Report to the W.T. Grant Foundation: An Evaluation of the Effects of High School Governance on Students' Moral Judgment and Action. Center for Moral Development and Education, Harvard University.

Higgins, A., Power, C., and Kohlberg, L. (1984). The relationship of moral judgment to judgments of responsibility. In J. Gewirtz and W. Kurtines (Eds.). *Morality, Moral Development, and Moral Behavior: Basic Issues in Theory and Research.* New York: Wiley-Interscience.

Jackson, P.W. (1968). *Life in the Classroom.* New York: Holt, Reinhart and Winston.

Kohlberg, L. (1970). The moral atmosphere of the school. In N. Overley (Ed.). *The Unstudied Curriculum.* Washington, D.C.: Association for Supervision and Curriculum Development.

Kohlberg, L. (1971). Indoctrination versus relativity in value education. *Zygon., 6,* 285-310.

Kohlberg, L. (1978). Preface to P. Scharf (Ed.). *Readings in Moral Education.* Minneapolis: Winston Press.

Kohlberg, L.(1980). High school democracy and educating for a just society. In R. Mosher (Ed.). *Moral Education: A First Generation of Research and Development.* New York: Praeger.

Kohlberg, L. (1981). *Essays on Moral Development. Volume I: The Philosophy of Moral Development.* San Francisco: Harper and Row.

Kohlberg, L. (1984). *Essays on Moral Development. Volume II: The Psychology of Moral Development.* San Francisco: Harper and Row.

Kohlberg, L. (1985). A just community approach to moral education in theory and practice. In M. Berkowitz and F. Ozer (Eds.). *Moral Education: Theory and Practice.* Hillsdale, New Jersey: Lawrence Erlbaum.

Kohlberg, L. and Candee, D. (1984). The relation of moral judgment to moral action. In J. Gewirtz and W. Kurtines (Eds.). *Morality, Moral Development, and Moral Behavior.* New York: Wiley-Interscience.

Kohlberg, L. and Mayer, R. (1972). Development as the aim of education. *Harvard Educational Review, 42,* 449-496.

Kohlberg, L., Hickey, J., and Scharf, P. (1980). The justice structure of the prison: A theory and intervention. *Prison Journal, 51,* 3-14.

Leming, J. S. (1976). An exploratory inquiry into the multifactor theory of moral behavior. *Journal of Moral Education, 5,2,* 179-188.

Leming, J. S. (1981). Curriculum effectiveness in moral/values education: A review of the research. *Journal of Moral Education, 10,* 147-164.

Lockwood, A.L. and Harris, D.E. (1985). *Reasoning with Democratic Values: Ethical Problems in United States History.* New York: Teachers College Press.

Minuchin, P. and Shapiro, E. (1981). The school as the context for social development. In P. Mussen (Ed.) *Handbook of Child Psychology,*

*Fourth Edition.* New York: Wiley.

Mosher, R. (1980). *Moral Education: A First Generation of Research and Development.* New York: Praeger.

Mosher, R. and Sullivan, P. (1976). A curriculum in moral education for adolescents. In D. Purpel and K. Ryan (Eds.). *Moral Education: It Goes with the Territory.* Berkeley: McCutchan.

Power, C. (1979). The moral atmosphere of a just community high school: A four year longitudinal study. Unpublished Ed.D. dissertation, Harvard University.

Power, C. and Reimer, J. (1978). Moral atmosphere: An educational bridge between moral judgment and moral action. In W. Damon (Ed.). *New Directions for Child Development: Moral Development, Volume 2.* San Francisco: Jossey-Bass.

Power, F. C., Higgins, A., and Kohlberg, L. (1989). *Lawrence Kohlberg's Approach to Moral Education: A Study of Three Democratic High Schools.* New York: Columbia University Press.

Snarey, J. (1985). Cross-cultural universality of social-moral development: A critical review of Kohlbergian research. *Psychological Bulletin, 97,* 202-232.

Tittle, C. K. (1986). Gender research and education. *American Psychologist, 41,* 1161-1168.

Walker, L. J. (1983). Sex differences in the development of moral reasoning: A critical review. *Child Development, 54,* 1103-1141.

Walker, L. J., DeVries, B., and Bichard, S. L. (1984). The hierarchical nature of stages of moral development. *Developmental Psychology, 20,* 960-966.

Wasserman, E. (1975). Implementing Kohlberg's "Just Community" in an alternative high school. *Social Education, 40,* 203-207.

Wasserman, E. (1979). The Fairness Committee: A Manual for Students and Teachers—A Community Approach to Grievances. Unpublished manuscript, Center for Moral Development and Education, Harvard University.

# Chapter 4

# Sexism in Kohlberg's Moral Psychology?

*LAWRENCE J. WALKER*
*University of British Columbia*

**Abstract**

This chapter provides an overview of theory and research regarding the issue of sexism in moral psychology and Kohlberg's theory of moral development in particular. The focus of the issue has been on moral reasoning because it is considered basic to moral functioning. At the center of the contemporary controversy regarding sex differences and sex bias have been the theories of Gilligan and Kohlberg. It has been claimed that there are sex-related moral orientations and that dominant theories of moral psychology have maligned females' mode of thinking. Conceptual issues regarding both theoretical perspectives are discussed and potential sources of sex bias noted. The research evidence regarding the claims about morality and the sexes are reviewed, both in terms of moral orientations and moral stages; and it is concluded that such claims, in general, cannot be substantiated.

This chapter will provide an overview of theory and research regarding the issue of sexism in moral psychology in general and Kohlberg's theory of moral development in particular. Rarely in the history of psychology has an issue been so controversial and so difficult to disentangle. Not only does it entail the empirical questions of whether or not there are sex differences in moral development and what form they might take, but this issue, of necessity, also involves questions regarding conceptions of morality and philosophy of science. The empirical findings regarding sex differences in moral development will be of minimal interest if the moral domain has been inadequately characterized and if methods of investigation are of questionable validity. Not incidentally, discussions regarding this issue have occurred in the context of contemporary feminism. It is not surprising that the issue has been contentious—not only within psychology, the other social sciences, and the humanities, but also outside of academia, in broader society—and rightly so! Claims and allegations regarding the sexes and morality have been widely voiced. Given that morality is so central to our self-definition (most people regard themselves as being moral), group comparisons of any kind on such an obviously value-laden dimension ought to be examined with extraordinary caution and scrutiny. It is hoped that a careful review of relevant psychological theories and research may contribute in a positive way to the dialogue on this issue.

## Theory

Morality is a fundamental and pervasive aspect of human functioning since it refers to one's basic goals and way of life; but it has been a formidable concept for psychology to handle. A fundamental issue for moral psychology is the definition of morality on which to base theory and research. In my view, morality refers to voluntary actions that (at least potentially) have social or interpersonal implications and that are governed by some intrapsychic mechanism. Morality is a multifaceted phenomenon which, of necessity, entails the interplay of behavior, thought, and emotion.

Unfortunately, theorists have regarded different aspects of human functioning as central to morality: the identification-internalization approach has emphasized emotion, the social-learning approach has emphasized behavior, and the cognitive-developmental approach has emphasized cognition. These differing emphases have created an artificial trichotomy (emotion, behavior, thought) that implies that these are independent aspects of moral functioning when indeed they are necessarily interdependent and interactive. In some sense, the concept of morality is trivialized when psychological research examines each aspect in isolation. Nevertheless, an examination of research in moral psychology over the last several decades reveals that most work has focused on the development of moral thought, and certainly the controversy regarding sex differences has primarily concerned this aspect of moral functioning. If moral behaviors are considered to be voluntary ones—governed by some intrapsychic mechanism—then an initial focus on moral reasoning seems warranted. Blasi (1984) argued that "reason is of the essence of morality and cannot be eliminated without destroying the moral phenomenon itself" (p. 134). Even Haan, a critic of the cognitive bias in contemporary moral psychology, acknowledged that "morality is constituted, considered, and decided in the minds of people. . . . Morality is based on reason" (Haan, Aerts, & Cooper, 1985, p. 54).

## Historical Perspectives

The current controversy regarding sex differences in moral reasoning revolves around the work of two contemporary theorists: Carol Gilligan (1982a) and Lawrence Kohlberg (1981, 1984). Despite the recent flurry of interest, it should be recalled that the issue is actually a very old one. Historically, women and men have often been accorded and claimed different moral qualities (and, not infrequently, different moral worth). The predominance of patriarchal societies is illustrative of the denial to women of *institutional* positions of moral leadership. Female leaders remain somewhat of a novelty in religious, political, judicial, management, academic, and other spheres (although admittedly these are rather questionable proxies for *moral* leadership!). Moral philosophers over the ages (e.g., Philo, Augustine, Aquinas, Descartes, Kant, Rousseau, Hegel) have perpetrated the notion that males have a more rational sense of morality and females, a more emotive one (see Lloyd's, 1983, review). Social scientists have sometimes also endorsed the view that the sexes differ in moral maturity.  Freud provides the most notorious example: "For women the level of what is ethically normal is different from what it is in men. . . . They show less sense of justice than men, . . . are less ready to submit to the great necessities of life, . . . [and] are more often influenced in their judgment by feelings of affection and hostility" (1927, pp. 141-142). Freud attributed females' lack of moral maturity to deficiencies in same-sex parental identification and consequent superego formation. In contradistinction to these claims of male moral superiority, the women's suffragist movement and the women's temperance movement earlier in this century were explicit attempts to impart females' stricter moral standards into public life. Similarly illustrative are contemporary feminists' positions on various social issues such as abortion, capital punishment, pornography, nuclear disarmament, and domestic violence. Clearly, both sexes have been guilty of expressing chauvinistic attitudes regarding morality. Thus, there is a significant historical context to the recently revived issue of sexism in moral psychology.

As noted earlier, the two contemporary theories that have been at the center of this debate are those of Gilligan and Kohlberg. The theoretical perspectives of each approach will be discussed in turn.

## Gilligan's Theory of Moral Orientations

Gilligan (1982a, 1986b, 1986c, 1987; Gilligan, Lyons, & Hanmer, 1990; Gilligan, Ward, & Taylor, 1988; Gilligan & Wiggins, 1987; also see Brown, Tappan, & Gilligan, Chapter 12, this volume) has propounded two separable claims: first, that there are two sex-related orientations for moral decision-making (justice/rights vs. care/response); and second, that influential theories of human development (e.g., Erikson, Freud, Kohlberg, Levinson, McClelland, and Piaget) have been insensitive to females' "different voice" on morality and have caricatured females as morally deficient and aberrant.

Her first claim is that the sexes typically differ in their basic life orientation, especially in conceptions of self and of morality, and that they follow different developmental pathways (Gilligan, 1982b, 1987). A moral orientation could be defined as a conceptually distinctive framework or perspective for organizing and understanding the moral domain. Gilligan claims that there is something of a gestalt shift in perspectives between orientations and sometimes uses the vase-face illusion as an illustration of the relationship between them.

In Gilligan's view, males typically have a *justice/rights orientation* because of their individualistic and separate conception of self, their detached objectivity, their basing of identity on occupation, and their proclivity for abstract and impartial rules and principles. She believes that this orientation has been well-represented in moral philosophy and moral psychology. On the other hand, females typically have a *care/response orientation* based on their perception of self as connected to and interdependent with others, their basing of identity on intimate relationships, their sensitivity not to endanger or hurt, their concern for the well-being and care of self and others and for harmonious relationships in concrete situations. It is this "feminine" moral orientation that she believes has not been adequately included in moral philosophy and theories of human development.

Gilligan has proposed that these orientations arise from young children's relational experiences of inequality and attachment. "We locate the origins of morality in the young child's awareness of self in relation to others and identify two dimensions of early childhood relationships that shape that awareness in different ways" (Gilligan & Wiggins, 1987, p. 280). One dimension is that of inequality/equality. Young children experience being powerless and dependent (relative to adults and older children), but with development progress to equality and independence. The other dimension is that of attachment/detachment and reflects children's love of those who care for them and their awareness of having an effect on others, of "connecting" with them. Gilligan argues that girls are both attached to, and identify with, their mothers. Thus, the experience of inequality is less salient, whereas the experience of attachment, of connecting with others, is more central to their self-definition. Boys, on the other hand, are attached to their mothers but identify with their fathers. Thus, the experience of inequality is more salient and the need for independence and separation more crucial for their self-esteem. "To the extent that biological sex, the psychology of gender, and the cultural norms and values that define masculine and feminine behavior affect experience of equality and of attachment, these factors presumably will influence moral development" (Gilligan & Wiggins, 1987, p. 282).

Gilligan (1977) originally proposed developmental stages in the response orientation (a three-level sequence). However, the status of these stages is unclear since no scoring system has yet been developed to assess such stages and they have been omitted from her more recent presentations of the theory.

Gilligan's second major claim is that influential theories of human development, but particularly the dominant one in moral psychology, that of Lawrence

Kohlberg, have missed or misconstrued females' "different voice" on morality (i.e., their response orientation). As a consequence, their reasoning has been denigrated to lower stages, and females falsely characterized as being morally deficient and aberrant. Gilligan argues that Kohlberg's conception of morality is *androcentric*—has a masculine bias—in that there is an emphasis (particularly at the higher stages) on what she describes as traditionally masculine traits and values such as rights, rationality, individuality, abstraction, detachment, impersonality, and principles of justice. Gilligan believes that traditional feminine concerns, such as maintenance of relationships, care, and commitment, when tapped, are typically relegated to the lower stages of moral development. Gilligan not only holds that Kohlberg's conception of morality is biased, but also his measure of moral reasoning—the Moral Judgment Interview (MJI). In the MJI, participants are asked to respond to a series of hypothetical moral dilemmas. Gilligan believes that these dilemmas focus on irrelevant issues, are devoid of contextual information, and are constructed as conflicts of rights. As such, she argues that, although these dilemmas may be suitable for tapping justice/rights reasoning, they mask care/response reasoning. Thus, Gilligan claims that Kohlberg's approach yields evidence that females (and those with a response orientation) are deficient in their level of moral development and that this sex difference is indicative of bias.

## Issues Concerning Gilligan's Theory

Gilligan's claims have been widely popularized and received; and it is now an appropriate time for evaluation. It should be recognized that Gilligan's theorizing represents a significant shift in feminist thought: from attempts to attain equality and minimize the significance of differences to attempts to discover and celebrate sex differences (Brabeck, 1989b). Undoubtedly, Gilligan has expanded our understanding of moral psychology and philosophy with her emphasis on care, response, interdependence, and commitment, and has also suggested alternate means to assess moral functioning. And she has clearly helped to focus attention on the need to examine and represent more carefully the experience of females in psychological theories. Nevertheless, many issues concerning her theory remain to be resolved.

  **1.** Gilligan's description of the origins of these orientations is troublesome, both in its lack of clarity and in its implications. (Locating the origins of moral orientations in young children's experiences with parents represents a surprising return to a psychoanalytic line of thought, given that psychoanalytic theory has been so roundly criticized for its treatment of women.) It is not yet clear to what Gilligan attributes this sex difference: anatomy or early socialization (i.e., nature vs. nurture). Do these orientations represent the essential quality of the sexes, inevitable because of their anatomy, or do they represent the product of social factors in contemporary society? The validity of her arguments, furthermore, will be relatively immune from empirical test given the inherent difficulty in assessing the particular constructs she has proposed. Untestable concepts have minimal explanatory value. Regardless of whether differences are innate or deeply socialized, her arguments imply a strong bifurcation between the sexes.

**2.** Gilligan's definition of moral maturity needs to be made explicit. As with other developmental theories, the description of the endpoint is the keystone to the evaluation of the approach. Gilligan has provided a variety of responses to this question (see Flanagan & Jackson, 1987, and Mason, 1990, for discussions).

   **a.** She sometimes implies that the response orientation is morally superior to the rights orientation, although this may represent more of a rhetorical device on her part to promote the value of care/response thinking.
   **b.** At other times, she argues that the two orientations are fundamentally incompatible alternatives, but ones which are equally valid and acceptable for the respective sexes.
   **c.** The orientations have also been described as being complementary perspectives that ideally would be maintained in some sort of dynamic tension.
   **d.** Finally, she has also suggested that each orientation is deficient without the other and that maturity is a synthesis or integration of rights and response reasoning (Gilligan, 1982a, p. 174).

It will not be possible to evaluate Gilligan's model adequately until her definition of moral maturity is clarified and defended.

**3.** Gilligan has yet to specify, as is essential for any psychological theory, a mechanism for development (Auerbach, Blum, Smith, & Williams, 1985; Puka, 1989b). Indeed, as noted earlier, it seems that her description of stages in the development of orientations has been abandoned (Gilligan, Brown, & Rogers, 1990; Brown et al., this volume). Thus, not only does the theory lack a mechanism for development, but it also lacks a valid description of development (Sichel, 1985). Assuming that some description of developmental stages can be provided and the definition of moral maturity defended, it will still be essential to explain how one attains moral maturity. What propels change? How can moral development be stimulated?

**4.** Gilligan's claim that the sexes typically differ in their basic life orientation is fraught with political dangers for women—dangers that Gilligan has seemingly ignored. While the value of a "woman-centered analysis" (Brabeck, 1989b) and of women's "epistemic privilege" to interpret sexist oppression (Boyd, 1990) are acknowledged, it should be recognized that Gilligan's work can also be taken as support for traditional stereotypes about the sexes (Henley, 1985), which simply re-presents old debates in moral philosophy (Sher, 1987). As such it preserves the status quo in a sexist society where significant inequality between the sexes remains and does not challenge either individuals or social structures to change (Hare-Mustin, 1987). Some commentators have argued that a care/response orientation represents the type of thinking that is adaptive for dealing with oppression—a sexist service orientation (Brabeck, 1987; Lykes, 1989; Puka, 1989a). It is argued that persons in power advocate rights and rationality, whereas persons in subordinate positions, of necessity, advocate connection and compassion (Hare-Mustin & Marecek, 1988). Gilligan's theorizing regarding the origins of these orientations comes close to implying a biological determinism (Lykes, 1989) and does not sufficiently recognize that sex differences may arise from a social hierarchy. Thus, her theory may serve to legitimize inequality—running the "risk of turning victimization into virtue" (Puka, 1989a, p. 19). Her work may represent "a misguided attempt to claim for women those very characteristics which have been traditionally attached to women and which have provided justification for treating them as inferior" (Seigfried, 1989, p. 65). Herein lies a potential paradox: If women's essential qualities, such as caring and compassion, are to be valued (as Gilligan argues), but arise primarily through subordination, how can these qualities be advanced without also endorsing inequality (Hare-Mustin & Marecek, 1988; Houston, 1989)? Concerns have also been expressed about the dangers of a "bandwagon" concept (such as a "different voice") for the status of women. Mednick (1989) argues, for example, that the extreme popularity of these notions represents more of a political than an intellectual event and is particularly worrisome given the relative lack of supportive empirical data. The political dangers of Gilligan's work for women need to be addressed directly.

5. There are some significant moral limitations to an ethic of care that need resolution. Although care may be essential for morality, it seems deficient in itself (Held, 1987). For example, it does not include the notions of impartiality and universalizability that have been regarded as essential to mature moral decision-making (Flanagan & Adler, 1983). The notion of impartiality has been much maligned by Gilligan and others. It does not imply that moral agents need be cold, detached, calculating, and blind to the context (Hill, 1987; Mason, 1990). As Sher (1987, p. 180) noted, "it is hard to see how all contextual features could ever be *irrelevant* to a moral decision, or how they all could be *relevant* to it." The real problem is how to determine what are the morally relevant features of a situation (Houston, 1989). Furthermore, the morality of response and care has no mechanism in itself to resolve conflicts of responsibility (inherent in everyday living) or to handle deficient or corrupt kinds of care (Flanagan & Jackson, 1987). Finally, its focus on interpersonal relationships implies an exclusion of moral responsibility to those beyond the sphere of personal interactions.

6. Gilligan's (1986c, 1987) theorizing advances the argument that the two moral orientations are both logically and psychologically incompatible (inequality vs. attachment) and she continues to argue "against the implication that these two perspectives are readily integrated or fused" (1987, p. 30). These two orientations are viewed as dichotomous, as fundamentally incompatible perspectives on morality. This notion precludes the possibility of some synthesis or integration reflecting a gender undifferentiated human morality (Stocker,

1987; Waithe, 1989). This dichotomization on the basis of sex caricatures human experience and reflects what Hare-Mustin and Marecek (1988) have labeled the "alpha bias," the tendency to exaggerate differences. The minimizing of within-sex variability and maximizing of between-sex differences creates a false dichotomy, and is worrisome in that "conflating rationality with masculinity and relatedness with femininity leads to their being construed as mutually exclusive" (Hare-Mustin, 1987, p. 265). Not all theorists agree with this dichotomous view. For example, Higgins (1989, p. 197) claimed that "justice and care are indivisible insofar as they are moral."

**7.** Gilligan's presentation of the justice/rights orientation seems rather deficient and a simplistic caricature to many commentators (Bebeau & Brabeck, 1989; Brabeck, 1989a; Puka, 1991; Sichel, 1985). Gilligan certainly has not provided any demonstration that her definition of the justice/rights orientation is a valid measure of Kohlberg's approach which she claims reflects such reasoning. Indeed, there is now some evidence (Walker, 1989; Walker, de Vries, & Trevethan, 1987), to be reviewed later, demonstrating that Gilligan's rights orientation does not accurately capture Kohlberg's moral stages. Furthermore, her criticisms of Kohlberg's theory, especially principled moral reasoning, seem to be based on arcane descriptions. Kohlberg has argued that principled moral reasoning entails the notion of "respect for persons" as ends, not means. This principle involves not only the adjudicating of conflicting interests and rights, but also a willingness to dialogue with others in seeking agreement, an attitude of identification and empathic connection with others (i.e., active sympathy), and an obligation to promote good and prevent harm (see Boyd, 1983; Kohlberg, 1984; Kohlberg, Boyd, & Levine, 1990). The "psychological postures" inherent in principled moral reasoning include open-mindedness, principledness (i.e., principle-seeking, not rigid rule-applying), humility, a sense of responsibility, and a sensitivity to the morally relevant features of the context (Boyd, 1979, 1989). Unfortunately, Gilligan has failed to represent Kohlberg's theory in this light.

## Kohlberg's Moral Stage Theory

Kohlberg's (1984) theoretical perspective on sex differences in moral development is considerably different from that of Gilligan. Kohlberg's approach neither predicts nor requires sex differences in either "developmental pathway" or rate of development. It should be noted, however, that Kohlberg and Kramer (1969), in an early review, noted the presence of sex differences in moral stages in some studies which they explained in terms of availability of role-taking opportunities.

Kohlberg argued that it was appropriate and useful to characterize moral reasoning in terms of (cognitive-developmental) stages. Thus, his model held that moral reasoning stages represent holistic structures that develop in an invariant, universal sequence and that constitute a hierarchy (Walker, 1988).

These well-known stages have been described earlier (see Gibbs, Chapter 2, this volume; Higgins, Chapter 3, this volume; see also, Colby & Kohlberg, 1987). As was noted, Kohlberg claimed empirical support for the first five stages in his typology, but regarded Stage 6 primarily as a theoretical construct given its absence in his longitudinal data (Colby, Kohlberg, Gibbs, & Lieberman, 1983). There have also been substantial revisions in both stage descriptions and scoring procedures over the years as the model was refined and validated (Colby & Kohlberg, 1987).

Kohlberg (1976) claimed that the order of development through the stages was invariant and universal, but predicted variability in rate and an eventual endpoint of development. One determinant of rate of moral development is the attainment of prerequisite levels of cognitive and perspective-taking development—in other words, moral reasoning has a basis in cognition. Isomorphic processes are involved in parallel stages in different domains of cognition. Evidence for this determinant is provided by studies that indicate the attainment of a moral stage requires the prior or concomitant attainment of the parallel cognitive and perspective-taking stages (Walker, 1988). The other major determinant of rate of moral development is exposure to appropriate social experiences—in other words, moral reasoning also has a basis in social interactions. These interactions provide the cognitive and social disequilibrium that induces development. These experiences arise both through interpersonal relationships with family and friends and through real participation in the economic, political, and legal institutions of society through education, occupation, citizenship, and such activities. These are emotional, personal experiences that involve responsibility, leadership, decision-making, dialogue, and commitment. Kohlberg's theory does not predict that any particular social experience is necessary for attainment of a given stage. The experiences that will affect moral development are those that induce rethinking of current modes of moral reasoning. A number of studies (e.g., Berkowitz, Gibbs, & Broughton, 1980; Haan, Smith, & Block, 1968; Walker, 1986a; Walker & Taylor, 1991) have confirmed that various social experiences predict moral development: education, occupation, political and social activity, household decision-making, and peer and family discussions.

Kohlberg (1984) argues that these determinants of rate and the endpoint of moral development will explain variability among individuals and between groups—including the sexes. Thus, his position is that, if sex differences on his measure are revealed, then they should be fully attributable to differences between the sexes in terms of these influences on moral development.

## Kohlberg's Theory of Moral Orientations

It is noteworthy that Gilligan's theorizing regarding moral orientations was actually predated by Kohlberg's (1976) proposal of four moral orientations. These orientations are somewhat more closely related to the content, rather than the structure, of individuals' reasoning and are held to be conceptually independent of Kohlberg's better known moral stages (although Walker, 1989, found some empirical relationships). It is possible to distinguish these orientations with the current scoring manual (Colby & Kohlberg, 1987), based on the classification of each moral judgment according to "element." The *normative orientation* emphasizes maintenance of the normative order, with a focus on duties and rights defined by adherence to prescribed rules and roles. The *fairness orientation* emphasizes justice, with a focus on liberty, equity and equality, reciprocity, and contract. The *utilitarianism orientation* emphasizes welfare and happiness consequences of moral actions for oneself or for others. Finally, the *perfectionism orientation* emphasizes attainment of dignity and autonomy, good conscience and motives, and harmony with self and others.

Kohlberg's typology of moral orientations seems to identify some similar themes and dimensions to those described by Gilligan in her typology. Given these similarities and Gilligan's claim of a pervasive sex difference, it seems reasonable to predict that sex differences would be evident in Kohlberg's typology as well. Males would be expected to use the normative and fairness orientations because of their presumed concern with rights, duties, and justice; whereas, females would be expected to use the utilitarianism and perfectionism orientations because of their presumed concern with relationships, welfare, and caring. It is important to note that neither Kohlberg nor Gilligan made predictions regarding sex differences in Kohlberg's typology of moral orientations, although Colby and Kohlberg (1987) argued that a care/response mode of moral reasoning is reflected in the utilitarianism and perfectionism orientations. Additionally, one would expect Gilligan to argue that her claims cannot be appropriately examined within the context of Kohlberg's approach.

## Sexism in Theories of Morality

Claims and allegations regarding sex differences in moral maturity and sex bias in moral theories have been widely circulated and discussed. It is important to recognize that the charge of sexism might be warranted for two reasons. First, a theorist could advocate or popularize the notion that the sexes are fundamentally different in moral orientation or in rate and endpoint of moral development when such a claim has no empirical validity. For example, it has been argued that Freud's (1927) theory could be characterized as sexist for this reason. Gilligan (1982a) is also vulnerable to such an allegation. Second, a theorist might make no claims regarding sex differences in morality, but define and/or assess moral maturity in ways that unintentionally favor one sex over the other and thus impart the false conclusion of real differences in moral maturity. For example, the allegations that Kohlberg's (1981, 1984) theory is sexist are primarily premised on this latter reason.

A variety of sources of sex bias in these two theories of moral psychology has been posited:

1. It has been suggested that the sex of the theorist represents a potential source of bias. If Gilligan's claims regarding a pervasive and fundamental sex difference in moral orientations are valid, then it is possible that a theorist may not be able to fully and adequately describe the moral thinking of persons of the other sex. This suggestion, of course, has profound implications for both psychology and the philosophy of science.

2. A second and similar possible source of bias is the ideological basis for the moral theory. The self-admitted intellectual roots of Kohlberg's theory, for example, lie in a tradition of Western moral philosophy and liberal social science (Kohlberg, 1984). Similarly, the ideological roots of Gilligan's theory are in contemporary feminism.

3. A third possible source of bias could be found in the measure of moral functioning advocated by the approach. For example, Kohlberg has been castigated for his reliance on hypothetical dilemmas that focus on what might be unfamiliar issues and that minimize emotional involvement. The MJI has also been criticized for the predominance of male protagonists in the dilemmas. However, Walker's (1991) review of the research on this claim indicates that sex of protagonist is not a reliable predictor of level of moral reasoning. Gilligan has similarly been criticized for her reliance on participants' recall and discussion of actual dilemmas from their personal experience. Such real-life dilemmas are idiosyncratic and, thus, the interpretation of individuals' reasoning is fraught with confounds.

4. The final possible source of bias to note is the original sample upon which the theories' constructs were derived and validated (although it is recognized that theories are not based exclusively on research data). Kohlberg's moral stage model and scoring system were constructed, in large part, from the longitudinal data provided by an exclusively male sample (Colby et al., 1983). Similarly, the data for Gilligan's (1977) original study of moral orientations were obtained from an exclusively female sample—women who were considering an abortion. This lack of representativeness is a potential threat to the generalizability of both theories of moral development.

It is now appropriate to review the empirical evidence regarding sex differences in both models of moral development. Before turning to that review, an important proviso should be mentioned. Some theorists (e.g., Baumrind, 1986; Gilligan, 1982a) have argued that findings of difference are indicative of bias. It is not that simple. Findings of sex difference will support the allegation of sexism only if they do not validly reflect reality. It is possible that sex differences may be a reflection of a sexist society that oppresses females rather than an indication of a biased theory. To illustrate: Males are taller than females on average, but this evidence does not necessarily call into question our systems of measurement. In any case, the foundation for an interpretive claim of bias against a theory would be provided by empirical evidence indicating that its claims regarding the sexes and morality cannot be substantiated.

# Research

## Research on Gilligan's Moral Orientations

As noted above, there remains considerable ambiguity regarding many aspects of Gilligan's theory; however, she has posited several testable claims regarding moral orientations:

1. The two moral orientations represent distinct frameworks and "most people . . . focus on one orientation and minimally represent the other" (Gilligan, 1986a, p. 10). In other words, individuals should be consistent in the use of a single orientation—there should be a high level of intra-individual consistency.
2. The care/response orientation is best revealed by reasoning about real-life moral dilemmas and that this orientation is masked by hypothetical dilemmas (such as those on Kohlberg's MJI) which are more likely to elicit justice/rights reasoning. It is noteworthy that this claim of variability in orientation usage across dilemma types (hypothetical vs. real-life) is in direct contradiction to the first claim of intraindividual consistency.
3. The third, and best known, claim is that these orientations are sex-related (females will tend to use care reasoning and males, justice reasoning). Although Gilligan is quite adamant that the orientations are sex-related, not sex-determined, her explanation of the origins of these orientations in girls' and boys' differential experiences with caregivers implies a strong association between orientations and sex.
4. Orientations are evident across the life-span, from early childhood on.
5. The origins of these orientations lie in young children's relational experiences with caregivers of inequality and attachment. Over the last few years, several studies have yielded data relevant to these claims.

### Intraindividual Consistency

Empirically, this claim means that a substantial proportion of an individual's reasoning should reflect one orientation with relatively little reasoning reflecting the other. What is a reasonable level of consistency? Since 50 percent represents the minimum possible (i.e., equal use of both orientations) and 100 percent represents perfect consistency (i.e., one orientation exclusively), Walker et al. (1987) proposed an arbitrary criterion of 75 percent+ (the percentage of reasoning reflecting the modal moral orientation, either care or justice)—a criterion also adopted by Gilligan and Attanucci (1988). Walker (1989; Walker et al., 1987) determined the percentage of subjects who met this criterion of consistency over a four-dilemma interview and found that very few (less than 20 percent) were consistent in the use of a single orientation. Even when examining a single real-life dilemma, only about half of the participants met the criterion. Similarly, Gilligan and Attanucci reported that less than two-thirds of their subjects met this criterion of consistency on a real-life dilemma. Pratt,

Golding, Hunter, and Sampson (1988) asked their subjects to discuss two real-life dilemmas and found that only 60 percent used the same orientation between dilemmas—a level not significantly different from chance. Walker (1989) also examined the stability of individuals' orientations in their discussions of a real-life dilemma over a two-year longitudinal interval, and found a low level of consistency over time—half of the participants evidenced a different orientation on the retest than the initial interview.

If a moral orientation represents a distinctive framework for understanding morality and is as basic to our functioning as has been proposed, then individuals should focus on one orientation or the other, a preference which generalizes across moral problems and is stable over time. The findings of these studies are uniform in indicating low levels of intraindividual consistency within dilemmas, across dilemmas, and over time. Most individuals use a considerable mix of both orientations.

### Dilemma-type Differences

Gilligan argued that hypothetical dilemmas obscure the care/response orientation because they are abstract, depersonalized, limited in contextual information, and preconstructed (by the researcher) as issues of conflicting rights. Personally generated real-life dilemmas, however, are held to be more appropriate contexts for expressing care reasoning. (It is surprising, then, that Gilligan (1982a) provides numerous anecdotes of care/response reasoning in response to Kohlbergian hypothetical dilemmas.)

The evidence regarding the relation between dilemma type and orientation is somewhat equivocal. Walker (1989) found that real-life dilemmas elicited more care reasoning than did hypothetical dilemmas, but only among adults; in two groups of children, the opposite pattern was found. Langdale (1986) reported that the justice orientation was more frequently used in discussing the hypothetical Heinz dilemma and a hypothetical abortion dilemma than a real-life dilemma. Rothbart, Hanley, and Albert (1986) found that the Heinz dilemma elicited more justice reasoning than did a real-life dilemma; however, the real-life dilemma in turn elicited more justice reasoning than did a hypothetical physical-intimacy dilemma. Walker et al. (1987) found significant differences in care reasoning across hypothetical Kohlbergian dilemmas (e.g., the Heinz dilemma elicited more care reasoning than did the Joe dilemma which concerns a father's failure to keep his promise). Derry (1989) reported that work-related real-life dilemmas were almost exclusively discussed in justice terms (although there was no comparison with other dilemma types in this study). Obviously, whether the dilemma format is hypothetical or real-life is not an important influence on orientation use; rather, the characteristics of the dilemma are of considerable significance.

The importance of the nature of the dilemma in influencing moral orientation has been illustrated in two studies (Pratt et al., 1988; Walker, 1989). In both studies, participants were asked to discuss real-life dilemmas from their own experience and their moral orientations were determined. The researchers conducted a content analysis of these real-life dilemmas: Walker distinguished between personal and impersonal dilemmas; Pratt et al., between relational and nonrelational dilemmas. Personal or relational dilemmas involve conflicts among people who have a significant, continuing relationship; whereas impersonal or nonrelational dilemmas entail conflicts among relative strangers, or with institutions or generalized others, or are intrinsic to self. Both Walker and Pratt et al. examined the relationship between dilemma content and orientation and found that personal/relational dilemmas tended to be discussed in terms of care and response, whereas impersonal/nonrelational dilemmas were more likely to be reasoned in terms of justice and rights. Thus, the nature of the dilemma exerts a considerable influence on the mode of moral reasoning used, and it seems that dilemma format (i.e., hypothetical vs. real-life) is, in general, of less significance.

### Sex Differences

Pivotal to Gilligan's theory is the claim that the sexes typically understand and resolve moral problems within the framework of different moral orientations. A reasonable amount of evidence has now been generated regarding this claim. Researchers have used three different paradigms to address this issue: (1) Sex differences in moral orientations have been examined in reasoning about real-life dilemmas and (2) standard hypothetical dilemmas; (3) sex differences in subjects' objective ratings regarding these orientations have also been examined. Lyons (1983) conducted the initial study in which moral orientations were analyzed in individuals' discussion of a real-life dilemma from their own experience. She reported support for Gilligan's claim of sex-related moral orientations: A focus on care reasoning was predominant among females, whereas a focus on justice reasoning was predominant among males. This pattern was replicated by Gilligan and Attanucci (1988) and Donenberg and Hoffman (1988). However, it is difficult to interpret Donenberg and Hoffman's finding that girls produced a greater number of care considerations than did boys since that may be an artifact of the finding that girls also produced more responses overall than did boys. Contrary evidence regarding sex differences in moral orientations in reasoning about real-life dilemmas has been reported in several studies. For example, both Rothbart et al. (1986) and Derry (1989) failed to find sex differences in their subjects' reasoning about real-life moral problems. Galotti (1989) asked subjects to list the considerations they would use in solving moral problems (note that they were not asked to describe a specific dilemma from their own experience) which were scored for masculine and feminine themes (following Gilligan). Sex differences were not found on 12 of the 13 themes analyzed.

There are two further studies which are of considerable importance in this context because they posit alternate explanations for moral orientations. Walker (1989; Walker et al., 1987) found a sex difference among a sample of parents, but not among children. Pratt et al. (1988, Study 1) reported a sex difference in orientation among a middle-aged sample of adults, but not among samples of younger and older adults. Pratt et al. speculated that middle-aged adults are more likely to be active in the parenting role, a situation which is conducive to sex-role polarization. In a second study they tested this hypothesis with two groups of adults of the same age, half of whom were parents and half, not. Only the parents evidenced the sex-related pattern in orientation usage. Thus, this indicates that the sex difference in moral orientations is of rather limited generality. There is also a significant methodological problem in all of these studies of moral orientations in real-life dilemmas: Participants simply recounted one of their own moral problems. Thus, these moral problems are idiosyncratic. This suggests the possibility that the findings of sex differences in moral orientation in some of these studies may be an artifact of the differing moral problems that the sexes encounter in everyday living or choose to relate, rather than a basic difference in moral framework (Walker, 1986a). This suggestion was examined in both Pratt et al.'s and Walker's studies. As noted in an earlier section, they conducted content analyses of real-life dilemmas (personal/relational vs. impersonal/nonrelational) and then examined sex differences when dilemma content was held constant. In both studies it was found that sex differences were no longer evident within types of real-life dilemmas, although as noted earlier, personal/relational dilemmas were more likely to be discussed with care reasoning than were impersonal/nonrelational dilemmas (regardless of individuals' sex). Thus, variability in moral orientations can be better attributed to the type of dilemma that subjects typically encounter than to their sex. Interestingly, Seigfried (1989) noted the philosophical and political advantages to women of such a finding.

If the sex difference in moral orientations is as pervasive and basic as Gilligan implies, then it should be evident in reasoning about standard, hypothetical moral dilemmas. Langdale (1986) analyzed moral orientations in response to Kohlberg's Heinz dilemma and a hypothetical abortion dilemma and found a sex-related pattern. Donenberg and Hoffman (1988) asked children to respond to two hypothetical interpersonal dilemmas and found a sex difference in the number of care considerations (but, as noted before, this is confounded with a sex difference in the number of responses made overall). Johnston (1988) examined orientations in children's responses to two of Aesop's fables, but found sex differences for only one of them. Garrod, Beal, and Shin (1990) replicated Johnston's study and found no sex differences at all. The absence of sex differences in moral orientations has also been reported in response to a hypothetical competitive-athletics dilemma (Crown & Heatherington, 1989), the Heinz dilemma and a hypothetical physical-intimacy dilemma (Rothbart et al., 1986), and the standard dilemmas of Kohlberg's MJI (Walker, 1989). Thus, the weight of the available evidence supports the view that sex differences in moral orientations are generally absent in responses to standard stimulus materials (consistent with the finding that sex differences are not found when the content of real-life dilemmas is held constant).

The third research paradigm used to examine sex differences in moral orientations involves subjects' rating their use or endorsement of either orientation. This represents a more objective methodology than analyzing responses to open-ended questions regarding dilemmas. Ford and Lowery (1986) failed to find sex differences in students' rating of the extent to which they used either orientation in thinking about a moral conflict. Friedman, Robinson, and Friedman (1987) similarly failed to find sex differences in students' rating of the importance of care and justice considerations in resolving dilemmas. Forsyth, Nye, and Kelley (1988) found no sex differences in endorsement of questionnaire items reflecting an ethic of care. Finally, Yacker and Weinberg (1990) found a marginally significant sex difference in graduate students' rankings of orientations used in childhood dilemmas. Thus, the findings of this paradigm, in which stimuli are standardized, are consistent with those studies in which responses to standard hypothetical dilemmas were examined.

### Developmental Trends
Gilligan (1982a) claimed that moral orientations will be evident across the lifespan, from early childhood on. She (1977) also proposed a three-level sequence in the development of care reasoning, but no scoring system nor supportive data have yet been provided. There are relatively little developmental data regarding moral orientations since most studies (discussed above) involve samples that are homogeneous in age. Furthermore, several studies that had cross-sectional designs did not examine age differences (e.g., Gilligan & Attanucci, 1988; Lyons, 1983; Pratt et al., 1988). However, Langdale (1986) reported no significant age differences across samples (of varying sizes) of children, adolescents, and adults. Donenberg and Hoffman (1988) also reported no age differences in their study with Grade 5/6 and 10/11 students; as did Garrod et al. (1990) in their study with Grade 1, 3, and 5 students. The most comprehensive examination of developmental trends was reported by Walker (1989) in a two-year longitudinal study with a large sample of children, adolescents, and adults (5-63 years). He found a developmental pattern with the proportion of care reasoning increasing across age groups, although there was no development over the longitudinal interval. Thus, these studies yield rather equivocal data regarding developmental trends, and point to the need for a better delineation of the levels and process of growth in moral orientations.

### Origins
Gilligan and Wiggins (1987) claimed that the origins of the two moral orientations are in young children's experiences with caregivers, especially in terms of the dimensions of inequality and attachment. Support for such a claim would require extensive longitudinal data and, not surprising, none has yet been reported.

## Research on Kohlberg's Moral Orientations

As noted in an earlier section, Kohlberg's (1976; Colby & Kohlberg, 1987) typology of moral orientations seems to tap dimensions related to those described by Gilligan—there are many similar themes and distinctions. Given these similarities and Gilligan's argument regarding a pervasive sex difference in moral orientations, it seems reasonable to predict that males would focus on the normative and fairness orientations, whereas females would focus on the utilitarianism and perfectionism orientations.

The extant data regarding sex differences on Kohlberg's moral orientations are limited. Pratt, Golding, and Hunter (1984) examined orientation use in response to Kohlberg's MJI with a sample of adults and found no sex differences overall on any of the orientations. However, among the small number of high-stage subjects, men oriented more to fairness than did women, whereas women oriented more to perfectionism than did men. In another study with adults, Walker (1986a) found no sex differences on either the utilitarianism or perfectionism orientations, but men were found to use the normative orientation more than women, but (contrary to predictions) women used the fairness orientation more than men. Three other studies failed to reveal any sex differences in orientation use in response to hypothetical moral dilemmas: Pratt et al. (1988) with a sample of adults; Walker (1989) with a sample of children, adolescents, and adults; and Walker and Moran (1991) with a sample of Chinese students and adults.

Gilligan might be expected to argue that sex differences in orientation use would be obscured by the use of hypothetical dilemmas. Two of the above-noted studies also examined moral orientations in reasoning about real-life dilemmas. Walker (1989) found no sex differences on any orientation, whereas Walker and Moran (1991) found that females oriented more to normative concerns and less to utilitarian concerns than did males, a pattern which contradicts the hypothesis that females have a care (i.e, utilitarianism and perfectionism) orientation and males, a justice (i.e., normative and fairness) one.

These studies indicate the almost complete absence of sex differences within Kohlberg's moral orientations, but when they occurred, they were typically inconsistent with the predictions derived from Gilligan's theory.

## Research on Kohlberg's Moral Stages

As discussed earlier, the second principal component of contemporary discussions regarding morality and the sexes is the claim that currently dominant theories of moral development (notably Kohlberg's) have failed to represent adequately the moral thinking of females and, as a consequence, down-score their level of moral maturity (Gilligan, 1982a). There is now a considerable body of evidence regarding sex differences in stage of moral development, but before examining these data, there is a cautionary point to note. The true incidence of sex differences is probably overestimated by the extant research literature, especially in areas of human development where such differences have not been of primary interest. This overestimation of sex differences has been labeled the "file-drawer problem" (Rosenthal, 1979) which arises from two biases against nonsignificant findings: a reporting bias (i.e., the failure of many researchers to report a test of sex differences, although participants were of both sexes), and a publication bias (i.e., the process of publication favors studies with significant findings, leaving the studies with nonsignificant differences unknown).

Walker (1984, 1986b) reported a review of the literature that included all studies using Kohlberg's measure in which sex differences in the development of moral reasoning were, or could be, examined. My review included 80 studies with 152 samples, and involved a total of 10,637 subjects. Of the 152 samples, a nonsignificant difference was reported for the vast majority, 130 (85.5 percent). Females had higher scores in 9 samples (5.9 percent), whereas males had higher scores in 13 samples (8.6 percent). The few differences favoring females tended to occur in homogeneous samples of school and university students. The rare differences favoring males either occurred in homogeneous samples of students or in heterogeneous samples of adults, heterogeneous in that the sexes differed in levels of education and occupation (which, of course, is reflective of contemporary society). It is interesting that in every case where researchers controlled in some manner for education and/or occupation, sex differences in moral reasoning disappeared. This is not an attempt to "explain away" these findings, but to illustrate Kohlberg's claim that such experiences are influential in stimulating moral development. Thus, the overall pattern yielded by Walker's review is one of nonsignificant sex differences. A few studies with particular samples did yield significant findings, but such a small number would be expected by chance.

It should be acknowledged that the traditional vote-counting method of integrating findings (i.e., significant or not), as in Walker's review, is limited because it makes no assessment of the size of an effect. If an effect is a moderate one, then differences may tend not to reach significance, although they cumulatively favor a given direction. Meta-analysis is a powerful and objective means to combine statistically the results of a set of studies, thereby overcoming some of the limitations of the traditional review method (Rosenthal, 1984). Walker (1984, 1986b) also reported a meta-analysis of the studies included in his review and found that the probability level for the overall pattern of findings did not reach significance. In subsidiary analyses the effect size was found to be extremely small: Sex explained only 1/20 of 1 percent of the variability in moral reasoning development. The minuscule effect size and nonsignificant meta-analysis clearly contradicts the claim that Kohlberg's approach down-scores the moral thinking of females.

There is another comprehensive meta-analysis of sex differences in moral reasoning to note. Thoma (1986) examined sex differences on Rest's (1979) Defining Issues Test (DIT), a measure derived from Kohlberg's theory (and thus, presumably, subject to Gilligan's criticisms), although based on somewhat different stage descriptions and quite different methodology. On the DIT, subjects rate and rank moral reasoning statements. Thus, the DIT is a recognition measure, whereas the MJI is a production measure. Thoma surveyed 56 samples in which sex differences on the DIT were examined and found a significant difference—favoring females. However, the magnitude of the effect was extremely small (sex accounted for less than 1/2 of 1 percent of the variance). Again, there is no support for the notion that Kohlberg's approach favors males.

### Moral Stages and Moral Orientations

Gilligan's (1982a) allegations of bias against Kohlberg's theory not only claimed that his approach down-scored females' moral reasoning, but also claimed that his approach tended to undervalue the care orientation, categorizing such reasoning at lower stages. "The primary use of the care orientation . . . creates a liability within Kohlberg's framework" (Gilligan, 1986b, p. 45). (For Gilligan, females' moral reasoning and the care orientation were essentially synonymous, but the evidence reviewed in an earlier section indicated that this is an unwarranted assumption.) Gilligan argued that Kohlberg's theory favors justice/rights reasoning, particularly at the principled stages. The research regarding this claim is quite limited, but very revealing. In Pratt et al.'s (1988) study, subjects responded to Kohlberg's MJI (providing a stage score) and discussed a real-life dilemma (indicating moral orientation). Gilligan predicts a negative relationship between use of care reasoning and moral stage, but Pratt et al.'s findings did not support this prediction. For women, higher-stage reasoning was associated with greater care reasoning, whereas for men, there was no significant relationship.

In Walker's (1989; Walker et al., 1987) study, subjects responded to both the MJI and a real-life dilemma at two different interview times (separated by a two-year longitudinal interval), and both types of dilemmas were scored for moral stage and for moral orientation. If Gilligan's arguments are correct, then individuals with a care orientation should score lower in moral stage than those with a justice orientation. The analyses for the relation between stage and orientation on the hypothetical dilemmas revealed no effects, failing to support Gilligan's claim. However, the analyses for the real-life dilemma revealed that individuals with a care orientation evidenced a higher level of moral development than did those with a justice orientation (at both interview times). Thus, the findings of both studies fail to support the notion that Kohlberg's theory and scoring system are biased against the care orientation—rather they indicate the opposite.

It was argued earlier that Gilligan's description of the justice/rights orientation seems rather deficient and simplistic. It is now clear that it is inappropriate to regard Kohlberg's moral stage theory as synonymous with Gilligan's justice/rights orientation. One finding of Walker's study is particularly provocative in this regard. It was found that individuals at the higher stages of moral development were more likely to be "split" in their moral orientations (i.e., to use care and justice reasoning equally). A split orientation suggests an attempt to integrate or coordinate both types of reasoning. The association with moral stage indicates that mature moral thinking does entail such an integration. This hypothesis is supported by Garrod et al.'s (1990) finding that the ability to explain both orientations and to switch between them was associated with advanced cognitive and perspective-taking development. These findings are also consistent with the notion that principled moral thinking, as conceptualized by Kohlberg, does reflect the reasoning of both the care and justice orientations (e.g., Kohlberg et al., 1990).

## *Application*

Over the last couple of decades moral education programs have been widely implemented in schools. Many of these programs have been based on Kohlberg's theory. Critics of Kohlberg's theory have expressed concerns that his paradigm of moral education focuses on a masculine view of morality and tends to silence females' "different voice." As the previous discussion of sex differences in Kohlberg's theory indicated, however, there is no empirical basis for the claim of sex bias in his approach. It is interesting that Kohlberg's initial recommendations for moral education entailed peer discussion of hypothetical moral dilemmas and that the approach has now evolved into the "Just Community" with an emphasis on the fostering of a sense of responsibility and community, student self-government, and the resolution of practical problems in everyday school life (Power, Higgins, & Kohlberg, 1989). Gilligan has yet to propose a paradigm for moral education (not surprisingly, given that the pattern and mechanism of development in moral orientations are, as yet, unspecified), except to note the value of studying narratives in history and literature instead of studying science (Brown et al., this volume). However, several scholars (e.g., Martin, 1987; Noddings, 1984) have emphasized the need to transform the process of education, in general, from a preoccupation with achievement to include care and connection.

Although it was argued that reasoning represents the core of moral psychology, it is acknowledged that other areas of human functioning are relevant to the moral domain. In this regard, the evidence regarding sex differences in ethical sensitivity (Bebeau & Brabeck, 1989), empathy (Eisenberg & Lennon, 1983), and prosocial and other behaviors (Blasi, 1980; Krebs, 1970) is of considerable interest.

In summary, then, what can be concluded about the issue of sexism in moral psychology? Some conceptual difficulties with Gilligan's formulation of two moral orientations were explored. Her primary empirical claim that these orientations are sex-related could not be clearly supported. The allegation that Kohlberg's theory down-scores females' care reasoning also was not substantiated. Claims regarding sex differences on a dimension so central to human functioning should be made with extreme caution, and only on the basis of considerable and valid research evidence.

## Recommended Readings

Brabeck, M. M. (Ed.). (1989). *Who cares? Theory, research, and educational implications of the ethic of care.* New York: Praeger.

Broughton, J. (Ed.). (1987). Women and moral development [Special issue]. *New Ideas in Psychology, 5*(2).

Gilligan, C. (1982). *In a different voice: Psychological theory and women's development.* Cambridge, MA: Harvard University Press.

Kittay, E. F., & Meyers, D. T. (Eds.). (1987). *Women and moral theory.* Totowa, NJ:

Rowman & Littlefield.

Nails, D., O'Loughlin, M. A., & Walker, J. C. (Eds.). (1983). Women and morality [Special issue]. *Social Research, 50*(3).

Noddings, N. (1984). *Caring: A feminine approach to ethics and moral education.* Berkeley, CA: University of California Press.

Walker, L. J. (1991). Sex differences in moral reasoning. In W. M. Kurtines & J. L. Gewirtz (Eds.), *Handbook of moral behavior and development* (Vol. 2, pp. 333-364). Hillsdale, NJ: Erlbaum.

## References

Auerbach, J., Blum, L., Smith, V., & Williams, C. (1985). Commentary on Gilligan's "In a Different Voice." *Feminist Studies, 11*, 149-161.

Baumrind, D. (1986). Sex differences in moral reasoning: Response to Walker's (1984) conclusion that there are none. *Child Development, 57*, 511-521.

Bebeau, M. J., & Brabeck, M. M. (1989). Ethical sensitivity and moral reasoning among men and women in the professions. In M. M. Brabeck (Ed.), *Who cares? Theory, research, and educational implications of the ethic of care* (pp. 144-163). New York: Praeger.

Berkowitz, M. W., Gibbs, J. C., & Broughton, J. M. (1980). The relation of moral judgment stage disparity to developmental effects of peer dialogues. *Merrill-Palmer Quarterly, 26*, 341-357.

Blasi, A. (1980). Bridging moral cognition and moral action: A critical review of the literature. *Psychological Bulletin, 88*, 1-45.

Blasi, A. (1984). Moral identity: Its role in moral functioning. In W. M. Kurtines & J. L. Gewirtz (Eds.), *Morality, moral behavior, and moral development* (pp. 128-139). New York: Wiley.

Boyd, D. R. (1979). An interpretation of prin-

cipled morality. *Journal of Moral Education, 8*, 110-123.

Boyd, D. R. (1983). Careful justice or just caring: A response to Gilligan. *Proceedings of the Philosophy of Education Society, 38*, 63-69.

Boyd, D. R. (1989). The character of moral education. In L. P. Nucci (Ed.), *Moral development and character education* (pp. 95-123). Berkeley, CA: McCutchan.

Boyd, D. R. (1990, April). *One man's reflection on a masculine role in feminist ethics: Epistemic vs. political privilege.* Paper presented at the meeting of the Philosophy of Education Society, Miami, FL.

Brabeck, M. M. (1987). Gender and morality: A response to Philibert and Sayers. *New Ideas in Psychology, 5*, 209-214.

Brabeck, M. M. (1989a, November). *Changing descriptions of the self and feminist moral visions.* Paper presented at the meeting of the Association for Moral Education, Newport Beach, CA.

Brabeck, M. M. (1989b). Introduction: Who cares? In M. M. Brabeck (Ed.), *Who cares? Theory, research, and educational implications of the ethic of care* (pp. xi-xviii). New York: Praeger.

Colby, A., & Kohlberg, L. (1987). *The measurement of moral judgment* (Vols. 1-2). New

York: Cambridge University Press.

Colby, A., Kohlberg, L., Gibbs, J., & Lieberman, M. (1983). A longitudinal study of moral judgment. *Monographs of the Society for Research in Child Development, 48*(1-2), Serial No. 200.

Crown, J., & Heatherington, L. (1989). The costs of winning? The role of gender in moral reasoning and judgments about competitive athletic encounters. *Journal of Sport and Exercise Psychology, 11*, 281-289.

Derry, R. (1989). An empirical study of moral reasoning among managers. *Journal of Business Ethics, 8*, 855-862.

Donenberg, G. R., & Hoffman, L. W. (1988). Gender differences in moral development. *Sex Roles, 18*, 701-717.

Eisenberg, N., & Lennon, R. (1983). Sex differences in empathy and related capacities. *Psychological Bulletin, 94*, 100-131.

Flanagan, O. J., & Adler, J. E. (1983). Impartiality and particularity. *Social Research, 50*, 576-596.

Flanagan, O. J., & Jackson, K. (1987). Justice, care, and gender: The Kohlberg-Gilligan debate revisited. *Ethics, 97*, 622-637.

Ford, M. R., & Lowery, C. R. (1986). Gender differences in moral reasoning: A comparison of the use of justice and care orientations. *Journal of Personality and Social Psychology, 50*, 777-783.

Forsyth, D. R., Nye, J. L., & Kelley, K. (1988). Idealism, relativism, and the ethic of caring. *Journal of Psychology, 122*, 243-248.

Freud, S. (1927). Some psychological consequences of the anatomical distinction between the sexes. *International Journal of Psycho-analysis, 8*, 133-142.

Friedman, W. J., Robinson, A. B., & Friedman, B. L. (1987). Sex differences in moral judgments? A test of Gilligan's theory. *Psychology of Women Quarterly, 11*, 37-46.

Galotti, K. M. (1989). Gender differences in self-reported moral reasoning: A review and new evidence. *Journal of Youth and Adolescence, 18*, 475-488.

Garrod, A., Beal, C., & Shin, P. (1990). The development of moral orientation in elementary school children. *Sex Roles, 22*, 13-27.

Gilligan, C. (1977). In a different voice: Women's conception of the self and of morality. *Harvard Educational Review, 47*, 481-517.

Gilligan, C. (1982a). *In a different voice: Psychological theory and women's development.* Cambridge, MA: Harvard University Press.

Gilligan, C. (1982b). New maps of development: New visions of maturity. *American Journal of Orthopsychiatry, 52*, 199-212.

Gilligan, C. (1986a, Spring). [letter to D. Baumrind]. *Newsletter of the APA Division on Developmental Psychology*, pp. 10-13.

Gilligan, C. (1986b). Remapping development: The power of divergent data. In L. Cirillo & S. Wapner (Eds.), *Value presuppositions in theories of human development* (pp. 37-53). Hillsdale, NJ: Erlbaum.

Gilligan, C. (1986c). Remapping the moral domain: New images of the self in relationship. In T. C. Heller, M. Sosna, & D. E. Wellbery (Eds.), *Reconstructing individualism: Autonomy, individuality, and the self in Western thought* (pp. 237-252). Stanford, CA: Stanford University Press.

Gilligan, C. (1987). Moral orientation and moral development. In E. F. Kittay & D. T. Meyers (Eds.), *Women and moral theory* (pp. 19-33). Totowa, NJ: Rowman & Littlefield.

Gilligan, C., & Attanucci, J. (1988). Two moral orientations: Gender differences and similarities. *Merrill-Palmer Quarterly, 34*, 223-237.

Gilligan, C., Brown, L. M., & Rogers, A. G. (1990). Psyche embedded: A place for body, relationships, and culture in personality theory. In A. I. Rabin, R. A. Zucker, R. A. Emmons, & S. Frank (Eds.), *Studying persons and lives* (pp. 86-147). New York: Springer.

Gilligan, C., Lyons, N. P., & Hanmer, T. J. (Eds.). (1990). *Making connections: The relational worlds of adolescent girls at Emma Willard School.* Cambridge, MA: Harvard University Press.

Gilligan, C., Ward, J. V., & Taylor, J. M. (Eds.). (1988). *Mapping the moral domain: A contribution of women's thinking to psychological theory and education.* Cambridge, MA: Harvard University Graduate School of Education.

Gilligan, C., & Wiggins, G. (1987). The origins of morality in early childhood relationships. In J. Kagan & S. Lamb (Eds.), *The emergence of morality in young children* (pp. 277-305). Chicago: University of Chicago Press.

Haan, N., Aerts, E., & Cooper, B. A. B. (1985). *On moral grounds: The search for practical morality.* New York: New York University Press.

Haan, N., Smith, M. B., & Block, J. (1968). Moral reasoning of young adults: Political-social behavior, family background, and personality correlates. *Journal of Personality and Social Psychology, 10,* 183-201.

Hare-Mustin, R. T. (1987). The gender dichotomy and developmental theory: A response to Sayers. *New Ideas in Psychology, 5,* 261-267.

Hare-Mustin, R. T., & Marecek, J. (1988). The meaning of difference: Gender theory, postmodernism, and psychology. *American Psychologist, 43,* 455-464.

Held, V. (1987). Feminism and moral theory. In E. F. Kittay & D. T. Meyers (Eds.), *Women and moral theory* (pp. 111-128). Totowa, NJ: Rowman & Littlefield.

Henley, N. M. (1985). Psychology and gender. *Signs, 11,* 101-119.

Higgins, A. (1989). The just community educational program: The development of moral role-taking as the expression of justice and care. In M. M. Brabeck (Ed.), *Who cares? Theory, research, and educational implications of the ethic of care* (pp. 197-215). New York: Praeger.

Hill, T. E., Jr. (1987). The importance of autonomy. In E. F. Kittay & D. T. Meyers (Eds.), *Women and moral theory* (pp. 129-138). Totowa, NJ: Rowman & Littlefield.

Houston, B. (1989). Prolegomena to future caring. In M. M. Brabeck (Ed.), *Who cares? Theory, research, and educational implications of the ethic of care* (pp. 84-100). New York: Praeger.

Johnston, D. K. (1988). Adolescents' solutions to dilemmas in fables: Two moral orientations—two problem solving strategies. In C. Gilligan, J. V. Ward, & J. M. Taylor (Eds.), *Mapping the moral domain: A contribution of women's thinking to psychological theory and education* (pp. 49-71). Cambridge, MA: Harvard University Graduate School of Education.

Kohlberg, L. (1976). Moral stages and moralization: The cognitive-developmental approach. In T. Lickona (Ed.), *Moral development and behavior: Theory, research, and social issues* (pp. 31-53). New York: Holt, Rinehart and Winston.

Kohlberg, L. (1981). *Essays on moral development: Vol. 1. The philosophy of moral development.* San Francisco: Harper & Row.

Kohlberg, L. (1984). *Essays on moral development: Vol. 2. The psychology of moral development.* San Francisco: Harper & Row.

Kohlberg, L., Boyd, D. R., & Levine, C. (1990). The return of Stage 6: Its principle and moral point of view. In T. Wren (Ed.), *The moral domain: Essays in the ongoing discussion between philosophy and the social sciences* (pp. 151-181). Cambridge, MA: MIT Press.

Kohlberg, L., & Kramer, R. (1969). Continuities and discontinuities in childhood and adult moral development. *Human Development, 12,* 93-120.

Krebs, D. L. (1970). Altruism—An examination of the concept and a review of the literature. *Psychological Bulletin, 73,* 258-302.

Langdale, C. J. (1986). A re-vision of structural-developmental theory. In G. L. Sapp (Ed.), *Handbook of moral development: Models, processes, techniques, and research* (pp. 15-54). Birmingham, AL: Religious Education Press.

Lloyd, G. (1983). Reason, gender, and morality in the history of philosophy. *Social Research, 50,* 490-513.

Lykes, M. B. (1989). The caring self: Social experiences of power and powerlessness. In M. M. Brabeck (Ed.), *Who cares? Theory, research, and educational implications of the ethic of care* (pp. 164-179). New York: Praeger.

Lyons, N. P. (1983). Two perspectives: On self,

relationships, and morality. *Harvard Educational Review, 53,* 125-145.

Martin, J. R. (1987). Transforming moral education. *Journal of Moral Education, 16,* 204-213.

Mason, A. (1990). Gilligan's conception of moral maturity. *Journal for the Theory of Social Behaviour, 20,* 167-179.

Mednick, M. T. (1989). On the politics of psychological constructs: Stop the bandwagon, I want to get off. *American Psychologist, 44,* 1118-1123.

Noddings, N. (1984). *Caring: A feminine approach to ethics and moral education.* Berkeley, CA: University of California Press.

Power, F. C., Higgins, A., & Kohlberg, L. (1989). *Lawrence Kohlberg's approach to moral education.* New York: Columbia University Press.

Pratt, M. W., Golding, G., & Hunter, W. J. (1984). Does morality have a gender? Sex, sex role, and moral judgment relationships across the adult lifespan. *Merrill-Palmer Quarterly, 30,* 321-340.

Pratt, M. W., Golding, G., Hunter, W., & Sampson, R. (1988). Sex differences in adult moral orientations. *Journal of Personality, 56,* 373-391.

Puka, B. (1989a). The liberation of caring: A different voice for Gilligan's "different voice." In M. M. Brabeck (Ed.), *Who cares? Theory, research, and educational implications of the ethic of care* (pp. 19-44). New York: Praeger.

Puka, B. (1989b). Caring—In an interpretive voice. *New Ideas in Psychology, 7,* 295-314.

Puka, B. (1991). Interpretive experiments: Probing the care-justice debate in moral development. *Human Development, 34,* 61-80.

Rest, J. R. (1979). *Development in judging moral issues.* Minneapolis: University of Minnesota Press.

Rosenthal, R. (1979). The "file-drawer problem" and tolerance for null results. *Psychological Bulletin, 86,* 638-641.

Rosenthal, R. (1984). *Meta-analytic procedures for social research.* Beverly Hills, CA: Sage.

Rothbart, M. K., Hanley, D., & Albert, M. (1986). Gender differences in moral reasoning. *Sex Roles, 15,* 645-653.

Seigfried, C. H. (1989). Pragmatism, feminism, and sensitivity to context. In M. M. Brabeck (Ed.), *Who cares? Theory, research, and educational implications of the ethic of care* (pp. 63-83). New York: Praeger.

Sher, G. (1987). Other voices, other rooms? Women's psychology and moral theory. In E. F. Kittay & D. T. Meyers (Eds.), *Women and moral theory* (pp. 178-189). Totowa, NJ: Rowman & Littlefield.

Sichel, B. A. (1985). Women's moral development in search of philosophical assumptions. *Journal of Moral Education, 14,* 149-161.

Stocker, M. (1987). Duty and friendship: Toward a synthesis of Gilligan's contrastive moral concepts. In E. F. Kittay & D. T. Meyers (Eds.), *Women and moral theory* (pp. 56-68). Totowa, NJ: Rowman & Littlefield.

Thoma, S. J. (1986). Estimating gender differences in the comprehension and preference of moral issues. *Developmental Review, 6,* 165-180.

Waithe, M. E. (1989). Twenty-three hundred years of women philosophers: Toward a gender undifferentiated moral theory. In M. M. Brabeck (Ed.), *Who cares? Theory, research, and educational implications of the ethic of care* (pp. 3-18). New York: Praeger.

Walker, L. J. (1984). Sex differences in the development of moral reasoning: A critical review. *Child Development, 55,* 677-691.

Walker, L. J. (1986a). Experiential and cognitive sources of moral development in adulthood. *Human Development, 29,* 113-124.

Walker, L. J. (1986b). Sex differences in the development of moral reasoning: A rejoinder to Baumrind. *Child Development, 57,* 522-526.

Walker, L. J. (1988). The development of moral reasoning. *Annals of Child Development, 5,* 33-78.

Walker, L. J. (1989). A longitudinal study of moral reasoning. *Child Development, 60,* 157-166.

Walker, L. J. (1991). Sex differences in moral reasoning. In W. M. Kurtines & J. L. Gewirtz (Eds.), *Handbook of moral behavior and development* (Vol. 2, pp. 333-364).

Hillsdale, NJ: Erlbaum.

Walker, L. J., de Vries, B., & Trevethan, S. D. (1987). Moral stages and moral orientations in real-life and hypothetical dilemmas. *Child Development, 58,* 842-858.

Walker, L. J., & Moran, T. J. (1991). Moral reasoning in a Communist Chinese society. *Journal of Moral Education, 20,* 139-155.

Walker, L. J., & Taylor, J. H. (1991). Family interactions and the development of moral reasoning. *Child Development, 62,* 264-283.

Yacker, N., & Weinberg, S. L. (1990). Care and justice moral orientation: A scale for its assessment. *Journal of Personality Assessment, 55,* 18-27.

# In a Communitarian Voice: The Sociological Expansion of Kohlbergian Theory, Research, and Practice

*JOHN SNAREY*
*Emory University*

## Abstract

This chapter proposes that Kohlberg's theory does not sufficiently take into account social class and cultural variations in moral reasoning. The validity of this critique is evaluated by a review of both quantitative and qualitative Kohlbergian research. Finally, the critique is extended to Kohlberg's application to educational practice. This three-part analysis reveals that genuine forms of moral reasoning are incompletely represented in Kohlberg's theory, empirical method, and educational practice. These missing values are consistent with what sociologist Ferdinand Tönnies described as the communitarian voice commonly found in working-class communities and folk, or nonurban, cultural groups.

This chapter considers the possibility that Kohlbergian theory, research, and educational practice do not sufficiently take into account social class and cross-cultural differences in moral reasoning. To set the stage for this analysis, I would like to begin by challenging you to see the connections between Kohlberg's work and two sociological observations.

First, my experience and field research overseas and in the U.S. have shown me that "doing favors" is a primary means of building and maintaining relationships within folk (village) and working class communities (Snarey, 1987, 1993). This favor-doing forms a complex social system that is governed by clear social norms; reciprocity is expected to be mutual, equitable, and nonexploitive. It is assumed that all persons deserve mutual respect, balanced exchanges, and fair honest deals. Working-class people typically view such informal *quid pro quo* (Latin, "something for something") exchanges as expressions of good citizenship, faithfulness, and loyalty. Members of the middle class, however, typically view such *quid pro quo* exchanges suspiciously, characterizing them as "shocking" (i.e., explicit), "crude" (i.e., unconcealed), and "political in the worst (i.e., non-middle class) sense."

Second, Sample (1984) has noted one of the bases for these contrasting class perspectives:

> Reciprocity is a basic ingredient in blue-collar lifestyles, [but] it is understood differently by working-class people than by middle-class people because middle-class life operates on a different basis. The middle classes emerged at the end of the feudal period and had to make the case for their status on the basis of universal laws and civil rights. They claimed the right to own property as a basic human and civil right. . . . This combination of values and interests, proclaimed and sustained by the middle class, contributed to the shape of the modern world. . . . The major beneficiary of this bourgeois contribution has also been the middle class. It is no secret that the laws of the Western world have been written on behalf of those who own property. And, except for more recent history when working-class people have owned their own homes, these laws have not benefitted them very much. (p. 137)

Sample (1984) also concludes that an outcome of such differences is that middle- or upper-class "universalistic" ideas of society and morality are regarded suspiciously by working-class people because, especially with regard to economic equality or educational opportunity, working-class people believe they have learned who actually benefits by such high-sounding appeals—the more privileged classes. Working-class people typically view formal contracts as "legal" justifications for the continuation of upper-class Machiavellian deceit, selfishness, and pomposity (cf. Turner & Martinez, 1977); thus, working-class folks tend to enter contract negotiations with historically grounded suspicions.

Now, of course, Kohlberg's model of moral development defines *quid pro quo* reasoning as primarily characteristic of Stage 2, and legalistic contractual reasoning as primarily characteristic of Stage 4. What is conventional reasoning in a working class subculture, therefore, can be misinterpreted as preconventional reasoning. Such misinterpretations may potentially occur at any stage level. In this chapter, examples will also be provided of postconventional reasoning among working-class people and folk cultural groups. This observation is also reminiscent of Carol Gilligan's (1982) feminist critique, of course, which suggested that Kohlberg's "universal" model had left out the voices of women. Similarly, I will provide examples in this chapter that point out how using the privileged classes' and elite cultural groups' moral values as the universal criteria for modeling, researching, and promoting all human moral development ironically mistreats people from working-class and folk subcultures because it promotes a misunderstanding of their ethical values and a silencing of their claims against the status quo of inequality.

The chapter will now turn, in successive sections, to considerations of Kohlbergian theory, research, and educational practice.

## Theory

In *The Philosophy of Moral Development,* the first volume of his collected essays, Kohlberg (1981) summarized his theoretical claim of universality as follows:

> All individuals in all cultures use the same thirty basic moral categories, concepts, or principles, and all individuals in all cultures go through the same order or sequence of gross stage development, though they vary in rate and terminal point of development. (p. 126)

Kohlberg (1981) maintained, in brief, that the development of moral reasoning follows a universal invariant sequence, toward the same universal ethical principles, in all social classes and cultural groups (p. 116). This particular element of Kohlberg's theory has, in fact, been the most difficult for many social scientists to accept (cf. Edwards, 1986; Haan, Aerts, & Cooper, 1985; Shweder, 1982; Simpson, 1974; Snarey, 1985; Sullivan, 1977).

To gain a measure of theoretical leverage on Kohlberg's theory, this first section of the chapter will review the classic theoretical work of sociologist Ferdinand Tönnies (pronounced "two-neez") in order to clarify the contrasting basic values that characterize working-class versus middle-class communities and folk versus urban cultural groups. This perspective will then be used to evaluate the thesis that Kohlberg's model incompletely represents the communitarian voice that is typical of working class and folk communities.

## Tönnies's Background

Ferdinand Tönnies (1855-1936) was a founding contributor to the rise of socio-logical theory. Born into a wealthy farm family, Tönnies spent his childhood in rural Germany and, throughout his life, he remained passionately bonded to the land and was known for having an easy way with rural village and work-ing-class people (Cahnman & Heberle, 1971). After studying at several German universities, he received his doctorate of philosophy from Tuebingen in 1877 and went on to establish a distinguished career as Professor of Sociology at the University of Kiel and as the president of the German Sociological Society from 1909 to 1933, a group he founded with Georg Simmel, Max Weber, and others. Despite his influential theoretical work, however, Tönnies was not popular with some of his contemporaries. "His . . . socialist leanings, his support of working class movements [e.g., trade unions and consumer cooperatives], and . . . his membership in the Ethical Culture Society," for instance, "made him *persona non grata* with the powerful chief of personnel of the central university of Prussia" (Cahnman & Heberle, 1971, p. xv). Tönnies also joined the Social Democrat Party in 1932 as a statement against the rising influence of Nazism. "This and his public denunciation of Nazism and anti-Semitism in the winter of 1932/33 led to his illegal discharge by the Hitler government from his position as professor emeritus" in 1933 (Heberle, 1968, p. 99). He died 3 years after his eviction by the Nazi regime, having nearly attained the age of 81.

## Tönnies's Community versus Society Typology

Tönnies established his place among the founders of modern social theory with his typology of *Gemeinschaft* (German, "community") versus *Gesellschaft* (Ger-man, "association" or "society"). He begins his book (1887) *Gemeinschaft und Gesellschaft* (Community and Society) by creating a series of comparisons. In a *Gemeinschaft* or communitarian type of social order relationships are construed as "real," "organic," and as "ends" in themselves. In a *Gesellschaft* or associa-tional type of social entity relationships become "imaginary," "mechanical," and "means" to an end. Community has to do with "all intimate, private and exclusive living together." Society involves "public life—it is the world itself" (p. 33). One lives in community "from birth on, bound to it in weal and woe." One enters society as "into a strange country" (p. 34). Community is associated with language, folkways, and mores, while society involves business, travel, science, and commerce. In community, "will by feeling" is revealed in custom; in society, "will by thought" is reflected in statute law and a formally ordered system of government. Community is rooted in the whole of humankind. It is the old, lasting, and genuine form of living together, likened to a living organ-ism itself. Society is based on coexistence. It is the new, urban, transitory, and superficial mode of social existence, likened to a mechanical conglomeration. A communitarian social order remains united despite superficial separations; an associational social order is divided despite superficial unity.

It is clear that the everyday use of the terms *community* and *society* are not synonymous with Tönnies's community versus society; a neighborhood community, for instance, may be more or less communitarian (*Gemeinschaft*) or associational (*Gesellschaft*) in character. Tönnies notes, furthermore, that neither *Gemeinschaft* or *Gesellschaft* exists in absolutely pure form. They are to be understood as ideal types, that is, as intentional idealizations which are useful because they allow one to compare or analyze actual societies relative to the ideal model. Therefore, one can only speak of communitarian-like or association-like social entities, and of communitarian-oriented or association-oriented persons, in the knowledge that all societies and all individuals manifest, at least to some degree, elements of both types and that the relative balance between the two poles may change at different times during the life history of any particular society or person.

### Community and Society Variations

Tönnies described a variety of subtypes or variations within each pole of his typology.

There are three subtypes of *Gemeinschaft*: Community of Blood (kinship), Community of Locality (neighborhood), and Community of Mind (friendship) (p. 42). One's house is the realm of kinship, where one is among one's own. In the neighborhood, relationships are reinforced by the fact of physical proximity. Between friends, when the dimension of locality is missing, relationships are maintained by habits of reunion or sacred customs. Memory, habit, love, gratitude, trust, understanding, and faithfulness are critical to community. "Only as long as mutual furtherance and affirmation exist can a relation really be considered *Gemeinschaft*" (Tönnies, 1887/1957, p. 44). In the preceding description, the interconnectedness of the community is evident. It is bound together by an understanding that is tacit, inexpressible, never ending, and incomprehensible. The highest expressions of community, according to Tönnies, can be found in such forms as guilds, fraternities, fellowships of workers, and religious communities.

One also could conceivably construct three subtypes of *Gesellschaft* or associational social orders. For instance, in contrast to a community of kinship or family, Tönnies writes that in an associational society, "the family becomes an accidental form for the satisfaction of natural needs, neighborhood and friendship are supplanted by special interest groups and conventional society life" (Tönnies, 1887/1957, p. 168). Tönnies, however unsystematically, also implies two additional distinctions, which I will term: (a) society as explicitly associational and (b) society as pseudo-community. Both versions represent "artificial" constructions (Tönnies, 1887/1957, pp. 64, 65). In explicit associational society, persons unashamedly acknowledge that there are "no actions that can be derived from an a priori and necessary existing unity; no actions therefore, which manifest the will and the spirit of the unity even if performed by the individual" (p. 65). That is, it is commonly understood that there is nothing that has common value. Things derive their value on the basis of the parties participating in a given transaction. There is an artificial common will that exists only as long as the transaction is taking place. For something to be of value in society, it is only necessary that someone has something that someone else wants. In contrast, this social fact is camouflaged in society-as-pseudo-community. Each person is working for the self, while superficially appearing to work for the good of the other. As he states:

> Here in the *Gesellschaft*, in that which is useful to you and essential for your ends and purposes, you must limit your freedom in such a manner as to respect the freedom of others, because only thus can you maintain your own sphere or enlarge it. You must keep yourself in the esteem of others; they must fear and have a good opinion of your strength. Therefore, it is helpful to appear morally good and noble, fair and just, if and for so long as the appearance of these values has value for you. (Tönnies, 1887/1957, p. 160)

Each person is working for the self, while superficially appearing to work for the society. Tonnies's nominee for "the most . . . *Gesellschaft*-like state" in the modern world was the United States of America (p. 221), although there are also significant *Gemeinschaft* elements in U.S. society which have moved into and back out of the foreground at different points in our society's history (see Laupa and Turiel, Chapter 17, this vol.).

### Means versus Ends

Tönnies was explicit about the construction of pseudo-community means for actual-society ends. The distinction between means and ends is also crucial for understanding the contrast between communitarian versus associational ethical perspectives. Tönnies's distinction between the nature of means and ends in the two social forms, that is, is crucial for understanding his vision of an ethical *telos* (Greek, "end point"):

> I have thought of the possible kinds of positive relations among human beings, including the relations of the individual to the social unit. My types are: First, the unit is felt and thought of as an end, that is, as a natural whole, and second, the unit is felt and thought of as means to the ends of the individual and therefore as something that is made, an instrument. (Tönnies, 1893/1973, p. 253)

He elaborates on the relationship between will and means and ends as follows:

> Essential will definitely comprises what psychologists would call volitional actions insofar as they affirm means and ends as an organic whole, that is, as belonging together. The concept of arbitrary will arises, as it were, only when and to the extent that means and ends

become separated (become alienated from each other), to the point even of becoming outright antagonistic to each other. (Tönnies, 1925/1971, p. 66)

In sum, the basic ethical question of Tonnies' perspective is whether people and relationships are simply means to other ends or are also ends in themselves in terms of will and action (Heddendorf, 1969). Community maintains a unity of means and ends.

Tönnies's typology has become an archetypal formulation of the differences between modern, industrial, urban societies, on the one hand, and traditional, agrarian, rural societies, on the other. His theory is a carefully wrought critique of Western modernity and, by extension, of the upper social classes. The theoretical descendants of Tonnies's communitarian versus associational social types include Emile Durkheim's "mechanical" versus "organic" solidarity, and "sacred" versus "profane" social realms; Robert Redfield's "folk-urban" continuum; Pitrim Sorokin's "familistic" versus "contractual" relations; and many others (cf. Loomis & McKinney, 1957, pp. 12-29).

## *Tönnies on Kohlberg*

Tönnies's sociological typology is of particular relevance for evaluating the social class and cross-cultural inclusiveness of Kohlbergian theory for several reasons. Tönnies's typology effectively: (1) addresses ethical, psychological, and sociological dimensions of the relationship between the individual and society; (2) avoids the reductionism of theories that view the individual as solely determined by the group; (3) tends to take a developmental approach to society; and (4) is critical of Western rationalism and middle class individualism, offering a carefully nuanced but tantalizingly simple paradigm for analyzing the differences between Western modernity and other social constructions.

Kohlberg's theory, of course, is primarily associational or *Gesellschaft*-like. Convention and rationality, central elements of his theory, are central society qualities. In fact, several of Kohlberg's critics accuse him of precisely this limitation, that is, of having constructed an individualistic, elitist, Western theory that is incomplete in terms of the voices of women, people from non-elite social classes, and people from non-Western cultural groups (cf. Edwards, 1986; Gilligan, 1982; Simpson, 1974; Sullivan, 1977). Although empirical research has not provided straightforward support for these critiques, there are striking parallels between the groups Tönnies associates with community or *Gemeinschaft* and the groups Kohlberg's theory is purported to misunderstand or exclude. It is also important to note that Kohlberg's research method is patently *Gesellschaft*-like. The society-oriented formal legal structures embedded within Heinz-like dilemmas, for instance, cannot be easily reconciled with the communitarian-like values of communal interconnectedness, harmony, and suspicion of formal legal structures. The association-like moral dilemmas, that is, are at odds with communitarian moral reasoning.

The quantitative and qualitative empirical data relevant to this thesis will be evaluated in the next section.

## Research

In *The Psychology of Moral Development*, the second volume of his collected essays, Kohlberg (1984) justifies his claim for universality against critiques that his theory is not culturally inclusive (cf. Shweder, 1982; Simpson, 1974). As part of his defense, he draws upon the results of longitudinal research conducted in "the United States, Turkey, and Israel"and cross-sectional research conducted in "India, Turkey, Taiwan, Zambia, and other non-Western societies" (p. 324-325). This and other quantitative and qualitative empirical evidence will be reviewed in this second section in order to evaluate the support for two of the major theoretical assumptions underlying Kohlberg's claim—the representation of the full range of stages in diverse sociocultural settings and the general applicability of the stages to all moral judgments made by people from diverse social classes and cultural groups.

### Review Questions and Method

Two questions are addressed in order to evaluate the universality claim of Kohlberg's stage theory, and to develop the theory toward greater social class and cross-cultural inclusiveness.

#### Full Stage Range and Quantitative Research

Are all stages of moral development described by Kohlberg, including the highest, represented in all types of cultural groups and social classes? The full range of moral stages, including the highest, should be found in all types of cultural groups. The consistent absence of some stages in particular types of societies, that is, would suggest that the missing stages are not universally applicable. To be perfectly clear, the claim is not that every individual should reach the highest stage, and it is not even that the highest stage should be found in every society studied. Rather, the claim is that adequate and representative samples from all *types* of cultural groups, including both communitarian or *Gemeinschaft* and associational or *Gesellschaft*, should evidence all levels of moral reasoning in Kohlberg's model to establish its universality.

I (1985) previously reviewed the quantitative empirical data relevant to this question, and in this section I will give an abridged but updated summary of quantitative findings: This report is based on a systematic review of all known English-language cross-cultural studies of moral reasoning that had used Kohlberg's model and measure. To help ensure that the interviews had been reliably scored and, otherwise, to make the studies as comparable as possible, only studies that had used the standardized scoring manual (Colby & Kohlberg, 1978/1987) were reviewed. One caveat is obvious. Studies that include only children could not be required to find the most mature stages present, just as studies that include only adults could not be required to find examples of the earliest stages. The best test cases for the postconventional stages would be samples of adult subjects from non-Western, nonurban populations chosen because the other adult members of their society considered them to be examples of unusual moral maturity.

### General Stage Applicability and Qualitative Research

Do all instances of genuine moral reasoning in all social classes and cultural groups correspond to one of the modes or stages of moral reasoning described by Kohlberg? According to Kohlberg, no genuine moral judgments should be found for which none of the available stages or stage transitions is applicable; in other words, there is no wastebasket category. It is, of course, possible that moral statements may be found for which either the subject gives no explanation or the explanation is vague and very brief. Here, the available categories cannot be applied, not because they are inadequate as a set but because no clear or genuine moral judgment can be interpreted. However, clear criteria must be provided to determine whether the information given is inadequate or whether the available stage categories are insufficient. Otherwise, the meaning of *vague* or *incomplete* may be interpreted in such a way that Kohlberg's set of categories could never be proven false.

Snarey and Keljo (1991) previously reviewed the qualitative empirical data relevant to this question, and an abridged but updated summary of the qualitative findings will be reported in this section. This summary is based on a systematic review of all known studies and available interview transcripts for specific examples of moral judgments that were difficult to score. The presence of such material could call this final assumption into question in that qualitative analysis of cultural patterns in the theoretically unconventional or anomalous judgments would help define particular areas of inadequacy in Kohlberg's theory.

## Overview of Quantitative Research Findings

In order to review all known cross-cultural studies that had used Kohlberg's standardized scoring manual, the subjects from the various studies were first organized by age groups and cultural groups. This involved 6 age categories and the following 10 countries or cultural regions:

Finland (Helkama & Ikonen, 1986),

India (Vasudev & Hummel, 1987),

Israel (Bar-Yam & Abrahami, 1982; Linn, 1987a, 1987b; Snarey, Reimer, & Kohlberg, 1985a, 1985b),

Kenya (Harkness, Edwards, & Super, 1981),

New Guinea (Tietjen & Walker, 1985),

Poland (Niemczynski, Czyzowska, Pourkos, & Mirski, 1988),

Taiwan (Lei & Cheng, 1984),

Tibet (Huebner, Garrod, & Snarey, 1990; Huebner & Garrod, 1991),

Turkey (Nisan & Kohlberg, 1982), and the

United States (Colby, Kohlberg, Gibbs, & Lieberman, 1983; Cortese, 1984; Lee & Snarey, 1988; Shulik, 1988).

This procedure yielded a total of 59 age-by-culture sample subgroups: 5 late-adulthood subgroups, 11 middle-adulthood subgroups, 13 early-adulthood subgroups, 13 late-adolescence subgroups, 9 middle-adolescence subgroups, and 8 early-adolescence or late-childhood subgroups. These sets of data were then examined quantitatively to address the question of the full stage range.

A survey of the moral development stage scores for all 59 populations showed that, overall, the full range of stages was represented—from 77 percent of the 10- to 12-year-old Turkish village children at Stage 1 or Stage 1/2, to 83 percent of a selected sample of senior kibbutz members at Stage 4/5 or 5. One also noted that, as progressively older age groups were considered from early adolescence to middle adulthood, the stage scores also consistently increased. A slight fall in scores during later adulthood was primarily due to the fact that, in contrast, the middle-adulthood subgroup included several intentionally selected elite samples, many of which had exhibited exemplary moral behavior (see also Narvaez & Rest, Chapter 14, this vol.). Stage 1 or Stage 1/2 was present among 6 of the 8 young-adolescent samples. Presumably, if younger Taiwanese and kibbutz children were interviewed, Stage 1 would also be found in these two exceptions. Stage 1 disappeared after middle adolescence, and Stage 2 and Stage 3 were well represented among both older adolescents and adults. Stage 4 first appeared during late adolescence and became common in the young-adult samples. Stage 4/5 was first seen in an 18-year-old Taiwanese high-school student and was represented in 9 of the 13 young-adult samples and 10 of the 11 middle-adulthood samples. Stage 4/5 was found only among 1 of the 5 older-adult samples, although these age groups also often represented only non-advantaged people. Stage 5, in particular, proved to be quite rare among all adults. All subjects who scored as fully Stage 5 were 30 years or older in age and came from only 3 countries. These included 2 socially elite subjects in India, 15 moral activists in Israel (kibbutz members or war protestors), and 10 subjects in the United States.

A more critical scrutiny of the cultural distribution of the stages within each age range showed that subjects in urban societies always had a faster rate and reached a higher end point of development than did subjects from traditional folk societies. When only the adult samples were considered, Stage 4/5 or 5 was present to some degree in 100 percent of the modern *Gesellschaft*-like urban samples, both Western and non-Western (Finland, India, Israel, Poland, Taiwan, and the United States). Stage 4/5 or 5 was also present among the members of two modern but also communitarian kibbutz communities, one of which was a rural village and the other a small town. In contrast, Stage 4/5 or 5 was absent from 100 percent of the three traditional *Gemeinschaft*-like folk or village communities (rural Kenya, Papua New Guinea village, Turkish village).

Another approach to the question of the full range of stages is to examine social class subcultures within the various societies studied and ask whether the subgroups differ significantly. Kohlberg's original 20-year longitudinal study in the United States had shown significant social class differences in the rate of moral development: Middle-class subjects had a faster rate of development than their working-class peers (Colby, Kohlberg, Gibbs, & Lieberman, 1983). This pattern was replicated in 100 percent of the cross-cultural studies under review for which social class was known: Upper middle- and middle-class subjects always showed a faster rate of development than working- or lower-class subjects within the same society.

In sum, as one surveys the samples within each of the six age-level categories, one observes that the mean scores of consistently urban or middle-class samples are always higher than those of consistently nonurban or non-middle-class samples. Stage 5, in particular, was found to be a rare empirical phenomenon, and its distribution was skewed toward particular types of social entities. From a methodological perspective, one could argue that part of the reason for these findings lies with the size of the adult samples; 6 of the 13 populations in the oldest age-group included fewer than two-dozen subjects each. It might, in fact, be unreasonable to expect such small samples of adult moral reasoning to represent the population of moral reasoning instances. However, 9 of the 13 samples in the oldest age range were intentionally selected because they were thought to have a higher probability of including some subjects at the higher stages. Of these 9 samples, 7 did in fact include a substantial number of subjects at Stage 4/5 or 5 (5 Israeli samples, 1 Taiwanese sample, 1 Indian sample), but the other 2 selected populations did not go beyond Stage 3 or 3/4 (Kenyan village leaders, New Guinea village leaders). It is noteworthy that both of the selected samples that failed to score beyond the conventional level were the most consistently traditional folk societies. Village leaders in Kenya and New Guinea did score significantly higher than nonleaders, however, suggesting that their fellow villagers recognized characteristics related to moral development as relevant to village leadership. Yet, the fact that no members of traditional folk societies, including leaders, used Stage 4/5 or 5 reasoning suggests the additional possibility that the theory itself is incomplete. Specific patterns of omissions in the theory are considered in the following section.

## Overview of Qualitative Research Findings

Do all instances of moral reasoning, regardless of a subject's cultural background, correspond to one of the finite modes of moral reasoning described by Kohlberg? A growing number of cases of genuine moral judgments that were not scorable have been included in research reports. Snarey and Keljo (1991) reprinted examples from research conducted in Israel (kibbutz), India, Kenya (rural village), Papua New Guinea (Maisin village), Taiwan, Turkey, and the United States (working class). Based on this material, Snarey and Keljo (1991) formulated descriptions of post-conventional *Gemeinschaft*-like thought as it might be expressed on different norms. These include the following six concepts: happiness, tradition, understanding, reciprocity, role relationships, and the unity of life.

### Happiness

In community, the principle of happiness relies on the conviction that people live out their existence in the context of both their personal innate characteristics and their relationships in the web of the community. Happiness thus construed is the fulfillment of potentials inherent in the individual and the social context. A postconventional construction of happiness recognizes that while the traditions and norms are generally conducive to happiness, they are also subject to the principle of happiness. The happiness of the individual which is integrally linked to the well-being of the community is a value that functions as a principle for evaluating a given societal construction or a moral decision.

### Tradition

Tradition seems to fulfill the role of law in communitarian moral reasoning. For those who live in *Gemeinschaft*-like societies, that is, tradition seems to stand as either a parallel or superior system to the *Gesellschaft* legal system and decisions are guided more by tradition than they are by law or rationality. It is important to note, however, that in a postconventional construction of tradition, it will also be recognized that tradition represents an approximation of the nature of being. Tradition is a respected and trustworthy approximation of the nature of being which lies beyond it.

### Understanding

A central value in community, understanding is a characteristic of the organic unity of a community. Concord or mutual understanding is not a means to some end but, rather, is integral to the community. In a postconventional formulation, concord or understanding becomes a principle adjudicating both the means and the end of resolving moral conflict. While this principle may be expressed in the norms or traditions of a given society, it derives its force from a position outside or above those systems.

### Reciprocity

As noted in the introduction, "doing favors" is a primary means of building and maintaining relationships within working-class communities and folk cultural groups. These complex systems of doing favors take various forms, but all are governed by clear social norms. Reciprocity is expected to be mutual, equitable, and nonexploitive; it is assumed that all persons deserve mutual respect, equal transactions, and fair deals. If these assumptions are breached (e.g., when promises are not kept, or when someone is "used" under the facade of a gift) both the person and the community are understood to have been violated.

### Role Relationships and Solidarity

More than simply means to some end, role relationships are part of the fabric of being. Each individual has a role in the context of the larger whole, and there are norms and customs associated with each role. In a postconventional construction of this concept, it is recognized that every individual has knowledge needed by the group, whatever her or his role. Moreover, the roles do not derive fundamentally from societal assignments. They, too, have their basis in being and in principles of responsibility. When an individual's role does not correspond with the person's being, or an individual does not live up to the responsibilities of a given role, normative role relationships are subject to modification.

### Unity of All Life

A final concept in the world view of community is that of the unity of all life. While this is related to the concepts of understanding and concord, it is also distinct. Communitarian ethics are based on the premise of the unity of all being. In a postconventional construction, it would be argued that all life is fundamentally connected. Undergirding social construction and moral decision-making is the principle of the organic connection and solidarity of all forms of life.

These formulations of postconventional communitarian thought must be qualified as being tentative theoretical formulations. To illustrate their social reality, however, excerpts from interviews with subjects from two populations (Israeli kibbutzniks and U.S. workers) will now be presented.

### Examples from an Israeli Kibbutz

A longitudinal study of moral development among kibbutz-born kibbutz members in Israel showed that all of Kohlberg's stages, including the postconventional, were present among kibbutz members, but that Kohlberg's scoring manual failed to capture some elements of kibbutz postconventional reasoning (Snarey, Reimer, & Kohlberg, 1985a). To identify what might be missing from the model and manual, all interview judgments on which the blinded scorers had given a "guess" score, indicating that the material was a genuine moral judgment but not easily scored according to the standardized manual, were clinically examined. It was observed that the lower-stage statements were usually difficult to score because of the incompleteness of that particular judgment by the subject, but that the higher-stage judgments that were difficult to score were usually complete, and that they reflected the *Gemeinschaft* working-class values of the kibbutz. Some judgments scored as guess Stage 4 or guess Stage 4/5 could be understood as full postconventional Stage 5 judgments if one took a communitarian rather than a middle-class individualistic perspective to the data. The following excerpts from two kibbutz-born subjects' interviews illustrate some of these principled judgments.

### Excerpt 1 (Kibbutz Female):

*Q.* It is against the law for Moshe to steal the drug. Does that make it morally wrong?

*A.* It will be illegal or against the formal law, but not against the law which is the moral law. Again, if we were in a utopian society, my hierarchy of values, and the hierarchy of others, through consensus, would be realized.

*Q.* What are those values?

*A.* Socialism. But (laughter) don't ask me to explain it.

*Q.* What is wrong with a nonsocialistic society that makes it unjust?

*A.* In a utopia . . . everyone will be equal. . . . It is our dream, our ideal. In one way it is ridiculous since this utopia will never be achieved, of course. . . .

*Q.* Should people still do everything they can to obey the law in an imperfect world?

*A.* Yes, unless it will endanger or hurt another important value. . . . But generally speaking, people should obey the law. The law was created in order to protect . . . from killing, robbery, and other unjust uses of power. . . . I believe everyone has the right to self-growth and the right to reach happiness. . . . People are not born equally genetically and it is not fair that one who is stronger physically should reach his happiness by whatever means at the expense of one who is weaker because the right to happiness is a basic human right of everyone, equal to all. A nonkibbutz society that is based on power negates the right and possibility of those who are weaker to get their happiness. . . .

### Excerpt 2 (Kibbutz Male):

*Q.* Should Moshe steal the drug?

*A.* Yes. . . . I think that the community should be responsible for controlling this kind of situation. The medicine should be made available to all in need; the druggist should not have the right to decide on his own . . . the whole community or society should have the control of the drug.

*Q.* Is it important for people to do everything they can to save another's life?

*A.* If I want to create a better community, a nice and beautiful one, an ideal world, the only way we can do it is by cooperation between people. . . . We need this cooperation among ourselves in order to achieve this better world. . . . The happiness . . . principle underlies this cooperation—the greatest happiness for the greatest number of people in the society.

*Q.* Should people try to do everything they can to obey the law?

*A.* In principle, yes. It is impossible to have any kind of state, country, society without laws. [Otherwise,] it will be complete anarchy and those who have the power will dominate the weaker.

*Q.* Why is that wrong?

*A.* I am [not] strong. (Laughter.) But really, you can see in the totalitarian countries today in contrast to, for example, the kibbutz. You damage the principle of democracy and, most importantly, you destroy the principle of equality. Which is why I [have chosen to] live on a kibbutz. (Snarey, Reimer, & Kohlberg, 1985a, p. 14)

Collective equality and happiness principles are common to these interviews. In a *Gemeinschaft* outlook, happiness is not an end to be attained by some means, as in the goal of "life, liberty, and the pursuit of happiness," but, rather, represents the fulfillment of individual being, which is understood in the context of an organic community. Similarly, equality is a part of community when it reflects, and is born out of, the interconnectedness of the community and the unity of all life. There is a sense in which these values are more mature than Kohlberg's definition of Stage 4, even though they are missing from Kohlberg's definition of Stage 5. The kibbutz functions for some subjects as an imperfect embodiment of a more utopian ideal. In declaring that the kibbutz is the basis for their moral argument, kibbutzniks are making a Stage 5 rather than a Stage 4 judgment to the extent that they view kibbutz membership as based on a commitment to cooperative equality and the equal right to happiness by all persons. Allusions in some interviews to the social system becoming dysfunctional are also not necessarily conventional system-maintenance judgments when the reason they are protecting the social system is also to protect the principle of collective equality and happiness. This is consistent with the working-class value of solidarity, for instance, but it is not fully consistent with Kohlberg's model.

### Examples from the U.S. Working Class

A subject from Kohlberg's longitudinal study in the United States (the son of a steel worker who himself works for the Post Office) also illustrates a working-class communitarian voice. In terms of Kohlberg's stage model, his interviews at age 28 were scored at Stage 4 on the original form of the interview and Stage 3/4-Guess on an alternate form of the interview. I would suggest that the "guess" and "unscorable" designations reflect the difficulty of a *Gesellschaft*-like model to make sense of a *Gemeinschaft*-like mind. This is transparent in the introductory autobiographical portion of the interview. He describes his wife as follows: "It seems like we make a good team, and it seems we tend to stick up for each other and we are backing each other up in all sorts of ways." Here is seen a communitarian a priori unity of wills. The way he describes his best friend also has a clear communitarian character:

> I've got a friend that I would do just about anything for . . . we have been quite close and we have stood up for each other many times. . . . I would do just about anything for him, and I never ever even discussed anything with the guy but I imagine that if Larry Kohlberg goes to . . . [location] and checks with him, he would probably say the same thing about me.

His friendship reflects an organic-unity orientation. Communitarian perspectives are also apparent in his comments regarding his job:

I am obligated to do the best job I can in the Post Office, even though I am so pissed off at the way it is going. It is getting worse.

*Q.* So what is it that makes you feel obligated. If the Post Office is not doing such a good job?

*A.* I have always been an admirer of tradition. . . . The Post Office itself is probably one of the oldest companies in the country, the Post Office started way back when, and I get a deep sense of dedication to it. . . .

*Q.* If it were private enterprise, would you have the same feeling of obligation?

*A.* I don't know. . . .

In this excerpt the subject expresses a sense in which he is bonded to his job through both good and bad. This bond seems to have its roots in a sense of tradition. Both the sense of organic belonging and the dimension of tradition are typical of community. Tradition seems to fulfill the role of law.

The last question asked by the interviewer can be understood as inquiring whether it would make any difference if the company were more associational. The subject is not sure. He is intuitively attracted by the relatively more community-like quality of the Post Office. Yet the Post Office has changed during his work career; as he went on to explain, its mission has evolved from that of being a service-providing agency to that of being a profit-making business. His work role has also changed. After serving as a letter carrier for many years, he was promoted to the equivalent of a foreman, a position caught in the rub between labor and management. The Post Office seems to have originally appeared to be a resolution to the tension between his need for upward mobility and his fundamentally communitarian values.

Later in the interview, when asked about a mercy killing dilemma, the subject indicates that he wishes that there would be a way "that we could circumvent the court system or the legality of shutting off the machine." This effort to keep things out of the courts is characteristic of communitarian reasoning; societal legality is foreign to pure *Gemeinschaft*. The closest this subject comes to making a postconventional judgment is at the end of the moral interview:

*Q.* Does that leave you to question your own moral expectations or standards?

*A.* Yeah, it leaves me wondering why I am beating my brains against the wall because it does no damn good. You wonder, "for the good of mankind," sometimes. Sometimes you wonder what the hell is mankind. They walk all over you.

*Q.* What do you think does keep you acting in a more or less moral way, if there is no set of rewards?

*A.* I don't know; it is same intangible inner drive.

The subject's reference to an "intangible inner drive" is a classic communitarian moral statement. While this subject may not have developed to the point of postconventional reasoning, there are several indications that the raters' difficulties in scoring the interview reflect their attempts to assimilate a *Gemeinschaft*-like interview to a *Gesellschaft*-like theory.

In sum, prior research has presented evidence from the Israeli kibbutz, India, Kenya, New Guinea, Taiwan, Tibet, Turkey, and the United States to suggest that communitarian-oriented moral judgments are misconstrued by Kohlberg's theory or scoring manual (Snarey & Keljo, 1991). As also illustrated by the interview excerpts from kibbutz and working-class subjects presented in this chapter, the language, basic values, and logical constructions of these judgments all reflect a communitarian voice.

## Application

Kohlberg and his colleagues, in *Lawrence Kohlberg's Approach to Moral Education* (Power, Higgins, & Kohlberg, 1989), describe and evaluate Kohlberg's practice of moral education. It reports "just community" interventions and their outcomes at the lower- and working-class Cluster School in Cambridge, MA, the upper-class Scarsdale Alternative High School in Scarsdale, NY, and the middle class School-Within-A-School in Brookline, MA.

### Kohlberg's "Just Community" Model

Kohlberg's original stage model of moral development remained remarkably consistent over the years, inattentive to cross-cultural critiques, but radical changes characterized the evolution of his approach to moral education. Drawing unexpectedly from the ideas of Emile Durkheim, Kohlberg came to believe that the unit of education was the group, not simply the individual, and that moral education should change the school's moral culture, not just develop the person's moral reasoning. Moral education, thus revised, involved both the collective socialization of moral content and the developmental promotion of moral reasoning. Kohlberg hoped to give priority to the power of the collective in a way that also protected the rights of the individual. To turn this new understanding of the requirements for effective moral education into practice, Kohlberg drew upon another source: the Israeli kibbutz—collective communities in Israel governed by direct participatory democracy. In 1969 he began a study of a kibbutz that had established a joint high school for their own kibbutz-born children and for nonadvantaged adolescents from Israeli cities (Kohlberg, 1971; Reimer, 1977; Snarey, 1987; Snarey, Reimer & Kohlberg, 1985a, 1985b). He and his colleagues concluded from the research findings that the kibbutz practice of group education was superior to anything that had been conceived from moral development theory, and that the kibbutz provided not just improvements in the manner of practicing of moral education, but also corrections in the manner of theorizing about moral education. The kibbutz became for Kohlberg and his colleagues a real-life model that had the power to shape, correct, and guide moral development theory and application.

Kohlberg called his new kibbutz-like approach to moral education the "just community" approach. It was deceptively simple—a return to the progressive ideals of educational democracy but within a communitarian mode. The keystone of any genuine just community school is a kibbutz-like weekly community meeting—a gathering of students and staff to decide school policies and practices that deal with issues of fairness. The general aim of the meetings is for students to achieve a sense of community solidarity and, within this context, to democratically arrive at fair decisions, to carry out these decisions and, as necessary, to democratically change their decisions. The just community educator's role is similar to that of the kibbutz *madrich* (youth leader): both function as both Durkheimian socializers and Piagetian facilitators. The teachers serve as moral leaders by advocating their own positions within the constraints of students' democratic participation and by being invested in "what" students decide to do and in "why" they decide to do it. The sense of group solidarity also allows the peer group to function as a moral authority for its members' behavior. In sum, Kohlberg and his educator colleagues claimed that "the just community approach purposely fosters *Gemeinschaft* as the principal project of the school" (pp. 106-107).

## Developmental Outcomes

Does Kohlberg's approach actually promote the moral reasoning of students or the moral culture of schools? Comparing each of the three just community schools with their parent high school, Kohlberg and his colleagues (Power, Higgins & Kohlberg, 1989) report that the students in each of the just community schools were significantly higher than their contemporaries attending the parent high schools on all moral culture variables, including degree of collectiveness and level of community valuing. The results on individual moral judgment development were also in the expected direction; the average moral stage scores for the students in the just community programs were significantly higher than for the students in the traditional programs. The stage gains were smaller than expected, but still respectable (e.g., Cluster students' two- and three-year longitudinal follow-up interviews showed that they had gained, on average, about a half-stage in moral development). It is also noteworthy that the evaluation studies found no statistically significant gender differences in any of the analyses of moral culture or moral stage variables.

Each of the three intervention schools made important gains compared to their parent schools, but how do the three just community schools compare with each other? The results surprised Kohlberg and his colleagues (1989, Table 8.4). The lower and working class "Cluster" just community school achieved lower mean scores on 100 percent of the six measures of moral and community development when compared to the upper-class "Alternative" school and the middle class "School-Within-A-School." These comparisons are complicated by the fact that the three interventions were not fully equivalent (e.g., Kohlberg, Power, and Higgins were more personally involved in the Cluster school), but these findings do suggest that Kohlberg's approach to moral education is more effective among middle- and upper-class students.

## Social Class Limitations

Just community schools are counter-cultural in a U.S. community, in contrast to their acceptability and goodness of fit within an Israeli kibbutz. Kohlbergian just-community schools, however, tend to ignore the importance of students' different social class experiences and to underplay the tension between the intervention's ideal of social equality and the larger reality of social inequality. Two examples from *Kohlberg's Approach to Moral Education* illustrate this.

When Cluster just-community school students' discussion comments revealed an awareness of social class inequality, their comments often were portrayed by Kohlberg and his colleagues (1989) as a regrettable tendency of the students to engage in nonmoral "practical" digressions (e.g., pp. 85-88). Consider the comments of Bev, a student, at a weekly community meeting in response to a real dilemma involving property damage by a minority of her fellow students during a just community school retreat:

> Two things. One, the reason I think the whole community is in it together is that we all went on a trip together and sort of agreed to be liable for everyone else, and we agreed to be part of the community. But obviously a lot of kids can't pay it, so maybe we'll have to do something, have a fund-raiser, I don't know. Not many people can pay $7.50 or whatever it is. (1989, p. 87)

Bev's fund-raiser proposal is interesting from a kibbutz perspective in that it is consistent with the principle of "from each according to his or her ability, to each according to his or her need," which is central to a kibbutz method of resolving moral dilemmas. Although her classmates eventually adopted her proposal as the most fair, the analysis implicitly classifies her "practical" ability-to-pay plea as a nonmoral digression (pp. 85-88). The analysis explicitly focuses only on the first half of the quote, indicating that "Bev offers a Stage 4 elaboration" (p. 139) that clarifies the "social contract involved in going on a retreat together" (p. 88). Most strikingly, when the original quote is repeated (pp. 88, 139), the text literally omits her practical concern with inequality from the quotation, ignoring the very orientation the community aims to promote.

Social class differences also appear to have influenced the very types of injustice that became "issues" in the schools studied by Power, Higgins, and Kohlberg (1989). "Stealing and property loss" were major issues among the lower- and working-class Cluster School students but not among the affluent Scarsdale Alternative High School students. "Cheating," in contrast, was a major issue among academically-focused Scarsdale students but not among vocationally-oriented Cluster students. The analysis notes that the transgressions are ethically analogous in that both involve the violation of trust (p. 213). What is ignored is how blue-collar students' theft of money versus white collar students' theft of test answers involve a response to the injustices of their particular social class and also reflect significant inequalities between their future life-chances.

While a kibbutz model inspired Kohlberg's just community schools, the model was not consistently translated in ways that addressed the special characteristics of education in the United States. Most just community educators simply were not well grounded in kibbutz educational practice, let alone in the complexities of adapting the kibbutz model to their unique situation. Thus, in the one and only working-class just community school, Kohlberg's ideal of turning an "undemocratic" school into a "kibbutz-like" school became operationalized as turning a "bad" school into a "middle-class" school.

## Conclusion

Kohlberg's developmental theory, empirical method, and pedagogical application all miss or misunderstand significant aspects of the moral reasoning of people from working class and folk cultural backgrounds.

### Theory

Tönnies's typology proved to be a powerfully inclusive method for interpreting the problems with Kohlberg's theory related to social class and cross-cultural inclusiveness. The general theoretical construct of a communitarian or *Gemeinschaft*-like voice has the potential for subsuming the values and concepts that are now omitted from Kohlberg's theory. Hence, it may yet prove possible to demonstrate the cross-cultural validity of a structural construct of Stage 5, if the theory is expanded to include more elements of communitarian judgments.

## Research

The review of quantitative research among 59 age-by-culture subgroups showed that Stages 1 to 4 were in evidence virtually universally when one considered the age range and sample size of the populations under study. Although the presence of Stage 4/5 or 5 was very rare in all populations (see also, Gibbs, Chapter 2, this vol.), it was evident to some degree in approximately two-thirds of the subcultures sampled that included subjects in the 18 to 80 age range. An examination of the presence or absence of the higher stages in different types of cultural groups and social classes, however, indicated that in nearly all samples, adults from urban cultural groups or middle-class populations exhibited some principled reasoning but that all samples of adults from folk cultural groups failed to exhibit any postconventional reasoning, and all samples of working-class populations evidenced lower levels of postconventional reasoning as defined by Kohlberg.

The review of qualitative hard-to-score interview data representing eight cultural groups revealed that there are legitimate forms of conventional and postconventional reasoning that seem to be missing from the current theory and scoring manual. Moreover, these forms of reasoning were consonant with or characteristic of *Gemeinschaft*, suggesting that values commonly stressed in *Gemeinschaft*-like folk cultural groups and working-class communities were missing from the theory's explication and the scoring manual's examples of reasoning at the higher stages.

## Application

While Kohlberg's just community schools were inspired by a communitarian kibbutz model, the kibbutz model was not always thoughtfully adapted for life in a highly associational society like our own. In particular, Kohlberg's just community translation of a kibbutz model to actual educational settings in the United States tended to overlook the importance of students' prior social class backgrounds and the class-oriented structure of our society. Nevertheless, just community schools still seem to me to have greater potential for class and cultural inclusiveness than anything else available. If operationalized with genuine social class and cultural inclusiveness, the just community approach clearly has the potential to provide a way for teachers and administrators to embody justice and care in their treatment of students from non-middle class and diverse cultural backgrounds.

## Gilligan Revisited

Carol Gilligan's (1982) feminist analysis of developmental theories is directly relevant to our thesis of an inadequately represented communitarian or *Gemeinschaft* voice in Kohlberg's theory. Kohlberg (1984) previously responded to Gilligan, for instance, by pointing out that most studies of adults have not found gender differences and, among those that do, most do not control for social class and, for those few that statistically control for education and job status, the initial gender differences disappear. Kohlberg concluded that gender differences are spurious because he theoretically expected social class differences. Baumrind (1986) insightfully pointed out, however, that Kohlberg failed to see that Gilligan's documentation of a missing developmental ethic of care in his model still has not been refuted, even if the care orientation's origins are more likely to be found in the context of class or culture rather than gender. It seems that Gilligan insightfully identified a missing voice in Kohlberg's model but inappropriately primarily linked it to gender. Gilligan's thesis, however, can be recast in a context of class and culture. To focus on social class, for instance, it would be important to begin by acknowledging that the life experiences and values of most members of the working class differ from those of the middle class. A serious problem arises when psychologists define maturity to correspond to their own elite class values, leaving the working class in a position of apparent evolutionary retardation. Developmental psychologists have repeatedly built their models of development upon their own upper-class experiences and their observations of middle-class subjects. When members of the working class then do poorly on the psychologists' class-biased tests of development, these same psychologists conclude that there must be something wrong with working people rather than trying to unravel the apparent puzzle that their development presents. This, in turn, leads to an even more serious problem: These psychological theories are then used to generate or justify class-biased educational practices.

To move toward a class-inclusive and culture-inclusive Kohlbergian model of moral development, future researchers would do well to reflect in a sustained and explicit way on social class and cross-cultural differences in the equally principled moral orientations of people from working-class and folk cultural backgrounds. This need to expand Kohlberg's work should not, however, overshadow its remarkable achievements.

## Recommended Readings

Blasi, J. (1986). *The communal experience of the kibbutz*. New Brunswick, NJ: Transaction Books.

Edwards, C. (1986). Cross-cultural research on Kohlberg's stages: The basis for consensus. In S. Modgil & C. Modgil (Eds.), *Lawrence Kohlberg: Consensus and controversy* (pp. 419-430). Philadelphia: Falmer Press.

Power, F. C., Higgins, A., & Kohlberg, L. (1989). *Lawrence Kohlberg's approach to moral education*. New York: Columbia University Press.

Sample, T. (1984). *Blue-collar ministry: Facing economic and social realities of working people.*

Valley Forge, PA: Judson Press.

Shweder, R., & Miller, J. (1987). Culture and moral development. In J. Kagan & S. Lamb (Eds.), *The emergence of morality in young children* (pp. 1-83). Chicago, IL: University of Chicago Press.

Snarey, J. (1987). Promoting moral maturity among adolescents: An ethnographic study of the Israeli kibbutz. *Comparative Education Review*, 31(2), 241-259.

Snarey, J. (1993). *How fathers care for the next generation*. Cambridge, MA: Harvard University Press.

# *References*

Bar-Yam, M., & Abrahami, A. (1982). Sex and age differences in moral reasoning of kibbutz adults. Unpublished manuscript, School of Education, Boston University.

Baumrind, D. (1986). Sex differences in moral reasoning: Response to Walker's conclusion that there are none. *Child Development*, 57, 511-521.

Blasi, J. (1986). *The communal experience of the kibbutz.* New Brunswick: Transaction Books.

Blatt, M. (1969). Studies on the Effects of Classroom Discussion upon Children's Moral Development. Doctoral dissertation, University of Chicago, Chicago, IL.

Blatt, M., & Kohlberg, L. (1975). Effects of Classroom Discussion on Children's Level of Moral Judgment. *Journal of Moral Education* 4(2):129-161.

Cahnman, W. J. (1973). Tönnies and Spencer: Evaluation and excerpts. In W. J. Cahnman (Ed.), *Ferdinand Tönnies: A new evaluation* (pp. 207-218). Leiden, Netherlands: E. J. Brill.

Cahnman, W. J., & Heberle, R. (Eds.) (1971). *Ferdinand Tönnies on sociology: Pure, applied, empirical.* Chicago: University of Chicago Press.

Colby, A., & Kohlberg, L. (1987). *The measurement of moral judgment, Volume Standard issue scoring manual.* Cambridge, England: Cambridge University Press. (Originally available in 1978.)

Colby, A., Kohlberg, L., Gibbs, J., & Lieberman, M. (1983). A longitudinal study of moral judgment. *Monographs of the Society for Research in Child Development*, 48(1-2), 1-124.

Cortese, A. J. (1984). Moral judgment in Chicano, Black, and White young adults. *Sociological Focus*, 17(3), 189-199.

Edwards, C. (1986). Cross-cultural research on Kohlberg's stages: The basis for consensus. In S. Modgil & C. Modgil (Eds.), *Lawrence Kohlberg: Consensus and controversy* (pp. 419-430). Philadelphia: Falmer Press.

Gilligan, C. (1982). *In a different voice.* Cambridge, MA: Harvard University Press.

Haan, N., Aerts, E., & Cooper, B. (1985). *On moral grounds.* New York: New York University Press.

Harkness, S., Edwards, C., & Super, C. (1981). Social roles and moral reasoning: A case study in a rural African community. *Developmental Psychology*, 17, 595-603.

Heberle, R. (1968). Tönnies, Ferdinand. In *International Encyclopedia of the Social Sciences* (Vol. 16, pp. 98-103). New York: Macmillan.

Heddendorf, R. (1969). The community: Tönnies typology. Unpublished lectures delivered at Geneva College, Beaver Falls, PA.

Helkama, K., & Ikonen, M. (1986). Some correlates of maturity of moral reasoning in Finland. *Behavior Science Research*, 20, 110-131.

Huebner, A., & Garrod, A. (1991). Moral reasoning among Tibetan monks: A study of Buddhist adolescents and young adults in Nepal. *Journal of Cross-Cultural Psychology*, 24, 167-185.

Huebner, A., Garrod, A., & Snarey, J. (1990). *Moral reasoning among Tibetan Buddhist monks: A cross-cultural study of adolescence.* Paper presented at the biennial meeting of the Society of Research on Adolescence, March 22, Atlanta, GA.

Kohlberg, L. (1958). The development of modes of thinking and choice in the years 10 to 16. Unpublished doctoral dissertation, University of Chicago.

Kohlberg, L. (1971). Cognitive-developmental theory and the practice of collective moral education. In M. Wolins & M. Gottesman (Eds.), *Group care: An Israeli approach* (342-371). New York: Gordon & Breach. (a)

Kohlberg, L. (1971). Indoctrination versus relativity in value education. *Zygon* 6:285-310. (b)

Kohlberg, L. (1978). Moral Education Reappraised. *The Humanist* 38 (Nov./Dec.): 13-15.

Kohlberg, L. (1981). *Essays on moral development: Volume I: The philosophy of moral development.* San Francisco, CA: Harper & Row.

Kohlberg, L. (1984). *Essays on moral development: Volume II: The psychology of moral development.* San Francisco, CA: Harper & Row.

Lee, L., & Snarey, J. (1988). The relationship between ego and moral development: A theoretical review and empirical analysis. In D. Lapsley & C. F. Power (Eds.), *Self, ego and identity: Integrative approaches* (pp. 151-178). New York, NY: Springer-Verlag.

Lei, T., & Cheng, S.W. (1984). An empirical study of Kohlberg's theory and scoring system of moral judgment in Chinese society. Unpublished manuscript, Harvard University, Center for Moral Education, Cambridge, MA.

Linn, R. (1987a). Moral reasoning and behavior of striking physicians in Israel. *Psychological Reports, 60*(2), 443-453. (a)

Linn, R. (1987b). Moral disobedience during the Lebanon war: What can the cognitive-developmental approach learn from the experience of the Israeli soldiers. *Social Cognition, 5*(4), 383-402. (b)

Loomis, C. P., & McKinney, J. C. (1957). Introduction. In F. Tönnies, *Community and society* (pp. 1-29). East Lansing: The Michigan State University Press.

Niemczynski, A., Czyzowska, D., Pourkos, M., & Mirski, A. (1988). The Cracow study with Kohlberg's moral judgment interview: Data pertaining to the assumption of cross-cultural validity. *Polish Psychological Bulletin, 19*(1), 43-53.

Nisan, M., & Kohlberg, L. (1982). Universality and cross-cultural variation in moral development: A longitudinal and cross-sectional study in Turkey. *Child Development, 53*, 865-876.

Power, F. C., Higgins, A., & Kohlberg, L. (1989). *Lawrence Kohlberg's approach to moral education.* New York: Columbia University Press.

Reimer, J. (1977). A study in moral development of kibbutz adolescents. Unpublished doctoral dissertation, Harvard University, Cambridge, MA.

Sample, T. (1984). *Blue-collar ministry: Facing economic and social realities of working people.* Valley Forge, PA: Judson Press.

Shulik, R. (1988). Faith development in older adults. *Educational Gerontology, 14*, 291-301.

Shweder, R. (1982). Beyond self-constructed knowledge: The study of culture and morality. *Merrill-Palmer Quarterly, 28*, 41-69.

Simpson, E. L. (1974). Moral development research: A case study of scientific cultural bias. *Human Development, 17*, 81-106.

Snarey, J. (1985). The cross-cultural universality of social-moral development: A critical review of Kohlbergian research. *Psychological Bulletin, 97*(2), 202-232.

Snarey, J. (1987). Promoting moral maturity among adolescents: An ethnographic study of the Israeli kibbutz. *Comparative Education Review, 31*(2), 241-259.

Snarey, J. (1993). *How fathers care for the next generation.* Cambridge, MA: Harvard University Press.

Snarey, J., & Keljo, K. (1991). In a *Gemeinschaft* voice: The cross-cultural expansion of moral development theory. *Handbook of moral behavior and development: Volume 1. Theory* (pp. 395-424). Hillsdale, NJ: Erlbaum.

Snarey, J., Reimer, J., & Kohlberg, L. (1985a). The development of social-moral reasoning among kibbutz adolescents: A longitudinal cross-cultural study. *Developmental Psychology, 20*, 3-17. (a)

Snarey, J., Reimer, J., & Kohlberg, L. (1985b). The kibbutz as a model for moral education: A longitudinal study. *Journal of Applied Developmental Psychology, 6*(2), 151-172. (b)

Sullivan, E. (1977). A study of Kohlberg's structural theory of moral development: A critique. *Human Development, 20*, 352-376.

Tietjen, A., & Walker, L. (1985). Moral reasoning and leadership among men in a Papua New Guinea village. *Developmental Psychology, 21*(6), 982-992.

Tönnies, F. (1957). *Community and society* (C. P. Loomis, Trans.). New York: Harper & Row. (Original work published 1887).

Tönnies, F. (1971). The concept of Gemeinschaft. In W. J. Cahnman & R. Heberle (Eds.), *Ferdinand Tönnies on sociology: Pure, applied, and empirical* (pp. 62-72).

Chicago: University of Chicago Press. Original work published 1925).

Tönnies, F. (1971). Social Norms: law. In W. J. Cahnman & R. Heberle (Eds.), *Ferdinand Tönnies on sociology: Pure, applied, and empirical* (pp. 199-211). Chicago: University of Chicago Press. (Original work published 1931).

Tönnies, F. (1973). Durkheim, Emile: De la division du travail social. In W. J. Cahnman (Ed.), *Ferdinand Tönnies: A new evaluation* (pp. 252-254). Leiden, Netherlands: E. J. Brill. (Original work published 1893).

Turner, C., & Martinez, D. (1977). Socioeconomic achievement and the Machiavellian personality. *Sociometry, 40*(4), 325-336.

Vasudev, J., & Hummel, R. (1987). Moral stage sequence and principled reasoning in an Indian sample. *Human Development, 30*, 105-118.

# Part *II*

## *Behavioral/Learning Perspectives*

### *Prologue*

The behavioral tradition has produced a more diverse and distinguished array of theorists and researchers than perhaps any other tradition in the history of psychology. Beginning with the work of Ivan Pavlov and J. B. Watson and continuing through the work of B. F. Skinner, a complete list of contributors to the behavioral tradition would have to include some of the most notable names in psychology. Needless-to-say, in this book we will only be able to touch on some of the work that has been done in the behavioral tradition. More specifically, in this part of the book we will focus on the contribution of the behavioral tradition to the moral development field.

The behavioral tradition is sometimes depicted as behavioristic and environmentalistic in the extreme. This is the case, in part, because some of the most notable theorists in this tradition have adopted positions that were extreme. J. B. Watson, for example, actively sought to discredit Freudian clinical theory, with its emphasis on the instinctual and biological basis of behavior. Impressed by Ivan Pavlov's work on classically conditioning involuntary physiological responses such as salivation, Watson sought to demonstrate that phobias (or any other psychopathology) could be induced environmentally. In a widely cited study (Watson & Rayner, 1920), he classically conditioned an eleven-month infant (Albert) to display extreme anxiety in the presence of a white rat that had previously been a neutral stimuli, thereby directly challenging the Freudian doctrine of unconscious processes. B. F. Skinner was similarly an outspoken critic of theories that attribute human behavior to inner causes. Skinner did *not* claim that inner states do not exist, but only that they play no causal role in determining behavior. He therefore argued that the scientific analysis of behavior has to be restricted to observable events (either behavioral or environmental). His radical behaviorism frequently resulted in Skinner adopting controversial positions on a number of issues. He has argued, for example, against the notion of free will in favor of a strong version of determinism as well as against all theoretical views that postulate inner structures, drives, instincts, or processes.

The radical (and controversial) nature of the extreme behaviorism and environmentalism of some of the leading spokepersons for the behavioral tradition is an important and fascinating part of the behavioral tradition in U.S. psychology, and it has helped to color public perception of the field. By itself, however, it presents an incomplete picture of the behavioral tradition. The modern behavioral tradition, like the discipline of psychology itself, has become increasingly more pluralistic. A growing number of behaviorists now recognize the role of human inner states, particularly cognitive processes. In addition, although the behavioral approach continues to emphasize the importance of environmental determinants of behavior, there is also a growing recognition that the organism does not simply respond to environmental events, but also plays an active role in shaping those events, i.e., the bidirectional influence of organism and environment. Consequently, many modern behavioral approaches representing current trends in the behavioral tradition are actually considerably more eclectic then the behavioral tradition is sometimes popularly portrayed.

In the moral development literature, as in psychology in general, the behavioral perspective has been defined by a diversity of theorists and researchers representing theoretical perspectives that range from operant theory to social learning, social conditioning, cognitive behavioral, and cognitive social learning theory (e.g., Burton, 1984; Gewirtz & Paláez-Nogueras, 1991; Liebert, 1984; Mischel & Mischel, 1976). Despite this diversity of theoretical perspectives, work within the behavioral approach tends to adopt a common set of meta-theoretical, theoretical, and methodological assumptions that are characteristic of what we have termed the mechanistic and the contextualistic traditions. In particular, in the moral development literature, this has resulted in an emphasis on importance of observable behavior rather than on moral reasoning. In addition, it has also resulted in a view of development as involving a continuous process of change that is under the control of environmental processes such as learning and conditioning rather than a discontinuous process that is the outcome of stages and sequence.

## Overview of Chapters in Part II

The chapters in this part provide a more detailed introduction to the behavioral/learning perspective. Chapter 6 provides an extensive history and overview of behavioral models of moral development. Chapter 7 focuses more specifically on the behavior analytic approach to moral behavior and development. The work described in the chapters in this part provides an alternative to the cognitive developmentalist's emphasis on moral reasoning and qualitative, stage-type change in moral reasoning. In contrast, the chapters in this part of the book highlight the importance of moral behavior, the continuous nature of behavior change, and the role of learning and conditioning in acquiring moral behavior.

Chapter 6, by *Roger Burton* and *Linda Kunce*, begins with a discussion of the importance of studying actual moral behavior as well as moral reasoning. The importance of studying moral reasoning in moral development depends on its relevance to determining or explaining moral conduct. Although moral reasoning and arguments may be powerfully persuasive in influencing others, actions speak louder than words in judging the morality of individuals. Within this framework, the chapter reviews a number of the major studies that have focused on moral behavior.

The review begins with an early psychological study that is frequently cited in the literature and widely regarded as a classic work. The study, conducted by Hartshorne and May, is usually referred to as the "Character Education Inquiry." Conducted during the 1920s, the study involved over 11,000 children and used state-of-the-art methods and procedures. The study included many behavioral tests of honesty, altruism, self-control, and moral attitudes. The best known conclusion from the study was labeled the "doctrine of specificity," namely, that moral behavior is primarily situationally determined rather than due to "unified character traits" such as honesty or altruism. Chapter 6, however, notes that a re-analysis of the data using more modern analytic techniques revealed the existence of a modest but cross-situationally consistent trait of honesty that distinguished individual children in their tendency to resist temptation. Hartshorne and May also explored the correspondence between verbal reports and overt actions, or words and deeds. The results, Chapter 6 points out, indicate that any valid assessment of moral development requires both types of measures.

Chapter 6 also discusses Piaget's classic study on moral judgment in children which was also conducted during the 1920s. Chapter 6 points out that although for most of the study Piaget questioned children about their moral concepts using hypothetical situations to explore their moral reasoning and logic, he also considered it necessary to begin his study by first observing their behavior. His initial explorations of children's conceptions of moral rules were therefore based on their responses to games they actually played rather than on hypothetical situations.

Other studies that focused on moral behaviors are also reviewed in Chapter 6. They include a discussion of the work that was done just before World War II that sought to integrate Freudian psychoanalytic theory with Hullian drive reduction theory and Skinnerian operant theory. In addition, observational social learning and cognitive-behavioral, cognitive dissonance and attributional, and physiological learning research is also reviewed. Finally, the application of behavioral theory and research is used to illustrate the process of creating a moral climate in the classroom.

Chapter 7, by *Martha Pelaez-Nogueras* and *Jacob Gewirtz*, focuses on the behavior analytic approach to moral behavior and development. Chapter 7 begins with a discussion of the importance of studying actual moral behavior. The focus on moral reasoning that has characterized much of the research on moral development has limited our understanding of the proximal causes of moral action. The behavioral-analytic approach described in this chapter emphasizes action and focuses on the underlying processes by which behavior is learned, i.e., the functional interrelations between environmental contingencies and the child's behavior in context. This approach draws on the contextualistic tradition and focuses on sequential and reciprocal influence in interaction between the individual's behavior and environmental stimuli. Thus, behavior analysis conceives both the organism and the environment as active, and to comprise an inseparable interdependent unit.

Chapter 7 examines some of the differences between cognitive-developmental and behavior-analytic theories of moral behavior. These differences include differing views of the nature of morality (i.e., universal versus contextual), of the underlying causes of behavior (i.e., mental structures versus observable contingencies), the relationship between moral reasoning and moral actions (i.e., should be correlated versus not necessarily correlated), and on how moral behavior is influenced by environmental stimuli and ultimately of rules. Chapter 7 also provides an overview of the principles and basic operations involved in the acquisition of moral behavior patterns, including the role of positive and negative reinforcement and the role of positive and negative punishment. The chapter also provides a discussion of the concepts of imitation, identification, and attachment and the role these processes play in the acquisition of moral behavior.

Finally, Chapter 7 provides a detailed description of the difference between direct-contingency versus rule-governed moral behavior. Direct contingency-shaped behavior is shaped directly by its consequences and comes under the control of environmental stimuli. Contingency-shaped behavior units ("operants") are given meaning and are strengthened by those of their *direct* consequences that function as reinforcing stimuli. Rule-governed behavior, on the other hand, is shaped by reinforcement of rule-following. Although the two types of behaviors are similar in form, their functional properties and controlling variables are different. For the most part, moral behavior is rule-governed rather than direct-contingency shaped. Rule-governed behavior has been distinguished theoretically and experimentally from behavior that is shaped and maintained by its direct consequences. Rule-governed behavior can be modified by altering either its antecedents, its consequences, or both. In contrast, contingency-shaped behavior is modified only by its consequences. The implications of the concept of rule-governed behavior for moral development in children is discussed. The important feature of the explicit rule is that it substitutes for typical consequences of behavior. Explicit rules stated by parents, teachers, and other prestigious figures can control the child's moral behavior in contexts where natural contingencies are ineffective, slow to be effective, or dangerous for the child. In addition, children can also verbalize self-formulated rules. Self-formulated rules develop at a later phase, when the child can describe verbally the consequences of behaviors.

## References

Burton, R. V. (1984). A paradox in theories and research in moral development. In W. Kurtines & J. L. Gewirtz (Eds.), *Morality, moral behavior and moral development*. New York: John Wiley & Sons, 178-192.

Gewirtz, J. L., & Peláez-Nogueras, M. (1991). Proximal mechanisms underlying the acquisition of moral behavior patterns. In W. M. Kurtines & J. L. Gewirtz (Eds.) *Handbook of moral behavior and development. Vol 1: Theory* (pp. 153-182). Hillsdale, NJ: Erlbaum.

Liebert, R. (1984). What develops in moral development? In W. Kurtines & J. L. Gewirtz (Eds.), *Morality, moral behavior, and moral development*. New York: John Wiley & Sons, 177-192.

Mischel, W. & Mischel, H. N. (1976). A cognitive-social learning approach to socialization and self-regulation. In T. Lickona (Ed.), *Moral development and behavior: Theory, research, and social issues*. New York: Holt, Rinehart & Winston, 84-107.

Watson, J. B. & Rayner, R. (1920). Conditioned emotional reactions. *Journal of Experimental Psychology, 3,* 1-14.

# Behavioral Models of Moral Development: A Brief History and Integration

*ROGER V. BURTON*
*State University of New York at Buffalo*

*LINDA KUNCE*
*State University of New York at Buffalo*

### Abstract

This chapter provides a history and overview of behavioral models of moral development and a hypothetical scenario of how the findings from them might be implemented. Although these "behavioral" models may appear disparate as often as they appear similar, they share the common assumption that research on moral development must go beyond an exclusive emphasis on reasoning and judgment to address actual conduct. The historical review is divided into six sections and covers the classic studies of Hartshorne and May and of Piaget, the studies generated by traditional behavioral, psychoanalytic, and operant theories, the social learning models that incorporate cognitive components, observational learning, and modeling, the cognitive dissonance and attributional models that rely on cognitive and behavioral feedback, and finally the physiological learning models. Despite this separation into different theoretical categories, we emphasize the influences and implications between and among the various studies. The hypothetical case study integrating the findings and conclusions of these various studies and theoretical models is heuristic and is intended to stimulate discussion and research to fill in the gaps between moral reasoning and moral conduct.

A Calvin and Hobbes cartoon (10-18-90) has Calvin asking Hobbes, "Hobbes, Do you think our morality is defined by our actions, or by what's in our hearts?" Hobbes responds, "I think our actions *show* what's in our hearts." After the full implication of Hobbes's retort finally hits him, Calvin screams, "**I RESENT THAT!**"

Our newspapers, magazines, and TV talk shows increasingly express concerns about the moral and ethical values of our society. As evidence for these concerns, the reports frequently cite the lying by elected officials about Watergate, Iran-Contra secret dealings, the Panama invasion, the current state of the deficit, and how the savings and loan debacle came about. Especially troubling for many commentators is the open justification by these representatives of public trust for their deception. Editorials also decry the cheating, fraud, and waste by federal defense contractors who take being found guilty occasionally and being fined several millions as merely the cost of doing business in billion dollar contracts. Daily newspapers cover details about fraudulent business transactions in "redoubtable" brokerage houses, the buying of influence from senators and representatives by PACs, and about companies that knowingly pollute our waters with deadly chemicals, again seeing such practices and being fined occasionally as "business as usual." Even our scientific journals carry an increasing number of cases of outright fraud, as well as instances of suspicious claims of authorship, discovery, and priority due to questionable record keeping and lab procedures. These practices may even get their start or have their models in our high school and college athletic programs that are regularly exposed for cutting corners and breaking the rules to win at any cost. A recent survey of studies by Josephson (1990) concludes that "an unprecedented proportion of today's youth lack commitment to core moral values like honesty, personal responsibility, respect for others and civic duty." The studies contributing to this survey indicate that most students in college admit having cheated on exams in high school and that after graduation 10-25 percent falsify their resumes.

What is it about these instances that evokes such concern? Clearly it is not the way our elected officials, Wall Street wizards, scientific colleagues, athletes and coaches, and our youth discuss and reason about moral issues. The concerns are evoked by their behavior and its implications. As Hobbes states, what's in their hearts is shown by their actions.

Moral development and research in morality must go beyond investigations of reasoning to address conduct. Even Madison Avenue recognizes that we must watch what we do and not just what we say by running full-page ads for Mercedes Benz: "DEEDS NOT WORDS." This behavioral emphasis does not devalue the roles of cognitions, decision-making, reasoning and judgments about moral conflicts. These factors are seen as components that may influence action or may themselves be determined by actions that have been taken. Their importance as measures of moral development, however, depends on their relevance in determining or explaining the moral conduct of individuals. Although moral reasoning and arguments may be powerfully persuasive in influencing others, actions speak louder than words in judging the morality of individuals.

Many investigators of moral development will take issue with this emphasis on conduct as the sine qua non for assessing the relevance of cognitions in moral development. Their argument assumes that reasoning guides (determines) what action one takes when in moral conflict and therefore cognitions take precedence over behavior. Our position is that, from a developmental perspective, reasoning about moral issues results from early behavioral training and that these judgments may eventually become guides to subsequent action as part of a feedback system. This position is very close to that of Piaget who argued that cognitive structures are not innate but are products of the child's interaction with the environment. As a moral rule develops, it may begin to influence subsequent action, which in turn strengthens or, if producing negative feedback (disequilibrium), leads to accommodation and change (development) of that rule. Because we see conduct and reasoning as interacting in this feedback manner, studies of determinants of moral reasoning are clearly important. However, the importance to the overall picture of moral development of studies that assess *only* reasoning and judgment awaits further evidence that shows how their findings relate to moral conduct. Citing Piaget, "the relations which exist between the practice and the consciousness of rules are those which will best enable us to define the psychological nature of moral realities" (Piaget, 1932, p.3).

We delimit our attention in this chapter to studies of moral development in which there is societal consensus about the morally required behavior in specific situations. These studies, in the main, examine cheating in games and on academic tests, lying, and stealing. Further, we address primarily those actions involving restraint from norm-violation, leaving for another chapter the prosocial moral conduct of altruism. It also should be noted that an area strongly associated with "moral" conduct by the lay public, sexual behavior, is not included in this review.[1]

This chapter is divided into two parts. The first section presents a brief history and descriptions of the behavioral theories of moral development. The research and theories included are classified under six headings: (1) the classic studies of Hartshorne and May; (2) the classic study of Piaget; (3) the interface of traditional behavioral, psychoanalytic, and operant theories; (4) the observational social learning and cognitive-behavioral models; (5) cognitive dissonance and attributional models; and (6) physiological learning models. The second section presents a hypothetical case study to illustrate how the empirical contributions from these various studies and their theoretical interpretations might be integrated in bearing upon a specific instance of moral training.

## *Historical Review of Behavioral Models*
## *Hartshorne and May: The Behavioral Classic*

A classic among psychological studies is Hartshorne and May's "Character Education Inquiry" (CEI), also called the *Studies in the Nature of Character*. This three-volume work set a high standard for many issues to be considered in conducting research, particularly with children, in the area of moral conduct. Their discussions on ethical issues, methodology, analytical procedures, interpretations, and limitations of implications are as meaningful and fresh today as they were over a half century ago. The first of the three volumes, *Studies in Deceit* (1928), addressed cheating, lying, and stealing. The second volume, *Studies in Service and Self-Control* (Hartshorne, May, & Maller, 1929) addressed altruism (cooperative and charitable acts called "service") and persistence and inhibition of distractions (labeled self-control). The last volume, *Studies in the Organization of Character* (Hartshorne, May, & Shuttleworth, 1930), explored the roles of moral knowledge, opinions, and attitudes, and finally how all these observed measures might be aggregated to reflect the general moral character of the individual.

These studies are the most well-known and certainly the most comprehensive to date addressing the development of moral conduct and character. The impetus for the CEI was concern in the 1920s by the Religious Education Association and the Institute of Social and Religious Research about evaluating the inculcation of moral and religious values in children. Among the panel of advisors, also close at hand at Teachers' College, Columbia, was E. L. Thorndike—the most famous U.S. psychologist at that time. The CEI was under his immediate supervision and conducted as a project within his Institute of Educational Research. Thorndike's imprint is clearly seen in the decisions to "study the actual experiences of children which have moral and religious significance" and to "apply the objective methods of the laboratory to the measurement of conduct under controlled conditions" as well as in the appointments of Hugh Hartshorne and Mark May as codirectors of the project.

Within five years these investigators had (1) surveyed the previous literature, (2) developed many behavioral tests of honesty, altruism, self-control, and of moral attitudes, (3) tested over 11,000 children, (4) developed and published statistical models for analyzing the data, (5) computed by hand or on very primitive hand calculators thousands of correlations and tests of group differences, and (6) wrote the three volumes—a remarkable feat!

In their studies of honesty the children were tempted to do something for personal gain that involved active deception by attempting to conceal their action or motives for the action. Development of specific honesty tests was based on clear, stringent criteria. First, they required the tests to be commonly occurring, naturalistic situations (currently called "ecologically valid") that placed the child in moral conflict. Second, they required the tests to have "face validity" such that there was a consensus by adults of what was the morally required behavior in that situation. That is, the ethical choice had to be clearly, unambiguously called for in the situational context in order to be reliably scored and classified. These requirements made it highly likely that every child had been exposed at sometime to training in resisting the temptation presented. After developing many tests and procedures for measuring deception, they sampled cheating, stealing, and lying in classroom, homework, athletic contest, and party game situations. Hartshorne and May applied the same approach, analytic procedures, and general kinds of conclusions to the other facets of character addressed. The "service" tests measured children's altruistic, self-sacrificing, charitable, helpful, and cooperative behavior. The "self-control" facets of persistence and inhibition measured how long a child persisted on insolvable tasks when other choices were available and resisted the distraction of a more interesting activity when assigned to work at a dull task. In addition to the observed behavioral measures, they created batteries of questionnaires to assess moral knowledge, opinions, and attitudes to assess familiarity with conventional moral codes and professed acceptance of them. To portray the scope of this classic work and its bearing on current research in moral development, let us briefly enumerate some of the findings.

The best-known conclusion, labeled the "doctrine of specificity" from the empirical findings in the CEI, is that behavior is primarily situationally determined rather than due to "unified character traits" (v. I, 411). With such impressive data challenging personality "traits," why is it that psychologists still speak of individual traits? It is essentially a difference in definition. The concept of "trait" evaluated by Hartshorne and May was a binary classification of character that would lead to labeling an individual as "honest" or "deceitful," "altruistic" or "selfish," etc. Their data, revealing a minimal consistency in honest behavior across the different measures, showed little support for such a concept of trait. To illustrate, observing a child cheat on an arithmetic test did not predict whether the child also would cheat on all tests, and certainly did not predict whether the child also would lie and steal. By contrast, the specific determinants in the test situations, such as level of risk, were very effective in producing differences in behavior. Their measures of character produced continuous, normal curves, not dichotomous, bimodal distributions. What Hartshorne and May rejected was the extreme concept of trait as "an inner entity operating independently of the situation in which the individual is placed" (v. I, p. 385).

A reanalysis of their data, using analytic procedures developed to show what different tests have in common, clearly revealed a unidimensional factor of honesty (Burton, 1963). Though modest, this factor, or "trait" as most current researchers define the term, is sufficient to distinguish individual children in their tendencies to resist temptation. This interpretation, incidentally, was in keeping with Hartshorne and May's noting that the "looseness" of the relations among their tests was not random, that the correlations among the tests were almost consistently positive. In fact, they developed an individual difference score of consistency across the facets of character that they labeled an "integration" score (see below).

Another notable finding was that a "group morale" developed in school units and became stronger the longer the children were together. This developing group code produced individual consistency in conduct by setting the range of acceptable moral choices for the unit's members. This collective standard was strongest for close friends in the same classroom, but was also present for entire classrooms and even for whole schools. Developing a group code was more powerful in bringing the individual pupil's conduct in line with the moral standards established for that social unit than simply relying on the teacher's attempting to instill standards in each child. The authors concluded that educators should focus on establishing a school atmosphere that permits individual students to achieve success through acceptable conduct while avoiding failure.

Hartshorne and May also explored the correspondence between verbal reports and overt actions, or words and deeds. Do individuals do what they profess they would do when they consider hypothetical situations? Does knowledge of right and wrong predict action in real temptation situations? They recognized that what others think of an individual, the individual's reputation, may influence what that person does and becomes. This foreshadows the expectancy and attribution effect in person perception that is of such current interest. Their results were complex and mixed as is still true of current research in the area (see section below).

There was little correspondence between knowledge of what one was supposed to do in a specific situation and what the child actually did. One questionnaire assessed the pupils' self-reported adherence to conventionally prescribed codes of conduct. The investigators established that only a "pious fraud" would answer all or even 75 percent of the items in the prescribed manner. This lie scale and the procedures for its development became the basis for most current scales measuring falsification and social desirability bias. Many current studies verify that correspondence between words and deeds is elusive, especially on the very measures of most interest where social desirability is apparent in the questions being asked. Nevertheless, Hartshorne and May believed that "consistency shown between knowledge and conduct is an aspect of life adjustment of great significance for individual strength and social harmony and peace" (v. III, p. 362). Analyses of aggregate measures supported this belief: General moral knowledge correlated positively with an integrated measure of moral conduct, a score averaged over a wide range of behavioral tests. Since so many factors influence correspondence between verbal responses and conduct measures, it follows that any valid assessment of the effects of moral training by parents and teachers requires both kinds of measures. Overt behavior in non-surveillance, non-coercive situations is the bottom line that exposes our real morality, the morality that's "in our hearts," and our verbal responses provide a context for understanding why we behaved that way.

Besides self-report measures, the CEI also obtained ratings of honesty and moral reputation from peers and teachers. Initially, Hartshorne and May planned to use these ratings as criteria for assessing the validity of the specific behavioral measures. They did find a significant association ($r = .34$) (v. III, p. 230) between total character (37 behavioral tests) and reputation (3 teacher ratings of each child and one peer rating by every child in a classroom of every other child) scores. It was necessary to have the extensive aggregate measures to obtain adequate reliabilities for both the behavioral and reputation scores and to produce the significant positive association. These requirements shed doubt on interpreting any single rating scale as an adequate predictor of what an individual will do in a specific situation. In other words, judgments from a single observation or reputation score that a child is dishonest or selfish are not good predictors of what that child will do in specific situations.

In their analyses of motivation, they manipulated both the motive to avoid detection and the incentive to deviate. A series of tests ordered for degree of risk showed that the greater the risk, the less likely the deception. Further, the tests formed a scale such that an individual child would cheat on all tests up to a certain degree of risk and then would not cheat on any test with greater risk.[2] Incentive was manipulated by supplying various false levels of performance supposedly attained by their peers. Falsely high standards increased deception to avoid odious comparison with peers. When asked why they might have cheated, two thirds of the children said it was to do well. Apparently a well-learned precept in school is, "If at first you don't succeed, cheat."

Many specific factors were also explored for their associations with honesty, altruism, persistence, and character integration: age, sex, intelligence, physical and emotional condition, socioeconomic and cultural background, race, religion, school status, school and teacher influences, and experimental attempts to increase honesty and altruism. Among the many findings, the negative association between cheating and intelligence ($r = -.49$; v. I, p. 183) is frequently cited as evidence that the more intelligent children are, the more honest they are. It was noted, however, that this association was due to the tests that were familiar and provided the children with expectations of how well they would do. On unfamiliar tests, such as stealing and party games, there was no connection between deception and intelligence. Therefore, the investigators tested the hypothesis that previous experience of success or failure with similar tasks accounted for the correlation in two ways. First, analyses showed that actual ability on the academic tests related to honesty, a finding in line with the hypothesis that children were less motivated to cheat if they expected to do well. Secondly, an experimental test showed that children "highest in ability cheated the most" (v. I, Bk. II, p. 241) on simple, unfamiliar clerical tasks when cheating was measured by the child's working past the allotted time. The authors concluded that expectations of success or failure on familiar tasks were significant determinants, but when there was no previous experience with the task, the more able "make more use of the opportunities to cheat" (v. I, Bk. II, p.

242). Thus, the positive association between intelligence and honesty was primarily due to an artifact of the academic content of the tests.

Another "finding" often cited, especially as contrasting with the developmental patterns of moral reasoning, is that moral conduct was unrelated to age. This conclusion does not consider all the data, however. The evidence does show that, when the situation is relevant to the maturity of the person, people of all ages may or may not cheat, steal, lie, or be selfish depending on the situation. However, the analyses of the integration score showed that consistency across situations was positively correlated with age, with some children becoming more consistently honest and others more consistently dishonest as they matured. As might be expected from a developmental, social learning perspective, people become more consistent in their moral conduct as they mature.

These findings are selective, representing only a small sample of the many presented in the CEI. The interested scholar will find much of value, not only in the other findings but also in the wise discussions of ethical, measurement, and interpretive issues in these three volumes.

## Piaget: The Cognitive Classic

In his monograph, *The moral judgment of the child* (1932), Piaget states that he investigated moral judgment, "not moral behavior or sentiments" (p. vii). For most of his data he questioned children about their moral concepts using hypothetical situations to explore their moral reasoning and logic. On the other hand, he also argued that it was necessary to begin his study by recording "how (children) observed rules at each age and level of mental development" and then how this observed behavior linked up with their conceptions of the rules (p. 13). That is, Piaget noted that to understand the development of conceptions of morality it was necessary to observe behavior first. Therefore, his initial explorations of children's conceptions of moral rules were based on their responses to games they actually played rather than on hypothetical situations.

While actually playing familiar games with children (marbles for boys and "hide-and-seek" for girls), Piaget pretended to be completely ignorant of the rules and procedures and had children instruct him in how to play. This procedure enabled him to observe directly their behavior. He distinguished four "stages" in the playing of these games: a *motor* stage in which the child physically manipulates and explores the marbles as new objects—an initial stage not considered in the analyses of hide-and-seek; an *egocentric* stage in which the child may imitate older children's play but doesn't observe any codified rules ("everyone can win"); a stage of incipient *cooperation* in which the child competes with others but is vague about exactly what the rules are; and, finally, a *codification of rules* in which the child plays by an agreed-upon set of rules known to all players.

After obtaining observations of their actions, he asked the children questions about the games' rules: What are the rules? Can they be changed? Have they always been the same? How did they begin? Piaget proposed three stages for children's understanding of rules: a first stage in which the observed constraints are essentially idiosyncratic rituals; a second stage in which rules are immutable and sacred, coming from God or omnipotent parent; and a final stage of seeing rules as agreed-upon codes of conduct that are modifiable by mutual agreement, created by children playing the game, and to be strictly adhered to out of mutual respect—in other words, the elements of a social contract.

Relating Piaget's considerations to our emphasis on linking action and cognition, we see that he considered behavior (e.g., rituals and practice) as the foundation for the later development of moral reasoning. He saw the infant as "bathed in an atmosphere of rules" (p. 43) due to parentally imposed routines (e.g., meals, bedtime, cleanliness). Compliance with the rules imposed as constraints by the child's elders—whether older children or adults—is seen as essential to the development of an elaborated hierarchy of moral values in adulthood. Although Piaget addresses how conceptions map on to practice, some issues are left unresolved: Why are the younger children who believe the rules are sacred so flexible in the observance of them? Why, in the final stages, when rules are seen as arbitrary and temporary, is there so much emphasis on strict adherence to them when playing? Piaget's major interest in intellectual development led him to turn his attention to the child's developing conceptions of moral judgments, leaving it for others to fill in the linkages between words and deeds.

## Behavioral/Psychoanalytic and Operant Studies

Just before World War II, some psychologists were being influenced by both learning theory—primarily Hullian drive reduction theory (Hull, 1943)—and Freudian psychoanalytic theory. Among the questions being asked in this theoretical blending was how are traits and skills acquired without direct instruction? Freud included this issue under his discussions of identification and superego development whereas the learning theorists (e.g., Tolman, 1932) addressed it under the heading of observational or latent learning. A major contribution was that of Miller and Dollard (1941) who addressed the processes involved when people, particularly children, acquire behaviors from others through imitation. Although this monograph presented stimulating and creative experimental data based on both animals and humans, the war temporarily diverted attention to other issues.

After the war, Sears and colleagues (Sears, 1951; Sears, Whiting, Nowlis, & Sears, 1953; Sears, Maccoby, & Levin, 1957; Sears, Rau, & Alpert, 1965) delineated a theoretical framework for investigating social development again drawing on both the behavioral and psychoanalytic theories. They explored many facets of the antecedents of moral development including aggression, resistance to temptation, and guilt. Results from these studies indicated that parental use of physical punishment is associated with generally undesirable characteristics in the child, including aggression and low moral development. On the positive side, the combination of parental warmth that establishes a context of secure love and some forms of psychological punishment, such as "time-out" and explanations the child can understand, is associated with low aggression and high conscience development. These findings generated numerous studies attempting to establish the influences of early child-rearing practices on moral development (e.g., Burton, Maccoby, & Allinsmith, 1961; Miller & Swanson, 1960).

The work of Whiting and colleagues (Burton & Reis, 1980; Whiting, 1959; Whiting & Child, 1953; Whiting & Whiting, 1975) expanded this testing of behavior theory, influenced by Freudian considerations, to cross-cultural comparisons. Typically, these studies sought to determine whether adult personality traits were determined by the use of specific child-rearing techniques, the intensity with which these techniques were administered, and the child's age when the technique was used. Illustrative is the finding that early warmth, indexed by indulgence in infancy, combined with later use of withdrawal of love disciplinary techniques results in high conscience (guilt) in adulthood (Burton & Reis, 1980).

These studies also show that societies around the world have social control devices for ensuring conformity to the society's rules and that these mechanisms are associated with different child-rearing antecedents. Western society tends to rely on the internalization of conscience, consisting of resistance to temptation and guilt, while other societies may rely on other mechanisms, such as sorcery, fear of ghosts, or shame. Besides confirming some conclusions that might be found from studies within our society, these cross-cultural studies provided greater confidence in the generalizability of the findings to all human socialization processes.

Much of the theory being developed and tested by the investigators above resulted from a reinterpretation of Freudian observations and theoretical depictions into behavioristic hypotheses to be tested empirically. Although much of the theoretical framework for assessing the effects of rearing on adult behavior is still influential, at the time there was growing dissatisfaction with the imprecision of the Freudian descriptions of the developmental processes underlying the observations. The concepts of "identification" and "superego" seemed too global, too vague, to carry too much extra baggage to be useful for precise analysis of the specific processes. This concern led some investigators to pull apart the global character of some of Freud's concepts into more precise, more tractable components for experimental analysis. Solomon's experimental studies and accompanying theoretical models, derived from both classical (Pavlovian) and operant conditioning theories, made notable contributions in delineating the specific variables involved in conscience formation, specifically the acquisition of resistance to temptation and guilt (Solomon, 1964; Solomon, Turner, & Lessac, 1968). His two experimental paradigms produced very different behaviors in his puppy subjects: Punishment administered prior to the infraction resulted in resistance to temptation whereas punishment after the deviation produced guilt behavior. The observation that most people show both resistance and guilt had led Freud to conclude that these components were parts of a unitary process. By analyzing the various parameters of punishment, Solomon was able to demonstrate that specific conditions led to quite different components of the development of conscience.

Other investigators with a strict Skinnerian (Skinner, 1953) orientation also addressed some of the issues. Gewirtz (1969; see also, Peláez-Nogueras & Gewirtz, this vol.) made significant theoretical contributions in reinterpreting modeling and the acquisition of initial imitation in behavioral terms, eschewing what was argued to be excess baggage of vague literary terms to describe psychological processes. It has also been noted that more research on the use of positive reinforcement alone, without punishment, to train moral standards would be valuable (Burton, 1976a). Although there are important considerations that indicate reliable resistance to temptation may require some punishment, careful manipulation of rewards and cognitive context (see below) may minimize the amount of punishment that is necessary. Evidence from animal experiments indicates that a combination of intermittent reward schedules and greater reward for a desirable response than is gained by a deviant act increase the likelihood of the desired behavior. Unfortunately, the possible applications to moral development have not yet been explored so that there is little empirical evidence with humans to support this suggestion.

## Observational Social Learning and Cognitive-Behavioral Models

The studies just cited called attention to the importance of learning by watching others—through observation, modeling, and imitation. Much of Freud's description of the identification process indicated the importance of imitation and learning by observation without direct tuition. Dissatisfied with hypotheses based on the conception of identification as a global process, investigators returned to the questions initially addressed experimentally by Miller and Dollard (1941). A major impetus for these studies was the work of Bandura and colleagues (Bandura, 1962; 1965, 1969, 1971; Bandura, Ross, & Ross, 1963a; 1963b; Bandura & Walters, 1963). These experimental studies explored many factors involved in imitation, including:

- Similarity of the model to the observer
- Status of the model
- Degree of nurturance of the model
- Control of desired resources
- Learning/performance distinction
- Vicarious learning by observing the outcomes of others' behavior
- The role of reward and punishment as motivating performance of what is learned by observation

- Live vs. symbolic (cartoon, TV, and film) models
- Preaching (only) vs. practicing/modeling (only) vs. the combination of preaching and practicing/modeling moral standards

This lists only some of the factors shown to affect learning and performance by observation. These studies clearly demonstrated that models (parents, siblings, teachers, peers) who practice as well as preach moral standards influence the observer to comply with those same high standards. An important point is that although parents consciously teach moral standards when they "preach" to their child, they are often unaware that they also "teach" by their actions. The evidence indicates that a child is more likely to imitate a respected model's actions than conform to his/her verbalized exhortations of standards. In addition to exploring the general parameters involved in imitation, the effect of modeling on moral standards was investigated directly and shown to increase moral judgments (Bandura & McDonald, 1963).

In attempting to account for these results many social learning theorists were increasingly aware of roles played by cognitive processes: attention to and interpretation of what was observed, memory for modeled behavior over time (delayed performance), selective imitation such as sex-appropriate behavior, generalization to disparate contexts by semantic connections, and cognitive level necessary for encoding the modeled act. Therefore, the theoretical models increasingly included cognitive components in their explanations. Bandura (1971) and others with similar interpretations (e.g., Mischel & Mischel, 1976) rejected the learning models that explained all observational learning and imitation due directly to a history of contingent rewards and punishments, as was argued by theorists with a more strict, operant orientation (e.g., Baer & Sherman, 1964; Gewirtz & Stingle, 1968). Instead they argued that the effects of contingent rewards and punishments are cognitively mediated.

The major components of Bandura's model (the most fully formulated of these social learning theories) are *attention* (register the model's action), *retention* (memory of what is observed, either by imaginal or verbal representation), *motoric reproduction* (expressing the cognitive representations behaviorally), and *motivation* (the effects of reward and punishment on prompting the observer to attend, encode carefully, rehearse symbolically, and finally to perform the observed act overtly). Although cognitive components play a significant role in the theory, the required evidence for assessing whether observational learning and imitation are affected by these variables is overt performance of an action. An important point in Bandura's model is that to demonstrate that observational learning has occurred, the imitated action must consist of a newly organized pattern of behavioral responses not previously in the observer's repertoire.

Much of the research and theoretical accounts in these cognitive-social learning models are based on children who already demonstrate imitation and cognitive representation. But how to account for the origin or acquisition of imitation itself? Does the evidence in older children of delayed imitation, the performance of modeled behavior after a period of time and when the model is no longer present, require a theoretical interpretation that includes cognitive representation and mediation even for newborns? It is this issue of the origin of imitation, whether it is innate, part of a maturational process, or is acquired through environmental experience, that may best distinguish the thrust of the operant models (e.g., Gewirtz & Stingle, 1968) versus the models invoking cognitive mediation. As Bandura (1971) noted, it is possible that cognitive mediation is not an essential component of imitation by young infants when the reproduction of the model's behavior may be much more under the control of immediate rewards and punishments. Later studies suggest that imitation and intermodal matching (visually observing and then motorically performing an act) may be innate, at least in normal infants (Meltzoff & Moore, 1983). Whether these very early acts of reproducing modeled behaviors are evidence of innate, reflex-like acts, or evidence of a human predisposition to acquire a generalized, imitative action if highly likely environmental events occur, is not yet clear. For understanding the implications for moral development, the cognitive learning model may be most applicable for older, normal children. The operant models, by contrast, may be most relevant in accounting for the origin of the initial act of imitation, assuming that imitation is not an innate action pattern. The operant model has been especially useful as a guide for intervention strategies with children who do not imitate social models, such as autistic children (Loovas 1967). What is clear from these studies of observational learning is that modeling moral standards increases the likelihood of compliance to these standards in observers.

Other behavioral models also introduce cognitive mediation as essential for understanding how moral rules are acquired and internalized. Burton (Burton 1976a, 1976b; 1984; Burton, Maccoby, & Allinsmith 1961; Casey & Burton 1982) has proposed that the level of cognitive development of the child, particularly linguistic development, is critically important in determining the effectiveness of training techniques for teaching moral standards. The teacher must tailor techniques to the child's level of understanding. Providing a good verbal argument to a six-month-old infant for why she should not put her fingers in the electric outlet is obviously ineffective, whereas saying, "no! no!" and physically moving the child away is appropriate. At the same time, however, the visual stimulus of the outlet, the parent's verbal cue, tone of voice, and facial expression are all being classically conditioned and associated with punishment for the forbidden action.

A critical component of the punishment is an arousal of negative affect (fear or anxiety) that is also being conditioned to these situational cues. As these cues are associated with numerous restrictive situations, they gain generalized power to inhibit forbidden behavior. The parent does not have to use the immediate, physical control techniques, and can rely more on the acquired verbal commands, and even very subtle facial gestures, for controlling the child's behavior. With the acquisition of language, the initial verbal cues that acted as simple conditioned stimuli take on semantic meaning. If the parents provide explanations and reasons that make clear what factors define the situation as moral, they are providing the cognitive context for the child's developing moral concepts. Particularly important are the labels the parents use in identifying these situations (Burton, 1976b; Casey & Burton, 1982). These labels are hierarchically arranged. Some are so specific that they apply to only a few, very similar situations, and others are so broad that they include a large number of quite physically different situations connected only by the concept. We illustrate with samples of teaching moral behavior. At the lowest level, telling a child who is taking her sister's candy, "don't do that," teaches the child to suppress a particular response (taking candy) in a specific situation (her sister's room). The label "stealing" is broader but still restricted in that it applies only to situations of taking another person's property. "Cheating," an even broader term, can apply across specific behaviors and situations, such as the breaking of rules in games or the sharing of answers in classroom tests. At a much more inclusive level, "honesty" includes lying, stealing, and cheating. The critical label must be attached to the situational context. If the child does not recognize that a situation calls for a moral response, he or she will likely not resist the temptation. However, if the child has learned to label situations as "stealing," and this concept has been associated with punishment and therefore with affect arousal, he or she may resist taking another child's toy in many different contexts, whether on the playground, in a house, or in the back yard. If "cheating" is used, the child may comply with the rules of many games or not peek at the answers in a classroom test. If the broad concept of "honesty" is applied in various situations, he or she may resist whatever deception would have resulted in immediate but tabooed gain.

These semantic discriminations map on to the primary stimulus generalization gradients learned as an infant. What the child does in a new situation depends not only on similarity of physical stimuli, but also on whether the context permits the child to classify it with a critical label used when moral training occurred. The cognitive structuring by the parent's "reasoning" aids the child in learning the concept in order to generalize to subsequent situations. The arousal of negative affect by this classification acts to deter deceptive behavior.

Aronfreed (1968) has shown that punishment combined with explanations for why an initially preferred act should not be performed increases the child's compliance to the imposed restriction. Especially effective were explanations stating that even the thought or intent to perform the forbidden act was not allowed. Aronfreed (1976) suggests that the cognitive representations of these strictures are more "mobile" than the physical cues, a suggestion that seems parallel to Burton's (1963) hypothesis of a semantic generalization of concepts. Also, the effectiveness of the explanation for why an act is taboo can be increased by portraying the harm that the act may have for others (Hoffman, 1976).

In general, the more immediate and the greater the intensity of punishment, the more the suppression of the forbidden behavior. However, some studies indicate that providing a clear cognitive context when teaching the required moral behavior may cancel and even reverse these effects (Cheyne, 1971; Parke, 1969). These studies indicate that high-intensity punishment administered early in the response sequence may produce less suppression of a prohibited response than a low intensity of delayed punishment if the same level of reasoning accompanies both punishment conditions. A study by Andres and Walters (1970) also shows the effects of cognitive mediation in verbally recreating a situation in which the child had earlier deviated but the parents have just discovered it. Recreating the situation, verbally or by having the child role play what actually happened, and then administering punishment at the appropriate time when the deviation has taken place was shown to be an effective procedure in deterring future infractions. Taken together, these findings provide welcome relief to parents. From the animal studies one might conclude that to ensure effectiveness parents should use a high level of punishment from the start to prevent the child's adapting to gradually increasing intensities. Further, since delayed punishment is so ineffective in these animal experiments, the conclusion would be that if you didn't discover the child's infraction very soon after it was committed, there would be little use in disciplining the child after a lengthy interval. These human studies indicate that under some conditions punishment can be effective when it is both mild and delayed. The cognitive structuring of the situation appears to be critical. The level of punishment does need to be sufficient to suppress the forbidden behavior, but optimum intensity may be quite mild when the child is being taught a complex, conceptual discrimination. The effectiveness of recreating the occasion of the infraction is particularly important as many occasions for teaching standards arise long after the commission of the unacceptable behavior. These learning models rely strongly on the cognitive ability of humans to represent "in their heads" past events and to associate situations by their similarities in semantic categories. These memories and cognitive processes then act as internal monitors to evoke the affective arousal, originally produced by the discipline, that the learning model indicates is necessary for the inhibition of the forbidden act.

The models we've discussed here have evolved from basic behavioral learning theories. The cognitive elements in the theories tended to be introduced to account for behavior that seemed to depend on human representational systems, particularly language. Other models have their roots more directly in human studies addressed to cognitive processes. Let us turn to those now.

## Cognitive Dissonance and Attributional Models

Various social-psychological theories propose that humans strive to maintain consistency in their beliefs, attitudes, values, and behavior (e.g., Festinger, 1957; Heider, 1958; Lerner, 1970). Similar theories hypothesize that we also strive to maintain consistency in ourselves and others by attributing global personality characteristics to individuals based on insufficient, incomplete, and selective observations (e.g., Bem, 1972; Berscheid & Walster, 1967; Dix, Ruble, Grusec, & Nixon, 1986; Jones, Kanouse, Kelley, Nisbett, Valins, & Weiner, 1972). The data generated by the development and testing of these theories bear significantly on the inculcation of moral standards.

Festinger's cognitive dissonance theory (Festinger, 1957; Festinger & Freedman, 1964) has demonstrated conditions under which cognitions (attitudes, beliefs, self-attributions) are modified to conform to behavior. It is necessary that there be no adequate alternative justification for how one has behaved other than to attribute the action to one's own attitudes, beliefs, motivational system, or personality traits. Neither rewards nor threat of punishment should be so salient that they justify the behavior. For example, in an experiment by Festinger and Carlsmith (1959), college students participated in some very boring tasks. They were then paid either $1 or $20 to tell another student waiting to participate that the tasks were interesting. When later asked how they really felt about the tasks, students paid $1 said the tasks were somewhat interesting whereas those paid $20 said they were boring. The interpretation is that, if the pressure to perform the behavior is objectively sufficient to inhibit but psychologically insufficient to justify the action taken, the cognitions will come in line with the action, i.e., "dissonance reduction." How could the students paid so little justify their having been dishonest in their reporting about the tasks? They seem to say to themselves, "Well, maybe they weren't so boring but could really be quite interesting." Those paid the large amount can justify to themselves why they did it (for the money) and don't change their initial evaluations. An alternative interpretation is that the subjects change their evaluation of the task when paid the small amount to protect their feelings of self-worth (Steele, 1988). That is, if they believe that they lied unjustifiably, their perceptions of self-integrity are threatened; therefore, to obviate this threat subjects may reinterpret the situation to reaffirm their views of themselves as adaptively and morally adequate individuals.

A similar effect of inadequate justification as found in the Festinger studies occurs with strong and mild punishment. If a child is inhibited from committing an infraction with a very mild threat of punishment or risk of being caught, the likelihood of resisting the temptation the next time is increased. However, if the inhibition of the tabooed behavior is due to high level of risk and threat of severe punishment, the child is likely to commit the infraction when the risk of getting caught is withdrawn (Aronson & Carlsmith, 1963). A similar change in cognitions was seen in an experiment in which four-year-old children completed deviation doll-play stories both a week before and immediately after being in a temptation test (Burton, 1971). The doll-play stories presented the children with a doll's committing a deviation (e.g., not watching a baby who falls off a couch) and then asked the child to complete the story. Children who cheated during the temptation test decreased in the frequency of portraying punishment in their stories and increased in portraying parental nurturance and permissiveness. Children who resisted the temptation, by contrast, increased in their portrayals of punishment following deviation and decreased in parental permissiveness. These results show that the children's attitudes came into line with how they had behaved in the temptation test.

Festinger (Festinger & Freedman 1964) hypothesized that a feedback system in these situations contributed to moral development. When the child acts honestly and resists the temptation to deviate for some immediate gain under what he perceives to be low threat of punishment, he may attribute to himself the trait of honesty or devalue what would have been gained by the deceptive act. If the subsequent temptations just happened to be graded so that they gradually increase in incentives and decrease in risk but never so abruptly as to elicit a deviation, the self attribution of honesty increases. The stronger this positive self-attribution, the less likely the giving in to subsequent temptation. Lepper (1982) has labeled this attribution process the *minimal sufficiency hypothesis:* The minimal pressure that is just sufficient to inhibit the proscribed behavior increases the likelihood that the child attributes her behavior to self-control, that she complied willingly rather than from coercion. But can parents and teachers affect these attributions developing in the child directly? The following studies suggest the answer is yes.

Dix et al. (1986) found that parents who made stronger dispositional attributions for child misbehavior also tended to perceive the misbehavior as more intentional, stable, and general. Parents who see the misbehavior as caused by "internal" character traits of the child instead of by aspects of the situation also reported feeling greater anger and "need to respond." Experimental studies have shown that these attributions coming from the parents and others do affect the child's behavior and development, particularly the child's self-concept. Behavior such as tidiness (Miller, Brickman, & Bolen, 1975), cooperative behavior (Jensen & Moore, 1977), and altruism (Grusec & Redler, 1980) have been increased by attributing to the child the positive trait associated with those behaviors ("you're very neat"; "you really get along well with others"; "you're very generous and sharing"). It is also likely that the attribution of negative qualities to the child contributes to a negative self-concept and increases misbehavior. For example, saying, "You're always a naughty child" attributes an internal, global, and stable trait to the child, attributions that may be particularly deleterious for their developing a healthy self-concept and emotional adjustment (Abramson, Seligman, & Teasdale, 1978; Weiner, 1980). By saying, "That was a naughty thing you did," the parent labels the act, not the child, as unacceptable. By adding, "I'm surprised that you would have done that. I know you are very honest and trustworthy. That is just not like you at all," the parent distinguishes the act from the child's character and also enhances the child's positive self-concept while actually punishing him.

In combination with more general studies of expectancy effects (e.g., Rosenthal & Jacobson, 1968), these attributional studies indicate that children are subject to being shaped by others' expectations about them. Swann (1983) suggests that adults strive to maintain their self-conception, even to the extent of distorting information to verify their self-view. In adults, the self-view is a product of a long history of feedback from one's own behavior and the attributions of others. By contrast, children's self-concept is being formulated, indicating that they may be more vulnerable to these expectancies and attributions—for better or for worse.

Parents are responsible for setting limits on their children, teaching them to delay gratification, to abide by rules, and to respect the rights of others. These studies indicate that the astute parent accomplishes this socialization process most effectively by arranging the context so that it appears that a minimum of pressure resulted in the child's compliance to the required standard. Choices of what to do may be offered the child, but all of them are acceptable. After the child chooses, the parent can attribute a positive trait to the child for the choice. As Maccoby (1982) has pointed out, however, such attributions must have the ring of truth or the child will see through the strategy quickly and discount it. As she suggests, the surest way to ensure that children feel they have exercised free choice is to allow them as much free choice as is appropriate for their age.

## *Physiological Learning Models*

In the Solomon (Solomon et al., 1968) model based on experiments with puppies (described above), it is essential that the subject experience the physiological arousal of anxiety at specific temporal points in the sequential flow of the moral conflict situation in order to develop either a resistance or guilt reaction. This model, giving a central role to both innate and acquired emotional responding, stands in contrast to the more cognitively oriented theories that tend to treat motivation as just another cognitive component. This emotional arousal is produced, according to the theory, by Pavlovian conditioning during the initial punishment for misbehavior so that the stimuli present during the discipline are conditioned to this negative affective arousal. When these same stimuli are presented after the training sessions, they elicit the conditioned anxiety. This arousal then acts as an internal cue, prompting the puppy to learn an operant response, which is to avoid the negative sanctions by not misbehaving.

This model has been influential in the design and interpretation of research dealing directly with children and the effects of child-rearing practices (Aronfreed, 1976; Burton, 1963; 1976a; 1976b; 1984; Burton et al., 1961; Casey & Burton, 1982; Cheyne, 1971; Cheyne & Walters, 1969; Parke, 1969; Parke & Walters, 1967; Walters, Parke, & Cane, 1965). These studies show that training children with the same procedures used with the puppies produces parallel results. However, as mentioned earlier, when verbal context or cognitive structure accompanies the punishment, the effects of intensity and timing of punishment are different and can reverse: low intensity and delayed punishment can produce most compliance to the rule. Furthermore, the attribution studies also extend the complexity of the basic model when cognitive processes are considered. Nevertheless, the basic hypothesis that negative affect must be attached to the linguistic categories used to classify the situation and to interpret the physiological arousal receives much support in these studies.

In most of these studies, the affective arousal was assumed to be occurring rather than having been measured directly. Some early attempts were made to assess the physiological responses and their timing in the sequence. The results were suggestive and generally in line with the theory, but these efforts were not pursued due to methodological difficulties, mainly unreliable measures and apparatus (Black, Solomon, & Whiting, 1954; Cheyne & Walters, 1969). Later studies with adults experimentally manipulated affective arousal directly by administering drugs or placebos. Schachter and colleagues (Nisbett & Schachter, 1966; Schachter, 1964; Schachter & Latane, 1964; Schachter & Singer, 1962) demonstrated that the labeling of one's emotional state or mood had an impact on how one behaved when drugs were used to increase or depress arousal of the sympathetic nervous system. Administering an arousal drug and then having a confederate act either angry or euphoric led the experimental subject to imitate the reaction to the drug modeled by the confederate. Even telling the subjects that they were receiving a drug that would make them feel either aroused or depressed when they actually received a placebo produced differential behavior.

These findings were then extended to experiments on moral development. Schachter and Ono (in Schachter & Latane, 1964) hypothesized that sympathetic arousal would facilitate avoidance responses (resistance to temptation) whereas a tranquilizer (sympathetic inhibiter) would decrease learned avoidance responses and result in more cheating. Consonant with their predictions, they found that chlorpromazine (a tranquilizer) increased cheating over a control group. Extending these findings to an attribution model, Dienstbier and Munter (1971) gave subjects a placebo but told them that it was either an arousing or depressing drug. Males who believed they had received a stimulant cheated more than males who believed that the pill was a depressant. Dienstbier and Munter interpreted the results as demonstrating that men who attributed their emotional reactivity to the drug rather than to arousal from the moral conflict, perceived themselves as less inhibited regarding cheating and increased their infractions. Men who believed their emotional responding had been chemically depressed perceived the emotional conflict they felt in the test as being less than they would normally feel and increased their compliance to the rules. However, women were not affected by these manipulations leading to rather strained explanations for this lack of effect.

These experiments that directly manipulate emotions and cognitions to assess their effects on behavior are complex and elicit different interpretations. For example Zajonc (1980) hypothesizes that because our emotional reactions to events occur faster than our cognitive interpretations of them, emotions take precedence over thought as determinants of action. Instead of a top-down process (i.e., our thoughts determine what emotions we experience), Zajonc argues that our cognitions rationalize what we are feeling and doing. Possibly, theory is ahead of hardware in that the apparatus has not yet been developed that is sensitive enough to pick up the slight traces of affective arousal that operate as the internal cues. What has been made clear is that emotions and cognitions interact in complex ways in determining what behavior occurs and whether that behavior is perceived as having been performed willfully or from external pressure. In the context of moral development, this differential perception (attribution) may be critical in whether the child internalizes the rule complied with or just sees the compliance as forced on him by another's (parent, teacher, or peer) surveillance (Maccoby & Martin, 1983).

This review has provided a history and overview of behavioral models of moral development. Although these "behavioral" models may appear disparate as often as they appear similar, they share the common assumption that research on moral development must go beyond an exclusive emphasis on reasoning and judgment to address actual conduct. We now present a hypothetical case study of an intervention strategy derived from the empirical findings and theoretical conclusions presented in these studies. Our attempt is to show how these findings may be integrated in a real world case involving the inculcation of moral standards in a specific child.

## Creating a Moral Climate in the Classroom: Application of Research and Theory

In addition to the inculcation of moral standards in the home by parents and siblings, the development of moral character has been a central goal of public education from its beginning in the United States. This goal is strongly supported by parents who consistently have indicated in national polls that they want moral training in the schools. For example, the 1980 Gallup poll showed that 84 percent of the parents endorsed moral training in schools whereas only 12 percent were opposed to such direct instruction.

If we accept that schools have a role in buttressing or, if necessary, directly training the consensual moral rules of our society, how might an individual teacher implement the training of ethical standards in a specific student? The following case study does not attempt to package principles derived from the above review in a unified theoretical model. Instead, this illustration is eclectic, deriving from the various studies applications of controlling the child's environment to bring about desired changes in his behavior.

Our hypothetical student, Billy, is a seven-year-old second-grade boy who has been observed to engage repeatedly in cheating on classroom tests, in lying about his unacceptable actions when confronted by Ms. Jones, the teacher, and finally in stealing out of her purse. In each of these situations there is clear consensus in our society of what is required for proper moral conduct. There is no ethical relativism here; Ms. Jones knows what is right and wrong in each of these instances. Ms. Jones does not have to be an expert in ethics and moral philosophy to inculcate these basic moral standards.

Whatever action Ms. Jones takes is done with the intent to internalize standards for each of these specific types of infractions as well as to inculcate a general standard of honesty. Ms. Jones agrees with the perspective of all current theories of moral development that the learning and acceptance as right (internalization) of these simple standards of ethical conduct in early childhood is the necessary base for developing a mature system of moral standards. Although adult morality may involve much more complex ethical decisions, such as the type of conflicts assessed in measures based on reasoning about moral dilemmas (Kohlberg, 1976; Rest, 1983), Ms. Jones believes that without the inculcation of basic behavioral standards that tend to be performed automatically in adequately socialized adults advanced levels of moral decision-making that lead to moral conduct are blocked (Burton, 1984).

## School Environment as Matrix for Moral Development

Whatever Ms. Jones may do directly will be supported or thwarted by the moral atmosphere of the total school context (Hartshorne & May, 1928). Schools develop distinctive morales that spread throughout the administration, faculty, and student body. Although difficult to delineate precisely how these qualities of administrative structure interact with many other variables in school settings, the school atmosphere influences the moral code of the students. School principals, in their policies and behavior toward faculty and students, set the model for what their teachers see as appropriate attitudes and ways of treating pupils. Teachers who are treated in an authoritarian style by a school administrator are likely to model after their boss and to establish authoritarian classroom structures. Teachers who see their suggestions about school structure and policies being seriously considered and implemented when appropriate, feel a personal responsibility for implementing the policies. The teacher-pupil interaction is the final link in a system in which all levels of the administration and staff share in the responsibility for establishing an environment in which ethical standards are practiced as well as preached.

A classroom climate that models the democratic process of establishing goals, rules, rewards, and sanctions by group discussion, arriving at a group charter and code of conduct perceived as clear, fair, and representative of the students' inputs as well as of the teacher's, is superior in developing self-control in the individual student compared with a permissive or authoritarian classroom organization (Lewin, Lippitt, & White, 1939). The democratic, authoritative teacher understands her responsibility for inculcating moral standards and doesn't hesitate to set limits on unacceptable behavior. His or her imposed sanctions, however, are the legitimized forms of discipline established by the classroom and school charter and codes of conduct that manifest respect for the inherent dignity of the misbehaving child.

## Modeling: Practicing versus Preaching

By contrast, consider a recently observed disciplinary episode in a classroom for the model it portrays: A classroom rule was to keep desks neat, but one child kept crumpled up papers stuffed in hers. Noting the papers, the teacher turned the desk over, dumping the entire contents on the floor. The child appeared stunned, standing motionless as the other children laughed. When asked about this form of discipline, the teacher said it was very effective. No doubt it is—in the short run.

But what are the long-term effects? It does not contribute to the child's developing a positive self-concept, nor does it help develop an attitude of mutual respect and a mature concept of justice, two qualities related to developing ethical standards. How effective can this teacher be when she appeals to this child's notion of fairness and respect for others as the rationale for honesty involving lying, stealing, and cheating? As our review above shows, modeling disrespect speaks louder than preaching consideration of others. The most effective conditions are provided when preaching is consonant with and buttresses actions. An awareness of the subtle and cumulative process involved in the formation of moral values makes us recognize that these seemingly trivial events are the raw stuff from which moral standards develop.

## Teacher/Pupil Personal Relationship

Ms. Jones knows that most of her charges form a positive attachment to her, wanting to please her and to receive her warm approval. She sees this likelihood as a valuable means to render more effective her occasional disapproval of a child's unacceptable behavior. She establishes pupil relationships based on warmth and trust and provides clear and fair reasons to justify the sanctions she imposes for misbehavior. If she punishes, it is to shape moral behavior in the child, not administered out of frustration, for revenge, or just to hurt. At the same time, she appreciates that negative perceptions and attributions of peers, parents, and teachers accrue to a child who regularly engages in unethical conduct. These deleterious consequences may render the skilled use of punishment (see below) to insure the development of moral conduct a humane alternative. A few well-timed punishments might obviate much more prolonged aversive and painful consequences later in life.

## Sequencing Moral Training

To intervene and modify established behavior in Billy, Ms. Jones plans out situations in which performance of the desired moral behavior is assured. She tailors these situations to conform to principles that can be derived from the results of the studies reviewed above. First, Ms. Jones will want to arrange situations that permit Billy to practice resisting the temptations to cheat, lie, and steal. Having seen Billy steal other children's toys, candy, and finally money from her purse, she decides to work on changing this behavior first. To provide for his practicing honesty, she appoints Billy to be the money collector for various school events. Initially, she arranges situations which involve much surveillance as she wants to insure that Billy does not deviate in these planned situations. At first, she walks around with Billy and records the money being put into the money box. When the collection is done, she attributes honesty to account for his behavior. Billy is learning from his peers on the playground that being called a "stealer," "liar," or "cheater" are serious accusations to be denied. Ms. Jones capitalizes on this peer teaching to link "dishonesty" and "untrustworthiness" with "stealing" so that these labels also become negative appellations, and the opposites, "honesty" and "trust" acquire positive value. In her verbal structuring of the situation and Billy's behavior, she intentionally associates these concepts: "I know I can trust you not to steal. You're honest" (Burton, 1984).

After several practices with such surveillance, she begins to leave some distance between where she is and where Billy is collecting, but still watching closely. If any money is held without being put into the box immediately, she moves near and reminds Billy that it is best to put the money in the box right away or it might get lost. This mild form of punishment is being associated with the anticipation of actually stealing the money, the best conditions initially for developing resistance to the temptation (Aronfreed, 1968; Solomon et al, 1968). She makes sure he is not rewarded by succeeding in any attempt to keep the money. Later she can say that someone might think that some money was stolen if it were lost and that he would certainly not want anyone to think that he ever stole things. She stresses "How terrible a person would feel if others thought he or she were a stealer. Don't you feel good when other people know you're not a stealer and that they can trust you to be honest?" She structures her statements to have Billy say that he knows that stealing anything is not right and that he would never do it. In these teaching episodes, she gradually reduces her apparent surveillance until she can remain near her desk during the entire collection. Each time she compliments Billy on his honesty and trustworthiness.

Consideration of attribution effects are also brought to bear. At first Billy is likely to interpret his not stealing to the high risk of being caught. With each step in appearing to withdraw surveillance, Ms. Jones is presenting conditions that are likely to lead to Billy's attributing his honesty to his own decision, starting to build the self-concept of being an honest person. The practice of resisting temptation and being honest that is followed by positive social reinforcement is increasing the strength and likelihood of that behavior.

The next step is to have Billy take the money to the office. To insure that this new challenge is not too great for Billy's current level of resistance to temptation, Ms. Jones reduces the chances of Billy's taking any of the money by counting the money, putting it in a sealed box, and attaching a large note on the outside of the box indicating how much it contained. She adds preventative pressure by having another child she knows is very trustworthy and popular to accompany him. His being chosen with a high status peer for such responsible jobs also enhances his status and adds to his positive self-esteem. The person in the office who receives the money has been informed to read the note aloud, open the box and count the money, write a note back to Ms. Jones that she must be pleased to have such trustworthy children, and then compliment the children on their honesty. Ms. Jones then reads the note aloud to Billy and the other child while the rest of the class is listening. The other children are forming expectations of Billy that add to the shaping of his moral behavior.

Ms. Jones's strategy is to provide many natural situations for Billy to practice being honest, providing her with the occasions to reinforce his overt behavior and to attribute the trait of honesty to him. The sequencing of these episodes is scheduled to withdraw external risk gradually until he perceives he has acted honestly without risk of being caught. He credits himself with determining his own actions, attributing to himself the decision not to steal but to act honestly. The reinforcement for honest behavior is more frequent and has become more valued than what would be gained by the acts of stealing. In having the other children participate and share in the attribution process, she is establishing the group code for honesty that she knows is so influential in establishing the norms for her class's standards.

## Punishment's Role

Punishment for unacceptable behavior is also administered during this training. When Billy misbehaves, such as shoving another child, talking during a lesson, or not taking turns, Ms. Jones shows her displeasure and disciplines him. She demonstrates that her approval is earned or withdrawn by his behavior. Her creating verbal scenarios in her casual talking with Billy, in which stealing is portrayed as being objectionable and punished, provides vicarious avoidance learning for that infraction. These scenarios, using plots based on the collection situations Billy engages in, permit Ms. Jones to associate the punishment of the fictitious deviator of the story with the terms of "stealing," "untrustworthy," and "dishonest." This vicarious learning adds to the association of negative affect with these terms (Casey & Burton, 1982) and decreases the likelihood of Billy's committing the punished behavior in similar situations (Bandura, 1965).

## Semantic Generalization

Ms. Jones also begins to work on Billy's cheating and lying. Now she chooses a strategy that takes advantage of having associated the term "honesty" with Billy's learning to resist temptations to steal. For cheating, she adopts a strategy similar to her strategy for stealing. The temptation in such planned situations should initially be weak by having a low incentive, no sense of failure in performance, and sufficient risk to insure that cheating is inhibited. Ms. Jones makes sure that Billy's not cheating results in a positive outcome rather than a negative experience of failure and possible ridicule by other children for a low grade. She can note those parts he did well on and indicate that she'll go over some other parts with him alone. Gradually, the obvious risk is lessened until it is no more than the regular classroom supervision experienced by all the children. As with stealing, Ms. Jones notes that Billy did not cheat and that he can be trusted not to cheat because he is an honest boy.

Ms. Jones provides Billy additional practice in succeeding honestly by tailoring situations for public success. For example, when sending children to the blackboard to do arithmetic or when having spelling bees, she can engineer the problems for Billy to ensure at least average success. She would not undercut the credibility of the episodes by obvious differences in the demands for Billy compared with the other children (Maccoby, 1982). Letting him succeed as an average child in the class lessens his need to cheat to avoid being seen as a "dummy." Billy needs to practice being honest in these ecologically valid situations to consolidate seeing himself as a moral person (Bem, 1972). The stronger his self-concept as an honest boy, the more likely he will decide when in a moral conflict that inasmuch as he is an honest person he will not yield to the temptation. His resisting the temptation adds to his self-concept of honesty, and the feedback loop escalates.

## Labeling Act, Not Child, As Unacceptable

But all is not likely to go so smoothly. If the surveillance was removed too quickly and Billy cheats by copying on a test, Ms. Jones shows her displeasure by saying, "Billy, that was cheating. I'm very disappointed in you that you would do that. It's not like you at all. That was a dishonest thing and you're a very honest boy. Do you understand that cheating is wrong?—Do honest boys cheat?—Aren't you honest?—Well, I think you're honest, too, so are you going to cheat any more?" Here Ms. Jones attributes a positive trait to the child while labeling the act as unethical. Billy is not bad but his action was. She includes the immediate act of cheating as an instance of dishonesty, increasing generalization of this instance of punishment for cheating along a semantic gradient to also inhibit stealing and lying (Burton, 1963; Casey & Burton, 1982). Ms. Jones demonstrates that dishonesty results in punishment. She arranges the discussion so that Billy commits himself to complying with the moral standard, an overt act that increases the likelihood of such compliance (Fischer, 1970).

## Reducing Fear of Failure

She follows up her confronting Billy by having him take the test again. Ms. Jones knows that most children cheat to avoid failure. Before having him retake the test, therefore, she inspects the test to see where Billy needs extra help in understanding how to succeed on the problems. She can go over the problems she will ask and coach him some to be sure he understands. Then she administers the test under conditions in which it is almost impossible to cheat. After looking over the test, Ms. Jones says, "That's what I expect of you. You did well on the test and you didn't have to cheat. You took the test just the way an honest and trustworthy person takes tests. I'm proud of you, Billy."

## *"Punishment" May Not Be Punishing*

Ms. Jones knows that her actions are punishments only if they suppress the unacceptable behavior. She is sensitive to the possibility that the above treatments actually may be very reinforcing for Billy's *misbehavior*. Her confrontation of his deception may provide attention that he wants. Possibly he has learned from his parents and other teachers that he receives attention when he misbehaves but is ignored when he acts positively, conditions that perpetuate and increase the very behavior the adults are intending to inhibit (Scott, Burton, & Yarrow, 1967). Even the attention from being reprimanded is better than being ignored. Scolding Billy makes him contrite, promising not to do it again. His resolve, however, is weak and fleeting compared with the usual classroom pressures to avoid failure combined with the reinforcement from having gained the teacher's total focus. Ms. Jones understands that not responding to unacceptable behavior can be effective punishment, and is especially effective if terminated by the desired behavior. Ending her unpleasant demeanor contingent on Billy's acceptable behavior serves to reinforce that desired action.

This principle of not responding, or "time out," is particularly applicable to Billy's lying. Ms. Jones knows that all children commit moral infractions at times and that at other times comply with the moral code (Hartshorne & May, 1928). With this awareness, she is sympathetic and understanding when Billy slips up in complying with all the rules. Although carefully monitoring Billy's progress, she is not rigid in moral condemnation. Aware that even the group of children most extreme for behaving immorally act morally a third of the time (Hartshorne et al., 1930), Ms. Jones builds more on reinforcing those positive occurrences than on punishing minor misbehavior. From this perspective, Ms. Jones occasionally chooses to ignore, not to respond to an infraction, particularly in cases of Billy's not telling the truth. When Billy denies his responsibility for accidental harm to a person or property, or blames another child for something he has done, Ms. Jones just looks at Billy, not changing her expression, until he begins to own up to his responsibility. Then she softens her demeanor, nods, and compliments him for telling the truth and being honest. To prevent his learning that "confession" is a good way to avoid punishment, Ms. Jones labels the action Billy denied as unacceptable and imposes whatever sanctions are appropriate.

In planning these experiences, Ms. Jones is careful to avoid placing Billy in situations that are too tempting for his stage of development. Were he to succeed in stealing and cheating, and in avoiding accountability for his actions by lying, he would be immediately rewarded. Ms. Jones tries to negate this intrinsic reinforcement for deception by withdrawing anything gained by the misbehavior and by trying to provide stronger rewards for the moral conduct that is incompatible with the deception.

## Preparing for Return to Regular Classroom Treatment

As Billy's behavior comes into line with the socially required moral codes, Ms. Jones prepares to withdraw her special awareness of his actions. She knows that if she abruptly withdraws a high rate of positive responding for his moral conduct he is very likely to backslide. To prevent this, she begins to respond less than every time Billy is honest, instead gradually increasing the number of occasions of his proper conduct before she gives him her approval. Called intermittent reinforcement, this procedure places Billy on a schedule of approval that is finally the same as occurs in the normal classroom situation. Ms. Jones carefully monitors this procedure to insure that the honest behavior is maintained. If Billy should start returning to his previous ways, she assumes that she went too fast and returns her rate of approval to a more frequent ratio.

## Endnotes

1. Perhaps, one reason for the paucity of developmental studies of this facet of morality is that it is not easily addressed developmentally. Another possibility is that until the rise of AIDS, sexual behavior was not seen as a problem area by most behavioral scientists investigating moral development. Certainly attempts to study sexual activity in children and adolescents have been hindered and blocked by parents, school authorities, human subjects review committees, and government officials. The strength of the taboo against obtaining behavioral data even in adults is currently reflected in the blocking for over a year by the Surgeon General's office of the Survey of Health and AIDS Risk Prevalence, a national survey of sexual behavior in adolescents and adults.

2. The authors recognized this feature of unidimensional scaling applied to attitudes in general and published a separate article on it (Hartshorne & May, 1926). Overlooked for nearly 20 years, the significance of the procedure was rediscovered by Guttman and is now known as the Guttman scale (Guttman, 1944).

3. The cognitive learning theory of Tolman (1932) and its emphasis on learning as associations between observed events was certainly influential in some of these formulations.

## References

Abramson, L. Y., Seligman, M. E. P., & Teasdale, J. D. (1978). Learned helplessness in humans: Critique and reformulation. *Journal of Abnormal Psychology, 87*, 49-74.

Andres, D., and Walters, R. H. (1970). Modification of delay of punishment effects through cognitive restructuring. *Proceedings of the 78th Annual Convention of the American Psychological Association*, 483-484.

Aronfreed, J. (1968). *Conduct and conscience: The socialization of internalized control over behavior.* New York: Academic Press.

Aronfreed, J. (1976). Moral development from the standpoint of a general psychological theory. In T. Lickona (Ed.), *Research in moral development and behavior* (54-69). New York: Holt, Rinehart & Winston.

Aronson, E., & Carlsmith, J. M. (1963). Effect of the severity of threat on the devaluation of forbidden behavior. *Journal of Abnormal and Social Psychology, 66*, 584-588.

Baer, D. M., & Sherman, J. A. (1964). Reinforcement control of generalized imitation in young children. *Journal of Experimental Child Psychology, 1*, 37-49.

Bandura, A. (1962). Social learning through imitation. In M. R. Jones, (Ed.) *Nebraska Symposium on Motivation: 1962*. Lincoln: Univ. of Nebraska Press.

Bandura, A. (1965). Influence of models' reinforcement contingencies on the acquisition of imitative responses. *Journal of Personality and Social Psychology, 1*, 589-595.

Bandura, A. (1969). *Principles of behavior modification*. New York: Holt, Rinehart & Winston.

Bandura, A. (1971). *Social learning theory*. New York: General Learning Press.

Bandura, A., & McDonald, F. J. (1963). The influence of social reinforcement and the behavior of models in shaping children's moral judgments. *Journal of Abnormal and Social Psychology, 67*, 274-281.

Bandura, A., Ross, D., & Ross, 5. A. (1963a). Imitation of film-mediated aggressive models. *Journal of Personality and Social Psychology, 66*, 3-11.

Bandura, A., Ross, D., & Ross, S. A. (1963b). A comparative test of the status envy, social power, and secondary reinforcement theories of identificatory learning. *Journal of Personality and Social Psychology, 67*, 527-534.

Bandura, A., & Walters, R. H. (1963). *Social learning and personality development*. New York: Holt, Rinehart & Winston.

Bem, D. J. (1972). Self-perception theory. In L. Berkowitz (Ed.), *Advances in experimental social psychology* (Vol. 6, pp. 1-62). New York: Academic Press.

Berscheid, E., & Walster, E. (1967). When does a harm-doer compensate a victim? *Journal of Personality and Social Psychology, 6*, 435-441.

Black, A., Solomon, R. L., & Whiting, J. W. M. (1954). Resistance to temptation as a function of antecedent dependency relationship in puppies. *American Psychologist, 9*, 579 (Abstract).

Burton, R. V. (1963). Generality of honesty reconsidered. *Psychological Review*, 70, 481-499.

Burton, R. V. (1971). Correspondence between behavioral and doll-play measures of conscience. *Developmental Psychology, 5*, 320-332.

Burton, R. V. (1976a). Honesty and Dishonesty: The research reconsidered. In T. Lickona (Ed.), *Research in moral development and behavior* (173-197). New York: Holt, Rinehart & Winston.

Burton, R. V. (1976b). Assessment of moral training programs: Where are we going? Invited address to Division 7, Developmental Psychology, at the Annual Convention of the American Psychological Association, Washington, D.C.

Burton, R. V. (1984). A paradox in theories and research in moral development. In W. M. Kurtines & J. L. Gewirtz (Eds.), *Morality, moral development and moral behavior* (193-207). New York: Wiley & Sons, Inc.

Burton, R. V., Maccoby, E. E., & Allinsmith, W. (1961). Antecedents of resistance to temptation in four-year-old children. *Child Development, 32*, 689-710.

Burton, R. V., & Reis, J. (1980). Internalization. In Munroe, R. H., Munroe, R. L., & Whiting, B.B. (Eds.), *Handbook of cross-cultural human development* (675-687). New York: Garland Publishing, Inc.

Casey, W., & Burton, R. V. (1982). Training children to be consistently honest through verbal self-instructions. *Child Development, 53*, 911-919.

Cheyne, J. A. (1971). Some parameters of punishment affecting resistance to deviation and generalization of a prohibition. *Child Development*, 1971, *42*, 1249-1261.

Cheyne, J. A., & Walters, R. H. (1969). Intensity

of punishment, timing of punishment, and cognitive structure as determinants of response inhibition. *Journal of Experimental Child Psychology, 7,* 231-244.

Dienstbier, R. A., & Munter, P. O. (1971). Cheating as a function of the labeling of natural arousal. *Journal of Personality and Social Psychology, 17,* 208-213.

Dix, T., Ruble, D., Grusec, J., & Nixon, S. (1986). Social cognition in parents: Inferential and affective reactions to children of three age levels. *Child Development, 57,* 879-894.

Festinger, L. (1957). *A theory of cognitive dissonance.* Stanford: Stanford University Press.

Festinger, L., & Carlsmith, J. M. (1959). Cognitive consequences of forced compliance. *Journal of Abnormal and Social Psychology. 58,* 203-210.

Festinger, L., & Freedman, J. L. (1964). Dissonance reduction and moral values. In P. Worchel & D. Byrne (Eds.), *Personality change.* New York: Wiley.

Fischer, C. T. (1970). Levels of cheating under conditions of informative appeal to honesty, public affirmation of values, and threats of punishment. *The Journal of Educational Research, 64,* 12-16.

Gewirtz, J. L. (1969). Mechanisms of social learning: Some roles of stimulation and behavior in early human development. In D. A. Goslin (Ed.), *Handbook of socialization theory and research* (57-212). Chicago: Rand-McNally.

Gewirtz, J. L., & Stingle, K. G. (1968). Learning of generalized imitation as the basis for identification. *Psychological Review, 75,* 374-397.

Grusec, J. E., & Redler, E. (1980). Attribution, reinforcement, and altruism: a developmental analysis. *Developmental Psychology, 16,* 524-534.

Guttman, L. (1944). A new approach to factor analysis: The radex. In P. F. Lazarsfeld (Ed.), *Mathematical thinking in the social sciences* (258-348). Glencoe, Ill.: Free Press.

Hartshorne, H., & May, M. A. (March, 1926). First steps toward a scale for measuring attitudes. *Journal of Educational Psychology.*

Hartshorne, H., & May, M. A. (1928), Studies in the nature of character. Vol. I. *Studies in deceit.* New York: Macmillan.

Hartshorne, H., May, M. A., & Maller, J. B. (1929). Studies in the nature of character. Vol. II. *Studies in service and self-control.* New York: Macmillan.

Hartshorne, H., May, M. A., & Shuttleworth, F. K. (1930). Studies in the nature of character. Vol. III. *Studies in the organization of character.* New York: Macmillan.

Heider, F. (1958). *The psychology of interpersonal relations.* New York: Wiley.

Hoffman, M. L. (1976). Empathy, role taking, guilt, and development of altruistic motives. In T. Lickona (Ed.), *Moral development and behavior* (124-143). New York: Holt, Rinehart, & Winston.

Hull, C. L. (1943). *Principles of behavior.* New York: Appleton-Century-Crofts.

Jensen, R. E., & Moore, S. G. (1977). The effect of attribute statements on cooperativeness and competitiveness in school-age boys. *Child Development, 48,* 305-307.

Jones, E. E., Kanouse, D., Kelley, H. H., Nisbett, R. E., Valins, S., & Weiner, B. (Eds.) (1972). *Attribution: Perceiving the causes of behavior.* Morristown, NJ: General Learning Press.

Josephson, M. (1990). *Ethics of American youth.* Marina Del Rey, CA: Josephson Institute of Ethics.

Kohlberg, L. (1979). Moral stages and moralization: The cognitive-developmental approach. In T. Lickona (Ed.), *Moral development and behavior.* New York: Holt, Rinehart, and Winston.

Lepper, M. R. (1982). Social control processes, attributions of motivation, and the internalization of social values. In E. T. Higgins, D. N. Ruble, & W. W. Hartup (Eds.), *Social cognition and social behavior: Developmental perspectives.* Cambridge, Eng.: Cambridge Univ. Press.

Lerner, M. J. (1970). The desire for justice and reactions to victims. In J. McCauley & L. Berkowitz (Eds.), *Altruism and helping behavior.* New York: Academic Press.

Lewin, K., Lippitt, R., & White, R. (1939). Patterns of aggressive behavior in experimentally created social climates. *Journal of Social Psychology, 10,* 271-299.

Loovas, O. I. (1967). A behavior therapy approach to the treatment of childhood schizophrenia. In J. P. Hill (Ed.), *Minnesota symposia on child psychology* (Vol.l). Minneapolis: University of Minnesota Press.

Maccoby, E. E. (1982). Let's not over-attribute to the attribution process. In E. T. Higgins, D. N. Ruble, & W. W. Hartup (Eds.), *Social cognition and social behavior: Developmental perspectives.* Cambridge, Eng.: Cambridge Univ. Press.

Maccoby, E. E., & Martin, J. A. (1983). Socialization in the context of the family: Parent-child interaction. In E. M. Hetherington (Ed.), *Handbook of child psychology: Volume 4. Socialization, personality, and social development* (pp. 1-101). New York: John Wiley & Sons.

Meltzoff, A. N., & Moore, M. K. (1983). Imitation of facial and manual gestures by human neonates. *Science, 198,* 75-78.

Miller, D. R., & Swanson, G. E. (1960). *Inner conflict and defense.* New York: Holt.

Miller, N. E., & Dollard, J. (1941). *Social learning and imitation.* New Haven, CT: Yale Univ. Press.

Miller, R. L., Brickman, P., & Bolen, D. (1975). Attribution versus persuasion as a means for modifying behavior. *Journal of Personality and Social Psychology, 31,* 430-441.

Mischel, Y., & Mischel, H. N. (1976). A cognitive social-learning approach to morality and self-regulation. In T. Lickona (Ed.), *Moral development and behavior: Theory, research and social issues* (pp. 84-107). New York: Holt, Rinehart and Winston.

Nisbett, R. E., & Schachter, S. (1966). Cognitive manipulation of pain. *Journal of Experimental Social Psychology, 2,* 227-236.

Parke, R. D. (1969). Effectiveness of punishment as an interaction of intensity, timing, agent nurturance, and cognitive structuring. *Child Development, 40,* 213-235.

Parke, R. D., & Walters, R. H. (1967). Some factors influencing the efficacy of punishment training for inducing response inhibition.

Monographs of the Society for Research in Child Development, 32, (1, Serial No. 109).

Piaget, J. (1932). *The moral judgment of the child* (M. Gabain, Trans.). London: Routledge & Keegan Paul.

Rest, J. R. (1983). Morality. In J. Flavell and E. Markman (Eds.), *Handbook of child psychology: Vol. 3: Cognitive Development* (pp. 556-629). New York: John Wiley & Sons.

Rosenthal, R., & Jacobson, L. (1968). *Pygmalion in the classroom.* New York: Holt.

Schacter, S. (1964). The inter-action of cognitive and physiological determinants of emotional states. In L. Berkowitz (Ed.), *Advances in experimental social psychology* (Vol. 1, pp. 49-80). New York: Academic Press.

Schachter, S., & Latane, R. (1964). Crime, cognition and the autonomic nervous system. In M. R. Jones (Ed.), *Nebraska Symposium on Motivation.* Lincoln, NE: Univ. Nebraska Press.

Schacter, S., & Singer, J. E. (1962). Cognitive, social and physiological determinants of emotional states. *Psychological Review, 69,* 379-399.

Scott, P., Burton, R. V., & Yarrow, M. R. (1967). Social reinforcement under natural conditions. *Child Development, 38,* 53-63.

Sears, R. R. (1951). A theoretical framework for personality and social behavior. *American Psychologist, 6,* 476-483.

Sears, R. R., Maccoby, E. E., & Levin, A. (1957). *Patterns of child rearing.* Evanston, IL: Row, Peterson.

Sears, R. R., Rau, L., & Alpert, R. (1965). *Identification and child rearing.* Stanford, CA: Stanford Univ. Press.

Sears, R. R., Whiting, J. W. M., Nowlis, V., & Sears, P. S. (1953). Some childrearing antecedents of aggression and dependency in young children. *Genetic Psychology Monographs, 47,* 135-234.

Skinner, B. F. (1953). *Science and human behavior.* New York: Macmillan.

Solomon, R. L. (1964). Punishment. *American Psychologist, 19,* 239-253.

Solomon, R. L., Turner, L. H., & Lessac, M. S. (1968). Some effects of delay of punishment on resistance to temptation in dogs. *Journal of Personality and Social Psychology, 8*, 233-238.

Steele, C. M. (1988). The psychology of self-affirmation: Sustaining the integrity of the self. In L. Berkowitz (Ed.), *Advances in Experimental Social Psychology, 21*, (pp. 261-302). San Diego, CA: Academic Press.

Swann, W. B. (1983). Self-verification: Bringing social reality into harmony with the self. In J. Suls & A. G. Greenwald (Eds.), *Psychological perspectives on the self* (Vol. 2, pp. 33-66). Hillsdale, NJ: Lawrence Erlbaum.

Tolman, E. C. (1932). *Purposive behavior in animals and men.* New York: Appleton-Century-Crofts.

Walters, R. H., Parke, R. D., & Cane, V. (1965). Timing of punishment and the observation of consequences to others as determinants of response inhibition. *Journal of Experimental Child Psychology, 2*, 10-30.

Weiner, B. (1980). A cognitive (attribution)-emotion-action model of motivated behavior: An analysis of judgments of help-giving. *Journal of Personality and Social Psychology, 39*, 186-200.

Whiting, J. Y. M. (1959). Sorcery, sin, and the superego: A cross-cultural study of some mechanisms of social control. In M. R. Jones (Ed.), *Nebraska Symposium on Motivation: 1959* (174-195). Lincoln: Univ. Nebraska Press.

Whiting, J. W. M., & Child, I. (1953). *Child training and personality: a cross- cultural study.* New Haven, CT: Yale U. Press.

Whiting, B. B., & Whiting, J. W. M. (1975). *Children of six cultures.* Cambridge, MA: Harvard U. Press.

Zajonc, R. B. (1980). Feeling and thinking: Preferences need no inferences. *American Psychologist, 35*, 151-175.

# Chapter 7

# The Learning of Moral Behavior: A Behavior-Analytic Approach

*MARTHA PELÁEZ-NOGUERAS*
*Florida International University*

*JACOB L. GEWIRTZ*
*Florida International University*

**Abstract**

This chapter describes the *principles* and *operations* involved in the acquisition and control of moral behavior. Various learning *processes* for moral behavior in preverbal and verbal children are presented, focusing on overt behaviors that connote altruism, empathy, sharing, caring, justice, or virtue. The cognitive-developmental and behavior-analytical approaches to moral development are contrasted. A distinction is made between direct contingency-shaped behavior and rule-governed behavior. Moral behavior is viewed initially as being under the control of nonverbalizable direct contingencies in prelinguistic children. Later in development, with advances in children's language skills, much moral behavior is viewed as coming under the control of rules (including both rules that are self-generated and those provided by others). While the analysis presented emphasizes the determinants of moral action, it also attempts to fill in the details that cognitive-developmental postulates seem to require, and provides some leads on how to relate moral reasoning to moral action.

The behavior-analytical approach presented here recognizes that moral behavior is determined by *both* organismic and environmental factors, and that human beings may be born with the potential for developing different patterns of moral conduct. The present analysis, however, will focus only on moral-behavior patterns that are *learned*; our assumption is that moral behavior can be shaped and maintained, modified, managed, and even reversed or eliminated by environmental factors. The various processes that appear responsible for the learning of overt moral acts are described without taking a particular moral-value position, distinguishing "good" from "evil" actions, or appealing to absolute value principles and developmental stages.

In the literature, psychological research on young children's moral reasoning and actions has focused on: (1) *behaviors* like lying or cheating, as well as prosocial, altruistic, and empathic behaviors and their determinants (e.g., Eisenberg & Mussen, 1989; Ekman, 1989; Hartshorne & May, et al., 1928, 1929, 1930; Hoffman, 1988); and (2) *reasoning* and *judgments* about hypothetical moral dilemmas (e.g., Colby, Kohlberg, Gibbs & Lieberman, 1983; Kohlberg, 1969; Piaget, 1932) and hypothetical cultures (Wainryb, 1993). In recent years, cognitive-developmental approaches to moral development, based in particular on the work of Piaget (1932) and Kohlberg (1969, 1981, 1984; Kohlberg & Diessner, 1991), have given the area of moral development much of its tone. One problem, however, with some cognitive-developmental theories is that, for the most part, they have not concentrated on moral acts per se, but on expressed judgments or reasoning about hypothetical acts under different moral dilemmas. This reliance on moral reasoning and judgment of the child has limited an understanding of the proximal causes of moral *action*, particularly in cases where verbal judgments and reasoning are neither precursors, nor concomitants, of overt moral action.

To date, most investigators in the field of moral development have subscribed to cognitive explanations and thus have devoted little attention to the study of overt moral action. One result of this intellectual trend is that the learning principles and processes that account for the early acquisition of moral behavior, such as *reinforcement and punishment*, *imitation*, and *generalization processes*, as well as *rule governance* have, for the most part, been overlooked by theorists and researchers.

In this chapter, a behavioral approach to moral development that emphasizes action and focuses on the processes underlying action is outlined. The present analysis concentrates on the functional interrelations between environmental contingencies and the child's behavior in context. The examination is of extrinsic stimuli and observable responses, as we describe how variations in environmental factors and contingencies comprising the *social context* can influence the child's socio-moral behavior, and vice versa. From this perspective, moral development refers not only to progressive changes in the child's behavioral patterns, but also to progressive changes in interrelated social-stimulus patterns interacting with the child's behavior. In other words, the environmental stimuli mediated by the behavior of others (e.g., parents, peers) are also subject to change (or influence) as a result of their *interaction* with behaviors of the child in a *reciprocal influence process.*

## Contextualism: The World View of Behavior Analysis

Kurtines and Gewirtz (Chapter 1, this vol.) have outlined five different theoretical models, systems, traditions, or world views that provide the foundation for the organizational structure of this book: organismic, psychoanalytic, mechanistic, contextualistic, and dialectic. The researcher's assumptions about moral behavior and interpretations of observations depends on the theoretical model or world view adopted. For instance, the behavior-analytic approach is often considered to be in the mechanistic tradition. However, the behavior-analytic approach to moral development presented here is not viewed as mechanistic; rather behavior analysis has come to be recognized increasingly as being in the *contextualistic* tradition (see Hayes, 1988; Morris, 1988, 1992, 1993). Even so, to date many nonbehavioral developmentalists (e.g., Dixon & Lerner, 1988; Sameroff, 1983) continue to misclassify all behavioral approaches as mechanistic. One problem with mechanistic models is that the individual is seen as passive and inherently at rest. That is, the external environmental forces applied to the organism are taken to be the efficient and immediate causes of behavior.

Behavior analysis, however, does *not* see the child as a passive organism, as one who does *not* contribute to his or her own development, or as molded by the environment without assuming any particular direction to development (Lerner, 1976; Mussen, Conger, & Kagan, 1974). The focus of behavior analysis is on *sequential* and *reciprocal* influence in interaction between the individual's behavior and environmental stimuli. Thus, behavior analysis conceives *both* the organism and the environment as *active,* and to comprise an inseparable interdependent unit (Bijou, 1979; Gewirtz & Peláez-Nogueras, 1991; 1992b; Morris, 1988). Even though the experimental analysis in behavioral approaches is typically made in terms of stimulus and response units, the results of which are sequences of stimuli and responses, the main focus of behavior analysis is on (a) the *functional* and *reciprocal* interrelations of those stimuli and responses in context and (b) their *bidirectional* influences. Responses are in continuous dynamic interaction with the stimuli that constitute the child's functional environment. That is, both environment and child behaviors are active. The environment units in turn act upon and modify the child's responses while the child's responses act on and modify the environmental units (Bijou, 1979; Gewirtz, 1978).

Context is what gives behavior its functional meaning (Morris, 1988). Because moral behavior occurs in context and has a history of contingencies with environmental stimuli, it must be studied in context. On this basis, the behavior-analytic approach to morality is contextualistic in world view, with its goal being the *study of the moral act in context.* This means that each interaction is the unique product of past activity in current context, and provides, as well, the historical context for the next interaction. In this way, present contingencies become the past determinants of future behavior. The ongoing behaviors, constituted of stimulus and response functions in context, are continuously interactive. It is in this sense that behavioral development is said to be a *continuous process*; the individual's behavior evolves on a moment-to-moment basis rather than in terms of qualitatively-distinct macro changes.

In sum, the study of moral development must recognize the historical context: that an individual's social-contingency history for particular moral actions would be the major determinant of the individual's subsequent moral actions. The unique history of contingencies for each individual's behavior results in interindividual differences in moral action patterns and in the development of the rules governing those moral actions.

## Differences between the Cognitive-Developmental and Behavior-Analytic Theories of Moral Behavior

Even while the *cognitive-developmental* and the *behavior-analytic* approaches to moral development have similar implications for studying the direction of effects in interaction (Gewirtz & Peláez-Nogueras, 1991), they differ in at least four respects:

1. The cognitive-developmental and behavior-analytic approaches to moral development diverge on their epistemological and normative orientations, the first being *absolutistic*, the latter *relativistic* (Kurtines & Gewirtz, 1984; Wainryb, 1993). Theories of moral development, like that of Kohlberg (1969), are absolutist, in that they stress the universality of moral principles (e.g., justice) and the thinking based on those principles. Morality is thought to be universal and moral judgments are thought to be generalizable and prescriptive across social contexts and situations. In contrast, the behavior-analytic approach can be seen as relativistic in that it stresses the specific contexts and consequences of moral and immoral actions. We believe that, at all ages, individuals tend to contextualize and relativize their moral judgments when they refer those judgments to groups and cultures with different informational beliefs and social contexts (Wainryb, 1993).

From the present learning perspective, prosocial behavior and moral actions and judgments are viewed as under the influence of beneficial or detrimental consequences experienced or predicted by the individual. Judgments and actions termed "moral" are not taken to involve romantic expressions of moral "goodness" or "principled" thinking, but rather to involve an increasingly-sophisticated sense of how to further one's long-term interests based on the predicted consequences of one's actions (Liebert, 1984). (An analysis of different theoretical perspectives and their epistemological and normative orientations to moral development can be found in Kurtines, Alvarez, & Azmitia, 1990.)

**2.** The cognitive-developmental and behavior-analytic perspectives also differ in how they explain the underlying "causes" (or processes) of action, and whether or not a universal invariant progression of "stages" is required to order moral development hierarchically. Evidently, the cognitive-developmental theories have been imprecise in accounting for the acquisition of, and changes in, the child's moral behavior patterns. They have advanced heuristic mental structures termed "schemas" as devices for explaining the child's moral behavior. Whether these "schemas" reside in the individual or are constructs of the theories, remains unclear. On the other hand, behavior analysis assumes that the determinants of moral action can be isolated by an analysis of context and observable contingencies. Thus, the context and consequences and their interrelations provide the basis for understanding and predicting moral actions without recourse to unobservable causes, inner activities, or complex theoretical constructs.

In this frame, cognitive-developmental theories use mentalistic, intra-psychic, cognitive structures to explain moral and other behavior. Mentalistic abstractions like schemas, moral self, and stages (Kohlberg, 1969; Kohlberg & Diessner, 1991) and decentration (Flavell 1985; Gibbs, Chapter 2, this vol.) have been advanced to index processes or causes of the behavioral patterns observed, even while little is known about "facts" in the moral realm, namely functional (cause and effect) relations between interacting environmental and behavior variables. Cognitive theories tend to use these constructs to explain the development of moral behavior, which they seem to arrive at by what Schlinger (1991) has termed "logical error." Schlinger's argument is that:

> First, the behavioral class is given a name. The name is then reified and itself becomes the object of study. And, finally, the name becomes the explanation, usually with the help of syntactic rearrangement. Much of the Piagetian approach to development illustrates this (p. 5).

An illustration is found in the study by cognitive-developmental theorists of verbal responses denoting moral reasoning and judgments about hypothetical actions under moral dilemmas. Later, if individuals respond verbally according to the criteria of a higher moral stage, the explanation given may be that they do so because they have now "achieved a higher moral stage." Clearly, there is circularity if not tautology in this argument. The "stage" of moral development, which was originally based on the ordered grouping of certain verbal responses or judgments of the child, is now transformed into a causal "structure" that is conceived to be responsible for those same verbal moral responses. The abstract structure is regarded as a material cause.

In sum, whether or not moral behavior can be ordered in terms of stages can be of interest for behavior analysis, but circularly-defined stages can not provide the required proximal explanation of moral behavior. When a progressive order of behavioral change is detected among children, manifested by a changed organization at different developmental levels, behavior analysts should attempt to explain these behavior patterns in terms of common learning experiences and contextual determinants or setting factors (Peláez-Nogueras,

1994) and not in terms of invariant universal stages. The concept of developmental stages may be useful for its heuristic, descriptive, or classificatory value. Nevertheless, "stages" have very limited, if any, explanatory value as "causes" of observed behavioral changes.

3. The two approaches to moral development also differ in their conception of how the child's reasoning relates to moral action. For instance, Kohlberg (1981, 1984) has advanced the general proposition that moral judgments generally should correlate with, and hence predict, overt moral action. Even so, his theory of moral development has not demonstrated *if* and *how* reasoning processes lead to moral action. Our assumption is that overt moral reasoning and judgments can occur as antecedents of, concurrently with, or consequent to moral action. However, reasoning/judgment and moral action often could be *un*correlated.

When moral reasoning and judgment are transformed into observable verbal-behavior indices, they can be studied and related to moral actions. There may be some difficulties with such a transformation analysis, however. One problem for the researcher is to detect by which means the verbal judgment of the child has been reached. For instance, verbal judgments can be reached through problem-solving skills, by the emergence of stimulus equivalence relations, as a result of imitation, rule-governed processes, or simply via a memorized verbal response of the child (like in delayed imitation). In such analyses, then, it is often not possible immediately to ascertain true "judgment" on the basis of the verbal report itself. Such verbal responses could be concurrent reflections of the process, or independent learned responses, rather than proximal causes or predictors of moral acts. Moreover, even when verbal behavior indices of moral reasoning and judgment are employed, they do not necessarily have to correlate with overt moral acts. Before the researcher makes any assumptions of cause and effect between reasoning and action, it is always important in behavior analysis to make a historical analysis of the determinants of the verbal responses involved.

4. The cognitive-developmental and behavior-analytic approaches also differ on how moral behavior can be influenced by environmental stimuli and ultimately by *rules*. According to the organismic (constructivist) views of Kohlberg (1969) and Piaget (1932), the organism's "cognitive structures" refer to rules for connecting experienced events. In behavior analysis, rules are seen as *verbal behavior* describing environmental contexts, behavior units and environmental contingencies. Verbal rules can maintain behavior for long periods without individuals directly experiencing the consequences of their actions. Thus, verbal behavior can have a history of reinforcement exclusively through the direct or indirect mediation of other persons. This point will be elaborated in a later section.

To sum up, behavior analysis is concerned with lawful relations among observable events—the behavior of individuals in interaction with environmental factors. The analysis can be extended to private events, like problem solving and thinking, but *only* after overt behaviors reflecting those private events are analyzed and understood (Schlinger, 1991). The advantage of behavior analysis is that, by emphasizing *extrinsic* variables and *observable* moral actions, the analysis moves away from those "inner" events that are inaccessible to the investigator. Emphasis on these unobservables can only complicate analyses of the actual processes and contextual factors responsible for the child's moral behavior or, for that matter, of any other behavior.

## Commonalities and Convergences of Ideas between the Approaches

This section searches for commonalities and the convergence of ideas between the cognitive-developmental approach and the behavior-analytical approach outlined in this chapter. An attempt is made to integrate (or at least compare) Piaget's types of moral thinking with a behavioral approach to the moral judgment of the child.

Piaget (1932) distinguished between two types of moral thought: *effective* and *verbal* moral thought. Based on Piaget's distinction, and on the control that *implicit* and *explicit* rules could exercise over behavior, we speculate that there may exist two types of moral judgment in the child. *First*, there appears to be *effective* moral judgment, controlled by implicit moral rules. Piaget recognized that the child's moral experience is built up gradually by actions as the child comes into contact with the environment. The effect of the environmental contingencies on the child's effective moral behavior is what leads the child to form implicit judgments that eventually can operate as rules to guide the individual's action. *Second,* there is *verbal* moral judgment, that involves the child evaluating his/her actions explicitly (i.e., there is a verbal recognition of exposed relationships). This overt verbal behavior appears whenever the child is called upon to make a judgment on other people's moral actions or dilemmas. Even when verbal judgment constitutes a reflection of moral activity, the relationship between judgment and action is far from being simple to observe and measure. However, when the child's verbal moral judgment turns into a generalized response (e.g., of a universal type), that verbal response might not correspond at all either to effective moral judgment or to the child's moral actions.

In addition, a researcher may have difficulty distinguishing between conventional moral behavior and "true" moral behavior. When asked to make a moral judgment in a given situation, the child may simply state the learned rule. Children typically conform to the explicit ideas and conventions that they have learned during socialization, which often emphasize explanations for moral acts. In making a distinction between conventional moral acts and "true" moral acts, it is conceivable that the former is governed by the enforcement of parental or authority instructions and social constraints, and that the latter is under the control of implicit rules derived exclusively from direct (self-generated) experience and not manifested verbally.

Another type of judgment that can be identified is the *verbal imitative judgment* that occurs when the child is simply copying or matching verbal statements to those of an influential model, without necessarily ever experiencing or deriving the moral rule. Another type of moral judgment can be identified as just being *verbal exploratory responses,* as when a child's behavior is oriented to receiving approval or avoiding disapproval from an audience (e.g., an interviewer). Such verbal explanatory responses may be inconsistent with the child's actions. Piaget (1932) also noticed that verbal morality appears whenever the child is asked to judge other people's actions that do not interest him directly. Based on this, neither the behavioral approach nor the Piaget-Kohlberg theory would assert that the child's "reflective moral reasoning" in a hypothetical moral dilemma is invariably reflected in, or predicts, real-life moral action.

The stated moral judgment of the child in response to hypothetical moral dilemmas can vary with the specific context and the child's history of experiences. The conducting of research on the child's process of *decision-making* in hypothetical situations (e.g., in the moral dilemmas), in which the researcher describes an ambiguous moral situation and asks the child to state what he would do and why, necessarily requires a separate functional analysis from what the child's actions are in life circumstances. One reason for separating these analyses is that the verbal judgments of hypothetical dilemmas do not necessarily predict actions in life circumstances. If a repertoire of verbal moral judgments is already present in the child, generalization to similar contexts might occur. Moreover, in actual situations, the child may respond quite differently since his behavior is a function of different discriminative stimuli leading to different consequences. Here, then, the context for the child's moral action varies from that context of the child's verbal responses to hypothetical moral dilemmas.

## Moral Judgment and Moral Action: Independent or Dependent?

In this chapter, no inquiry is made into the structure and mechanisms of reasoning, for the obvious reason that any probing must necessarily be indirect and possibly artifactual. An indirect method relies mainly in the child's verbal explanations of his moral judgements for possible actions.

Cognitive-developmental theorists influenced by the work of Baldwin (1911), Piaget (1932) and Kohlberg (1969, 1976) have conceived ethical/moral stages in terms of the formal properties of moral judgment focused upon by various moral philosophers. They have emphasized verbalizations of moral judgments and reasoning, giving scant attention to moral action per se, and much less to the socialization antecedents of moral action. In contrast, behavior-oriented theorists routinely approach action directly, and to a lesser extent moral reasoning and judgement.

The assumption made here is that a verbal moral judgment occurring in advance of, concurrently with, or after an action could be a correlated outcome of the same process governing the action. A proper process analysis of moral tendencies must focus on overt moral-behavior outcomes; these include actions and verbal judgments as well. (An exception to this norm is conceivable when research attempts systematically to probe the basis or reasons underlying either judgments or actions.)

In contrast to the later work on moral reasoning done in the traditions of Piaget and Kohlberg, is the earlier research by Hartshorne, May, and their associates (Hartshorne & May, 1928; Hartshorne, May, & Maller, 1929; Hartshorne, May, & Shuttleworth, 1930). These researchers emphasized overt moral behaviors, such as those denoting honesty, deceit, or self control. They concluded that a moral behavior represented situational conformity to group norms and was also influenced by the consequences of that behavior (for reviews, see Burton & Kunce, Chapter 6, this vol.; Kohlberg, 1984; Kohlberg & Diessner, 1991). There is a substantial difference in emphasis between the dependent variables used by cognitive-developmental theorists, namely verbal reasoning and judgment, and those employed by behavior analysts, primarily action. That difference maintains for the moral-development research on prosocial phenomena in the moral realm, under such labels as altruism, empathy, caring, sharing, and helping (e.g., Eisenberg & Mussen, 1989).

Ideally, the verbal judgment of the child should be studied under controlled conditions. Such verbal-judgment responses have antecedents and consequences, and may be emitted alone or concurrently with other potentially-relevant behavior indices. Hence, verbal judgment should lend itself to experimental control and an analysis into causal concurrent and historical variables could be profitable. As overt communicative responses denoting end-of-process, verbal judgments would result from features of the antecedent reasoning process, they could constitute a beginning in establishing the relationship between a range of verbal stimuli comprising moral dilemmas and children's verbal judgments to those dilemmas. In this context, Bandura and McDonald (1963) found that the child's judgment responses are readily modifiable, particularly through the utilization of adult "modeling" cues (or reinforced matching-to-sample, as we interpret the process in a later section of this chapter). While interpretations of the meaning of these results have been controversial and the theory behind them inadequate under the conceptions of an operant-learning analysis (Gewirtz, 1971b, Gewirtz & Peláez-Nogueras, 1992b), the implications of the data are clear: Modes of moral reasoning and verbal judgments are subject to social influence, and are thus modifiable.

## Operations in the Acquisition of Moral Behavior

A brief schematic survey of the principles and basic operations involved in the acquisition of moral behavior patterns are presented in this section.

### Reinforcement

The term *reinforcement* is descriptive rather than explanatory. It describes a functional relation between a response and its environmental consequences, but it does *not* explain that relation (Catania, 1984). The concept of reinforcement under the functional analysis employed in operant learning is straightforward (Catania & Harnad, 1988; Skinner, 1938, 1953, 1969).

Four major operations are relevant:

**1.** The operation wherein the *presentation* of a contingent environmental event results in a systematic response *increase* is termed *positive reinforcement*, and the contingent event is termed a *positive reinforcer*.

**2.** The operation wherein the *presentation* of a contingent environmental event results in a systematic response *decrease* (or leads to avoidance or escape) is termed *positive* or *Type I punishment*, and the contingent event is termed a *positive punishing stimulus* or *punisher*.

**3.** The operation wherein the *removal* of an environmental event contingent on a response results in a systematic response *increase* is termed *negative reinforcement*, and the event contingently removed is termed a *negative reinforcer*.

**4.** The operation wherein the *removal* or elimination of environmental events contingent on a response results in systematic response *decrease* is termed *negative* or *Type II punishment*, and the contingent event is termed a *negative punishing stimulus* or *punisher*.

These four basic operations are involved in the acquisition of moral behaviors and operate at all developmental levels from the earliest phases of the child's life. These operations occur separately at first, and then provide the bases for rule-governed behavior. In this chapter, we will focus primarily on the role of differential positive reinforcement.

The answer to the question, "Why is a reinforcer reinforcing?" is given by the functional relations among antecedent environmental events and contextual factors that can lower or enhance the efficacy of reinforcing stimuli. To the degree that a nonreductionistic reply is required, the answer to this question may lie in an explanation in evolutionary species-history terms. In other words, unconditioned stimuli (like food) and functional reinforcers for diverse species responses (like mating), can be conceived to have acquired their value due to the survival contingencies in the evolutionary history of the species (Skinner, 1966, 1981; Petrovich & Gewirtz, 1985). As recognized also by sociobiologists, as selection processes these species' contingencies are involved in mating and rearing practices, as well as in foraging for and consuming food (Wilson, 1975; Dawkins, 1976).

Reinforcing or punishing stimuli need not function as such under *all* conditions for every response of an individual. For example, a contingent event that functions as a reinforcer or punisher for one response of the child need not function as a reinforcer or punisher for the same response in a different setting, for a different response in the same setting, or for the same response of another individual in the same setting. Also, the fact than an environmental event functions as a reinforcing stimulus for a response in a particular context does not preclude its functioning in different stimulus roles in other contexts for the same, or for another, response unit. In the case of *social reinforcement*, the intended social reinforcer may operate differently across individuals. For example, in early acquisition of the child's moral behavior, adult attention or approval may function as a positive reinforcer for the act of one child, as a negative reinforcer for a second child emitting the same act, as a neutral stimulus for a third child, or even as a punisher for a fourth child (Bijou & Baer, 1961). Therefore, when making a functional analysis of moral behavior, careful consideration of individual differences is recommended in the selection of reinforcing stimuli.

Two aspects of an environmental event of primary interest in operant learning are, first, to cue or evoke a response that is the function of a *discriminative stimulus* and, second, to be a contingent occurrence or consequence for a response (that produces some change in a response measure) that is the function of a *reinforcing* or *punishing stimulus*. Under a functional analysis, the child's *responses* are related to the environmental *stimuli* of the past and present, and no comprehensive empirical account of behavior can be attained if the interrelationship between them is not understood. The analysis attends to systematic changes in some attribute (e.g., rate, amplitude, duration, intensity, latency) of the response as a function of the environmental contingencies. In terms of behavioral functions, a functional analysis of moral action establishes what effects the individual's responses have on the environment.

In the section that follows, several learning processes that involve a functional analysis of stimulus control, behavior, and reinforcement (or punishment) are described.

## Processes in the Acquisition of Moral Behavior

### Imitation

Infants first perform imitative acts that are matched to the behavior of significant models (parents). *Reflexive* imitation occurs immediately following birth and then seems to decrease with development. *True* imitation, however, develops later during the first year and subsequently (Uzgiris, 1981). The child's imitative responses can be reinforced by the behaviors of these models and other adults, such as by contingent smiles, attention, praise, approval, reciprocal imitation, and the like. Such reinforcement contingencies, occurring at least intermittently, can establish the first learned prosocial behaviors in the infant.

The acquisition of these imitative responses is thought to follow operant-learning principles (Skinner, 1938).

In the younger child, the matching responses are normally emitted immediately after the model's behavior. In the older child, imitation can be delayed. But the child's prosocial responses, like sharing and helping, are controlled similarly in both *immediate* and *delayed* imitation. In the immediate imitation case, the child's behavior is controlled by the discriminative stimuli in the situation and the response is performed shortly after in that same situation. In the delayed imitation case, the child's response matched to the model's behavior may be emitted after lengthy delays, or in the model's absence. The child's behavior is controlled by the discriminative matching of those stimuli present in the immediate context with stimuli that were present in an earlier context in which the model's actions were emitted originally. In other words, the discriminated stimuli serve, as it were, to prompt and to reinstate part of the original situation. Delayed imitation is involved in a process of *pervasive imitation* and is commonly seen in more developmentally-advanced children acting in wider social contexts; also there are the processes of rule acquisition, rule generalization, and role taking, where the social-conditioning process can involve more elaborate forms of social interaction.

## *Pervasive Imitation*

Much of the child's moral behavior, values, judgments, moral rules, and moral roles are acquired through the process of *pervasive imitation*. A substantial proportion of the phenomena grouped under the concept of *identification* can be ordered by the concept of pervasive imitation. (That is, the distinction between identification and pervasive imitation is, to a large degree, an arbitrary semantic one, with no fundamental differences in the way in which they are learned.[1]) In pervasive-imitation learning, a child acquires the range of the behavior repertory of a parent (usually the parent of the same gender as the child), including behaviors connoting moral values, attitudes, and standards. Pervasive imitation involves conditional responding, with imitation a functional matching-response class comprised of diverse responses matched to a parent/model's behaviors. The conditional moral responses can be emitted by the child after lengthy delays or in the model's absence, and could be acquired and maintained by extrinsic reinforcing stimuli usually provided intermittently by the parent's or other adult's contingent reactions to the child's moral actions. Insofar as Kohlberg (1969; Kohlberg & Diessner, 1991) has postulated identification to be the basis for early rule learning and, therefore, later moral reasoning and behavior, and this process can be reduced parsimoniously to the concept of pervasive imitation, the cognitive-developmental and the behavior-analytic theoretical approaches can be conceived to be congruent in this arena.

The present behavior-analytical approach to moral development views the phenomena of pervasive imitation as involving: (1) the child's moral and other behavior being matched to those of a specific other with whom the child has a salient relationship and, in that sense, has formed an *"attachment"* (Gewirtz & Peláez-Nogueras, 1991), and (2) the tendency of the child to imitate the moral behaviors of that person across relatively long periods of time. The child's behavior pervasively becomes like that of the influential model (the attachment figure), matching most of the model's moral actions, as well as verbal judgments and values. In this way, imitative prosocial/moral behaviors can be emitted and reinforced intermittently by various others in the absence of the model. As noted, the child focuses his/her pervasive imitation on at least one model and imitates not only a range of the model's overt moral behaviors, but also the behaviors implied in such general dispositions as moral values, principles, style, motives, as well as moral judgments.

In sum, the child's pervasive imitation of the model's behavior can occur in the absence of environmental consequences. The behavior occurs due to the consequences produced during training and subsequently, usually on intermittent reinforcement schedules. If imitation is to be seen as a learning process in development, the child's imitative repertoire must be generative, as in generalized imitation, rather than dependent on direct reinforcement for each response (Baer & Deguchi, 1985; Poulson, Kymissis, Reeve, Andreatos, & Reeve, 1991).

### The Match-to-Sample Paradigm

An efficient operant paradigm to account for imitative matching phenomena can be provided by a conditional-responding conception such as that of the *matching-to-sample paradigm* (Cumming & Berryman, 1965; Gewirtz & Stingle, 1968; Gewirtz, 1971a, 1971b). In a simple discrimination learning task, the presence of a single discriminative-stimulus ($S^D$) sets the occasion for reinforcement of an instance of the "correct" response. In a conditional-discrimination task, the correct response for reinforcement is defined on the basis of the relationship of the attributes of *two* or *more* stimuli. For instance, the subject's moral response must match a conditional sample stimulus (in this case, successive responses of the parent) in a particular setting for reinforcement to occur. The discriminative stimulus for the child's response thus can vary across discrimination trials, depending on the conditional stimulus. The conditional stimulus comes to function not as a simple, but rather as a differential, cue for responding. Under this paradigm, a child acquires the pattern of matching his moral responses to those of the parent model across occasions, as a result of these matched responses being extrinsically reinforced by the model or others (e.g., a father saying to his child, "You are as kind and just as your mother").

As earlier stated, the matching moral responses of the child will often occur in the apparent absence of reinforcing contingencies. The observers can be unaware of the conditioning history (historical context) of the matching-response class and, in particular, of the wider intermittent extrinsic-reinforcement matrix in which that response class is embedded. This is why intermittently-reinforced child imitations of moral behaviors can appear often to be instances of the "observational" or "vicarious learning" for which Bandura (e.g., 1969, 1971; Bandura & McDonald, 1963) has argued. But there are many problems concerning the application of Bandura's social-learning conceptualizations, as well as other cognitive approaches to moral development. The concept of "observational learning" and "vicarious reinforcement" cannot be meaningful within an operant learning frame. This is because the *target behavior* in the observer, together with its controlling *antecedent* and *consequent stimuli* (i.e., the three-term contingency pattern of *stimulus-response-reinforcement* in context), typically are *not* identified. Specifically, the so-called "vicariously-learned" matching response of the observer is *not* emitted nor, by definition, can that nonemitted response ever be reinforced extrinsically. (For a detailed critique of such problems with Bandura's model, see Gewirtz, 1971a, 1971b.)

## Moral Role Playing

*Moral role playing* consists primarily of the individual learning (through differential contingencies for compliance and noncompliance of role-pertinent behaviors, or through rules) to discriminate the characteristics of, and exhibit specific behaviors required for, a particular moral *role* (e.g., a "good son/daughter," a "responsible student," a "loyal friend," a "faithful spouse," a "devoted parent," an "honorable politician," a "caring nurse/doctor," an "honest judge," a "fair boss"). *Moral role taking* is somewhat different. It involves the reinforced imitation of a set of actions of an influential model directly relevant to the response class. These responses could include those that denote altruism, loyalty, empathy, justice, as well as prosocial behaviors such as sharing, helping and cooperating in a variety of social settings. With developmental advances, the role-pertinent behaviors of the child may be controlled by a subset of specific rules operating in some given contexts.

Behavior denoting moral standards such as honesty, justice, loyalty, conscience, and public or private virtue such as altruism, caring, sharing, or empathy, can be fostered in appropriate environmental contexts by the child being exposed repeatedly to behaviors of role models that can be characterized as "honest," "altruistic," "just," and provide reinforcing consequences contingent upon the child's matching responses. In the same way, behavior denoting standards such as dishonesty, greed, corruption, or selfishness can be fostered by exposing the child repeatedly to the model's behavior patterns characterized as "dishonest," "greedy," "corrupt," and provide reinforcing contingencies on the child's *matching* (imitating) those responses (e.g., as in the case of "gang" or "terrorist" leaders functioning as models for the members of the group). All these imitative behaviors then would become part of the individual's repertory of moral and immoral behaviors. Later in development (e.g., during adolescence) the overt imitative behaviors of the young adult can occur in the absence of the original model(s) and be maintained by consequences mediated by the behaviors of diverse others (e.g., peers) conforming to group norms and societal standards.

# Direct-contingency and Rule-governed Moral Behavior

## Direct Contingency-Shaped Behavior

Direct contingency-shaped behavior is behavior shaped directly by its consequences, and can come under the control of nonverbal discriminative stimuli. Contingency-shaped behavior units ("operants") are given meaning and are strengthened by those of their *direct* consequences that function as reinforcing stimuli. On the other hand, rule-governed behavior, as described by Skinner (1966, 1969), is discriminative responding shaped by reinforcement of rule following. Although these two types of behaviors could be similar in form, their functional properties and controlling variables are different (Cerutti, 1989).

The acquisition of stimulus control over behavior termed "moral" is reinforced by diverse contingent consequences for that behavior in the presence of the discriminative controlling stimuli ($S^D$). Often the contingencies applied to the moral actions refer to, or specify, rights, duties, or obligations, and are typically dispensed by reinforcing or punishing agents based on societal or reference-group standards. Because of a history of an operant response class having been repeatedly followed by reinforcing-stimulus contingencies, the response class becomes more frequent in the presence of a discriminative stimulus. As a result of this history, the consequences for that response class in a particular environmental context could be anticipated or predicted by a child.

The child's behavior patterns that have been termed "moral" or prosocial (e.g., sharing, caring, helping) typically involve responses that have been shaped and maintained by direct positive social consequences (e.g., approval, acceptance, praise, affection) or direct nonsocial consequences (e.g., privileges, activities, tokens). Also, many moral behaviors can avoid or eliminate aversive social consequences (e.g., disapproval, rejection, reprimands) and/or aversive nonsocial consequences (e.g., removal of material privileges or activities). Parents play a most important role in the training of moral behavior and judgment of their children. The contingent behaviors of parents and caregivers provide the reinforcing or punishing consequences for the child's actions in a given context, thus directly shaping those classes of moral responses.

As the child's behavioral repertoire becomes more complex, and language is acquired, the child's actions come more under the control of *verbal rules* (both formulated by others and self-formulated) and of the *remote* or *indirect* consequences implied in those rules, compared to the control of direct reinforcing or punishing contingencies. As the child's behavior repertoire increases, the child is able to discriminate both the immediate and the delayed long-term consequences of his/her actions. That is, the child learns to predict the consequences of a given action, *which* consequences prevail in a particular setting, and *how, when,* and *by whom* these consequences would be applied. Thus, in the study of moral behavior, a systematic focus on environmental/controlling variables is essential, and requires the study of stimulus-response processes in past and current contexts. Our emphasis thus far has been on overt prosocial behavior shaped by direct consequences in children with nonverbal skills, and similar behavior learned through imitative processes. Next, we will examine how the child's actions come increasingly to be controlled by *rules*, both formulated or prescribed by others and self-derived rules.

## Rule-governed Behavior

For the most part, moral behavior is rule-governed rather than direct-contingency shaped. Rule-governed behavior has been distinguished theoretically and experimentally from behavior that is shaped and maintained by its direct consequences (Catania, 1985; Catania, Shimoff, & Matthews 1989; Cerutti, 1989; Hineline & Wanchinsen, 1989; Skinner, 1966, 1969; Vaughan, 1989; Zettle & Hayes, 1982). Rule-governed behavior can be modified by altering either its antecedents, its consequences, or both. In contrast, contingency-shaped behavior is modified only by its consequences.

In Skinner's account, rule-governed behavior is often determined by verbal behavior and, therefore, only *indirectly* by its consequences (1969). Skinner identified rules as "contingency-specifying stimuli" (1966), that is, the rule specifies (explicitly or implicitly) the consequences for the behavior. Hence, the acquisition of verbal language is required. The child must have acquired verbal skills and receptive and expressive language to be able to comply with specific instructions and requests. The child must also differentiate between the meaning of short- and long-term consequences.

A rule differs from a simple discriminative stimulus ($S^D$) in that the rule is a verbal statement that specifies the contingency between stimulus and response; the effectiveness of the rule in controlling behavior will ultimately depend on the consequences for following or not following the rule. Rules can be provided by an instructional agent or can be self-derived. But it is important to emphasize that the contingencies for the behavior exist before the rules are formulated (Skinner, 1966). Even though both contingency-shaped and rule-governed behavior are established by contingencies, their controlling variables and functional properties differ, even in those cases where the behavior is similar, if not identical, in form.

Various difficulties in the distinction and diverse interpretations have led to confusion and controversy in the field of rule-governed behavior (e.g., Catania, 1989; Glenn, 1989; Ribes, 1987; Schlinger, 1990). Most behavior theorists, however, seem to agree on the notion that rule-governed behavior involves discriminative responding that is shaped by the reinforcement of rule following. In our analysis of moral behavior, the concept of rule-governed moral behavior is important because it accommodates the description of *complex* moral behavior that is under the control of, and can be modified only by, antecedent verbal stimuli. Crucial to the distinction between direct contingency-shaped and rule-governed moral behaviors is that the latter involves *two* sets of contingencies, those related directly to the behavior of interest and those related to the verbal antecedents of that moral behavior. For verbal stimuli to function as a rule, they must have ready-made discriminative attributes (i.e., by virtue of the listener's verbal history) that do not require new conditioning on every new occasion in which they appear. The important distinction is that rule-governance allows individuals ". . . to behave from the outset in accordance with contingency requirements they have never before encountered" (see Andronis, 1991, p. 230).

When a rule is presented in complete form, it may be seen as a *prescription*—moral, practical, or juridical (see Reese, 1989, for an analysis of normative forms of rules). In a behavior-analytical frame, however, a rule specifies the three-term contingency: the interdependency between three components—antecedent stimulus, behavior, and consequence ($S^D$-R-$S^R$). As will be illustrated next, sometimes the rule is incomplete, in that the consequence for the behavior is not specified explicitly or even specified at all. In such instances, the consequent stimuli are implicit in the verbal statement presented to the subject (i.e., the subject has a history with components of that or similar verbal statements or concepts).

The distinction between direct-contingency shaped and rule-governed behavior may be clarified in the following example. Consider the case of two boys fighting. One of the children is hurt as a *direct* result of engaging in the fight and the other gets away with what he originally demanded. Due to the natural consequences for fighting (punishment for the behavior of one, reinforcement for the behavior of the other), it is likely that both children would modify their behavior in subsequent disagreements. Thus, the child who was hurt may act more submissive subsequently and the child who succeeds may act more dominant subsequently. These response changes may be seen as direct contingency-shaped behavior (because the children experienced the direct consequences of their fighting). On the other hand, consider the parent saying to these children, "Don't fight with each other, that's a very *bad* thing to do; if you don't stop *you will be punished.*" If the children *stop* fighting right after the parent makes such a declaration, the behavior can be said to be rule-governed. (Notice that the *parent statement* specifies the consequences.) However, one can conceive of instances in which behavior that is rule-governed is not necessarily under the control of consequences specified verbally in that instruction, for example in "you may hurt each other." This instruction may imply consequences that are not necessarily those controlling the behavior. In other words, the boys need not experience the consequences specified in the instruction (i.e., hurting each other) for their behavior to be controlled or to stop occurring. One possibility could be that the boys have had experience with the same instruction in the past, did not follow it, and their fighting was punished by the parent (e.g., by removing such privileges as TV viewing or friends visiting). In this example, the children's behavior is under the control of parental instruction (i.e., "don't fight") and disapproval (as stimulus control) or punishment (as the consequence for not following the instruction).

*When Moral Behavior Becomes Insensitive
to Direct Consequences*

Moral rules may often override the possible effects of direct consequences produced by the behavior in question (as in the preceding example). When one attempts to control the child's behavior through instructions, that behavior might become insensitive to diverse other contingencies that could operate at a given moment through direct experience. This insensitivity of a response to direct consequences has been demonstrated in laboratory settings (Catania, Matthews & Shimoff, 1982; Kaufman, Baron, & Kopp, 1966; Lowe, Beasty, & Bentall, 1983; Matthews, Catania, & Shimoff, 1985; Matthews, Shimoff, Catania, & Sagvolden, 1977).

Insensitivity to direct consequences involves a relative absence of control over the response by *collateral* consequences. Collateral consequences are those produced after the behavior has been generated and that accompany, or are in accordance with, the consequences specified in the rule or instruction. According to Cerutti (1989), the role of these collateral consequences in determining the initial form of responding is minimal when the behavior is under the control of the rule because the behavior is assumed to be sensitive to contingencies of rule-following that shaped it. In addition, when accompanied by subject verbal descriptions, behavioral performance becomes more rule-governed than direct contingency-shaped (Catania, Mathews, & Shimoff, 1982; Catania, Shimoff, & Mathews, 1989).

In sum, the paradox has been noted that accompanying verbal behavior (descriptions) can make other human actions less rather than more sensitive to their direct consequences. It has been noted also that rule-governed behavior is sensitive to contingencies only to the extent that verbal rules are consistent with them. When this is not so, the contingencies that maintain the rule-following behavior may override some direct consequences by getting in the way (see Catania et al., 1982). That is, a rule, self-formulated or formulated for the individual, can insulate the individual's moral actions from direct natural consequences. (In an analysis of how self-rules are formulated, Zettle and Hayes, 1982, noted the problem of determining whether a particular self-formulated rule governs the behavior, or whether the rule is simply a collateral response.)

## *The Child's Moral Behavior as Rule-governed*

When children acquire language, much of their moral behavior becomes guided by rules rather than by direct contingency shaping. Moral behavior is trained by parents, caregivers, teachers, and peers, who, for instance, foster empathy through modeling, prompting, and reinforcing behavior patterns such as those denoting helping, caring, kindness, sharing, responsibility, loyalty, and justice. Thus, in our analysis, there is an essential distinction between the process of shaping and maintaining the child's moral responses via *direct* consequences *and* the process of *indirect* or *remote* consequences prescribed by the rule.

As described earlier, in *rule-governed behavior* the child's moral actions are controlled differently. A child carrying out or not carrying out a given instruction might bring on a consequence that differs from that specified by the rule to follow the action. Further, a request, instruction, or command may specify behavior that implies consequences (aversive or punishing in the command, pleasant or reinforcing in the request). For instance, consider a child who has been told by the parent not to leave school settings without permission or supervision because it could be dangerous. When a group of peers attempts to influence the child to skip classes and leave the school setting to go with them, the child chooses not to do so. This child could be more concerned about the consequences of disobeying parental instructions and the school rules than about the possible direct consequences of leaving the school settings with his peers (e.g., having fun with them, missing classes, getting behind academically, or being on the street unsupervised). In this case, that child's behavior is actually under the control of the parental/school rules and not the natural contingencies. In such an instance, it can be said that rule-governed behavior became "insensitive" to direct, natural contingencies, since *indirect* consequences of rule-following acquired greater control over the child's behavior and precluded the interaction of such behavior with otherwise natural direct consequences. This is an instance in which parental rules *insulate* the child from experiencing the natural consequences of the behavior in question.

In many cases, the verbal instructions given to the child on how to behave in a particular situation may describe for the child the consequences involved for that action in that situation. Parents and teachers often relate to their children the consequences of their actions in a given circumstance under the assumption that the description of these consequences for alternative acts will produce/induce the "right" pattern of moral behavior. One way rules may acquire control over the child's behavior is through conditioning; that is, when the child acquires and exhibits conditioned moral actions in association with antecedent parental instructions together with verbal rationales provided during, or immediately after, the behavior. An explanation given by the parents after the child's action typically specifies why the action was "right" or "wrong" (according to the parents' moral values) while reminding the child of the steps and consequences that were involved.

The differential functions of verbal stimuli (in the form of a self-made rule) in the acquisition of a conditional-discrimination task have been investigated (Ribes & Martinez, 1990; Ribes, Penaloza, Moreno, Hernandez, & Hickman, 1988). Ribes et al. (1988) highlighted the importance of *verbal recognition* by the child of *exposed* relations (resulting from prompts to facilitate the child's explicit evaluation of his or her responses) to appreciate how the responses relate to their consequences.

Thus, it is possible that the parents' moral *rationales*, and value labels (e.g., "right," "wrong") for the action during or after the child's acts may increase the effectiveness of a rule on subsequent occasions. A simple illustration follows: A mother says to the child contingent on an undesirable action: "Why did you destroy your sister's homework? That was *wrong* (value label). Now, you see, your sister is upset because she has to redo her homework. *Don't* ever do it again! For your transgression, you will not be allowed to play outside today." After several pairings of the value label ("It was *wrong* to do that") and the instruction ("*Don't* do it again") with the consequence (not being able to play outdoors), when the rule precedes any action in future it may influence the child's responses in that context. On new occasions, predicting the consequence would lead the child to reconsider before acting. In such cases, the behavior seems to be under the control of a higher-order class of self-provided rule. For instance, a child may say to himself: "I should not destroy my sister's work. My mother says doing that is wrong and, if I do it, I won't be able to play outdoors today." Thus, a distinction between rules provided or stated to the child and rules that are self-provided and formulated is often useful.

## Rules Stated to the Child

An advantage of *explicit* verbal rules for training aspects of child moral behavior is that such rules facilitate behavior coming under the control of verbal descriptions of contingencies. This is often a more convenient (and safe) training procedure than exposing behavior to direct consequences. The important feature of the explicit rule is that it can *substitute* discriminative stimuli for typical consequences of the behavior. Moreover, the advantage of their use is that explicit rules stated by parents, teachers, and other prestigious figures can control the child's moral behavior in contexts where natural contingencies are ineffective, slow to be effective, or dangerous for the child. Hence, stating the rule becomes a discriminative stimulus for the action prescribed by the rule (Bijou, 1976; Catania, 1984). This control is particularly effective when those explicit verbal instructions are given by a parent who ordinarily mediates reinforcing contingencies. It should be remembered that the response of following a stated rule must be reinforced, at least occasionally, for that stated rule to function effectively.

## Self-formulated Rules

Self-formulated rules are verbalizable statements arrived at by the child through different processes. They can derive from other verbal statements (or other rules) that specify appropriate behaviors with their consequences in similar contexts. During response acquisition, rule-governed behavior is influenced by adult verbal rationales and commentaries that specify present or future consequences of an act. Self-formulated rules, however, emerge at a later developmental phase, when the child can describe verbally social interactions, and may become manifest in a series of steps. First, a description of a given moral act may be a preliminary form of its explanation. Second, the verbalized explicit rule can become discriminative to instruct and control the child's moral responses. Third, based on an extensive repertoire of other existing rules, the child can formulate or generate a new rule. New rules, implicitly formulated, can emerge via the processes of *transfer, response generalization, concept formation, stimulus equivalence,* and/or *relational frames.* Thus, linguistic knowledge is instrumental in creating, substituting, and transforming the verbal contingencies into functional acts.

## Generalized Rule Control and Response Generalization

*Generalized rule control* occurs when novel classes or rearrangements of components of earlier rules come to control effectively a behavior, even when the individual has had no experience with that new rule (Malott, 1989). Thus, due to the transfer of stimulus properties, new rules can come to exert control over behavior that was earlier controlled by a different rule. In those instances, some stimulus components, like words or labels (e.g., "wrong") stated in the new rule, may overlap. The phenomenon of rule *transfer* can occur when the original training stimuli and consequences for the moral response are identical or very similar to those in another context. The ease with which such explicit rules are acquired is assumed to depend on the extent to which the child has experienced similar moral rules in earlier learning. Association value, meaningfulness, frequency, duration, tone, and intensity are some of the variables likely to affect this process. Thus, when the transfer process is operating, the acquisition of a first moral rule may affect the acquisition of a second rule, and so on.

One mechanism that is involved in this transfer of learning is *stimulus generalization,* under which a child's moral response, reinforced in a particular discriminative-stimulus context, may occur also, over short-time spans or few trials, in situations that are *similar* to the original training situation. The mechanism refers to the spread of effects to other stimulus settings when the original behavior was reinforced in the presence of a particular stimulus setting. However, in those new settings, the initial response occurrences also may need to be reinforced (at least intermittently), so that the response might recur often.

*Response generalization* (also known as *induction*) refers to the spread of effects to other classes of behavior when originally one class of behavior was reinforced. For instance, the way a person indicates he/she would behave in a moral dilemma can have some similarity to moral behavior reinforced in the past, but is not identical with it (i.e., is not of the same class). There are practical advantages of instructions from parents and other adults in providing verbal stimuli that can come to control the child's behavior of following rules in a *wide* activity range.

### Response Discrimination
Children may also show consistent moral conduct if the range of situations that they confront is restricted to the original learning setting or to very similar

settings (Hartshorne & May, 1928). In those cases, when the setting is changed, the child's moral behavior may be inconsistent. The pattern of conduct differs from one situation to another when the discriminative stimuli differ. The presence of a particular discriminative event evokes the rule that governs the behavior in question. For instance, children learn to discriminate different contingencies associated with different adults. Some adults can provide differential discriminative stimuli for reinforcement. The child learns to respond differentially to adults (father, mother, grandparent) depending upon the behaviors that have been differentially reinforced by the adult. When the child's moral behavior is under the control of an adult's presence, we may have a clear case of response discrimination. However, when there are no supervising adults in a particular situation, the child's adherence to moral practices can be a function of discriminative-stimulus similarity. As described earlier, stimuli that resemble the original conditioned stimulus demonstrate the functional capacity to evoke members of a class of operant moral responses, over a few occasions in the absence of reinforcement contingencies.

As the child's experiences increase and his verbal abilities become more complex, the child's moral behavior may change in form and content, with the discriminative stimuli that set the occasions for moral responses to occur also becoming more variegated and complex. The developmental changes in the child's moral judgments and actions will result from their consequences, some of which strengthen (i.e., reinforce) new forms of moral action, while other unacceptable forms of moral behavior will be weakened or eliminated by the punitive consequences. These changes will, of course, conform to moral practices and rules of the family and culture.

## Moral Development

The child's moral *development* is based on an extensive repertoire of acquired moral rules. A developmental level is manifested in the child's understanding and compliance with such moral rules. In the cognitive-developmental literature, the child's rule-governed behavior, and the pattern, quality, and extensiveness of his moral repertoire, are often characterized as the child being more or less "mature," being at a higher or lower "stage" level of moral development (Kohlberg, 1969, 1976; Piaget, 1932), or as having a relativistic or universal moral style of solving moral dilemmas (Kurtines, 1987). Research data on the child's changes in perceptions of, or compliance with, moral rules are often inappropriately related to a developmental *stage* level and also to chronological *age* as explanatory causal variables. The problem is that neither stage nor age variables can provide a *causal* explanation for behavior—as noted earlier. This is because stage refers merely to the ordinal level of the child's behavior pattern within a sequential-classification matrix. In itself, age manifestly indexes neither causal nor process variables for behavior (Baer, 1970; Gewirtz, 1969, 1978; Gewirtz & Peláez-Nogueras, 1992b). For a process analysis within the behavior-analytical perspective, neither developmental stage nor chronological age can provide the required proximal indices of causes or processes underlying moral development. These variables provide only incidental conceptual leverage over the sequential phenomena comprising changes in the child's moral patterns.

In conclusion, *"morality"* can be conceived to be a system of rule-governed behavior, with the developmental question being how rules (implicitly or explicitly formulated) come to acquire discriminative control over the individual's moral actions. On the basis of rule acquisition and an extensive history of contingencies, we believe that the child eventually abstracts out a *second-order* rule and forms a *moral concept*, which is knowledge of stimulus attributes that control action in diverse contexts. Hence, the effectiveness of the acquired rule will be based on its past success in controlling the moral behavior in question, on how explicitly and completely it describes the current situation and the contingencies for the child's behavior, and on how it relates to *other* currently-controlling rules.

## Summary

In this chapter, basic operations and learning processes were proposed for the acquisition of moral behavior in the pre-verbal and verbal child. The analysis was done with a focus on overt behaviors that typically connote altruism, sharing, empathy, and justice. Differences and commonalities between the cognitive-developmental and behavior-analytic theories of moral development were discussed. The basic learning processes of immediate, delayed, and pervasive imitation were detailed. Pervasive imitation was equated with Kohlberg's notion of "identification" as the basis for early child learning and later moral reasoning. The matching-to-sample paradigm was proposed as an efficient operant model to explain the imitative-matching behavior that occurs in pervasive imitation. Direct contingency-shaped moral behavior was distinguished from rule-governed moral behavior in later development. Generalization, transfer, and stimulus equivalence processes were thought to be involved in the emergence of new rules which appear to be "self-formulated" by the child. Throughout the chapter, it was emphasized that morality might be conceived as a system of rule-governed behavior with the developmental question being how (explicit or implicit) rules come to govern moral action.

## Endnote

1. In our analysis, the major reason we use the term *pervasive imitation* is to preclude misinterpretations and to facilitate the fitting of existing and future data on identification processes into a framework that allows us more easily to tie in other important aspects of the learning process (Gewirtz & Stingle, 1968). Identification has been used variously to refer to the process by which moral values, motives, ideas, roles and conscience of an important

other person (the model, a parent usually of the same gender) are acquired/adopted by the child. Freud (1933) regarded identification as the process by which "one ego becomes like another one, which results in the first ego behaving . . . in certain respects in the same way as the second; it imitates it and, as it were, takes it into itself (p. 90)." Earlier, Freud (1920) used imitation as the outcome index of identification (Gewirtz, 1991).

## References

Andronis, P. (1991). Rule-governance: Enough to make a term mean. In L. J. Hayes & P. N. Chase (Eds.). *Dialogues on verbal behavior*, (pp. 226-235). Reno, NV: Context Press.

Baer, D. M. (1970). An age irrelevant concept of development. *Merrill-Palmer Quarterly, 16*, 238-245.

Baer, D. & Deguchi, H. (1985). Generalized imitation from a radical-behavioral viewpoint. In S. Reiss & R. Bootzin (Eds.), *Theoretical issues in behavior therapy* (pp. 179-217). New York: Academic Press.

Baldwin, J. M. (1911) *Thought and things* (Vol. 3). London: Swan Sonnenschein.

Bandura, A. (1969). Social-learning theory of identificatory processes. In D.A. Goslin (Ed.), *Handbook of socialization theory and research* (pp. 213-262). Chicago: Rand-McNally.

Bandura, A. (1971). Vicarious and self-reinforcement processes. In R. Glaser (Ed.), *The nature of reinforcement*, New York: Academic Press.

Bandura, A., & McDonald, F. J. (1963). The influence of social reinforcement and the behavior of models in shaping children's moral judgments. *Journal of Abnormal and Social Psychology, 67*, 274-282.

Bijou, S. (1976). *Child development: The basic stage of early childhood*. Englewood Cliffs, NJ: Prentice–Hall.

Bijou, S. (1979). Some clarifications on the meaning of a behavior analysis of child development, *Psychological Record, Vol. 29*, 3-13.

Bijou, S. & Baer, D. M. (1961). *Child development: Vol 1. A systematic and empirical theory*. New York: Appleton-Century-Crofts.

Catania, A. C. (1984). *Learning* (2nd ed.). Englewood Cliffs, NJ: Prentice-Hall.

Catania, A. C. (1985). Rule-governed behavior and the origins of language. In C. F. Lowe, M. Richelle, D. E. Blackman, & C. M. Bradshaw (Eds.), *Behavior analysis and contemporary psychology* (pp. 135-156). London: Erlbaum.

Catania, A. C. (1989). Rules as classes of verbal behavior: A reply to. *The Analysis of Verbal Behavior, 7*, 49-50

Catania, A. C., & Harnad, S. (Eds.) (1988). *The selection of behavior: The operant behaviorism of B.F. Skinner—Comments and consequences*. New York: Cambridge University Press.

Catania, A. C., Matthews B. A., & Shimoff, E. (1982). Instructed versus shaped human verbal behavior: Interactions with nonverbal responding. *Journal of the Experimental Analysis of Behavior, 38*, 233-248.

Catania, A. C., Shimoff, E., & Matthews B. A. (1989). An experimental analysis of rule-governed behavior. In S.C. Hayes (Ed.), *Rule-governed behavior: cognition, contingencies and instructional control*. New York: Plenum Press.

Cerutti, D. T. (1989). Discrimination theory of rule-governed behavior. *Journal of Experimental Analysis of Behavior, 51*, 259-276.

Colby, A., Kohlberg, L., Gibbs, J., & Lieberman, M. (1983). A longitudinal study of moral judgment. *Monographs of the Society for Research in Child Development, Vol. 48* (1, Serial No. 200).

Cumming, W. W., & Berryman, R. (1965). The complex discriminated operant: Studies of matching-to-sample and related problems. In D.I. Mostofsky (Ed.), *Stimulus generalization* (pp. 284-330). Stanford: Stanford University Press.

Dawkins, R. (1976). *The selfish gene*. London: Oxford University Press.

Dixon, R. A., & Lerner, R. M. (1988). A history of systems in developmental psychology. In M. H. Bornstein & M. E. Lamb (Eds.), *Developmental psychology: An advanced textbook*. Hillsdale, NJ: Lawrence Erlbaum Associates.

Eisenberg, N., & Mussen, P. H. (1989). *The roots of prosocial behavior in children*. New York: Cambridge University Press.

Ekman, P. (1989). *Why kids lie: How parents can encourage truthfulness*. New York: Charles Scribner's Sons.

Flavell, J. H. (1985). *Cognitive development* (2nd ed.) Englewood Cliffs, NJ: Prentice-Hall.

Freud, S. (1920). (J. Riviere, Trans.) *A general introduction to psychoanalysis*. London: Hogarth.

Freud, S. (1933). *New introductory lectures on psychoanalysis*. London: Hogarth.

Gewirtz, J. L. (1969). Mechanisms of social learning: Some roles of stimulation and behavior in early human development. In D. A. Goslin (Ed.), *Handbook of socialization theory and research* (pp. 57-212). Chicago: Rand-McNally.

Gewirtz, J. L. (1971a). Conditional responding as a paradigm for observational, imitative learning and vicarious reinforcement (pp. 273-304). In H.W. Reese (Ed.), *Advances in child development and behavior, Vol 6*. New York: Academic Press.

Gewirtz, J. L. (1971b). The roles of overt responding and extrinsic reinforcement in "self" and "vicarious-reinforcement" phenomena and in "observational learning" and imitation. In R. Glaser (Ed.), *The nature of reinforcement* (pp. 279-309). New York: Academic Press.

Gewirtz, J. L. (Ed.) (1972). *Attachment and dependency*. Washington, DC.: Winston.

Gewirtz, J. L. (1978). Social learning in early human development. In A.C. Catania & T. Brigham (Eds.), *Handbook of applied behavior research: Social & instructional processes* (pp. 105-141). NY.: Irvington Press.

Gewirtz, J.L. (1991). Identification, attachment, and their developmental sequencing in a conditioning frame. In J. L. Gewirtz & W. M. Kurtines (Eds.), *Intersections with attach-*

*ment* (pp. 247-255). Hillsdale, NJ: Erlbaum.

Gewirtz, J. L., & Peláez-Nogueras, M. (1991). Proximal mechanisms underlying the acquisition of moral behavior patterns. In W. M. Kurtines & J. L. Gewirtz (Eds.) *Handbook of moral behavior and development. Vol 1: Theory* (pp. 153-182). Hillsdale, NJ: Erlbaum.

Gewirtz, J. L. & Peláez-Nogueras, M. (1992a). Infants' separation difficulties and distress due to misplaced maternal contingencies. In T. Field, P. McCabe, & N. Schneiderman (Eds.), *Stress and coping in infancy and childhood* (pp. 19-46). Hillsdale, NJ: Erlbaum.

Gewirtz, J. L., Peláez-Nogueras, M. (1992b). B. F. Skinner's legacy to human infant behavior and development. *American Psychologist, 47,* 1411-1422.

Gewirtz, J. L., & Stingle, K. G. (1968). Learning of generalized imitation as the basis for identification. *Psychological Review, 75,* 374-397.

Glenn, S. (1989). On rules and rule-governed behavior: A reply to Catania's reply. *The Analysis of Verbal Behavior, 7,* 51-52.

Hartshorne, H., & May, M. A. (1928). Studies in the nature of character. *Vol. 1: Studies in deceit*. New York: Macmillan.

Hartshorne, H., May, M. A., & Maller, J. B. (1929). Studies in the nature of character. *Vol. 2: Studies in self control*. New York: Macmillan.

Hartshorne, H., May, M. A., & Schuttleworth, F. K. (1930). Studies in the nature of character. *Vol. 3: Studies in the organization of character*. New York: Macmillan.

Hayes, S. (1988). Contextualism and the next wave of behavioral psychology. *Behavior Analysis, 23,* 7-22.

Hineline, P. N., & Wanchisen, B. A. (1989). Correlated hypothesizing and the distinction between contingency-shaped and rule-governed behavior. In S.C. Hayes (Ed.), *Rule-governed behavior: Cognition, contingencies and instructional control*. New York: Plenum Press.

Hoffman, M. L. (1988). Moral development. In M. H. Bornstein & M. L. Lamb (Eds.), *Developmental Psychology: An advanced textbook*

(2nd. ed.), pp. 205-260. Hillsdale, NJ: Erlbaum.

Kaufman, A., Baron, A., & Kopp, R. E. (1966). Some effects of instructions on human operant behavior. *Psychonomic Monograph Supplements. 1* (11), 243-250.

Kohlberg, L. (1969). Stage and sequence: The cognitive developmental approach to socialization. In D. A. Goslin (Ed.), *Handbook of socialization theory and research* (pp. 347-480). Chicago: Rand McNally.

Kohlberg, L. (1976). Moral stages and moralization: The cognitive–developmental approach. In T. Lickona (Ed.), *Moral development and behavior: Theory, research and social issues* (pp. 31–53). New York: Holt, Rinehart & Winston.

Kohlberg, L. (1981). *Essays on moral development: Vol. 1 The philosophy of moral development.* San Francisco: Harper & Row.

Kohlberg, L. (1984). *Essays on moral development: Vol 2. The psychology of moral development.* San Francisco: Harper and Row.

Kohlberg, L., & Diessner, R. (1991). A cognitive developmental approach to moral attachment. In J.L. Gewirtz & W.M. Kurtines (Eds.), *Intersections with attachment* (pp. 229-246). Hillsdale, N.J.: Erlbaum.

Kurtines, W. M. (1987). Sociomoral behavior and development from a rule-governed perspective: Psychosocial theory as a nomotic science. In W. M. Kurtines & J. L. Gewirtz (Eds.), *Moral development through social interaction*, (pp. 149-194). New York: Wiley.

Kurtines W. M., Alvarez, M., & Azmitia, M. (1990). Science and morality: The role of values in science and the scientific study of moral phenomena. *Psychological Bulletin, 107*, 1-13.

Kurtines, W. M., & Gewirtz, J. L. (1984). Certainty and morality: Objectivistic versus relativistic approaches. In W. M. Kurtines & J. L. Gewirtz (Eds.), *Morality, moral behavior, and moral development* (pp. 3-23). New York: Wiley.

Lerner, R. M. (1976). *Concepts and theories of human development.* Reading, MA: Addison–Wesley.

Liebert, R. (1984). What develops in moral development? In W. Kurtines & J. L. Gewirtz (Eds.), *Morality, moral behavior, and moral development* (pp. 177-192). New York: Wiley.

Lowe, C. F., Beasty, A., & Bentall, R. P. (1983). The role of verbal behavior in human learning: Infant performance on fixed-interval schedules. *Journal of Experimental Analysis of Behavior, 39*, 157-164.

Malott, R. (1989). The achievement of evasive goals: Control by rules describing contingencies that are not direct acting. In S. C. Hayes (Ed.) *Rule-governed behavior: Cognition, contingencies, and instructional control* (pp. 269-319). New York: Plenum Press.

Matthews, B.A., Catania, A. C., & Shimoff, E. (1985). Effects of uninstructed verbal behavior on nonverbal responding: Contingency descriptions versus performance descriptions. *Journal of Experimental Analysis of behavior, 43*, 155-164.

Matthews, B. A., Shimoff, E., Catania, A. C., & Sagvolden, T. (1977). Uninstructed human responding: Sensitivity to ratio and interval contingencies. *Journal of Experimental Analysis of Behavior, 27*, 453-467.

Morris, E. K. (1988). Contextualism: The world view of behavior analysis. *Journal of Experimental Child Psychology, 46*, 289–323.

Morris, E. K. (1992). The aim, progress, and evolution of behavior analysis. *The Behavior Analyst, 14*, 3-29

Morris, E. K. (1993). Behavior analysis and mechanism: One is not the other. *The Behavior Analyst, 16*, 25-34.

Mussen, P. H., Conger, J. J. & Kagan, J. (1974). *Child development and personality* (4th ed.). New York: Harper.

Overton, W. F., & Reese, H. W. (1973). Models of development: Methodological implications. In J. R. Nesselroade & H. W. Reese (Eds.), *Life-span developmental Psychology: Methodological issues* (pp. 65–86). Orlando, FL: Academic Press.

Pepper, S. C. (1942). *World Hypotheses: A study in evidence.* Berkeley: University of California Press.

Petrovich, S. B., & Gewirtz, J. L. (1985). The attachment learning process and its relation to cultural and biological evolution: Proximate and ultimate considerations. In M. Reite & T. Filed (Eds.), *The psychobiology of attachment* (pp. 259-291). San Diego, CA: Academic Press.

Piaget, J. (1932). *The moral judgment of the child* (M. Gabain, Trans.). London: Routledge & Keegan Paul.

Poulson, C. L., Kymissis, E., Reeve, K. F., Andreatos, M., & Reeve, L. (1991). Generalized vocal imitation in infants. *Journal of Experimental Child Psychology, 51,* 267-279.

Reese, H. W. (1989). Rules and rule-governance: Cognitive and behavioristic views. In S. C. Hayes (Ed.), *Rule-governed behavior: Cognition, contingencies, and instructional control,* (pp. 3-84). New York: Plenum Press.

Reese, H., & Overton, W. F. (1970). Models of development and theories of development. In L. R. Goulet & P. B. Baltes (Eds.), *Life-span developmental psychology: Research and theory* (pp. 115-145). Orlando, FL: Academic Press.

Ribes, E. (1987). Some thoughts on thinking and its motivation. *Mexican Journal of Behavior Analysis, 13,* 317-335.

Ribes, E. & Martinez, H. S. (1990). Interaction of contingencies and rule instructions in the performance of human subjects in conditional discrimination. *Psychological Record, 40,* 565-586.

Ribes, E., Penaloza, E., Moreno, D., Hernandez, M. L., & Hickman, H. (1988, June). Perceptual, instructional and perceptual-verbal recognition variables in the performance in complex conditional discrimination in children and adults. Paper presented at *The Eleventh Symposium on Quantitative Analysis of Behavior,* Harvard University, Cambridge, MA.

Sameroff, A. J. (1983). Developmental systems: Context and evolution. In P. H. Mussen (Ed.), *Handbook of Child Psychology* (4th

ed.). W. Kessen (Ed.) Vol 1. *History, theory and methods* (pp. 237-294). New York: Wiley.

Schlinger, H. (1990). A reply to behavior analysts writing about rules and rule-governed behavior. *The Analysis of Verbal Behavior, 8,* 77-82.

Schlinger, H. (1991). Theory in behavior analysis: An application of perceptual development. Paper presented at the annual meeting of the Association for Behavior Analysis, Atlanta, GA.

Skinner, B. F. (1938). *The behavior of organisms.* New York: Appleton-Century-Crofts.

Skinner, B. F. (1953). *Science and human behavior.* New York: Macmillan.

Skinner, B. F. (1966). An operant analysis of problem solving. In B. Kleinmuntz (Ed.), *Problem solving: research, method and theory.* New York: Wiley.

Skinner, B. F. (1969). *Contingencies of reinforcement: A theoretical analysis.* New York: Appleton–Century–Crofts.

Skinner, B. F. (1981). Selection by consequences. *Science, 213,* 501-504.

Uzgiris, I. C. (1981). Two functions of imitation during infancy. *International Journal of Behavioural Development, 4,* 1-12.

Vaughan, M. (1989). Rule-governed behavior in behavior analysis: A theoretical an experimental history. In S. C. Hayes (Ed.), *Rule-governed behavior: Cognition, contingencies, and instructional control,* (pp. 97-118). New York: Plenum Press.

Wainryb, C. (1993). The application of moral judgments to other cultures: Relativism and universality. *Child Development, 64,* 924-933.

Wilson, E. D. (1975). *Sociobiology: The new synthesis.* Cambridge, MA: Belknap-Harvard University Press.

Zettle, R. D. & Hayes, S. C. (1982). Rule governed behavior: A potential theoretical framework for cognitive-behavior therapy. In P. C. Kendall (Ed.), *Advances in cognitive-behavioral research and therapy* (Vol. 1, pp. 73-118). New York: Academic Press.

# Part III

# *Personality Perspectives*

## *Prologue*

The personality tradition in psychology, like other major traditions, has a number of roots. Although modern personality theory has a number of roots, it is a branch of psychology that perhaps more than any other owes its origins to the work of a single individual—Sigmund Freud. For all practical purposes Freud invented the modern field of personality theory. With the publication of his *Interpretation of Dreams* (Freud, 1900/1965), Freud launched a whole branch of psychology. Published in the first year of the 20th century, Freud's earliest major book set the stage for the new age. In the years that followed, Freud published a remarkable number of books that not only fostered the emergence of modern personality psychology, but also played a central role in transforming Western conceptions of human nature. Freud's psychoanalytic theory, with its emphasis on the unconscious and irrational determinants of human behavior, stood in direct contrast to the intellectual legacy of the preceding century. In contrast to the "Enlightenment's" view of human beings as basically rational, Freud painted a darker, more sinister picture, one that explored the nonrational or irrational side of human nature. In the course of a lengthy and productive career, Freud expanded his theory to include, in addition to a theory of dreams and dream interpretation, a theory of human motivation, a theory of human development, a theory of the origins of psychopathology, a widely used theory of psychotherapy, and a theory of moral development. The influence of Freud's work proved to be enormous. His psychoanalytic theory served as a prototype for a vast array of subsequent personality theories. Moreover, even those theories that are antithetical to psychoanalytic theory can be viewed, in part, as a reaction to Freud's theory. Modern behaviorism, we noted, had its origins in Watson's attempt to refute Freud's clinical theory.

Although his contribution to the personality tradition was enormous, any introduction that stopped with Freud would be incomplete. Like the other perspectives covered in this book, a list of the contributors to the personality tradition would include some of the most notable names in psychology. In addition to Freud, we have already mentioned Jung and Erikson. To that list we could add other names such as Anna Freud, Erik Fromm, Gordon Allport, Abraham Maslow, Carl Rogers, Raymond Cattell, and George Kelly, and we would have only touched on the range of people who have contributed to the personality tradition. The full range of contributors to the field represents an enormous and diverse array of perspectives and approaches. Modern personality theory thus continues to play a central role in contemporary psychology.

Although the field is characterized by an enormous and diverse array of perspectives and approaches, the personality tradition has tended to be most closely allied with organicism in its metatheoretical assumptions. The psychoanalytic tradition, we noted earlier, is clearly in the organicist tradition. This is also true of many nonanalytic approaches to personality theory. Although not all adopt the view of developmental change as qualitative rather than quantitative, personality theories have tended to adopt the holistic view characteristic of organicism. Personality theories have tended to define themselves as alternatives to other traditions such as the cognitive and behavioral in adopting a view of the total person, i.e., personality as the totality of what it means to be a person. The focus has not been the person's behavior, cognition, or affect—the focus has been on the total person.

In focusing on the total person, personality theories have tended to address a diverse array of issues and employ a variety of types of explanatory models. In this frame, personality theories have been defined as sharing in common three basic themes (Hogan, 1976). First, personality theories are concerned with the ways people are all alike; second, they are concerned with the ways all people are different; and third, they provide a means for explaining particular, enigmatic, and puzzling actions. Explanations of the first type are normally phrased in terms of distinctive features or qualities that all human beings share (i.e., what constitutes the nature of human nature). Explanations of the second type typically combine elements of the first type of explanation (e.g., propositions about the nature of human nature) with statements of the antecedent conditions that characterize the particular phenomena to be explained. Individual differences, for example, are often explained by appealing to general laws of human development and the specific developmental history of the person or persons in question. Explanations of the third type (i.e., of specific behaviors, puzzling symptoms, etc.) typically involve interpretation. Interpretation involves demonstrating in various ways that the behaviors in question are meaningful in terms of the context in which the behavior occurs. Interpretive explanations are almost never predictive, nor are they subject to experimental verification. They are intended to render meaningful particular actions that occur in particular contexts. Personality theories have thus traditionally tended to serve the same functions: They account for the nature of human nature and for individual differences among people; and they explain anomalous, idiosyncratic behavior problems.

From its very beginnings in the works of Freud, the process of moral development has been at the core of the personality perspective. Freud considered understanding the relationship between the individual and society to be complex and difficult and devoted considerable time to this question. For example, he wrote an extremely thoughtful reflection, entitled *Civilization and Its Discontents*, on what it meant to be a human being in civilized society. Freud found the relationship between the individual and society to be complex and difficult, in part, because he considered morality to be a cornerstone of civilization and at the same time he considered morality to be at odds with our basic instinctual needs and desires. Consequently, Freud viewed an understanding of how morality comes to be an integral part of the structure of our personality to be one of the core challenges he faced in developing his theory of personality. Freud found his solution to this problem in his often cited (and controversial) account of the development of a conscience or superego.

Although Freud found his account to be satisfactory, not everyone has agreed. In the past century, the particulars of Freud's theory of moral development (and many other particulars of his personality theory) have been questioned, disputed, and challenged on assorted grounds from a variety of perspectives. Moreover, as the contents of this part of the book indicate, no broad consensus has emerged. Thus, the problem that gave rise to Freud's theory of moral development has yet to be resolved. The understanding of how morality comes to be an integral part of the structure of our personality remains one of the core challenges of modern personality theory. This challenge is reflected in the works of a number of modern personality theorists representing diverse personality traditions (Blasi, 1984; Erikson, 1964; Hogan, 1984; Waterman, 1984) and, as you will see in reading the chapters in Part III, it remains a core challenge for the moral development field.

## Overview of Chapters in Part III

The personality perspective presented in this part of the book represents a highly individualistic tradition—the focus is on the understanding of the total individual person. Although the personality perspective is rooted in an individualistic tradition, it is also a perspective that has historically been (and continues to be) self-conscious of the importance of understanding the complex relationship that exists between the individual and the social context within which the individual is embedded. The chapters in Part III reflect this tradition. The relationship of the individual and society is a theme common to all of the chapters. Moreover, as the chapters will illustrate, the concept of "identity," which provides an important conceptual link between the individual and society, is one that has emerged as central to the field. Chapter 8 begins with a historical overview of Freud's contribution to the field and the contribution of the psychoanalytic tradition that he pioneered. Chapter 8 then goes on to provide a perspective on how morality comes to be an integral part of the structure of our personality. The socioanalytic perspective that Chapter 8 describes builds on Freud and other social theorists to present a view of the links between personality, identity, and reputation. Chapter 9 addresses the question of how morality comes to be an integral part of the structure of our personality from a perspective that draws on both the personality and cognitive developmental traditions. The chapter also provides an overview of a series of studies that aim at answering the question of the integration of morality and identity. Chapter 10 seeks to reconcile the individual and society from the perspective of psychological individualism. Psychological individualism aims to reconcile the individual and society by demonstrating that individualistic psychological functioning yields beneficial outcomes both to the individual and society.

Chapter 8, by *Robert Hogan* and *Nicholas Emler*, begins with an overview of the work of Freud and the psychoanalytic tradition. The focus of this overview is on Freud's description of the origins of conscience—which he called the most significant event in human development. The internalized image of its parents that the child acquires during this process becomes a child's "superego" or conscience. According to Freud, the superego serves to control the biological urges or impulses (essentially sexual and aggressive) that motivate human behavior. The development of a means for controlling these relentlessly selfish and antisocial instincts is necessary for human civilization. The uninhibited gratification of these instincts would result in a breakdown of society.

Although the particulars of Freud's theory of moral development have been disputed, Chapter 8 notes that many of its assumptions and implications are quite insightful and are well worth remembering. The socioanalytic perspective on moral development described in Chapter 8 draws on these insights as well as on the those of Durkheim, Mead, and Erikson in outlining three major milestones in the moralization process. These milestones represent psychological transformations in the relationship between the individual and the social groups to which the individual belongs. The first transformation, which draws on Freud, occurs in early childhood and involves the identification with our parents and the development of respect for authority. This transformation results not only in respect for authority, but also generalizes to include respect for the customs, rules, and traditions of one's society or culture. The second transformation, which draws on the work of the U.S. social theorist George Herbert Mead, occurs in middle childhood and early adolescence and involves role playing and perspective taking. This transformation results in an identification with one's social groups and becoming responsive to the expectations of other. The third transformation, which draws on the work of the French sociologist Emile Durkheim and the U.S. psychologist Erik Erikson, occurs in late adolescence and young adulthood as the individual assumes adult roles in society and involves the identification of themes that define the self, that is, the development of a personal sense of identity—a sense of who one is and what one stands for *vis-à-vis* the adult community. This transformation results in the ability to provide a philosophical justification for one's group membership and obedience to its rules.

The socioanalytic perspective provides an alternative to Freud's view that the interests of the individual and society are in conflict and that moral development involves the "internalization" of constraints on our basic nature. The socioanalytic perspective considers human beings to have evolved as social organisms, and adapted for social life. The most important problems that confront human beings, therefore, do not have to do with renouncing our basic nature because the basic nature of human beings is social. Thus, from a socioanalytic perspective, "internalization," is not a problem; rather the two great problems of life concern getting along with others (because we must live with and depend on them) and achieving some status (or not losing status) in the group in which we live. From a socioanalytic perspective, the most useful concepts for understanding how an individual solves the problem of getting along and getting ahead are *identity* and *reputation.* Having a viable identity (a role that we play in society) is critical to achieving the goals of getting along and getting ahead. An identity is the idealized version of ourselves that we hope others will understand, believe, accept, and give us credit for. Each of us develops an identity which we use to tell others who we are, how we expect to be treated, and how much status and respect are due to us. Our personal identity (including our moral identity), however, is private and subjective and unavailable to observation. Our reputation, in contrast, is the public record of our identity. Reputations are judgments that communities make about the character of their individual members. From a socioanalytic perspective, reputations are important because they provide an accurate estimate of character. They provide an accurate assessment of character because reputations reflect the pooled observations of an entire community, which is a larger and more representative sample of a person's conduct than any one person alone could accumulate by direct observation. Chapter 8 provides examples of the links between moral identity and moral reputation.

Chapter 9, by *Augusto Blasi* provides an introduction to the concept of integration as an alternative to that of internalization. The chapter begins with a critique of the concept of "internalization." The chapter notes that it seems generally safe to say that human beings are born without any knowledge of what is considered to be morally right and wrong in their communities and without any specific tendency to follow these guidelines. This view, however, does not necessarily entail the view that we are innately selfish and aggressive as Freud argued. Others, for example, have argued that we are born with empathic and altruistic proclivities. Whether human beings are innately selfish or altruistic, it seems fairly obvious that mature morality is not simply a result of refining our natural tendencies—pro- or anti-social—because there are times when it appears to be no more morally desirable to be overly empathic than it is to be overly aggressive. According to the concept of internalization, morality is initially "external," at least with respect to the individual's natural impulses (of whatever type). The process of socialization includes as one of its main tasks the assimilation on the part of the individual, the bringing in, of these external demands, the creation of a "second nature," which unfortunately, even in successful cases, remains in a state of uneasy truce with the "first" nature. The concept of internalization was created to indicate, if not to explain, this particular aspect of socialization.

"Internalization," Chapter 9 proposes, is predominantly a motivational concept: That is, its purpose is not to explain the acquisition of beliefs about right and wrong, for which learning concepts should be sufficient, but to account for the development of action tendencies, and perhaps desires, which did not previously exist in the individual—tendencies that override our "innate" tendencies. The psychoanalytic and behavioral traditions differ in their explanation of how controls are internalized, but agree that what was initially external becomes internal. "Integration," on the other hand, is used in this chapter as a substitute for internalization. One important advantage of the concept of integration is that it gets away from the spatial metaphor of inner and outer and relies on the basic metaphor of both biology and logic, thus opening to the organismic side of human beings and to their cognitive-structural capacities. In this respect, the concept of moral integration would allow us to view those phenomena that internalization was expected to clarify in ways that are consistent with the organismic and cognitive traditions in developmental psychology. The metaphor of integration assumes that personality, in all its complexity, is a unity or has a pull toward unity and that this unity has a functional center, a principle of subordination and coordination that has frequently been called ego.

Morality is an issue whenever our motivation (i.e., our needs and desires, whether intrinsic or otherwise) come in conflict with our moral knowledge or understanding. According to the perspective proposed in Chapter 9, the integration of moral knowledge and motivation can be thought of as involving two complementary components. The first concerns the ability to bring one's moral understanding to bear on one's already existing motives. Following this process, needs and desires acquire, in specific situations, additional meanings: Some become an obstacle for the realization of what one knows to be good and right; others become subjectively and formally right and acquire the power of objective standards. A second component of the integration of moral understanding and motivation concerns the investing of moral understanding with motivational force. This is literally the way the issue was seen in classical psychoanalytic and learning theories: A person would be motivated to follow moral precepts and beliefs, because these would be instrumental to the satisfaction of pre-existing needs—narcissistic needs, social acceptance, relief from anxiety, or rewards of various kinds. The basic problem with these accounts is that they attempt to explain moral functioning by eliminating what is most characteristic of morality, as we commonly understand it, namely, the independence of values from, and their irreducibility to, personal needs.

Therefore, this chapter assumes that moral understanding eventually acquires its own motivational power, one, namely, that is intrinsic to the nature itself of morality. When this occurs, moral understanding begins to make its own specific claims and becomes a part of one's motivational system, in interplay with and sometimes in opposition to the other motives of the system. At this point, a person may still choose not to follow his or her understood values in action, particularly when the competing motives have a high degree of urgency. In this case the integration of moral understanding and motivation should be manifested in such emotions as regret, sadness, or guilt. The absence of these or similar feelings can be taken as an indication that one's moral understanding is isolated from the rest of personality.

The highest degree of moral integration is achieved when one's moral understanding and concerns become a part of one's sense of identity, of the specific way one views and defines oneself. When this occurs, morality not only becomes, at least in principle, one aspect of the total conscious organization of personality, but is also invested with additional motives and emotions. The term *identity* refers to a mature form of self-concept, one that is characterized by a strong sense of unity, by its salience in the person's consciousness, and by its ability to anchor the person's sense of stability, individuality, and purpose. The starting assumption of the research described in this chapter is that morality and identity or the self-concept are separate psychological systems which only slowly, and sometimes imperfectly, come together and become integrated. A very important advantage of this position is to protect the autonomy of morality, namely, to accept that moral understanding and its validity are in principle independent of the person's psychological make-up. This assumption carries an equally important implication, which could be considered as an extension of the cognitive-developmental approach to moral development: a cognitively valid moral system should have the capacity, perhaps a very limited one, to affect the shape of one's personality. The series of studies briefly reviewed in this chapter have as their ultimate goal answering the question of the integration of morality in identity.

Chapter 10, by *Alan Waterman* seeks to bring psychological theory and research to bear on the debate over the moral priorities of individual and collective interests. It does do so from a particular philosophical perspective, *eudaimonism*, a philosophy in which the moral priority is assigned to the individual in terms of promoting self-realization. Eudaimonism is an ethical theory that calls upon people to recognize and live in accordance with the *daimon* or "true self." The theory extends at least as far back as classic Hellenic philosophy where it received its most notable treatment by Aristotle. The value assumptions of eudaimonism provide the foundation for many strands of contemporary personality theory.

As the term is used in Chapter 10, the daimon refers to those potentialities of each person, the realization of which represents the greatest fulfillment in living of which each is capable. These include both the potentialities that are shared by all humans by virtue of our common specieshood and those unique potentials that distinguish each individual from all others. The daimon is an ideal in the sense of being an excellence, a perfection toward which one strives and, hence, it can give meaning and direction to one's life. The efforts a person makes to live in accordance with the daimon, to realize those potentials, can be said to be personally expressive. According to the ethics of eudaimonism, each individual is obliged to know and to live in truth to his daimon, thereby progressively actualizing an excellence that is his innately and potentially. It requires that a commitment be made both to the principles by which one chooses to live and the goals toward which one's life is to be directed. This commitment involves a conscious recognition and acknowledgement of personal truths already known intuitively.

Eudaimonism provides the means for reconciling the interest of the individual and of society. Finding the center of strength within ourselves is in the long run the best contribution we can make to our fellow human beings. Advancements in the evolution of civilization, whether in the arts, the humanities, the sciences, technology, or other fields, have come from the striving of individuals to find solutions to the problems of the human situation experienced on a personal level. The creations brought forth through the expression of unique individual potentials are not just for private use and appreciation, but may be to the benefit of all. Such creativity appears to be facilitated by the social conditions that provide personal freedom and encourage the difficult task of self-realization.

The psychological perspective on the daimon that Chapter 10 advances is psychological individualism. The philosophical definition of the daimon or "true self" in terms of potential excellences does not readily lend itself to use within the paradigms of empirical social science. Potentialities are not observable. Psychological individualism seeks to operationalize the concept of the daimon. The psychological construct that corresponds to the philosophical concept of the daimon is "personal expressiveness." The personal qualities that are used to denote personal expressiveness are a sense of personal identity, self-actualization, an internal locus of control, and principled moral reasoning. Evidence is presented, based on an extensive literature review, regarding the benefits to both the individual and society that are derived from each of the qualities of personal functioning. Implications for moral education are discussed in terms of application to counseling aimed at improving career choices and the quality of interpersonal relationships.

## References

Blasi, A. (1984). Moral Identity: Its Role in Moral Functioning. In W. Kurtines & J. L. Gewirtz (Eds.), *Morality, moral behavior, and moral development*. New York: John Wiley & Sons, 128-139.

Erikson, E. H. (1964). *Insight and responsibility*. New York: Norton

Freud, S. (1900/1965). *The interpretation of dreams*. New York: Avon Books.

Hogan, R. (1976). *Personality theory: The personological tradition*. Englewood Cliffs, NJ: Prentice-Hall.

Hogan, R. & Busch, C. (1984). Moral conduct as auto-interpretation. In W. Kurtines & J. L. Gewirtz (Eds.), *Morality, moral behavior and moral development*. New York: John Wiley & Sons, 227-240.

Waterman, A. S. (1984). *The psychology of individualism*. New York: Praeger.

Chapter *8*

# Personality and Moral Development

ROBERT HOGAN
*University of Tulsa*

NICHOLAS EMLER
*University of Dundee*

### Abstract

This chapter provides a perspective on how morality comes to be an integral part of the structure of our personality. The socioanalytic perspective described in this chapter builds on Freud and other social theorists to present a view of the links between personality, identity, and reputation. According to this socioanalytic perspective, the moralization process involves three major milestones. These milestones represent psychological transformations in the relationship between the individual and the social groups to which the individual belongs. The first transformation, which draws on Freud, occurs in early childhood and involves the identification with our parents and the development of respect for authority. This transformation results not only in respect for authority, but also generalizes to include respect for the customs, rules, and traditions of one's society or culture. The second transformation, which draws on the work of George Herbert Mead, occurs in middle childhood and early adolescence and involves role playing and perspective taking. This transformation results in an identification with one's social groups and becoming responsive to the expectations of other. The third transformation, which draws on the work of Emile Durkheim and Erik Erikson, occurs in late adolescence and young adulthood as the individual assumes adult roles in society and involves the identification of themes that define the self, that is, the development of a personal sense of identity—a sense of who one is and what one stands for *vis-à-vis* the adult community. This transformation results in the ability to provide a philosophical justification for one's group membership and obedience to its rules. From a socioanalytic perspective, the most useful concepts for understanding the social and moral life of the individual are identity and reputation. This chapter provides examples of the links between moral identity and moral reputation.

Morality is a subject that lies at the intersection of philosophy and psychology. Philosophers try to provide logical justifications for regarding particular actions as moral or immoral; psychologists try to explain why people act in moral or immoral ways. Many philosophers, but especially Aristotle and Nietzsche, argue that goodness means human goodness and that conceptions of morality depend on conceptions of human nature.

Personality theory is the subdiscipline within academic psychology that is explicitly concerned with analyzing the nature of human nature. Following Aristotle and Nietzsche, one might think that models of moral development would draw heavily on personality theory, but that is not the case. The psychology of moral development has been most heavily influenced by cognitive developmental theory (e.g., Kohlberg, 1984) and social learning theory (e.g., Bandura, 1971). In these models moral conduct is explained in terms of cognitive structures or situational influences rather than intra- and interpersonal dynamics.

The purpose of this chapter is to provide an account of moral development that is directly related to the ideas of Freud, Jung, Murray, and Erikson—i.e., traditional personality psychology. We will make three primary claims. First, stable individual differences in personality are related to stable individual differences in moral behavior. Second, moral orientations evolve through specifiable stages that reflect age-appropriate social demands, and individual differences in moral orientations reflect these experiences. And third, moral conduct in adulthood can be largely understood in terms of the concepts of identity and reputation management. Part of our task will be to clarify the links between personality, identity, and reputation.

## Freud and Psychoanalysis

Freud's writings are not well-respected today in academic psychology and, in a real sense, that is as it should be—science should constantly outgrow its pioneers. Nonetheless, although many aspects of psychoanalysis *are factually wrong*, many of its assumptions and implications are quite insightful and we forget them at our peril.

The theory is well-known. We will only sketch it briefly here, so that we may expand upon its implications. Accoording to Freud, from birth onward people are motivated, at an unconscious level, by the instincts of sex and aggression. The uninhibited gratification of these instincts is pleasurable for individuals but the stable operation of society requires that they be suppressed; suppressing them, however, causes tension and distress. Consequently, tension and distress are the prices we pay for the benefits of civilized living.

Because the tendencies of the instincts are relentlessly selfish and antisocial, they must be controlled, and this is what psychoanalysis is largely about; i.e., it concerns the processes by which the instincts are brought under control. The story goes as follows. In normal circumstances, infants become quickly attached to their parents by bonds of respect and affection. Freud suggests that young children take a special interest in their same-sexed parent, whom they tend to idolize, and whom they wish to emulate.

Sometime after age 3, according to Freud, children begin to experience erotic and incestuous desires aimed at their opposite-sexed parent. These desires become stronger over time and bring children increasingly into conflict with their same-sexed parents, whom they begin to see as sexual rivals. Each child is caught in a conflict that increases over time. On the one hand, it loves its parents; on the other hand, it becomes increasingly jealous and afraid of one of those parents.

The conflict and tension become quite intense around age five and, according to Freud, are resolved dramatically. Small boys suddenly think that their fathers will castrate them for their incestuous desires; the reason boys believe this has to do with Freud's ideas about human evolution (cf. *Totem and Taboo*, 1913, a fascinating and wildly provocative book). Fearing castration, boys: (a) internalize the image of their father; (b) renounce sexual desires for their mother; and (c) repress all conscious memory of these events. Small girls suddenly think their mothers will abandon them as punishment for their incestuous desires. Fearing abandonment, girls: (a) internalize the image of their mother; (b) renounce sexual desires for their fathers; and (c) repress all conscious memory of these events.

The internalized image of its parents becomes a child's "superego" or conscience. The superego consists of moral commandments, prescriptions about what the child should and should not do, and self-punitive tendencies if a child should break (or think about breaking) a parental rule. After a child has internalized a superego, both its thoughts and its actions will be judged and evaluated by the inner parent. Violations of parents' expectations and commandments (including their rules against incest) will be punished by feelings of guilt. Even thinking about forbidden actions will evoke guilty feelings.

The parental image that a child internalizes represents a five-year-old's view of its parents and their rules. This view is quite punitive. A child's conscience, therefore, is aggressive, authoritarian, harsh, and judgmental. In adulthood, a conscience makes a person self-critical and that self-criticism erodes self-esteem. Moreover, because conscience stifles the expression of sex and aggression, and because the instincts can't be entirely suppressed, these impulses tend to "leak out," to appear in disguised ways, usually as neurotic symptoms. The psychoanalytic process concerns training the superego to be more tolerant and reasonable. Civilization requires that the instincts be repressed; maturity requires that they be partially acknowledged—but not directly acted upon.

The foregoing is a quick overview of Freud's description of the origins of conscience—which he called the most significant event in human development. The theory has been roundly criticized, often correctly, and has been largely dismissed by academic psychologists. But, once again, there are certain assumptions of the theory that are worth remembering. We will mention seven.

First, Freud's conclusions regarding the origins and role of conscience are based on his ideas about human evolution, which he borrowed from Darwin. Here we agree with him; that is, we also assume that any scientifically valid account of the development of morality must be consistent with the principles of evolutionary theory (cf. Buss, 1991; Dawkins, 1989). Many modern writers seem not to know this (but see Campbell, 1976, for a thoughtful discussion). The specific implications of an evolutionary approach are open to debate. Thus, Campbell and Freud argue that the development of civilization depended on the capacity of society to control individual selfishness, which is a product of evolution. On the other hand, the sociobiologists (Wilson, 1975) argue that society is part of the survival mechanisms of our species and directly serves individual selfish interests. But the general implications of evolutionary theory are beyond dispute: (a) humans are products of an evolutionary process that selected behavioral tendencies and capabilities with survival value for individuals; (b) individual human beings differ from one another in the strength of these various tendencies and capabilities; and (c) moral tendencies also reflect the evolutionary process.

Second, Freud equates "morality" with the rules and conventions of one's society. To do this usually makes one a moral relativist (i.e., a person who takes the view that what is moral depends entirely on where one lives). But Freud is too sophisticated to be a simple relativist; he argues that there is a universal human nature and conventional morality usually affects that nature in a negative way. Freud's point is that conventional morality saves us from the negative aspects of human nature—the instincts of sex and aggression; these instincts are negative in the sense that they tend to disrupt social order and harmony. But at the same time, morality is painful for us as individuals. And there is nothing for it. There is nothing beyond conventional morality that can serve as an organizing principle for society—certainly not Kohlberg's (1976) "individual principles of conscience."

Third, Freud suggests that one's orientation to authority is the first non-biological structure of personality to develop, and because it is the first it is also the most significant. Attitudes toward authority (one's superego) can be readily assessed with measures of normal personality. The Socialization scale of the California Psychological Inventory (Gough, 1987) is a superb measure of attitudes toward authority; it is also a measure with remarkable validity defined in terms of the number of inferences one can make on the basis of a single test score (cf. Gough, 1965).

Our point is that the personality assessment literature provides overwhelming support for the notion that a person's orientation to authority is one of the most, if not *the* most, significant structures of personality, as Freud predicted. Research on attitudes toward authority also shows that individual differences in this disposition are both stable and quite general (Emler, 1990; Rump, Rigby, and Walters, 1985).

Fourth, Freud proposes that certain patterns of child rearing produce desirable outcomes, and that deviations from these patterns produce less desirable outcomes. Specifically he suggests that optimum superego development is a function of the degree to which both parents are simultaneously warm and controlling in their parenting styles. Research on child development since the late 1940s confirms this implication (cf. Baumrind, 1971; Hoffman, 1977). Conversely, parents who are arbitrary, harsh, unloving, and inconsistent in the standards that they enforce have children with weak or non-existent superegos. Our general point, often neglected in cognitive developmental analyses of moral development, is that how parents behave as parents has long-term consequences for the character of their children.

Fifth, implicit in Freud's discussion of superego development (cf. *Totem and Taboo*) is a realistic view of justice that contrasts sharply with the Piagetian view found in John Rawls' famous book, *The Concept of Justice*. For the Piaget/Rawls model of "justice as fairness," the concept of justice emerges from childhood experiences of peer cooperation; children discover, in social interaction, that they can only resolve conflicts of interest, such as how to share a pizza or a preferred toy, by adopting the principle of distributive justice. In contrast, Freud argues that society is repressive and requires painful renunciations from its members; life in society requires that we share burdens and privations as well as benefits. Consequently, for Freud, a just society is one in which everyone suffers equally. Moreover, an appreciation for justice develops from experiencing injustice at the hands of peers and adults. Children discover that they only get their fair share when they can force their peers to give it to them or when adults are willing to make other children "play fair." They also discover that they must protect their fair share by being willing to retaliate against peers who do not respect their rights (Hogan & Emler, 1981). The reader might ask him or herself about what life was like in his or her childhood peer group and which definition (i.e., Piaget vs. Freud) of justice corresponds with his or her experience.

Sixth, although Freud argues that the superego is the principle cause of neurosis in human society and, therefore, something to be overcome, he is neither a hedonist nor a libertarian. He does not advocate self-expression, or a Dionysian celebration of the Id and the biological side of human nature. Freud was a stern Victorian moralist who insisted that we replace the repression of our instincts with their condemnation. Immature people can't bear to acknowledge the "animal" side of their nature; mature people can acknowledge it, but they condemn it. Freud recommends conformity to conventional morality because he believes even more suffering would occur in the absence of such conformity.

Finally, as we noted above, because Freud defines morality in terms of the rules and conventions of society and because he defines moral conduct as compliance with those rules and conventions, he is typically classified as a moral relativist (cf. Kohlberg, 1971). But Freud endorsed an interesting, universal moral principle that is not well understood today. Freud thought that we have a moral obligation to pursue self-awareness, that we should (in a moral sense) strive to overcome self-deception. To the degree that we are unaware of the reasons for our actions, Freud argued, we are at the mercy of forces we don't understand. And these unacknowledged forces are typically egocentric, selfish, and self-serving. Freud was not a moral relativist. However, the universal moral ideal that he advocated is no longer popular in our society, perhaps because it is too morally demanding.

We take the foregoing points as axiomatic and try to build on them.

## Durkheim & Mead

By and large psychologists tend to ignore sociology. But if one is interested in moral development, this is a mistake because sociology has some very important things to say about the moralization process. In particular, Durkheim's book *Moral Education* (1925), and Mead's book *Mind, Self, and Society* (1934) contain insights that: (a) augment Freud's analysis; (b) can be empirically evaluated.

Durkheim (1925) suggests that there are three desirable outcomes for the process of moral education; i.e., he describes three psychological attributes that characterize a moral person. The first is a sense of discipline which includes respect for authority as such, which generalizes to respect for the customs, rules, and traditions of one's society or culture (this is essentially what one gets with a well-developed Freudian superego). The second outcome of effective moral education, according to Durkheim, is a feeling of attachment to the social groups of which one is a member. This feeling makes one sensitive to the wishes and expectations of the other members of the group, but also makes one an enthusiastic and committed contributor to group goals. The third outcome is the ability to provide a philosophical justification for one's group membership and obedience to its rules. This justification is often available in one's culture in the form of religious or political doctrine. Durkheim was less comfortable with people who make up their own justifications (as Kohlberg, 1984, requires). Nor did he believe this third outcome would free one from disciplined compliance with the rules; rather it provides an intellectual explanation for the necessity of that compliance.

Durkheim has provided a good *description* of the outcome of normal moralization, defined in terms of three psychological "transformations." Beyond that he tried to spell out how these outcomes could be achieved through formal education, but he didn't explain why these transformations occur, and that is the next question. Freud's theory deals with the first transformation; it concerns the origins of our attitudes toward authority. Mead's (1934) book concerns the second, the processes by which people identify with their social groups and become responsive to the expectations of others. In brief, Mead emphasizes the importance of peer play in games in childhood as a moralizing process. In order to participate in even simple games (e.g., jump rope), children must fulfill complementary roles (rope turner vs. rope jumper) and mutually coordinate their actions in accordance with certain norms associated with their respective roles (turn the rope at the right speed, jump in time with the rope). This role-taking process teaches a child to consider its actions from the perspectives of its counter players. This experience both reduces a child's natural egocentrism and sensitizes a child to the expectations of others. Because games are played over and over with many of the same partners, this also fosters a solidarity with one's fellow players and attachment to the peer group. Finally, children begin to see themselves as others see them, to accept that they have certain talents (e.g., are good at playing particular roles) but lack others, and begin to accept a particular identity within the social group.

We noted earlier that the personality assessment literature, especially the literature surrounding the Socialization scale of the California Psychological Inventory (Gough, 1965), provides strong support for the notion that attitudes toward authority are an essential and universal component of moral orientations. The personality assessment literature also supports Mead's notion that role-taking ability—sensitivity to social expectations—is also an important component of moral character. Specifically, Hogan (1968; Grief & Hogan, 1973; Hogan & Kurtines, 1972) developed a reliable and valid measure of individual differences in role-taking ability. He then provided evidence that this construct: (a) is a source of individual differences in social sensitivity; (b) is independent of attitudes toward authority; and (c) is associated with a range of pro- and anti-social behaviors.

Erikson's writings on the concept of identity (cf. *Childhood and Society*, 1950) deal with Durkheim's third transformation. Erikson, who tried to synthesize psychoanalysis and classic sociology, suggests that personality development proceeds through eight "psychosocial" stages. The crucial stage that bridges the transition from adolescence to adulthood concerns developing a sense of identity, a sense of who one is and what one stands for *vis-à-vis* the adult community. Erikson argues that the problem of identity is typically resolved when a young person adopts an ideology—a political, religious, or historical world view. This ideology serves to explain to oneself and one's community who one is morally; it provides the individual with a moral identity.

The moral reasoning literature, which studies young people's moral theories, is an important potential source of data regarding the link between moral ideology and moral conduct. The source is untapped, however, because that tradition studies the structure rather than the content of moral reasoning. Nonetheless, that data could, in principle, be used to evaluate the link that Durkheim proposed between moral ideology and moral action.

## Socioanalytic Theory

Our perspective on moral development is based in three general assumptions. First, most contemporary accounts of moral development are decontextualized and incomplete because they analyze moral development *per se*. We believe moral development is a byproduct of personality development; like Freud, G.

H. Mead, and Erik Erikson, we think about moral development in the context of personality development more generally.

Second, we believe that Freud, Durkheim, Mead, and Erikson identified the major milestones of the moralization process. Specifically, people differ in terms of their moral character in three primary ways. They differ in terms of their attitudes and orientations to authority (as Freud suggested). They differ in terms of their responsiveness to the needs and expectations of others (as Mead suggested). And they differ in terms of the nature and coherence of the arguments they use to justify their moral orientations (as Durkheim and Erikson proposed). The primary issue in the study of moral development, therefore, is to identify the developmental origins of these three categories of differences.

Third, although the process of becoming moral has major consequences for the lives and careers of individuals, morality is, in reality, a group or collective phenomenon, and ultimately should be understood in those terms. Stop for a moment and ask yourself why there are moralities in the first place. One answer is that they were created by individuals to protect their rights and interests. However, we believe the answer has less to do with individual's private interests than with preserving the groups and collectivities in which individuals live. The function of moralities is to facilitate the survival of groups by regulating the behavior of the group members.

Given that other species have evolved viable societies without using moralities to control their members (Wilson, 1975), there must be something unique about the human species that requires regulation. This is a topic about which there has been little professional discussion; the unique human practice of morality may have to do with our capacity for language, our high level of intelligence (compared to ants, bees, and wolves), the unique social organization that language and intelligence allow us to develop, and the capacity that language and intelligence give us for deception and betrayal.

Because humans depend heavily on verbal information, they are especially vulnerable to deceptive messages (cf. Hockett, 1958). Chimpanzees are Machiavellian (de Waal, 1982; Whiten & Byrne, 1988) but they lack our capacity for lies, deceit, slander, and concealment. People routinely make false accusations and promises, betray trusts, loyalties, and confidences, and engage in a variety of linguistically mediated mayhem, manipulation, and treachery. This suggests that language should be a focal concern of moralities and, indeed, many rules for personal relationships (Argyle, 1988) refer to language use: we should share secrets with close friends, not criticize friends behind their backs, defend them when they are criticized, etc.

If the function of morality is to sustain society in the face of human waywardness, then this raises another issue. People differ in the degree to which they are routinely virtuous. Because both individuals and their communities suffer from delinquent behavior, it is obviously useful for people to be able to judge the character of others, and for communities to limit the damage done by their undersocialized members. Groups improve their chances of survival if they assign responsibilities and opportunities to those least likely to abuse them. Our point is that moral development not only produces individuals capable of self-control and amenable to social control (cf. Emler & Hogan, 1991), it also teaches them how and when to control the behavior of others. Although the issue is neglected in the moral development literature, one important outcome of moral development is the capacity to detect malefactors and delinquents and to be able to deal with them sensibly.

The health of a group or society can be evaluated by the degree to which the members observe the group's rules and standards (societies torn by internal violence, adultery, larceny, or corruption are unlikely to survive for long), by the solidarity of the group (societies lacking solidarity risk being overrun by their more cohesive neighbors), and by the vitality of its moral traditions. These conditions do not imply or depend on rigid consensus or tradition in the sense of Edmund Burke's dead hand of the past; rather, they depend on free public debate about the nature of goodness and virtue (cf. MacIntyre, 1985). Thus, yet another important outcome of moral development is the capacity to participate in the public debates that characterize social life; this requires becoming familiar with the moral arguments, ideas, ideologies, and doctrines that circulate within one's society. As with orientation to authority and attachment to the collective, this characteristic will also vary considerably across individuals.

To summarize the foregoing, moral psychology tends to focus on individuals and individual development and to overlook the larger social significance of the moralization process. The concept of group survival highlights the moral contributions that socialized adults must make; these contributions include following rules, attending to social expectations, participating in public moral debates, reviewing moral standards, modifying unfair rules, and monitoring and sanctioning the conduct of others.

We turn now to a brief review of our ideas about personality and personality development (see also Emler & Hogan, 1981; Hogan, Johnson, & Emler, 1978). We start with two generalizations about human nature that the reader can quickly confirm or disconfirm. On the one hand, people always live in groups; on the other hand, every stable group is organized in terms of a status hierarchy, with a few people at the top, some in the middle, and the majority at the bottom. These generalizations suggest that two great problems in life concern getting along with others (because we must live with and depend on them) and achieving some status (or not losing status) in the groups in which we live.

Humans appear to have evolved as group hunting animals. The fossil record shows that our ancestors were successful mass killers of other animals. The same capabilities make it possible for us to kill one another. Ethnographic data also reveal high homicide rates among modern hunter-gatherers. In view of our proclivity and talent for violence, the ability to attract supporters and allies, to avoid creating enemies, and to be able to repair damaged social relationships, has substantial survival value.

Persons who are socially accepted and have status enjoy a number of advantages over those who lack social acceptance and status. These advantages include better diet, better living conditions, greater choice of sexual partners, enhanced reproductive success, better health, less stress, greater security, and longer life. It seems reasonable to assume, therefore, that people are in some sense motivated to pursue social acceptance and status. People differ from one another primarily in terms of the means they use to pursue these goals and in the success they have achieving them.

Everyone wants social approval and status, but how do they get them? Small children, during the first 2 or 3 years of life, are normally cared for and cherished as a matter of course. Thereafter, however, social acceptance and status must increasingly be earned or negotiated, especially when a child moves beyond its family and into peer society. Other children rarely love you as much as your parents do.

Children enter their peer groups differing in natural advantages—health, looks, physical prowess, size, intelligence—which they may squander or successfully exploit. The quality of the parenting they have received will equip them more or less adequately for the task of dealing with their peers. As suggested above, a person's orientation to authority and social rules is strongly shaped by early experience; secure attachment to loving parents who consistently set and enforce limits will produce a positive orientation to rules and authority. This has other important implications for personality development. Children who are positively attuned to rules and authority are also educable, insofar as education requires complying with the instructions, judgments, and wisdom of one's elders. Moreover, educational attainment is powerfully related to attitudes to authority (e.g., Digman, 1990; Emler, in press). Educational attainment is also related to moral status within the community; Havighurst and Taba (1949) report a correlation of .74 between educational achievement in a group of adolescents and ratings of their moral reputations. A child's orientation to authority strongly influences his or her success in attaining status. But there is more to negotiating social acceptance and status than complying with authority. Three other components are crucial for understanding this process.

The first is having a viable identity, one that can be successfully sustained and defended. In order to interact with others, we must have a part to play—everybody has to be somebody. An identity is the generic part we play in society; it is the idealized version of ourselves that we hope others will understand, believe, accept, and give us credit for. Some identities are reasonably easy to support—e.g., cowboy, deviant, rock fan. Other identities require more personal resources to sustain—e.g., brain surgeon, symphony conductor, Olympic athlete. Within this range of choices, each of us develops an identity which we use to tell others who we are, how we expect to be treated, and how much status and respect are due to us. Outside of our identities, however wretched or noble they may be, we have little to say to one another.

The second concept necessary for understanding social (and moral) conduct is reputation. Each of us has one; moreover, our reputations are a matter of public record. Consequently, reputations are the bottom line in social interaction. At first glance the variety of reputations that people may claim seems endless, but a careful analysis reveals that all reputations can be scaled or classified along two dimensions. One dimension concerns the amount of social acceptance accorded that identity: *viz* a homeless person vs. Mother Teresa. The second dimension concerns the amount of status associated with the reputation: *viz* a homeless person vs. the Pope. Generally speaking, we are (or should be) concerned with maintaining or enhancing our reputations; conversely, we normally try to avoid a decline in our reputations. Although it is unseemly to appear overly concerned with one's reputations, every normal person is in fact keenly interested in reports regarding how he or she is perceived in his or her community and keenly sensitive to any attacks on his or her good name (Eibl-Eibesfeldt, 1989).

The third concept necessary for understanding social behavior and moral conduct is interpersonal skill. Choosing identities, managing reputations, and negotiating status and social acceptance all require skill. Individual differences in this skill are apparent as early as 3 1/2 years and little girls are usually more advanced than little boys. Differences in interpersonal skill mean that some people are more charming, persuasive, charismatic, and socially effective than others. Interpersonal skill is crucial for the attainment of one's goals in life. Because low status people—felons and delinquents—are characterized by poor interpersonal skills (reflected in hostility, arrogance, impulsivity, egocentrism, and social insensitivity), interpersonal skill also has implications for understanding immoral conduct. That felons or delinquents are deficient in interpersonal skill might seem obvious; perhaps less obvious is the fact that good interpersonal skills are also associated with the ability to lie, dissemble, and deceive.

To summarize the foregoing, people need attention, approval, and social acceptance; at the same time they need status, power, and control. Conversely, people strive to avoid losing social acceptance and status. Acceptance is usually achieved through affiliative behaviors; status is usually achieved through competitive behaviors. People do many things in the pursuit of status and acceptance, and while they do those things, others record and evaluate their efforts in terms of their reputation.

But what are reputations and why do people have them? First, reputations are judgments that communities make about the character of their individual members. Reputations are ". . . judgments, about vices and virtues, strengths and weaknesses, based on accumulating patterns of evidence which societies constantly process and reprocess (Emler, 1990, p. 178)." These judgments depend on certain conditions. There must be communities with some continuity of membership, in which individual persons are known, in which their conduct is observed, and in which community members exchange observations about their conduct. As language-using animals, humans know one another by repute, which is to say on the basis of verbally transmitted evidence. Communities of humans can, and routinely do, form and disseminate collective judgments about individuals during conversations. As to why this happens, we have already noted that individuals and communities need to be able to make sound judgments about the character of group members. If reputations reflect the pooled observations of an entire community, which is a larger and more representative sample of a person's conduct than any one person alone could accumulate by direct observation, then reputations offer an accurate and effective estimate of character.

There is also an important connection between reputations and identities: "reputations link individuals to social identities insofar as the latter serve as prototypes of virtue (Emler, 1990, p. 181)." In other words people are not evaluated in the abstract but in terms of the extent to which they live up to the standards or virtues implicit in the identities that they choose for themselves. One is judged to be not merely a more or less good person but a more or less good mother, warrior, brain surgeon, Catholic, or scholar. In the process of being evaluated by others, actors acquire moral as well as social reputations.

Other people's reputations tell us what these people are like and what we can expect from them in the various identities they claim. But their reputations also provide us with an instrument of social control. The socioanalytic perspective assumes that people try to manage or control their reputations, although there are wide variations in the energy and talent they bring to this task, and wide variations in their awareness of the reputations they have and how these reputations affect their lives. Nonetheless, people normally conduct themselves in public in ways that will at best enhance, or at worst not damage, their reputations.

Some readers may regard this as an overgeneralization and argue that some people are more spontaneous than others, that some people care little for the opinions of others, that some people are simply "themselves." It is the case that people who are highly self-conscious about the process of identity negotiation and reputation enhancement will tend to be less successful at these activities. But, it is also the case that, whether or not one pays attention to the evaluation of others, one will nevertheless be evaluated and these evaluations will have consequences. But more to the point, Darby and Schlenker (1989) demonstrate that being unconcerned with others' evaluations is a relatively conscious interpersonal strategy too; people who are unconcerned with how they are evaluated have taken being unconcerned as part of their identities.

To return to our primary theme—the link between personality and moral conduct—consider the question, "What does it mean to be moral?" One of the things it means is to be perceived as moral, to have a reputation in one's social community as a moral person. Few people are privately moral and publicly immoral, and though the reverse may be more common, it is still rarer than one might imagine. It turns out that, even in contemporary mass society, individual lives are seldom anonymous and very little conduct of any consequence is either concealable or concealed (Emler, 1990; Emler, Reicher, & Ross, 1987). To be seen by others as a moral person requires a certain kind of conduct not on one or two occasions but routinely, day in and day out, year after year. Reputations are remarkably stable. The behaviors that generate and support reputations, therefore, must also be quite stable over time and across situations. What does it mean to be immoral? Again, one of the things it means is to be perceived as immoral, to have a reputation for immorality. And there are particular things one must do consistently to maintain an immoral reputation.

We need to restate the point that one's moral or immoral reputation is an outcome of one's typical style of interacting with others. The process of pursuing or maintaining status and social acceptance using one's social identity to guide social interaction is what creates one's reputation. Judgments about one's morality or immorality are relative to the community or communities one inhabits. The degree to which moral reputation is a central and conscious aim of social interaction and not just an incidental and unconscious byproduct depends on the person involved. We believe reputation management requires skilled social behavior and thus to some degree it must be automatic and unconscious. On the other hand, we believe people are characteristically sensitive to their reputations and will often take deliberate steps either to avoid damage or to make repairs.

There is now general agreement in the personality research community that people's reputations can be defined in terms of five broad dimensions (cf. Digman, 1990). That is, descriptions or ratings of individuals by their peers reveal five clusters of attributes or dimensions along which these descriptions or ratings vary. One dimension concerns how bright, curious, and imaginative one seems. A second dimension concerns how self-confident and resilient one seems. A third dimension concerns how energetic and outgoing one seems. A fourth dimension concerns how charming and likeable one seems. And the final dimension concerns how "moral" one seems. So moral reputation is one of the five major themes that comprise a person's reputation as a whole.

What is gained by having a reputation for being moral? Being regarded as moral is typically associated with being trusted and well-liked. It is largely independent of status. Morality buys us credit in the area of social acceptance rather than in the area of power and control.

What is gained by having a reputation for immorality? Generally speaking, being perceived as immoral is associated with being mistrusted. It can also be associated with being feared. Although being regarded as untrustworthy has no obvious advantages, being feared does. On the one hand, such people gain a measure of intimidation in social interaction; on the other hand, the capacity to intimidate others is associated with status in certain communities. Prisons, like universities, have status hierarchies, and being seen as vicious and vindictive is a useful attribute in the former if not in the latter.

History suggests that great moral figures (Jesus of Nazereth, Martin Luther, Gandhi) normally live in reduced or impoverished circumstances. On the other hand, great immoral figures (Cesare Borgia, Joseph Stalin, Nikolai Ceausescu) often live rather well. Moreover, people seem endlessly fascinated by the truly evil, which fascination itself reflects a kind of status. In contrast, people's interest in great moral figures is largely confined to searching for signs of hidden moral flaws.

Finally, what precisely must we do if we want to be perceived by others as moral? What kinds of social performances support a reputation for being a moral (or immoral) person? There seem to be three broad categories of performances that are associated with moral reputations.

In the first case, one will be regarded as moral if one is scrupulous about adhering to the rules of one's culture, society, and social group. Conscientious observance of religious and institutional rules denotes integrity, conscientiousness, fidelity, piety, and even saintliness—perhaps because we find perfect conformity of the orthodox kind beyond the reach of most of us, and because most people do break rules to some degree. In any case, people who "keep the faith" (Marines, Catholic Priests, Orthodox Jews) "are an inspiration to us all" as symbols of discipline, self-denial, and dedication. However, such people can also seem rigid and overly zealous.

Rule following often involves various forms of abstinence and self-denial; i.e., it involves not doing things that others like to do. A moral reputation based on avoiding certain activities raises what Goffman (1959) calls difficulties of dramatic realization—because the absence of action is undramatic. In medieval Europe, individuals whose moral reputations were based on the extent and severity of their self-denial would typically make elaborate public displays of penitence by wearing the proverbial sackcloth and ashes, thereby insuring that others could see how self-denying they were. Because abstinence is undramatic, people who abstain as part of their moral identity also need to proselytize.

Perfect conformity is difficult. Most of us occasionally succumb to strong temptations or provocations and perhaps transgress or give offence. But periodic lapses do not necessarily damage our reputations, because during moral socialization we learn, in varying degrees, strategies for making repairs. These include a variety of emotional expressions—remorse, regret, sympathy for the victim—and verbal reactions—apologies and other self-justifying "accounts"—(cf. Blumstein, 1974)—as well as direct reparations to victims. Even young children know how to say "sorry" or explain that an offence or injury was "an accident" (Walton, 1985).

Most successful adults have complex and sophisticated strategies of reputation repair. Compare Gary Hart, a former U.S. Senator and presidential candidate, with Gilbert Ronson, head of Britain's second largest private company. Hart's reputation and career was ruined after certain details of his private life were leaked to the press, although his offenses were relatively minor and no charges were ever brought against him. Ronson was convicted and imprisoned for involvement in a major fraud, but his reputation was saved by a vigorous campaign mounted by an array of prominent figures who attested to Ronson's otherwise impeccable moral credentials. Gary Hart seems either to have been unaware of these repair strategies, or to have had no capacity to use them. One's success in life may substantially depend on one's ability to accumulate support powerful enough to defend one's reputation. And how much power is necessary will depend on the scope of one's ambitions.

The foregoing concerns rule following and moral reputations. As a second route to a moral reputation, a person will be regarded as moral if he or she takes a conspicuous interest in the welfare of others or the common good. This attitude is expressed in John Donne's line, "Seek not to know for whom the bell tolls, it tolls for thee." People who behave in this way (Mother Teresa, Albert Schweitzer) often dedicate their lives to helping others. Compassion, charity, concern, *agape, engagement, sorge* are all words we use to denote behaviors that reflect this moral orientation. Please note that one can be preoccupied with the welfare of others and at the same time not be deeply concerned about observing rules. Indeed, these requirements may at times conflict.

This second approach to building a moral reputation also requires consistency and effort. An occasional act of kindness is not enough, and daily life affords few opportunities for dramatic and unambiguous acts of selflessness. This kind of reputation depends on routine sacrifice and an enduring program of action directed at promoting the welfare of others.

In the third case, one's moral reputation will be enhanced if one endorses a moral philosophy, if one takes stands on principle, if one "talks a good moral game." This is the style of the great moral leaders. One thinks here of Gandhi preaching non-violence, Martin Luther King preaching racial tolerance, Abraham Lincoln preaching against slavery, and Nelson Mandela preaching against apartheid. People who consistently articulate a strong public moral position acquire reputations for being moral. Most of us, of course, are not great moral leaders; it is a stage only a few can occupy. However, there are some less demanding ways to establish moral credentials in this tradition. One is to criticize or condemn the behavior of others (limited moral philosophy is needed for this). Another is publicly to support certain moral causes (Save the Whales, Band-Aid, Greenpeace, etc.). A third is to support particular policies of social reform or particular political parties (cf. Emler & Hogan, 1981). All of these are symbolically equivalent to taking a public moral posture.

To sum up, if one is concerned with one's moral reputation, then he or she has three options; closely observe the rules of one's group; actively promote the welfare of others; or publicly endorse a principled moral position.

It is interesting to ask what a person must do in order to be perceived or described as immoral. An immoral reputation also depends on three kinds of behaviors. The first thing one might do is flagrantly defy the ordinary rules, conventions, and standards of conduct. Being known as a (non-psychotic) person who willfully disregards the accepted norms of behavior (by fighting, cheating, stealing, lying, etc.) will create an immoral reputation.

A second path to immorality is to be perceived as ruthless, uncaring, cold, and unfeeling. It is also useful consistently to ignore the plight or suffering of others, and to be relentlessly self-centered and indifferent to the injurious consequences of one's actions. Such behavior may be rational if one lives in an inner city ghetto and wants to be left alone, but it is not rational if one wants to climb the corporate ladder or be invited to work in Washington. In these latter cases such behavior will ruin one's reputation unless one is careful only to treat the relatively powerless in an uncaring way.

The third way to create an immoral reputation is publicly to advocate an immoral philosophy, to endorse Satanic practices, to applaud wicked principles or praise illegal behavior. One might think that no one would behave this way, but this is a more popular identity choice than one might suspect. Real life examples include British soccer thugs, Ku Klux Klansmen, Hell's Angels and skinheads, not to mention soldiers of fortune, drug dealers, pimps, and pornographic filmmakers.

## Conclusion

Once again, we believe that Freud, Durkheim, G. H. Mead, and Erikson were perceptive interpreters of social behavior and that the psychology of moral conduct needs to build on their valid insights. Consequently, we would like to end this chapter by noting how our perspective resembles psychoanalysis and how it differs.

First, we agree with Freud that the fundamental motives for social action (and therefore moral conduct) are biological and largely unconscious. Freud thought these biological impulses would disrupt normal social life; in contrast we believe these impulses are the source of social life—people are, in a sense, compelled to do social interaction as they seek companionship and acceptance or, alternatively, power and status.

Second, we agree with Freud that the first significant non-biological structure of personality develops in response to the demands of adult authority. Following Mead, Durkheim, and Erikson, however, we believe there are at least two subsequent non-biological structures in personality that: (a) are products of social development; and (b) regulate social (and moral) conduct. These structures promote responsiveness or sensitivity to the social expectations of peers and the larger social community, and foster the ability to interpret one's social experience in terms of a religious, philosophical, or political theory. We also agree with Freud that these non-biological personality structures influence our behavior in ways that are outside of consciousness. Few of us can accurately describe how we orient ourselves to authority, or how responsive we are to others' expectations, or what our religious and political value assumptions really are.

Third, we agree with Freud that our typical goals and agendas in social life concern solving problems caused by our biology and that, consequently, we rarely set out to "be moral." Our moral reputations are based on how others evaluate us during social interaction and they concern how we pursue our goals (i.e., with respect for rules, with respect for the welfare of others, with regard to "higher moral principles"). Consequently, our moral reputations are byproducts rather than conscious goals of social interaction.

Fourth, we disagree with the "internalization" metaphor that seems to have been invented by Freud. According to the metaphor, children are at birth amoral and antisocial. Certain experiences transform the structures of a child's personality; post-transformation children are qualitatively different from pre-transformation children. In the case of psychoanalysis, the transformation consists of internalizing the image of one's parents—hence the internalization metaphor. In our view delinquents differ from non-delinquents in a number of ways but these differences do not include lacking unobservable internal structures. To say that delinquents ignore rules, violate other people's expectations, and endorse degraded moral principles because they lack certain internal control structures is to prejudge the issue and foreclose subsequent discussion.

We do know, however, that delinquents and non-delinquents have different reputations because they conduct themselves in different ways. This observation is not as superficial as it sounds. It says that their public conduct differs; but that does not mean that their private desires also differ or that they differ in the strength of their self-control. We think they differ primarily in terms of the identities they have chosen and the means they use to support their identities.

Finally, we agree with Freud that moral development must be understood in the context of personality development more generally considered. Moral orientations are only one aspect of interpersonal behavior; people also differ in terms of friendliness, shyness, self-confidence, assertiveness, curiosity, self-absorption, and so on. It is an error to study moral development as a phenomena in and of itself.

Writers in the Kohlberg tradition will note that we define moral character in terms of reputation, which means that moral conduct consists of conforming to certain collective notions of social appropriateness. They will note that acting in accordance with social rules is cultural conformity rather than *true morality*, and that socioanalytic theory is another version of moral relativism.

There are two responses to this criticism. First, no satisfactory definition of true morality has been or is likely to be discovered, and this has been the consensus of philosophers and scientists for at least 100 years. This is because there are no absolute standards on which a "true morality" can depend.

Second, the socioanalytic model contains some universal themes: all normal people share the same motives; all developing children must accommodate themselves to the demands of parents, a community of peers, and group traditions; the basic dimensions of reputation seem universal; consequently, the parameters of moral development are universal. On the other hand, some of the content of morality (what specifically is right or wrong) tends to be relative to local culture and economy, and to the individual's position in his or her social hierarchy. Even at the level of content, however, viable social groups endorse and prohibit the same kinds of behaviors—truth telling, reciprocity, respect for custom and authority. Beneath the surface differences are remarkable uniformities.

## References

Argyle, M. (1988). Social relationships. In M. Hewstone, W. Stroebe, J.P. Codol, & C.M. Stephenson (Eds.) *Introduction to social psychology.* Oxford: Blackwell.

Bandura, A. (1971). *Social learning theory.* New York: General Learning Press.

Baumrind, D. (1971). Current patterns of parental authority. *Developmental Psychology*

Monographs, 4, No. 1, Part 2.

Blumstein, P.W. (1974). The honoring of accounts. *American Sociological Review, 39*, 551-556.

Buss, D.M. (1991). Evolutionary Personality Psychology. *Annual Review of Psychology, 42*, 459-491.

Campbell, D.T. (1976). On the conflicts between biological and social evolution and between psychological and moral tradition. *American Psychologist, 30*, 1103-1126.

Darby, R.W., & Schlenker, B.R. (1989). Children's reactions to transgressions: Effects of the actor's apology, reputation and remorse. *British Journal of Social Psychology, 28*, 353-364 .

Dawkins, R. (1989). *The selfish gene.* 2nd ed. Oxford: Oxford University Press.

Digman, J.M. (1990). Personality structure: Emergence of the five-factor model. *Annual Review of Psychology,* Vol. 41, (pp. 417-440). Palo Alto, CA: Annual Reviews.

Doherty, K. & Schlenker, B.R. (1991). Self-consciousness and strategic self-presentation. *Journal of Personality, 59*, 1-18.

Durkheim, E. (1925/1961). *Moral education.* Glencoe, Ill.: The Free Press.

Eibl-Eibesfeldt, I. (1989). *Human ethology.* New York: Aldine.

Emler, N. (1990). A social psychology of reputation. In W. Stroebe & M. Hewstone (Eds.) *European review of social psychology.* Vol. 1. Chichester: Wiley, pp. 173-193.

Emler, N. (in press). The young person's relationship to the institutional order. In S. Jackson & H. Rodriguez-Tome (eds.) *The social worlds of adolescents.* Hillsdale: Erlbaum.

Emler, N. & Hogan, R. (1981). Developing attitudes to law and justice. In S.S. Brehm, S.M. Kassin, & F. X. Gibbons (Eds.) *Developmental social psychology.* New York: Oxford University Press, pp. 298-314.

Emler, N. & Hogan, R. (1991). Moral psychology and public policy. In W. Kurtines (Ed.) *Handbook of moral psychology,* Vol. 3. Hillsdale, NJ: Erlbaum, pp. 69-93

Emler, N., Reicher, S., & Ross, A. (1987). The social context of delinquent conduct. *Journal of Child Psychology and Psychiatry, 28*, 99-109.

Erikson, E.H. (1950). *Childhood and society.* New York: Norton.

Erikson, E.H. (1968). *Identity: Youth and crisis.* New York: Norton.

Freud, S. (1913/1950). *Totem and taboo.* New York: Norton.

Goffman E. (1959). *The presentation of self in everyday life.* New York: Doubleday.

Gough, H.G. (1965). Conceptual analysis of psychological test scores and other diagnostic variables. *Journal of Abnormal Psychology, 70*, 294-302.

Gough, H.G. (1987). *Manual: The California Psychological Inventory.* Palo Alto, CA: Consulting Psychologists Press.

Grief, E.B. & Hogan, R. (1973). Theory and Measurement of Empathy. *Journal of Counseling Psychology, 20*, 280-284.

Havighurst, R. & Taba, H. (1949). *Adolescent character and personality.* New York: Wiley.

Hockett, C. (1958). *A course in modern linguistics.* New York: Macmillan.

Hoffman, M. (1977). Moral internalization: Current theory and research. In L. Berkowitz (Ed.) *Advances in experimental social psychology,* Vol. 10. New York: Academic Press.

Hogan, R. (1968). Development of an Empathy Scale. *Journal of Consulting and Clinical Psychology, 33*, 307-316.

Hogan, R., & Emler, N. (1981). Retributive justice. In M. Lerner & S. Lerner (Eds.), *The justice motive in social behavior.* New York: Plenum, pp. 125-143.

Hogan, R., Johnson, J., & Emler, N. (1978). A socioanalytic theory of moral development. *New Directions in Child Development, 2*, 1-18.

Hogan, R., & Kurtines, W. (1972). Sources of Conformity in Unsocialized College Students. *Journal of Abnormal Psychology, 80*, 49-51.

Kohlberg, L. (1971). From is to ought: How to commit the naturalistic fallacy and get away with it in the study of moral development. In T. Mischel (Ed.), *Cognitive development and epistemology*. New York: Academic Press.

Kohlberg, L. (1976). Moral stages and moralization: The cognitive developmental approach. In T. Lickona (Ed.), *Moral development and behavior: Theory, research, and social issues*. New York: Holt, Rinehart, & Winston.

Kohlberg, L. (1984). *The psychology of moral development: Essays on moral development*, Vol. 2. San Francisco, CA: Harper & Row.

MacIntyre, A. (1985). *After virtue: A study in moral theory*. London: Duckworth.

Mead, G.H. (1934). *Mind, self, and society*. Chicago: University of Chicago Press.

Rawls, J. (1971). *A theory of justice*. Cambridge, Mass: Harvard University Press.

Rump, E.E., Rigby, K., & Walters, L. (1985). The generality of attitudes to authority: Cross cultural comparisons. *Journal of Social Psychology, 125*, 307-312.

de Waal, F. (1982). *Chimpanzee politics*. London: Jonathan Cape.

Walton, M.D. (1985). Negotiation of responsibility: Judgments of blameworthiness in a natural setting. *Developmental Psychology, 21*, 725-736.

Whiten, A. & Byrne, R.W. (1988). The manipulation of attention in primate tactical deception. In R.W. Byrne & A. Whiten (Eds.), *Machiavellian intelligence: Social expertise and the evolution of intellect in monkeys, apes and humans*. Oxford: Clarendon Press.

Wilson, E.O. (1975). *Sociobiology: The new synthesis*. Cambridge, Mass: Belknap/Harvard.

# Chapter 9

# Moral Understanding and the Moral Personality: The Process of Moral Integration

*AUGUSTO BLASI*
*University of Massachusetts at Boston*

## Abstract

This chapter addresses the question of how morality comes to be an integral part of the structure of our personality from a perspective that draws on both the personality and cognitive developmental traditions. The chapter also provides an overview of a series of studies that aim at answering the question of the integration of morality and identity. This chapter assumes that moral understanding eventually acquires its own motivational power, one, namely, that is intrinsic to the nature of morality itself. When this occurs, moral understanding begins to make its own specific claims and becomes a part of one's motivational system, in interplay with and sometimes in opposition to the other motives of the system. The highest degree of moral integration is achieved when one's moral understanding and concerns become a part of one's sense of identity, of the specific way one views and defines oneself. When this occurs, morality not only becomes, at least in principle, one aspect of the total conscious organization of personality, but is also invested with additional motives and emotions. The term *identity* refers to a mature form of self-concept, one that is characterized by a strong sense of unity, by its salience in the person's consciousness, and by its ability to anchor the person's sense of stability, individuality, and purpose. The research described in this chapter is based on the assumption that morality and identity or the self-concept are separate psychological systems which only slowly, and sometimes imperfectly, come together and become integrated. The ultimate goal of this research is that of answering the question of the integration of morality in identity.

It seems generally safe to say that human beings are born without any knowledge of what is considered to be morally right and wrong in their communities and without any specific tendency to follow particular guidelines. It has been argued that we are not simply born with aggressive and selfish tendencies, but also with empathic and altruistic proclivities, as rudimentary as they may be at life's beginnings (Hoffman, 1977; Matthews, Batson, Horn, and Rosenman, 1981; Wilson, 1975). Whatever the verdict on this issue will eventually be, it seems fairly obvious that mature morality is not simply a result of refining our natural tendencies. The natural tendency to strike back after being injured may be the basis of justice, both as an individual sense and as a social institution (Solomon, 1990); and yet one must learn to suppress the desire for revenge when it runs against what our culture and we define as fair. A similar case can be made for controlling, and at times suppressing, spontaneous empathy.

In sum, morality, as we know it, is initially "external," at least with respect to the individual's natural impulses. The process of socialization includes as one of its main tasks the assimilation on the part of the individual or the bringing in of these external demands. This leads to the creation of a "second nature," which unfortunately, even in successful cases, remains in a state of uneasy truce with the "first" nature. The concept of internalization was created to indicate, if not to explain, this particular aspect of socialization.

In this chapter the concept of internalization will be briefly and critically discussed and then the alternative concept of integration will be introduced. The meaning and some of the main aspects of moral integration will be elaborated and illustrated with some empirical data.

## Internalization

What is perhaps the most striking thing about the term *internalization* is that its frequent use in the psychological literature on moral behavior and emotions is accompanied by a high degree of conceptual vagueness. One would think that its meaning is so clear and so widely shared that it can be taken for granted. In reality, the concept is imprecise and theoretically ambiguous. Moreover, internalization may simply be the inappropriate metaphor for the kind of phenomena that it was meant to clarify. Such problems have already been pointed out within psychoanalysis (Behrends and Blatt, 1985; Meissner, 1981). Schafer (1972), in fact, suggested that the term simply be abandoned.

Of course, there have been attempts to attach relatively precise meanings to "internalization," particularly within psychoanalysis and learning theories. These meanings, however, are typically incompatible with that understanding of morality that is socially shared and guides ordinary evaluations and control of behavior. This point deserves some elaboration.

"Internalization" is predominantly a motivational concept: That is, its purpose is not to explain the acquisition of beliefs about right and wrong, for which learning concepts should be sufficient, but to account for the development of action tendencies, and perhaps desires, which did not previously exist in the individual.

The model constructed by psychoanalysis, or at least by important currents in it, to account for the origin of these internal tendencies is at the same time paradoxical and utopian. It is, therefore, deeply unsatisfactory from the perspective of everyday understanding. The paradox, from the perspective of psychoanalysis, is that internalizations, if they should be effective and become a part of personality, can only be built on instinctual foundations and must contribute to the gratification of one's instinctual needs (Behrends and Blatt, 1985; Havens, 1986; Sandler, Holder, and Meers, 1963). But these instinctual needs are precisely what moral internalizations are supposed to control and what to some extent must be renounced for values to remain values, without becoming functionalized (for the idea of functionalization of values, see Odier, 1947).

The psychoanalytic view is also utopian. On the one hand, moral values can be considered to be genuinely integrated in personality only if one deeply loves and desires them with one's whole being, to the point that conflict and disharmony are no longer experienced. Of course, as was already mentioned, this state could only occur if moral values and ideals were built on what is most "true" about oneself, namely, instinctual impulses and narcissistic pleasure (Havens, 1986; Winnicott, 1965). In this respect, psychoanalysis participates in the romantic vision: Truth and perfection are in the state of nature, in the ultimate integration and simplicity. On the other hand, this ideal state is no longer possible, if it ever was: Paradise and mother's womb have been lost forever. What is available, the morality that people manage to construct through their internalizations, is not only inadequate but inevitably flawed. The ideals we give ourselves through knowledge and philosophy are artificial and false, a product of defensive rationalization and intellectualization.

At the other end of the theoretical spectrum, behavioristic approaches of any kind have little use for such distinctions as between false and true aspects of personality. For those approaches that have been influenced by classical learning theory (including the social-learning and the cognitive ones), the concept of internalization was meant to answer a more practical question: How can we explain that certain socially approved behaviors, though not easy to come by spontaneously, continue to be performed in the absence of reinforcements and external controls? Obviously external controls must have become "internal." (This is not the solution of operant theories, for which internalization is a scientifically meaningless answer to a non-question.) Typically what is postulated inside the person is the creation of cues—perceptual memories, words, statements, or other "cognitive" elements—having the power to elicit the same kinds of emotion (fear, pleasure, etc.) that were initially associated with the external reinforcements that controlled socially desirable behavior (a careful theoretical analysis can be found in Aronfreed, 1968; recently the concept was briefly discussed by Grusec and Goodnow, 1994; Hoffman, 1994; Kochanska, 1994; and Perry, 1994).

One point about the concept of internalization in psychoanalysis and learning theories needs to be clearly understood. Internalization works if it controls socially desirable action. This control is exercised by emotions such as fear, anxiety, guilt, self-esteem, etc. Cognitive cues (e.g., the psychoanalytic "introjects") may be necessary, but only insofar as they reliably elicit the required emotions. Therefore their cognitive value is largely irrelevant to the functional definition of internalization. It is conceivable that complex ideas are more effective than simple ones; that structure-embedded ideas more reliably elicit the controlling emotions than simple verbal cues, images, or memory flashes. Even in these cases, however, whether these ideas are true or not, logically coherent or not, the characteristics emphasized by the cognitive-developmental approach to moral development play no role whatsoever in internalization. What matters, instead, are the functional capacities of these "cognitive" elements to persist for longer periods of time and to generalize across many situations.

## The Concept of Integration

*Integration* is used in this chapter as a substitute for *internalization*. One must admit at the outset that the concept of integration is neither less ambiguous theoretically nor less confounded by commonsense meanings than its rival. But it has one important advantage, namely, to get away from the spatial metaphor of inner and outer and to rely on the basic metaphor of both biology and logic, thus opening to the organismic side of human beings and to their cognitive-structural capacities. In this respect (and perhaps only in this respect), the concept of moral integration would allow us to view those phenomena that *internalization* was expected to clarify in ways that are consistent with the organismic and cognitive traditions in developmental psychology. The metaphor of integration assumes that personality, in all its complexity, is a unity or has a pull toward unity and that this unity has a functional center, a principle of subordination and coordination. This center has frequently been called ego, from which derived the notion of ego involvement to represent the hierarchical nature of our motives (e.g., Allport, 1961; Ausubel, 1952).

A more precise meaning of *integration*, particularly as it affects moral functioning, will hopefully emerge from the various discussions in this chapter. In a preliminary and general sense, when looking at different aspects of personality, it is possible to speak of *degrees* of integration. A similar statement can be made when comparing the way the same psychological aspect fits in different personalities. The degree of integration is here assumed to depend on two criteria: the degree of coordination of one aspect with the other subsystems that constitute personality; and the level of superordination of the aspect in question in the hierarchy of one's personality organization. Thus, when a piece of information (as the sum of the internal angles of any triangle is 180°) is stored in somebody's memory system, it becomes integrated, in a real sense, into his or her personality. For many, however, integration is minimal in this case: in fact, this information is not likely to engage one's emotions, sense of self, sense of responsibility; it does not guide daily decisions, the selection of friends, or the way one leads one's life; it does not stimulate dreams and fantasies nor does it elicit hopes and future plans. The basic assumption of this chapter is that very meaningful questions in psychologically studying morality concern its degree of integration, in the sense presented here, and the developmental or other variables on which moral integration depends.[1]

Before embarking on a more detailed discussion, the distinction between unintended and cultivated integration needs to be elaborated. The type of integration that is described in biological organisms occurs outside the domain of consciousness and is not a result of intentional regulation. It is rather the effect of automatic and genetically based processes of adaptation and internal regulation: in this sense it could be called "natural." Many instances of integration at the behavioral and psychological level are also unintentional and natural. For instance, the kind of structuring that Piaget theorized for the sensorimotor stages must certainly be unintentional. Even beyond infancy, Piagetian cognitive structures and language structures do not seem to be acquired consciously and intentionally. The same should be said of those personality syntheses that psychoanalysis attributes to the ego and of those integrations that are maintained by defense mechanisms.

Next to unintentional and "natural" integration, there seem to be attempts at personality integration that are consciously and intentionally pursued; the resulting integration, therefore, could be called "cultivated." A useful analogy may be provided by an important episode in Roman history. When during the 2nd century B.C. Rome, till then simply a powerful Etruscan city, began to pursue its territorial expansion around the Mediterranean Sea, it found itself in the midst of the Hellenistic civilization. What happened is sometimes presented as the territorial conquest of Greece by Rome and the spiritual and cultural conquest of Rome on the part of Greece. However, as historians have pointed out (e.g., Veyne, 1987), Rome did not experience this process as the adoption of the culture of a powerless foreign nation. To the Romans Hellenistic civilization was civilization itself, its values and truths were *universal* values and truths: "The Romans were determined not to leave a monopoly of that civilization to the Greeks" (Veyne, 1987, p. 3). They started then, consciously and purposefully, their own transformation. In the process, they did not feel they were giving up anything important or were taking in a foreign body, since their adopted guidelines for development and greatness were objective universal standards.

In a similar way, or so it seems, people, even young children with the help of their families and societies, consciously and intentionally, frequently with effort and persistence, pursue their own progressive moralization. Values are apprehended in their objective validity; are integrated with one's motivational and emotional systems; are made the object of agentic processes, including responsibility; and are finally taken as a basis for the construction of one's self-concept and identity. These are the main themes of this chapter. These themes should not be seen as defining sequential developmental steps, but, rather, as being dialectically interrelated throughout one's life.

Of course, the borders between unintentional and cultivated integration cannot be drawn too sharply. Both in history and in personal life what happens outside consciousness affects the limits and the possibility of what can be consciously achieved. On the other hand, it may be possible, in principle, to have some kind of indirect control over one's unconscious integrating processes. For example, one may decide to undergo psychotherapy in order to deal with those unconscious needs that have become an obstacle for achieving the desired type of moral integration.

Finally the "natural" mode of integration, with its promise of a spontaneous, effortless total harmony of heart and mind, of knowledge, emotions, and desires may offer us a seductive image and lead us to believe that only there can one find true morality. Freud, I think, was right on this point: Civilization has introduced a split in nature and the split is irreparable. He went wrong, however, in believing that attempts to heal the split from above, that is, operating from reason, can only be superficial, artificial, and ultimately distorting. This is the only solution available to us for achieving some kind of moral integration. Some degree of moral harmony in personality may still be possible, but it would never be the result of spontaneous natural processes. Whatever moral integration we can obtain, instead, would be forever fragile, requiring constant attention, and a lengthy, sometimes painful, ascesis inhibiting and suppressing some of the impulses that feel most natural to us.

## The Integrating Power of Understanding

Following the pendular movement of concerns, interests, and fashions, it has become increasingly common to criticize and even to dismiss the cognitive approach to moral development. It may be easy to forget, then, the achievements of theories like Piaget's and Kohlberg's or, more seriously, to lose sight of the conceptual constraints and of the undisposable requirements that cognitive-developmental theories were designed to address.

Morality, as is understood in everyday language, has an essential objective component.[2] Thus, not all solutions to social problems that people could imagine can also be considered moral, nor are all moral solutions equally valid from a moral perspective. In fact, people tend to perceive values in general as involving a central objective aspect; it is this aspect that differentiates values from preferences and tastes and explains why values are seen as making a claim on us (Nisan, 1988). If this is true, then cognition and cognitive development must be important for morality and moral development. This recognition, of course, does not prejudge the further question of how moral cognition and understanding should be explained from a psychological perspective. Existing theories cannot foreclose the search for more adequate answers.

These observations are sufficient to justify the choice of moral understanding as the starting point and the foundation in the process of moral integration. Here, however, I wish to stress a different point, namely, the integrating capacity of understanding as such. This characteristic was well known to Medieval and Renaissance philosophers, who tended to view the possession, symbolic for sure, of objects and reality as the most central feature of knowledge; it is still reflected in such metaphors as apprehending, comprehending, grasping, getting, holding, by which the process of understanding is conveyed in everyday language. This same idea, of course, is reflected in the Piagetian concepts of assimilation and structure: in this case, to understand means to assimilate a new object or a new experience, that is, to integrate it in an already existing structure.

Unfortunately this view of knowledge and understanding is widely absent in contemporary cognitive psychology, which focuses instead on impersonal, automatic, largely nonconscious information processes. Even more thoroughly lost, also in Piagetian theories, is the idea that knowledge belongs to, is an intrinsic possession of the conscious person, who intentionally pursues it and is responsible for its correctness and truth (Blasi, 1983).

When the agentic view of knowing disappears, then the distinctions among image, idea, belief, concept, notion, thought, opinion, sentiment, judgment, and knowledge also begin to blur and disappear. But the distinctions among cognitive processes and products are particularly important from the perspective of integration. Some of these processes, for instance, judgment, knowledge, and conviction, seem to have deeper roots (another organismic metaphor) in one's personality than others.

As far as I know, there is no research on this issue, but one could formulate relatively precise and testable hypotheses. For instance, one could hypothesize that an isolated moral belief, one that is not related to other beliefs, or a belief that can hardly be articulated, is less integrated in one's personality (other things being equal) than a moral belief that is related to and supported by other beliefs. A similar hypothesis can be made for beliefs, for which one cannot give reasons to oneself or to other people, or those that one received ready-made, and were not acquired as a result of a personal effort to sift various opinions, to compare arguments and evidence, and to defend one's choice against competing beliefs. As plausible indices of integration one could use the capacity of moral beliefs to survive under difficult conditions—social isolation or social pressure, persecution, dramatic societal and cultural changes—and to remain an important factor in various facets of one's life.

## *Moral Understanding, Motivation, and Emotions*

Is it possible for a person to perform an action that he or she knows and understands to be wrong, without experiencing regret, sadness, shame, guilt, or some kind of negative emotion? More generally, can one have a genuine, though perhaps simple, understanding of morality which is not accompanied by the appropriate emotions?

The question is partly conceptual. Some philosophers (e.g., Rich, 1986) argue that certain emotions are constitutive of moral concepts and that, therefore, "an absence of appropriate constitutive emotion when committing a morally wrong act shows that the person does not fully have a concept of what is morally right in the situation" (Rich, 1986, p. 212). This view may have some merit, even though it seems to stretch the ordinary meaning of "understanding" beyond its commonly accepted boundaries. In any event, the questions that should interest psychologists are of another sort: whether, for instance, two different kinds of understanding—with and without the appropriate emotions—do in fact exist in people; and what could be, for each kind, the psychological contexts and the behavioral consequences.

One could hypothesize, with some plausibility, that the child's moral knowledge and understanding, when first acquired and for some time afterwards, do not have much of a motivational power. Vice-versa, it is possible that those spontaneous desires and impulses that lead a child towards empathic and altruistic acts are not in fact moral, when they are viewed from the perspective of the child's own understanding of morality. Children approach the moral world, where actions are not simply pleasant or unpleasant, useful or useless, but also right and wrong, with an already rich system of needs, impulses, desires, and wants. Some of these motives are very powerful, others are less so; some appear to be totally natural and spontaneous, others have already been shaped by the culture. In either case the sense of value and goodness that the child appreciates in the early moral judgments is no match for the motivational system that most frequently determines his or her intentions and goals. This is not to say that children's spontaneous desires are all competitive, aggressive, and selfish. But even empathic and altruistic impulses may guide children's action simply because they are their impulses, because they want the actions they engage in and not because actions or impulses are good. In pursuing their "nature" children are not acknowledging and submitting to certain standards of right and good behavior.

In sum, the integration of moral understanding in one's motivational system may not be an automatic affair that could be taken for granted. Rather, disjunctures and disarticulations between these two aspects of personality should be expected, either as a normal characteristic of the developing process or as a result of dynamic processes of isolation.

The integration of moral knowledge and motivation can be thought of as involving two complementary components. The first concerns the ability to bring one's moral understanding to bear on one's already existing motives. Following this process, needs and desires acquire, in specific situations, additional meanings: some become an obstacle for the realization of what one knows to be good and right; others become subjectively and formally right and acquire the power of objective standards. Thus, a girl may share a toy not simply because she wants to, but because, knowing that the gesture is good, she wants to conform her action to her standards of goodness. It should then be possible to compare children's altruistic and empathic behaviors and to distinguish those that are a result of spontaneous tendencies and those that are a formal response to moral knowledge. Only in the latter case is there genuine integration of understanding and motives.

A study on the development of responsibility (Blasi, 1984) suggested that this type of integration is still weak among first graders. These children were presented with a hypothetical dilemma (one of five), in which the protagonist was confronted with the choice between obeying mother's rule or helping a younger child who seemed to be lost and was crying. The large majority (73 percent) chose the altruistic alternative. In justifying their decisions, these children resorted to four main kinds of considerations: what the protagonist wants or likes to do (26 percent), what is nice and normal (18 percent), the younger child's needs (80 percent), the possibility to be found out and punished (60 percent). The last type of consideration was neither the most frequent nor the most effective, as it convinced only 27 percent of the children that obedience was the right alternative.

However, what is interesting from the perspective of this chapter is that only 12 percent of those first graders that opted for the altruistic alternative recognized an obligation to do so in answer to the question, "does the protagonist have to do what he thinks is right?" The pattern of responses of 6th and 11th graders was strikingly different: whatever alternative they chose, 86 percent of 6th graders and 78 percent of 11th graders acknowledged the strict obligation to act according to it. A plausible interpretation of these findings is that the choice of the altruistic alternative among first graders corresponds to a spontaneous tendency (in this respect, similar to egocentric impulses and to fear of punishment), which has not been invested yet with the value and the claims of objective standards.

A second component of the integration of moral understanding and motivation concerns the investing of moral understanding with motivational force. This is literally the way the issue was seen in classical psychoanalytic and learning theories: A person would be motivated to follow moral precepts and beliefs, because these would be instrumental to the satisfaction of pre-existing needs—narcissistic needs, social acceptance, relief from anxiety, or rewards of various kinds. The basic problem with these accounts is that they attempt to explain moral functioning by eliminating what is most characteristic of morality, as we commonly understand it, namely, the independence of values from, and their irreducibility to, personal needs.

Therefore, it is simply assumed in this chapter that moral understanding eventually acquires *its own* motivational power, one, namely, that is intrinsic in the nature itself of morality.[3] When this occurs, moral understanding begins to make its own specific claims and becomes a part of one's motivational system, in interplay with and sometimes in opposition to the other motives of the system. At this point, a person may still choose not to follow his or her understood values in action, particularly when the competing motives have a high degree of urgency. In this case the integration of moral understanding and motivation should be manifested in such emotions as regret, sadness, or guilt. The absence of these or similar feelings can be taken as an indication that one's moral understanding is isolated from the rest of personality.

In a series of studies, Nunner-Winkler and her collaborators (Asendorpf and Nunner-Winkler, 1992; Nunner-Winkler, 1983; Nunner-Winkler and Sodian, 1988) relied on this kind of index (i.e., the type of emotions that are attributed to a wrongdoer) to infer whether or not moral understanding produces in children a sense of personally binding obligation. These investigators reported that, while practically all children from the age of four on had some understanding of the intrinsic validity of moral norms, many of the younger children attributed positive emotions to wrongdoers. For instance, in two stories concerning theft, only 20 percent of four-year-olds and 48 percent of six-year-olds, but 88 percent of eight-year-olds thought that the protagonist was sad and felt bad after stealing. In addition, 35, 70, and 90 percent respectively in each of these three age groups decided that the protagonist who was happy after stealing was worse than the protagonist who was sad in the same situation.

The attribution of positive emotions to wrongdoers was observed among four- and five-year-olds also when the offense produced serious physical harm in another child, even when no tangible gain derived from it. What seemed to determine children's emotional attribution is whether or not the action achieves what they think the protagonist of the stories desires and intends. The implication is that, for these children, following one's moral understanding is not what one typically intends. In agreement with this interpretation, Asendorpf and Nunner-Winkler (1992) found that moral emotion attribution was related, in five- to six-year-old boys but not in girls of the same age, to the ability to resist the temptation to cheat.

It is possible that the integration of moral understanding and motivation is not achieved at approximately the same age for the whole body of moral norms and virtues, but must be worked out separately for different issues. Plausibly this kind of integration depends on the general expectations of obligation and on the intensity of the motives that are in competition with moral motives. In Nunner-Winkler et al.'s (1988) study, 88 percent of eight-year-olds made a moral emotion attribution in a situation of theft; however, when a group of seven- and eight-year-olds was presented with three different situations concerning sharing and helping, 40 to 64 percent (across the three situations) gave a wish-oriented attribution, even though the large majority (80 to 94 percent) understood the intrinsic validity of the relevant norms (Nunner-Winkler, 1993).

In an unrelated study, Davis (1990) interviewed first, fourth, and eighth grade children (there were 10 boys and 10 girls in each group) and asked them to predict the emotion that would be experienced by the protagonist of the worst of three hypothetical cases of revenge, as judged by each child. The coding categories combined the positive or negative quality of the emotions and the reasons given for them. Davis found that 20 percent of first graders, 50 percent of fourth graders, and 78 percent of eighth graders made a moral emotion attribution, that is, justified the attributed emotions, whether positive or negative, on moral grounds.

In sum, the obligation for altruistic behavior is normally less stringent than the obligation to refrain from stealing. Therefore, even older children made fewer moral emotion attributions in the first than in the latter situation. In the case of revenge, the desire to strike back and get even can be felt very intensely, even when one understands revenge to be morally wrong. It is not surprising, then, that the integration of moral understanding and motivation is acquired later for this issue and may remain somewhat uncertain.

## Moral Understanding, Temptation, Effort, and Responsibility

Most of us experience, on occasion, the "willingness of the spirit" and the "weakness of the flesh," instances when the rationality of morality and the beauty of the ethical ideal move our desire, but we are ultimately unable to express in action what we know and wish. Even when understanding, emotions, and motivation are reasonably well integrated, there may be a significant split between our desires and what could be called the agentic system of our personality.

This system can be thought of as a complex organization of skills and attitudes, including the capacity to translate desires into intentions, to focus one's attention on the goal and away from distracting objects and ideas, to inhibit and control contrary impulses and to delay gratification, to create time-ordered plans and to persist on one's tasks. Essentially what is called here *agentic system* corresponds to what, in times past, was referred to as strength of the will or character, the mark of a trustworthy and reliable person. From the perspective of this chapter, the integration of moral understanding and motives with the agentic system should produce a very important result, namely, the sense of mastery and ownership of one's moral demands and, therefore, the acceptance of moral accountability toward oneself and others. Ideally one ought to be able to approach one's actions, whether one judges them to be morally right or wrong, with the feeling that they are precisely what one intended to do and that one is fully responsible for them.[4]

There is a rich body of research concerning various components of the agentic system, for instance, the development of intentionality (e.g., Piaget, 1932/1965; Keasey, 1978), of the understanding of causality in general and of psychological causality in particular (e.g., Poulin-Dubois and Shultz, 1988; Shultz and Kastenbaum, 1985), of impulse control (e.g., Mischel, 1981), and resistance to temptation (e.g., Casey and Burton, 1986; Wright, 1971). By and large these processes have been studied in isolation from each other and without relating them, in any direct way, to the development of moral understanding and of moral functioning in general (the exceptions are the Piagetian study of intentionality and the study of resistance to temptation). In sum, there is no clear sense of how these different aspects may come together to produce a functionally coherent psychological system and how this agentic system may take different forms with development. However, it seems intuitively obvious that, for instance, the capacity for self-control, or the sense of responsibility and accountability continue to develop long past childhood. In addition, one may expect situational, individual, and developmental variations in the extent to which the agentic system is integrated with moral understanding and values.

An attempt was made to study one specific aspect of moral agency, namely, the development of the understanding of accountability, in the context of a broader project on responsibility development (Blasi, 1984). Three groups of children and adolescents from first, sixth, and eleventh grade were presented, in a series of individual interviews, with hypothetical moral situations (the situations varied from five for first graders to seven for eleventh graders and, while differing in age appropriate details, were of the same general nature across the grades). In the last section of the interview, participants were told what the protagonist ended up doing and what the consequences of the action were (one or another form of punishment); then they were asked questions about the protagonist's accountability: Whose fault was it that all this happened? Who should be blamed for the consequences? Children were asked to explain their thinking and their answers were carefully probed.

Some of the participants' reasons concerned the moral evaluation of the actions; others had to do with the degree and limits of the protagonists' accountability and indicate subjects' understanding of moral agency. The latter considerations were grouped in categories: these and the extent of their use by each grade are reported in Table 9-1.

If it can be assumed that what one understands broadly corresponds to what one experiences, then we must conclude that children of different ages have significantly different agentic systems and, therefore, experience their moral actions in very different ways.

The large majority of first graders, at least for some of the stories, externalized blame. In the language of this chapter, they did not always seem able to integrate their moral understanding and their agentic system. About half of the sixth graders and practically none of the eleventh graders manifested this kind of difficulty.

Approximately 50 percent of the first-grade group was able to acknowledge, at least sometimes, the accountability of the protagonists; in doing so, these children used only three main criteria: the physical causation of the action, knowledge of the norms or of the consequences, and intention. In other words, their agentic system seems to be still relatively simple; and yet, since knowledge and intention exclusively belong to the agent and clearly differentiate the agent from other potential causes, these processes allow for a better integration of moral norms and for a genuine, though limited, ownership of morality.[5]

**TABLE 9-1    Understanding of Moral Accountability: Percentage of Use of the Response Categories by Grade**

| Categories of Justifications in Attributing Responsibility | Percentage of Use | | | p-Values | | |
|---|---|---|---|---|---|---|
| | Gr. 1 (N=46) | Gr. 6 (N=30) | Gr. 11 (N=32) | 1-6 | 1-11 | 6-11 |
| 1. Others or the circumstances are to be blamed for triggering the action | 78 | 50 | 6 | + | *** | * |
| 2. The physical author of the action is to be blamed | 35 | 83 | 47 | * | | ++ |
| 3. Intention and knowledge are criteria for blame | 48 | 93 | 81 | * | +++ | |
| 4. Responsibility is limited by temptation, impulse, others' manipulation | 4 | 57 | 31 | ** | +++ | * |
| 5. Effort, willpower, ingenuity are a part of responsibility | 0 | 63 | 50 | *** | ** | |
| 6. Decision determines and increases responsibility | 9 | 87 | 94 | *** | *** | |
| 7. Psychological traits, social background limit responsibility | 4 | 10 | 59 | | ** | * |
| 8. One is responsible for the type of person one is | 0 | 10 | 56 | | ** | * |

*Note:* The figures indicate the percentage of children, in each age group, using a specific category at least once across all dilemmas; they were obtained by dividing the number of children using a category at least once by the total number of children in the group.

[a]P-values are based on two-tailed $X^2$ tests; symbols indicate respectively:

| | | | |
|---|---|---|---|
| + | .05 | * | .001 |
| ++ | .01 | ** | .0001 |
| +++ | .005 | *** | .00001 |

As manifested in the interviews, the agentic system of sixth graders includes, in addition to the above attitudes, certain characteristics that are completely absent in the younger group: There is a shift in focus from the action itself to the psychological environment in which the action is born; this environment is seen in a dramatic way, as a battle between moral values and other impulses; in this context, the determining factors and the bases for accountability are the agent's ingenuity, effort, and final decision. Many sixth graders, therefore, bring to morality several of their psychological resources: morality is thus theirs in a way that would have been unthinkable in earlier years.

Most adolescents in the oldest group did not differ from sixth graders in their understanding of accountability. In about half of them, however, there were indications that the domain of accountability was broadened even further to include, to some extent, one's personality traits. In this case, having a certain kind of personality is not seen as a limit of one's moral responsibility.

In sum, there seem to be two parallel developments from middle childhood through adolescence: the first concerns the increasing complexity of the agentic system and the broadening of the domain that the agentic system is called to master; the second is the integration with it of one's moral understanding and moral motivation. To what extent are these two developmental lines independent of each other; in what measure is the development of moral understanding (as reflected, for instance, in Kohlberg's stages) accompanied by, and a factor in, the increasing moral integration, are questions that still need to be addressed.

## Moral Understanding and Moral Identity

On purely conceptual grounds it seems likely that the highest degree of moral integration is achieved when one's moral understanding and concerns become a part of one's self-concept, of the specific way one views and defines oneself. When this occurs, morality not only becomes, at least in principle, one aspect of the total conscious organization of personality, but is also invested with additional motives and emotions. For instance, an adolescent girl would be interested in moral issues, try to find adequate moral solutions, and desire to do the morally right thing, not only because she understands the objective importance of altruism and justice, but because she views herself as a certain kind of person and wants to remain faithful to the ideal she has for herself.

Self-concepts, however, do vary and not simply in the specific contents that differentiate people from each other. They also vary, from age to age and from person to person, in their more formal characteristics, namely, in the degree of internal unity and coherence or in the "structural tightness" of the organization, and also in the degree of subjective importance that a self-concept has for the person. The term *identity,* as it is frequently used in psychology, refers to a particularly mature form of self-concept, one that is characterized by a strong sense of unity, by its salience in the person's consciousness, and by its ability to anchor the person's sense of stability, individuality, and purpose.

Erikson (e.g., 1959, 1968) who, more than anyone else in psychology, contributed to the description of identity and its development and inspired a large body of research on the topic, argued that ideals and ideology, particularly political, religious, and moral, are an essential component of identity. He had a theoretical reason for this claim: on one hand, ideology is a central aspect of any society; on the other, identity is expected to function as the critical link between society and personality; namely, it would allow society and culture to become constitutive of the conscious personality and the person to become a consciously integrated member of society. But the realization that the ideals one has for oneself are essential for a mature identity is a result of common observation and could be explained in different ways. Damon (1984), for example, operating from a rather different perspective than Erikson's, showed that, starting somewhere in mid-adolescence, morality becomes increasingly integrated with the self-concept.

Within Erikson's framework, several studies (Cauble, 1976; Podd, 1972; Poppen, 1974; Rowe and Marcia, 1980) tested the hypothesis of a significant correlation between the development of identity (typically using Marcia's, 1966, operationalizations) and stages of moral reasoning as described by Kohlberg. The findings are not consistent with each other. But even if it could be concluded that the development of moral reasoning and the development of identity proceed in a parallel way, this kind of research would tell us very little about the relations between moral development and identity, and even less about the integration of morality in one's identity.

In recent years, Gilligan (1982) approached the relation between morality and identity in a way that, in some respects, is opposite to Erikson's. She claims that there are two different orientations in morality: the first, characterized by a concern for care and responsibility, would be more typical of women; the second, characterized by an emphasis on social norms and justice, would be more frequent in men. She also claims that the psychological foundation for these two divergent moralities lies in the different sense of self and identity that women and men tend to have, a connected and relational self for women, and a separate, individualistic sense of self for men. Therefore, whereas Erikson was interested in the constitutive role that morality, and other ideals, play in identity, Gilligan stresses the role of identity in determining the nature of one's morality. Of course, this approach guarantees a certain degree of continuity and consistency between morality and identity. However, the problem of integration and of its various degrees still remains to be studied. In addition, Gilligan's solution presents a potential conceptual difficulty: in making morality dependent on psychological identity, the question of its rationality becomes so much harder to answer.

In the past few years I and my collaborators have been engaged in a series of studies with the ultimate goal of answering the question of the integration of morality in identity. Even though this project is still far from its goal, some aspects of the answer begin to appear.

The starting assumption, also shared with Damon (1984), is that morality and identity or the self-concept are separate psychological systems which only slowly, and sometimes imperfectly, come together and become integrated. From my viewpoint, a very important advantage of this position is to protect the autonomy of morality, namely, to accept that moral understanding and its validity are in principle independent of the person's psychological make-up. This assumption carries an equally important implication, which could be considered as an extension of the cognitive-developmental approach to moral development: a cognitively valid moral system should have the capacity, perhaps a very limited one, to affect the shape of one's personality. This is precisely what is involved in selecting moral understanding as the starting point and the cornerstone of moral integration.

The present project attempts to raise two broad questions: After its first appearance during adolescence, does identity (in the stronger sense adopted here) change and acquire different developmental forms, varying from each other in their degree of unity and coherence as well as in the importance that they have for the sense of self? Are there individual differences in the choice of morality as constitutive of one's identity?

The first question required a shift of emphasis toward the phenomenological aspect of identity and the construction of a new set of empirical definitions (Blasi, 1988). This work (initially guided by a reinterpretation of Loevinger's ego developmental categories—Loevinger, Wessler, and Redmore, 1970) has led us so far to the empirical verification of three different identity modes, which seem to follow each other in a developmental sequence (Blasi, 1993; Blasi and Milton, 1991; Glodis and Blasi, 1993).[6]

Each of these identity modes consists of a set of characteristics (in our studies these characteristics were assessed, independently of each other, from interview material), which tend to empirically cluster together and to form a psychologically coherent portrait. The first one, Social Role Identity, seems to precede the type of identity that Erikson (1959) considered to be a developmental milestone of adolescence. Here the self seems to be experienced as diffused in one's body and in one's typical or preferred actions. No inner psychological substance has yet been constructed that one can identify as the core aspect of oneself. To be sincere, then, simply means to tell the truth about one's actions and to behave in one's typical way. Finally, one's personality characteristics are not the object of special attachment and affective responses.

At the next identity mode, Identity Observed, the experience of self is dominated by the inner self, mostly spontaneous emotions and beliefs. This inner world is felt as personal, individual, unaffected by and perhaps inaccessible to other people, and therefore is seen as the true self. Insincerity now means to behave in a way that does not correspond to one's inner feelings and evokes strong self-condemnation. One's inner identity is seen as a natural given and as basically unchangeable. And yet one is affectively attached to it and feels responsible to faithfully express it. The third identity mode, Management of Identity, while still anchored in one's inner personality, works an important shift from the previous one: identity is now experienced as made up of values, ideals, and commitments, rather than of spontaneous emotions and thoughts. One's responsibility covers not only sincerity in expressing feelings, but, even more so, the construction of one's beliefs and values and the control of one's emotions. Self-betrayal is then understood as a serious violation of one's ideals and commitments: their hypothetical loss would be felt as the loss of one's identity.

Several samples were interviewed and classified according to these identity modes: a group of 24 sixth-grade boys and girls; two groups of high-school seniors, one of 15 women and another of 24 men and women; a group of 15 college-educated women in their thirties. According to our findings, two-thirds of our sixth graders expressed themselves according to the description of Social Role Identity; overall, Identity Observed was the modal mode (41 percent) of high-school seniors (the rest were either in transition from the lower mode or to the higher mode); only about 40 percent of the adult women were fully at the Management of Identity Mode, the others being at lower modes. Particularly relevant to the topic of this chapter is that these identity modes differ from each other in the degree of centrality that each has in the overall personality and in the sense of ownership and self-possession that each seems to involve. As a result, people who construct their identity on the basis of moral concerns may still differ significantly in their moral integration, depending on the mode with which they experience identity.

A small study (Blasi and Glodis, 1990) provided a preliminary confirmation of this expectation: a group of high-school seniors and one of young adults, all women (we had already assessed their identity mode and inquired about the ideal that they considered to be essential to their sense of self), were presented with the hypothetical case of a person who made a decision contradicting her ideal—the same ideal that each participant had chosen for herself. Subjects were asked to make an effort to experience the decision as their own and then to report their emotions and explain their reasons for the emotions. Those who had been classified at the Management of Identity Mode or in transition to it differed from the others in important respects: they expressed more intense negative emotions, referred more frequently to the chosen ideal, and more frequently justified their response in terms of self-inconsistency and lack of integrity.

The second question, about the ways people differ in the use of moral concerns for the construction of identity, has not been approached yet in any systematic manner. It seems clear, though, that only some people tend to shape their identity around moral values and that this difference does not exclusively depend on age, education, or identity mode. In one sample including high-school seniors and adults, all women, approximately 60 percent, chose either compassion and caring or a concern for justice as one of their two most central ideals from a list of ten (Blasi, 1993); in another sample of high-school seniors and adults, men and women, the same two moral ideals were chosen by 25 percent of the subjects as one of the two most essential for their identity.

However, the question concerning the factors that account for these choices—life experiences, models one was exposed to, personality characteristics, etc.—still remains to be answered. On the basis of our subjects' replies to the interview questions, people seem to have objective reasons for choosing a specific ideal for themselves, acknowledging, that is, its validity and objective importance, independent of subjective preferences. None of our subjects claimed to have chosen his or her ideal for purely subjective psychological reasons or for no reason at all. However, our subjects gave objective reasons for all the ideals on the list, and not only for the moral ones, and recognized the appeal that most of the ideals had for them. In addition, they tended to insist that objective considerations alone are insufficient; there has to be a degree of subjective resonance, a sense of fitness between the ideal and the sense of who they are, of their capacities and limits.

One can state the same conclusion in somewhat different terms: morality appears to have been understood and to have been considered as important by practically everyone, including those who did not select it as the basis of their identity. In other words, moral concerns do not seem to require this strong identity integration in order to be effective in one's life. This much could be predicted from cognitive-developmental theory. But cognitive-developmental theory cannot account for the choice of moral ideals over other ideals, when many ideals are grounded on objective considerations of social and community living. As many of our subjects argued, many ideals need to be pursued for the common good, but they cannot and need not be pursued all by every person; the fact that people select different ideals for their identity leaves each person free to pursue what seems to be most consonant with what one is and thus to develop his or her individual identity.

## Moral Self-Deception and Its Disintegrating Power

It is a truism that moral ideals and moral intentions provide frequent opportunities for distortion, self-deception, and defensive maneuvers, and that it is almost impossible, at times, to extricate the ones from the others. According to some theories, the whole moral enterprise is nothing but a disguise for very different motives, ranging from aggression and hostility, power and greed, to the more acceptable but still mundane need to compensate for one's inferiority and lack of self-esteem. This understanding of the nature of morality, cynical or realistic as it might be judged, has been with us at least since Socrates' times, but has received renewed support in contemporary culture, particularly through Nietzsche's (e.g., 1887/1956) and Freud's (e.g., 1923/1961) arguments.

The problems with this view are well-known: while it is not difficult to list instances of distorting uses of morality, there is no evidence for the belief that morality is nothing but disguise and pretense. In fact this belief is such a radical departure from everyday language and common understanding that, if correct, it would require a complete reformulation of those accepted meanings that regulate social exchange and social life in general.

It seems much more useful, instead, to inquire about the *specific factors* that lead to and explain the distorting use of morality. Some of these may have to do with situations and life conditions, others may be related to personality characteristics. Two general hypotheses could be stated about the latter:

1. Self-deception concerning morality can only occur in a person who understands morality and for whom morality has a genuine motivational power. The presence of moral self-deception, then, could be taken as an indication

that moral understanding has been integrated, to some extent, in one's personality.

2. Moral self-deception is less likely to occur, the stronger is the motivational power of morality and the more central are moral concerns and ideals to a person's sense of self.

These two propositions, which will be left here unelaborated and unargued, together tie the probability of self-deception to the degree of moral integration.

From the opposite perspective, not only does moral self-deception depend on moral integration, but, in its turn, it can have the effect of seriously limiting and even reversing the integration of morality in personality. On the one hand, in fact, moral integration, as understood here, seems to be driven by conscious intentions. On the other, the very function of self-deceptive and defensive processes is to limit the accessibility to awareness of whatever information could be experienced as threatening, to isolate it and make it unavailable for overall integration.[7]

Moral self-deception can occur at several levels, in fact, at any one of the levels at which moral integrity is worked out. At the level of general moral understanding self-deception could prevent access to that information which potentially could compel a revision of one's ideas. More frequently self-deception seems to operate on the process of applying our general moral understanding to specific instances. Depending on whether a certain course of action is seen to facilitate or hinder the satisfaction of our desires, we can manipulate the overall construction of the situation to make it either relevant or irrelevant to the way we understand moral obligation.

Similar distortions could be present at the level of emotional and motivational integration: for instance, one could reinterpret an emotional response as nonmoral or simply isolate it from one's consciousness, whenever that response would provide a clue for one's obligation; similarly, in processing the various motives that are elicited by a specific situation, one could focus on one and deemphasize another, or exaggerate the subjective or objective importance of nonmoral motives.

Perhaps the most frequently used, and the best documented, moral distortion consists of splitting one's moral understanding and sense of obligation from one's agentic system. One could convince oneself that one did not intend one's behavior or its consequences, that the temptation was overwhelming or one's impulses too strong (once again, see Shapiro's, 1965, description of the impulsive style); that others should be blamed for the events; that one is weak and incompetent, saddled by other responsibilities, and, in any case, only following orders.

Self-deception, finally, also could creep in at the level of one's self-concept and identity. The most obvious examples may be the belief that one is a moral compassionate person or that one deeply cares about other people, when reality is quite different; or the successful attempt to maintain a high degree of self-satisfaction while frequently disregarding the ideals with which one identifies. A different case, less obvious but perhaps no less frequent, concerns the person who intellectually understands the importance of morality, but succeeds in divorcing this understanding from the construction of ideals for self and of identity—because moral concerns are impractical, unrealistic, old-fashioned; because one is burdened with powerful contrary impulses; because one cannot change one's personality, etc.

The assumption underlying this discussion is that moral integration can only be achieved within a genuine understanding of what morality involves in the real world of people—a point with which this chapter was started—and that, in addition, it requires the perception, in daily practice, of how moral concerns and ideals affect the reality of one's emotions and self-concept.

Unfortunately very little empirical work has been done on the use of defensive maneuvers in the context of morality. Haan, Aerts, and Cooper (1985) inquired about the effect of using coping or defensive ego strategies on the adequacy of moral understanding in concrete group situations; they reported that the absence of isolation—defensively separating related ideas and feelings—of displacement, and of defensive intellectualization, all made significant contributions to the level of moral understanding in middle and late adolescents. Hart and Chmiel (1992), working on Kohlberg's longitudinal data, similarly found a relationship between the use of coping strategies (as opposed to defense mechanisms) and progression in moral stage. Perhaps the most promising attempt to capture distortions in morality is the ongoing project by Krebs and colleagues (Denton and Krebs, 1990; Krebs, Denton, Carpendale, Vermeulen, Bartek, and Bush, 1989). While their interest is in describing variations in moral reasoning under different conditions, some of the observations have the unmistakable flavor of self-deception.

There are no empirical data relevant to the hypotheses presented above, concerning the role of individual differences in self-deception and the effect of self-deception on moral integration and functioning. Of course, the problems of methodology and operationalization are overwhelming. And yet it seems impossible to study the way people actually experience their moral life, without an accurate description of moral self-deceptions and of the strategies used to avoid them.

## Concluding Remarks: Moral Integration and Moral Action

In these pages I tried to articulate a concept of moral integration not so much by describing its abstract characteristics, but by discussing various nodal points through which morality slowly becomes a central aspect of one's personality: the role of personal understanding; the investment of emotions and motives with moral meanings and, vice-versa, the insertion of morality in one's motivational system; the development of the agentic system—intentions, self-control and effort, responsibility, and commitment—at the service of moral concerns; finally, the incorporation of moral understanding and ideals in one's self-concept and sense of identity.

I said nothing here about moral behavior and its prediction. This may seem surprising, particularly in view of my earlier emphases (Blasi, 1980, 1983). It may also be seen as a serious neglect, both because of the practical importance that the issue has for society and because of the way psychology typically defines itself as a scientific enterprise.

While the emphasis on behavior is understandable, there is something deeply odd about psychology's goal to predict moral action. If the nature of moral action, as I argued, must be defined by common social understanding and everyday language, and if, from this perspective, individual freedom and responsibility are essential prerequisites of moral praiseworthiness and blameworthiness, then a project of scientific prediction, assuming as it must the absence of individual freedom, does not seem to be compatible with the nature of the action that it attempts to predict.

The emphasis of this chapter on moral integration and on the moral personality attenuates the sharpness of this problem. Even if some day psychologists were able to isolate those variables and conditions that are reliably related to different kinds of moral personality, the link between personality and specific moral actions would remain to a large extent indeterminate. Of course, I do not mean to suggest that people's moral personality is irrelevant to the way they conduct their life. If a person, time after time, were to behave contrary to his or her moral beliefs, one could question the extent to which these beliefs have been successfully integrated. However, in studying the relation of moral integration to moral conduct, the appropriate unit cannot be the individual action, but must be expanded to comprise a stretch of a person's life.

The shift in emphasis from moral action to moral personality would have, then, the additional advantage of introducing the time dimension in the questions one asks and the kind of information one pursues, remedying perhaps some of the triviality that mars much empirical work in this field. For instance, we may become more sensitive to the fact that the way a person responds to his or her behavior and to its consequences would be quite pertinent to the assessment of moral integration in addition to behavior itself. Whether or not one resists the temptation to rationalize the action or to externalize blame and the extent to which one accepts the responsibility; whether one attempts to compensate for the damages inflicted on other people, accepts to experience guilt, analyzes the circumstances and tries to figure out more realistic plans to deal with similar problems in the future, are all relevant in determining the full meaning of the action. At the limit, only a life can fully clarify the quality of moral integration: its various events and experiences could then be seen (as in the biographical data reported by Colby and Damon, 1992) for the role they play in affecting the integration of the person's morality.

## Endnotes

1. In their recent work on self-determination theory, Deci and Ryan (e.g., 1985, 1991), starting from a broad organismic perspective, articulated a concept of integration that is rather congenial with the approach of this chapter. Particularly relevant are the relations that Deci and Ryan established with intrinsic motivation and autonomy and the different levels of integration that they described.

2. The importance of commonsense and everyday understanding for the definition of morality is discussed by Berlin (1979), Winch (1958), and many others (see also Blasi, 1990).

3. For a general theory of motivation that does not reduce motives and interests to basic needs, but makes them dependent on the nature of their specific objects, see Nuttin (1984).

4. Shapiro (1965), in his description of the impulsive neurotic style, provides an interesting portrait of what could be considered as the extreme expression of a poor agentic system.

5. These findings suggest a much slower development of moral intentionality than is typically reported in Piagetian literature (e.g., Keasey, 1977). One should keep in mind, however, that the methodology followed in the study reported here would tend to underestimate the child's capacities and to bring out, instead, the child's more typical way of thinking. Our stories, in fact, did not provide any clues about the factors that could be relevant in accountability while the questions required that children construct, entirely on their own, an explanation that readily made sense to them.

6. A fifth mode, Identity as Authenticity, was also derived from Loevinger's categories. In our project we did not attempt to independently study this mode.

7. Defense mechanisms seem to present a double face with regard to integration: while they do work against a more encompassing synthesis, they do so in order to protect a fragile and narrower ego integrity.

## References

Allport, G. W. (1961). *Pattern and growth in personality*. New York: Holt, Rinehart, and Winston.

Aronfreed J. (1968). *Conduct and conscience. The socialization of internalized control over behavior*. New York: Academic Press.

Asendorpf, J. B., and Nunner-Winkler, G. (1992). Children's moral motive strength and temperamental inhibition reduce their immoral behavior in real moral conflicts. *Child Development, 63*, 1223-1235.

Ausubel, D. P. (1952). *Ego development and the personality disorders*. New York: Grune and Stratton.

Behrends, R. S., and Blatt, S. J. (1985). Internalization and psychological development through the life cycle. *Psychoanalytic Study of the Child, 40*, 11-39.

Berlin, I. (1979). *Four essays on liberty*. Oxford: Oxford University Press. (Original work published 1969).

Blasi, A. (1980). Bridging moral cognition and moral action: A critical review of the literature. *Psychological Bulletin, 88*, 1-45.

Blasi, A. (1983). The self and cognition: The roles of the self in the acquisition of knowledge and the role of cognition in the development of the self. In B. Lee and G. G. Noam (Eds.), *Psychosocial theories of the self* (pp. 189-213). New York: Plenum Press.

Blasi, A. (1984). Autonomie im Gehorsam: Die Entwicklung des Distanzierungsvermogens im sozialisierten Handeln [Autonomy in obedience: The development of distancing in socialized action]. In W. Edelstein and J. Habermas (Eds.), *Soziale Interaktion und soziales Verstehen* (pp. 300-347). Frankfurt an Main: Suhrkamp.

Blasi, A. (1988). Identity and the development of the self. In D. K. Lapsley and F. C.

Power (Eds.), *Self, ego, and identity: Integrative approaches* (pp. 226-242). New York: Springer-Verlag.

Blasi, A. (1990). How should psychologists define morality? or, The negative side effects of philosophy's influence on psychology. In T. E. Wren (Ed.), *The moral domain: Essays in the ongoing discussion between philosophy and the social sciences* (pp. 38-70). Cambridge, MA: MIT Press.

Blasi, A. (1993). The development of identity: Some implications for moral functioning. In G. G. Noam and T. E. Wren (Eds.), *The moral self: Building a better paradigm* (pp. 99-122). Cambridge, MA: MIT Press.

Blasi, A., and Glodis, K. (1990). *Response to self-betrayal and the development of the sense of self.* Unpublished manuscript, University of Massachusetts at Boston.

Blasi, A., and Milton, K. (1991). The development of the sense of self in adolescence. *Journal of Personality, 59,* 217-242.

Casey, W. M., and Burton, R. V. (1986). The social-learning theory approach. In G. L. Sapp (Ed.), *Handbook of moral development: Models, processes, techniques, and research* (pp. 74-91). Birmingham, AL: Religious Education Press.

Cauble, M. A. (1976). Formal operations, ego identity, and principled morality: Are they related? *Developmental Psychology, 12,* 363-364.

Colby, A., and Damon, W. (1992). *Some do care: Contemporary lives of moral commitment.* New York: Free Press.

Damon, W. (1984). Self-understanding and moral development from childhood to adolescence. In W. M. Kurtines and J. L. Gewirtz (Eds.), *Morality, moral behavior, and moral development* (pp. 109-127). New York: Wiley.

Davis, S. A. (1990). *Children's concepts of revenge and justice.* Unpublished Seniors Honors Thesis, University of Massachusetts at Boston.

Deci, E. L., and Ryan, R. M. (1985). *Intrinsic motivation and self-determination in human behavior.* New York: Plenum.

Deci, E. L., and Ryan, R. M. (1991). A motiva-

tional approach to self: Integration in personality. In R. Dienstbier (Ed.), *Nebraska Symposium on Motivation: Perspectives on motivation* (Vol. 38, pp. 237-288). Lincoln, NE: University of Nebraska Press.

Denton, K., and Krebs, D. (1990). The effect of alcohol and social context on moral judgment. *Journal of Personality and Social Psychology, 59,* 242-248.

Erikson, E. H. (1959). Identity and the life cycle. *Psychological Issues, 1,* No. 1.

Erikson, E. H. (1968). *Identity: Youth and crisis.* New York: Norton.

Freud, S. (1961). The ego and the id. In J. Strachey (Ed. and Trans.), *The standard edition of the complete psychological works of Sigmund Freud* (Vol. 19, pp. 3-66). London: Hogarth Press. (Original work published 1923).

Gilligan, C. (1982). *In a different voice.* Cambridge, MA: Harvard University Press.

Glodis, K., and Blasi, A. (1993). The sense of self and identity among adolescents and adults. *Journal of Adolescent Research, 8,* 356-380.

Grusec, J. E., and Goodnow, J. J. (1994). Impact of parental discipline on the child's internalization of values: A reconceptualization of current points of view. *Developmental Psychology, 30,* 4-19.

Haan, N., Aerts, E., and Cooper, B. A. B. (1985). *On moral grounds: The search for practical morality.* New York: New York University Press.

Hart, D., and Chmiel, S. (1992). Influence of defense mechanisms on moral judgment development: A longitudinal study. *Developmental Psychology, 28,* 722-730.

Havens, L. (1986). A theoretical basis for the concepts of self and authentic self. *Journal of the American Psychoanalytic Association, 34,* 363-378.

Hoffman, M. L. (1977). Empathy, its development and prosocial implications. In C. B. Keasey (Ed.), *Nebraska Symposium on Motivation* (Vol. 25, pp. 169-217). Lincoln, NE: University of Nebraska Press.

Hoffman, M. L. (1994). Discipline and internalization. *Developmental Psychology, 30,* 26-28.

Keasey, C. B. (1978). Children's developing awareness and usage intentionality and motives. In C. B. Keasey (Ed.), *Nebraska Symposium on Motivation* (Vol. 25, pp. 219-260). Lincoln, NE: University of Nebraska Press.

Kochanska, G. (1994). Beyond cognition: Expanding the search for the early roots of internalization and conscience. *Developmental Psychology, 30,* 20-22.

Krebs, D. L., Denton, K., Carpendale, J. I., Vermeulen, S., Bartek, S., and Bush, A. (1989). The many faces of moral judgment. In M. A. Luszcz and T. Nettelbeck (Eds.), *Psychological development: Perspectives across the life-span* (pp. 97-105). New York: Elsevier Science Publishers.

Loevinger, J., Wessler, R., and Redmore, C. (1970). *Measuring ego development: II. Scoring manual for women and girls.* San Francisco: Jossey-Bass.

Marcia, J. E. (1966). Development and validation of ego identity status. *Journal of Personality and Social Psychology, 3,* 551-558.

Matthews, K. A., Batson, C. D., Horn, J., and Rosenman, R. H. (1981). "Principles in his nature which interest him in the fortune of others. . .": The heritability of empathic concern for others. *Journal of Personality, 49,* 237-247.

Meissner, W. W. (1981). *Internalization in Psychoanalysis.* New York: International Universities Press.

Mischel, W. (1981). Metacognition and the rules of delay. In J. H. Flavell and L. Ross (Eds.), *Social cognitive development: Frontiers and possible futures* (pp. 240-271). Cambridge: Cambridge University Press.

Nietzsche, F. (1956). *The genealogy of morals: An attack* (F. Golffing, Trans.). New York: Doubleday. (Original work published 1887).

Nisan, M. (1988). The child as a philosopher of values: Development of a distinct perception of values in childhood. *Journal of Moral Education, 17,* 172-182.

Nunner-Winkler, G. (1993). The growth of moral motivation. In G. G. Noam, and T. E. Wren (Eds.), *The moral self: Building a better paradigm* (pp. 269-291). Cambridge, MA: MIT Press.

Nunner-Winkler, G., and Sodian, B. (1988). Children's understanding of moral emotions. *Child Development, 59,* 1323-1328.

Nuttin, J. (1984). *Motivation. planning and action: A relational theory of behavior dynamics* (R. P. Lorion and J. E. Dumas, Trans.). Hillsdale, N.J.: Erlbaum.

Odier, C. (1947). *Les deux sources. consciente et inconsciente. de la vie morale* [The two sources, conscious and unconscious, of moral life]. Neuchatel, Switzerland: Editions de la Baconnière.

Perry, D. (1994). Comments on Grusec and Goodnow (1994) model of the role of discipline in moral internalization. *Developmental Psychology, 30,* 23-25.

Piaget, J. (1965). *The moral judgment of the child.* New York: The Free Press. (Original work published 1932).

Podd, M. H. (1972). Ego identity status and morality. *Developmental Psychology, 6,* 497-507.

Poppen, P. J. (1974). *The development of sex differences in moral judgment for college males and females.* Unpublished Doctoral Dissertation, Cornell University.

Poulin-Dubois, D., and Shultz, T. R. (1988). The development of the understanding of human behavior: From agency to intentionality. In J. W. Astington, P. L. Harris, and D. R. Olson (Eds.), *Developing theories of mind* (pp. 109-125). Cambridge: Cambridge University Press.

Rich, J. M. (1986). Morality, reason, and emotion. In S. Modgil and C. Modgil (Eds.), *Lawrence Kohlberg: Consensus and controversy* (pp. 209-222). London: Falmer Press.

Rowe, I., and Marcia, J. E. (1980). Ego identity status, formal operations, and moral development. *Journal of Youth and Adolescence, 9,* 87-99.

Sandler, J., Holder, A., and Meers, D. (1963). The ego ideal and the ideal self. *Psychoanalytic Study of the Child, 18,* 139-158.

Schafer, R. (1972). Internalization. *Psychoanalytic Study of the Child, 27,* 411-436.

Shapiro, D. (1965). *Neurotic Styles.* New York: Basic Books.

Shultz, T. R., and Kastenbaum, N. R. (1985). Causal reasoning in children. *Annals of Child Development, 2,* 195-249.

Solomon, R. C. (1990). *Passion for justice.* Reading, MA: Addison-Wesley.

Veyne, P. (1987). Introduction. In P. Aries and G. Duby (Gen. Eds.), *A history of private life: I. From pagan Rome to Byzantium* (pp. 1-3). Cambridge, MA: Harvard University Press.

Wilson, E. O. (1975). *Sociobiology: The new synthesis.* Cambridge, MA: Harvard University Press.

Winch, P. (1958). *The idea of a social science and its relation to philosophy.* London: Routledge and Kegan Paul.

Winnicott, D. W. (1965). Ego distortion in terms of true and false self. In D. W. Winnicott, *The maturational processes and the facilitating environment* (pp. 140-152). London: Hogarth Press.

Wright, D. (1971). *The psychology of moral behavior.* Baltimore, MD: Penguin Books.

# Chapter 10

# Eudaimonic Theory: Self-Realization and the Collective Good

ALAN S. WATERMAN
Trenton State College

## Abstract

This chapter seeks to reconcile the individual and society from the perspective of psychological individualism. Psychological individualism aims to reconcile the individual and society by demonstrating that individualistic psychological functioning yields beneficial outcomes both to the individual and society. This chapter seeks to bring psychological theory and research to bear on the debate over the moral priorities of individual and collective interests. It does do so from a particular philosophical perspective, *eudaimonism,* a philosophy in which the moral priority is assigned to the individual in terms of promoting self-realization. As the term is used in this chapter, the daimon refers to those potentialities of each person, the realization of which represents the greatest fulfillment in living of which each is capable. The daimon is an ideal in the sense of being an excellence, a perfection toward which one strives and, hence, it can give meaning and direction to one's life. According to the ethics of eudaimonism, each individual is obliged to know and to live in truth to his daimon, thereby progressively actualizing an excellence that is his innately and potentially. Eudaimonism provides the means for reconciling the interest of the individual and of society. Finding the center of strength within ourselves is in the long run the best contribution we can make to our fellow human beings. Evidence is presented, based on an extensive literature review, regarding the benefits to both the individual and society that are derived from each of the qualities of personal functioning. Implications for moral education are discussed in terms of application to counseling aimed at improving career choices and the quality of interpersonal relationships.

One of the perennial controversies within moral philosophy concerns the relative priorities to be assigned to the individual and to society in the determination of what constitutes moral action. There are philosophers who have made individual self-interest the measure of all things moral, for example, the hedonism of Aristippus of Cyrene (Tatarkiewicz, 1976), the egoism of Stirner (1973), and the nihilism of Nietzsche (1954). Others have decried this emphasis on self, for example, Hobbes (1651/1957) for whom self-interest produces a war of all against all that is antithetical to civilized functioning, or the Bhuddists for whom the self is an obstacle that must be transcended. Correspondingly, there are philosophers who have assigned moral priority to the collective, the maintenance and advancement of which is the prime, if not sole, end to be pursued, for example, the utilitarianism of Bentham (1789/1948) and the dialectical materialism of Marx (1867/1932). These, in turn, have had their implacable critics for whom the benefit of the collective is seen as bought at the cost of the trampling of individual rights (Hayek, 1948; Rand, 1964). But even when moral priority has been set at one end of the continuum of individual vs. collective interests, it is not unusual for philosophers to argue that the interests at the other end of the continuum will be advanced as well. For example, Adam Smith (1797/1981) reasoned that each individual pursuing personal self-interest will, through the invisible hand of the market, be producing benefits for the society as a whole. On the other side of the philosophical debate, Marx (1867/1932) argued that working for the good of the collective was the surest way improve the lot of individuals.

In this chapter, I will be seeking to bring psychological theory and research to bear on the debate over the moral priorities of individual and collective interests. I will do so from a particular philosophical perspective, *eudaimonism*, a philosophy in which the moral priority is assigned to the individual in terms of promoting self-realization. I have chosen this philosophical perspective because its value assumptions provide the foundation for many strands of contemporary personality theory, including the psychosocial analysis of Erikson (1963, 1968), the psychological humanism of Maslow (1968, 1970a), key constructs in the social learning perspectives of Bandura (1982) and Rotter (1966), and the cognitive-developmental theorizing of Kohlberg (1969) and Gilligan (1982). In advancing a position in which moral priority is assigned to individual interests, I am not unmindful of the value of collective interests. Indeed, a central tenet of my work in the development of a theory of psychological individualism has been the proposition that promoting self-realization "greatly enhances the likelihood that persons will engage in productive and satisfying interdependent behavior" (Waterman, 1981, p. 762). If maintaining a dialectical dichotomy between individual and societal interests is neither conceptually necessary nor predictively useful, then the advancement of a philosophical ideal entailing the compatible incorporation of both interests is a plausible objective.

Before turning to the specifics of eudaimonistic philosophy, its embodiment in contemporary theories of personality, and research on self-realization and moral functioning, it will be helpful to address briefly the ways in which psychological theories and empirical research can appropriately be employed in the process of ethical inquiry (Waterman, 1988). To advance the claim that the moral priority should be assigned to the individual in terms of promoting self-realization is to make a normative ethical statement, that is, it is a statement as to what ought to be done. Normative ethical statements can be justified either on the basis of teleological considerations or on deontological grounds.

Philosophical teleologists claim that a behavior has moral value because of its consequences. In doing so, they are making two types of assertions: (a) The behavior has certain specifiable consequences, and (b) those consequences are to be valued. The former is an issue of fact and is open to empirical confirmation or disconfirmation. It is here that psychology as an empirical science can make a useful contribution to the process of ethical inquiry. Can the behavior in question be shown to actually yield the benefits claimed for it? The latter assertion is not empirical, however, but criteriological. The adequacy of any statement that some types of consequences constitute a better criteria of moral value than do other types of outcomes can be judged only in philosophical terms.

To advance a deontological moral position is to reason on an a priori basis, that is, to claim that an act or a rule is right without respect to the consequences it produces. The results of empirical psychological investigations can play no direct role in the evaluation of deontological analyses. The adequacy of deontological claims can be judged only by philosophical criteria.

The eudaimonistic claim that moral priority should be assigned to the individual in terms of promoting self-realization can be advanced on either teleological or deontological grounds. As a psychologist working in the domain of morality, my efforts here will be addressed to evaluating the teleological analysis used to support the claim, that is, I will address questions of the consequences of actions to further self-realization. I am hypothesizing that such actions yield beneficial outcomes both to individuals and to the interdependent relationships providing the context in which individuals function. If empirical research results show benefits to the individual but not to others, then the controversy continues over whether moral priority should be assigned to the individual or to society. But if both parts of this hypothesis can be sustained by research findings it will suggest that eudaimonist moral philosophy offers us a means to transcend the conflict of individual vs. collective interests.

With respect to deontological justifications for eudaimonism, the outcome of the empirically based analysis to be offered here is not germane. However, even a deontologist may wish to know whether the right (as derived from reason or intuition) is also the beneficial (as determined empirically). A finding that the right and the beneficial coincide offers the possibility of a rapprochement between deontological and teleological approaches to moral philosophy.

## Theory

### The Philosophy of Eudaimonism

Eudaimonism (pronounced yōo dē' mən iz''m) is an ethical theory that calls upon people to recognize and live in accordance with the *daimon* or "true self." The theory extends at least as far back as classic Hellenic philosophy where it received its most notable treatment in Aristotle's (1985) *The Nicomachean Ethics*. Contemporary presentations of eudaimonistic ethics are provided by May (1969) and Norton (1976).

As the term will be used here, the daimon refers to those potentialities of each person, the realization of which represents the greatest fulfillment in living of which each is capable. These include both the potentialities that are shared by all humans by virtue of our common specieshood and those unique potentials that distinguish each individual from all others. The daimon is an ideal in the sense of being an excellence, a perfection toward which one strives and, hence, it can give meaning and direction to one's life. The efforts a person makes to live in accordance with the daimon, to realize those potentials, can be said to be personally expressive.

According to the ethics of eudaimonism, each individual "is obliged to know and to live in truth to his daimon, thereby progressively actualizing an excellence that is his innately and potentially" (Norton, 1976, ix). This spirit underlies two famous classical Greek injunctions: "Know thyself" and "Become what you are." To choose in Norton's (1976) phrase, "to live freely the life that is one's own" is an affirmation of personal responsibility and a statement of personal integrity. It requires that a commitment be made both to the principles by which one chooses to live and the goals toward which one's life is to be directed. This commitment involves a conscious recognition and acknowledgment of personal truths already known intuitively.

### The Nature and Scope of the Daimon

To define the daimon in terms of potential excellences would seem to suggest that it is something characteristic of only a few great men and women. If one accepts the view that there is a natural lottery of abilities, the potentials of some people may be claimed to be "better" than the potentials of others. But such a position was not intended by either the classical or contemporary proponents of eudaimonism. Rather, the daimon is seen as universal, possessed in varying forms by all, though expressed in widely varying degrees. As Norton (1976) has shown, there is no way of demonstrating the existence of unequal potentialities, only unequal performances can be observed. While each individual has his or her own distinctive potential excellences, thereby allowing for the possibility of a great diversity of excellent accomplishments, it is unclear what standards could be applied to judge some excellences as being of more worth than others.

When it is claimed that the daimon is universal, the assumption is made that there exist for each person some actions, which because they actualize personal potential excellences, will yield greater self-expression and self-fulfillment than could be derived from activities in any other direction. The relevant set of norms for understanding daimonic potentials is not external, using others as a basis for comparison, but internal, comparing the relative possibilities of progressively actualizing the potentials for excellence among the myriad of goals that might be pursued. It is with respect to the areas of the individual's highest potentials that philosophers refer when they speak of potential excellences toward which the person is morally obligated to strive.

Still, the actual range of expression of daimonic potentials will be very broad indeed. This is a result both of the difficulty of the tasks that some may feel called to undertake and as a result of people defaulting on their potentials in varying degrees. They may be limited by their environment to activities necessary for the satisfaction of needs that take precedence over the pursuit of self-fulfillment (e.g., those associated with survival). They may succumb to external social pressures directing them into other channels. They may allow themselves to be distracted by pleasures incompatible with the pursuit of their unique excellences. Or they may turn aside because of the arduous nature of the tasks that are theirs to do.

To speak of the daimon as personal potentialities capable of guiding action in the direction of self-fulfillment seems to invite granting it reified status. In part this is a carryover of its philosophical origins. Like the Roman genii, or tutelary gods, the daimon was conceived as originating externally to the individual as a kind of guiding spirit provided at birth. But the concept was later internalized, as reflected in the view of Heraclitus that "man's character is his daimon" (May, 1969, p. 133). To be consistent with the standards of contemporary theories, the daimon should be interpreted as being a number of interrelated psychological processes. If it is accepted that individuals by virtue of their physiology and/or experiences possess particular potentialities for excellence, some universal, some unique, then the daimon is constituted by those processes, both intuitive and reasoned, by which such potentialities are recognized and come to attain the status of personal goals to be actualized.

This is not the place to elaborate on a series of questions that are important to the understanding of the nature and scope of the daimon. These questions include (a) whether there is only one daimonic potential for each person or several, (b) whether there are daimonic potentials for destructive talents as well as those that are personally and socially productive, (c) the extent to which potential excellences are genetically determined and/or can be acquired in our lifetime, (d) the extent of malleability of daimonic potentials, (e) the role of agency in efforts toward the realization of such potentials, and (f) how we come to recognize our potential excellences and the means toward their realization. I have endeavored to provide at least a preliminary analysis of these questions elsewhere (Waterman, 1984a, 1984b, 1986).

*happiness — virtue — eikellie*

### Eudaimonia

When an individual is succeeding in living in truth to his or her daimon, it gives rise to a condition the Greeks called *eudaimonia*. The usual translation of eudaimonia in Aristotle's (1985) *The Nicomachean Ethics* is as happiness, but there is a controversy within philosophy over whether this is indeed a proper translation (Cooper, 1975; Kraut, 1979; Telfer, 1980).

In contemporary usage, the term "happiness" is generally considered to refer to hedonic happiness, a subjective experience that includes "the belief that one is getting the important things one wants, as well as certain pleasant affects that normally go along with this belief" (Kraut, 1979, p. 178). The most thoroughly consistent expression of hedonism as an ethical theory was advanced by Aristippus of Cyrene in the third century B.C., who held "that pleasure is the sole good, but also that only one's own physical, positive, momentary pleasure is a good and is so regardless of its cause" (Tatarkiewicz, 1976, p. 317).

Aristotle clearly rejected this Cyrenaic view of happiness. "The many, the most vulgar, seemingly conceive the good and happiness as pleasure, and hence they also like the life of gratification. Here they appear completely slavish, since the life they decide on is a life for grazing animals" (Aristotle, 1985, p. 7). Against this view of hedonic happiness Aristotle (1985) offers the proposition that eudaimonia (happiness) is "activity expressing virtue" (p. 284) where virtue may be variously considered to be the best thing, the best within us, or excellence (Ackrill, 1973; McDowell, 1980). According to Telfer (1980), eudaimonia embodies the idea, not that one is pleased with one's life, but that one has "what is worth desiring and worth having in life" (p. 37). This is to be taken as an objective statement as to the proper ends of each person.

### Reconciling the Individual and Society

May (1953) puts forth the eudaimonistic principle that "finding the center of strength within ourselves is in the long run the best contribution we can make to our fellow men" (p. 79). Advancements in the evolution of civilization, whether in the arts, the humanities, the sciences, technology, or other fields, have come from the striving of individuals to find solutions to the problems of the human situation experienced on a personal level. The creations brought forth through the expression of unique individual potentials are not just for private use and appreciation, but may be to the benefit of all. Such creativity appears to be facilitated by the social conditions that provide personal freedom and encourage the difficult task of self-realization.

The creativity of others benefits us not only through our access to their creations but in the psychological effect their work has on our activities in our own spheres of endeavor. This idea is described philosophically in the principle of the complementarity of excellences. "It affirms that every genuine excellence benefits from every other genuine excellence. It means that the best within every person calls upon and requires the best within every other person" (Norton, 1976, p. 10). This involves, in part, the value of having as models those who are succeeding in the expression of their individuality. The availability of models worthy of emulation is instructive both of what constitutes the fullest potential of human life and of the pathways by which it may be approached. No less important is the power of such models to inspire faith in our own potentials.

Eudaimonistic philosophy also embodies the ethical principle of universality (Norton, 1976). Each person is viewed as an end in himself or herself and not as a means toward the fulfillment of the interests of someone else. Every person has an equal right to strive for the attainment of personal goals, and hence there is the requirement that one not interfere with the rights of others in their similar strivings. Striving for self-realization contributes to the development of active awareness of the ethical value of respecting the integrity of others.

Norton (1976) describes the eudaimonist perspective on the reconciling of individual and social interests when he writes:

> The self-actualizing individual who knows his destiny [daimon] knows as well his dependence upon the excellence of others, and the worth of his excellence to them. It is true that neither the good society nor the good of others is his explicit aim, but that the good society is attained by the fulfillment of individuals would occasion in him no surprise, but only the confirmation of what he knew. (p. 143)

May (1969) goes a step further when he identifies the confluence of personal goals and "the expansion of interpersonal meaning" as the criterion for recognizing the moral aspects of one's daimon.

## A Theory of Psychological Individualism

### Psychological Perspectives on the Daimon

The philosophical definition of the daimon or "true self" in terms of potential excellences does not readily lend itself to use within the paradigms of empirical social science. Potentialities are not observable. One avenue for developing a psychological perspective on the daimon is through the concepts of aptitudes and talents. Aptitudes are observable, present performance indicators providing a basis for prediction of future performance that, with appropriate training and/or relevant experiences, a person can develop a high level of proficiency at particular skills. Aptitudes, then, are fallible predictors of the person's potentials. By extension, talents (or skills) represent the progress an individual has made in the development of his or her aptitudes. To develop a talent is to further the realization of a potential. As previously indicated, the relevant set of norms for assessing potential excellences are intraindividual, comparing each set of aptitudes and talents the person possesses with other aptitudes and talents that are also present. In other words, a person can potentially go farther in life by pursuing some avenues of activity than by pursuing others.

While furthering the development of one's aptitudes and talents is clearly one aspect of self-realization, the self cannot be reduced to a set of technical accomplishments. The value of a person's talents resides in the purposes to which those talents are employed. The same talents can be directed toward the achieving of a wide variety of ends, some laudable, others censurable. Thus, the second aspect of the daimon is constituted by the purposes in living to which the individual is committed. Whereas aptitudes and talents are, in themselves, morally neutral, purposes in living are inherently moral choices and a reflection of one's character.

For a eudaimonistic social science, then, the daimon can be translated into two sets of observable variables, the aptitudes and talents of the individual, and the purposes in living to which the person is committed. While for any given individual, it will not be possible to make a definitive statement regarding the degree of correspondence between the daimon, defined in philosophical terms, and the person's observable qualities, in terms of aptitudes, talents, and purposes in living, the approach taken here opens the possibility of empirically evaluating hypotheses drawn from the philosophy of eudaimonism.

### Experiences of Personal Expressiveness

The psychological construct that corresponds to the philosophical concept of eudaimonia, I have termed *personal expressiveness.* Experiences of an activity as personally expressive for an individual occur when there is (a) an unusually intense involvement in an undertaking, (b) a feeling of a special fit or meshing with an activity that is not characteristic of most daily tasks, (c) a feeling of being intensely alive, (d) a feeling of being complete or fulfilled while engaged in an activity, (e) an impression that this is what the person was meant to do, and (f) a feeling that this is who one really is (Waterman, 1990a, b). Such experiences of personal expressiveness appear conceptually linked with the feelings associated with intrinsic motivation (Deci & Ryan, 1985), flow (Csikszentmihalyi, 1975), and peak experiences (Maslow, 1968, 1970b). In line with eudaimonistic philosophy, the activities giving rise to feelings of personal expressiveness are believed to be those in which an individual experiences self-realization through the fulfillment of personal potentials either in the form of the development of one's aptitudes and talents and/or through the advancing of one's purposes in living.

### The Individualistic Personality

As I stated in the opening of this chapter, eudaimonistic value assumptions can be shown to provide the foundation for constructs drawn from diverse theoretical orientations within psychology. Four such personal qualities I (Waterman, 1984b) have sought to integrate under the label *psychological individualism* are: (1) a sense of personal identity, (2) self-actualization, (3) an internal locus of control, and (4) principled moral reasoning.

A sense of personal identity can be defined as "having a clearly delineated self-definition comprised of those goals, values, and beliefs to which the person is unequivocally committed. These commitments evolve over time and are made because the chosen goals, values, and beliefs are judged worthy of giving a direction, purpose, and meaning to life" (Waterman, 1984a, p. 331). The person's sense of identity thus constitutes an approximation of the daimon. Whereas the daimon embodies one's true potentials, in terms of both aptitudes and talents and purposes in living, the content of one's sense of identity does not necessarily match these closely. Identity elements may be chosen based on the models available, parental expectations, social rewards, or a variety of other factors unrelated to eudaimonistic considerations. When identity commitments are well chosen, that is, are consistent with one's endowment and consistent with one's purposes in living, activities based upon them will be experienced as personally expressive. When they are poorly chosen, the result is likely to be a frustration of purpose, with competence difficult or impossible to achieve, and interest difficult to sustain.

Whereas the sense of personal identity involves efforts to recognize one's "true self" or daimonic potentials, self-actualization refers directly to the efforts to fulfill those potentials. Thus Maslow (1968) defines self-actualization as the "ongoing actualization of potentials, capacities and talents, as fulfillment of mission (or call, fate, destiny, or vocation) as a fuller knowledge of, and acceptance of, the person's own intrinsic nature, as an unceasing trend toward unity, integration or synergy within the person" (p. 25). Or again as "intrinsic growth of what is already in the organism, or more accurately of what is the organism itself" (Maslow, 1970a, p. 134). (The psychological term "self-actualization" can be taken as equivalent to "self-realization," the term used in most philosophical writings.) In line with the eudaimonistic philosophical assumptions underlying Maslow's theorizing, the potential to become self-actualizing is universal. However, difficulties encountered in achieving and sustaining satisfaction of more basis needs (those taking priority over self-actualization) constitute a major limiting factor on the number of people actually engaging in self-actualizing behavior and the extent of such activity. Both at the level of skill development and goal attainment, self-actualization may be experienced tentatively, sporadically, to a mild degree, or in a stronger and more sustained fashion. The intensity, frequency, and duration of self-actualization will depend on the degree of progress made or success achieved in one's undertakings. Similarly, living up to one's ideals, as embodied in the sense of personal identity, will be experienced as self-actualizing in varying degrees, depending in part on the levels of effort and difficulty involved in putting those ideals into action.

The dimension of an internal vs. external locus of control is a construct reflecting the degree to which individuals accept personal responsibility for what happens to them (Rotter, Seeman, & Liverant, 1962). Efforts will be made to recognize one's personal potentials and act toward self-realization only if there is the perception that freedom of choice exists within a situation and that the outcomes obtained will be a function, at least in part, of the choices that are made. To act agenticly toward eudaimonistic goals thus requires the presence of an internal locus of control. The outcomes of activities experienced as personally expressive will be attributed primarily to the actor's own personal qualities, that is, as reflecting an internal locus of control. When an external locus of control is present, for example, in the absence of perceived choice, or where outcomes are not contingent on personal actions, activities are not likely to be perceived as personally expressive and events in life will be viewed as mere happenings to which neither credit nor blame can properly be attached.

The ethical principle of universality that is part of eudaimonistic philosophy is a key tenet in the cognitive-development theorizing that has been done regarding the development of moral judgment (Gilligan, 1982; Kohlberg, 1969, 1976). Principled moral reasoning, the highest developmental level of moral functioning, emerges from a process involving increasing reintegration, equilibration, and universalizability. Whereas Kohlberg (1969, 1976) demonstrated such development with respect to the virtue of justice, Gilligan (1982) described the progression with respect to the virtue of care and responsiveness. It is plausible that the same developmental process exists with respect to each of the more than 60 virtues identified by Pincoffs (1986). If this is the case, then individual differences with respect to acting in a principled fashion on the basis of different virtues is a statement of personally expressive preference. The preference may be justified to others on either rational or intuitive grounds, but either way, at another level it is a decision about how the individual wishes to define himself or herself on the level of moral values. Such values are aspects of personal identity and ideally are chosen because they are reflective of those existing potentials the person wishes to actualize.

### Reconciling the Individual and Society

There is general agreement among both the proponents and critics of psychological individualism that individualistic values underlie such personal qualities as a sense of personal identity, self-actualization, internality, and principled moral reasoning. The critics of psychological individualism have presumed that such values result in unscrupulous competition, atomistic self-containment, and alienation, and thus that individualistic personal qualities are antithetical to positive social functioning (Cushman, 1990; Hogan, 1975; Lasch, 1975; Sampson, 1977; Slater, 1976). The proponents of psychological individualism, in contrast, advance the view that the values at issue contribute not only to personal well-being but promote cooperative interdependence.

It should be evident that when individuals strive toward self-realization they do not have either the time or talents to develop all of the knowledge, skills, and personal qualities that could be enjoyed or found useful in the pursuit of personal goals. Thus, a person acting in the pursuit of self-interests is motivated to join together with others having compatible desires so that by working toward their common interests, all may increase the probability of achieving the quality of life that each desires. Such cooperation develops not just for material gain but also for the satisfaction of other needs, for example, in the areas of aesthetic pursuits, athletics, and recreation.

The incentives for cooperation inherent in an individualistic value system extend beyond exchanges convenient for mutual benefit. Among the eudaimonic potentials that individuals may possess are aptitudes and talents associated with relating to others in ways that are caring, supportive, nurturant, and loving. The goals and purposes in living that an individual adopts may include ones that are to the benefit of his or her family, community, country, or humankind as a whole. When these aptitudes, talents, and purposes in living come together, productive, caring, mutual interdependence will be experienced as personally expressive.

## Research

I began this chapter with the claim from eudaimonistic philosophy that striving to discover and live in terms of the daimon, that is, striving for self-realization, yields beneficial outcomes both to the individual and to the interdependent relationships providing the context in which the individual functions. This is a teleological moral claim in that the rationale offered in support of the philosophy is couched in terms of the consequences that follow from the actions given moral priority. It is an empirical research question as to whether behaviors associated with self-realization actually yield the benefits claimed for them. It is to the research record on this question that I now turn.

As previously discussed, there is no methodology by which the daimon can be assessed directly. There are, however, at least two approaches for evaluating propositions drawn from eudaimonistic philosophy that can be utilized. The first involves studying the nature and consequences of eudaimonia, as this is operationalized in terms of experiences of personal expressiveness. The second involves looking at the implications of psychological functioning with respect to the various aspects of the individualistic personality, including the qualities of a sense of personal identity, self-actualization, an internal locus of control, and principled moral reasoning. Empirical research data is available utilizing each of these approaches.

### Research on Personal Expressiveness

In order to investigate the nature and consequences of experiences of personal expressiveness (eudaimonia), I developed the Personally Expressive Activities Questionnaire with scales for assessing levels of both personal expressiveness and hedonic enjoyment (Waterman, 1989). Activities can be logically grouped into four categories based on the presence or absence of each of the two conceptions of happiness: (a) activities giving rise to both experiences of personal expressiveness and hedonic enjoyment, (b) activities that are hedonically enjoyed but that are not personally expressive, (c) activities that are personally expressive but not hedonically enjoyed, and (d) activities that do not yield either form of happiness. (According to Telfer [1980], eudaimonia is a sufficient but not a necessary condition for hedonic enjoyment, so that the third category above is theoretically null.) Because there are activities that are hedonically enjoyed, but not personally expressive (presumably because they do not involve self-realization), it was possible to develop a series of hypotheses drawn in part from eudaimonistic philosophy to distinguish between the two conceptions of happiness.

Research with both undergraduate and graduate students (Waterman, 1993) revealed, as expected, that across an array of activities selected by the respondents, experiences of personal expressiveness were significantly and strongly correlated with hedonic enjoyment (r's ranging from .71 to .86). With this degree of association between the two conceptions of happiness, it might be anticipated that it would be quite difficult to document differential relationships with other variables. However, numerous differences between them were observed, with the pattern of outcomes consistent with expectations.

Feelings of personal expressiveness and hedonic enjoyment were both described as highly positive cognitive-affective states, but with significant differences between the two conceptions of happiness in the strengths with which many of the components were represented. Feelings of personal expressiveness were more strongly associated with (a) investing a great deal of effort (in an activity), (b) knowing how well one is doing, (c) having clear goals, (d) having a high level of concentration, (e) feeling competent, (f) feeling challenged, and (g) feeling assertive. (Experiences of hedonic enjoyment were also characterized by each of these components except feeling challenged, though not as strongly). These cognitive-affective components are the types of experiences one would be likely to have while developing one's aptitudes and talents and working toward furthering one's purposes in living.

Experiences of hedonic enjoyment deriving from activities were more strongly characterized by (a) feeling happy, (b) feeling relaxed, (c) feeling excited, (d) feeling content, (e) feeling in harmony with my surroundings, (f) losing track of time, and (g) forgetting personal problems, though each of these cognitive-affective components was associated with experiences of personal expressiveness as well. None of these components would appear to have a close connection with the development of personal potentialities. Also, experiences of hedonic enjoyment were modestly, but significantly, negatively correlated with a variety of negative-affective components that were unrelated to feelings of personal expressiveness—(a) feeling angry, (b) feeling restless, (c) feeling anxious, (d) feeling confused, and (e) feeling self-conscious. This finding is consistent with prior research indicating that positive and negative affects are distinct and relatively unrelated dimensions (Bradburn, 1969).

There were also a number of cognitive-affective components significantly related with comparable intensity to feelings of personal expressiveness and hedonic enjoyment. These were (a) feeling good about oneself, (b) feeling alert, (c) feeling confident, (d) feeling in control, and (e) feeling it [the activity] is always different.

Evidence of the link between experiences of personal expressiveness and the development of personal potentials was also found when the types of opportunities for satisfaction arising from activities were studied. Consistent with the hypothesis drawn from eudaimonistic philosophy, experiences of personal expressiveness were significantly more strongly associated with the extent to which activities were perceived as affording opportunities for the development of one's best potentials than were feelings of hedonic enjoyment. Differences between the two conceptions of happiness were also found for their associations with perceptions of activities as affording opportunities to share experiences with others and competitive opportunities. Although the stronger relationships were for feelings of personal expressiveness, they did not approach the strength of the effect for opportunities to develop one's best potentials. Differences between the two conceptions of happiness were not significant with respect to the effects for perceptions of spiritual opportunities, aesthetic opportunities, or opportunities for the satisfaction of one's drives.

In other analyses, a stronger relationship was found between experiences of personal expressiveness and the rated importance of activities than was found for feelings of hedonic enjoyment. No differences between the two conceptions of happiness were found regarding the frequency with which activities were performed.

The results of the research on personal expressiveness summarized here support the hypothesized differences between eudaimonia and hedonic enjoyment, most importantly with respect to the association of personal expressiveness and the development of personal potentials. These findings support the view that activities directed toward self-realization yield notable benefits to the individual. While the research reported here was not designed to address the benefits of self-realization for the promoting of collective interests, evidence on the point was also obtained. Out of 14 content groupings of the activities described by the respondents, social activities (with family, friends, etc.) were given the highest scores on personal expressiveness, and activities involving helping others were next highest. With respect to the opportunities to develop one's best potentials, activities involving helping others received the fourth highest scores, while social activities were in the sixth position on the list. Finally, as previously cited, correlations between personal expressiveness and the opportunities to share experiences with others were significantly stronger than were correlations with hedonic enjoyment. Taken together, these findings indicate that individuals perceive that through sharing experiences with others and helping others they experience self-realization.

## *Research on the Individualistic Personality*

In *The Psychology of Individualism* (Waterman, 1984b), I reviewed 574 research findings pertaining to the individualistic personal qualities of a sense of personal identity, self-actualization, an internal locus of control, and principled moral reasoning. The purpose of this review of the literature was to evaluate ten hypotheses regarding potential benefits to both the individual and society to be derived from individualistic psychological functioning.

Each of the four individualistic personal qualities is deemed optimal within a different theoretical system. In Hypothesis 1, the expectation was advanced that individuals scoring high on one of these optimal qualities would be high on each of the others as well. Out of 41 tests of this hypothesis, there were 15 significant positive results, 26 null outcomes, and 0 significant negative outcomes. Evidence for the relationships between pairs of individualistic qualities was strongest for (a) a sense of personal identity and self actualization, (b) a sense of personal identity and an internal locus of control, (c) a sense of personal identity and principled moral reasoning, and (d) self-actualization and an internal locus of control. Weak support for the association of self-actualization and principled moral reasoning was found, and no relationship was observed between an internal locus of control and principled moral reasoning.

In Hypothesis 2, functioning in terms of the four individualistic qualities was predicted to be associated with low levels of debilitating affective states, such as anxiety, depression, and alienation. This hypothesis was confirmed with the findings arranged as follows: 83 outcomes significant in support of the hypothesis, 32 null outcomes, and only one outcome significant in the opposite direction. Support for this hypothesis was observed across all four personal qualities, though only limited research has been carried out with respect to principled moral reasoning.

Hypothesis 3 dealt with the relationship between the individualistic personal qualities and the presence or absence of various forms of psychopathology and social deviance. Evidence for the benefits of individualistic functioning, in terms of mental health, were found for a sense of personal identity, self-actualization, and an internal locus of control, with 32 of 65 outcomes across the four qualities significant in the expected direction, 31 null outcomes, and two outcomes in the reverse direction. (Only one test of the mental health implications of principled moral reasoning was found in the literature review and that yielded a null outcome.)

Hypothesis 4 was concerned with the relationship between the individualistic personal qualities and levels of self-acceptance and self-esteem. As expected, an individualistic personality was associated with psychological well-being, with 38 out of 54 findings significant in the positive direction, 17 null findings, and only one outcome significant in the negative direction. The strongest evidence in support of this hypothesis was found for an internal locus of control and a sense on personal identity, moderate support was found for self-actualization, and modest support was obtained for principled moral reasoning.

In Hypothesis 5, it was hypothesized that the four individualistic personal qualities would be associated with use of more sophisticated and efficient modes of cognitive functioning. Strong evidence in support of this hypothesis was found for the quality of principled moral reasoning and, in limited research, for the quality of self-actualization, moderate support was found with respect to a sense of personal identity, and the evidence was modest with respect to an internal locus of control. Out of 83 tests of this hypothesis, 29 were significant in the positive direction, 52 were null, and 2 were significant in the negative direction. (These totals would appear to underestimate the support for the hypothesis, since 51 of the 83 tests involved an internal locus of control, the quality for which the relationship is weakest.)

The topic for Hypothesis 6 was the relationship between the individualistic personal qualities and achievement motivation. For the quality of a sense of personal identity the evidence in support of this hypothesis was moderate, though the number of studies involved was relatively small, while the more extensive research on an internal locus of control provided only modest support for the hypothesis. Only one null finding was obtained in research on self-actualization while principled moral reasoning had not been studied in this regard. The summary numbers for this hypothesis were 8 positive outcomes, 21 null findings, and zero negative outcomes.

In Hypothesis 7, a relationship was postulated between the four individualistic qualities and such work-related variables as job involvement and job satisfaction. In the literature review, strong evidence in support of the hypothesis was found for the quality of an internal locus of control with 17 outcomes significant in the expected direction, 5 null outcomes, and none significant in the negative direction. In the only study of self-actualization pertinent to this hypothesis, a negative outcome was observed, and no studies were located regarding the qualities of a sense of personal identity and principled moral reasoning.

Hypotheses 1 through 7 pertaining to individualistic psychological functioning were concerned with outcomes bearing on individual interests. While the research record showed varying levels of support among the hypotheses, and among the individualistic personal qualities, taken together the research record provides clear and consistent support for the claim that individualistic psychological functioning is associated with notable personal benefits. Hypotheses 8 through 10 bear on the relationship of individualistic psychological functioning and collective interests.

In Hypothesis 8, it was predicted that the individualistic personal qualities would be associated with the holding of social attitudes reflecting tolerance for a diversity of social viewpoints and a non-manipulative acceptance of other people. Individuals scoring high on measures of psychological individualism were expected to score high on indices of such variables as tolerance, social interest, and interpersonal trust, and score low on measures of authoritarianism, dogmatism, and Machiavellianism. Support for this hypothesis was found across all four individualistic qualities, although the evidence with respect to principled moral reasoning was of only modest strength. The summary statistics for this hypothesis were 43 outcomes in the expected direction, 2 null outcomes, and zero outcomes in the reversed direction.

Hypothesis 9 was concerned with the relationship obtaining between individualistic psychological functioning and the willingness to engage in cooperative and helping behaviors. As predicted, those individuals most characterized by the individualistic personal qualities were also the most willing to work for collective interests, and to help others under circumstances where no personal benefits were involved. Out of 65 tests of the hypothesis, 39 significant out-comes were observed in the expected direction, 26 null outcomes were ob-tained, and zero outcomes were found in the reverse direction. Support for this hypothesis was obtained across all four of the individualistic qualities.

Finally, in Hypothesis 10, it was predicted that those persons most charac-terized by the individualistic psychological qualities would have closer, more mutually supportive, and satisfying friendship and romantic love relation-ships. Again substantial support for the hypothesis was obtained with 21 of 31 outcomes significant in the positive direction, while the remaining 10 were null findings. The evidence for the relationship was strongest for a sense of personal identity, and moderate for self-actualization and an internal locus of control. (Only one finding pertinent to the hypothesis was found regarding principled moral reasoning, and that was null.)

The research record existing with regard to Hypotheses 8 through 10, thus supports the second part of the claim derived from eudaimonistic philosophy, pertaining to the benefits to others deriving from efforts at self-realization. Based on the evidence available, if one wishes to promote collective interests, in the form of pluralistic social attitudes, prosocial behaviors such as cooperation and helping, and mutually rewarding interpersonal relationships, it appears advisable to promote the development of a sense of personal identity, self-actualization, an internal locus of control, and principled moral reasoning.

## Applications

### Moral Education

If, as the research evidence strongly indicates, striving for self-realization pro-vides notable benefits both to the individual and to others in the social commu-nity, then there is a need to re-examine how self-interest is handled in the task of moral education. The approach usually taken has been to treat self-interest as equivalent to egoism, specifically an egoism in which the object is competitive advantage over others. Such egoism is based on the model of a zero-sum game (in which if one person wins, the other loses) where winning by any means is the only goal. With respect to the task of moral education, this version of egoism has justly earned the opprobrious treatment it has received. But the nature of self-interest associated with the concept of self-realization, as ad-vanced from the perspective of eudaimonistic philosophy, is not based on the model of a zero-sum game. The standards for self-realization are internal, not comparative, such that it is possible for many (theoretically all) individuals in a community to have success in their efforts at self-realization. Consistent with the principle of the complementarity of excellences (Norton, 1976), the suc-cesses of one person in self-realization will increase the likelihood that others will progress toward that goal. Further, under the principle of universality (Norton, 1976), the use of any means in the pursuit of self-realization is not ethically permissible. The research record reviewed here provides empirical evidence that individuals most characterized by individualistic psychological qualities are not structuring their social world in terms of zero-sum games. Eudaimonism is thus a version of philosophical egoism to which the usual ethical objections to egoism do not appear to apply.

The task of moral educators now becomes one of conveying an understanding of the various meanings of self-interest and the ways in which it may be permissibly pursued. Specifically, students need to become acquainted with the concept of self-realization as a philosophical goal, and learn to identify in their own experiences the nature of the activities that are associated with progress toward that goal. Helping students to develop a recognition of their aptitudes and talents, as well as develop their purposes in living, becomes part of the task for moral educators. Students need to develop an understanding of the principle of the complementarity of excellences, that is, how they benefit from the excellences of others and how their own excellences contribute to the collective good. And they need to develop an appreciation of the principle of universality, as providing limits on the means that may be ethically employed in the pursuit of self-realization.

## Career Choice

When individuals think of the development of their aptitudes and talents and the furthering of their purposes in living, they are apt to think of them in terms of career choices and vocational development. This a very narrow construing of the concept of self-realization (see below), but career does represent one direction in which self-realization may be pursued. It is typical practice within the field of career counseling to help people identify their aptitudes, through aptitude testing, and their values, through interest testing, and then to assist them in using this information in the process of career selection. In this regard, vocational counselors have been acting on eudaimonistic philosophical assumptions without necessarily being aware of the ethical implications involved in their use.

The analysis offered here provides still another construct to aid in choosing a career affording possibilities for furthering self-realization. Feelings of personal expressiveness (eudaimonia) experienced in association with varying life activities can be used as a source of information regarding personal potentials the individual may seek to further in the context of vocational activity. Feelings of personal expressiveness offer a type of input into the process of vocational choice, different from either aptitude testing or values assessment. Aptitude tests are behavioral measures whose predictive power is strongly shaped by the nature of the specific tasks assigned or items asked on the particular tests. Interest tests call for principally cognitive responses to the values associated with various careers and compare the values of the individual with those of persons already in a variety of different careers. Interest tests are thus potentially subject to a variety of response set biases, including social desirability assumptions, and they lack the flexibility to identify when an idiosyncratic fit may exist for particular value-career pairings. Feelings of personal expressiveness involve experiences of cognitive-affective states arising in connection with everyday life activities, presumably under circumstances where the activities are associated with the development of aptitudes and talents and/or the furthering of purposes in living. As such, they serve as a useful, but fallible, predictor of the directions in which self-realization may be furthered. Used in combination with aptitude and interest tests, utilization of information regarding experiences of personal expressiveness may increase the quality of vocational counseling.

## Choosing to Care

Our eudaimonistic potentials relating to career choice represent only a part of our aptitudes and talents and our purposes in living. Among our most important potentials are those relating to the development and maintenance of satisfying social relationships. Indeed, the research evidence indicated that social activities and prosocial activities generated the highest average scores for personal expressiveness. It is possible that one component of feelings of friendship and love is the presence of experiences of personal expressiveness. When people talk about being with a friend or love partner, they frequently use the expression "I can be myself." A plausible interpretation of that phrase is in terms of self-realization, that is, one can do those things that are personally expressive rather than acting on the basis of social expectations.

Yet the closest of social relationships, marriage, is perceived as one of the most problematic in our society. The eudaimonist theory advanced here has the potential for applications in the area of marriage counseling. The model of love relationships implicit in eudaimonistic philosophy is one in which each person acts in ways to further both his or her aptitudes and talents and purposes in living and to facilitate the partner in his or her comparable efforts. Since the eudaimonistic potentials of each partner have the same level of importance (no matter what form they may take), relationships in which one person's strivings for self-realization take precedence over those of the other are contrary to the model. Further, the principle of universality renders the use of power tactics in marriage relationships ethically unacceptable.

It should be noted that eudaimonistic principles are concerned with establishing and maintaining mutual, egalitarian love relationships, but do not specify particular activities in which the partners should engage. The extent to which there is a division of labor within relationships may vary widely depending on the types of activities experienced as personally expressive by the partners. The more similar the aptitudes and talents of each person and the more similar the content of the goals associated with self-realization, the more similar will be the roles and activities of the partners. Where the eudaimonistic potentials of the partners are widely divergent, though compatible, a marked division of labor will occur, and each can experience self-realization. And where the aptitudes, talents, and purposes of the partners are incompatible, dissolution of the relationship is the appropriate course to take.

## Choosing Avocational Activities

Beyond the realms of career and relationships, self-realization may be pursued in terms of a person's leisure-time activities. The wider the range of avocational activities that individuals try, the more likely they are to find ones accompanied by experiences of personal expressiveness. From a eudaimonistic perspective, leisure-time activities need not necessarily be pastimes, that is, ways to pass time, but rather afford opportunities for furthering one's aptitudes, talents, and purposes in living. Such a perspective should not be viewed as turning play into work since activities in line with the daimon are strongly associated with both experiences of personal expressiveness and feelings of hedonic enjoyment. While it might be thought that self-realization through leisure-time activities is of lesser importance than that achieved through career or relationships, there is no basis in eudaimonistic philosophy for such a conclusion. The development of excellence consistent with the potentials of the daimon, and in ways consistent with the principle of universality, is valued independently of the vehicle through which it is advanced.

## Reprise: The Individual and Society

From the perspective of eudaimonistic philosophy, the making of a dialectical dichotomy between individual and collective interests is not conceptually necessary, and the research record summarized here indicates that such a dichotomy is not predictively useful. This makes a societal ideal entailing the compatible incorporation of both interests appear increasingly plausible.

An initial exploration of such a societal ideal has been provided by Ruth Benedict. In contrasting societies that differed markedly in levels of aggression, she made the following observations:

> From all comparative material, the conclusion that emerges is that societies where non-aggression is conspicuous have social orders in which the individual by the same act and at the same time serves his own advantage and that of the group. . . . Non-aggression occurs (in these societies) not because people are unselfish and put social obligations above personal desires, but when social arrangements make these two identical. . . . I shall speak of cultures with low synergy where the social structure provides for acts which are mutually opposed and counteractive, and cultures with high synergy where it provides for acts which are mutually reinforcing. (Benedict, cited in Maslow, 1972, p. 202)

It is of interest to observe that the synergistic societal ideal has become incorporated into the work of psychologists with widely differing orientations. Kanfer (1979), in his discussion of an applied psychological altruism, cites Hardin's cardinal rule of policy "Never ask a person to act against his own self-interest" and concludes that what is needed to facilitate helping is "to train persons to act for the benefits of another because it is in their own self-interest" (p. 237). Similarly, Erikson (1964), proceeding from his psychoanalytic perspective, has stated,

> Truly worthwhile acts enhance a mutuality between the doer and the other—a mutuality which strengthens the doer even as it strengthens the other. . . . Understood this way, the [Golden] Rule would say that it is best to do to another what will strengthen you even as it will strengthen him—that is, which will develop his best potentials even as it develops your own. (p. 233)

The research record is so consistent in indicating that those individuals functioning in ways to promote self-realization are also the ones most able and willing to engage in mutually supportive, prosocial interdependencies, that the question arises as to how critics of individualism (and eudaimonism) could have arrived at conclusions so at variance with the empirical evidence. I believe that their error stems from the mistaken belief that the eudaimonisitc values implicit in our psychological theories are the same as those embodied in our contemporary social institutions. A few examples of the discrepancies between the two should suffice. Where eudaimonism places a value on the disciplined pursuit of excellences requiring sustained effort toward personal expression through creativity, the message in our media is one of short-run hedonism, of happiness through material consumption. Where the values of eudaimonism include personal freedom and personal responsibility, our society has established a network of social service bureaucracies that, while intended to be helpful, actually serve to limit both freedom and responsibility. Where the eudaimonistic principle of universality contains the view that each person is an end in himself or herself (rather than the means to fulfill the interests of someone else), the practices of our political system foster competition among special interests for governmental favors at taxpayer expense. Given these discrepancies, it is not surprising that our society is not promoting self-realization, but rather is fostering narcissism.

There is more than a little irony in the observation that the proponents of eudaimonistic philosophy and psychology can so readily agree with the critics of individualism regarding the problems in contemporary society. If, as Cushman (1990) contends, the essence of contemporary social problems has been the creation of an "empty self," then two solutions suggest themselves. Either efforts should be made to foster the withering away of the self or to foster the development of the self as "full." But if the self is to be encouraged to whither away, from what source is effective action on behalf of community interests to arise? If "I" do not do it, who will? Alternatively, if the self is to become full, from what source is the substance of the self to come. Cushman (1990) is correct that to fill the self from external sources, through material consumption promoted by modern advertising or through "lifestyle" psychotherapy, has ultimately proven unsatisfactory. Similarly, the filling of the self through the reliance on external authorities or upon traditions has been rejected as the emergence of modern societies attests. But the essence of eudaimonistic philosophy and psychology is that the self is full and fulfilled internally. Indeed, the self is never empty, even when its nature is ignored. By promoting techniques to foster self-realization through the recognition of personally expressive activities serving to advance our aptitudes and talents and further our purposes in living, we can contribute to the establishment of a synergistic society, serving both individual and collective interests.

## Recommended Readings

Csikszentmihalyi, M. (1975). *Beyond boredom and anxiety.* San Francisco: Jossey-Bass.

May, R. (1969). *Love and will.* New York: Norton.

Norton, D. L. (1976). *Personal destinies: A philosophy of ethical individualism.* Princeton, NJ: Princeton University Press.

Waterman, A. S. (1984b). *The psychology of individualism.* New York: Praeger.

Waterman, A. S. (1990a). Personal expressiveness: Philosophical and psychological foundations. *Journal of Mind and Behavior, 11,* 47-74.

## References

Ackrill, J. L. (1973). *Aristole's ethics.* London: Faber and Faber.

Aristotle. (1985). *The Nichomachean ethics.* (T. Irwin, Trans.). Indianapolis, IN: Hackett.

Bandura, A. (1982). Self-efficacy mechanism in human agency. *American Psychologist, 37,* 122-147.

Bentham, J. (1948). *An introduction to the principles of morals and legislation.* New York: Hafner. (Original work published 1789)

Bradburn, N. M. (1969). *The structure of psychological well-being.* Chicago: Aldine.

Cooper, J. (1975). *Reason and human good in Aristotle.* Cambridge, MA: Harvard University Press.

Csikszentmihalyi, M. (1975). *Beyond boredom and anxiety.* San Francisco: Jossey-Bass.

Cushman, P. (1990). Why the self is empty: Toward a historically situated psychology.

*American Psychologist, 45,* 599-611.

Deci, E. L., and Ryan, R. M. (1985). *Intrinsic motivation and self-determination.* New York: Plenum.

Erikson, E. H. (1963). *Childhood and society* (2nd ed.). New York: Norton.

Erikson, E. H. (1964). *Insight and responsibility.* New York: Norton.

Erikson, E. H. (1968). *Identity: Youth and crisis.* New York: Norton.

Gilligan, C. (1982). *In a different voice.* Cambridge, MA: Harvard University Press.

Hayek, F. A. (1948). *Individualism and the economic order.* Chicago: University of Chicago Press.

Hobbes, T. (1957). *Leviathan.* (M. Oakeshott, Ed.). Oxford: Blackwell. (Original work published 1651.)

Hogan, R. (1975). Theoretical egocentrism and

the problem of compliance. *American Psychologist*, 533-540.

Kanfer, F. H. (1979). Personal control, social control, and altruism: Can society survive the age of individualism? *American Psychologist, 34,* 231-239.

Kohlberg, L. (1969). Stage and sequence: The cognitive-developmental approach to socialization. In D. A. Goslin (Ed.), *Handbook of socialization theory and research* (pp. 347-480). Chicago: Rand McNally.

Kohlberg, L. (1976). Moral stage and moralization: The cognitive-developmental approach. In T. Lickona (Ed.), *Moral development and behavior: Theory, research, and social issues* (pp. 31-53). New York: Holt, Rinehart & Winston.

Kraut, R. (1979). Two conceptions of happiness. *Philosophical Review, 87,* 167-196.

Lasch, C. (1975). *The culture of narcissism: American life in an age of diminishing expectations.* New York: Norton.

Marx, K. (1932). *Capital: The communist manifesto and other writings.* (Max Eastman, Ed.) New York: Modern Library. (Original work published 1867.)

Maslow, A. H. (1968). *Toward a psychology of being* (2nd ed.). Princeton, NJ: Van Nostrand.

Maslow, A. H. (1970a). *Motivation and personality* (2nd ed.). New York: Harper and Row.

Maslow, A. H. (1970b). *Religions, values, and peak-experiences.* New York: Viking Compass.

Maslow, A. H. (1972). *The farther reaches of human nature.* New York: Viking Press.

May, R. (1953). *Man's search for himself.* New York: Dell.

May, R. (1969). *Love and will.* New York: Norton.

McDowell, J. (1980). The role of eudaimonia in Aristotle's ethics. In A. O. Rorty (Ed.), *Essays on Aristotle's ethics* (pp. 359-376). Berkeley, CA: University of California Press.

Nietzsche, F. (1954). *The philosophy of Nietzsche.* New York: Modern Library.

Norton, D. L. (1976). *Personal destinies: A philosophy of ethical individualism.* Princeton, NJ: Princeton University Press.

Pincoffs, E. L. (1986). *Quandaries and virtues: Against reductivism in ethics.* Lawrence, KS: University Press of Kansas.

Rand, A. (1964). *The virtue of selfishness. A new concept of egoism.* New York: New American Library.

Rotter, J. B. (1966). Generalized expectancies for internal versus external control of reinforcement. *Psychological Monographs, 80* (1, whole No. 609).

Rotter, J. B., Seeman, M., & Liverant, S. (1962). Internal versus external control of reinforcement: A major variable in behavior theory. In N. F. Washburne (Ed.). *Decisions, values, and groups* (Vol. 2). London: Pergamon.

Sampson, E. E. (1977). Psychology and the American ideal. *Journal of Personality and Social Psychology, 35,* 767-782.

Slater, P. E. (1976). *The pursuit of loneliness: American culture at the breaking point* (Rev. ed.). Boston: Beacon Press.

Smith, A. (1981). *An inquiry into the nature and causes of the wealth of nations.* R. H. Campbell & A. S. Skinner, Gen. Eds.). Indianapolis, IN: Liberty Classics.

Stirner, M. (1973). *The ego and his own: The case of the individual against authority.* (S. T. Byington, Trans.). New York: Dover.

Tatarkiewicz, W. (1976). *Analysis of happiness.* The Hague: Martinus Nijhoff.

Telfer, E. (1980). *Happiness.* New York: St. Martin's Press.

Waterman, A. S. (1981). Individualism and interdependence. *American Psychologist, 36,* 762-773.

Waterman, A. S. (1984a). Identity formation: Discovery or creation? *Journal of Early Adolescence, 4,* 329-341.

Waterman, A. S. (1984b). *The psychology of individualism.* New York: Praeger.

Waterman, A. S. (1986, August). Parameters of the self in a theory of self-realization. In J. A. Meacham (Chair), Issues of agency and malleability in theories of the self. Symposium presented at the Symposium meeting of the American Psychological Association, Washington, D.C.

Waterman, A. S. (1988). On the uses of psychological theory and research in the process of ethical inquiry. *Psychological Bulletin, 103,* 283-298.

Waterman, A. S. (1989, August). Two conceptions of happiness: Research on eudaimonia and hedonic enjoyment. In B. Slife (Chair), Aristotle and contemporary psychology: Empirical investigations. Symposium presented at the meeting of the American Psychological Association, New Orleans.

Waterman, A. S. (1990a). Personal expressiveness: Philosophical and psychological foundations. *Journal of Mind and Behavior, 11,* 47-74.

Waterman, A. S. (1990b). The relevance of Aristotle's conception of eudaimonia for the psychological study of happiness. *Theoretical and Philosophical Psychology, 10,* 39-44.

Waterman, A. S. (1993). Two conceptions of happiness: Contrasts of personal expressiveness (eudaimonia) and hedonic enjoyment. *Journal of Personality and Social Psychology, 64,* 678-691.

# Part IV

# Social Constructivist/ Interpretative Perspectives

## *Prologue*

The chapters in this part draw on diverse and distinguished roots that span a broad range of traditions in the social sciences. Two traditions, however, stand out in particular. The first is the social constructivist tradition (Gergen, 1982) and the second is interpretative tradition (Packer, 1987). Both traditions have played a central role in shaping the direction of developments that have taken place in the moral development literature, and their influence is reflected in the work of a diverse array of scholars and researchers (Brown, Tappan, Gilligan, Miller, & Argyris, 1989; Kurtines, Alvarez, & Azmitia, 1990; Packer, 1987; Shweder & Much, 1987; Youniss, 1987). The work described in the chapters in this part draws on these traditions. An introduction to social constructivist/ interpretative perspectives will be helpful in understanding this work.

Although there are a number of differences between them, the social constructivist and the interpretative traditions share many common metatheoretical assumptions. Both traditions are concerned with the social construction of reality and the interpretation of the shared meaning of that reality. In this sense, both differ from the "individualistic" orientation of traditional personality, behavioral, and cognitive perspectives, which has been the subject of a number of critical reviews (Hogan & Emler, 1978; Sampson, 1981). In contrast to the view that human behavior can be understood in a decontexualized, ahistorical way, the social constructivist and interpretative traditions view all human action or conduct as embedded in a complex network of human relations, and human relations, in turn, embedded in a socio-historical context and subject to a variety of alternative interpretations at all levels. The social constructivist and interpretative perspectives thus belong most clearly in the contextualist metatheoretical tradition.

Contextualism, we noted, can be traced to the emergence of the pragmatic tradition in American philosophy (Peirce, James, Dewey). The contextualist shares with the organicist the view of the organism as active, but it does not share the organicist view of developmental change as teleological. For the contextualist, individual developmental change is viewed as interacting with the socio-historical change. According to this view, the individual's behavior must be interpreted in the context of a multiplicity of influences that include both developmental and socio-historical processes. The meaning and significance of human behavior and developmental change cannot be interpreted independent of the background or framework in which it occurs. The contextualist tradition, therefore, is concerned with the explanation of human action in context.

The social constructivist perspective clearly falls within this tradition. Following Gergen (1982), social constructivist inquiry can be viewed as principally concerned with explicating the process by which people come to describe, explain, or otherwise account for the world (including themselves) in which they live. It attempts to articulate common forms of understanding as they now exist, as they have existed in prior historical periods, and as they might exist should creative attention be so directed. Historically, social constructivism stands in contrast to two major competing epistemological[1] traditions that Gergen (1982) calls exogenic and endogenic. The exogenic perspective, on the one hand, views knowledge as concerned with representation of events in the real world. From such a perspective, knowledge maps or mirrors the actualities of the real world. The endogenic perspective, on the other hand, views knowledge as dependent on characteristics endemic to the organism (i.e., the processes by which information is categorized, organized, processed, etc.). In this case, knowledge depends upon inherent human tendencies rather than features of the world itself. In philosophy, this difference is captured in the contrast between realism (the view that reality is mind independent) versus idealism or subjectivism (the view that reality is mind dependent), and in the contrast between empiricism (the view that knowledge is obtained through external sense experience) versus rationalism and institutionism (the view that knowledge is obtained through rational, logical, or intuitive processes and *not* dependent upon sense experience). In psychology, the difference can be seen in the contrast between the behavioral learning tradition versus the cognitive and affective traditions.

Social constructivism seeks to transcend the subject-object dualism and all its attendant problems by rejecting both the purely subjective and the purely objective basis of knowledge in favor of a view of knowledge as a social construction. From this perspective, knowledge is not located in either external objective reality or inner subjective reality; rather, knowledge is viewed as something that human beings share. Knowledge is a shared social construction. From a social constructivist perspective, knowledge is part of the reality that is constructed in the context of ongoing and continuing social practices. Knowledge is part of the negotiated reality that defines the complex web of human interrelations. One important implication of such a perspective is that it calls attention to the limitation of the natural sciences and experimental methodology as models of understanding. From a social constructivist perspective, the focus becomes one of the interpretation of human meaning systems (Rabinow & Sullivan, 1979).

In this frame, there has been increasingly interest in the interpretative or hermeneutic methodology (Packer, 1985). Hermeneutics involves an attempt to describe and study meaningful human phenomena. Historically, hermeneutics was a set of techniques for interpreting written text, particularly biblical text. During the middle ages, medieval scholars refined methods for interpreting the Bible, which they believed to be the literal word of God. In recent years, hermeneutics has been expanded to include not only text, but also human action. When adopted to the study of human action, the action is treated as though it has a semantic and "textual" structure instead of a causal or logical structure. Hermeneutics, then, stands in contrast to empiricism and rationalism. The object of study in hermeneutic inquiry is neither an abstract system of logical relations or a mechanical system of causal relations but rather the semantic or textual structural of everyday practical activity.

## *Overview of Chapters in Part IV*

The chapters in this part of the book draw on the themes and issues that have helped to define the social constructivist and interpretive traditions. Chapter 11 provides an account of moral development from a social constructivist perspective. The social constructivist perspective that Chapter 11 describes builds on George Herbert Mead's interactivist view of the relationship between the individual and society, but extends it to include a more bi-directional model of social process. Chapter 12 describes an alternative to the theoretical traditions that have predominated the moral development field. This perspective uses an interpretative methodology in studies in which men and women describe experiences of moral conflict and choice that has proved useful for listening to the different voices that emerge in such contexts. Chapter 13 describes a co-constructivist perspective on moral development that emphasizes the formative process of the subjective construction and intersubjective co-construction of human reality. The focus of this perspective is on the human capacity to choose the goals and values that give human behavior and development its direction and purpose, and the moral responsibility that accompanies this capacity.

Chapter 11, by *Philip Davidson* and *James Youniss*, describes moral development from a social constructivist perspective. Chapter 11 seeks to provide an alternative to theories of moral development that emphasize socialization into existing adult value systems and those emphasizing children's cognitive construction of moral concepts like justice and obligation. The social constructivist approach to moral development seeks an authentic balance between the child's own constructive activities and the contribution of the social environment.

This perspective draws on the work of George Herbert Mead (1863-1931) who had proclaimed a social-interactivist theory of mind that influenced a generation of social scientists, and introduced numerous important concepts, such as "role taking" and "generalized other." Mead's interactivism is a theory about *process*. Among thinkers of his generation, Mead was singularly possessed by a vision of the seething complexity of human experience. Social and mental phenomena are intricately interwoven and therefore must be analyzed within a single framework. The key idea in Mead's psychology is that persons are objects to themselves: One can act toward the self in exactly the same sense as one can act toward another social object, and this is indeed what it means to be a self. Most important is the ability to converse with the self, because this is how humans construct meaning. Rather than merely reacting to the world of experience, humans interpret it and reflect on their interpretations through an internal conversation. In this way, they actively create meaning for all objects of thought, including their own meaning. Moreover, because behavior is guided by these meanings rather than by raw stimuli, humans construct *action* rather than emitting responses.

Humans also engage one another in the very same process of forging meanings and actions. Society brings together a multiplicity of individuals with separate backgrounds who must continually negotiate the definition of themselves and of every element in their shared environment. Mead recognized the mutual influence between self-reflective thought and social interaction. However, Mead's developmental theory was unidirectional. Mead considered reflective thought derived from literally taking an *external* viewpoint with respect to the self. For Mead, thought is an internalized social dialogue, and it develops by a progressive transfer to the internal plane of what originally were external forms of interchange. The proposal that cognition is an internalization of external processes leads to theoretical difficulties that detract from Mead's overall contribution. Mead does not satisfactorily show how universal judgments, cognitive or moral, could arise within his theory.

Chapter 11 describes a bi-directional model of social process designed to address issues unresolved by Mead's approach. Chapter 11 proposes that although it is probably not what he intended, Mead's description of social process would actually lead to individuals who are uninvolved in abstracting moral ideas, and uncommitted to moral ideas except insofar as other individuals compel adherence. A more adequate moral agent would be one who upholds principles through inner obligation rather than through conformity, presumably because of having had a stake in constructing these principles. Chapter 11 seeks to remedy this shortcoming by building on Piaget's model of morality as socially constructed through interpersonal exchange. According to this view, morality, consisting in respect for persons, depends on the historical fact that persons have together cooperated in the construction of norms of social interaction. The weight of these norms comes from the validation that their practice allows. The norms are principled and nonarbitrary, not because they can be defended by a detached logical argument, but because they actually express the invariant forms of equilibrated social relations. Moral knowledge is responsive to cultural content because it exists in the realm of intersubjectivity; but it is not mechanistically determined by that content because intersubjectivity itself is a norm or ideal. Through practice of the norms, individual experience is transformed so that each person's view of reality is changed by participating with the other. More importantly, each discovers that the other is necessary and that each must cooperate in a principled way if mutual understanding is to be achieved.

A theory that grounds knowledge and morality in social interactions has implications for the relation between the individual and society or culture. Such a theory would maintain, for example, that in co-constructing moral norms, persons come to see each other as mutually dependent and to identify with social processes that transcend the individual. Morality is as much a matter of identity as of knowledge, because the two are indissociably linked in development. The conception of morality advanced in this chapter accepts and embraces all culturally distinct backgrounds, while denying that morality derives from backgrounds. Rather, Chapter 11 suggests that morality derives from process. From social processes within a given context, one derives normative conceptions of communication, intersubjectivity, and respect. Encountering the other, one can then expect any number of differences in the content of backgrounds, but one can also assume the other has experienced similar social processes with similar social constructions of norms.

Chapter 12, by *Lyn M. Brown*, *Mark B. Tappan*, and *Carol Gilligan*, describes an approach to the study of moral development that originated in observations made in earlier studies. These observations resulted in a shift in focus from people's thinking about hypothetical dilemmas to their construction of actual life choices they faced and decisions they made. This change in approach made it possible to see how people describe moral problems in their lives and to explore the relationship between their understanding of moral problems and the strategies they used to resolve them. The use of this approach resulted in the discovery that a "different voice" often guides the moral thoughts, feelings, and actions of women. More specifically, this research suggested that the interpretation of observed differences in moral reasoning—particularly gender differences—has historically been constrained by the assumption that there is a single moral perspective—i.e., a male-defined "justice" perspective. The focus on women's moral judgments, however, has clarified an alternative approach to moral decision-making, called a "care" perspective. The identification of these two perspectives or orientations points to a more complex conception of moral thinking, feeling, and acting, and provides a new framework for understanding moral development across the lifespan.

Chapter 12 aims to describe such a framework, and to outline the ways in which it can be applied to the study of human/moral development. This theoretical framework is premised on a distinction between two perspectives that define two different ways of understanding and responding to problems, conflicts, and dilemmas in relationship: the "relational voices" or "moral orientations" of justice and care. The distinction between justice and care thus reflects different dimensions of human relationship that give rise to moral concern. Specifically, these two voices/orientations are generated by particular visions of ideal human relationship: the *justice* orientation reflecting an ideal of equality, reciprocity, and fairness between persons; the *care* orientation reflecting an ideal of attachment, loving and being loved, listening and being listened to, and responding and being responded to. These ideal visions are experienced as being undercut, in the case of *justice*, by oppression, domination, inequality, and/or unfairness of treatment; in the case of *care*, by detachment, abandonment, inattentiveness, and/or lack of responsiveness. In other words, actual or potential experiences of vulnerability in relationship are characteristically expressed in these different moral terms.

Central to the research efforts conducted within this framework has been the development of a method for reading and interpreting interview narratives of real-life moral conflict and choice for the voice of the self-speaking in the narrative, and for the relational voices/moral orientations of justice and care. This "reading guide" highlights both care and justice as relational voices, as well as the sense of tension people often convey in their stories of lived moral experience. In other words, it is a voice-sensitive method that attempts to record the complexity of narratives of conflict and choice, and attempts to capture the personal, relational, and cultural dimensions of psychic life—including language and voice, perspectives and visions, and the relationship between the narrator's and the reader's ways of seeing and speaking.

Such a method, focusing as it does on the reading process and the creation of an interpretive account of a narrative, raises questions both about a reader's subjectivity and perspective, and about how a reader can understand the subjectivity and perspective of the person whose narrative he or she reads. The reading guide explicitly acknowledges, therefore, the interpretive nature of the reading process. It is designed to teach the reader to read for care and justice in narratives of conflict and choice, highlighting in this process the way in which self is represented in these two voices. That is, it attunes the reader's ear to a person speaking in an interview text about themselves and talking about a personal moral conflict in terms of concerns about care and/or justice. Thus, this method outlines a particular way of interpreting texts. It does not preclude other readings, but rather clarifies one theoretical frame and highlights what it provides the researcher interested in self, relationships, and morality.

Research findings using this method clearly indicate that neither voice (justice or care) is *gender-specific*. They do, however, suggest that the two voices tend to be *gender-related*: males orient toward justice more frequently than females, while females orient toward care more frequently than males. Although the gender-relatedness of these two voices is important to stress, particularly in light of ongoing work on female development and the development of a care voice, the significance of the fact that a majority of subjects manifested a plurality of voices should by no means be overlooked. This research demonstrates that human beings not only speak in multiple voices, but they can and frequently do oscillate from one voice to another in their moral discourse. Indeed, it would appear that human beings are both polyphonic in switching from one voice to another over time, and polyphonic in their utterances at any one time.

In application, this theoretical framework focuses on three areas. The first concerns fostering and facilitating the development of both the care voice and the justice voice in children and adolescents. A second area of focus concerns the educative and developmental effect of providing children and adolescents the opportunity to tell their own stories about their real-life moral experiences. Such a narrative approach to moral development and education provides students with the opportunity, by telling their own moral stories, to express and enhance their own authority and responsibility through the process of "authoring." By thereby representing the cognitive, emotional, and active dimensions of their own moral experience through narrative, students are encouraged to reflect on their own experience from the standpoint of their own moral perspective. This leads not only to an increased sense of authority and authorization on behalf of that perspective, but also an increased sense of responsibility for action. Finally, recent theoretical and empirical work on girls' development from childhood to adolescence raises concern with respect to the role that women teachers can play in facilitating the healthy psychological development of girls, by encouraging girls to resist a loss of voice, unauthentic relationships, and capitulation to damaging norms and models of female development.

Chapter 13, by *William M. Kurtines, Steven L. Berman, Angela Ittel*, and *Susan Williamson*, describes moral development from a co-constructivist perspective that evolved in the context of an ongoing program of research. This co-constructivist perspective builds on the work that has been done in the area of developmental theory, but it also seeks to extend our understanding of human behavior and development in a number of different directions and at a number of levels. This co-constructivist perspective seeks to broaden our understanding of the process of personal and historical change, and to use this understanding to extend our capacity to control the forces that touch our individual and shared lives. This perspective also seeks to broaden and expand the way we think about human morality *and* human responsibility. It includes an ethical theory that contains some ideas about ways of deciding what is the right thing to do and doing the right thing. This co-constructivist ethic holds that the freedom to choose that comes with the capacity for critical and democratic decision-making carries with it the responsibility for our choices. It is an ethic that holds us responsible for the quality of our lives. The goal of this perspective is thus to change how we, as human beings, think about ourselves to include an explicit recognition of our essential dignity and worth.

This co-constructivist perspective views human beings as self-directed, goal-oriented biopsychosocial organisms with complex, higher order cognitive and communicative capacities that enable them to engage in the most complex forms of theoretical and practical problem-solving and decision-making. With the development of these higher order competencies, human beings acquire the *capacity* to engage, individually and collectively, in decision-making and problem-solving activities that affect the quality of their lives, and the *responsibility* for the consequences or outcomes of their decisions and actions.

Chapter 13 illustrates how a co-constructivist perspective can be applied to making the right choice when faced with an individual or group moral dilemma and provides some guidelines for moral decision-making and problem-solving from a co-constructivist perspective. According to this view, the same decision-making and problem-solving processes that make the freedom to choose possible also have the potential for helping us to live up to the responsibility for the moral quality of our choices. The guidelines for moral decision-making and problem-solving outlined in Chapter 13 are derived from a co-constructivist ethic that views human morality and responsibility as concerned with deciding what is the right thing to do and doing the right thing. "Moral" decision-making and problem-solving involve making a judgment about what is the right thing to do. Doing the right thing, in turn, involves acting on our judgment. Chapter 13 outlines a view of what is the best or most useful *methods* for deciding what is the right thing to do, namely, the use of critical and democratic decision-making and problem-solving. The use of critical and democratic decision-making does not guarantee making the right choice, but it does help to ensure that individual and collective choices most closely approximate the right choice.

## Endnote

1.  Epistemology is the branch of philosophy concerned with the study of knowledge.

## References

Brown, L., Tappan, M., Gilligan, C., Miller, B., & Argyris, D. (1989). Reading for self and moral voice: A method for interpreting narratives of real-life moral conflict and choice. In M. Packer & R. Addison (Eds.), *Entering the circle: Hermeneutic inquiry in psychology* (pp. 141-164). Albany: State University of New York Press.

Gergen, K. J. (1982). *Toward transformation in social knowledge.* New York: Springer-Verlag.

Hogan, R. & Emler, N. P. (1978). The biases in contemporary social psychology. *Social Research, 45* 478-534.

Kurtines, W., Alvarez, M., & Azmitia, M. (1990). Science and Morality: The role of theoretical and meta-theoretical discourse in the psychological study of moral phenomena. *Psychological Bulletin, 107,* 283-295.

Packer, M. J. (1985). Hermeneutic inquiry in the study of human conduct. *American Psychologist, 40,* 1081-1093.

Packer, M. J. (1987). Social interaction as practical activity: Implications for the study of social and moral development. In W. M. Kurtines and J. L. Gewirtz (Eds.), *Moral development through social interaction.* New York: John Wiley & Sons, pp. 245-280.

Rabinow, P. & Sullivan, W. M. (Eds.). (1979). *Interpretive social science.* Berkeley: University of California Press.

Sampson, E. E. (1981). Cognitive psychology as ideology. *American Psychologist, 36,* 730-743.

Shweder, R. A. & Much, N. C. (1987). Determination of meaning: Discourse and moral socialization. In W. M. Kurtines and J. L. Gewirtz (Eds.), *Moral development through social interaction.* New York: John Wiley & Sons, pp. 197-244.

Youniss, J. (1987). Social construction and moral development: Update and expansion of an idea. In W. M. Kurtines and J. L. Gewirtz (Eds.), *Moral development through social interaction.* New York: John Wiley & Sons, pp. 131-148.

# Chapter *11*

# *Moral Development and Social Construction*

*PHILIP DAVIDSON*
*Catholic University of America*

*JAMES YOUNISS*
*Catholic University of America*

## Abstract

This chapter provides an account of moral development from a social constructivist perspective. The social constructivist perspective described in this chapter builds on George Herbert Mead's interactivist view of the relationship between the individual and society, but extends it to include a more bidirectional model of social process. This chapter seeks to provide an alternative to theories of moral development that emphasize socialization into existing adult value systems and those emphasizing children's cognitive construction of moral concepts like justice and obligation. The social constructivist approach to moral development seeks an authentic balance between the child's own constructive activities and the contribution of the social environment. This chapter proposes that Mead's description of social process would lead to individuals who are uninvolved in abstract moral ideas, and un-committed to moral ideas except insofar as other individuals compel adherence. A more adequate moral agent would be one who upholds principles through inner obligation rather than through conformity, presumably because of having had a stake in constructing these principles. This chapter builds on Piaget's model of morality as socially constructed through interpersonal exchange. A theory that grounds knowledge and morality in social interactions has implications for the relation between the individual and society or culture. Such a theory would maintain, for example, that in co-constructing moral norms, persons come to see each other as mutually dependent and to identify with social processes that transcend the individual. Morality is thus as much a matter of identity as of knowledge, because the two are indissociably linked in development.

Most explanations of how children acquire morality can be classified into two types: those that emphasize socialization into existing adult value systems, and those emphasizing children's cognitive construction of moral concepts like justice and obligation. The former approach has been criticized because it leads to an inadequate conception of morality as conformity (Kohlberg, 1971). The latter position has been criticized for leading to an overly detached and idealistic conception of the person (Gilligan & Murphy, 1979).

The social constructivist approach to moral development seeks an authentic balance between the child's own constructive activities and the contribution of the social environment. This endeavor is not new, since it goes back at least as far as James Mark Baldwin's writings. In the present paper, we do not expect to improve on Baldwin's (1906) synopsis of the basic social constructivist hypothesis:

> [The] 'dialectic of social growth' is a circular movement of give-and-take between society and the individual. The form of collective organization cannot be social (general) without having first been individual (particular); and the matter of social organization cannot be individual (particular) without having first been social (general). There must always be, therefore, at every stage of social progress, a balance of ungeneralized form in the individual, and a balance of unparticularized material in society. And the rules of the one cannot express the balance found on the side of the other. (Baldwin, 1906, p. 570)

Such expressions of the basic position are familiar and, we trust, not especially controversial. However, complications have arisen when the components of social constructivism are articulated in sufficient detail for systematic scrutiny and empirical evaluation. Some attractive proposals turn out to be incomplete, while more comprehensive approaches turn out to be easily misunderstood. The result is that today there is no clear authoritative formulation of moral development from the social constructivist point of view. Our goal in this chapter is first to clarify the issues that have plagued this viewpoint, and then to propose a model that can serve as a basis for further theoretical and empirical work.

## A Standard Model of Social Process

We begin with a case study of George Herbert Mead (1863-1931), who studied and worked with William James, Charles Horton Cooley, and John Dewey, to name only the most prominent influences. He first made his mark in physiological psychology (Mead, 1895) before turning to issues of social and mental development. In his popular lecture course at the University of Chicago, Mead proclaimed a social-interactivist theory of mind that influenced a generation of social scientists, and introduced numerous important concepts, such as "role taking" and "generalized other," into the lexicon.

There are several reasons Mead's work should be featured prominently and evaluated carefully in the present context. First, it is a major contribution to the study of self-society interaction and its implications for development. Second, it is also a complete developmental theory, in the sense that it is not just a theory about social or moral development, but relates moral interpretations and judgments to general cognitive functioning. Third, Mead's and closely related theories are as relevant today as ever. The main assumptions have been absorbed into what one could call a standard model of social process held by many contemporary scholars. For all these reasons, Mead's theory provides an appropriate background for what follows. Summarizing the theory allows us to delve immediately into some basic issues, and to identify clearly the most viable points and the areas where new approaches are needed.

## Mead's Interactivism

If it is possible to describe G. H. Mead's theory in a word, one might say it is a theory about *process*. Among thinkers of his generation, Mead was singularly possessed by a vision of the seething complexity of human experience. Social and mental phenomena are intricately interwoven and therefore must be analyzed within a single framework. Mead describes this dynamic interaction as follows:

> Since organism and environment determine each other and are mutually dependent for their existence, it follows that the life-process, to be adequately understood, must be considered in terms of their interrelations. (Mead, 1934, p. 130)
>
> The organized structure of every individual self within the human social process of experience and behavior reflects, and is constituted by, the organized relational pattern of that process as a whole; but each individual self-structure reflects, and is constituted by, a different aspect or perspective of this relational pattern, because each reflects this relational pattern from its own unique standpoint. . . . (Mead, 1934, p. 201)

The key idea in Mead's psychology is that persons are objects to themselves: One can act toward the self in exactly the same sense as one can act toward another social object, and this is indeed what it means to be a self. Most important is the ability to converse with the self, because this is how humans construct meaning. Rather than merely reacting to the world of experience, humans interpret it and reflect on their interpretations through an internal conversation. In this way, they actively create meaning for all objects of thought, including their own meaning. Moreover, because behavior is guided by these meanings rather than by raw stimuli, humans construct *action* rather than merely emitting responses.

Humans also engage one another in the very same process of forging meanings and actions. Society brings together a multiplicity of individuals with separate backgrounds who must continually negotiate the definition of themselves and of every element in their shared environment. Individuals also continually coordinate their own actions to produce social acts—joint endeavors in the work place, in a marriage, in politics, religion, or in science. The implicit aim of persons who merge their endeavors is to reach mutual understanding about who they are and what they are about. Nevertheless, these transactions are always open-ended and subject to various uncertainties. Hence, each level of social organization, from the individual to society as a whole, must be viewed as being in flux and formation.

## Mead's Developmental Model

What has been said so far captures what we might call Mead's "intuition" of an equilibrium or mutual influence between self-reflective thought and social interaction. However, Mead's explanation of how this situation comes about is decidedly unidirectional:

> We attempt to explain the conduct of the individual in terms of the organized conduct of the social group. . . . The whole (society) is prior to the part (the individual), not the part to the whole; and the part is explained in terms of the whole, not the whole in terms of the part. (Mead, 1934, p. 7)

Foremost in Mead's developmental explanation is the idea that reflective thought derives from literally taking an *external* viewpoint with respect to the self:

> I know of no way in which intelligence or mind could arise or could have arisen, other than through the internalization by the individual of social processes of experience and behavior . . . as made possible by the individual's taking the attitudes of other individuals toward himself. (Mead, 1934, p. 191-192)

This role-taking ability originates in early childhood through adopting the attitude of distinct persons such as the parents (the "play stage"). It expands in later childhood into an ability to take the viewpoint of specific organized groups, such as a team (the "game stage"). And ultimately it evolves into an ability to take the perspective of society itself, the "generalized other," (Mead, 1934, pp. 152-164). Thought is an internalized social dialogue, and it develops by a progressive transfer to the internal plane of what originally were external forms of interchange: "Our so-called laws of thought are the abstractions of social intercourse. Our whole process of thought, technique and method is essentially social" (Mead, 1934, p. 90). We can hardly present this summary of Mead's psychology without noting in passing how congruent it is with Vygotsky's (1986) views on the origin of mind (see Wertsch, 1987).

Much of Mead's work reads like a manifesto against the mechanistic determinism that dominated both psychology and sociology in his day—particularly because he deals rather extensively with issues such as consciousness, mind, self, and reflectivity. However, closer inspection reveals that his developmental model roots knowledge in pre-existing external conditions, and hence is actually consistent with the standard empiricist assumptions of the time. The proposal that cognition is an internalization of external processes leads to theoretical difficulties that detract from Mead's overall contribution. Although these difficulties lie in his account of cognition, they have direct consequences for social relations and morality. Accordingly, before we turn to Mead's moral theory, we need to make a brief detour to clarify the implications of the internalization idea.

## Problems with the Internalization Construct

We will focus on two cognitive activities that are fundamental both in a general sense and for morality in particular. One is the ability to interpret or give meaning to events, and the other is the abstraction of rational norms. By the abstraction of norms, we mean the human capacity to "isolate the logical constants which are essential for any process of thinking" (Mead, 1934, p. 260). As noted, Mead proposes that these cognitive processes are internalized through role taking. Accordingly, the theory needs to explain the origin of role taking. It does not suffice merely to stipulate that role taking ability itself is abstracted from social experience, because that still leaves a question about the cognitive processes involved in abstracting role taking from social experience.

### Role Taking and the Internalization of Meanings
The problem with invoking internalization to explain cognition is that there must first be a functioning cognitive system to do the internalizing. Since Mead does not specify the workings of that system, his theory basically claims that internalization explains internalization, which is circular. In a very few passages, Mead seems to recognize this problem, and mentions a deeper explanation for the cognitive activity that underlies internalization. In these passages he resorts to preformed neurological capabilities: "The process is made possible by the mechanism of the central nervous system, which permits the individual's taking the attitude of the other toward himself" (Mead, 1934, p. 100). However, this ad hoc solution begs the question and doesn't actually deal with cognitive development.

The role-taking construct itself may obscure real issues of psychological explanation. To interpret another person's subjective states, such as attitudes, intentions, and so forth, one must have an existing knowledge base, or theory, pertaining to persons and psychological phenomena. This knowledge has been constructed over one's lifetime through innumerable interpersonal exchanges and hypothesis testing. "Role taking" is an abbreviated way of referring to one's use of this knowledge to produce a judgment in a given instance. To identify this ability with a label, "role taking," is often convenient but does not actually clarify the inferential processes involved in building the relevant knowledge system, nor does it explain how the knowledge system produces judgments about other persons' inner states. On the contrary, to invoke role taking may actually add confusion to psychological explanation, by suggesting a special mechanism that bypasses the usual activities of interpretation and inference, and somehow grants a direct apperception of reality—including even the covert states of other persons.[1]

### *The Isolation of Rational Norms and Necessity*

Mead's psychology also contains an account of rationality, which involves constructing universals: "The reaching of universal ways of acting that you can depend upon, and the application of these ways to particular instances, represents the phase of thinking with which logic has primarily to do" (Mead, 1938, p. 82). As shown in the following passage, Mead attributes these logical universals to empirical regularities:

> This organized group reaction of the individual over against himself I have termed the generalized other. In the wide field of logic and mathematics this represents the universally common attitudes of members of human society in significant conversation and reaction to the environment, in so far as the environment of the race is uniform. This uniform response of all men to the common environment, or the environment in so far as it is uniform, finds its expression in a Euclidean space. . . . (Mead, 1938, p. 432)

Mead must raise the question of universal concepts in order to explain a fundamental hallmark of human reason—*necessity*. Continuing with Mead's example, for a normal adult who possesses a Euclidian concept of space, it is necessary, not just probable, that walking straight from A to B is shorter than any trajectory touching a point lying outside the line A-B. A psychological theory that does not deal with the pervasive phenomena of necessary reasoning would certainly be incomplete.

The problem with Mead's explanation is that universals do not exist empirically; rather, they are forms imposed upon reality by the mind. For instance, the physical environment does not directly present itself as a Euclidean space with orthogonal dimensions and units of distance. Rather, the mind (of the older child and adult, but not of the young child) organizes physical space according to a dimensional and metric framework. The developmental sequence in constructing these mental constants clearly shows that abstraction from experience is required; but, from what aspect of experience? As just noted, universals or necessity cannot be generalized directly from empirical reality because they are not part of empirical reality. And considering our preceding remarks, it is not likely that necessity can be internalized directly from other minds.

What is the missing factor in Mead's model, which leads to his emphasis on the internalization of existing meanings and norms? A major clue is found in passages such as this: "If mind or thought has arisen in this way, then there neither can be nor could have been any mind or thought without language, and the early stages of the development of language must have been prior to the development of mind or thought" (Mead, 1934, p. 192). In a word, Mead's model simply omits cognitive development in infancy. If he did not see the internalization mechanism as problematic, he also would not have realized that meanings can only originate in previous meanings, a process that must ultimately be traced back to infants' construction of meanings-in-action (Langer, 1980; Piaget, 1991).[2]

## Mead's Ethics

Given the foregoing overview of Mead's theory, we can turn to his views on morality. This is a natural topic for his theory, as it is a theory about social relations and social relations are the substance of morality. It seems that Mead could take either of two approaches. On the one hand he might argue that his theory accounts for "isolating the logical constants" in social relations that become the basis of principled thought. On the other hand, he might argue that his theory leads to a fundamentally relativistic conception of morality that does not include universal or principled thought. In fact, he takes neither course.

Mead's position (Mead, 1934, pp. 379-389; 1938, pp. 460-465) is remarkably Kantian in emphasizing universal judgments, and in subordinating morality to rationality:

> We can agree with Kant that the "ought" does involve universality.... Wherever the element of the "ought" comes in, wherever one's conscience speaks, it always takes on this universal form. Only a rational being could give universal form to his act. (Mead, 1934, p. 380)
>
> You cannot lay down in advance fixed rules as to just what should be done. You can find out what are the values involved in the actual problem and act rationally with reference to them.... The moral act must take into account all the values involved, and it must be rational— that is all that can be said. (Mead, 1934, p. 388)
>
> Clear thinking in the face of a problem is a value itself, and it is a value which is always essential to this phase of right conduct. (Mead, 1938, p. 465)

However, Mead does not satisfactorily show how universal judgments could arise within his system, which as we have seen is founded on the mechanism of empirical internalization. The same shortcoming applies to his proposals about autonomous reason:

> The group advances from old standards toward another standard; and what is important from the standpoint of morality is that this advance takes place through the individual, through a new type of individual— one who conceives himself as individuals have not conceived themselves in the past. . . . By asking what is right, we are in that same situation, and we are helping in this way toward the development of the moral consciousness of the community. Values come into conflict with each other in the experiences of the individual; it is his function to give expression to the different values and help to formulate more satisfactory standards than have existed. (Mead, 1934, pp. 386-387)

These points highlight inconsistencies in Mead's analysis. In appealing to autonomous thought, he assumes what needs to be explained. It is hard to see how autonomy could arise in either his moral theory or his general psychological theory. His theory is actually more consistent with the idea of morality as conformity, because it assumes that at any point in ontogeny, further development depends on adopting some external viewpoint that is more adequate than the one the self now has.

Mead makes additional points that would be difficult to articulate without his analysis of the self and its development. Thus, he proposes that the universality of moral judgment "arises from the fact that we take the attitude of the entire community, of all rational beings" (Mead, 1934, p. 379). He describes further how the development of morality is related to the development of self: "This should lead to the development of a larger self which can be identified with the interests of others. I think all of us feel that one must be ready to recognize the interests of others even when they run counter to our own, but the person who does that does not really sacrifice himself, but becomes a larger self" (Mead, 1934, p. 386).

In sum, Mead has made a valuable contribution in pointing out connections among moral, cognitive, and self-development, although we must conclude that his theory itself does not account for the developmental outcome he envisions. We have gone into the theory in some depth to indicate why this is so, and in order to identify the ingredients that would be required in a more complete account of moral development.

## A Bi-directional Model of Social Process

Although it is probably not what he intended, in our view, Mead's description of social process would actually lead to individuals who are uninvolved in abstracting moral ideas, and uncommitted to moral ideas except insofar as other individuals compel adherence. A more adequate moral agent would be one who upholds principles through inner obligation rather than through conformity, presumably because of having had a stake in constructing these principles. In this section, we seek to remedy this shortcoming by building on Piaget's model of morality as socially constructed through interpersonal exchange. Our discussion draws on several previous expositions of Piaget's contributions to social constructivism (Chapman, 1986, 1988; Damon, 1978, 1988; Youniss, 1980, 1981; Youniss & Damon, 1991).

Introducing Piaget requires a few remarks about his methodology, and we limit ourselves to the most basic points. Piaget's core interest is the nature of knowledge and its development, which seems obvious enough but can lead to some confusion because knowledge has two distinct aspects and he is equally diligent in pursuing each. On the one hand, knowledge is a sui generis phenomenon, which allows Piaget to seek the general or ideal forms of its development by means of converging evidence from biological evolution, ontogenesis, and history of science, a program he calls "genetic epistemology." On the other hand, Piaget is equally concerned with what real people do in real environments to acquire these forms of knowledge. These developmental facts are then fed back to refine the generalizations about the nature of knowledge. To give a specific example, Piaget (1932a) seems to have started with the general proposition that "all morality consists in a system of rules, and the essence of all morality is to be sought for in the respect which the individual acquires for these rules" (p. 13), but he rejected this view after studying developmental processes in real children. His epistemological and psychological projects are therefore interdependent, but conceptually distinct.

This methodological point can be related to what we said in the introduction about moral theories that tend to be either too idealized or too contextualized. By addressing the epistemological or universal questions in conjunction with the psychological or contextual questions, a theory can better do justice to both aspects. This implies not only a need for balance in the amount of attention given to each, but also that the epistemological and psychological interpretations should be mutually compatible.

These prefatory remarks have now returned us to the focal point we reached in discussing Mead's theory, where we found a problem with the compatibility between the psychological model and the generalizations about morality. We will now show how Piaget attempts to bridge this gap.

## Reflective Abstraction

Our conclusion in the previous section was that meanings, especially universals, cannot be internalized directly from empirical reality nor from others' opinions. In what is arguably his most important psychological contribution, Piaget shows how meanings are abstracted, not from the environment, but from the actions the person introduces into the environment. Piaget calls this process of isolating the general form of action *reflective abstraction*. Abstraction from actions is possible, because actions are accessible to the inferential system; so the hypothesis does not lead to the theoretical difficulties associated with internalization. Abstraction from actions is also sufficient, because action systems already contain concrete versions of the mental invariants we are interested in. For instance, implications among actions such as rotating, inverting, and displacing can be abstracted into the invariants of Euclidean space; implications among actions like joining, separating, and negating can be abstracted into logical operations. Although not recognized in Mead's time, this process has by now been extensively investigated (Piaget, 1976, 1977, 1978, 1985). The main point is that reflective abstraction is a distinct mechanism for isolating the invariant aspects of interactions, not a process for acquiring knowledge about the specific content of interactions.

In the social realm, children's actions necessarily connect with and elicit new actions from other individuals. Such actions are simultaneously social interactions. Reflections on these social interactions create anticipatory coordinations for subsequent actions. This implies that the invariants abstracted from social relations are mutual invariants, having a similar significance for each participant. Persons contribute to the construction in unison, not just as individuals, and each has the opportunity of isolating a shared conception of the interaction's invariant properties. Therefore, according to Piaget, the construction of social knowledge involves give-and-take exchanges in which ideas are offered, criticized, and reformed. There is no social knowledge, in the sense of acquiring generalized concepts that transcend the here and now, without social construction.

### Forms of Interaction

In his study of moral judgment, Piaget (1932a) differentiated two prototypical forms of interaction, or person-person relationship. The first, unilateral authority, is exemplified by adult-child relationships. In this form, the child's contribution to interactions is constrained by the adult's vision of what the interaction and outcome should be. The formal basis of the relationship is a type of reciprocity which Hinde (1976) has called complementary. This refers to the child's contribution being a completion of and limited by the adult authority. For clarity, it helps to realize that constraint does not imply a negative condition but may arise from positive motivations. It is precisely because adults want to protect children and help them learn about society that they frame children's behavior with standards that are intended to short-circuit the tedious process of trial-and-error learning.

The second form, cooperative relationship, is based on symmetrical reciprocity (Gouldner, 1960; Hinde, 1976). In this form, each person can contribute to an interaction exactly as the other person has or is likely to contribute. Unlike unilateral authority, cooperative relationships cannot be dominated by one person, because each person is behaviorally equal to the other. When a father, for instance, tells his daughter the rules for playing a game, the daughter may disagree but in most cases the father's rules ultimately will prevail. In cooperative relationships between peers, on the other hand, one child's assertion of rules is not binding. It must be weighed with another child's assertion, and what ultimately holds as the binding rule is that to which the two equal parties can agree, after using fair procedures.

## Norms

One of the usual arguments against social construction in moral theories is that any two persons or separate groups of persons might construct rules or principles that suit their taste and circumstances, but their agreement might not be moral in any principled sense. Piaget (1932a) addresses this criticism directly. His proposal is that social construction procedures have inherent constraints which, if understood, lead to principles that are logical and necessary.

Consider cooperative relationships that originate in the practice of symmetrical reciprocity. Piaget calls this practice the constitutive element that guides children's interactions. He argues further that when children later reflect on their practices together, they reconstitute them into a known principle. Hence, the sheer practice of tit-for-tat is conceptually transformed into a principle of reciprocity such that children judge it is fair to treat others as they themselves want to be treated (Youniss, 1980). As a sheer practice, reciprocity allows that if child A hits child B, child B can retaliate. It also entails that if A helps B, B should help A in return. And it specifies that if child A asserts a rule for a game, child B might assert a different rule.

These three possibilities help to show how a constitutive practice might be reconstituted into a generalized principle. It is apparent that these practices can lead, respectively, to agonistic quarrelling, positive relations, or stalemate. The question is, then, how the practice of reciprocity can be grounds for a stable cooperative relationship. The answer lies in the properties of reflective abstraction, referred to above. In the first place, the process of reflectively reconstituting a particular practice as a principle requires the participants to interact in a continuous and mutually beneficial manner. Persons who cooperate in reconstructing the principle would try to treat one another fairly and to be treated fairly by one another. Second, the principle that would emerge from this process reflects the properties of the process itself including its tendency toward social equilibration or equal treatment. Hence, Piaget argues that the compelling moral principle of fair treatment can arise developmentally from the elemental practice of reciprocity. The development of this norm depends on prior interactions, which are reconstructed, and thereafter serve as moral constraints in the maintenance of cooperative relationships.

### The Norm of Communication
It is obvious that fairness alone is inadequate to explain processes underlying morality. Piaget, consequently, offers a second norm, called *objective discussion,* which merits careful explication. Recall that one of the natural outcomes of tit-for-tat practice is stalemate, such as when two children assert that different rules apply to a given situation in a game. Piaget proposes that children con-

tinuously come up against such impasses in their daily interactions and therefore infer from an early age that solutions are possible through communication.
The norm of objective discussion is children's recognition of the need to express
ideas clearly, listen to counter-arguments, revise ideas in light of criticism, and,
in short, to communicate in order to be understood as well as to understand.
Piaget suggests that this norm also is a reconstituted principle that is co-
constructed from everyday interactions. The raw data for the abstraction consist in the following kinds of interactions: arguments, debates, compromises,
discussions, and negotiations. These communication events, it is said, become
normative when children realize that they can be utilized at the level of principle to sustain cooperative relationships. At that level, they are no longer mere
practices, but become essential norms for coordinating relationships.

### The Norm of Intersubjectivity

Recall the problem with the internalization account of meaning, which, as we
understand it, is predicated on the "transmission" model which assumes one
person in an interaction possesses meanings that have priority and should be
adopted by the other person. For example, the former could be an adult who
holds the standard meaning shared by adults in a society. In such a case it
seems reasonable to say that adults should transmit and children should adopt,
or internalize, this meaning.

In Piaget's theory, both parties contribute to the formation of meanings. In
the case of cooperative relationships, the meaning each person brings to an
interaction is open to revision on three counts. First, it must be expressed
clearly to another person. Second, the other person in expressing a point of
view, serves as a critic of the first person. And third, the two persons may enter
a sequence of give-and-take co-constructions that lead to a series of revisions
which result in a meaning neither party imagined at the outset.

The general term for this framework is *intersubjectivity*. It refers to the
location of knowledge at the juncture of the communicative meeting of persons.
Rather than posit "objective" meaning, say in society, as a starting point, this
position sees meaning as an *understanding constructed through the norms of reciprocity and communication*. The relocation in the interpersonal realm distinguishes this position from Mead's without abandoning the possibility of
validity. While objectivity is no longer a refuge, validation of meanings through
reciprocity and open discussion is a grounded substitute.

A fuller view of this perspective can be gotten by reconsidering
intersubjectivity from the vantage of the unilateral relationship. From the
stance of internalization, such a relationship should be optimal for the transmission of the adult's "objective" views to children. According to Piaget, this is
a mistake, because without reciprocity and open discussion, neither adults nor
children could internalize the other's viewpoint. This is not to deny that adults
try to understand children and children try to understand adults. But given the
lack of shared experience, each ends with mainly a self-concocted version of the
other's viewpoint. Indeed, Piaget argues that the likely outcome of unilateral

exchange is misunderstanding. For instance, what the child thinks the adult means is probably more closely associated with the child's version of society than the adult's. Interaction outside the norms of reciprocity and communication, hence, deters intersubjective understanding because it lacks the procedures through which mutuality can be established.

### The Norm of Respect for Persons

In his 1930s writings, Piaget expressed skepticism of naive "rationality" as did other European scholars who were dealing with the disillusionment of World War One. In his 1932 monograph on moral judgment, Piaget took special effort to disassociate himself from Kant's position that morality consists in respect for principles derived through detached reflection. As we noted above, Piaget may have started with the view that morality is based on respect for rules, but he ended by identifying respect for persons as the key. Specifically, his alternative was that principles derive from respect for persons, because persons have cooperated in establishing and maintaining beneficial social relations.

Respect for persons can be exemplified with the case of a true moral dilemma in which two persons hold opposed positions. How is this difference to be resolved? Piaget's scheme of Kant's position would have each person revert to an overarching principle that should settle the issue. Presumably, if the argument from this principle is valid, the conclusion should be compelling for both persons. Piaget's own position is quite different in that the focus of each person's justification is on the other person, not on an abstract principle. Making one's justification understandable entails first of all understanding the other person's perspective and reasoning. This model of moral justification actually rectifies a flaw in the Kantian approach: Arguments from an abstract principle can eliminate behavioral choices that are incompatible with the principle, that is, arguments can determine what should not be done; whereas, such arguments cannot identify a unique appropriate choice of what should be done. By combining a principled decision procedure with a contextualized consideration of persons, the Piagetian model better explains how moral judgment can arrive at optimally appropriate decisions in real life.

Accordingly, Piaget transforms the usual relation between logic and morality that one finds in many theories. For him, morality is the logic of interpersonal relations: "Apart from our relations to other people, there can be no moral necessity. The individual as such knows only anomie. . . . Autonomy therefore appears only with reciprocity, when mutual respect is strong enough to make the individual feel from within the desire to treat others as he himself would wish to be treated" (Piaget, 1932a, p. 196).

At this point we are able to bring this section on process full circle to a close. Morality, consisting in respect for persons, depends on the historical fact that persons have together cooperated in the construction of norms of social interaction. The weight of these norms comes from the validation that their practice allows. The norms are principled and nonarbitrary, not because they can be defended by a detached logical argument, but because they actually express the invariant forms of equilibrated social relations. Moral knowledge is responsive to cultural content because it exists in the realm of intersubjectivity; but it is not mechanistically determined by that content because intersubjectivity itself is a norm or ideal, or as McCarthy puts it, a "procedural realization of universalizability" (1978, p. 314). Through practice of the norms, individual experience is transformed so that each person's view of reality is changed by participating with the other. More importantly, each discovers that the other is necessary and that each must cooperate in a principled way if mutual understanding is to be achieved.

## *Culture and Moral Identity*

One of the more interesting aspects of a theory that grounds knowledge and morality in social interactions is its implications for the relation between the individual and society or culture. Both Mead and Piaget recognize this fact and take care to outline their positions carefully. In the case of Mead's writings, the notion of the generalized other serves to highlight the importance of culture as that thing through which the individual gains identity. According to Mead (1934), "the organized community or social group which gives to the individual his unity of self may be called the 'generalized other'" (pp. 262-263). This cultural aspect of self is not something added to an individual but a necessary component of an identity. The self is not just an individual, in some abstracted sense, but an individual sharing identity with others in a particular time and place.

This side of identity comes from the individual's discovery of self through interactions with other persons. Through searching for regularity in social interactions, children construct ideas about order which allow them to proceed with reasonable anticipation of subsequent interactive events. As Piaget has noted, young children believe that the order they find already pre-exists in the domain of culture. Piaget depicts this idea clearly with an example from his own children: "When I ask my children not to touch my worktable, this rule becomes one of the laws of their universe . . ." (Piaget, 1932a, p. 379). For Piaget, the child's understanding of rules holds that they are not arbitrary but: "Are eternal, due to the authority of the parents, of the Gentlemen of the Commune, and even of an almighty God" (p. 61).

It is only recently that researchers have begun to recognize this point and deal with it as an essential aspect of social life. Corsaro (1985; see also Corsaro & Eder, 1990) has developed this idea quite well through the study of peer relations. He proposes that children's participation in peer interactions leads them to acquire what they believe to be the gist of peer *culture*. It consists of rules about interacting which have two related functions. On the one hand, children believe that by learning ruleful interactive procedures, they discover peer culture as it is. On the other hand, by this same discovery they believe they acquire means to reproduce peer culture through participation in subsequent interactions.

What do Corsaro and others who think similarly mean by peer culture? It consists primarily in shared interpretations for interactions so that members of this culture know how to produce knowledge that can be mutually understood and know how to negotiate those issues that are sources of interpersonal differences (Cook-Gumperz & Corsaro, 1977). When children share this knowledge, they become part of the culture they construct and their self definitions are inextricably tied to that culture. Citing Giddens, Corsaro and Eder (1990) emphasize the dual functions of this definition: "The structural properties of social systems are both medium and outcome of the practices they recursively organize" (p. 200). Children acquire culture by interacting according to known rules. When they interact according to these rules, they reproduce the culture and reinforce their identity in it.

Corsaro's work has been mainly concerned with children's construction of peer culture: "How children, through their participation in communicative events, become part of and collectively reproduce their interpersonal relations and cultural patterns" (Corsaro & Rizzo, 1988, p. 879). Miller (1982; see also Miller & Sperry, 1987) has outlined a similar position for parent-child interactions. Miller suggests that these interactions comprising communicative events become cultural forms that children understand as means for participation in adult culture. The language routines that children and parents employ, when seen from children's viewpoints, become means for them to know about and take part in adult culture. For example, children seem to view parents' handling of emotional expressions as instructions for ways adults express and react to anger with hostility or humor and direct or indirect aggression (Miller & Sperry, 1987; Semin & Papadopoulou, 1989).

One of Miller's additional contributions has been to describe the role of narratives in this process. It is not just that a parent may get angry at something the child did, but that parents place these individual actions within a richer scenery so that the acts appear to belong to an ongoing, cultural whole. Miller and Sperry (1987) describe mothers' telling their daughters stories about fights they have had with bosses and boyfriends. The stories depict angry exchanges in which the parties insult, counteract, and seek redress. But Miller and Sperry also note that the mothers' stories are coincident with aspects of interactions with their daughters. Hence, actual and narrative expressions are woven together so that daughters are likely to conclude that there are right cultural ways to express and deal with the interpersonal dynamics of emotional expression.

Winegar, Renninger, and Valsiner (1989) offer a similar analysis of what they call the school culture. Using basic school events such as forming lines or following rules for obtaining and drinking juice, Winegar et al. observe children's rapid accommodation to rules and willingness to accept the rules as the correct way to participate in school culture. These three cases with peers, parents, and schools offer concurring examples which demonstrate the general point. It is the societal component that gives rules authority. Children believe that rules are shared by all persons who belong to society. In adopting rules, children become members of this imagined society (Damon, 1988; Furth, 1990). And in learning how to cooperate to construct norms, children become agents who can reproduce society.

Some readers, on first discovering the structure of Piaget's 1932 monograph on moral judgment, have asked why the initial 108 pages are devoted to children's understanding of how rules for games of marbles came about, why they are binding, and how they should be negotiated. It may be recalled that children regularly asserted that rules for games have a long history. For example, Fal, a 5-year-old boy, stated that he learned the rules from his older brother who learned, in turn, from his father (pp. 55-56). Piaget was interested in games as a means to assess children's cultural identification. In agreeing to play by the rules, children are not simply submitting to another child but are acknowledging the societal order to which they want to belong, what Mead and Piaget recognize as the "more than I."

Mead and Piaget agree that the cultural dimension behind rules for interaction gives them the transcendent force through which they gain their authority. Mead grounds the notion of the universality of moral judgments in the ability to take the "attitude of the entire community, of all rational beings" (Mead, 1934, p. 379). This attitude is inextricably connected to the individual's notion of self because the self also gains identity through this same social order. Mead then denies that submission of the self to the generalized other would possibly detract from the self, by pointing out that "the person who does that does not really sacrifice himself, but becomes a larger self" (Mead, 1934, p. 386). And he argues:

> Every human individual must, to behave ethically, integrate himself with the pattern of organized social behavior, which, as reflected or prehended in the structure of his self, makes him a self-conscious personality. . . . The sense which the individual self has of his dependence upon the organized society or social community to which he belongs is the basis and origin, in short, of his sense of duty (and in general of ethical consciousness). (Mead, 1934, p. 320)

What Mead calls duty, Piaget calls respect which he sees as the basis for universal morality. Of course, for Piaget the developmental path to respect differs because it emanates from relationships of cooperation. "As soon as A identifies himself morally with B, and thus submits his own point of view to the laws of reciprocity, the product of this mutual respect is bound to be something new, because the norms admitted from now onwards will necessarily be contained within this very reciprocity" (Piaget, 1932a, p. 385). As with Mead, Piaget does not believe that full acknowledgment of one's dependence on social relationships minimizes the self. "The morality of autonomous conscience . . . simply obliges individuals to 'place' themselves in reciprocal relationship with each other without letting the laws of perspective resultant upon this reciprocity destroy their individual points of view." (p. 397)

A theory of social construction clearly argues that morality is not solely a product of the individual and cannot be so. From the outset, children manifest the sense that rules for behavior fit within a social order that existed before they existed. While young children hold that rules gain authority from adults who know society better than they, subsequent development through cooperative relations leads to a different conception. A morality based on cooperation consists in mutual respect among persons who can establish and validate norms of social interaction regarding reciprocity and communication. The individuals who share this sense of morality do not give up having a creative self, but actively participate with other selves to whom they are morally responsible and with whom they share the same norms.

## *Moral and Personal Autonomy*

We have seen that both Mead and Piaget weight the notion of autonomy quite heavily as an index of adequate moral thought.[3] Accordingly, we ought to ask whether our social constructivist model generates any novel perspective, or in any way enriches the concept of autonomy as it pertains to morality. The preceding remarks suggest how in co-constructing moral norms, persons come to see each other as mutually dependent and to identify with social processes that transcend the individual. Mead goes so far as to say that the self is nothing more than a reflection of these social processes, an interpretation we do not share. Nonetheless, it does follow from our position that part of the self is a *reconstruction* of a "trans-individual" reality. This part is what we have called the "moral identity" in a previous essay (Davidson & Youniss, 1991).

Morality is as much a matter of identity as of knowledge, because the two are indissociably linked in development (Blasi, 1984). Identity and knowledge are both a question of "What can I do?" and part of what a person can do is to act as a moral agent. We have described how participation in reciprocal relations enables thought to reconstruct an operational model consisting of idealized procedural norms abstracted from those relations. This reconstruction may vary in its degree of completion across ontogeny and across persons, but as it gradually attains functional stability it increasingly becomes a reliable structure of thought, or equivalently, a part of the self. What makes it unique is its *autonomy* from other aspects of the self, those that are intrinsically and quite adaptively self-protective or egoistic. In contrast, the moral or autonomous self is intrinsically nonegoistic, because it expresses the form of interindividual or cooperative activity. This autonomous self corresponds, we believe, to Piaget's conception of personality:

> Cooperation is really a factor in the creation of personality, if by personality we mean, not the unconscious self of childish egocentrism, nor the anarchical self of egoism, but the self that takes up its stand on the norms of reciprocity and objective discussion, and knows how to submit to these in order to make itself respected. Personality is thus the opposite of the ego. . . . (Piaget, 1932a, p. 95)

We have previously proposed that levels of moral development can be understood as steps in the consolidation of the egoistic and the autonomous identities with progressive ascendency of the latter (Davidson & Youniss, 1991).

This interpretation of autonomy deals directly with the connections among morality, cognition, and self. Yet, not once does it rely on what has become a standard construal of autonomy, as the self's attainment of, detachment from, and logical superiority to its broader social context. Instead, our conception of autonomy is the liberation of thought from ego. Not that the ego is "bad"; on the contrary, it is the source of much that is positive in mental, especially affective, life. Rather, the condition of being tied down to this single perspective is what impedes development.

Our position does not attribute the universal properties of moral thought to some advanced stage of reasoning in which there is a conceptual transcendence of cultural boundaries, but rather attributes universalizability to each step in the development of morality and moral identity. What thought abstracts from social experience is not the specific (e.g., cultural) content, but the general forms of interaction, which are species-wide. Hence, at every step there is some potential, which as we have said increases with development, for going beyond cultural or other particularistic constraints. Turiel's (1983) research, in particular, demonstrates that even young children apply universalistic judgments to explicitly moral issues.

In summary of the present section, we have gone a long way toward a synthesis of Mead and Piaget. On the one hand, we agree with Mead in attributing universal moral judgments to identification with an abstract class of rational persons, the "generalized other." On the other, Piaget's constructivism explains how this moral identity comes about, not through internalization but by reflective reconstruction of idealized norms implicit in the interactions of cooperating individuals.

## Conclusion

The essence of morality, as we have said, is the formation of an identity that goes beyond the self and the capacity this conveys to make judgments that go beyond the self. This capacity includes, on the one hand, the obligation to treat others with care, and, on the other hand, is the basis for one's moral authority to pass judgment on other's acts. Developmentally, this "going beyond" originates with reference to primary groups like family and peers, and as one's sphere of interaction grows, it expands with reference to increasingly diverse others: persons from different neighborhoods, religions, languages, and ever more remote geographical and cultural origins.

Hence, every exposure to new others is a renewed challenge to the conservation of one's norms of reciprocity and respect, demanding the acceptance of a broader class of persons as moral equals, or in other words, requiring a redefinition of the concept of "person" with which one identifies or which constitutes one's moral identity. Moral growth is not a trivial matter precisely because it exacts a change of identity, which is always threatening to some degree.

The progressive expansion of moral identity is hence the problematic aspect of moral growth. It may be almost inevitable for normally functioning children, raised without crushing abuse, and exposed to peer culture, to develop a stable nucleus of morality with the various normative qualities we outlined in preceding sections. It is far from inevitable that all persons will extend this nucleus at similar rates, ultimately to embrace an equally inclusive concept of person.

We end this essay by recalling that the study of moral development is not an academic exercise with the goal of elaborating a conceptual system. It is fundamentally about understanding the nature of morality itself, with the goal of helping people get better at living with others, who by definition are always different from the self. In today's global village containing such cultural diversity across and even within national boundaries, the most significant question to be addressed to a theory of moral development is a practical one: Does the theory offer an explanation for, and advice for promoting, the phenomenon of rising above one's particularistic roots to reach understanding with the other?

We have seen that a theory which grounds morality in the internalization of existing external arrangements is a prescription for the opposite result. On encountering the other, an individual with such a predetermined morality would merely be befuddled. A kind of compromise could result from this encounter, namely an agreement not to consider each other as moral agents, which we recognize in various cliches: "Let's agree to disagree"; "You can't legislate morality"; "It's all relative"; or, "Judge not lest ye be judged." The relativistic implications of this conception of morality are thus not merely a matter for theorists to discuss; they have real consequences that are familiar in everyday life, and which amount to an abrogation of morality. The conception is at odds with the reality that persons are obligated to treat each other as moral agents, a fact that is exemplified in the need for institutions like local and national justice systems, and most tellingly, in international forums such as the World Court.

The conception we have advanced in this chapter is of course different. It accepts and embraces all culturally distinct backgrounds, while denying that morality derives from backgrounds. Rather, we have suggested that morality derives from process. From social processes within a given context, one derives normative conceptions of communication, intersubjectivity, and respect. Encountering the other, one can then expect any number of differences in the content of backgrounds, but one can also assume the other has experienced similar social processes with similar social constructions of norms.

Accordingly, the present approach explains how at each developmental step it is possible to conserve one's moral identity while also making it more inclusive. And more importantly, the approach also prescribes a means to promote moral understanding in today's world, a means that was sketched by Piaget 60 years ago and seems as true now as it was then:

We certainly should not prescribe a new social ideal for the child, for we do not know what society will be like tomorrow. Nor is it for us to inculcate any precise political or economic or social creed. What we should help children to acquire is simply a method, a psychological instrument, based on the principles of reciprocity and cooperation. (Piaget, 1932b, p. 25)

## Endnotes

1. Apropos of the internalization idea, readers may recall that various philosophers have raised some version of the following argument: Assume that new knowledge arises as an internal copy of reality. Of course, the mind must already possess the means to understand this copy, otherwise it could not be called knowledge. But if this understanding is already present, the knowledge is not new after all. Therefore, the premise that knowledge is an internal copy of reality entails a contradiction. For instance, see Plato (the *Meno)*; Vico (in Gash & VonGlasersfeld, 1978); and Fodor (1980). Davidson (1991) summarizes similar arguments presented by psychologists.

2. In being susceptible to these critiques, Mead is certainly in good company. For instance, in the first two sections of their work on the social construction of reality, Berger & Luckmann (1966) provide a penetrating and influential description of the social basis of meaning. Explanations of the psychological activities involved are provided in the third section, where we learn that

> The beginning point of this process is internalization: The immediate apprehension or interpretation of an objective event as expressing meaning, that is, as a manifestation of another's subjective processes which thereby becomes subjectively meaningful to myself. . . . The ontogenetic process by which this is brought about is socialization, which may thus be defined as the comprehensive and consistent induction of an individual into the objective world of a society or a sector of it. (Berger & Luckmann, pp. 129-130)

It is quite remarkable how many theorists have adopted some version of the idea that cognition imports preformed knowledge from external sources, without considering how such a process would work or whether it is even possible.

3. The same is true, although we do not have space here to elaborate, of moral theorists with such diametrically opposed positions as Durkheim (1961) and Kohlberg (1971), and of others who approach morality through the framework of character or personality development rather than that of judgment (Loevinger, 1976; Peck & Havighurst, 1960).

## References

Baldwin, J.M. (1906). *Social and ethical interpretations in mental development* (4th ed.). New York: MacMillan.

Berger, P. & Luckmann, T. (1966). *The social construction of reality*. Garden City, NY: Anchor Books.

Blasi, A. (1984). Moral identity: Its role in moral functioning. In W. Kurtines & J. Gewirtz (Eds.), *Morality, moral behavior and moral development* (pp. 128-139). New York: Wiley.

Chapman, M. (1986). The structure of exchange: Piaget's sociological theory. *Human Development, 29*, 181-194.

Chapman, M. (1988). *Constructive evolution.* Cambridge: Cambridge University Press.

Cook-Gumperz, J. & Corsaro, W.A. (1977). Social ecological constraints on children's communicative strategies. *Sociology, 11,* 411-434.

Corsaro, W.A. (1985). *Friendship and peer culture in the early years.* Norwood, NJ: Ablex.

Corsaro, W.A. & Eder, D. (1990). Children's peer cultures. *Annual Review of Sociology, 16,* 197-220.

Corsaro, W.A. & Rizzo, T.A. (1988). Discussion and friendship: Socialization processes in the peer culture of Italian nursery school children. *American Sociological Review, 53,* 879-894.

Damon, W. (1978). *The social world of the child.* San Francisco: Jossey-Bass.

Damon, W. (1988). *The moral child.* New York: Free Press.

Davidson, P.M. (1991). The role of social interaction in cognitive development. In L.T. Winegar & J. Valsiner (Eds.), *Children's development within social contexts.* Hillsdale, NJ: Erlbaum.

Davidson, P.M. & Youniss, J. (1991). Which comes first, morality or identity? In W. Kurtines & J. Gewirtz (Eds.). *Handbook of moral behavior and development* (Vol. 1). Hillsdale, NJ: Erlbaum.

Durkheim, E. (1961). *Moral education.* Glencoe, IL: Free Press. (Original work published 1925).

Fodor, J. (1980). Fixation of belief and concept acquisition. In M. Piattelli-Palmarini (Ed. ), *Language and Learning* (pp. 143-149) . Cambridge, MA: Harvard University Press.

Furth, H. (1990). The "radical imaginary" underlying social institutions: Its developmental base. *Human Development, 33,* 202-213.

Gash, H. & VonGlasersfeld, E. (1978). Vico (1668-1744): An early anticipator of radical constructivism. *Irish Journal of Psychology, 4,* 22-32.

Gilligan, C. & Murphy, J.M. (1979). Development from adolescence to adulthood: The philosopher and the dilemma of the fact. In D. Kuhn (Ed.), *Intellectual development beyond childhood.* San Francisco: Jossey-Bass.

Gouldner, A.W. (1960). The norm of reciprocity: A preliminary statement. *American Sociological Review, 25,* 161-178.

Hinde, R.A. (1976). On describing relationships. *Journal of Child Psychology and Psychiatry, 17,* 1-19.

Kohlberg, L. (1971). From is to ought. In T. Mischel (Ed.), *Cognitive development and epistemology.* New York: Academic.

Langer, J. (1980). *The origins of logic: Six to twelve months.* New York: Academic.

Loevinger, J. (1976). *Ego development: Conceptions and theories.* San Francisco: Jossey-Bass.

McCarthy, T. (1978). *The critical theory of Jürgen Habermas.* Cambridge, MA: M.I.T. Press.

Mead, G.H. (1895). A theory of emotions from the physiological standpoint. *Psychological Review, 2,* 162-164.

Mead, G.H. (1934). *Mind, self and society from the standpoint of a social behaviorist.* Chicago: University of Chicago Press.

Mead, G.H. (1938). *The philosophy of the act.* Chicago: University of Chicago Press.

Miller, D.J. (1982). *Amy Wendy and Beth: Learning language in south Baltimore.* Austin: University of Texas Press.

Miller, D.J. & Sperry, L.L. (1987). The socialization of anger and aggression. *Merrill-Palmer Quarterly, 33,* 1-31.

Peck, R.F. & Havighurst, R.J. (1960). *The psychology of character development.* New York: Wiley.

Piaget, J. (1932a). *The moral judgment of the child.* London: Routledge & Kegan Paul.

Piaget, J. (1932b). *Social evolution and the new education.* London: New Education Fellowship.

Piaget, J. (1976). *The grasp of consciousness.* Cambridge, MA: Harvard University Press. (Original work published, 1974.)

Piaget, J. (1977). *Researches sur l'abstraction reflechissante* (2 Vols.). Paris: Presses Universitaires de France.

Piaget, J. (1978). *Success and understanding.* Cambridge, MA: Harvard University Press. (Original work published, 1974.)

Piaget, J. (1985). *The equilibration of cognitive structures.* Chicago: University of Chicago Press. (Original work published 1975.)

Piaget, J. (1991). *Toward a logic of meanings.* Hillsdale, NJ: Erlbaum. (Original work published 1987.)

Semin, G.R. & Papadopoulou, K. (1989). The acquisition of reflexive social emotions: The transmission and reproduction of social control through joint action. In G. Duveen & B.B. Lloyd (Eds.), *Social representations and the development of knowledge.* Cambridge: Cambridge University Press.

Turiel, E. (1983). *The development of social knowledge.* Cambridge: Cambridge University Press.

Vygotsky, L.S. (1986). *Thought and language.* Cambridge, MA: MIT press.

Wertsch, J. (1987). *Vygotsky and the social forma-tion of mind.* Cambridge, MA: Harvard University Press.

Winegar, L.T., Renninger, K.A., & Valsiner, J. (1989). Dependent-Independence in Adult-Child Relationships. In D.A. Kramer & M.J. Bopp (Eds.), *Transformation in clinical and developmental psychology* (pp. 157-168). New York: Springer-Verlag.

Youniss, J. (1980). *Parents and Peers In social development.* Chicago: University of Chicago Press.

Youniss, J. (1981). An analysis of moral development through a theory of social construction. *Merrill-Palmer Quarterly, 27,* 385-403.

Youniss, J. & Damon, W. (1991). Social construction in Piaget's theory. In H. Beilin & P. Pufall (Eds.), *Piaget's Theory: Prospects and possibilities.* Hillsdale, NJ: Erlbaum.

*Chapter* $12$

# Listening to
# Different Voices

*LYN M. BROWN*
*Colby College*

*MARK B. TAPPAN*
*Colby College*

*CAROL GILLIGAN*
*Harvard University*

## Abstract

This chapter describes an alternative to the theoretical traditions that have predominated the moral development field. This perspective uses an interpretative methodology in studies in which men and women describe experiences of moral conflict and choice that has proved useful for listening to the different voices that emerge in such contexts. Such a perspective results in a shift in focus from people's thinking about hypothetical dilemmas to their construction of actual life choices they faced and decisions they made. This change in approach made it possible to see how people describe moral problems in their lives and to explore the relationship between their understanding of moral problems and the strategies they used to resolve them. The use of this approach resulted in the discovery that a "different voice" often guides the moral thoughts, feelings, and actions of women. More specifically, this research suggested that the interpretation of observed differences in moral reasoning—particularly gender differences—has historically been constrained by the assumption that there is a single oral perspective—i.e., a male-defined "justice" perspective. The focus on women's moral judgments, however, has clarified an alternative approach to moral decision-making, called a "care" perspective. The identification of these two perspectives or orientations points to a more complex conception of moral thinking, feeling, and acting, and provides a new framework for understanding moral development across the lifespan. This chapter outlines the ways in which it can be applied to the study of human/moral development.

Our approach to the study of moral development originated in observations made in the course of research on the relationship between moral judgment and moral action in the early 1970s. Two studies—one of college students describing experiences of moral conflict and choice (Gilligan and Murphy, 1979; Murphy & Gilligan, 1980), and one of pregnant women who at the time were considering abortion (Gilligan, 1977, 1982; Gilligan & Belenky, 1980)—shifted the focus of our research from people's thinking about hypothetical dilemmas (see Kohlberg, 1981, 1984) to their construction of actual life choices they faced and decisions they made. This change in approach made it possible to see how people describe moral problems in their lives and to explore the relationship between their understanding of moral problems and the strategies they used to resolve them.

In the interviews conducted in the course of this research some *men* who scored at the highest levels of Lawrence Kohlberg's (1981, 1984) scale of moral development defined moral conflicts in their lives as problems of justice, but found principles of justice and fairness to dictate solutions that they considered in some sense to be morally problematic (see Gilligan & Murphy, 1979; Gilligan, Murphy, & Tappan, 1990). Furthermore, some *women*, especially when describing their own experiences of moral conflict and choice, defined and resolved moral problems in ways that differed from those described in the existing theories of moral development, and in the measures traditionally used for its assessment (see Gilligan, 1977, 1982). This latter discovery that a "different voice" often guides the moral thoughts, feelings, and actions of women called attention to a major design problem in previous research on moral development: namely, the use of all-male samples as the empirical basis for theory construction.

The selection of all-male samples as the basis for generalizations that are applied to both males and females is logically inconsistent. As a research strategy, the decision to begin with a single-sex sample is problematic because the categories of analysis will tend to be defined on the basis of the initial data gathered, and subsequent studies will thus tend to be restricted to those categories. Piaget's (1932/1965) work of the moral judgment of the child clearly illustrates these problems, since he charted the evolution of children's consciousness and practice of rules on the basis of his study of boys playing marbles, and then undertook a study of girls to assess the generality of his findings.

Thus, girls were of interest to Piaget (1932/1965) only insofar as they were similar to boys and confirmed the generality of his findings. The differences he ultimately noted with respect to girls' games, which included greater tolerance, a greater tendency toward innovation in solving conflicts, a greater willingness to make exceptions to rules, and a lesser concern with legal elaboration, were not seen as germane to the "psychology of rules," and were regarded, therefore, as insignificant for the study of children's moral judgment. Given the confusion that continues to surround the discussion of sex differences in moral judgment (see Baumrind, 1986; Walker, 1984, 1986), it is important to emphasize that the differences observed by Piaget did not pertain to girls' understanding of rules per se, or to the development of the idea of justice in their thinking, but rather to the way girls structured their games and their approach to conflict resolution—that is, to their use rather than their understanding of the logic of rules and justice.

Kohlberg's (1958, 1981, 1984) research on moral development encountered similar problems—he, too, not only used an all-male sample as the basis for theory and test construction, but he also equated moral development exclusively with the development of justice reasoning. In response to his critics, Kohlberg (1984) has modified his initial claims somewhat, renaming his test a measure of "justice reasoning" rather than "moral maturity," and acknowledging the presence of a "care" perspective in people's moral thinking. But the continuing use of Kohlberg's measure as a measure of "moral" development, together with the tendency to equate justice reasoning with "moral" judgment, leaves the problem of gender and moral orientation differences still unresolved. Moreover, Kohlberg's efforts to assimilate thinking about love and care to the six-stage developmental sequence he derived and defined by analyzing changes in justice reasoning (relying centrally on his all-male longitudinal sample) underscores the continuing importance of: (1) distinguishing between differences in developmental stage within a single orientation (for example, a "justice orientation") and differences between orientations; and (2) recognizing the significance of the fact that the moral thinking of girls and women was not examined in establishing either the meaning or the measurement of moral judgment.

In other words, the interpretation of observed differences in moral reasoning—particularly gender differences—has historically been constrained by the assumption that there is a single moral perspective; i.e., a male-defined "justice" perspective (see Freud, 1925/1963; Kohlberg, 1981, 1984; Piaget, 1932/1965). Our focus on women's moral judgments, however, has clarified an alternative approach to moral decision-making—what we have called a "care" perspective (see Gilligan, 1977, 1982). Furthermore, we would argue that the identification of these two perspectives or orientations points to a more complex conception of moral thinking, feeling, and acting, and provides a new framework for understanding moral development across the lifespan.

Our aim in this chapter, therefore, is to describe such a framework, and to outline the ways in which it informs our approach to the study of human/moral development.[1] Our presentation is organized as follows: We begin with an overview of our theoretical framework, key to which is the distinction between the "relational voices" or "moral orientations" of *justice* and *care*. We then provide a brief review of the research that has been conducted over the course of the past decade under the rubric of this framework, including a consideration of the main trends and findings of this research. And finally, we conclude with a consideration of the implications of this work for those interested in supporting and encouraging the development of children and adolescents, particularly in educational contexts.

## Theory

The theoretical framework that guides our research is premised on a distinction between two perspectives that define two different ways of understanding and responding to problems, conflicts, and dilemmas in relationship; we have called these two perspectives the "relational voices" or "moral orientations" of justice and care.[2] The distinctions between justice and care thus reflect different dimensions of human relationship that give rise to moral concern. Specifically, these two voices/orientations are generated by particular visions of ideal human relationship: the *justice* orientation reflecting an ideal of equality, reciprocity, and fairness between persons; the *care* orientation reflecting an ideal of attachment, loving and being loved, listening and being listened to, and responding and being responded to. These ideal visions are experienced as being undercut, in the case of *justice*, by oppression, domination, inequality, and/or unfairness of treatment; in the case of *care*, by detachment, abandonment, inattentiveness, and/or lack of responsiveness. In other words, actual or potential experiences of vulnerability in relationship are characteristically expressed in these different moral terms (Brown, 1989; Gilligan, 1982, 1987a, 1987b).

Central to our view of moral development, therefore, is the assumption that a perspective on relationships underlies any conception of morality. Recent research on infancy, for example, provides compelling evidence that the foundations of morality are present early in child development—in the infant's responsiveness to the feelings of others and the young child's appreciation of standards (Kagan, 1984; Stern, 1985). But to explain the nature of these moral feelings and standards, it is necessary to consider how these capacities become organized, and thus to consider the infant's experience of his or her relationships with other people.

As such, we locate the origins of the voices/orientations of justice and care in the young child's awareness of self in relation to others, and we identify two dimensions of early childhood relationships that shape this awareness in different ways. One is the dimension of inequality, reflected in the child's awareness of being smaller, less capable, and less powerful than adults and older children. This dimension of relationship has been stressed by theorists of moral development in both the cognitive and psychoanalytic traditions, and is reflected by the emphasis placed on the child's feelings of helplessness and powerlessness in relation to others, feelings tied to the fact of his or her dependence on others who are bigger, stronger, and more powerful. Focusing on the constraint of the young child's situation, psychologists have defined morality as *justice* and aligned development with the child's progress toward a position of equality and independence (see Freud, 1925/1963; Piaget, 1932/1965; Kohlberg, 1981, 1984).

But the young child also experiences *attachment*, and the dynamics of attachment relationships create a very different awareness of self—as capable of having an effect on others, as able to move others and to be moved by them (see Bowlby, 1969). Characteristically, young children come to love the people who care for them, desiring to be near them, wanting to know them, being able to recognize them, and feeling sad when they leave. In the context of attachment, therefore, the child discovers the patterns of human interaction and observes the ways in which people both care for, and hurt one another. Like the experience of inequality, although in different ways, the experience of attachment profoundly affects the child's understanding of human feelings and how people should act toward one another. The moral implications of attachment relationships have generally been overlooked in theories of moral development, in part because the passivity of early childhood love has been stressed, rather than the child's activity in creating and sustaining connections with others, and in part because the emergence of self-awareness during this time has been tied exclusively to separation and detachment. Yet we would argue that the experience of attachment generates a perspective on relationships that underlies the conception of morality as *care*.

Thus, the different dynamics of early childhood inequality and attachment lay the groundwork for two moral visions—one of justice and one of care. The growing child's experience of inequality and of attachment, sometimes but not always convergent, grounds a distinction between the dimensions of inequality/equality and attachment/detachment that characterize his or her relational world. Although the nature of the attachment between child and parent varies across individual and cultural settings, and although inequality can be heightened or muted by familial and societal arrangements, all children are born into a situation of inequality, and no child survives in the absence of adult connection. Since everyone is vulnerable, therefore, both to oppression and abandonment, two stories about morality recur in human experience.

Children know both stories and test them in a variety of ways. Children in the United States appeal to justice in the face of unequal treatment by claiming "That's not fair!" or "You have no right to do that!" They also assess the strength of care by stating "You don't care!" or "I don't love you anymore!" In this way children discover the efficacy of moral standards and injunctions—the extent to which justice offers protection to the unequal and powerless in the face of oppression, and the extent to which care protects attachment against threats of detachment or abandonment.

The lessons learned about justice and care in early childhood relationships, furthermore, generate expectations that are confirmed or modified in later childhood and adolescence. Two moral injunctions—not to treat others unfairly and not to turn away from others in need—thus define two lines of moral development, providing different standards for assessing moral thoughts, feelings, and actions, and pointing to changes in the understanding of what fairness means and what constitutes care. By tracing moral development across these two intersecting but orthogonal dimensions of relationship, it is possible to differentiate transformations that pertain to equality (and justice) from transformations that pertain to attachment (and care).

We would argue, therefore, that observations of gender differences in moral thinking, feeling, and acting reflect a tendency for problems of inequality and problems of detachment to be differentially salient, or to be differentially organized, in male and female development. The gender difference question, when framed in this way, neither carries the implication that one sex is morally superior, nor implies that moral judgment or moral behavior is biologically determined. Instead, it draws attention, once again, to two perspectives on morality. To the extent that biological sex, the psychology of gender, and the cultural norms and values that define masculine and feminine behavior affect experiences of inequality/equality and attachment/detachment, these factors will presumably influence moral development.

For example, the experience of attachment in early childhood may attenuate the experience of inequality by empowering the child in relation to the parent, who otherwise seems unmovable and all-powerful. If girls identify with their mothers, to whom they are attached and with whom they remain in closer proximity, the experience of inequality may be less overwhelming and the sense of efficacy gained by creating connections with others may be more central to the organization of their self-concept and self-esteem (see Chodorow, 1974, 1978). By adolescence, therefore, girls may be less attentive to the consequences of unequal relationships, and more apt to focus their attention on the nature or the strength of connection, especially when narrow conventions of feminine behavior impede strivings toward equality. As such, *care* may be more salient in their moral experience than justice.

In contrast, if boys are more strongly attached to their mothers but identify with their fathers and yet do not see beyond their father's authority and physical power, then the experience of inequality and the desire to overcome that status may become more central to the organization of self-concept and separation or independence more crucial for self-esteem (see Chodorow, 1974, 1978). If recurrent childhood experiences of inequality are less mitigated by experiences of attachment in boys' development, compounded by social inequality in adolescence and a high cultural valuation of male dominance, feelings of powerlessness may become heightened and the potential for violence may correspondingly increase. Consequently, *justice* may become more salient in the moral experience of boys than care.

These schematic observations are intended to suggest the ways in which experiences of inequality and experiences of attachment can interact with one another, leading one dimension of relationship—and morality—to overshadow the other. We have indicated how girls may tend to lose sight of the problems that arise from inequality and how boys may tend to lose sight of the problems that arise from detachment. Yet the tension between these two moral perspectives may best illuminate the psychology of moral development, by drawing attention to conflicts in relationships that give rise to genuine moral dilemmas.

When seen in terms of *either* care or justice, the following problems *appear* to have right, if difficult, answers; seen from *both* perspectives, however, their ethical ambiguity is obvious: a child who is uncertain whether or not to help a friend cheat on a test or to adhere to standards of fairness, or an adolescent who is torn between loyalty to a particular relationship and loyalty to ideals of equality and freedom, or an adult who wonders whether it is better to respond to the perception of need or to follow principles of justice when allocating scarce resources. Like the dilemma posed by Sartre (1948), concerning whether a young man should join the resistance or stay with his mother, or the dilemmas of mothers who wonder whether to join the resistance or stay with their children, these conflicts can be seen as paradigmatic human moral problems— problems that arise when the demands of justice and the demands of care clash.

The metaphor that best illuminates our perspective on moral development, therefore, is the ambiguous figure. When one looks at an ambiguous figure, like the drawing that can be seen either as a young or old woman, the image of the vase and the faces, or the figure that can be seen either as a rabbit or a duck, one initially sees it only one way. Yet, even after seeing it both ways, one way often seems more compelling—highlighting a human tendency to view reality as unequivocal, and thus to believe that there is one right or better way of seeing. Most important, however, from our perspective, the ambiguous figure simply illustrates how the same scene can be organized in at least two different ways, and how one way of seeing can lead another to disappear.

Before we conclude this section let us briefly highlight what we think are the most interesting and fruitful growing edges of our work. Over the past decade our attention has increasingly focused on studying girls' development during childhood and adolescence. This work began in 1981, partly in response to the observation, reiterated in the 1980 *Handbook of Adolescent Psychology*, that "girls have simply not been much studied" by researchers interested in adolescent development (Adelson and Doehrman, 1980), and partly as an outgrowth of previous work on women's conceptions of self and morality (Gilligan, 1977, 1982). Girls' development was empirically unexplored and theoretically of interest, raising difficult questions about differences and reopening to investigation the relationship between psychology and culture, development and education.

Initially, our research on girls' development focused on adolescent girls. Interviewing girls in early-, middle-, and late-adolescence, we were puzzled by a seeming disconnection of girls from their own knowledge. Extensive knowledge about human relationships and the socio-emotional world was apparent in many girls' descriptions of their lives, and this knowledge was often psychologically astute. Yet in describing actions they took or choices they made, girls often discounted or ignored their own experience (see, for example, Brown, 1990). At the time, however, as we have outlined above, we were primarily concerned with creating a developmental theory that registered the self as polyphonic, capable of speaking in different voices and involved in their orchestration. The creation of an enlarged, multidimensional developmental framework seemed prerequisite to mapping girls' development, and a shift away from the mutually exclusive categories of coding systems toward a *Reading Guide* (see below) that specifies multiple readings of any interview text seemed essential to speaking about observed differences without flattening those differences and arriving at caricatures of males and females.

With these theoretical and methodological advancements in place, our attention has returned in recent years to questions both about the psychology of women and about girls' development. The importance of connection or responsive relationship in girls' lives seems clear. Adolescent girls and adult women tend to elaborate an ethic of care, voicing the importance of responding to self and others and drawing attention to the dangers of detachment, disconnection, violation, and hurt (Gilligan, 1982; Gilligan & Attanucci, 1988). Yet it is also clear that girls in adolescence are tempted to solve problems in relationship by silencing themselves, thereby avoiding conflict and disagreement, but also removing themselves from relationship, and thus rendering connections inauthentic (see Brown, 1990; Gilligan, 1977, 1982, 1986; Gilligan, Lyons, & Hanmer, 1990; Miller, 1976; Stern, 1990). The tendency for adolescent girls and adult women to label caring for themselves "selfish," and to equate virtue with self-sacrifice, suggests the continuing power of constraining feminine norms of goodness in the lives of girls and women.

A decision to study younger, school-age girls at this juncture in our research has proven to be crucial, however, yielding unexpected findings of strength, courage, and healthy resistance in girls at the edge of adolescence (Brown, 1989; Brown & Gilligan, 1992, 1993; Gilligan, 1991; Gilligan, Rogers, & Tolman, 1991; Rogers, 1993; Rogers & Gilligan, 1988). These findings shed new light on the psychology of women and point to early adolescence as an especially critical time in girls' development. In particular, this research on younger girls prompted us to question the developmental sequence Gilligan had initially traced in women's descriptions of self and morality (Gilligan, 1977, 1982). This sequence, tracing three levels—survival, goodness, and truth—and two transitions—repairing relationships by correcting an exclusion of others or of self—did not reflect our observations of younger girls. In short, this sequence, which had been traced by following adolescent girls and adult women through time, did not seem to be rooted in childhood. Instead, it seemed to be a response to a crisis, and the crisis seemed to be adolescence. Adolescence thus appeared to pose a "problem of connection" for girls coming of age in Western culture, encouraging girls to solve this problem either by excluding themselves or by excluding others—that is, in the terms of this culture, by being a good woman, or by being selfish.

Consequently, the study of younger girls documented a struggle on the part of girls entering adolescence against a loss of voice and the relinquishing of authentic for inauthentic relationships—a struggle often observed in the public arena of the school classroom. The relationship between girls and women, and the role of women teaching girls, thus appears to be particularly critical both for girls and for women at this developmental juncture. These questions about girls' development in early adolescence and their relationship to women's psychology thus frame the growing edge of our theoretical and empirical work.[3]

## *Research*

Central to our research efforts, as we have indicated above, has been the development of a method for reading and interpreting interview narratives of real-life moral conflict and choice for the voice of the self speaking in the narrative, and for the relational voices/moral orientations of justice and care. We have called this method *A guide to reading narratives of conflict and choice for self and relational voice*; we refer to it as the *Reading Guide* (see Brown, et al., 1988; Brown, Tappan, Gilligan, Argyris, & Miller, 1989; Brown, Debold, Tappan, & Gilligan, 1991; Gilligan, Brown, & Rogers, 1990).[4] The *Reading Guide* highlights both care and justice as relational voices, as well as the sense of tension people often convey in their stories of lived moral experience. In other words, it is a voice-sensitive method that attempts to record the complexity of narratives of conflict and choice, and attempts to capture the personal, relational, and cultural dimensions of psychic life—including language and voice, perspectives and visions, and the relationship between the narrator's and the reader's ways of seeing and speaking.

Such a method, focusing as it does on the reading process and the creation of an interpretive account of a narrative, thus raises questions both about a reader's subjectivity and perspective, and about how a reader can understand the subjectivity and perspective of the person whose narrative he or she reads. The *Reading Guide* explicitly acknowledges, therefore, the interpretive nature of the reading process. It is designed to teach the reader to read for care and justice in narratives of conflict and choice, highlighting in this process the way in which self is represented in these two voices. That is, it attunes the reader's ear to a person speaking in an interview text about themselves and talking about a personal moral conflict in terms of concerns about care and/or justice. Thus, this method outlines a particular way of interpreting texts. It does not preclude other readings, but rather clarifies one theoretical frame and highlights what it provides the researcher interested in self, relationships, and morality.

By attending to the reader and the reading process, the *Reading Guide* thus contrasts with coding manuals that are designed to teach coders to match key code words or phrases or target sentences to a predetermined set of categories (see, for example, Colby & Kohlberg, 1987; Gibbs & Widaman, 1982; Loevinger & Wessler, 1970). This shift from a coding system to an explicitly interpretive method, from codifying statements to reading texts, entails several other important distinctions. Methods that rely either on counting considerations (see Lyons, 1983) or loosely matching justifications or reasons (see Colby & Kohlberg, 1987) may lose much of what seems relevant to understanding the choices people make. The sense of the story or narrative account, and therefore the experience of a person telling a story of sometimes unresolvable and therefore tragic conflict, cannot be captured by coding systems that excise certain passages or ideas from the overall narrative. That is, coding systems offer no provision for including the speaker's own reflection on the meaning of the conflict for him or her. The physical reality of a speaker who, because of certain circumstances or life experiences or material conditions, takes certain thoughts or feelings to be of major or minor importance is lost in such systems. Also lost is the engagement and response of the interpreter in his or her life context to such stories. Thus, one of our aims in creating the *Reading Guide* was to provide a way to acknowledge and explore the relationship between reader and text, and thus to move away from claims to an "objectified" and therefore decontextualized psychology.

The *Reading Guide* takes as its starting point the premise that a person, appearing in an interview text as a speaking voice telling a narrative or story, experiences relationships both in terms of attachment and in terms of equality. The care and justice voices are, as we have indicated above, relational voices— that is, they are characterized by the telling of different narratives about relationship. A care voice describes relationships in terms of attachment/ detachment, connection or disconnection. *Care narratives*, consequently, focus on the vulnerability of people to isolation and abandonment, and are concerned with the complexities of creating and sustaining human connection. A justice voice describes relationship in terms of inequality/equality, reciprocity, or lack of respect. *Justice narratives* thus focus on the vulnerability of people to oppression, and are centrally concerned with standards or principles of fairness.

The *Reading Guide* thus allows a reader to track the voices of justice and care and to specify the ways in which a person orchestrates or chooses between them. The reader first locates a narrative of relational conflict; he or she then reads this story a total of *four* different times. Each reading considers the narrative from a different standpoint; that is, in each the reader attends to a different aspect of the narrative deemed to be relevant in locating self and relational voice.

We have assumed in developing the *Reading Guide* that a narrative of moral conflict can be heard and understood by a careful reader. We have partially assured the coherence of such stories, however, by using a sequence of questions about moral conflict and choice (see Table 12-1) and by training interviewers to ask the narrator additional clarifying or activating questions about her or his construction of the dilemma, resolution of the problem, and evaluation of his or her action. It is important to note, though, that while we have used questions about moral conflict and choice to elicit stories of relational conflict in the majority of our studies, the *Reading Guide* is designed to enable interpretation of any such stories. That is, it can be used to interpret responses to other interview questions. Since concerns for care and justice emerge from experiences in relationship, any story of conflict in relationship can be read for these two voices.

The first of the four readings is designed simply to establish the story told by the narrator. The reader's goal is to understand the story, the context, the drama (the who, what, when, where, and why of the story). The reader, like a literary critic or a psychoanalyst, is also asked to look for recurrent words or images, central metaphors, emotional resonances, contradictions, or inconsistencies in style, revisions and absences in the text, as well as shifts in narrative

**TABLE 12-1    Real-Life Conflict and Choice Interview**

All people have had the experience of being in a situation where they had to make a decision, but weren't sure of what they should do. Would you describe a situation when you faced a moral conflict and you had to make a decision, but weren't sure what you should do?

What was the situation? (Be sure to get a full elaboration of the story.)

What was the conflict for you in that situation?

Why was it a conflict?

In thinking about what to do, what did you consider? Why?

Anything else you considered?

What did you decide to do?

What happened?

Do you think it was the right thing to do? Why/why not?

What was at stake for you in this dilemma?

What was at stake for others?

In general, what was at stake?

How did you feel about it?

How did you feel about it for the other(s) involved?

Is there another way to see the problem (other than the way you described it)?

When you think back over the conflict you described, do you think you learned anything from it?

Do you consider the situation you described a moral problem? Why/why not?

What does morality mean to you?

What makes something a moral problem for you?

position—the use of first, second, or third person voice. Such close attention to the text helps the reader locate the person telling the story in the narrative told, sets the scene, and establishes the flow of events. In addition, this first reading asks the reader to locate him or herself as a person in the privileged position of interpreting the life events of another and to consider the implications of this act. The reader is asked to reflect on his or her own feelings and thoughts about the story and to consider the issues of commonality and difference with the story's narrator.[5]

The next three readings focus specifically on the ways in which self and the voices of care and justice are represented in the interview-narrative. In the second reading the reader attends to "self": the "I" represented in the story or, in other words, the "I" who appears as an actor in the narrator's story of moral conflict. In the third reading the reader attends to a care voice—the speaker's expressed concerns for attachment, attention, and responsiveness to people. In the fourth reading the reader attends to a justice voice—concerns that people be treated fairly and with equal respect.[6]

One can think of the activity of each reading as looking through a different interpretive lens, each lens brings into focus different aspects of the narrative. To switch metaphors, each listening amplifies a different voice. Looking first through one interpretive lens and then another, listening first for one voice and then another, the interpreter can appreciate the way in which a narrator can see a situation differently, from different perspectives, and can tell a story told from more than one angle, or in different terms. A given statement may therefore have different meanings depending on the lens through which it is seen, and a meaning may become apparent with one lens that is hidden from view by another.[7] In this way the *Reading Guide* highlights what the Russian literary critic Mikhail Bakhtin (1981) calls the "polyphonic" nature of texts—in this case, interview texts.[8]

After each reading for self, care, and justice, the reader is asked to fill in summary worksheets. The worksheets provide a place for the reader to document relevant pieces of the text and to make observations and interpretive remarks. The worksheets are designed to highlight the critical move from the narrator's actual words to a reader's interpretation or summary of them, since they require the reader to substantiate his or her interpretation with quotes from the interview text itself. As such, the worksheets stand between the reader and the interview text; they provide a trail of evidence for the reader's interpretations of the narrative (see Brown, Tappan, Gilligan, Argyris, & Miller, 1989; Brown, Debold, Tappan, & Gilligan, 1991).

Our systematic research on relational voice as a dimension of moral thinking, feeling, and acting initially addressed three questions: (1) Do people articulate concerns about justice and concerns about care in discussing moral dilemmas?; (2) Do people tend to focus their attention primarily on one voice and minimally represent the other?; and (3) Is there an association between moral voice and gender? Evidence from a review of several studies that included matched samples of males and females, and used an early prototype of the method described above, provides affirmative answers to all three questions.

Gilligan and Attanucci (1988) report that when asked to describe a moral conflict they had faced, 55 out of 80 (69 percent) educationally advantaged U.S. adolescents and adults (high school students, college students, medical students, and adult professionals) raised considerations of *both* justice and care in their narratives of real-life experiences of moral conflict and choice. This suggests that individuals are not limited to a monotonic voice or single orientation in dealing with their conflicts and attempts at resolution.

Despite this plurality of voices exhibited by individual subjects, however, Gilligan and Attanucci also note that almost two-thirds of the subjects in the studies they reviewed (51 out of 80) manifested a clear *dominance* of one voice over the other—with *dominance* defined as 75 percent or more of the moral considerations raised in recounting a real-life experience framed in terms of either justice or care. Thus, for example, the individual who presented two care considerations discussing a moral conflict was more likely to give a third and fourth rather than to balance care and justice concerns—a finding consonant with the assumption that justice and care constitute organizing frameworks for moral decision-making. The men and women involved in these studies were equally likely to demonstrate this *dominant focus* phenomenon.[9] This finding suggests that individuals tend to "prefer" one or the other voice, even though they are capable of using both.

Finally, Gilligan and Attanucci observe that the *dominant focus* for males and females were strikingly different. Although not all women with a dominant focus showed a preference for the care voice, where the care voice was dominant, it was manifested almost exclusively by females in these samples. Thus, more than half of the women who showed a dominant focus preferred the *care* voice (12 out of 22); in contrast, of the 31 men who manifested a dominant focus, 30 showed a preference for the *justice* voice.

How can these findings be interpreted? They clearly indicate that neither voice (justice or care) is *gender-specific*. They do, however, suggest that the two voices tend to be *gender-related*: males orient toward justice more frequently than females, while females orient toward care more frequently than males (see also Gilligan & Wiggins, 1987; Lyons, 1983; Rogers, 1988).[10]

Additional research has not only supported this finding, but has also generated new insights about the interplay of the voices of justice and care. Johnston (1985, 1988) explored the relationship between moral orientation and problem-solving strategies by creating a standard method for identifying justice and care in response to two of Aesop's fables. In particular, she was interested in the voice spontaneously used to frame the solution to the fables, whether individuals could switch from one voice to the other, and what voice individuals would use to frame the "best" solution to the problem posed by the fables.

Johnston asked 60 eleven- and fifteen-year-old boys and girls to state and solve the problem posed by the fables, and then she asked "Is there another way to solve this problem?" The majority of her subjects initially framed the problem in each fable in terms of either justice or care—that is, either they assumed a detached position and appealed to a rule or principle for resolving the competing claims in the fable, or they took personal interest in the situation in an effort to discover or create a way of taking care of all the characters in the story, in an attempt to respond to all of their needs. Furthermore, roughly one-half of her subjects spontaneously switched voice when asked if there was another way to solve the problem; the rest did so when the interviewer provided cues to the form such a switch might take. Finally, Johnston asked her subjects which of the solutions they described was the best solution, and most answered in terms of one voice or the other.

Johnston found gender differences with respect to relational voice/moral orientation similar to those reported by Gilligan and Attanucci (1988). Boys more often spontaneously used and preferred justice solutions to the fables she posed, while girls more often spontaneously used and preferred care solutions.

More importantly, however, the fact that children and adolescents can shift perspectives and speak in both voices, when invited to do so, raises a number of very interesting and provocative questions relevant to understanding how and why individuals change in the ways in which they morally think, feel, and act. Specifically, the demonstration that children know both voices and can frame and solve moral problems in at least two different ways means that the choice of moral standpoint is an element of moral decision. The role of the self in moral judgment thus includes the choice of moral standpoint, and this decision, whether implicit or explicit, may become linked with self-respect and self-definition. Especially in adolescence, when choice becomes more self-conscious and self-reflective, moral standpoint may become entwined with identity and self-esteem. Johnston's finding that spontaneous voice and preferred voice are not always the same also raises a number of questions regarding why and under what conditions a person may adopt a problem-solving strategy that he or she sees as a less than ideal way to solve the problem.

Thus, although the gender-relatedness of these two voices is important to stress, the significance of the fact that a majority of Gilligan and Attanucci's and Johnston's subjects manifested a plurality of voices should by no means be overlooked. This research demonstrates that human beings not only speak in multiple voices, but they can and frequently do oscillate from one voice to another in their moral discourse. Indeed, as Bakhtin (1981) has argued, it would appear that human beings are both "polyphonic" in switching from one voice to another over time, and polyphonic in their utterances at any one time (see also Clark & Holquist, 1984; Emerson & Morson, 1987). Insofar as any conception of the moral development of "individuals" is dependent, at least in part, on a specific conception of the person, a reconception of human beings as fundamentally polyphonic must therefore lead to a significant reconsideration of our conception of what constitutes moral development (and moral education).[11]

Finally, as we have indicated above, our most recent work has focused on studying girls' development. Listening to the voices of nearly one hundred school-age and adolescent girls from a private school for girls outside Cleveland, Ohio speak over the course of five years about themselves, their relationships, and their experiences of moral conflict and choice, we have begun to explore the development of girls' psychological, social, and moral understanding (Brown, 1989, 1991; Brown & Gilligan, 1992, 1993). While most of the girls we spoke with—ranging in age from 6 to 18—came from middle-class or upper-middle-class families and the majority were white, 20 percent of the girls were from working-class families, attending the school on scholarship, and 14 percent were girls of color. In this group of girls, color was not associated with low social class, and low social class was not associated with educational advantage.

An analysis of interview texts revealed clear evidence that, in the transition from childhood to adolescence, these girls showed the kind of developmental progression that has been traditionally defined and measured by cognitive developmentalists (see Piaget, 1967; Kohlberg, 1984; Selman, 1980): They became less dependent on external authorities, less egocentric or locked in their own experience or point of view, more differentiated from others in the sense of being able to distinguish their feelings and thoughts from those of other people, more autonomous in the sense of being able to rely on or to take responsibility for themselves, more appreciative of the complex interplay of voices and perspectives in any relationship, more aware of the diversity of human experience and the differences between societal and cultural groups.

Yet we found this developmental progression went hand in hand with evidence of a loss of voice, a struggle to authorize or take seriously their own experience, increased confusion, sometimes defensiveness, as well as evidence for the replacement of genuine with inauthetic or idealized relationships. If we consider responding to oneself, knowing and expressing one's feelings and thoughts, clarity, courage, and free-flowing connections with others and the world as signs of psychological health, as we do, these girls were showing evidence of loss and struggle and signs of an impasse in their ability to act in the face of conflict. Thus, while in one sense, the girls we studied were progressing steadily as they moved from childhood to adolescence, girls at the edge of adolescence, our study suggests, face a central relational dilemma: to speak what they know through experience creates political problems—disagreement with authorities, disrupting relationships—while not to speak leaves a residue of psychological problems: false relationships and confusion as to what they feel and think, and where they stand.

## *Application*

We would like to conclude this chapter by considering the implications of our work for those who are interested in supporting and encouraging the development of children and adolescents, particularly in educational and clinical contexts. In this regard, there are three areas of focus to which we would like to direct our attention.

The first concerns the implications of our work for those interested in fostering and facilitating the development of both the care voice and the justice voice in children and adolescents. While much has been written about efforts to foster moral development defined as thinking and reasoning about justice and fairness (see Kohlberg, 1981, 1984; Mosher, 1980; Power, Higgins, and Kohlberg, 1989), very little has been written about how to foster the development of care and responsiveness (see, however, Noddings, 1993). Kohlberg's (1981, 1984) theory of moral development has provided a model for moral education (the "just community" approach) that is guided exclusively by the concerns of a justice voice—fairness, reciprocity, rights, and rules. The just community approach, however, appears to provide little opportunity, at least explicitly, to address the concerns of a care voice—for example, being morally bound to others, being responsive and caring to others, and avoiding harm to persons who break the rules.

In its broadest sense our research suggests that morality itself is dialectical; hence the development of an understanding of both justice and care is fundamental to mature moral functioning. Consequently, we would argue that education aimed and fostering and facilitating moral development must not only accord equal recognition to a care voice *vis-à-vis* a justice voice, it must also regard it as *essential* and must foster its development in both females and males. Such an aim suggests, therefore, that an assessment of the degree to which the development of both of these voices are encouraged by curriculum and educational policies and practices is in order. Seen in this light, it may not be an exaggeration to suggest that the separate self/knower who reasons deductively (see Belenky, Clinchy, Goldberger, & Tarule, 1986), and is regarded as a rational moral agent (hallmarks of the justice voice), is also the student we traditionally have in mind when we place priorities on science, mathematics, "individualized instruction," and the "rights" of students in our schools.

The focus on the particularities of a situation and an understanding of others which mark the care voice suggest, in contrast, a more narrative mode of thinking and a more contextual way of knowing. This calls for a renewed emphasis, in schools, on the communication and understanding that comes through the following: the activity of writing; the reading of fictional and historical accounts of human lives, societies, and cultures; the demonstration, through art, of how meaning depends on context; the dialogue of classroom discussion; and the construction of meaning in interactions between readers and texts—all aspects of education that have yielded, over the past decades, to a fascination with the abstraction of truth from life, the subordination of relationships to rules, and the increasingly impersonal technology of education.

We would suggest, therefore, that the study of history and literature, which have been relegated to a subordinate position in our schools in this science-dominated century, provide examples of subject areas that reflect the concerns of a care voice. They are premised on the narrative language of the connected self/knower who reasons inductively (see Belenky, Clinchy, Goldberger, & Tarule, 1986), and who sees herself or himself fit into a contextual world of interconnected relationships. So, if we were to elevate history and literature to a position of equality with mathematics and science, would the school curriculum successfully foster the development of both a justice voice and a care voice? Perhaps. But we should take heed that we do not limit our understanding of the power of a care voice to represent a different way of thinking, feeling, acting, and knowing that can be brought to bear not just in the study of history and literature, but to all areas of the curriculum (see McIntosh, 1983).

Finally, to explore the broader implications of this research, educators will need to look beyond the curriculum to the general patterns of learning fostered in our schools. In so doing, they may call into question, for example, whether a system in which each student is encouraged to learn separately from others—instead of collaboratively with others—may limit opportunities for the development of care and responsiveness in both males and females, thereby further limiting opportunities for students to come to understand and appreciate an ethic of care.

A second area of focus concerns the educative and developmental effect of providing children and adolescents the opportunity to tell their own stories about their real-life moral experiences. Such a narrative approach to moral development and education (see Tappan & Brown, 1989) provides students with the opportunity, by telling their own moral stories, to express and enhance their own authority and responsibility through the process of "authoring." By thereby representing the cognitive, emotional, and active dimensions of their own moral experience through narrative (see Tappan, 1990), students are encouraged to reflect on their experience from the standpoint of their own moral perspective. This leads, we would argue, not only to an increased sense of authority and authorization on behalf of that perspective, but also an increased sense of responsibility for action.

This opportunity for students to author their own moral stories can, and should, take several forms. One is to provide the opportunity for students to be formally interviewed, by teachers, fellow students, or, perhaps, even outside interviewers, so they can tell their stories of real-life conflict and choice in great detail. Such interviews can be guided by interview protocols designed to elicit such stories, like the one we use in our own research (see Table 12-1, above).

One of the reasons why an in-depth interview designed to evoke stories of moral experience, guided by a formal protocol like that presented above, is a powerful means of enhancing authorship is that it provides a real-live *audience*, in the form of a sympathetic and engaged listener, to whom the student can tell her story.[12] The presence of a real audience serves to encourage authoring, as the author/interviewee seeks to arouse and fulfill desires and expectations in the mind of her audience/interviewer. This is because, unlike someone who simply lists a sequence of events, the author of a story has a particular moral perspective on behalf of which she wants to claim authority, and, therefore, on behalf of which she wants to argue. Consequently, her role as an author is to convince her audience of both the legitimacy of her moral perspective, and the righteousness of her actions in the story she tells. Thus the author must engage the "psychology of the audience" (Burke, 1931) in ways that enable her to make her case most convincingly and authoritatively. This, again, is the process of *authoring* (see Tappan & Brown, 1989).

Students can also be given the opportunity to author their own moral stories in written form, by keeping a journal or through essay assignments that focus on the moral decisions they have made in their own lives. Here, again, the teacher is the primary audience for these stories; hence she must not only be sensitive and sympathetic, but she must also provide students with the kind of response to their stories that indicates that she has heard and understood them. While this response can be either oral or written, it must acknowledge the author's own moral perspective, and encourage the continued authorization of that perspective.

Finally, students may even be given the opportunity to dramatize their own moral stories, through skits and plays or through video productions. Such an option would necessarily involve sharing a story with a peer audience in a way not required by the first two approaches. While this may be uncomfortable for some, it may also provide the opportunity for students to learn important lessons from the stories of their peers—lessons that may not be learned in any other way.

Needless to say, in order for any of these options to succeed they must occur in the context of a relationship with a sensitive and caring teacher. The power of this approach comes from the authority students can gain by authoring their moral stories and sharing them with an audience; the danger of this approach is the vulnerability that goes along with sharing difficult, painful, and perhaps even tragic stories. Teachers, therefore, must recognize both the opportunities and the risks inherent in such an approach, and be prepared to respond accordingly.

In practice, teachers can exhibit their concern for and involvement with their students by taking great care in how they interpret and understand the stories they are told. This means that teachers must neither automatically assume they know what a student's story means, nor be too quick to judge a particular story as "inappropriate," "immoral," or, simply, "wrong." Rather, teachers must cultivate an openness to and a tolerance of the stories—and the voices—they hear, and they must be willing to work with their students so that both come to understand and appreciate the lessons inherent in these stories. Then, and only then, will students' authorship of their own stories—hence their authorization of their own moral perspective—be encouraged and enabled.[13]

Finally, we would like to return to our recent work on girls' development from childhood to adolescence. The implications of this work for educational theory and practice revolve primarily around the new light it sheds on the relationship between women and adolescent girls—particularly with respect to the role that women teachers can play in facilitating the healthy psychological development of girls, by encouraging girls to resist a loss of voice, inauthentic relationships, and capitulation to damaging norms and models of female development (see Dorney, 1991; Gilligan, 1991). In particular, with respect to the shift described above, from the openness and self-confidence of pre-adolescent girls to the more closed and self-protective posture of adolescent girls, it would seem important that teachers, particularly women teachers, establish connection with girls before they feel a need to protect or withdraw what they know about the relational world from adults. It would also appear that girls in fifth and sixth grades are at a pivotal point in this respect. At ten and eleven, these girls speak about what they feel and think and portray a complex relational world in rich detail—a world of difference in which there is disagreement and people get hurt; a world constructed from personal experience and observation. Yet, these girls are also beginning to feel the pressure to adapt to idealized notions of femininity at odds with their experiences and desires, a pressure that threatens to silence their realistic and forthright descriptions of the social world. In the midst of this struggle, however, these pre-adolescents seek out and listen attentively to advice from female adults; they observe how adults treat each other and how relationships are negotiated; they note inconsistencies and discrepancies; they recognize differences in interpretation and they wish to talk about them.

Thus, teachers who would engage the observations of these girls, who would stay with them as they struggle with discrepancies and confusion, and who would encourage them to face the risks of publicly speaking about what they know, may offer them a productive alternative to the protective move "underground." That is, teachers might join with their female students to transform the secret "underground" into a public "resistance" to negative sex-role stereotypes, to idealized or inauthentic relationships. Yet, since part of what these girls struggle with has to do with their critical observations of the behavior of female adults themselves, those who would engage these girls in genuine relationships must be willing to honestly confront themselves as women and teachers; that is, to consider their own value assumptions about being female in a male-defined society and what it then means to educate girls for success in this culture at this time.

Meeting at this crossroads between girls and women thus creates an opportunity for women to join girls and by doing so to reclaim lost voices and lost strengths, to strengthen girls' voices and girls' courage as they enter adolescence by offering girls resonant relationships, and in this way to move with girls toward creating a psychologically healthier world and a more caring and just society.

In reporting work which in its very nature is relational and therefore open-ended or incomplete, we bring to others the evidence from our work with girls and women—voices which we believe are worth listening to, in part because of the questions they raise. From this work, we take the strong conviction that resonant relationships between girls and women are crucial for girls' development, for women's psychological health, and also for bringing women's voices fully into the world so that the social construction of reality—the construction of the human world that is institutionalized by society and carried across generations by culture—will be built by and will be acoustically resonant for both women and men.

## Recommended Readings

Brown, L., & Gilligan, C. (1992). *Meeting at the crossroads: Women's psychology and girls' development.* Cambridge: Harvard University Press.

Gilligan, C. (1982). *In a different voice.* Cambridge: Harvard University Press.

Gilligan, C., Lyons, N., & Hanmer, T. (Eds.). (1990). *Making connections: the relational worlds of adolescent girls at Emma Willard School.* Cambridge: Harvard University Press.

Gilligan, C., Rogers, A., & Tolman, D. (Eds.). (1991). *Women, girls, & psychotherapy: Reframing resistance.* Binghamton, NY:

Haworth Press.

Gilligan, C., Ward, J., & Taylor, J. (Eds.). (1988). *Mapping the moral domain: A contribution of women's thinking to psychological theory and education.* Cambridge: Harvard University Press.

Noddings, N. (1993). *The challenge to care in schools.* New York: Teachers College Press.

Tappan, M. (1992). Texts and contexts: Language, culture, and the development of moral functioning. In. L. T. Winegar & J. Valisner (Eds.), *Children's development within social contexts: Metatheoretical, theoretical, and methodological issues.* Hillsdale, NJ: Lawrence Erlbaum.

Tappan, M., & Brown, L. (1989). Stories told and lessons learned: Toward a narrative approach to moral development and moral education. *Harvard Educational Review, 59* (2), 182-205.

## Authors' Note

Preparation of this chapter was supported, in part, by grants from the Cleveland Foundation, the George Gund Foundation, the Lilly Endowment, and the Spencer Foundation.

## Endnotes

1. We follow Bernard Kaplan (1983, 1986) in believing that any conception of development is fundamentally and inescapably value-laden. The concept of development is, in other words, a *prescriptive* concept, used to refer to an *ideal progression* toward some specified goal, endpoint, or *telos* that has been imbued with value:

> Development, as distinct from change, has been and ought to be an axiological and normative notion. It has been, and ought to be, comprehended as "movement toward perfection," "movement toward liberation," "movement toward the Good or God." (Kaplan, 1983, p. 204)

Consequently, we would argue that any conception of development is essentially a conception of *moral* development.

2. While we tend to use these two concepts interchangeably, in practice, they can be theoretically distinguished as follows: A *relational voice* represents the first-order forms of speech, language, and discourse a person uses when speaking about his or her thoughts and feelings about, and experiences in, relationships. A *moral orientation* is a second-order *interpretation* of a relational voice using categories and concepts taken from moral philosophy and ethical discourse. In our research, therefore, we have repeatedly identified two different *relational voices* (there are undoubtedly others) that we have identified using the *moral* categories of "justice" and "care."

3. This shift toward understanding girls' psychological development has entailed a corresponding shift away from an exclusive focus on the study of moral development per se, at least in the way it is often distinguished from social or psychological or emotional development. Rather, we have become interested in the ways morality, or the voices that speak of how one should or would like to act in relationships, carry the force of institutionalized social norms and cultural values into relationships and psychic and emotional life.

4. Over time, we have also come to call our method a *Listener's Guide*, to highlight the responsive nature of our method, the degree to which it is centered on voice and listening, and to more accurately represent the relational experience of speaking and being listened to (see Brown & Gilligan, 1991, 1992, 1993). Four questions thus attune one's ear to the polyphony of voice and the complex harmonics of relation-

ship: (1) Who is speaking? (2) In what body? (3) Telling what story or stories about relationship—from whose perspective or from what vantage point? (4) In what societal and cultural frameworks?

5. While we emphasize the reader's/listener's need to appreciate how commonalities and differences in such critical areas as race, cultural background, social class, gender, and sexual orientation might effect his or her understanding of a narrator's story, we also wish the reader to consider other reasons or experiences that could facilitate or interfere with his or her ability to listen well. One might imagine, for example, an intense emotional resonance with or reaction to a particular event or story that could lead the reader/listener either to over-identify with or dismiss the story.

6. The Reading or Listening Guide is designed to be open-ended and thus useful to those who wish to listen for voices other than those of justice and care. While the first two readings/listenings seem to us critical for bringing the interpreter into responsive relationship with the person speaking, more recently we have, ourselves, shifted our attention to girls' voices of capitulation or resistance to conventions of femininity and womanhood as they are culturally defined (Brown & Gilligan, 1992; Rogers, Brown, & Tappan, 1994; Taylor, Gilligan, Sullivan, & Tolman, in press).

7. In fact, the reader uses colored pencils to mark passages on the interview text to indicate each reading—colors that represent self (green), care (red), and justice (blue). Thus, to mix metaphors, this visual technique of representation attunes the reader at once to the specific languages or voices of the narrator without losing sight of the larger story or the way these voices are orchestrated to convey the conflict.

8. Polyphony [in Bakhtin's sense] goes beyond the mere juxtaposition or sequential sounding of contrary voices and ideas. The musical metaphor implies that many voices are heard at the same time, uttering the same voice differently. Thus, the same word simultaneously exhibits different values, "pitches," and "rhythms." By repeating this process in the course of a work, the orchestrator—the novelist [or the narrator]—can make the unrepeatable particularity of each utterance resonate. Voices join other voices to produce the timbre and intonation of a given communication. (Emerson & Morson, 1987, p. 49)

9. Two-thirds of both sexes fell into one of the pure focus categories, while the remaining one-third showed no focus, but rather a mixture of justice and care.

10. It is important to stress, however, that these findings are based, by and large, on samples of educationally and economically privileged, predominantly white, U.S. residents. Further research on diverse cultures and subcultures will thus be necessary to determine whether this dominant focus phenomenon is truly gender-related, or whether it is a result of some kind of gender/class/race/education interaction.

11. This research also underscores the socially constructed nature of morality as we have come to understand it, as distinct from biologically determined (Freud, 1963) or rationally reconstructed (Kohlberg, 1984) conceptions.

12. It is important to note, however, that stories elicited in a formal interview differ in fundamental ways from stories told spontaneously, in either oral or written form. The interviewer asks questions of the storyteller, thereby both interrupting his or her narrative, and perhaps even directing in ways the narrator might not have otherwise chosen to go. Thus it is important to acknowledge that stories told in such interviews are clearly *co-constructed*, in the context of the *dialogue* that necessarily occurs between interviewer and interviewee.

13. We do not, however, advocate a completely relative or subjective approach to moral education, where each and every story is accepted without judgment. We need only consider, for example, the kind of personal moral authority that Adolph Hitler claimed for himself to see the potential risks of authorship that is completely unconstrained and out of relationship. As such, we would argue that a dialogical and relational conception of authority

and responsibility—in which authorship is necessarily constructed in genuine dialogue between self and others, and thus informed by both compassion and respect—provides a powerful way to critique unilateral, totalitarian, and oppressive abuses of authority.

## References

Adelson, J., & Doehrman, M. (1980). The psychodynamic approach to adolescence. In J. Adelson (Ed.), *The Handbook of Adolescent Psychology*. New York: John Wiley & Sons.

Bakhtin, M. (1981). *The dialogic imagination* (M. Holquist, Ed., C. Emerson & M. Holquist, Trans.). Austin: University of Texas Press.

Baumrind, D. (1986). Sex differences in moral reasoning: Response to Walker's (1984) conclusion that there are none. *Child Development*, *57*, 511-521.

Belenky, M., Clinchy, B., Goldberger, N., & Tarule, J. (1986). *Women's ways of knowing: The development of self, voice, and mind*. New York: Basic Books.

Bowlby, J. (1969). *Attachment and loss, Vol. I: Attachment*. New York: Basic Books.

Brown, L. (1989). *Narratives of relationship: The development of a care voice in girls ages 7 to 16*. Unpublished doctoral dissertation, Harvard University.

Brown, L. (1990). When is a moral problem not a moral problem?: Morality, identity, and female adolescents. In C. Gilligan, N. Lyons, & T. Hanmer (Eds.), *Making connections: The relational world of adolescent girls at the Emma Willard School*. Cambridge: Harvard University Press.

Brown, L. (1991). A problem of vision: The development of voice and relational knowledge in girls ages 7 to 16. *Women's Studies Quarterly*, *19*, 52-71.

Brown, L., Argyris, D., Attanucci, J., Bardige, B., Gilligan, C., Johnston, K., Miller, B., Osborne, D., Tappan, M., Ward, J., Wiggins, G., & Wilcox, D. (1988). *A guide to reading narratives of conflict and choice for self and relational voice* (Monograph No. 1). Cambridge: Harvard Graduate School of Education, Project on Women's Psychology and Girls' Development.

Brown, L., Debold, E., Tappan, M., & Gilligan, C. (1991). Reading narratives of conflict and choice for self and moral voice: A relational method. In W. Kurtines & J. Gewirtz (Eds.), *Handbook of moral behavior and development: Theory, research, and application*. Hillsdale, NJ: Lawrence Erlbaum.

Brown, L., & Gilligan, C. (1991). Listening for voice in narratives of relationship. In M. Tappan & M. Packer (Eds.), *Narrative and storytelling: Implications for understanding moral development* (*New Directions for Child Development*, No. 54). San Francisco: Jossey-Bass.

Brown, L., & Gilligan, C. (1992). *Meeting at the crossroads: Women's psychology and girls' development*. Cambridge: Harvard University Press.

Brown, L., & Gilligan, C. (1993). Meeting at the crossroads: Women's psychology and girls' development. *Feminism and Psychology, 3*, 11-35.

Brown, L., Tappan, M., Gilligan, C., Argyris, D., & Miller, B. (1989). Reading for self and moral voice: A method for interpreting narratives of real-life moral conflict and choice. In M. Packer & R. Addison (Eds.), *Entering the circle: Hermeneutic investigation in Psychology*. Albany: SUNY Press.

Burke, K. (1931). *Counter-statement*. Berkeley: University of California Press.

Chodorow, N. (1974). Family structure and feminine personality. In M. Rosaldo & L. Lamphere (Eds.), *Women, culture, and society*. Stanford, CA: Stanford University Press.

Chodorow, N. (1978). *The reproduction of mothering: Psychoanalysis and the sociology of gender*. Berkeley: University of California Press.

Clark, K., & Holquist, M. (1984). *Mikhail Bakhtin.* Cambridge: Harvard University Press.

Colby, A. & Kohlberg, L. (1987). *The measurement of moral judgment.* New York: Cambridge University Press.

Dorney, J. (1991). *'Courage to act in a small way': Clues toward community and change among women teaching girls.* Unpublished doctoral dissertation, Harvard University.

Emerson, C., & Morson, G. (1987). Penultimate words. In C. Koelb & V. Lokke (Eds.), *The current in criticism.* West Lafayette, IN: Purdue University Press.

Freud, S. (1963). Some psychological consequences of the anatomical distinction between the sexes. In P. Rieff (Ed.), *Sigmund Freud: Sexuality and the psychology of love.* New York: Collier Books. (Original work published 1925)

Gibbs, J. & Widaman, K. (1982). *Social intelligence: Measuring the development of sociomoral reflection.* Englewood Cliffs, NJ: Prentice-Hall.

Gilligan, C. (1977). In a different voice: Women's conceptions of self and morality. *Harvard Educational Review, 47,* 481-517.

Gilligan, C. (1982). *In a different voice: Psychological theory and women's development.* Cambridge: Harvard University Press.

Gilligan, C. (1986). Exit-voice dilemmas in adolescent development. In A. Foxley, M. McPherson, & G. O'Donnell (Eds.), *Development, democracy, and the art of trespassing: Essays in honor of Albert O. Hirschman.* Notre Dame, IN: University of Notre Dame Press.

Gilligan, C. (1987a). Moral orientation and moral development. In E. Kittay & D. Meyers (Eds.), *Women and moral theory.* Totowa, NJ: Rowman & Littlefield.

Gilligan, C. (1987b). Remapping the moral domain: New images of the self in relationship. In T.C. Heller, M. Sosna, & D. Wellber (Eds.), *Reconstructing individualism: Autonomy, individuality and the self in western thought.* Stanford, CA: Stanford University Press.

Gilligan, C. (1990). Teaching Shakespeare's sister: Notes from the underground of female adolescence. In C. Gilligan, N. Lyons, and T. Hanmer (Eds.), *Making connections: The relational worlds of adolescent girls at Emma Willard School.* Cambridge: Harvard University Press.

Gilligan, C. (1991). Joining the resistance: Psychology, politics, girls, and women. *Michigan Quarterly Review, 29,* 501-536.

Gilligan, C. & Attanucci, J. (1988). Two moral orientations: Gender differences and similarities. *Merrill-Palmer Quarterly, 34,* 223-237.

Gilligan, C., & Belenky, M. (1980). A naturalistic study of abortion decisions. In R. Selman & R. Yando (Eds.), *New directions for child development, Volume 7: Clinical-developmental Psychology.* San Francisco: Jossey-Bass.

Gilligan, C., Brown, L., & Rogers, A. (1990). Psyche embedded: A place for body, relationships, and culture in personality theory. In A. Rabin, R. Zucker, R. Emmons, & S. Frank (Eds.), *Studying persons and lives.* New York: Springer.

Gilligan, C., Lyons, N., & Hanmer, T. (Eds.). (1990). *Making connections: The relational worlds of adolescent girls at Emma Willard School.* Cambridge: Harvard University Press.

Gilligan, C., & Murphy, J. M. (1979). Development from adolescence to adulthood: The philosopher and the dilemma of the fact. In D. Kuhn (Ed.), *New directions for child development, Volume 5: Intellectual development beyond childhood.* San Francisco: Jossey Bass.

Gilligan, C., Murphy, J. M., & Tappan, M. (1990). Moral development beyond adolescence. In C. Alexander & E. Langer (Eds.), *Higher stages of human development.* New York: Oxford University Press.

Gilligan, C., Rogers, A., & Tolman, D. (Eds.). (1991). *Women, girls, & psychotherapy: Reframing resistance.* Binghamton, NY: Haworth Press.

Gilligan, C., & Wiggins, G. (1987). The origins of morality in early childhood relationships. In J. Kagan & S. Lamb (Eds.), *The emergence of morality in young children.* Chicago: University of Chicago Press.

Johnston, D. K. (1985). *Two moral orientations—two problem-solving strategies: Adolescents' solutions to dilemmas in fables.* Unpublished doctoral dissertation, Harvard University.

Johnston, D. K. (1988). Adolescents' solutions to dilemmas in fables: Two moral orientations—two problem solving strategies. In C. Gilligan, J. Ward, & J. Taylor (Eds.), *Mapping the moral domain.* Cambridge: Harvard University Press.

Kagan, J. (1984). *The nature of the child.* New York: Basic Books.

Kaplan, B. (1983). A trio of trials. In R. Lerner (Ed.), *Developmental psychology: Historical and Philosophical Perspectives* (pp. 185-228). Hillsdale, NJ: Lawrence Erlbaum.

Kaplan, B. (1986). Value presuppositions in theories of human development. In L. Cirillo & S. Wapner (Eds.), *Value presuppositions in theories of human development* (pp. 89-103). Hillsdale, NJ: Lawrence Erlbaum.

Kohlberg, L. (1958). *The development of modes of moral thinking and choice in the years ten to sixteen.* Unpublished doctoral dissertation, University of Chicago.

Kohlberg, L. (1981). *Essays on moral development, Vol. I: The philosophy of moral development.* San Francisco: Harper & Row.

Kohlberg, L. (1984). *Essays on moral development, Vol. II: The psychology of moral development.* San Francisco: Harper & Row.

Loevinger, J. & Wessler, R. (1970). *Measuring ego development, Vol I: Construction and use of a sentence completion test.* San Francisco: Jossey-Bass.

Lyons, N. (1983). Two perspectives: On self, relationships, and morality. *Harvard Educational Review, 53,* 125-145.

McIntosh, P. (1983). *Interactive phases of curricular re-vision: A feminist perspective.* Wellesley, MA: Wellesley College, Center for Research on Women.

Miller, J. B. (1976). *Toward a new psychology of women.* Boston: Beacon Press.

Mosher, R. (Ed.). (1980). *Moral education: A first generation of research and development.* New York: Praeger.

Murphy, J. M., & Gilligan, C. (1980). Moral development in late adolescence and adulthood: A critique and reconstruction of Kohlberg's theory. *Human Development, 23,* 77-104.

Noddings, N. (1993). *The challenge to care in schools.* New York: Teachers College Press.

Piaget, J. (1965). *The moral judgment of the child.* New York: The Free Press. (Original work published 1932)

Piaget, J. (1967). *Six psychological studies.* New York: Vintage Books.

Power, F. C., Higgins, A., & Kohlberg, L. (1989). *Lawrence Kohlberg's approach to moral education.* New York: Columbia University Press.

Rogers, A. (1988). *The question of gender differences: A validity study of two moral orientations.* Unpublished manuscript, Harvard University.

Rogers, A. (1993). Voice, play, and a practice of ordinary courage in girls' and women's lives. *Harvard Educational Review, 63,* 265-295.

Rogers, A., Brown, L., & Tappan, M. (1994). Interpreting loss in ego development in girls: Regression or resistance? In R. Josselson & A. Lieblich (Eds.), *The narrative study of lives, Vol. 2.* Newbury Park, CA: Sage.

Rogers, A., & Gilligan, C. (1988). *Translating the language of adolescent girls: Themes of moral voice and stages of ego development* (Monograph No. 6). Cambridge: Project on Women's Psychology and Girls' Development, Harvard Graduate School of Education.

Sartre, J. P. (1948). *Existentialism and humanism.* London: Methuen.

Selman, R. (1980). *The growth of interpersonal understanding.* New York: Academic Press.

Stern, D. (1985). *The interpersonal world of the infant.* New York: Basic Books.

Stern, L. (1990). *Disavowing the self in female adolescence: A case study analysis.* Unpublished doctoral dissertation, Harvard University.

Tappan, M. (1990a). Hermeneutics and moral development: Interpreting narrative representations of moral experience. *Developmental Review,* 239-265.

Tappan, M., & Brown, L. (1989). Stories told and lessons learned: Toward a narrative approach to moral development and moral education. *Harvard Educational Review, 59,* 182-205.

Taylor, J., Gilligan, C., Sullivan, A., & Tolman, D. (in press). *Sustaining hope: Women and girls, race and relationship.* Cambridge: Harvard University Press.

Walker, L. (1984). Sex differences in the development of moral reasoning: A critical review. *Child Development, 55,* 677-691.

Walker, L. (1986). Sex differences in the development of moral reasoning: A rejoinder to Baumrind. *Child Development, 57,* 522-526.

# Chapter 13

# Moral Development: A Co-constructivist Perspective

WILLIAM M. KURTINES
*Florida International University*

STEVEN L. BERMAN
*Florida International University*

ANGELA ITTEL
*University of California, Santa Cruz*

SUSAN WILLIAMSON
*Florida International University*

## Abstract

The co-constructivist perspective that provides the framework for the work on moral development described in this chapter evolved in the context of an ongoing program of research. This perspective builds on the work of others in the area of developmental theory in seeking to extend our understanding of human behavior and development. This co-constructivist perspective views human beings as self-directed, goal-oriented biopsychosocial organisms that in the process of development acquire complex, higher order cognitive and communicative capacities. These capacities enable human beings to engage in the most complex forms of theoretical and practical problem-solving and decision-making, including "moral" decision-making and problem-solving. The development of these higher order competencies enables human beings to engage in both individual and group decision-making and problem-solving activities that affect the quality of their lives. With the development of these higher order competencies human beings acquire the *capacity* to choose the goals and values that give their

*(continued)*

**Abstract** *(continued)*

lives direction and purpose, and the *responsibility* for the consequences or outcomes of their choices. This perspective thus seeks to extend our understanding of human behavior and development to include an explicit recognition of the essential dignity and worth of *all* human beings. In the process of providing an introduction to this co-constructivist perspective, we will illustrate how it can be applied to making the right choice when faced with an individual or group moral dilemma and provide some guidelines for moral decision-making and problem-solving from a co-constructivist perspective.

Difficult life choices involve making decisions about what is the right thing to do. Sartre (1955), in his *Existentialism and Humanism*, tells the story of a former student. The young man came to Sartre for advice during World War II. He was faced with the choice of staying with his mother or joining the Resistance. Part of his dilemma was that he had to evaluate the consequences of his decision. If he left his dependent mother, she might suffer and possibly die. However, if he stayed in Nazi-occupied France to protect his mother, others would be fighting and dying on his behalf. He was faced with making a decision that had serious consequences and he had to evaluate those consequences (e.g., the probability that they would occur, their extent or severity, their desirability or undesirability, etc.). However, his decision was more difficult than simply evaluating consequences. It was more difficult because it involved evaluating consequences in the context of conflicting or competing moral obligations, and he also had to evaluate those obligations—in this case, the relative importance of his obligation to his mother and his obligation to his country. His dilemma was that he had to decide what was the right thing to do in the context of complex and conflicting consequences *and* obligations, and it was not clear what was the best or most useful method for making this decision. Methods that have traditionally helped us in making these decisions (e.g., religion, philosophy, etc.) could not provide him with a clear-cut choice.

> What could help him to choose? Could the Christian doctrine? No. Christian doctrine says: Act with charity, love your neighbor, and so forth. But which is the harder road? To whom does one owe the more brotherly love, the patriot or the mother? Which is the more useful aim, the general one of fighting in and for the whole community, or the precise aim of helping one particular person to live? Who can give an answer to that *a priori*? No one. Nor is it given in any ethical scripture. The Kantian ethic says, Never regard another as a means, but always an end. Very well; if I remain with my mother, I shall be regarding her as the end and not as a means: but by the same token I am in danger of treating as means those who are fighting on my behalf; and the converse is also true, that if I go to the aid of the combatants I shall be

treating them as the end at the risk of treating my mother as a means. (Sartre, 1955, p. 296)

The young man was indeed faced with an agonizing set of alternatives. Neither choice was an easy one. Moreover, the young man could not even choose not to choose, for that would be a choice with the full moral consequences of any other choice. Although dramatic, the type of moral dilemma that Sartre's story illustrates represents the types of dilemmas that we all have to confront sooner or later—conflicts of consequence and obligation. Moreover, there are many means or methods that might be used to resolve these types of dilemmas. In this chapter we will describe and illustrate some methods for making such choices. We will describe and illustrate what we consider to be the best or most useful methods for moral decision-making and problem-solving.

## Moral Development from a Co-constructivist Perspective

One important focus of our work in the area of moral development has been on the development *and* use of the skills and competencies that enable human beings to make the types of decisions that we illustrated in Sartre's dilemma. These competencies provide the foundation for the methods for resolving moral dilemmas that we will describe in this chapter. It will be helpful in illustrating how these methods can be used in resolving moral dilemmas if we begin by providing you with an introduction to the framework that has served as the foundation for our work in the area of moral development.

The co-constructivist perspective that provides the framework for our work evolved in the context of an ongoing program of research. This co-constructivist perspective draws on work that we have done over the past decade. In the course of this work we have found that we have had to address a number of difficult issues that go beyond moral development. Issues that raise fundamental questions about the nature and quality of human development itself, and about the context in which it takes place.

One of the issues we have had to confront as our program of research and our co-constructivist perspective evolved is the question of the conceptual tools that developmental psychologists have available for understanding human behavior and development. The theoretical tools one has available, in our view, defines the strengths (and limitations) of one's understanding. The co-constructivist perspective that provides the framework for our work builds on the work the has been done in the area of developmental theory, but it also seeks to extend our understanding of human behavior and development in a number of different directions and at a number of levels. We seek, however, to do more than simply extend developmental theory. We also seek to *change* the way we, as psychologists and educators, think about human behavior and development—change it to include an explicit recognition of the essential dignity and worth of human beings. Moreover, as will become clear as we outline the details of our efforts in this area, our work has implications that extend beyond psychology and education.

Developmental theory, for example, is concerned with the explanation of change. It is concerned with the explanation of a particular type of change, namely, intraindividual change—change in the individual over time. One goal of our co-constructivist perspective is to broaden and extend the way we think about developmental theory—about how we think about individual or personal change. Developmental theories have historically focused on the environmental, biological, and cultural processes that shape and influence individual change. Such theories have been successful in deepening our understanding of how such processes shape and influence human behavior and development. One of the consequences of this success, however, has been the tendency to limit or confine the range of our understanding to the type of processes these theories focus on. We have come to understand in great detail how environmental, biological, and cultural forces shape and influence individual or personal change, but in the process the role that human beings play in determining the direction of their development has received little attention. By comparison, we know relatively little about the human capacity to guide and direct personal change—to choose the goals and values that give our decisions and actions direction and purpose. In focusing on environmental, biological, and social processes, we have tended to overlook the role that human beings play in shaping and determining their own behavior and development.

Human beings are unique as a species in this respect. The human species is unique in its capacity to understand and control the forces that influence its behavior and development. Consequently, the developmental theory outlined in this chapter includes an account of how, with the development of a full range of competencies (including the capacity for critical decision-making and problem-solving), human beings acquire the capacity to choose the goals and values that give their personal decisions and actions direction and purpose. Our co-constructivist perspective thus seeks to broaden our understanding of the process of individual change, and to use this understanding to extend our capacity to control the forces that touch our individual lives.

So far we have talked about developmental theory. Our goal, however, is to do more than extend the way we think about developmental theory. Developmental theory is concerned with the explanation of individual change. Change, however, is ubiquitous—its pervasive quality extends beyond the lives of individuals to include a historical dimension. Our own age, for example, has been a time of great change. Not only the past several decades, but the past several centuries have been a time of tremendous change and transition—change that has touched all of our lives. Our co-constructivist perspective is also about this type of change—the social and historical change that has an impact on all of our lives. Our co-constructivist perspective is about the changing individual in a changing world, and the human capacity to shape and influence the direction and purpose of historical change itself. It is about how forms of social life can (and do) facilitate (or constrain) collective participation in decision-making processes. It is about how the evolution of democratic forms of life has changed the way we think about collective decision-making and, in the process, transformed the quality of life in the modern world. Consequently, our co-constructivist perspective also includes an account of how, with the social evolution of democratic institutions (including the capacity for democratic decision-making and problem-solving), human beings (as a species) acquired the institutional capacity to choose collectively and democratically the goals and values that give group or institutional decisions and actions their direction and purpose. Our co-constructivist perspective thus also seeks to broaden our understanding of the process of social and historical change, and to use this understanding to extend our capacity to control the forces that touch our shared lives.

Our co-constructivist perspective, however, is about even more than the development and evolution of the individual and institutional capacity to choose the goals and values that give our lives direction and purpose. It is also about the responsibility for the quality of our lives that accompanies this capacity. Our co-constructivist perspective touches on the unique moral dimension of human experience. It seeks to broaden and expand the way we think about human morality *and* human responsibility, which is concerned with deciding what is the right thing to do and doing the right thing. Morality and responsibility, which have always been difficult issues, have become increasingly more problematic. The extraordinary changes that have taken place over the past several centuries not only touched our lives but also challenged our sense of morality and responsibility. Our co-constructivist perspective addresses this problem—the challenge to our sense of morality and responsibility. It does not solve this problem, but it does contain some ideas about the nature of morality and responsibility. Our co-constructivist perspective includes an ethical theory that contains some ideas about ways of deciding what is the right thing to do and doing the right thing. This co-constructivist ethic holds that the freedom to choose that comes with the capacity for critical and democratic decision-making carries with it the responsibility for our choices. It is an ethic that holds us responsible for the quality of our lives. This co-constructivist ethic serves to bridge the gap between our developmental and social evolutionary theories and our efforts to apply these theories to enhance the quality of life. Our co-constructivist ethic holds that the use of critical and democratic decision-making not only enables human beings to make choices, but that the use of such decision-making capacities is helpful in making the *right* choices. That is, our move from theory to practice is grounded in our view that the use of the same decision-making and problem-solving processes that make the freedom to choose possible also have the potential for helping us to live up to the responsibility for the moral quality of our choices.

The aim of our work thus goes beyond broadening and expanding the way psychologists and educators think about human behavior and development. The goal of the co-constructivist perspective outlined in this chapter is to test or challenge the limits or boundaries of the way *we* think about human behavior and development. That is, the goal of this perspective is to change how we, as human beings, think about ourselves to include an explicit recognition of our essential dignity and worth. Thus, what is significant about our work is that it presents a new way of thinking about human behavior and development, a way of thinking about how and why people change, about how and why societies and cultures change, and about our responsibility for the quality of our lives. Our co-constructivist perspective views human beings as self-directed, goal-oriented biopsychosocial organisms with complex, higher order cognitive and communicative capacities that enable them to engage in the most complex forms of theoretical and practical problem-solving and decision-making. With the development of these higher order competencies, human beings acquire the *capacity* to engage, individually and collectively, in decision-making and problem-solving activities that affect the quality of their lives, and the *responsibility* for the consequences or outcomes of their decisions and actions.

Our goal in this chapter is to provide you with an introduction to our co-constructivist perspective. In the process, we will illustrate how a co-constructivist perspective can be applied to making the right choice when faced with an individual or group moral dilemma and provide some guidelines for moral decision-making and problem-solving from a co-constructivist perspective.

## Theory—Psychosocial Development

In this part of the chapter we will outline our developmental theory. This theory builds on the work of many others. Like other theories, our developmental theory is about the forces (environmental, biological, cultural, etc.) that influence organismic or intraindividual change. In this respect, our developmental theory is similar to other developmental theories. Ours, however, differs from other theories in a number of ways. Consequently, we will begin outlining our developmental theory with a brief overview of some of the ways it is similar to and differs from other developmental theories.

### The Mechanistic, Organicistic, and Contextualistic Traditions

Over the past half century, developmental theory has been defined by a diversity of perspectives. Two broad theoretical traditions, however, have played a central role in the historical emergence of developmental psychology: the behavioral (Bandura, 1986; Bijou & Baer, 1976; Gewirtz, 1969; 1977; 1991; Watson, 1913; Watson & Raynor, 1920) and the cognitive developmental (Piaget, 1932, 1936; Kohlberg, 1969; 1976; 1984) traditions. Both are representative of core meta-theoretical traditions that have helped to define the field. The behavioral tradition is representative of that "family" of theories that define what has been called the "mechanistic" meta-theoretical tradition; the cognitive developmental tradition is representative of what has been called the "organicist" meta-theoretical tradition (Reese & Overton, 1970; Overton & Reese, 1973). Although not the only traditions, these have been among the most influential in modern developmental theory. Each has contributed greatly toward our understanding of the forces that shape and influence human behavior and development, and our work in the area of psychosocial development draws on both traditions.

Although the mechanistic and organicist meta-theoretical traditions differ along numerous dimensions, our concern is with how they differ with respect to their explanatory models of organismic change. The mechanistic tradition takes the machine as its model for explaining organismic change, and emphasizes the influence of external antecedent causal events in shaping human behavior and development. The organicist tradition, on the other hand, takes the growing or unfolding organism as its model for explaining organismic change, and emphasizes the influence of biological and maturational processes in shaping human behavior and development. Our work on psychosocial development draws on both traditions. It shares with these theories a recognition of the important role that antecedent causal events (e.g., environmental contingencies, learning/conditioning, etc.) *and* maturational processes (e.g., stage and sequence) play in shaping human behavior and influencing the direction of human development.

Our work, however, also draws on a third tradition, which has been called the contextualist meta-theoretical tradition. The contextualist tradition takes the historical event as its model for explaining organismic change, and emphasizes the *interaction* between the organism and its environment. The contextualist tradition more specifically emphasizes in the human organism the interaction between individual change and social change, i.e., the changing individual in a changing world. It is in this sense that we understand our developmental theory to be a "psychosocial" theory similar in some respects to other social psychological theories such as those of Fromm (1947), Lewin (1935), Sullivan (1953), and the psychosocial developmental theory of Erikson (1950). It shares with these theories an emphasis on social and cultural processes as environmental forces, and an emphasis on the role that the interaction of social and psychological processes play in shaping and influencing human behavior and development.

Although we draw on behavioral, cognitive-developmental, and psychosocial traditions in formulating our theory of psychosocial development, we also seek to extend and refine this work. Each of these traditions looks for (and finds) different types of processes (environmental, biological, cultural) that influence human behavior and development. Each tradition finds what it is looking for because it is there. Environmental, biological, and cultural processes *do* shape human behavior and development. Moreover, work within each theoretical tradition has been successful in deepening our understanding of how such processes influence human behavior and development. Because of the work of the behavioral tradition we have come to understand in more detail how environmental contingencies shape and maintain behavior. Because of the work of the cognitive developmental tradition we have come to understand in more detail how the stages and sequences of development shape the direction of the evolution of our understanding. Because of the work in the psychosocial tradition we have come to understand in more detail how culture and society influence human behavior and development. As we noted, however, in focusing on environmental, maturational, and social processes, we have tended to overlook the role that human beings play in shaping and determining their own behavior and development.

The human species is unique in the extent of its capacity for self-directed, goal-oriented behavior (Frese & Sabini, 1985) and its capacity to understand and control the forces that influence its development. Thus, although our developmental theory (like other developmental theories) is concerned with the forces (environmental, biological, cultural, etc.) that influence human behavior and development, it differs in that providing an account of these forces is not its primary aim. Rather the principal aim of our developmental theory is to provide an account of the capacity of human beings to influence the forces that shape and determine their development. That is, our developmental theory is about the capacity of human beings to guide and direct their own behavior and development, and the responsibility human beings have to live up to this potential.

## *Psychosocial Development*

In formulating our theory of the psychosocial development we have drawn on work in a variety of areas including Chomsky's work on theoretical linguistics (Chomsky, 1965), Piaget's genetic epistemology (Piaget, 1932; 1936), Habermas's communication theory (Habermas, 1971; 1979; 1981), and Erikson's psychosocial developmental theory (Erikson, 1950; 1964). Our theory of psychosocial development thus builds extensively on work that has been done in many areas of developmental theory. To this work we have added our own view of human behavior as rule governed behavior and our interest in human freedom, creativity, and responsibility (Kurtines, 1984; 1986; 1987; 1993) and our ongoing program of psychosocial theory and research (Kurtines, Mayock, Pollard, Lanza and Carlo, 1991; Pollard, Kurtines, Carlo, Dancs, and Mayock, 1991).

For our work in this area we have defined psychosocial development in terms of four interrelated *domains* of competence and four *levels* of development. Figure 13-1 presents an overview of the four domains of competence (linguistic, cognitive, communicative, and sociomoral) and the four levels of development (infancy, childhood, pre-adolescence, and adolescence/adulthood) that make up the core of our developmental theory. The *domains* of competence depicted in Figure 13-1 are representative of the type of universal (i.e., species-wide) competencies that all human beings acquire in the process of becoming competent members of sociocultural systems. We conceptualize these competencies as similar in form but different in function from the special-

*COMPETENCIES*

| *LEVELS* | **Linguistic** | **Cognitive** | **Communicative** | ***Sociomoral*** |
|---|---|---|---|---|
| **1 (0-2) Infancy** | Pre-Verbal | Sensori-Motor | Non-normative GOA | *Pre-moral* |
| **2 (2-7) Childhood** | Language ↳ | Pre-Operational ↳ | Normative GOA, SGA ↳ | ↓ *Heteronomous* (External) |
| **3 (7-12) Pre-Adolescence** | | Concrete Operations ↳ | Normative GOA, SGA DCA ↳ | ↓ *Autonomous* (Internal) |
| **4 (12+) Adolescence/ Adulthood** | | Formal Operations ↓ Critical/ Hypothetic → | Discourse ↓ Critical/ Discursive → | ↓ *Critical* (Hypothetical/ Discursive) |

**FIGURE 13-1 Psychosocial Development: Domains of Competence and Developmental Levels**

ized competencies, abilities, capacities, resources, talents, potentials, etc. (e.g., artistic, investigative, social, enterprising, etc.) that particular individuals acquire in the process of developing their individual modes of personal expressiveness (see Waterman, Chapter 10, this vol.). Because each individual's specialized competencies are unique, the acquisition of modes of personal expressiveness follow developmental pathways that are unique for each individual. The *levels* of development depicted in Figure 13-1, in contrast, are descriptive of the species-wide process by which all human beings acquire competence in the universal domains of language, thought, communication, and morality.

We have described our theory of psychosocial development in detail elsewhere (Kurtines, 1993), including our view of developmental change in all four domains. We focus here on the domains of cognition and communication because they have the most direct bearing on our work in the area of moral development and moral decision-making. With respect to our theory of moral development, the most important of these developmental changes involves the emergence of the capacity to engage in critical-hypothetical cognition (i.e., critical thinking) in the domain of cognitive development and the capacity for critical-discursive communication (i.e., critical discussion) in the domain of communicative development. The development of these higher order cognitive and communicative competencies enables human beings to engage in the most complex forms of theoretical and practical problem-solving activities, including moral decision-making and problem-solving. Our theory of psychosocial development thus serves as a framework for our theory of moral development.

## Moral Development

Within this framework, our theory of moral development views the process of moral development as involving two basic types of intraindividual change. The first type of change involves the acquisition of the content of the individual's sociomoral understanding. The content of our sense of morality includes the goals and values, standards and norms, and rules and principles that give our choices their moral meaning and significance. According to our theory, the basic content of the child's sense of morality is acquired from the child's culture early in life through a process of learning (conditioning, imitation, modeling, etc.).[1] The sociomoral rules and rule systems we acquire in the process of moral development are thus not purely subjective constructions. They are shared co-constructions that exist in a historical context and find expression in the language, logic, laws, customs, and conventions of particular societies and cultures. They also find expression in art and literature and myth, where they take on their deeply human significance, in part, because they touch on the dreams and visions that provide our lives with direction and purpose. Most of all, however, they find expression in the complex network of goals and values, standards and norms, and rules and principles that we live by and that make up our individual and collective sense of morality. The process of moral development thus involves the acquisition of the moral traditions and obligations—the sense of right and wrong—that gives our decisions and actions their direction and purpose.

The second type of change involves the individual's orientation toward the content of morality, i.e., the type of cognitive and communicative processes the individual uses in making moral decisions. This type of change involves predictable developmental transformations in the individual's capacity to adopt a critical orientation toward the goals and values, standards and norms, and rules and principles that we acquire in the process of development. A critical sociomoral orientation involves the capacity to use critical thinking and critical discussion in moral decision-making and problem-solving. With the development of a full range of competencies (including critical cognitive and communicative competence), the individual acquires the capacity to use critical decision-making and problem-solving skills in the most complex types of theoretical and practical activities, including individual and group moral decision-making and problem-solving. The development of what we call a critical sociomoral orientation thus involves the development of the capacity to use such skills in resolving conflict that arises with respect to not only the consequences or outcomes of decisions and actions, but also in resolving conflicting moral traditions and obligations and the goals and values that give them direction and purpose.

In our theory of moral development, the development of a critical sociomoral orientation is viewed as linked to the development of more underlying critical cognitive and communicative competencies. Consequently, once a child acquires a basic mastery of the sociomoral rule system of its culture, subsequent sociomoral development does not involve predictable developmental transformations in the content of the individual sociomoral understanding.[2] Rather, the predictable developmental transformations that take place involve the child's capacity to adopt an increasingly more critical orientation toward sociomoral rules and rule systems. With the acquisition of a critical orientation, the individual can use critical thinking in making decisions about goals and values, standards and norms, and rules and principles now capable of being viewed as hypothetical. The individual can also use critical communication in solving problems and making decisions about conflicting normative claims, now viewed as open to critical examination, negotiation, discursive redemption, and co-construction. A critical sociomoral orientation not only enables the individual to engage in moral decision-making and problem-solving within the context of existing moral traditions and obligations, it also enables the individual to question and challenge those traditions and obligations and the goals and values that give them direction and purpose. The development of a critical sociomoral orientation thus enables human beings to make decisions, solve problems, and resolve difficulties with respect to the utility and/or validity of goals and values, standards and norms, and rules and principles, and to transform or reconstruct them and/or to invent or create new ones when necessary.

Our work in the area of psychosocial development thus draws on diverse programs of research in formulating the view that, as part of the process of psychosocial development, the human organism acquires a complex set of higher order competencies. The development of the capacity to use higher order problem-solving activities such as critical thinking and critical discussion is basic to the adaptability of the human species because they are types of problem-solving skills that facilitate successful goal-oriented behavior. The development of these complex, higher order competencies enables human beings to successfully adapt to an extraordinarily wide range of changing conditions.

Human beings, however, do more than adapt to changing conditions. Human beings are unique in the extent to which human goal-oriented behavior is self-directed, and in the extent to which human beings are capable of making the decisions that guide and direct personal and historical change. Other species engage in goal-oriented behavior, but the human species is unique in the extent to which it has the critical skills and competencies necessary to transform or reconstruct and/or invent or create the goals and values that gives human activity its direction and purpose. Change in the human organism is thus shaped and influenced by multiple determinants, one of which includes the human capacity for intentional, self-directed behavior.

Thus far we have described our view of the development of a full range of psychosocial competencies (including the capacity for critical decision-making and problem-solving) and the capacity to adopt a critical sociomoral orientation. We have as yet, however, said nothing specific about how human beings use these competencies to make the decisions that guide and direct their behavior and development. We have said nothing about what human beings *do* with these capabilities. We have said that human beings are unique in their capacity for intentional, "self"-directed behavior. We have, however, said nothing about the "self" that provides the sense of direction and integration we experience as part of the process of growth and development.

## The Development of the Self and the Formation of an Identity

Within the framework of our developmental theory, it is the formation of a sense of identity that provides the individual's decisions and actions (and ultimately, their lives) with direction and purpose. Our understanding of the concept of identity draws on Erikson's work and the large and growing literature that has emerged in the area (Adams, Bennion, & Hugh, 1987; Adams, Shea, & Fitch, 1979; Blasi, 1984; Chapter 9, this vol.; Grotevant & Adams, 1984; Marcia, 1966; 1980; Waterman, 1982; Chapter 10, this vol.). Like Erikson, we understand a sense of identity to be defined by the individual's sense of direction and purpose. Identity is the sense of who we are and what we want to do with our lives. A sense of identity is the self's sense of direction and purpose. As Blasi (Chapter 9, this vol.) has noted, the term *identity* refers to a particularly mature form of self-concept, one that is characterized by a strong sense of unity, by its salience in the person's consciousness, and by its ability to anchor the person's sense of stability, individuality, and purpose.

The concept of identity, which has emerged as central to the field, also plays a key role in our developmental theory. As can be seen from Table 13-1, at the early levels of development, the self's goals and values are expressed in terms of the satisfaction of immediate needs and interests and hence tend to be variable. However, with the development of a full range of competencies (including specialized competencies, abilities, capacities, resources, etc. that define the development of modes of personal expressiveness and higher order critical decision-making and problem-solving skills), the individual's needs and interests become increasingly more defined in terms of long-range goals and values, eventually including life goals and values. A life goal is the end or purpose in life that the individual aims to reach or accomplish. Values are those things that the individual considers desirable, good, right, useful, or important.

With the development of the capacity for critical decision-making and problem-solving, the individual acquires the capacity to make decisions about the life goals and values that give direction and purpose to the individual's specialized competencies, abilities, capacities, and resources. The formation of a sense of identity involves making decisions or choices with respect to one's life goals and values. The complex constellation of self-chosen life goals and values that the individual internalizes during the formation of an identity is the core of one's sense of identity. The self-chosen life goals and values that are internalized during this formation facilitate the process of making the decisions that shape and influence personal change. The formation of a sense of identity not only provides the self with a sense of direction and purpose, it also helps to provide the individual with a sense of continuity over time. The internalization of a core of life goals and values anchors and stabilizes the subjective experiences of the self.

The levels of identity formation that we have been using in our work, defined in terms of the psychosocial competencies and psychosocial perspective associated with each level, are briefly summarized in Table 13-1. *Psychosocial perspective* refers to the integrating theme that defines the individual's identity at each level of psychosocial development. The hypothesized levels of psychosocial development are viewed as providing only an approximate outline of the developmental sequence and the age ranges involved. These levels are viewed as necessarily tentative and our data only provides for a partial test of the hypothesized levels.

## Development and Beyond

The competencies and levels of development outlined in Figure 13-1 and Table 13-1 provide the main elements of our account of the development of the capacity to shape and influence the process of personal change. As can be seen from Table 13-1, we view human freedom and creativity as rooted in the development of a full range of unique *and* universal competencies (including critical competencies) and the development of a sense of direction and purpose. That is, we view psychosocial *development* as a "developmental" process with the endpoint of development (psychosocial maturity) predefined as a full range of competencies and a sense of direction and purpose. Change, however, does not cease with psychosocial maturity. Although it does not cease, the processes that influence intraindividual change shift. With the development of the capacity for critical thought and discussion and the formation of a sense of identity at Developmental Level 4 (see Table 13-1), the individual acquires a sense of direction and purpose and the capacity to understand *and* to shape and influence the direction and purpose of personal *and* historical change.

As a consequence, the nature of personal change is transformed. Intraindividual change is no longer "developmental" change in the sense of change toward some predetermined endpoint, i.e., an endpoint predefined by the nature of development. As Baltes and Goulet (1970) have noted, "When used as

### TABLE 13-1   Levels of Psychosocial Development and Identity Formation

Psychosocial Developmental Level 1: (Infancy: 0-2)

*Identity Formation Level: Pre-subjective Identity*

At this level the infant is linguistically pre-verbal and in the sensorimotor stage of cognitive development. During this period, the infant is in the process of acquiring basic linguistic and sensorimotor competencies. The infant's communicative actions tend to be primarily non-normative goal-oriented actions organized around sensorimotor activities. The sociomoral orientation associated with this level is pre-moral. The *psychosocial perspective* associated with this level is pre-subjective, a perspective rooted in the initial emergence of a separate and distinct sense of self.

Psychosocial Developmental Level 2: (Childhood: 2-7)

*Identity Formation Level: Egocentric/Subjective Identity*

At this level the child has acquired the basic linguistic competence necessary for verbal interaction. Cognitively, the child is at the pre-operational stage. At this level the child is acquiring basic role taking and role playing skills and is in the process of moving from egocentric thought to sociocentric thinking. In terms of communicative competence, the child is capable of engaging in ordinary communicative action, but has not yet achieved the capacity for critical discussion. Sociomoral competence, at this level, is defined by an orientation that is heteronomous and uncritical. The child acquires a basic understanding of sociomoral rules and concepts, but the rules are viewed as externally imposed. The *psychosocial perspective* that defines identity formation at this level tends to be *egocentric* (i.e., a perspective rooted in the ego's or self's understanding) and is typically oriented to *subjective* needs, interests and expectations, either of the self or others, but not to shared needs, interests and expectations. Life roles tend to be defined primarily in terms of familial roles and secondarily in terms of peer relationships. The goals of the self tend to be defined in terms of short-range intentions and objectives.

Psychosocial Development Level 3: (Preadolescence: 7-12)

*Identity Level: Sociocentric/Inter-subjective Identity*

At this level the child's linguistic competence becomes fully developed. The child's cognitive competence includes the capability for concrete operational thinking as well as the capacity for decentered thinking. The child's goal-oriented behavior becomes increasingly more intentional and self-directed. Along with the capacity for decentered thought, the child acquires basic role-taking and role-playing skills and the child's thinking tends to be sociocentric. In terms of communicative competence, at this level, the child can engage in ordinary communicative action and, at later ages, has some capacity for critical discussion. Sociomoral competence is defined by an orientation that is autonomous. Sociomoral rules are no longer viewed as externally imposed, but as inter-subjectively shared constructions. The *psychosocial perspective* that defines identity formation at this level tends to be *sociocentric* (i.e., a perspective rooted in shared understanding) and is typically oriented to *inter-subjectively* shared goals and values, standards and norms, and rules and principles now understood as collective co-constructions. Life roles tend to be defined increasingly more in terms of peer/friendship roles and relationships and more secondarily in terms of familial roles. This period of development is characterized by rapid and significant development in all domains of competence, and the goals of the self tend to become increasingly more defined in terms of long-range objectives.

Psychosocial Developmental Level 4: (Adolescence/Adulthood: 12+)

*Identity Level: Critical Identity*

Psychosocial Developmental Level 4 (Adolescence/Adulthood) defines, for our developmental theory, *psychosocial maturity*. At this level the youth/adult is cognitively at the stage of formal operations. The youth/adult's cognitive competence includes the capacity for formal, critical hypothetical thinking that is characteristic of this stage. Goal-oriented behavior becomes fully intentional and self-directed. The capacity for critical thinking enables the individual to not only engage in goal-oriented behavior, but also to challenge or question the utility and/or the validity of goals and ends and the means or methods for achieving them, and to transform or create new ones when necessary. In terms of role-taking skills, the individual now not only can take the perspective of the potential other in interactions, but can also take the perspective of an objective neutral third person. In terms of communicative competence, the individual acquires the capacity for critical discussion. The capacity for critical discussion enables the individual to challenge or question the utility and/or validity of group goals and the means for achieving them, and to transform or create new ones when necessary. With the development of critical thinking and discussion skills, the individual becomes capable of engaging in the most complex forms of theoretical and practical problem-solving activity. The individual can fully understand and contribute to the subjective construction and inter-subjective co-construction of social reality, and intra-individual change becomes more self-directed. Sociomoral competence at this level is defined by a critical orientation in that the individual can now use critical thinking and discussion in moral decision-making and moral problem-solving.

The *psychosocial perspective* that defines identity formation at this level tends to be *critical*, a perspective rooted in the capacity for *critical thought* and *critical communication*. With the onset of psychosocial maturity, the youth leaves adolescence and begins to assume adult roles. With the development of the capacity for critical thought and communication, the youth/adult acquires the capacity to distance him/herself from socially constructed roles and conventions as well as norms and values, and takes responsibility for the determination of the direction and purpose of his/her development. With the development of the capacity for critical decision-making and problem-solving, the individual acquires the capacity to make decisions about the life goals and values that give direction and purpose to the individual's specialized competencies, abilities, capacities, resources. Life goals and life roles begin to merge and the issue of integration of life goals and roles emerges as a central theme in the formation of an identity. Occupational, gender, familial, and peer roles come to be viewed more in terms of long-range objectives, now increasingly defined in terms of self-chosen life goals and values. The attainment of the level of critical identity confronts the youth/adult with the complex and difficult challenge of choosing *and* fulfilling the goals and values that provide the individual's life with direction and purpose.

---

a theoretical concept, the term development typically implies some essential ideas about the nature of change, such as change toward a higher level of complexity or an end state of organization." (p. 10) With the attainment of a full range of competencies and a critical level of identity, intraindividual change is no longer change toward a predetermined goal or end state; rather, the direction of intraindividual change is toward self-determined goals or a self-determined endpoint.

The development of a full range of competencies and the formation of a sense of identity results in a shift in the processes influencing intraindividual change. In early development, the formation of a sense of identity is dependent upon the development of a full range of competencies (i.e., linguistic, cognitive, communicative and sociomoral), which are themselves dependent upon maturation and learning. However, once we have developed a full range of competencies (including critical decision-making and problem-solving skills) and have acquired the capacity to choose our life goals and values, the nature of personal change and growth is transformed. It is no longer dependent upon the "development" of competencies. Maturational and learning processes play an increasingly less influential role and formative co-constructive social processes play an increasingly more central role. At the same time, with the expansion of the self and the development of a sense of identity, social, maturational, and learning processes *all* play an increasingly less important role in shaping and influencing the direction of intraindividual change. The nature of intra-individual change, as a consequence, undergoes a transformation. Personal change becomes a more intentional and self-directed process, with the endpoint of the process defined increasingly more in terms of life goals and life roles that are selected as part of the process of the formation of an identity.

We have thus come to one of the core theoretical claims underlying our efforts to change the way we think about ourselves. This claim provides the foundation for our efforts to foster the recognition of the essential dignity and worth of all human beings, viz., **that with the development of a full range of competencies (including critical competencies) and the formation of an identity, human beings acquire the capacity and freedom to choose the goals and values that give their lives direction and purpose and the responsibility for the quality of their lives.** The development of a full range of competencies and the formation of an identity is thus one of the most potentially liberating transformations that occurs in human development. It is also one of the most challenging transformations that the individual confronts. The development of the capacity to choose the goals and values that give our lives its direction and purpose raises the challenge of accepting the responsibility for the quality of our personal lives, i.e., the responsibility for *using* this capacity in choosing and fulfilling the goals and values that give our individual lives their direction and purpose.

## Research—Moral Identity

In the first section of this chapter, we outlined in broad terms some of the theoretical constructs and hypotheses that provide the framework for our empirical work. In this section, we provide a brief introduction to the direction that our program of research in operationalizing and testing these constructs has taken. As we turn to a discussion of our research program we would point out that although we have divided the chapter into three relatively distinct parts (theory, research, and application) for purposes of presentation, this is *not* how our work evolved. In reality, theory, research, and application went hand in hand. As our theories evolved, we sought to develop research strategies for operationalizing and applying them, and our efforts in the areas of research and application, in turn, influenced further development in our theory. Our work thus involved a continuous interplay of theory, research, and application.

Our program of research has played an important role in the evolution of our co-constructivist perspective because we view our work on developing methods and procedures for operationalizing and testing our concepts to be an essential extension of our theoretical work. In moving from theory to research, it was necessary to move from a broad framework to a more clearly defined and operationalizable set of concepts consistent with this framework. Central to this program of research was the development measures and research procedures that have proved to be useful in testing some of our theoretical claims. The focus of our measurement work has thus been on the development of theoretically based measures with adequate psychometric properties for use in our research program. We have also done work on refining experimental procedures and research methods.

Because of the central role that our measures have played in our program of research, we present a brief discussion of them in the *Appendix of Measures* at the end of this chapter. The summaries are intended to provide the reader interested in particular aspects of the research with ready access to enough of details of the measures to gauge their potential utility. Complete copies of the measures, including description of their psychometric properties and implementation and administration manuals are available. We would note that, although our measures appear to have adequate psychometric properties and our experimental procedures and methods have adequate validity, we have continued to work on refining both the theoretical concepts and measures/procedures.

## *Moral Identity*

A primary focus of our empirical work has been in the area of psychosocial development. Within this frame, our focus has been on sociomoral competence in general and the formation of moral identity in particular. We did not choose to focus on sociomoral competence and moral identity because we consider these domains more important in human affairs than other domains. Nor do we consider the development of sociomoral competence to be more central to psychosocial development than other universal competencies such as linguistic, cognitive or communicative, *or* the unique competencies that define our modes of personal expressiveness. On the contrary, we consider all domains of competence to be central to psychosocial development and we recognize the complex, interactive relationship that exists between development across domains.

Our reasons for focusing on moral identity were essentially pragmatic. In order to establish our program of research it was necessary to set some initial limit on the domains the research would encompass and to delimit issues and problems. We began our research with sociomoral competence and moral identity because our theoretical interest was in the nature and origins of sociomoral understanding. We viewed the work of developing methods and procedures for operationalizing the concepts of moral identity to be essential for establishing a foundation for our program of theoretical and applied research. As we said, in the evolution of our program of research, theory and application went hand in hand with research. As our theoretical framework evolved and expanded, we have continued to develop research strategies for operationalizing it. These developments, in turn, influenced (and continue to influence) further developments in theory.

The focus of our work in the area of moral development has been on the content of the individual's sociomoral understanding—the specific goals and values, norms and standards, and rules and principles that make up the individual's sense of morality. The content of the individual's sociomoral understanding makes up an important component of the individual's identity. In the process of the formation of an identity, the individual internalizes a complex constellation of self-chosen life goals and values. These internalized life goals and values define the individual's sense of identity and give his/her decisions and actions their direction and purpose. In a similar way, the formation of a moral identity provides the individual with a sense of morality (a sense of right and wrong, good and bad, etc.). In the formation of a moral identity, the individual internalizes a complex constellation of self chosen goals and values, norms and standards, and rules and principles that give the individual's moral decisions and actions their direction and purpose. In our work on moral identity we use the term *values* as a generic label for what we mean by a sense of morality. In this frame, the life "goals" that are internalized as part of the formation of an identity consist of the self-chosen ends or purpose in life that the individual aims to reach or accomplish. The life values that are internalized as part of the formation of an identity, on the other hand, consist of the self-chosen values, norms and standards, and rules and principles that make up the individual's sense of morality. Thus, life values make up that component of our identity that we refer to as our moral identity.

Our work in this area has focused on the structure of moral identity and the role that the use of critical thinking and critical discussion play in the formation of our moral identity. This effort has been thus far successful in generating a number of preliminary measures that are summarized in the *Appendix of Measures*. We have done extensive work on developing methods for assessing moral identity. We have also initiated efforts to develop and refine methods and procedures for measuring critical competencies, and have developed a method for assessing the use of critical decision-making and problem-solving in the sociomoral domain (i.e., a "critical" sociomoral orientation). As part of our ongoing program of research in the area of psychosocial development, we are currently in the process of developing a more multidimensional measure of identity that encompasses life goals as well as life values. The results of our efforts have up to this point provided some preliminary evidence for our view of identity formation as the outcome of a process of intersubjective co-construction as well as subjective construction and for the role that critical competencies play in identity formation.

Because this is a book about moral development we have mainly focused on introducing you to our work on the formation of moral identity. Our work, however, has involved a continuous interplay of theory, research, *and* application that has involved more than moral development. At the same time that we were establishing our program of theoretical research in the area of psychosocial development, we were also initiating a program of applied research that extended beyond psychosocial development. Our work on the role of critical thinking and discussion in moral problem-solving and decision-making has focused on the role of critical thinking and discussion in individual change. In our work on applying our co-constructivist perspective we have moved beyond the role of critical decision-making and individual change to include the role of critical modes of thought and communication in institutional change. In doing so, we have undertaken what we consider an even more difficult task, one that has provided a test of the limits of the utility of our perspective. We have begun to bring our co-constructivist perspective to bear on the problem of democratic decision-making and institutional change. The thrust of our applied work in this area has been on fostering the social evolution of democratic forms of life as a means for enhancing the quality of life at the individual and institutional levels. The primary focus of this work has been on the role of education in preserving and promoting democracy. In moving into the domain of social evolution we extend our work beyond individual change to include institutional change, and the role that such change plays in fostering the emergence of democratic forms of life. The focus of our work in this area has been on the role of education in this process.

## Application—Making Life Choices

Now that we have talked about our theory and research, we turn to the implications that this work has for our everyday life. We have described how human beings acquire the capacity to choose the goals and values that give their lives direction and purpose. Now we will illustrate how we can use this capacity in making the choices that shape and influence the direction and purpose of our lives. Because this is a book about moral development, we will illustrate how critical decision-making can be used in "moral" decision-making and problem-solving, although we consider critical decision-making to be the best or most useful method for making *any* life choice.

In outlining our theory of psychosocial development we proposed that with the development of a full range of competencies (including the capacity for critical decision-making and problem-solving), human beings acquire the individual capacity to choose the goals and values that give their personal lives direction and purpose. Our move from theory to practice, however, extends beyond this theoretical claim to include the practical claim that **the use of critical decision-making not only enables human beings to make choices, but that the use of such decision-making processes is helpful in making the *right* choices.** That is, our move from theory to practice is grounded in our view that the use of the same processes that make the freedom to choose possible also have the potential for helping us to live up to the responsibility for the moral quality of our choices.

The co-constructivist ethic that we describe in the next section provides the normative foundation for our view that, with the development of a full range of competencies, human beings not only acquire the capacity to choose the goals and values that give their lives direction and purpose, but also the responsibility for the moral quality of their choices. Our co-constructivist ethic holds that human beings not only *can* evaluate the moral quality of the goals and values that give their lives direction and purpose, but also that they *should* (ought to) evaluate the moral quality of their lives.

## A Co-constructivist Ethic

The guidelines for moral decision-making and problem-solving that we will outline in this section are derived from a co-constructivist ethic that we have described in detail elsewhere (Kurtines, 1993). This co-constructivist ethic provides the cornerstone for our view of the nature and origins of human morality and responsibility. According to this ethic, human beings not only make choices and are responsible for them, they also evaluate some choices as better, more right, or more moral than others. Human morality and responsibility is concerned with deciding what is the right thing to do and doing the right thing. "Moral" decision-making and problem-solving involves making a judgment about what is the right thing to do. Doing the right thing, in turn, involves acting on our own judgment. Our co-constructivist ethic is thus comprised of a view of the nature of human morality *and* human responsibility. It is an ethic that holds human beings responsible for the moral quality of their lives.

In formulating this co-constructivist ethic we have drawn on what might be broadly termed the existential pragmatic tradition in Western thought. From the existential tradition we adopt the view that human beings, unlike other things or objects in the world, are morally responsible for their decisions and actions. From the pragmatic tradition we adopt the view that deciding what is the right thing to do is essentially a problem-solving process that involves evaluating the value (i.e., desirability, rightness, usefulness, goodness, etc.) of the outcomes of human decisions and actions in the context of existing goals and values and, when necessary, testing the boundaries of the cultural and historical horizon that defines the limits of those goals and values. We not only adopt the pragmatist's problem-solving approach, we also adopt the pragmatist's optimism concerning the nature of both personal and historical change. The pragmatist not only thinks that things change, but also that things can (and do) change for the better. That is, the pragmatist thinks that as things change human beings can understand how and why they change, and human beings can (and do) come up with better ideas and ways of doing things.

Our co-constructivist ethic provides the normative underpinning for the work that we have done in applying our co-constructivist perspective to the problem of enhancing the quality of life. In the next section, we will extend our discussion of our co-constructivist ethic to include a view of the role that critical and democratic decision making plays in enhancing the moral quality of our lives. More specifically, we will illustrate how critical and democratic decision-making can be applied to the process of resolving the types of dilemmas that arise in the context of everyday moral decision-making at the individual and group or institutional levels. In describing the use of critical and democratic decision-making in resolving moral dilemmas, we move beyond the issue of *whether* human beings can and should evaluate the moral quality of their decisions and actions to address the issue of *how* human beings can and should evaluate the moral quality of their lives.

## Critical and Democratic Decision-Making in Resolving Moral Dilemmas

Although we recognize that resolving real life moral dilemmas (individual *or* group) is often complex and difficult, the most basic guidelines this co-constructivist ethic offers are relatively simple. From the perspective of this co-constructivist ethic, resolving a moral dilemma ultimately involves making a decision with respect to the value (desirability, rightness, usefulness, goodness, etc.) of the consequences or outcomes of competing or conflicting alternatives *and* the value (desirability, rightness, usefulness, goodness, etc.) of competing or conflicting moral traditions and obligations (i.e., the goals and values, norms and standards, rules and principles, etc. that make up our sense of morality). Resolving a moral dilemma also involves accepting the responsibility for our decision. Resolving both individual and group moral dilemmas, in other words, involves deciding what is the right thing to do and doing the right thing.

In illustrating the application of our co-constructivist ethic our goal is not to tell you *what* is the right thing to do when faced with a moral dilemma. That decision is up to you. Rather, our goal is to outline what we consider to be the best or most useful *methods* for deciding what is the right thing to do, namely, the use of critical and democratic decision-making and problem-solving. As we will describe in more detail as we go along, we consider critical and democratic decision-making to be the best method for evaluating the value (desirability, rightness, usefulness, goodness, etc.) of the consequences or outcomes of competing or conflicting alternatives *and* the value (desirability, rightness, usefulness, goodness, etc.) of competing or conflicting moral traditions and obligations in a particular context.[3]

### Moral Problem-Solving

Resolving a moral dilemma can be complex, but the process is basically no different than solving any other type of problem. In this case, the problem involves deciding what is desirable or right and the means for achieving this goal in the context of competing or conflicting moral traditions and obligations. The same basic types of activities that are helpful in solving any type of theoretical or practical problem are also helpful in solving moral problems and making moral decisions, and the three types of activities that we illustrate here draw on the literature on interpersonal problem-solving (Spivack, Platt, & Shure, 1976; Spivack & Shure, 1977). We will begin our discussion of the process of making a moral decision with a brief review of these basic problem-solving activities (i.e., identifying the problem, generating potential alternatives for solving the problem, and choosing the best alternative), followed by a discussion of our responsibility for acting on our decisions.

First, resolving a moral dilemma involves recognizing when a problem exists and identifying what the problem is. In the case of a moral dilemma, recognizing when a problem exists includes acknowledging the existence of conflicting alternatives *and* moral traditions or obligations. Identifying what the problem is involves identifying the actual and foreseeable consequences or outcome of the alternative choices and the specific moral traditions or obligations that the alternatives bring into conflict. This phase of problem-solving also includes evaluating the practical significance of the problem. This involves evaluating the time and effort likely to be required to solve the problem relative to the actual difference that it will make for the person or persons experiencing the problem.

Successfully resolving a moral dilemma, however, requires more than recognizing that a problem exists and identifying what the problem is. It also includes generating potential alternatives for resolving the problem. Generating alternatives involves the creative construction of alternatives for reconciling or integrating existing moral traditions and obligations that are in conflict or coming up with new and better goals and values to give our ideas and activities direction and purpose.

Finally, successfully resolving a moral dilemma involves selecting the best (most valuable, desirable, right, useful, good, etc.) alternative, choice, or resolution. This involves evaluating the value of the alternative consequences or outcomes, the relative validity of the goals or values in conflict, and the relative utility of the means or method for fulfilling the goals or values. This process involves not only testing the practical significance and value of the actual or potential consequences or outcomes in the context of existing goals and values, it also involves (when necessary) testing the limits of existing goals and values and testing the boundaries of the cultural and historical horizon that define the limits of those goals and values.

## *Moral Responsibility*

Now that we have briefly discussed some of the types of basic problem-solving activities that are helpful in solving moral problems and making moral decisions, we continue our description of the application of a co-constructivist ethic with a discussion of moral responsibility. Our co-constructivist ethic includes an account of human responsibility because one of the possible choices that comes with the freedom to choose is that of choosing *not* to take responsibility for our actions. This is, after all, one of the potential choices available to us. We *can* choose to attempt to avoid responsibility for our choices. Moreover, the possibility of avoiding responsibility is more than merely another possible choice; it is a choice that is itself difficult to avoid. It is difficult to avoid because, as we noted, human behavior and development *is* multi-determined. Consequently, it is difficult to avoid shifting responsibility for our decisions and actions to other things, qualities, or characteristics such as to the nature of human nature, to the environment, to culture, or to biology.

This issue (i.e., human responsibility) has played a central role in the existential tradition in ethics, and we draw on this tradition in formulating our account of human responsibility. Sartre, for instance, has written extensively on human responsibility, and the tendency to avoid responsibility. In fact, Sartre has a term for attempting to avoid responsibility. His term is *mauvais foi* or literally, "bad faith." For Sartre, to seek to escape responsibility for our actions is an act of bad faith. Kierkegaard similarly considered the awesome responsibility that accompanies human freedom to be a fundamental source of anguish or *angst*. For Kierkegaard, as for Sartre, we seek to avoid anguish by avoiding the responsibility for our choices. For the existentialist, however, we, as human beings, are ultimately responsible for the choices we make—*all* of our choices. Hence, even though we can choose to not take responsibility for our actions, we are ultimately responsible for even this choice. We are responsible for even this choice because it *is* a choice with the full moral consequences of any other choice. We can seek or attempt to escape our responsibility, but we can never succeed. We can no more escape our responsibility than we can escape our freedom. We can never succeed in escaping our responsibility because in the process of doing so we become not only responsible for our actions but we also become responsible for attempting to escape the responsibility for our actions, i.e., for acting in bad faith. Responsibility is an unavoidable consequence of the freedom to choose.

As it does in existential ethics, accepting responsibility for moral decisions also plays a central role in our co-constructivist ethic. From the perspective of a co-constructivist ethic, accepting the responsibility for moral decisions means that you have a responsibility to actively participate in decision-making processes (both individual and group) that result in moral decisions *and* a responsibility to act on those decisions.

What we mean by actively participating in decision-making processes is relatively simple and straightforward—making a decision to accept our responsibility and then living up to this responsibility by actually participating in all of the activities necessary to solve the problem of deciding what is the right thing to do, i.e., using critical and democratic decision-making and problem-solving in identifying the problem, generating potential alternatives for solving the problem, and choosing the best alternative.

## Deciding What Is the Right Thing to Do in Individual Moral Dilemmas

Now that we have reviewed the basic types of problem-solving activities that are helpful in resolving moral dilemmas and the nature of human moral responsibility, we continue our discussion of the application of a co-constructivist ethic with an illustration of how the use of "critical" decision-making and problem-solving is useful in making the *right* decision in an individual moral dilemma such as we illustrated with Sartre's young man. Using "critical" decision-making and problem-solving in resolving such dilemmas involves more than the use of the three basic types of problem-solving activities described above. "Critical" decision-making involves the use of critical thinking and critical discussion in the resolution of conflicting moral traditions and obligations, i.e., a critical sociomoral orientation as described earlier in this chapter. It will be helpful in illustrating why we consider critical decision-making to be the most useful means or method for making the right choice in an individual moral dilemma if we describe in more detail what we mean by "critical" thinking and discussion.

One thing that *critical* means is to be skeptical, to be willing to question and challenge the validity and utility of the alternatives and obligations in conflict. At the cognitive level, to be critical means to engage in critical thinking. *Critical thinking* in the resolution of a personal moral dilemma is thinking that involves adopting a "critical" (i.e., skeptical or questioning) stance. Adopting a critical stance involves both suspension of judgment and critical evaluation. It involves suspending judgment with respect to our own decision or action *and* moral traditions and obligations (goals and values, norms and standards, rules and principles, etc.) that justify them, and subjecting them to critical examination. To be critical (i.e., to think critically) means to be skeptical or at least willing to question your own decisions and actions and the validity of the personal goals, values, and principles that you use to justify them.

Critical discussion is similar to critical thinking in that it involves being willing to suspend judgment and being willing to be skeptical, to question, and to challenge. *Critical discussion* is "discussion" that critically examines or questions the individual's choices and the validity of the normative claims that justify them. It is important in individual moral decision-making because, as we will discuss next, it helps to guard against acting in bad faith.

In moral decision-making and problem-solving, it is relatively easy to suspend judgment and to be critical or skeptical toward the decisions and actions (and the moral traditions and obligations) of others. It is frequently much more difficult to adopt a critical stance with respect to one's own decisions and actions (and one's own moral traditions and obligations). Thus, although it is important to be aware of and be able to recognize the use of strategic means (including deception and manipulation) when used by others, it is also important (perhaps even more important) to be aware of and be able to recognize an extremely subtle form of deception, namely, *self*-deception, which occurs when you are uncritical of your own choices. Being uncritical of your own choices (and the normative claims that you use to justify them) promotes or encourages shifting responsibility from yourself to other people, things, or qualities. Thus, one of the most important safeguards against all forms of bad faith is to guard against self-deception, and one way to guard against self-deception in individual decision-making is to open your choices (and the normative claims that you use to justify them) to critical discussion. That is, to not only subject your choices to critical examination by yourself, but also to subject them to critical examination *and* discussion by others.

Guarding against self-deception not only helps to guard against individual acts of bad faith, but also institutional acts of bad faith. It helps to guard against institutional acts of bad faith because institutional decisions and actions derive their direction and purpose from the shared goals and values of the individuals who make up the institutions. Institutional acts of bad faith are ultimately rooted in individual acts of bad faith. Consequently, one of the most important safeguards against both individual *and* institutional forms of bad faith is to guard against self-deception, and the way to guard against self-deception is by being willing to subject your own choices and the normative claims that justify them to critical *thinking* and *discussion*.

From the perspective of a co-constructivist ethic, then, the best way to insure that you are making the right choice in an individual moral dilemma is to actively participate in the decision-making process and to be willing to subject your choices (and the goals, values, and principles you use to justify them) to critical *thinking* and *discussion*. The same is true for acting in bad faith. The best way to avoid acting in bad faith is to actively participate in the decision-making processes and to be willing to subject all the potential choices and the actual and potential normative claims that justify them to critical examination by yourself and others.

We thus consider critical decision-making to be the most useful means or method for evaluating the value (desirability, rightness, usefulness, goodness, etc.) of consequences or outcomes *and* the value (desirability, rightness, usefulness, goodness, etc.) of competing or conflicting moral traditions and obligations. We consider critical decision-making the most useful means or method for deciding what is the right thing to do even though we do not consider the evaluation of the value of outcomes or consequences (or moral traditions and obligations) that results from critical decision-making to be universally, absolutely, or objectively "right" (good, desirable, useful, etc.). This is so because we are doubtful or skeptical that *any* method can be used to make such a decision. Rather, we consider it more useful to regard values as contextual in significance. Thus, from the perspective of a co-constructivist ethic, methods for evaluating values, like values themselves, are contextual in significance. Although many different means or methods (e.g., logic, religion, science, intuition, reason, etc.) have been used in differing and diverse ways to attempt to identify or discover universal, absolute, or objective values, none has been successfully used to achieve this goal. Although their use is intended to yield an objective foundation for values, the use of such methods has historically yielded "objective" foundations with limits that are defined by the boundaries of particular cultural and historical horizons. That is, the "objective" foundations that the use of such methods yield ultimately reflect the contextual significance of the methods themselves and of the values the methods evaluate as desirable.

Critical decision-making, in contrast, is *not* a method intended to yield an "objective" foundation for values. On the contrary, critical decision-making is a method for doing exactly the opposite, namely, rendering explicit the contextual significance of values. Critical decision-making is a method for testing the practical significance and value of actual or potential consequences or outcomes in the context of existing goals and values, and (when necessary) testing the limits of existing goals and values and testing the boundaries of the cultural and historical horizon that define the limits of those goals and values.

If our co-constructivist ethic considers values as something that can never be determined with absolute certainty, does this mean that our co-constructivist ethic is *relativistic*? Does this mean that it is merely another example of what might be called moral or ethical relativism?

We think not. Our co-constructivist ethic is not relativistic because we are as doubtful or skeptical of the concept of relativism as we are of the concept of objectivism. Relativism is a term that is commonly used to describe the view that every belief is as good as every other (Rorty, 1985). Although our ethic views values as contingent and contextual, it does not view every belief or value as good as every other. Nor do we think that nothing can be evaluated as right or wrong and good or bad. On the contrary, the recognition of the contingent and contextual nature of values also results in a recognition that our understanding of value is particularistic and, in every case, necessarily rooted in the reality of specific cultural and historical contexts. For actual decisions made by real human beings in particular contexts, it is clearly not the case that every alternative, every goal or value, every belief, is as good as every other. Quite the opposite. Material realities such as scarcity and indeterminacy and the social and psychological constraints and limitations on human existence ensure that all alternatives, goals, values, beliefs, etc. are not equal. More importantly, when real human beings make actual decisions in specific historical and cultural contexts, it is always the case that not everyone will consider every alternative, goal, value, belief, etc. as good as every other. Nor is it the case that nothing can be evaluated as right or wrong and good or bad in specific historical and cultural contexts. In such contexts, existing hierarchies of goals and values can be (and are) used to evaluate the right and the good. Moreover, from the perspective of our ethic, there is no good reason for not accepting, at least provisionally, existing hierarchies.

Existing hierarchies, however, are not eternal or absolute. Existing hierarchies of goals and values do not define the ultimate endpoint of human action; rather, they constitute the starting point. The validity of existing means *and* ends can (and should) be evaluated with regard to their success in contributing to the successful solution to concretely experienced problems. And as conditions change (or as we create new conditions), ends as well as means can (and should) be evaluated with regard to their success in contributing to the solution of new problems. Goals that have been successfully achieved, in turn, become the means to achieve new goals and values—goals and values that formerly may have been not only unattainable but even unimaginable—thereby expanding the boundaries of cultural and historical horizons. There is always room for new and better ideas and ways of doing things—for improved belief.

Our co-constructivist ethic, consequently, is *not* relativistic. Quite the opposite, we are skeptical about the concept of relativism in the same way that we are skeptical about the concept of objectivism, only for a different reason. On the one hand, we object to the concept of an objective foundation for values because we think that things change and that, as they change, what is of value changes as does our understanding of value. On the other hand, we object to the concept that every belief is as good as every other because we, like the pragmatist, think that things not only change, but that things can (and do) change for the better. That is, we think that, as things change, human beings can understand how and why they change, and human beings can (and do) come up with better ideas and ways of doing things. Our ethic, consequently, not only objects to moral or ethical relativism because we believe that it is possible to come up with new and better ideas and ways of doing things, but also because we believe that it is possible to come up with new and better goals and values to give these ideas and activities their direction and purpose.

Thus, although the decisions or choices that result from critical decision-making are *not* objectively right (useful, desirable, good, etc.), they are *not* arbitrary or relativistic. Critical decision-making is not a means or method that considers every decision or choice as good as every other. Rather, our perspective considers some decisions or choices as actually or potentially better than others. In this frame, critical decision-making is more than a means or method for making the best possible decision or choice among actual or potential alternatives in a particular context. Because critical decision-making includes both actual *and* potential alternatives, it is more than a means or method for choosing the best alternative from an array of existing alternatives. It is also a means or method for using potential alternatives to test or challenge the limits of existing alternatives, thereby facilitating the creation, construction, or co-construction of new and better alternatives. Critical decision-making is in this sense itself a "better" idea or way of doing things. It is a better way of making decisions because it provides the most practical means or method presently available for testing the limits of the utility and validity of both actual and potential alternatives. Thus, although critical decision-making does not result in decisions or choices that are "objectively" right, individual decisions or choices in particular contexts that are arrived at through critical decision-making are, for all practical purposes, the closest approximation to right that is possible.

What does all of this mean for you as an individual when faced with making a moral choice or decision in a particular context? How can you know what is right? How can you avoid acting in bad faith? What it means is that you, as moral agent, actor, and decision-maker have to be willing to actively participate in decision-making processes and to subject your moral choices (and the goals, values, and principles that justify them, both actual and potential) to critical examination by yourself and to open them up to critical examination by others. Thus, one test of whether an individual moral choice is right is whether it can withstand your own critical examination. If a moral choice is personally defensible (and not simply a consequence of self-deception) then the next step is to test whether the moral choice is publicly defensible. Is it a choice that you would (or could) justify publicly? Is it a choice that you would be willing to open to critical examination? If you are uncertain, our advice is to open it to critical discussion. If your choice cannot stand up to critical thinking *and* critical discussion, then maybe you should reconsider it. Maybe it needs to change. If, on the other hand, you have actively and fully participated in the decision-making process and your moral choice (and the goals, values, and principles that justify it, both actual and potential) pass the test of critical examination by yourself and others (and all that implies) then, for all practical purposes, in that particular context, you have acted in good faith and have made the right choice.

## Deciding What Is the Right Thing to Do in Group Moral Dilemmas

We began this chapter by illustrating the type of difficult choices that individuals face in making a decision about what is the right thing to do. In Sartre's example the young man was faced with the choice of joining the Resistance or staying with his mother. Suppose, however, that the Resistance was itself faced with a moral dilemma. The Nazi campaign on the Eastern front was going poorly and it was clear that the allies would soon invade Western Europe. France would be free in the near future, and the dilemma that the Resistance faced was who they should support in the power vacuum that would follow when the Nazis left France. On the one hand, the government that was in power at the time of the Nazi occupation, which was very popular, had fled to England and continued to govern in exile. The Communist Party, on the other hand, which was less popular had stayed in France to continue the fight against the Nazis. The leaders of the government in exile and the Communist Party had both asked the leader of the Resistance for support in post-occupation France. The Resistance was faced with the choice of deciding which group to support. Part of their dilemma was that they had to evaluate the consequences of their decision. If the government in exile had lost their popular support, they might not be able to govern effectively in the chaotic and unstable times that would follow the departure of the Nazis. The Communist Party, on the other hand, was well-organized but might resort to oppression to impose order. This part of the dilemma involved evaluating consequences (e.g., the probability that they would occur, their extent or severity, their desirability or undesirability, etc.). However, the decision was more difficult than simply evaluating consequences. It was more difficult because it involved evaluating consequences in the context of conflicting or competing moral obligations, and they also had to evaluate those obligations—in this case, the relative importance of their obligation to the government in exile and their obligation to the party that had fought with them against the Nazis. This dilemma was even more complex, however, because it also involved the issue of *who* should make the decision. Should the leader of the Resistance make the decision for the group? Should the central committee make the decision? What role should the members of the Resistance play in making this decision? We complete the illustration of the application of a co-constructivist ethic with a discussion of how "democratic" decision-making is useful in making the *right* decision in the type of dilemma we have just described, namely, in a group or institutional moral dilemma.

A group or institutional moral dilemma is one in which more than one person has to make a decision involving conflicting obligations. The use of democratic decision-making in resolving group or institutional moral dilemmas involves the use of the same type of critical decision-making that we illustrated in the previous section. However, democratic decision-making includes more than critical decision-making. "Democratic" decision-making includes more because it takes place at the group or institutional level rather than at the individual level. An individual can make a personal moral decision, and this decision can be critical (or not critical), but an individual cannot make a democratic decision. Democratic decisions can only be made by more than one person. Groups or institutions make collective or shared decisions, and these decisions can be democratic (or not democratic). Democratic decision-making includes critical decision-making that is "democratic." By democratic we mean that it includes the opportunity for all to participate. Democratic decisions are collective or shared decisions that have been subjected to critical examination **in a context where all the individuals who are affected by the consequences or outcomes have the freedom and equality of opportunity to participate in the decision-making process.** A democratic decision is a decision in which the decision-making processes approximate the democratic "ideal." In groups or institutions that are "democratic," the democratic ideal requires that **all members have the freedom and opportunity to participate in all collective decisions; that no member's interests, goals, or values be excluded from any collective decision-making activity; and that all collective decisions be open to critical examination by all members of the group or institution.**

As an ideal, the democratic ideal is counterfactual. A "pure" democracy is a practical impossibility. No group or institution, no matter how small and intimate (or large and encompassing), could function if all members participated in every decision *and* if all members' interests, goals, and values were represented in all decisions, *and* if all decisions were subjected to critical examination by all members. Moreover, even if such a "pure" democracy were possible, the practical constraints of everyday life would limit its desirability. The social, psychological, and physical limitations and constraints of human existence effectively rule out the ideal of all individuals participating in every decision and subjecting all collective decision-making to critical examination. Nevertheless, this does not render the democratic ideal inappropriate or inadequate as an ideal. Although this ideal can never be perfectly realized in real life, it is an ideal that can be more *or* less closely approximated in real life. The democratic ideal thus serves as a guide or standard against which actual forms of social life can be evaluated. Consequently, we do not consider the democratic ideal as "ideal" in the sense of either "not real" or "unrealistic," but rather as an ideal in the normative sense, i.e., a criterion, standard, or value against which institutional forms of life can be evaluated.

Democratic groups or institutions are thus institutions that place no limits on participation in decision-making processes and no constraints on the use of critical thought and discussion, **as a matter of principle.** By this we mean to distinguish between procedural constraints or limitations on freedom and equality to participate that can or may be necessary in the practice of democracy, and constraints or limitations as a matter of principle. The type of practical constraints on the institutionalization of democratic processes that we described above, for example, can or may require procedural constraints or limitations on freedom and equality, either explicit or implicit. Democratic groups or institutions can or may involve full participatory democracies (as in the case of the scientific community and some sociomoral-political communities) or they can or may involve various forms of representative democracy (republic, parliamentary democracy, presidential democracy, etc.) with procedural limitations or constraints (majority rule, minority rights, etc.). However, in the case of participation, the democratic "ideal" requires that procedural constraints or limitations themselves be, as a matter of principle, open to public discussion and critical examination. In other words, constraints and limitations on participation must themselves be open to challenge by any or all participants and, under conditions of consensual agreement, subject to negotiation and revision. Democratic groups or institutions are groups or institutions that, in principle, include structures, methods, or procedures, either implicit or explicit, that provide the means for *all* members of the group or institution to participate in shared decision-making processes. It will be helpful in illustrating why we consider democratic decision-making to be the most useful means or method for making the right choice in a group or institutional moral dilemma if we describe the process in more detail.

In illustrating the process of democratic decision-making, we begin by noting that whether the methods or procedures that provide the means for all members to participate are implicit or explicit is less significant than whether the methods and procedures are implemented in practice. Democratic decision-making in groups or institutions is frequently accompanied by explicitly defined methods or procedures (e.g., constitutions, elections, bills of right, etc.) for implementing the democratic ideal (i.e., no limit or constraints on thought, discussion, or participation). Although the explicit articulation of the democratic ideal frequently reflects the extent to which the decision-making processes of a group or institution approximate the democratic ideal in practice, in many cases it does not. In fact, it is a tribute to the power of the democratic ideal that many of the most totalitarian political dictatorships in modern times—regimes that have been relentlessly oppressive and nondemocratic—have used the rhetoric of democracy in their constitutions and adopted what are called "democratic" procedures (e.g., one-party "elections") as part of their decision-making process (Ravitch & Thernstrom, 1992). The explicit articulation of the democratic ideal thus often reflects the institutionalization of practices that are democratic, but not always.

The democratic ideal is realized through the actual practices of groups or institutions rather than its explicit articulation. Many groups or institutions (or even relationships) that approximate the democratic ideal in practice, for example, do not have explicitly defined methods or procedures for implementing the democratic ideal. Modern science, for instance, is a social institution that closely approximates the democratic ideal in practice. The willingness to question, to challenge, and to criticize has been (and continues to be) the quintessence of the scientific spirit since the beginning of modern science. No scientific theory, no scientific fact, no scientific method is exempt from public discussion and critical examination by *all* members of the scientific community, from the most junior scientist to the most senior scientist.

Modern science thus closely approximates the democratic ideal in practice. The scientific community, however, neither uses the rhetoric of democracy nor has any explicitly defined methods or procedures for implementing the democratic ideal. The scientific community does not have a constitution or a bill of rights (written or otherwise); it does not conduct formal elections; it does not have a legislative or judicial branch, etc. What the scientific community does have is an implicit ethic or ideal, the "scientific spirit," that in actuality represents a shared value on the democratic ideal in collective decision-making (i.e., no limit or constraints on thought, discussion, or participation). The scientific ethic *is* thus a democratic ethic. More importantly, it is an ethic or ideal that is put into practice by its members when they are engaged in scientific activity. What makes modern science (or any other group or institution) a democratic institution is that its members value *and* practice democratic decision-making. It is thus the institutionalization of democratic practices (in science or any other form of social life) that represents the embodiment of the democratic ideal.

The evolution of democratic social institutions of all types (e.g., political, economic, intellectual, etc.) has tested the limits of the goals and values of our age. In the process, it has challenged and tested our ideas and ways of doing things. The institutional capacity for democratic decision-making that emerged with the evolution of democratic forms of life represents a new and better idea or way of doing things because it has opened up a possibility that was previously unavailable—a better way of making collective or shared decisions. Democratic decision-making provides a better way for making collective or shared decisions because it furnishes a means or method for achieving a rational consensus[4] with respect to group or institutional goals and values. The evolution of the institutional capacity for democratic decision-making has opened up the possibility of achieving a rational consensus with respect to value because the democratic ideal provides a standard by which to evaluate the rightness of group or institutional decision-making. To the degree to which decision-making processes in particular groups or institutional forms of life approximate the democratic ideal, the consensual decisions of such groups or institutions represent the closest approximation to what is the right thing to do that can be achieved.

We thus consider democratic decision-making to be the most useful method for resolving institutional moral dilemmas as well as for making institutional decisions about what is the right thing to do even though decisions concerning the evaluation of value that results from democratic decision-making are not any more "objectively" right (good, desirable, useful, etc.) than those that result from critical decision-making. Democratic decision-making, like critical decision-making, is *not* a method intended to yield an "objective" foundation for values. On the contrary, democratic decision-making, which includes critical decision-making, is a method for rendering explicit the contextual significance of values in a group or institutional setting. Democratic decision-making, however, is more than a useful method for resolving institutional moral dilemmas. The potential opened up by the evolution of democratic forms of life is that of enhancing the quality of life by enlarging and expanding the boundaries of our cultural and historical horizon to include the goal or ideal of providing the opportunity for *all* human beings to participate in the decision-making processes that affect the quality of their lives.

What does all of this mean for you as an individual member of a group or institution that is faced with making a collective or shared moral choice or decision in a particular context? How can you know what is right? How can you avoid acting in bad faith? What it means is that you, as a member of a democratic group or institution, have to actively participate[5] in decision-making processes and to subject the group or institution's choices (and the goals, values, and principles that justify them, both actual and potential) to critical examination that is open and public. In democratic forms of life, the freedom and equality of opportunity for *all* to participate in decision-making and the institutionalization of the use of critical decision-making does not guarantee making the right choice, but it does help to ensure that consensually agreed upon collective choices most closely approximate the right choice. If all members of an institutional form of life have the freedom and equality of opportunity to actively and fully participate in a decision-making process and competing or conflicting alternatives (and goals and values and the boundaries of the cultural and historical horizons that define the limits of those goals and values, both actual and potential) are open to a process of critical examination by all (and all that implies), then for all practical purposes, in that particular group or institutional context, the democratic choice is the right choice.

## Doing the Right Thing

Now that we have discussed the best methods for deciding what is the right thing to do, we turn to the issue of doing the right thing. Accepting responsibility for moral decisions, we noted, means that you have a responsibility to actively participate in decision-making processes that result in moral decisions *and* a responsibility to act on those decisions. We said that what we mean by actively participating in decision-making processes is relatively simple and straightforward. By this we mean making a decision to accept our responsibility and then living up to this responsibility by actually participating in all of the activities necessary to solve the problem of deciding what is the right thing to do.

What we mean by acting on our decisions is even more simple and straightforward. Acting on our decisions means *doing* what we have decided is the right thing to do.

## Discussion

The co-constructivist perspective that we have described in this chapter seeks to extend our understanding of human behavior and development. It seeks to change the way we think about human morality *and* human responsibility. It seeks to change it to include the idea that the freedom to choose that comes with the capacity for critical and democratic decision-making carries with it the responsibility for our choices. It is an ethic that holds us responsible for the quality of our lives. The practical implications of our co-constructive ethic are clear.

At the individual level, it is an ethic or ideal that holds that the individual should (ought to) live up to the responsibility for his/her decisions and actions. In practice this means that the individual should actively engage in decision-making processes *and* be willing to subject his/her choices (and the goals and values, norms and standards, rules and principles that justify them, both actual and potential) to critical examination. At the personal level, this translates into the internalization of a value on the use or practice of critical modes of thought and discussion in personal decision-making.

At the institutional level, it is an ethic or ideal that holds that institutions should live up to the responsibility for their collective or shared decisions and actions. In practice, this means that the members of the institution should actively participate in decision-making processes *and* be willing to subject their collective decisions and actions (and the goals and values, norms and standards, rules and principles that justify them, both actual and potential) to critical examination that is open and public. At the institutional level, this translates into the institutionalization of placing a value on the freedom and equality of opportunity to participate in decision-making processes and on the use of critical modes of thought and discussion, i.e., the institutionalization of the democratic ideal.

One goal in this chapter was to briefly outline the co-constructivist perspective that provides the framework for our work on human development. An additional goal was to illustrate how a co-constructivist ethic can be applied to making the right choice when faced with an individual or group moral dilemma—to provide some guidelines for moral decision-making and problem-solving from a co-constructivist perspective. The critical and democratic decision-making processes that we have illustrated in this chapter are helpful in making the right choice and living up to the responsibility for that choice. The guidelines that we have outlined, however, can at best only *help* to insure that we make the right choices and *help* to guard against acting in bad faith. They do not provide an absolute test for the rightness of our choices or the validity of the goals, values, and principles that justify them. As we noted earlier, however, it is not clear that it is either possible or desirable to identify or discover an objective foundation for values. For real human beings in particular contexts the question of deciding what is desirable and the means for achieving it is a practical problem, and practical problems have practical solutions. The contingent and contextual nature of such solutions does not detract from their usefulness. As Kierkegaard pointed out, the dilemma of human existence is that although we cannot avoid making choices, we can never be sure that we have made the right one—we can never be *certain* that we have made the right decision. Consequently, the best we can do is to make a commitment to take responsibility for our decisions and to be willing to subject our choices (and the goals, values, and principles that justify them) to the most critical tests possible. We can, in other words, seek to avoid acting and living in bad faith by making a commitment to accept the responsibility for the moral quality of our individual and shared lives. As Kierkegaard noted, a life without such a commitment is a life lacking direction and purpose. The co-constructivist perspective that we have described in this chapter thus seeks to change the way we think about human behavior and development to include an explicit recognition of the essential dignity and worth of *all* human beings—a recognition of the human capacity to guide and direct personal and historical change, and to choose the goals and values that give our lives direction and purpose, and the responsibility that accompanies this capacity.

## *Appendix of Measures*

This appendix presents summaries of the measures that we have developed as part of our program of research. We have continued to work on refining our measures/procedures, and a more detailed and up-to-date description of the measures, including more complete implementation and administration manuals, are available from the first author.

## The Moral Identity Scale—Production (MIS-P): Ages 5–Adult

The Moral Identity Scale-Production (MIS-P) is a measure of value orientation. The MIS-P is an individually administered interview that assesses five dimensions of value orientation: Relativism-Universalism, Teleological-Deontological, Individualistic-Social, Religious-Secular, Intuitive-Rational. The MIS-P is administered in an open-ended interview format that elicits the subject's self-generated categories or dimensions of understanding, hence the term production measure. The MIS-P can be used to identify unique dimensions of variability in value orientation in a specific research population. The MIS-P can also be used to assess the five dimensions of variability in value orientation. The manual describes administration and scoring procedures for each task. When used to identify dimensions of value orientation in a research population, the MIS-P is administered to elicit open-ended responses that can then be subjected to a content analysis. When used to assess variability in value orientation, responses to the MIS-P are coded using standardized rating scales to yield quantitative data for assessing individual and developmental differences in value orientation. The administration of the MIS-P takes approximately 40 to 50 minutes using a trained interviewer.

## Moral Identity Scale—Moral Issues (MIS-MI): Ages 11–Adult

The Moral Identity Scale-Moral Issues (MIS-MI) is a measure of value orientation. The MIS-MI is a group administered self-report measure that assesses two dimensions of value orientation: Relativism-Universalism and Teleological-Deontological. The items for the MIS-MI were constructed by developing paraphrases derived from the responses of the subjects to the items from the MIS-P. The paraphrases were intended to represent contrasting orientations for each of the value dimensions (e.g., a relativist versus a universalist value orientation). The MIS-MI asks subjects to suppose two people were talking about the issue. Each hypothetical person's "position" on the issue is presented and the subject is asked to indicate which person's position comes closest to their own and to indicate on a five-point Likert-type scale how much they agree with each person's position. Subject's responses are scored for two scales: the Relativism-Universalism (RU) value scale and Teleological-Deontological (TD) value scale. The administration of the MIS-MI takes approximately 15 to 20 minutes.

## Moral Identity Scale—Moral Dilemmas (MIS-MD): Ages 11–Adult

The Moral Identity Scale-Moral Dilemmas (MIS-MD) is measure of value orientation. The MIS-MD is a group-administered self-report measure that assesses one dimension of value orientation: Teleological-Deontological. The MIS-MD is designed to assess developmental and individual differences in the tendency to make moral decisions based on obligation (deontological moral choices) versus moral decisions based on consequence (teleological moral choices). The MIS-MD consists of six simulated moral decision-making situations, i.e., six hypothetical moral dilemmas involving fictional characters (Hobbits). Each of the six dilemmas involved a situation that contrasted a prima facie moral obligation (i.e., telling the truth, being fair, keeping a promise, not stealing, etc.) with a potential negative consequence (some potential harm to one of the characters). For each dilemma, the subject is asked to choose between two possible courses of action (e.g., telling the truth or not telling the truth). Subjects are also asked to rate how much they agree with each choice on a five-point scale. Subjects' responses are scored for a single scale: the Teleological-Deontological (TD) value scale. The administration of the MIS-MD takes approximately 15 to 20 minutes.

## Critical Decision-Making and Problem-Solving Scale—Moral Dilemmas (CPS-MD): Ages 13–Adult

The Critical Decision-Making and Problem-Solving Scale-Moral Dilemma (CDP-MD) is designed to assess the use of a "critical" sociomoral orientation, i.e., the use of critical thinking and discussion in individual and group moral decision-making and problem-solving. The MIS-MD dilemmas are used as test stimuli. The CDP-MD consists of two parts.

The Critical Thinking Subscale of the CDP-MD samples the "cognitive" decision-making and problem-solving operations and actions the subject uses in resolving individual or personal moral dilemmas. It is administered as a "standardized" interview, and the dilemmas are presented as an individual decision-making or problem-solving situation (i.e., the subject has to decide what to do). The interviewer elicits the subject's account of his/her choice, and the subject's responses represented in the narrative account are coded for the categories of decision-making and problem-solving operations and actions the subject uses.

The Critical Discussion Subscale of the CDP-MD samples the "communicative" decision-making and problem-solving operations and actions the subject uses in resolving a group or shared moral dilemma. It is administered as an "interactive" interview, and the dilemmas are presented as a shared decision-making or problem-solving situation (i.e., the subject *and* the interviewer have to try to agree about what to do). The interviewer engages the subject in a discussion or dialogue involving his/her choice, and the subject's responses represented in the discussion are coded for the categories of decision-making and problem-solving operations and actions the subject uses.

The administration of the CDP-MD takes approximately 40 to 50 minutes using a trained interviewer.

### Moral Development Scale (MDS): A Piagetian Measure of Moral Reasoning: Ages 5–13

The Moral Development Scale (MDS) is a Piagetian measure of moral judgment for use with children. The MDS is an individually administered interview that assesses moral reasoning within a Piagetian framework. The MDS uses dilemmas adopted from Piaget's original work on the moral judgment of the child. The MDS yields data on the two levels of moral reasoning Piaget identified: Heteronomous and Autonomous. The MDS yields a total Moral Development score that provides a composite measure of the child's attainment of an autonomous sense of responsibility and justice within a Piagetian framework. Additionally, the MDS also yields separate scores for Responsibility and Justice. The administration of the MDS takes approximately 40 to 50 minutes using a trained interviewer.

### Authors' Note

The work in this chapter was carried out at the Laboratory for Research on Psychosocial Development and Behavior, Florida International University. For further information about this work, contact William M. Kurtines, Department of Psychology, Florida International University, Miami, Florida 33199.

### Recommended Readings

Bandura, A. (1986). *Social foundations of thought and action: A social cognitive theory*. Englewood Cliffs, NJ: Prentice-Hall.

Bijou, S. W., & Baer, D. M. (1976). *Child development: The basic stage of early childhood*. Englewood Cliffs, NJ: Prentice-Hall.

Erikson, E. H. (1950). *Childhood and society*. New York: Norton.

Erikson, E. H. (1964). *Insight and responsibility*. New York: Norton.

Frese, M. & Sabini, J. (1985). (Eds.). *Goal directed behavior: The concept of action in psychology*. Hillsdale, N.J.: Erlbaum.

Fromm, E. (1947). *Man for Himself*. New York, Rinehart.

Gewirtz, J. L. (1969). Mechanism of social learning: Some roles of stimulation and behavior in early human development. In D. A. Goslin (Ed.), *Handbook of socialization theory and research* (pp. 57-212). Chicago: Rand-McNally.

Habermas, J. (1971). *Knowledge and human interest*. Boston: Beacon Press.

Habermas, J. (1979). *Communication and the evolution of society*. Boston: Beacon Press.

Kohlberg, L. (1969). Stage and sequence: The cognitive-developmental approach to socialization. In D. A. Goslin (Ed.), *Handbook of socialization theory and research*. Chicago: Rand-McNally.

Kohlberg, L. (1976). Moral stage and moralization: The cognitive developmental approach. In T. Lickona (Ed.), *Moral development and behavior: Theory, research, and social issues.* New York: Holt, Rinehart & Winston, 31-53.

Kohlberg, L. (1981). *Essays in moral development: The philosophy of moral development.*, Vol. 1. New York: Harper & Row.

Kohlberg, L. (1984). *Essays in moral development: The psychology of moral development.*, Vol. 2. New York: Harper & Row.

Kurtines, W. & Gewirtz, J. L. (Eds.) (1991). *Handbook of moral behavior and development, Vol. 1-3.* Hillsdale, New Jersey: Erlbaum.

McCarthy, T. (1981). *The critical theory of Jurgen Habermas.* Cambridge, Mass.: The MIT Press.

Piaget, J. (1932/1965). *The moral judgment of the child.* (M. Gabain, Trans.), New York: Free Press. (Originally published 1932).

Sartre, J. P. (1955). Existentialism is a humanism. In W. Kaufman (Ed. and Trans.), *Existentialism from Dostoyevsky to Sartre.* New York: World Publishing.

## Endnotes

1. We would note that the process of cultural transmission is an imperfect process. The child's culture influences the content of the child's morality, but the child also has an influence on the content of the culture's morality. More specifically, the developing child contributes to the transformation and creation of the cultural content of morality in the form of the transformation or reconstruction and the invention or creation of new or novel interpretations of sociomoral rules.

2. We would note that we do not mean to suggest that no further change or transformations occur in the content of the individual's sociomoral understanding, but only that such changes are not developmentally predictable. We have described in more detail elsewhere (Kurtines, 1993) the process by which the content of the individual's sense of morality is changed and transformed.

3. We consider critical and democratic decision-making to be more useful methods for evaluating values than other means or methods. However, means or methods for evaluating values, like values themselves, are open to evaluation. Moreover, it is always possible to come up with a better idea or way of doing things. Consequently, we only consider them more useful until a better way comes along.

4. Our use of the notion of "rational consensus" draws on Habermas' work on theoretical and practical discourse (McCarthy, 1981). Habermas' work has been directed toward articulating the features of the type of discourse community that provides the foundation for a rational consensus with respect to both truth and value.

5. Participation can be explicit or implicit. Many institutional decisions and actions are implicitly supported by the lack of participation. As we noted earlier, however, taking no action or not participating in decision-making processes (for *any* reason, e.g., forgetting, not knowing, being too busy, not having the time, etc.) is a choice with the full moral consequences of any other choice.

## References

Adams, G. R., Bennion, L., & Hugh, K. (1987). Objective measure of ego identity status: A reference manual. Unpublished manuscript.

Adams, G. R., Shea, J. & Fitch, S. A. (1979). Toward the development of an objective assessment of ego-identity status. *Journal of Youth and Adolescence, 8,* 223-237.

Baltes, P.B. & Goulet, L.R. (1970). Status and Issues of a Life-Span Developmental Psychology. In L. R. Goulet and P. B. Baltes (Eds.) *Life-span developmental psychology.* New York: Academic Press.

Bandura, A. (1986). *Social foundations of thought and action: A social cognitive theory.* Englewood Cliffs, NJ: Prentice-Hall.

Bijou, S. W., & Baer, D. M. (1976). *Child development: The basic stage of early childhood.* Englewood Cliffs, NJ: Prentice-Hall.

Blasi, A. (1984). Moral identity: Its role in moral functioning. In W. Kurtines & J. L. Gewirtz (Eds.), *Morality, moral behavior and moral development.* New York: John Wiley & Sons, 128-139.

Chomsky, N. (1965). *Aspects of a theory of syntax.* Boston: MIT Press.

Erikson, E. H. (1950). *Childhood and society.* New York: Norton.

Erikson, E. H. (1964). *Insight and responsibility.* New York: Norton

Frese, M. & Sabini, J. (1985). (Eds.). *Goal directed behavior: The concept of action in psychology.* Hillsdale, N.J.: Erlbaum.

Fromm, E. (1947). *Man for Himself.* New York: Rinehart.

Gewirtz, J. L. (1969). Mechanism of social learning: Some roles of stimulation and behavior in early human development. In D. A. Goslin (Ed.), *Handbook of socialization theory and research* (pp. 57-212). Chicago: Rand-McNally.

Gewirtz, J. L. (1977). Maternal responding and the conditioning of infant crying: Directions of influence within the attachment-acquisition process. In B. C. Etzel, J. M. LeBlance, & D. M. Baer (Eds.), *New development in behavioral research: Theories, methods, and applications* (pp. 31-57). Hillsdale, NJ: Erlbaum.

Gewirtz, J. L. (1991). Social influence on child and parent via stimulation and operant-learning mechanism. In M. Lewis & S. Feinman (Eds.), *Social influences and socialization in infancy* (pp. 137-163). New York and London: Plenum.

Grotevant, H. D. & Adams, G. R. (1984). Development of an objective measure to assess ego-identity in adolescents: Validation and replication. *Journal of Youth and Adolescence, 13,* 419-438.

Habermas, J. (1971). *Knowledge and human interest.* Boston: Beacon Press.

Habermas, J. (1979). *Communication and the evolution of society.* Boston: Beacon.

Habermas, J. (1981). *Legitimation crisis.* Boston: Beacon Press

Hogan, R. & Busch, C. (1984). Moral conduct as auto-interpretation. In W. Kurtines & J. L. Gewirtz (Eds.), *Morality, moral behavior and moral development,* (pp. 227-240). New York: John Wiley & Sons.

Kohlberg, L. (1969). Stage and sequence: The cognitive-developmental approach to socialization. In D. A. Goslin (Ed.), *Handbook of socialization theory and research.* Chicago: Rand-McNally.

Kohlberg, L. (1976). Moral stage and moralization: The cognitive developmental approach. In T. Lickona (Ed.), *Moral development and behavior: Theory, research, and social issues,* (pp. 31-53). New York: Holt, Rinehart & Winston.

Kohlberg, L. (1981). *Essays in moral development: The philosophy of moral development.,* Vol. 1. New York: Harper & Row.

Kohlberg, L. (1984). *Essays in moral development: The psychology of moral development.,* Vol. 2. New York: Harper & Row.

Kurtines, W. (1984). Moral behavior as rule governed behavior: A psychosocial role theoretical approach to moral behavior and development. In W. Kurtines & J. L. Gewirtz (Eds.), *Morality, moral behavior, and moral development.* New York: John Wiley & Sons, 303-324.

Kurtines, W. (1986). Person and situation effects on moral decision making: A psychosocial role-theoretical approach. *Journal of Personality and Social Psychology, 50,* 784-791.

Kurtines, W. (1987). Psychosocial theory as a nomotic science. In W. Kurtines & J. L. Gewirtz (Eds.), *Moral development through social interaction.* New York: John Wiley & Sons,

Kurtines, W. (1993). *Human behavior and devel-*

*opment: A co-constructivist perspective.* Unpublished Manuscipt.

Kurtines, W., Mayock, E., Pollard, S., Lanza, T., & Carlo, G. (1991). Social and moral development from the perspective of psychosocial theory. In W. M. Kurtines & J. L. Gewirtz (Eds.), *Handbook of moral behavior and development, vol. 1.* Hillsdale, New Jersey: Lawrence Erlbaum Associates.

Lewin, K. (1935). *A dynamic theory of personality.* New York: McGraw-Hill.

Marcia, J. E. (1966). Development and validation of ego identity status. *Journal of Psychology and Social Psychology, 3,* 551-558.

Marcia, J. E. (1980). Identity in adolescence. In J. Adelson (Ed.). *Handbook of adolescent psychology.* New York: Wiley

McCarthy, T. (1981). *The critical theory of Jurgen Habermas.* Cambridge, Mass.: The MIT Press.

Overton, W. W. & Reese, H. W. (1973). Models of development: Methodological implications. In J. R. Nesselroade, H. W. Reese (Eds.), *Life-span developmental psychology: Methodological issues* (pp. 65-86). New York: Academic Press.

Piaget, J. (1932/1965). *The moral judgment of the child.* (M. Gabain, Trans.), New York: Free Press. (Originally published 1932).

Piaget, J. (1936). *The origins of intelligence in children.* New York: International Universities Press.

Pollard, S., Kurtines, W., Carlo, G., Dancs, M., & Mayock, E. (1991). Moral education from the perspective of psychosocial theory. In W. M. Kurtines & J. L. Gewirtz (Eds.), *Handbook of moral behavior and development, vol. 3.* Hillsdale, New Jersey: Lawrence Erlbaum Associates.

Ravitch, D. & Thernstrom, A. (1992). *The democracy reader: Classic and modern speeches, essays, poems, declarations, and documents on freedom and human rights worldwide.* New York: Harper Collins Publishers.

Reese, H. W. & Overton, W. F. (1970). Models of development and theories of development. In L. R. Goulet and P. B. Baltes (Eds.), *Life-span developmental psychology* (pp. 115-145). New York: Academic Press.

Rorty, R. (1985). Solidarity or objectivity? In J. Rajchman and C. West (Eds.), *Post-analytic philosophy* (pp. 3-19). New York: Columbia University Press.

Sartre, J. P. (1955). *Existentialism is a humanism.* In W. Kaufman (Ed. and Trans.), *Existentialism from Dostoyevsky to Sartre.* New York: World Publishing.

Spivack, G., Platt, J., & Shure, M. (1976). *The Problem-Solving Approach to Adjustment.* San Francisco: Jossey-Baas.

Spivack, G. & Shure, M. (1977). The cognition of social adjustment: Interpersonal cognitive problem-solving thinking. In B. Lahey and K. A. Kazdin (Eds.), *Advances in Clinical Psychology.* New York: Plenum Press.

Sullivan, H. S. (1953). *The interpersonal theory of psychiatry.* New York: Norton.

Waterman, A. S. (1982). Identity development from adolescence to adulthood: An extension of theory and a review of research. *Developmental Psychology, 18,* 341-358.

Watson, J. B. (1913). Psychology as the behaviorist views it. *Psychological Review, 20,* 158-177.

Watson, J. B. & Rayner, R. (1920). Conditioned emotional reactions. *Journal of Experimental Psychology, 3,* 1-14.

# Part V

# Integrative Perspectives

## Prologue

In this part of this book we turn to a tradition that has played an important (indeed, central) role in the moral development literature. This tradition, however, does not fall neatly into any one of the meta-theoretical traditions (organicist, mechanistic, contextualist, etc.) that we have used to organize the previous chapters in the book. It does not fit into any *one* of these categories because it is a tradition that draws on *all* of these perspectives. More specifically, it is a tradition whose strength lies in a willingness to draw on what has proved to be useful and effective in diverse traditions, models, approaches, and perspectives.

The theoretical perspectives covered in this part of the book all share in common one of the characteristics that has enabled such theoretical orientations to make an important contribution to the continued strength and vitality of modern psychological theorizing, namely, they draw on the strengths of multiple traditions and combine and integrate them in highly original and creative ways. Developmental psychology, we noted, no longer appears to be predominately defined by any one theoretical orientation. On the contrary, the discipline has become increasingly more pluralistic. A similar trend has taken place in the moral development field. The phenomenal growth that has taken place over the past several decades has been fueled, in part, by the growing diversity that has taken place as the field has matured. Perspectives and traditions have been combined and recombined, integrated and reintegrated, and otherwise transformed in ways that have resulted in an extraordinary profusion of highly creative and original perspectives. As you will see in reading this part, the range of perspectives introduced in this part attests to the extent to which the field of moral development, like the larger discipline of psychology, has become defined by a multiplicity of theoretical alternatives, each an innovative integration of diverse traditions. The perspectives in this section not only integrate a diversity of traditions, but they also address a myriad of themes, topics, and issues.

## Overview of Chapters in Part V

The chapters in this part of the book all define original and unique theoretical perspectives that represent innovative integration that draws on diverse traditions. The first three chapters (14, 15, and 16) propose detailed descriptive models that integrate a variety of components, factors, variables, etc. that shape and influence moral outcomes. Chapter 14 provides an account of four components responsible for the production of *moral behavior*. Chapter 15 describes a multifaceted model of the factors (environmental, personal, cognitive, and emotional) that influence the performance of *prosocial behavior* (voluntary behavior intended to benefit others). Chapter 16 describes personal (social) goal theory, a theory of motivation and action, intended to account for the role of environmental, personality, culture, and socialization in influencing both *pro-* and *antisocial behavior*. Chapter 17 draws on extensive research on social domain theory in describing an alternative to the view that morality is a social construction specific to the make-up of each culture. Chapter 18 describes a model of moral choice that uses the concepts of limited morality, moral balance, and moral identity to account for why people may allow a personal consideration to override a moral one.

Chapter 14, by *Darcia Narváez* and *James Rest*, focuses on the complexity of psychological processes inherent in moral behavior which must work in concert in order for moral action to result. There are at least four processes that produce moral behavior: (1) moral sensitivity, (2) moral judgment, (3) moral motivation, and (4) implementation. These four processes or components comprise the *Four Component Model*. These are not personality traits or virtues. Rather, they are major units of analysis used to trace how a person responds in a particular social situation. The model depicts the four components as an *ensemble of processes*, not a single, unitary process. Therefore, behaving morally cannot be predicted from a single variable or single process. Behaving morally necessitates the effectuation of each process and the execution of the entire ensemble. This implies that the course of moral behavior may fail at any point due to a weakness in one skill or process. Some people may function well on one process but may be deficient in another. For instance, a person may demonstrate great sensitivity but poor judgment skills. Some people, on the other hand, make excellent judgments but fail in follow-through. Finally, there are those who have great tenacity but who make simple-minded judgments.

Each of the four component processes involves different kinds of *cognitive-affective interactions*. The Four Component model holds that there are no cognitions completely devoid of affect, no moral affects completely lacking in cognitive aspects, and no moral behavior separable from the affects and cognitions that prompted it.

Chapter 14 describes the four components that comprise the Four Component model.

Component 1: *Moral sensitivity* involves receptivity to social situations and the interpretation of the situation in terms of what actions are possible, who and what would be affected by each of the possible actions, and how the involved parties might react to possible outcomes.

Component 2: *Moral judgment* involves deciding which of the possible actions is most moral. The individual weighs the choices and determines what a person ought to do in such a situation.

Component 3: *Moral motivation* implies that the person gives priority to the moral value above all other values and intends to fulfill it.

Component 4: *Implementation* combines ego strength with the social and psychological skills necessary to carry it out.

Although the processes are presented in a logical sequence, the model does not assume that people perform each process in the order 1, 2, 3, then 4. Actually, there is evidence that the components interact with each other. For instance, notions about what is morally right or obligatory (Component 2) often influences one's sensitivity to possible actions and outcomes (Component 1).

Chapter 15, by *Nancy Eisenberg*, is concerned with the development of prosocial behavior in children, and the factors that affect this development. The work described in this chapter has examined several types of factors that appear to be relevant to children's prosocial responding: (a) children's moral reasoning about moral dilemmas in which someone can assist another (a sociocognitive ability), (b) the role of parents, teachers, and peers in prosocial development, (c) personality correlates of prosocial behavior, (d) emotional factors such as sympathy and empathy that may facilitate or preclude prosocial responding, and (e) situational factors that affect whether or not people help or share. In this work, it has become clear that all of these types of factors influence the development and performance of prosocial behavior.

The model of prosocial behavior described in Chapter 15 includes all of these factors. This model can used to try to integrate research findings emerging from a variety of perspectives (e.g., social learning theory, cognitive developmental theory, and the work on empathy and in social psychology).

Socialization influences and the individual's level of sociocognitive development are the starting points in the model. Such influences are the influences of cultural, parents, teachers, and peers, including the modeling of values and behaviors and disciplinary techniques; sociocognitive development is the development of cognitive skills used to understand and interpret social phenomena, skills such as perspective taking and moral reasoning. In a given situation in which someone may or may not assist another, characteristics of the situation are processed by individuals. The person's characteristics, mood, and interpretation of the helping context all may contribute to the individual's decision to assist.

Motivational factors make up the second step in the model. Whether or not people decide that they will help depends on a complex interaction of emotional and cognitive processes, as well as personal motivational factors. At some point in time, often after a decision-making process, a potential helper usually decides whether or not he or she *intends* to assist the potential recipient of aid. However, even when individuals decide that they intend to assist, they may not actually do so. This is for numerous reasons. First, their motivation may decrease due to the passage of time. In addition, people who intend to assist another may not actually do so due to real or perceived lack of competence to help. Also, some people may lack the social skills or social assertiveness to approach and assist someone else, even if they would like to do so. Finally, whether or not a person actually assists another may have consequences in regard to the probability of the individual enacting subsequent prosocial behaviors. Thus, the act of engaging in a prosocial behavior, especially an altruistic behavior, may affect the individual's self-perception, values and motives, sociocognitive capabilities, or behavioral repertoire in ways that impact on future prosocial responding. Research on those aspects of the model that are most pertinent to developmental analysis is discussed.

Chapter 16, by *Ervin Staub*, discusses the roots of prosocial and antisocial behavior in persons and groups. Research on both prosocial and antisocial behavior has focused on social-situational influences. But social-environmental conditions exert their influence by affecting people, by creating the psychological states and motivations that lead people to help or harm others. Their effects differ greatly depending on the characteristics of the people involved, like their self-concepts, values, or competencies. While it has become a truism that personality and situations jointly affect behavior, it is necessary to specify what characteristics of persons and what aspects of situations are important in influencing prosocial and antisocial behavior.

Chapter 16 describes a theory of action, which specifies how situations and personal characteristics join in giving rise to the psychological processes and motives that are the immediate influences on behavior. In addition to the characteristics of individuals, Chapter 16 also focuses on how the nature of societies and the characteristics of their culture and social institutions affect prosocial and antisocial behavior. These characteristics shape individuals, form their personalities, and also represent an ongoing environmental influence on their behavior.

The personal (social) goal theory described in Chapter 16 is a general framework for understanding social behavior, moral conduct, and specifically altruism and aggression. The theory identifies different kinds of motives, all of which, in their particular manifestations, are characteristics of individuals: *biologically based needs* like hunger and sex that press for satisfaction; *social rules, norms, and standards* that individuals adopt as their own, which guide our behavior, their influence becoming especially evident when another motive makes us want to deviate from them; *unconscious motives*, desires that have become unacceptable to us so that we have become unaware of them, which nonetheless continue to exert influence; and *personal goals* which are purposive, future-oriented, and the motivation they embody incentive-like.

Personal goals are desires for classes of outcomes, with associated networks of thought that identify the meaning and value of the desired outcomes. They are the most advanced motives; but all human motives can potentially become goallike in nature. Goals have ranges of applicability, that is, ranges of environmental conditions to which the goals apply and in which the goals can be satisfied. For example, an achievement goal, the desire to do well in comparison to standards of excellence, is for some people relevant to the domain of sports, for others to intellectual activity, for others to arts, for others to social situations. For some people, the achievement goal can be applicable to all situations.

Other-oriented or moral values are goallike in nature, with classes of desired outcomes and related networks of cognitions. The theory differentiates between self-related goals, and other-related goals which are values like prosocial and rule orientation. Other-oriented values also have ranges of applicability, and circumstances or people can be excluded from their range. Moral exclusion, which makes moral values inoperative in relation to certain groups of people or certain individuals, removes the inhibitions against harming and even killing people that most human beings acquire.

According to personal goal theory, altruism and aggression are the result of stimulating or instigating conditions and the characteristics of persons and groups. External conditions are seemingly the frequent initiators of people helping or harming others and have seemingly great power. This is due to shared characteristics among members of groups, and certain frequently existing but not inevitable human dispositions. Ultimately, it is the characteristics of the person (or members of a group) that determine the response to external conditions. Often enough, people will engage in prosocial or antisocial behavior that is internally instigated or initiated, a person's own thoughts or images giving rise to the psychological processes and motives that are the direct influences on their actions.

Chapter 16 describes some of the influences that lead people to help or harm others, or to remain passive bystanders to others who are suffering or to conditions that threaten or harm the social good. Understanding the origins of helping and harmdoing can help develop conceptions and practices for the creation of nonaggressive and caring persons and societies, and involved, responsible individuals.

Chapter 17, by *Marta Laupa* and *Elliot Turiel*, presents a theoretical approach based on the idea that moral and social judgments develop within distinct conceptual domains. Chapter 17 focuses on research that has uncovered the existence, starting in early childhood, of reasoning about three social domains. These are: (1) the *moral*, which pertains mainly to concerns with welfare, justice and rights; (2) the *social-conventional*, which pertains to understanding of social uniformities and regularities that are part of the smooth and efficient functioning of social organizations; and (3) the *personal*, which pertains to those individual prerogatives and entitlements considered to be exempt from social regulation.

This approach is intended to provide an alternative to the view that morality is a "social construction" specific to the make-up of each culture. Whereas morality is constructed through the traditions of a society by virtue of its history, individuals incorporate (not construct) morality by virtue of their socialization in the cultural setting. The domain-specific view, in contrast, is partially based on the idea that children generate or construct moral and social understandings of the world around them, not solely because of what is transmitted to them by adults, but also through their inference about events and social relationships directly experienced. Accordingly, moral judgments are not solely reflections of ready-made cultural codes and can entail solutions to problems that may exist across societal boundaries.

Heterogeneity in social orientations stems from the different domain-specific types of social judgments children make (i.e., judgments in the moral, conventional and personal domains). Social conventions are defined as behavioral uniformities which coordinate interactions of individuals within social systems. Conventions are relative to the societal context, and may be altered by consensus or general usage within a social system.

Unlike conventional prescriptions, moral prescriptions are not perceived to be alterable by consensus. Moral prescriptions are determined by factors inherent to social relationships. An individual's perception of an act such as the taking of a life as a transgression is not contingent on the presence of a rule, but rather stems from factors intrinsic to the event (e.g., from the perception of the consequences of the act). This means that moral issues are not perceived as relative to the societal context.

In contrast to both moral and conventional prescriptions, actions in the personal domain are those actions considered to be outside the jurisdiction of moral concern or social regulation. These actions are judged by individuals to be of a personal nature, and to be regulated by the personal preference of the actor, and not by moral concerns or the demands of social custom or convention.

Research has demonstrated that both children and adults respond differently to conventional and moral transgressions. In addition, a large body of research has shown that these domains are distinguished by children starting as young as three years of age. Consistent with the proposed distinction between the moral and conventional as qualitatively distinct domains of knowledge, children of varying ages have been shown to discriminate between events pertaining to different domains, and to reason about them differently depending on the specific domain to which they pertain.

In addition to the basic domain distinctions, researchers have investigated the development of children's reasoning (justifications) within domains. Studies have demonstrated development in each domain. Research on the social-conventional domain has described children's understanding of conventions as progressing through levels of affirmation and negation of conventions. Researchers have also found developmental change in the moral and personal domains as well.

The social environment which children experience while growing up is complex and heterogeneous. Children reflect on the social interactions and events which they experience, thus this heterogeneity is found in their judgments about their social world. The social-domain perspective and the research done from this perspective call into question the usefulness of stereotypes of different cultures and societies, or their members, in homogeneous terms.

Chapter 18, by *Mordecai Nisan*, describes a Moral Balance model. Based on everyday observations and on the findings of empirical studies, this model suggests that people (although probably not all people and not in all cultures) who accept the validity and force of moral imperatives do not *always* demand proper moral action of themselves. At certain times and under certain circumstances, they allow themselves to deviate to a certain degree. Moral perfection is generally not required, either of oneself or of others. Yet, a moral line is usually drawn beyond which one does not allow oneself to descend. This line, which is personal and rather flexible, allows the individual to view himself or herself as a moral person, and it serves as a barrier against unlimited transgressions.

This description of limited morality underscores its inherent contradiction: If we acknowledge the moral imperative and consider ourselves members of the moral community, how can we allow ourselves to deviate? In light of this, how can we understand a conscious decision to act against one's own moral judgment without relinquishing one's standing in the moral community? The Moral Balance model proposes that the very factor which explains why people behave in accordance with their moral judgment can also explain why they sometimes allow themselves to deviate from that judgment.

According to this approach, one of the major reasons that people choose to behave in accordance with their moral judgment is that they find it imperative to perceive themselves as moral people, i.e., to maintain their moral identity. The consideration of maintaining one's moral identity does not generally arise in response to a direct question, such as "Why don't you cheat?" Rather, the principle underlying moral choice can be said to revolve around the following question: Will the intended "improper" behavior hurt my self-image as a moral person to an unacceptable degree, or does it constitute a "tolerable" blow that my moral identity can withstand? Thus, judgments made from the perspective of moral identity generate evaluations which differ significantly from the impersonal moral judgment. A moral judgment relates to an act that is judged as either "right" or "wrong." In contrast, evaluation of a considered behavior in terms of its effect on one's moral identity is made along a continuum, ranging from very good behavior (which confirms and strengthens one's moral identity) to very bad behavior (which challenges and may even seriously damage that identity). Whereas a dichotomous evaluation forces the individual to take a clear stand, evaluation along a continuum allows for flexibility. An ideal is aspired towards, but it is not necessarily obligatory; people are more concerned with not falling too short of the ideal than they are with actually attaining it. They allow themselves a certain moral deviation, provided that their moral identity remains "satisfactory."

The model holds that individuals calculate a sort of moral balance for themselves, quantitatively weighing their morally relevant commissions and omissions within a given time span. According to this Moral Balance model, individuals compare their moral balance to their personal "level of acceptable morality"—a level below which we will not allow ourselves to descend. This level is usually lower than the ideal moral judgment, according to which we judge the rightness or wrongness of actions.

The Moral Balance model is based on the principle of "balanced identity," according to which the desire to maintain one's moral balance is part of a more general need to preserve one's personal identity. While the moral component of that identity plays a central role, its significance may be challenged by other identity components. Hence, when a moral choice involves a conflict between essential identity components, e.g., between the personal value of self-actualization and the moral value of duty to one's parents, people consider their current identity balance. In an attempt to maintain a balanced identity, personal considerations may outweigh moral ones.

# The Four Components
# of Acting Morally

*DARCIA NARVÁEZ*
*University of Minnesota*

*JAMES REST*
*University of Minnesota*

**Abstract**

The production of a moral act entails four inner psychological processes termed the *Four Component model.* These are (1) moral sensitivity, (2) moral judgment, (3) moral motivation, and (4) implementation. Analyzing the production of moral behavior in terms of the Four Component model is useful for explaining various failures in moral behavior, for providing a framework for organizing various research/theoretical traditions in the psychological study of morality, for understanding various theoretical controversies in the psychological literature, and for planning moral education interventions. Both cognition and affect are intertwined in each component, and the ensemble of four components are responsible for the production of moral behavior.

Do you wonder why people do bad things? Why does a terrorist kill innocent people? Do you ever ask yourself why people, who seem decent otherwise, treat you so insensitively? Why are people sometimes seemingly oblivious to the suffering of others? Or, have you wondered how some people can make such unfair decisions? And, have you thought about why it is so difficult for you to do what you think is right sometimes? When is the last time you thought about the complexity of morality? Was it yesterday or last week when you noticed someone cheating in class? Was it when the questionable actions of a media star or politician hit the front page? Or was it when someone you know struggled with the option of getting an abortion? Chances are, you have been thinking about moral behavior, or its lack thereof, a lot since you have been reading this book. This chapter will focus on the complexity of psychological processes inherent in moral behavior which must work in concert in order for moral action to result.

What are the psychological aspects of morality? Psychology has traditionally divided morality into three units: cognition, affect and behavior. According to this tripartite division of morality, the cognitive developmentalists study thinking while the psychoanalysts study emotion and the behaviorists or social learning researchers study behavior. It has been assumed that each area has its own separate track of development. While they are convenient distinctions, these traditional divisions do not represent theoretically clear units of analysis. For example, think of a dilemma you faced recently. Perhaps it involved whether to help someone out or not, how to divide your time among several demands, or how to approach a sensitive issue with someone. As you think about the situation, notice whether you can (or you did) clearly divide your feelings from your thoughts. If you are observant, you will notice that they are inseparable. Furthermore, would you say that your behavior had nothing to do with your feelings and thoughts? We all sense that there are interconnections here, but that they are complex. So how *can* we usefully analyze morality? There are at least four processes that produce moral behavior. These four processes or components comprise the Four Component model (see Table 14-1). Four internal psychological processes must occur for moral action to take place:

1. *Moral sensitivity* involves the receptivity of the sensory perceptual system to social situations and the interpretation of the situation in terms of what actions are possible, who and what would be affected by each of the possible actions, and how the involved parties might react to possible outcomes.
2. *Moral judgment* involves deciding which of the possible actions is most moral. The individual weighs the choices and determines what a person ought to do in such a situation.
3. *Moral motivation* implies that the person gives priority to the moral value above all other values and intends to fulfill it.
4. *Implementation* combines the ego strength with the social and psychological skills necessary to carry out the chosen action.

In order to produce moral behavior, our hypothetical person has to have both skills and persevering character in the face of opposition that arises during the course of the action's fulfillment. Before exploring each of the components in more detail, here are some general comments about the Four Component model.

The Four Component model represents the internal *processes* necessary to produce a moral act. These are not personality traits or virtues. Instead, these

## TABLE 14-1　Inner Processes Producing Behavior

| Major Functions of the Process | Cognitive-Affective Interactions |
|---|---|
| *Component 1* | |
| To interpret the situation in terms of how one's actions affect the welfare of others. | Drawing inferences about how the other will be affected and feeling empathy, disgust, and so on, for the other. |
| *Component 2* | |
| To formulate what a moral course of action would be; to identify the moral ideal in a specific situation. | Both abstract-logical and attitudinal-valuing aspects are involved in the construction of systems of moral meaning; moral ideals are composed of both cognitive and affective elements. |
| *Component 3* | |
| To select among competing value outcomes of ideals, the one to act upon; deciding whether or not to try to fulfill one's moral ideal. | Calculation of relative utilities of various goals; mood influences outlook; defensive distortion of perception; empathy impels decisions; social understanding motivates the choice of goals. |
| *Component 4* | |
| To execute and implement what one intends to do. | Task persistence as affected by cognitive transformation of the goal. |

are major units of analysis used to trace how a person responds in a particular social situation. The model depicts an *ensemble of processes*, not a single, unitary process. Therefore, behaving morally cannot be predicted from a single variable or single process. Behaving morally necessitates the effectuation of each process and the execution of the entire ensemble. This implies that the course of moral behavior may fail at any point due to a weakness in one skill or process. Some people may function well on one process but may be deficient in another. For instance, a person may demonstrate great sensitivity but poor judgment skills. Or, as another example, there are people you know who make excellent judgments but fail in follow-through. And there are those who have great tenacity but who make simple-minded judgments. See Table 14-2 for some examples from popular characters.

Each of the four component processes involves different kinds of *cognitive-affective interactions*. As we noted earlier, cognition and affect do not occur in separation. As Piaget contended, they are sides of the same coin. Unlike other

**TABLE 14-2    Real and Fictional Characters That Represent the Components**

| Component | Strong in Component | Weak in Component |
|---|---|---|
| Moral sensitivity | Mother Teresa<br>Mary Tyler Moore<br>Bill Moyers<br>The Tin Man (Wizard of Oz) | Archie Bunker<br>Spock<br>Bart Simpson |
| Moral judgment | King Solomon<br>The Scarecrow (Wizard of Oz) | Snow White<br>Ralph Cramden<br>Lucy (I Love Lucy) |
| Moral motivation | The Biblical Paul<br>Don Quixote<br>Eleanor Roosevelt | Hitler<br>Stalin<br>Saddam Hussein<br>Alex P. Keaton<br>Scrooge |
| Implementation | Moses<br>Hercules<br>John Wayne<br>The Virgin Mary<br>Dirty Harry<br>Scarlett O'Hara | Woody Allen characters<br>Garfield<br>Cathy |

theories and theorists, the Four Component model holds that there are no cognitions completely devoid of affect, no moral affects completely lacking in cognitive aspects, and no moral behavior separable from the affects and cognitions that prompted it.

The processes are presented here in a *logical sequence*. However, this sequence does not assume that people perform each process in the order 1, 2, 3, then 4. Actually, there is evidence that the components interact with each other. For instance, one's notions about what is morally right or obligatory (Component 2) often influences one's sensitivity to possible actions and outcomes (Component 1).

The goal of presenting such a model is multiple. It provides a framework for programmatic research and for moral education programs. In addition, the Four Component model has been useful in organizing existing research on the psychology of morality and as a tool in analyzing theoretical problems. It may also help you in examining your own behavior and those of others you know.

## Component 1

In order for a person to choose to respond to a situation in a moral manner, she must be alerted to the need for a particular action and be able to interpret the events adequately. In other words, the individual must be sensitive to the situational information and constructively imagine various possible actions.

One aspect of sensitivity concerns response to cues in the environment. Individual differences abound in arousal to environmental events. One person's alarm may not be activated until he sees blood flowing, while another person reacts to minute details, a glance or expression, and finds momentous moral implications in every act.

Critical to interpreting the situation is empathy. It is usually defined as distress felt by the self which is triggered by the perception of distress in another person. It is a primary affective response which can be aroused in very young infants and which requires little cognitive development for its activation. As a child matures, so does her response to her empathetic feelings. She is first moved to distress when she hears another infant cry. As she develops a clear distinction between herself and others, she feels sympathy for another in visible distress. She seeks to comfort that person in ways that would comfort her. For instance, she might take her teddy bear to her mother when her mother is upset, assuming that the teddy bear is as comforting to her mother as it is to her. At age two or three, the child begins to realize that others may have different needs than she does. She begins to make inferences from her world knowledge that enable her to give more effective help to others. In late childhood, she is aroused by a tragic life situation as well as by immediate distress. That is, she may feel sad for a person who lives in poverty and has much less than she does.

If you will recall our earlier statement about affect and cognition, you will note how affective development is inseparable from a cognitive understanding or conceptions of others. It is this gradual development of both affect and cognition together that helps the adult interpret difficult social situations. It assists the adult in deciding which actions are possible and what influence they might have on the parties involved. The emerging field of social cognition is exploring the complications not only in cue detection, but in information integration and inference-making as well.

Part and parcel of sensitivity are what we call "gut reactions." A particular situation can arouse strong feelings even prior to the perception of what the situation actually entails. One may feel instant empathy or an immediate antipathy for the person or persons involved. These primitive cognitions, which can be pre-verbal, are tacit and automatic. They can occur whether or not reflective judgment and consideration of the facts have taken place. These feelings may help or hinder our better judgment. When we sympathize with victims, we are more likely to come to their aid. But when we instantly recoil from a victim's looks or aspect, we may deny that person his full human rights. Affective arousal of this sort happens and must be taken into consideration when we are interpreting the social situation. First impressions are often poor guides for action but they must be recognized and dealt with responsibly if moral action is to ensue.

Proper interpretation of social situations is often difficult. Many years ago, a brutal killing in New York City captured the public attention for a while and spurred a great deal of psychological research. This was the case of Kitty Genovese. Now it is true that many violent killings occur every day in many cities. But what was seemingly unusual about the Genovese case was that the slaying took place while 38 people watched and did nothing. Kitty Genovese was walking home from work one evening when an assailant grabbed her purse and then stabbed her repeatedly with a knife. This was in a busy residential section of town. Kitty cried out when she was stabbed. Some lights in nearby apartments went on, some people looked out. But they did not respond. No one shouted out, no one called the police, no one went out to where Kitty was lying and tried to help her. The assailant ran off with her purse. Some time later, the assailant realized that Kitty was still alive and would be able to identify him. So he went back to where she was lying and stabbed her several times again. Kitty cried out again. And again, people peered from their windows and did nothing. Twenty minutes later the assailant came back for the third time and stabbed her some more to make sure she was dead. What is haunting about this event is the fact that 38 people witnessed a brutal and extended murder but did not attempt to intervene. At little personal expense, someone could have at least phoned the police.

There is evidence that people have trouble interpreting social situations, such as bystanders in emergency situations. When the 38 witnesses to the murder of Kitty Genovese were interviewed later, they indicated confusion about what had been happening. They were not completely clear that Kitty Genovese was being stabbed by a purse-snatcher; they thought perhaps they were observing a lovers' quarrel and would suffer embarrassment if they were to get involved. In other words, they were confused in their interpretation of the situation. This confusion led to inaction. Staub (1978) has reviewed many studies that demonstrate how helping behavior is determined by the level of cue ambiguity in the situation. If the subjects are not clear about what is happening, they do not help as much.

Once a person determines what is happening, he or she thinks about possible actions, who would be affected by the possible outcomes of these actions, and how these people would react. In emergency situations, these assessments often occur in split-second time, e.g., when an adult sees a child playing on a railroad track that holds an oncoming train. The adult quickly assesses the configuration of events: whether the child is old enough to understand a shout and to move obediently, how fast the train is moving, whether a physical intervention is necessary, whether the adult would be at risk of injury, what other options might be available, etc. On the other hand, in everyday life, these assessments may take a long time to make. For example, the ramifications of an abortion decision have implications not only for the fetus, but also for many aspects of the woman's life, her partner's life, her family and friends. This decision may take agonizing days of time to figure out.

Think about a time when you blamed yourself, afterwards, for lacking sensitivity to a situation. Were you preoccupied with something else at that time? Had the cues seemed irrelevant? Were you confused by what was happening? Did you experience strong gut reactions that pulled you in conflicting ways? These and likely other factors not yet identified help determine moral behavior. Let's consider another aspect.

## Component 2

Having identified possible lines of action in terms of the Component 1 process, the function of Component 2 is to judge which action possibility is morally right and which is wrong. Moral judgment has been researched more extensively in modern psychology than any of the other components. There are two major research traditions offering an explanation of the mechanisms involved in forming a judgment. The first has evolved from social psychology and postulates that *social norms* govern the judgment of what is morally correct in a particular situation. A social norm has the following form: "In a situation with X features, a person ought to do Y." A number of social norms have been proposed, such as social responsibility, equity, reciprocity, and giving. For example, the norm of social responsibility prescribes that when you perceive a need in a person who is dependent on you, you should help that person. As an illustration, let us apply this approach to Lawrence Kohlberg's widely-known dilemma, *Heinz and the drug.* Heinz' wife is dying and a druggist has a remedy that he is selling at a price beyond the means of Heinz and his wife. The question is, should Heinz steal the drug for his wife? Heinz faces a moral dilemma. He notices a particular configuration in the event. Applying the norm of social responsibility, Heinz notices that a person who is dependent on him is in need. The norm has been activated. Heinz then infers that he should steal the drug. According to the social norm approach, as a person matures, he acquires more and more social norms which are then activated in special situations under particular circumstances.

The second major research tradition concerned with moral judgment is cognitive-developmental research, beginning with Jean Piaget's work, *Moral judgment and the child,* followed by Lawrence Kohlberg's more systematic and detailed research program and continuing with other cognitive-developmental psychologists. There are two critical assumptions made by theorists of this tradition. First, people automatically reflect on their social experience and construct meaning structures in response to their experience. Making moral judgments seems to come easily to people. Even young children display moral outrage when they feel cheated or experience unfair treatment. Particularly striking is the fact that people's moral intuitions about right and wrong can be so drastically different from each other's and that these intuitions will be held with such zealous certitude. The cognitive developmentalist seeks to understand how people form their judgments, what makes these judgments so different and what comprises the fervor with which the beliefs and opinions are held.

Second, as people have social experience they develop more elaborate conceptions of the social world and a progressive understanding of the purpose, function, and nature of social arrangements. These shifting conceptual schemes of cooperation are termed "stages" of moral reasoning. Each of the stages is characterized by a distinctive notion of justice, that is, a conception of the possibilities and requirements for arranging cooperation among participants. Each stage is viewed as an underlying *general* framework of assumptions about how people ought to act toward one another, how people ought to cooperate together. Accompanying the particular conception of social organization is a distinctive sense of fairness. This concerns the reciprocity of cooperation—what is owed to others and what others owe to me. When a person is confronted with a decision about what is morally right in a social situation, the sense of fairness that is derived from a particular concept of organizing cooperation is the driving force behind the moral judgment.

At first, the young child is struck by the power and status of caretakers; he has the notion that the way to get along with these more powerful people is to do what you are told. According to this notion of getting along with others, being "good" is being obedient. This notion is referred to as *Stage One: Punishment and Obedience.*

But the child notices that each individual has personal likes and dislikes, interests and goals. The child begins to suspect that what the caretaker says is good is not necessarily what he considers to be good all of the time. "Mom and Popeye might say that eating spinach is good, but I don't agree. Why should I accept them or anyone else as my boss?" These new realizations undermine the earlier notion of blind obedience. In its place springs another idea: Even though people may have different opinions about what is good, they do not have to be at odds with each other all of the time. In fact, people can get along with each other by doing favors for each other. "You butter my bread and I'll provide you with jam." What is morally good is performing your favor in simple exchange for somebody else's favor. Morality is abiding by your part of the bargain. This is *Stage Two: Prudence and Simple Exchange.*

With further experience and reflection, the growing individual realizes that people do not simply get along by exchanging favors on an individual basis. Instead, there grows an understanding that people form enduring relationships in which the parties do not keep strict count of who owes what to whom; they orient toward understanding each other, maintaining the other's approval, caring, and support. Being morally good at this stage is to do those things that support and nurture caring relationships. Loyalty and being on the same wavelength are valued more than concrete favors. This is *Stage Three: Interpersonal Harmony and Concordance.*

Gradually, the circle of participants in the human being's conceptions of the social world expands; he grows into the awareness of more complicated schemes of cooperation as he becomes aware of the limitations of the Stage 3 notion, how to deal with strangers and groups of strangers with whom one will never be in relationship. Living in towns and cities, one must often deal with people on a short-term basis. Yet one also wants to be able to cooperate with them and have reasonable expectations about each other's behavior. Thus is conceived the idea of formal laws and formal organization. The law is publically set forth for all in a society to know; it prescribes behavior for everyone. Formal organizations have chains of command and role positions that circumscribe particular responsibilities and allow certain prerogatives. The morally right action is to keep within the law and to perform the allocated duties of your role, expecting that others in society are also obeying the law and fulfilling their duties. What would be unfair is for a person to think that she is above the law or to fail to fulfill the responsibilities of her duty within the society. This is *Stage Four: Law and Order.*

When the individual becomes aware of the limitations of the law and the status quo, he begins to think of other ways than the current structure to organize society-wide cooperation. The individual uses a guiding principle for conceptualizing role and rule systems. He seeks to balance the benefits and burdens of living together for mutual benefit and in avoidance of exploitation. The individual understands that specific laws, rules and roles are instruments, not ends in themselves, for achieving general human values. The use of moral principles is distinctive of *Stages Five and Six: the Principled Stages.*

Most research in this area has been centered around the conceptualization of justice, postulating it as a core concept that handles the balancing of benefits and responsibility within a cooperative scheme. Thus, development consists in the subject's increasing awareness of the possible kinds of cooperative arrangements. Some theorists disagree with this formulation and have suggested concepts to either replace justice or to accompany it. Such postulations include benevolence, honor, duty, and filial piety.

An interesting study that supports the contention that justice concepts are not the only way that people make moral judgments was conducted by Lawrence (discussed in Rest, 1979). She studied radically fundamentalist seminarians. After the seminarians had formulated judgments about moral dilemmas, they reported that they had set aside their own personal views about fairness. They stated that it was wrong for them to allow their own sense of justice to intrude on questions of value, which have all been previously adjudicated by the highest authority, God himself. The moral questions they faced were answered by church or Biblical teaching. This study indicates that allegiance to an ideology may override a person's own moral intuitions. As another instance of ideological commitment preempting one's intuitive sense of fairness, consider Abraham and Isaac in the book of Genesis. According to this story, Abraham understood that God wanted him to offer his only son as a sacrifice to the Lord God. Like any normal father, he abhorred the thought and intuitively thought the idea was unfair. But his religious sense of obedience was more powerful than his own intuitions. On the way up the mountain to the designated place, Isaac asked his father, what will we sacrifice? With a heavy heart, Abraham kept his silence while he prepared the altar. Then he bound his son and laid him on the altar. As he took the knife to slay his son, an angel interrupted him saying that his faith was evident and that he need not follow through. But the fact remains that Abraham had judged that the right thing for him to do was to sacrifice his son, against his own intuitions of justice.

Although some theorists in the field of morality have regarded research in moral judgment as comprising the whole of morality, the Four Component Model regards such work as only relevant to Component 2. Accordingly, moral judgment is not the whole of morality. It does not tell us how sensitive a person is or whether the person has the skills to implement her moral ideal. And it indicates nothing about Component 3, what other values may preempt a moral ideal.

## Component 3

Once a judgment has been formed about what is the most moral action there also arises the awareness of how the moral course of action may interfere with optimizing other values. Moral values are not the only values that people have. A person may value pleasure, career advancement, art, music, status, etc. These other values may conflict with the chosen moral value. For instance, you may decide to forego the new bicycle in favor of giving a donation to a needy cause. Or, you might think that a critic of your organization does have a justified complaint, yet you value the reputation of your organization and don't acknowledge the criticism. It often happens that choosing the moral course of action is in conflict with some other value.

Many of our religious, legendary, mythic, and folktale heroes have to undergo value conflicts. Consider the adventures and conflicts of Ulysses, Hercules, Jesus, John the Baptist, Luke Skywalker, and Pinocchio. Remember how Lancelot was attracted to the legendary Round Table of King Arthur. Lancelot was an outsider who proved himself to be not only outstanding in athletic and noble feats but in his pure upright character. To his misfortune, and that of the kingdom, he fell in love with the queen, Guinevere, and she with him. For years, they stayed silent and avoided each other's solitary company, out of love for Arthur and for the good of the Round Table and the kingdom. Arthur was aware of their feelings and never left them alone either. Through the plotting of Mordred, Arthur's heir, they finally discovered themselves together, alone. Another value, amorous fulfillment, took hold and got the best of their earlier resolve. They were discovered and brought the kingdom down with them.

More contemporary and true-to-life examples are often found in government circles. Consider John Dean, who, in his book, *Blind Ambition*, describes his activities as special counsel to President Nixon prior to and during the

Watergate scandal. He admits that he was motivated by ambition to succeed. Questions of morality and justice were circumnavigated by his desire to convince everyone else that he, too, could play "hardball."

An interesting illustration from research was performed by Damon (1977). He asked youngsters how they thought ten candy bars *ought* to be distributed as a reward to those who had worked on making bracelets. In their interviews, the children described various schemes for a fair distribution and explained why their particular scheme should be implemented. When these same children were subsequently given the ten candy bars to distribute, they deviated from their espoused schemes of fair distribution, giving themselves a disproportionate number of the bars. Thus, the children's moral intuitions and judgments were compromised by a more attractive value, the pleasure of eating those tasty bars.

Given that a person is aware of various courses of action and their outcomes in a particular situation, many of which hold alternative attractions, why is it that a person ever chooses the moral option? What is it that motivates the selection of moral values over other values?

Psychologists have come up with many theories to explain why moral values are ever chosen over other values. The following are among these theories:

1. People choose moral values because evolution favors species with inbred altruism. Creatures that help each other have a survival advantage. Parenting instincts and other altruistic behavior is demonstrable among animals, and is part of human genetic inheritance also.
2. Shame, fear, and guilt over transgression is what makes people do the right thing. Consider interactions among coaches and athletes, military officers and recruits, religious leaders and their congregants. These negative affects can be powerful controlling devices.
3. People learn to do the right thing through the pervasive mechanisms of social modeling and reinforcement. Behaviorists believe that moral behavior is just learned behavior. There is no special motivation to "be moral."
4. People choose to do the moral thing through allegiance to a higher power. Moral motivation is derived from a sense of awe for a deity, one's country, a crusade, etc.
5. People become motivated to choose moral values over other values from the experience of living in a just community and in caring relationships. Having these experiences leads a person to prize these relationships above other values.
6. People do the moral thing from a motive to maintain their own self-concept which includes a sense of integrity. Everyone has a notion of who they are and what they stand for. If I consider myself to be a moral person, I will want to act in moral ways. I want to preserve my identity.

7. People chose to do moral values through social understanding. Education is a broadening experience that can overcome prejudice and pettiness as it fosters social responsibility.

These are a few of the explanations that psychologists have given to account for the prioritizing of moral values over other values that a person may have. It may turn out that there is no one theory that explains all moral motivation, but that various and multiple motives account for some people's behavior some of the time. It is obvious, however, that moral motivation must be one component in the production of moral behavior.

## Component 4

Component 4 necessitates working around impediments and unexpected snags. It requires resisting distractions and other allurements. Envisioning and keeping in sight the final goal is vital. These characteristics of perseverance, resoluteness, and competence comprise what we call "character" or "ego-strength." Failure in these self-regulative behaviors has been termed weakness of the flesh, weak-willedness, and cowardliness. Ego strength is essential for any long-term task, irregardless of its morality. It is indispensable in preparing for a marathon, practicing for a recital, climbing a mountain, obtaining a degree, robbing a bank, or carrying out genocide. We observe failures in this process, and call them wimps or regard them as having weak characters.

Research is uncovering some compelling information about how to develop and enhance these skills. Individuals who cheer themselves on seem to be able to increase their perseverance at a task. Self-confidence and perceived efficacy at the task influence coping behavior, effort, and staying power. In one study of Stage 4 ("law and order") subjects, those with high ego strength cheated less than those subjects with low ego strength. Others suggest that what a person thinks about during the course of helping another may determine his persistence at the task. If an individual thinks of the task as fun, easy or satisfying, he is more likely to stick with it. One self-regulation technique studied involves cognitively transforming the goal object. In a study by Mischel (1976), children were instructed to think about their reward objects, marshmallows, as cotton balls, while others were told to consider the marshmallows as marshmallows, e.g., as soft, chewy, and sweet. The children who focused on the consummatory qualities were unable to wait as long as the children who focused on transforming the object in their minds. Again, as with the other components, it is obvious that cognition and affect interact in Component 4 also.

Think about the United States, as a nation, during the Second World War. Unlike during the Vietnam war, there was a national resolve to see the conflict through. The society as a whole was cheering on individual and united efforts to overcome the enemy. Women were encouraged to take traditionally male jobs in order to maintain the economy and the troops. The nation focused on winning, on keeping up the troops' morale. The positive emotions were rallied and prevailed upon the negative effects of the situation. People suffered rationing without undue complaint. Family losses were expected and honored. Most of all, the United States believed it could accomplish the task of defeating the enemy, who turned out to have perpetrated more evil than at first realized. This perseverance, grit, tenacity, strong character, and ego strength is what is distinctive about Component 4—a necessary component for doing good or doing evil.

## Interaction of the Components

We have noted that there is a multi-faceted complex of processes that must take place in order to engender moral action. In addition, the components must interact harmoniously until the action has been completed. Research and common sense indicate that sometimes one component compels so much attention that one or more of the other components is ineluctably slighted. For example, when emotions are manipulated, behavioral differences can result; being dutiful with one moral action can cause insensitivity to another situation that has sprung up in the midst of the first and before the first has been completed, i.e., steadfastness and resolve can interfere with sensitivity; as the personal costs of a moral action become more and more clear, there is often a reappraisal of the situation and the phenomenon called "blaming the victim" may result. All sorts of seemingly trivial changes in a situation can influence subsequent behavior, e.g., number of people in the vicinity, gender of those involved, immediate prior experience, attractiveness of the participants, and so on. The complexity of interactions often make it difficult to sort out the causal factors of non-moral behavior.

Consider a recent and stark event, the case of Brian Watkins. He, a 22-year-old, his parents, and older brother and wife were in New York City for the U.S. Tennis Open. One evening, they planned to go out on the town and were taking the subway. As they waited on the platform with a dozen or so other people, they were swarmed by a group of about 10 teenagers. The young people demanded the father's money. When he did not react fast enough, his pocket was slashed from his pants. The mother screamed and tried to intervene. She was pushed down and kicked in the face. Her younger son, Brian, jumped to her aid. At that moment, one of the youths pulled out a four-inch blade and plunged it into Brian's chest. The attackers grabbed the father's wallet and ran off. Brian ran after them, up two flights of stairs and then collapsed. His parents sought help from anyone and everyone. No one listened to their cries for help. They were astonished at the apathy. No one had tried to intervene. No one was jumping to their aid now, either. Even the token booth operator had turned his head away. When they finally caught someone's attention out in the street, paramedics were summoned. It was too late. Brian's severed pulmonary artery brought about his death but one half hour later. In this situation, it was obvious to witnesses what was happening. There was no confusion as in the Genovese case. What then was the matter? Staub (1978) has demonstrated that when people are concerned about themselves, they are less helpful. As is often the case in a large city, people were no doubt focused on their own safety. Staub noted that when a person is concerned about performance, achievement or self-representation, they are less likely to be sensitive to others. This is also true when a person has received negative feedback about herself. He concludes that when people are focused on the self, there is less attention and concern for the needs and welfare of others. On the other hand, when self-esteem or good feelings are boosted, there is apparent increased helpfulness. Thus, situational cues seem to be altered by psychological states. Component 3 (motivation) interferes with Component 1 (sensitivity) and prevents Component 2 (judgment) from taking place.

## Conclusion

In conclusion, there may be one or more reasons for moral failure. Moral behavior requires a complexity of processes—at least four. It is a mistake to portray the whole of morality as simply empathy, or simply concepts of justice, or merely genetic predisposition to be altruistic, or solely mimicking a model, etc. Attempts to predict moral behavior from just one of these components is likely to produce weak associations inasmuch as the link of one component with behavior leaves the other three components to vary randomly. Moral failure may occur at any point in the chain of processes as a "weak" link, sabotaging moral action. If moral behavior is the end goal of moral education, then moral education ought to be addressing all four components. Moral development entails gaining proficiency in all four component processes across all situations.

## References and Recommended Readings

Damon, W. (1977). *The social world of the child.* San Francisco: Jossey-Bass.

A body of work in the Piagetian tradition of moral judgment tradition done with younger children.

Mischel, W. and Mischel, H. (1976). A cognitive social-learning approach to morality and self regulation. In *Moral development and behavior.* T. Lickona (ed.) New York: Holt, Rinehart & Winston, 84-107.

This chapter considers some of the main constructs of a cognitive social-learning position and examines how they apply to the psychological analysis of moral judgments, moral or prosocial conduct, and self-regulation.

Piaget, J. (1965). *The moral judgment of the child.* M. Gabain, trans. New York: Free Press (originally published, 1932).

This is the classic work on moral judgment which pioneered the field of moral development for study and research.

Rest, J. (1979). *Development in judging moral issues.* Minneapolis, MN: University of Minnesota Press.

This book deals with instrument development (validity and reliability, test format) to test moral judgment (the Defining Issues Test) and a formulation of the moral judgment stages.

Rest, J. (1986). *Moral Development: Advances in research and theory.* New York: Praeger Press.

Drawing on about 500 studies, this book presents an overview of the Four Component model of moral behavior. It reviews studies relating moral judgment to age, education, and life experiences. It reviews gender and cultural differences and differences due to religion. It also focuses on the relation of moral judgment to behavior and provides a summary and meta-analysis of over 50 moral educational programs that have used the Defining Issues Test as a pre-post measure of effectiveness.

Staub, E. (1978, 1979). *Positive social behavior and morality, Volume 1-2.* New York: Academic Press.

A review of hundreds of studies that concern mostly prosocial behavior.

# Chapter 15

# Prosocial Development: A Multifaceted Model

*NANCY EISENBERG*
*Arizona State University*

## Abstract

The performance of prosocial behavior (voluntary behavior intended to benefit others) is complex, morally relevant behavior influenced by a variety of factors including environmental, personal, cognitive, and emotional influences. Thus, any theory or model designed to explain and predict prosocial behavior, including altruistically motivated prosocial behavior, must include discussion of the diverse factors that influence prosocial responding. However, current theories in developmental psychology tend to emphasize one type of factor (e.g., cognitive) while ignoring or deemphasizing others (e.g., emotional). Therefore, our approach has been to draw from a variety of theories and perspectives in developing a working model for thinking about and investigating the development and performance of prosocial actions. In this chapter, I briefly delineate this model and then focus primarily on aspects of the model for which developmental factors are of particular relevance. These factors include the following: sociocognitive skills such as perspective taking and moral reasoning; emotional reactions such as sympathy, personal distress, and guilt; and the socialization influences to which children are exposed. The model is viewed as a heuristic for exploring the variety of developmental and social psychological factors that influence prosocial behavior in children and adults.

Until approximately 20 years ago, few psychologists were interested in the development of positive behaviors such as sharing, helping, and providing comfort. Most of the researchers and theorists concerned with moral development during the decades previous to 1970 examined topics such as honesty, aggression, and moral reasoning or knowledge. However, in the late 1960s, social scientists started to turn their attention to issues such as "When do people help?" and "Why don't many people help during emergencies?" This emerging interest in helping behaviors seemed to be due in part to the humanitarian values embedded in both the anti-war movement of the 1960s and the "Great Society" politics of President Johnson in which education and welfare issues were prominent. In addition, social scientists' attention was drawn to the issue of the apathetic bystander in an emergency by a dramatic and well-publicized murder in which a young women was stabbed to death within the sight or hearing of 38 witnesses, none of whom helped (Latane & Darley, 1970).

Whatever the reasons for the sudden interest in prosocial behaviors (that is, voluntary behaviors intended to benefit another), numerous developmental and social psychologists began to study them around 1970. Thus, much of the literature concerning prosocial development is relatively recent, and theoretical perspectives on the topic are still emerging and changing. Grand theories such as psychoanalytic theory, learning theory, and cognitive-developmental theory can be used to explain parts of the body of knowledge regarding prosocial behaviors (Radke-Yarrow, Zahn-Waxler, & Chapman, 1983), but none appears to adequately explain much of what has been learned. Thus, various researchers have proposed new models and conceptual frameworks to try to organize and explain the research findings (e.g., Eisenberg, 1986; Piliavin, Dovidio, Gaertner, & Clark, 1981; Schwartz & Howard, 1984). However, no one model or framework deals with all of the issues and factors relevant to an understanding of prosocial behavior (e.g., Piliavin et al.'s model concerns helping in emergencies whereas Schwartz and Howard's work pertains to value- and norm-based helping).

My own work in the last 18 years has concerned the development of prosocial behavior in children, and the factors that affect this development. In this work, I have examined several types of factors that appear to be relevant to children's prosocial responding: (a) children's moral reasoning about moral dilemmas in which someone can assist another (a sociocognitive ability); (b) the role of parents, teachers, and peers in prosocial development; (c) personality correlates of prosocial behavior; (d) emotional factors such as sympathy and empathy that may facilitate or preclude prosocial responding; and (e) situational factors that affect whether or not people help or share. In this work, it has become clear that all of these types of factors influence the development and performance of prosocial behavior. Thus, my own framework for understanding prosocial behavior includes all of these factors. In addition, to try to make sense of what is known, I have drawn ideas and information from a variety of perspectives, including cognitive-developmental theory (Kohlberg,

1984), cognitive social learning theory (Bandura, 1986), social psychology (see Dovidio, 1984), and biological perspectives.

In this chapter, I present a brief overview of a model of prosocial behavior, and then review examples of findings that are relevant to the role of development in the model. This model is far from complete, and is merely a heuristic to help guide further research and thinking about prosocial behavior. Its merit, I believe, is that it focuses on both cognitive and affective processes that affect the decision to assist another, as well as situational, socialization, and personality factors that influence prosocial responding. Thus, the model can be used to try to integrate research findings emerging from a variety of perspectives (e.g., social learning theory, cognitive developmental theory, and the work on empathy and in social psychology).

In discussing prosocial behavior, it is important to keep a few points in mind. First, most people who are concerned with prosocial behavior—researchers, educators and other professionals, and laypersons—are usually most interested in one particular type of prosocial behavior, altruism. Altruistic behaviors often are defined as those prosocial behaviors motivated by other-oriented or moral concerns rather than social or material rewards or the desire to reduce or avoid aversive internal affective states such as guilt and anxiety. Thus, altruistic behaviors are those prosocial behaviors performed for unselfish, moral, or sympathetic reasons. Of course, many prosocial behaviors are not altruistic. For example, children often assist others merely to behave in a socially acceptable manner, to elicit approval, or to obtain some egoistic outcome (e.g., to induce another child into play). Unfortunately, because motives are internal states, it is often impossible to determine whether a given prosocial behavior is altruistic or not; moreover, the performance of non-altruistic prosocial behaviors may eventually lead to the development of altruistic tendencies (Eisenberg, Cialdini, McCreath, & Shell, 1987). Consequently, given the difficulty in discriminating between altruistic and non-altruistic behaviors, our model of prosocial behavior pertains to all types of prosocial behaviors, although altruistic behaviors are of special interest.

## The Model: An Overview

An overview of our model of prosocial behavior is depicted in Figure 15-1, and more detail is presented in Figures 15-2 to 15-4. I now briefly summarize the components of the model.

### The Initial Steps

As can be seen in Figure 15-1, socialization influences and the individual's level of sociocognitive development are seen as starting points in the model. Socialization influences are the influences of the culture, parents, teachers, and peers,

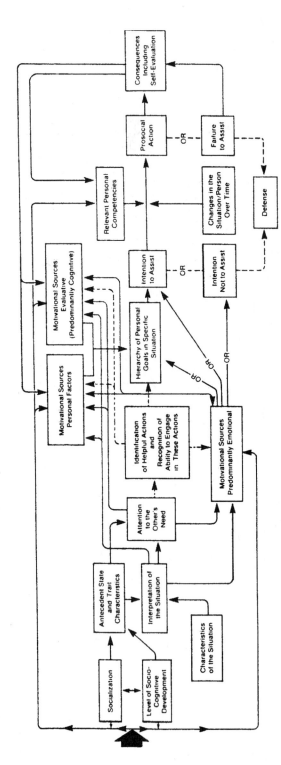

FIGURE 15-1    **A Model of Prosocial Behavior**

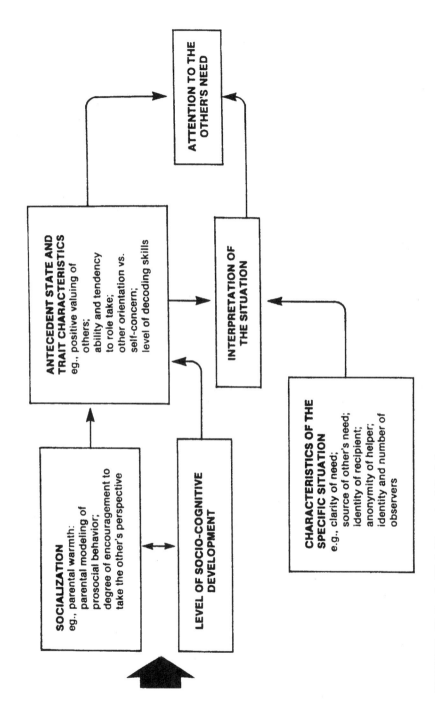

FIGURE 15-2   Initial Steps in Model

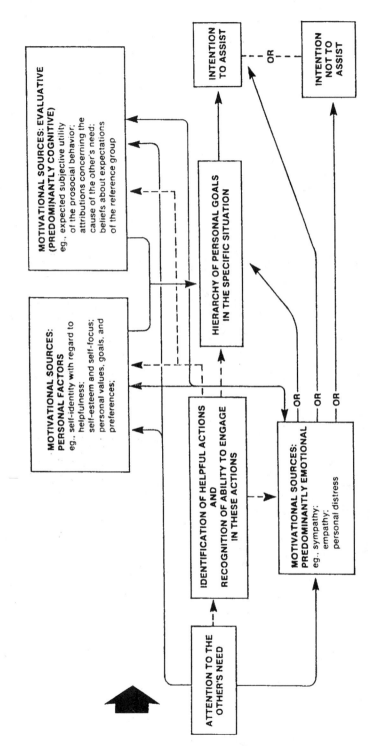

FIGURE 15-3   Motivational Portion of the Model

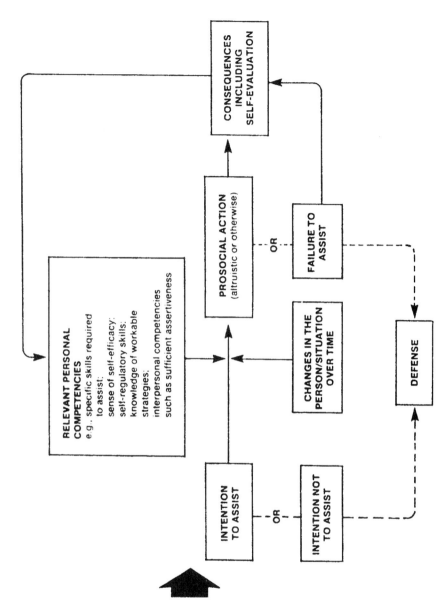

FIGURE 15-4   The Link between Intention and Behavior

including the modeling of values and behaviors and disciplinary techniques; sociocognitive development is the development of cognitive skills used to understand and interpret social phenomena, skills such as perspective taking and moral reasoning.

Socialization influences and the sociocognitive capabilities of the child influence one another. Socializers undoubtedly adapt their child rearing practices to the level of a child's ability to think about social interactions, and the child's thinking about the social world is influenced by his or her experience with socializers. Moreover, both socialization influences and the sociocognitive level of the child play a role in shaping the child's personality ("Antecedent State and Trait Characteristics" in the model), including the individual's personal values, preferences, needs, and affective responses, as well as how the child responds emotionally in various contexts ("Motivational Sources: Predominantly Emotional"). However, biological aspects of the child's personality such as his or her temperament (e.g., emotional reactivity and sociability) and the child's intelligence undoubtedly also affect how socializers deal with the child and how the child interprets his or her world.

In a given situation in which someone may or may not assist another, characteristics of the situation ("Characteristics of the Situation" in the model) are processed by individuals. For example, whether or not a person assists may be influenced by who it is that needs help, who else is present, and what type of help is needed (e.g., knowledge about changing a tire or money). In addition, potential helpers' interpretations of the situation are influenced by who they are—their values, needs, preferences, and so forth ("Antecedent State and Trait Characteristics"). For example, people's values, needs, and preferences undoubtedly affect how positively they respond to representatives from different charitable groups, and some people are more motivated than others to decipher cues concerning another's emotional state. Of course, as was noted previously, an individual's personal characteristics are themselves affected by their socialization experiences and their level of sociocognitive functioning.

Before a person can actually assist another in need, he or she usually must process and recognize the other person's need or desires (although nonaltruistic helping may occur without attending to another's needs). To do so requires that the observer attend to the person in need ("Attention to the Other's Need" in Figure 15-1). Whether or not an observer does so varies as a function of his or her interpretation of the situation. For example, if an observer believes that another person is simply clowning around when that person trips and falls, the observer may not perceive cues of distress. In addition, the individual's interpretation of the situation will affect whether he or she responds to the other person with sympathy, disgust, anxiety, or some other emotional response. For example, if a person is laying on the ground on the street, one observer may conclude that the person is a drunk, react with disdain and disgust, and decide that the fallen person does not need any immediate assistance. Another observer may decide that the person lying on the ground has had a heart attack and is in need of assistance. Yet another observer may believe the person on the ground is drunk, but due to their personal experience and value system, may feel sorry for the intoxicated person and view him or her as in need of assistance.

People will not help another person if they do not recognize that they are able to do so. For example, young children often may not view themselves as capable of assisting adults. Similarly, people who know nothing about cars may not view themselves as capable of helping someone whose car has broken down. The person's characteristics, mood, and interpretation of the helping context all may contribute to whether or not an individual believes that he or she can assist. If a person does not feel capable of helping, he or she may not proceed any further through the process of deciding whether or not to help.

## Motivational Factors

Even if people feel that they are capable of assisting another person, they may decide not to help. Whether or not people decide that they will help depends on a complex interaction of emotional and cognitive processes, as well as personal motivational factors. Emotional reactions such as sympathy or personal distress or guilt may or may not be activated ("Motivation Sources: Predominantly Emotional" in the model); moreover, motives related to personal factors (e.g., the need to maintain self-esteem and personal values related to helping) may come into play in the decision-making process ("Motivation Sources: Personal Factors" in the model). In addition, assuming that the prosocial behavior is not performed habitually (i.e., by habit without much conscious processing) or spontaneously without thought (e.g., as when a parent jumps into a pool to save his or her drowning child), cognitive evaluative processes would be expected to become relevant ("Motivation Sources: Evaluative" in the model). Specifically, the individual's assessments of the costs and benefits of a given helping action and factors such as the individual's beliefs regarding why the other person needs help may become important.

Thus, depending on the specifics of a given situation, a variety of cognitions, emotions, and personal values, needs, and preferences may be activated. Some of these factors may be consistent with the decision to assist the other person; some may not. For example, a person may feel sympathy for a needy other and value helpfulness, but also may think that the cost of helping in the given context is very high. Or a person may want to help tutor a friend in math because the friend will be pleased but also may feel the need to study for a test in English because of a high need to achieve. In such situations, individuals must prioritize their various motivations in regard to the importance of each motive in the given context.

How people prioritize motives will depend on their hierarchy of personal goals, that is, their motivational preferences for certain end-states and their aversions to others (Staub, 1978). For everyone, some needs, desires, values, and preferences are more important than others; however, the ordering of these varies across people. For some people, the approval of others is important; for others, it is not. Some people are concerned about monetary costs, whereas others are more concerned about self-condemnation for acting in a way that is not consistent with personal values. People come into situations with their own hierarchies of personal goals, which are shaped by a variety of factors (including socialization experiences, individual differences in personality, emotional responding, and sociocognitive skills, and even biologically based aspects of temperament).

However, in real-life situations, a person's hierarchy of personal goals varies as a function of not only the individual's a priori personal goals, but also the individual's evaluation of aspects of the particular situation (e.g., how needy the other person is and why) and the intensity of the person's emotional response to the situation ("Hierarchy of Personal Goals in Specific Situation" in Figure 15-1). For example, if the situation is very sympathy-evoking for a given individual, values related to altruism may become particularly salient. In contrast, if the needy other is viewed as manipulative and the help needed is costly, concerns about the cost of helping may become more salient than usual for the potential helper. Factors that are relevant in one situation (e.g., approval from parents) may not be relevant in another, and different personal goals may be salient in different contexts. The individual's reactions to, and interpretations of, a given situation partially influence the salience of various personal goals.

When various personal goals conflict, a social or moral dilemma is created (the dilemma is moral if moral concerns are involved, which is not always the case). For example, a person's prosocial values based on internalized values may conflict with the nonmoral goal of avoiding contact with certain types of people or obtaining material goods. The resolution of moral dilemmas of this sort is analogous to what has been assessed in the research on prosocial moral judgment.

As was just discussed, a potential helper's decision whether to assist or not generally is based on his or her hierarchy of personal goals in the given context. Occasionally, however, this decision may be made primarily on an emotional basis (e.g., in a very compelling emergency) or, if the situation involves no costs, on the basis of habit. In most instances, however, people are likely to engage in at least a brief consideration of the costs and benefits of assisting and the relation of a potential helping behavior to their personal goals.

## To Help or Not to Help

At some point in time, often after a decision-making process, a potential helper usually decides whether or not he or she *intends* to assist the potential recipient of aid ("Intention to Assist" and "Intention Not to Assist" in Figure 15-1). When people decide not to assist, they are likely to justify that decision by derogating the needy other, denying responsibility, minimizing the other's need, or some other defensive technique (Schwartz & Howard, 1984). They also may reinterpret the situation to avoid internal conflict regarding the decision to refuse assistance or guilt. People generally do not like to think of themselves as immoral, uncaring, or cruel, even if their actions appear to reflect such characteristics.

However, even when individuals decide that they intend to assist, they may not actually do so (see Ajzen & Fishbein, 1977). This is for numerous reasons. First, their motivation may decrease due to the passage of time. For example, emotional reactions such as sympathy diminish over time. Moreover, the situation may actually change with time; for example, the other person may become less needy or the costs for helping may change. In addition, people who intend to assist another may not actually do so due to real or perceived lack of competence to help. For example, some people who would like to donate blood cannot do so because they do not meet the necessary requirements (Pomazal & Jaccard, 1976), and young children may frequently lack the skills necessary to assist someone. In addition, some people may lack the social skills or social assertiveness to approach and assist someone else, even if they would like to do so (e.g., Barrett & Yarrow, 1977).

Finally, whether or not a person actually assists another may have consequences in regard to the probability of the individual enacting subsequent prosocial behaviors. Indeed, engaging in prosocial behaviors is associated with an enhanced probability of doing so in the future (Beaman, Cole, Preston, Klentz, & Steblay, 1983; Eisenberg, Cialdini, McCreath, & Shell, 1987; Staub, 1979). This may be for several reasons. Engaging in prosocial actions, or not doing so, may affect a person's self-image. Changes in one's self-image are important because people tend to act in ways consistent with their self-image (Grusec & Redler, 1980; Lepper, 1983). Moreover, the mere performance of a prosocial act may serve to shape moral values that may then influence future behavior. Because people seem to have a need to maintain consistency between their behaviors and beliefs (Festinger, 1957), they may alter their values and reasoning processes pertaining to altruism to be consistent with prior behavior. In addition, when individuals perform prosocial behaviors, they may receive material, social, or internal (e.g., emotional) reinforcements for doing so, which may increase the probability of enacting prosocial behaviors in the future. Finally, when people do assist others, they may have opportunities to role-take and to learn about others' feelings and perspectives or new ways of helping. Such learning would be expected to enhance the likelihood of assisting in future situations (Peterson, 1983; Underwood & Moore, 1982). Thus, the act of engaging in a prosocial behavior, especially an altruistic behavior, may affect the individual's self-perception, values and motives, sociocognitive capabilities, or behavioral repertoire in ways that impact on future prosocial responding.

## Development and Components of the Model

Additional research relevant to each of the components in the model in Figure 15-1 is reviewed by Eisenberg (1986). Thus, given constraints on the length of this chapter, only certain aspects of the model are discussed in this portion of the chapter. The aspects selected were those most pertinent to a focus on development and childhood.

## Initial Steps in the Model

In the initial portion of the model, we are concerned with pre-existing and ongoing aspects of the individual and his or her environment (socialization, level of sociocognitive development, and antecedent state and trait characteristics), as well as aspects of the situation and how it is interpreted by the individual. Much of the research concerning situational influences on prosocial behavior has been conducted by social psychologists with adult subjects (Bar-Tal, 1984); there is relatively little research on how children's prosocial behavior is affected by situational variables or how children's perceptions of the environment change with increasing age. However, there is a sizable literature concerning the socialization of prosocial predispositions and behavior, and the relation of sociocognitive functioning to prosocial development. Consequently, these aspects of the beginning section of the model are examined in more detail.

### Sociocognitive Level

There is abundant evidence that sociocognitive capabilities relevant to prosocial behavior change dramatically with age during childhood (e.g., Kohlberg, 1984; Shantz, 1983). For example, children's abilities to understand how another person feels or what another person is thinking increase throughout early childhood and the adolescent years (Selman, 1980; Shantz, 1975). Very young children appear to have difficulty differentiating their own thoughts and feelings from those of others and may become overwhelmed by exposure to another's distress (Hoffman, 1984; Radke-Yarrow et al., 1983). Moreover, young children are less able than older children to interpret subtle cues indicative of another's need (Pearl, 1985). Sociocognitive abilities such as these have been linked theoretically and empirically with altruistic behavior (e.g., Hoffman, 1984; Underwood & Moore, 1982). Children who are better able to detect and understand others' thoughts and feelings are more likely than other children to sympathize with, and appropriately assist, distressed or needy others.

Another sociocognitive ability that changes dramatically with age is moral reasoning—that is, how individuals reason when they resolve moral dilemmas. Moral reasoning typically is assessed by presenting children or adults with several hypothetical dilemmas about moral conflicts and then asking the individual to resolve the dilemmas. For example, a typical dilemma may concern a man's decision to steal a drug to save his wife's life or the decision whether or not a child should help another child who is being picked on by a bully. However, in some studies, people have been asked to reason about real-life moral dilemmas or have provided reasons for their own prior, morally relevant behaviors. The reasoning that is used by the respondent to resolve the dilemma is of central importance in all research of this sort (see Eisenberg, 1986; Kohlberg, 1984).

The moral dilemmas used by investigators concern a variety of moral issues, for example, lying, stealing, and breaking promises. In the past decade, a considerable amount of research has been conducted using dilemmas in which a person can assist another individual at a cost to the self in a context in which the role of authorities and their dictates, punishment, rules, laws, and formal obligations is minimal. These dilemmas sometimes are called prosocial moral dilemmas, and they have been useful for understanding how children's reasoning about helping and sharing changes with age (see Eisenberg, 1986).

Although there are individual differences in the way children of the same age reason about prosocial moral dilemmas, the sequence of change in reasoning that occurs with age seems to be somewhat similar across children. This sequence is outlined in Table 15-1. Briefly, young children tend to view moral conflicts in terms of outcomes for the self, although even preschoolers are capable of attending to others' needs when dealing with a conflict concerning helping another. With age, children's reasoning about prosocial moral dilemmas becomes less hedonistic, and in middle childhood, improving the quality of social relationships, social approval, and adherence to social norms become considerations in many children's moral reasoning. Beginning in early adolescence, issues related to internalized moral values, self-reflective empathic concerns (e.g., explicit perspective taking and sympathizing), responsibilities and duties, internalized guilt, and the welfare of the larger group start to emerge in some children's moral reasoning about prosocial dilemmas. Thus, in general, children's prosocial moral reasoning becomes less hedonistic and more socially oriented, value-oriented, and overtly other-oriented with age (Eisenberg, 1986; Eisenberg, Shell, Pasternack, Lennon, Beller, & Mathy, 1987).

These developmental changes in prosocial moral reasoning seem to reflect changes in children's needs, values, and preferences, and in the relative ordering in children's hierarchies of personal goals. In resolving a moral dilemma, the child must decide which of various personal goals are most important in a given situation. For example, children must decide whether winning a contest that would result in a cash prize as well as possible public recognition and praise is more important than whatever personal goals can be achieved by helping needy others (e.g., the desire to reduce another's distress, the desire for praise, the desire to live up to internalized values, or concern for the functioning of society). Thus, the research on prosocial moral reasoning can be viewed as providing evidence for the assertion that children's personal goals become more socially directed, other-oriented, and value-based with age.

The research concerning children's prosocial moral reasoning also supports the assumption that the changes in children's personal goals and values influence children's tendencies to assist others. Investigators frequently have found that higher level moral reasoning is associated with more and higher quality (more altruistic) prosocial behavior (Bar-Tal, 1982; Eisenberg, 1986; Underwood

## TABLE 15-1 Levels of Prosocial Reasoning

*Level 1*

*Hedonistic, self-focused orientation:* The individual is concerned with self-oriented conse-quences rather than moral considerations. Reasons for assisting or not assisting another include consideration of direct gain to the self, future reciprocity, and concern for others because one needs and/or likes the other (due to the affectional tie). (Predominant mode primarily for preschoolers and younger elementary-school children.)

*Level 2*

*Needs-oriented orientation:* The individual expresses concern for the physical, material, and psychological needs of others even though the other's needs conflict with one's own needs. This concern is expressed in the simplest terms, without clear evidence of self-reflective role taking, verbal expressions of sympathy, or reference to internalized affect such as guilt. (Predominate mode for many preschoolers and many elementary-school children.)

*Level 3*

*Approval and interpersonal orientation and/or stereotyped orientation:* Stereotyped images of good and bad persons and behaviors and/or considerations of other's approval and acceptance are used in justifying prosocial or non-helping behaviors. (Predominant mode for some elementary- and high-school students.)

*Level 4a*

*Self-reflecting empathic orientation:* The individual's judgments include evidence of self-reflective sympathetic responding or role taking, concern with the other's humanness, and/or guilt or positive affect related to the consequences of one's actions (predomi-nant mode for a few older elementary-school children and many high-school students).

*Level 4b*

*Transitional level:* The individual's justifications for helping or not helping involve internalized values, norms, duties, or responsibilities, concern for the condition of the larger society, or refer to the necessity of protecting the rights and dignity of other persons; these ideas, however, are not clearly and strongly stated. (Predominant mode for a minority of people high-school age or older.)

*Level 5*

*Strongly internalized stage:* Justifications for helping or not helping are based on internalized values, norms, or responsibilities, the desire to maintain indi-vidual and societal contractual obligations or improve the condition of society, the belief in the dignity, rights, and equality of all individuals. Positive or negative affect related to the maintenance of self-respect for living up to one's own values and accepted norms also characterizes this stage. (Predominant mode for only a small minority of high-school students and no elementary-school children).

Reprinted from Eisenberg (1986), with permission of Lawrence Erlbaum Associates.

& Moore, 1982). The relation of prosocial behavior to other-oriented modes of moral reasoning (i.e., those reflecting a focus on others' needs or perspective taking and sympathy) seems especially clear (Eisenberg, 1986). However, it is important to note that moral reasoning may be related to prosocial behavior only in contexts in which people go through an active decision-making process; in some situations, people may enact small acts of consideration without really thinking (such as helping pick up an object that was dropped) or by habit (e.g., contributing a small amount to the same charity every year). Nonetheless, the research on moral reasoning provides investigators with information concerning the types of reasoning a given person is likely to use when making real-life decisions regarding prosocial actions.

In addition, children's social skills in dealing with everyday social dilemmas often must be a reflection of their perspective-taking abilities, moral reasoning level, and other aspects of their understanding of the social world. For example, how well children can negotiate solutions to their conflicts depends in part on their understanding of others and their motives and perspectives (Shure, 1982). In brief, children's sociocognitive abilities seem to affect their interpersonal problem-solving skills, which in turn influence how cooperative and prosocial children are in their social interactions.

To summarize, sociocognitive capabilities influence how people understand and respond to other people. Consequently, because these skills change dramatically with age, they must be considered in models of prosocial development.

### Socialization

Developmental psychologists frequently have studied socialization techniques that are associated with prosocial responding. A variety of techniques have been used to investigate how adult socializers and peers shape children's prosocial tendencies, including laboratory studies involving experimental manipulations, studies in which parents or children are interviewed about parental practices, and observational studies. In general, somewhat consistent patterns have emerged from the body of data collected with these diverse techniques. Some of these patterns are now briefly reviewed (see Moore & Eisenberg, 1984; Radke-Yarrow et al., 1983, for more detailed information).

In general, prosocial children have been exposed to socializers who are themselves prosocial and empathic, who hold high standards for children, and who verbally communicate that prosocial behaviors are valued and expected. In addition, parents of prosocial children tend to reason with their children in disciplinary encounters rather than use excessive physical punishment and threats. If parents or teachers have a warm relationship with a child, their use of the aforementioned techniques seems to be enhanced, although warmth combined with a very permissive approach does not promote prosocial behavior.

Why are the aforementioned techniques associated with prosocial behavior in children? There are too many possible reasons to enumerate here; thus, I will focus on those most relevant to our model.

Children tend to imitate adults around them (Bandura, 1986). Parents, teachers, and other socializers (including TV characters!) that are warm, empathic, and prosocial themselves provide a positive model for children to imitate. Similarly, adults who verbalize prosocial values teach children the importance of such values, particularly if they provide reasons for their assertion that prosocial behavior is desirable. Thus, children exposed to prosocial, warm adults learn that caring and consideration for others is valuable and desirable. In addition, because of the positive relationship between the adult and child, the child is likely to feel loved and secure, which would be expected to result in the child being interested in other people and not being overly self-preoccupied (Kestenbaum, Farber, & Sroufe, 1989; Staub, 1979). Under such circumstances, the child is also likely to have relatively high self-esteem, which also may be associated with altruistic tendencies (Staub, 1979). Thus, exposure to adults who model, verbalize, and promote prosocial values and behaviors increases the probability that a child will attend to and be concerned about others, hold prosocial values, and develop other personality characteristics such as emotional stability that seem to be associated with altruism.

Socialization techniques also appear to influence children's ability or willingness to engage in perspective taking (which increases the probability of their behaving in a prosocial manner; see previous discussion). For example, children's level of perspective-taking skills seems to be enhanced by maternal warmth and support, low maternal use of physical punishment, a tendency for parents to avoid dominating or controlling the child, and mothers' emphasis on rationales that refer to people in a personal way rather than to roles or positional attributes (Light, 1979).

In addition, some specific child-rearing practices may alter the children's perceptions regarding themselves, which may in turn affect their prosocial predispositions. As noted previously, when children are subtly induced by socializers to engage in prosocial behaviors, they tend to be more prosocial in subsequent helping contexts (Eisenberg, Cialdini, McCreath, & Shell, 1987; Staub, 1979). Similarly, prosocial behavior is enhanced when adults provide children with altruistic explanations for why the children assisted others (i.e., tell the children that they assisted because they are helpful people and like to help others). When children are provided with such explanations, they are more likely to help or share on subsequent occasions than if socializers provide external attributions (e.g., say the child assisted only to please the adult) or no attributions at all (Grusec & Redler, 1980; Grusec, Kuczynski, Rushton, & Simutis, 1978). Apparently, when children engage in prosocial behaviors that appear to be voluntary and when children have reason to believe that their prosocial acts were altruistically motivated, they often come to view themselves as the type of person who helps others (Lepper, 1983). Thus, socializers' practices may alter children's characteristic self-perceptions, and these self-perceptions would be expected to influence children's motivation to assist in some circumstances (see Figures 15-1 to 15-4).

Developmental factors sometimes may affect whether a given socialization practice relevant to prosocial responding has an impact on the child. For example, parental use of reasoning that facilitates perspective taking may be more effective for younger children in the process of developing perspective taking capabilities than for adolescents (however, this hypothesis has not been tested). In addition, socializers' use of techniques that seem to promote an altruistic self-image may not be effective for children younger than seven or eight years of age (Eisenberg, Cialdini, McCreath, & Shell, 1987). This is because young children do not have a firm understanding that people have stable personality characteristics that endure across contexts and time; thus, young children are relatively unlikely to conceptualize themselves in terms of stable psychological dispositions (e.g., Rholes & Ruble, 1984). Moreover, children do not seem to base self-attributions (e.g., inferences about their own behavior) upon prior behavior until about age 7 (e.g., Ruble, Parsons, & Ross, 1976).

In summary, it appears that children's prosocial dispositions are shaped to some degree by their socialization experiences. Socializers undoubtedly can influence children's values and self-perceptions, as well as their behavioral preferences. However, the effect of socializers' practices may vary with the age of the children. Unfortunately, at this time, we know relatively little about the ways in which children's developmental status moderates the impact of socialization experiences.

## Empathy and Related Responses: Sources of Affective Motivation

Introspection will convince most people that more than cognition is involved in much prosocial behavior. Often we engage in prosocial behaviors because of what we *feel*, or what we think we will feel if we are kind or considerate. For example, feelings of concern or sadness for needy or distressed people frequently precede helping, sharing, or comforting. Thus, despite the assertions of philosophers such as Kant (1797/1964) and some psychologists (Kohlberg, 1984) who attribute moral actions primarily to cognitive factors, I believe that emotional reactions are an important component of any model of moral behavior. Indeed, people can cognitively comprehend another's need and choose to ignore it; worse, they can use their understanding of another person to exploit or manipulate that person.

Psychologists and philosophers interested in the role of emotion in morality frequently have discussed the role of empathy and sympathy in altruism (e.g., Batson, 1987; Blum, 1980; Eisenberg, 1986; Hoffman, 1984). As is discussed shortly, these emotional reactions seem to influence whether or not people help others in distress or need. Moreover, there appear to be developmental changes in empathy and sympathy. Thus, vicarious emotional responses such as empathy and sympathy play a major role in numerous models of prosocial development (e.g., Hoffman, 1984; Staub, 1979).

What are empathy and sympathy? Empathy and sympathy have been defined in many ways (see Eisenberg & Strayer, 1987; Wispe, 1986). Many developmental and social psychologists, however, define empathy in primarily affective or emotional terms. Thus, in this chapter, *empathy* is defined as an affective state that stems from another's emotional state or condition—one that is highly congruent with the other's state or condition. If a girl who observes a distressed peer feels sad or distressed herself, she is empathizing. Although empathizing is an emotional reaction, it frequently is based on cognitive skills such as the ability to label another's emotional state or role taking (Feshbach, 1978; Hoffman, 1984).

*Sympathy* is an emotional response that frequently results from empathizing. It is defined as an emotional response that stems from another's emotional state or condition, one that is not identical with the other's emotion but consists of feelings of sorrow or concern for another. Therefore, sympathy is not the matching of the other person's emotional state or condition; it is a distinct emotional reaction to another's condition.

### Age-Related Changes in Empathy and
### Related Emotional Responses

Martin Hoffman (1982, 1984) has proposed an intriguing theory in which he discusses how age-related changes in sociocognitive understanding may affect the development of empathy and prosocial responding. According to Hoffman, empathic distress, defined as "experiencing another's painful emotional state," develops early in infancy as a consequence of either built-in (that is, biologically determined) human tendencies toward empathy or early classical conditioning. Hoffman believes that infants are capable of experiencing empathic distress before they can differentiate themselves from others. Consequently, infants often are unclear about who is feeling the distress they witness and may, at times, behave as though what happens to others is happening to them.

Once babies cognitively differentiate themselves from others, their empathic distress "may be transformed at least in part into a reciprocal concern for the victim." That is, they may continue to feel uncomfortable and highly distressed themselves—but they also experience "a feeling of compassion for the victim, along with a conscious desire to help because they feel sorry for the victim and not just to relieve their own empathic distress" (Hoffman, 1984, p. 287). However, for some time, although aware of others as separate individuals, the toddler sees the world primarily from his or her own perspective. Consequently, the child attributes his or her own feelings to others, and therefore may use inappropriate means when attempting to relieve another's distress. For example, Hoffman has cited the examples of (a) a 13-month-old who brought his own mother to comfort a crying friend, even though the friend's mother was equally available, and (b) another toddler who offered his own favorite doll to cheer up an adult who looked sad.

According to Hoffman, at about the age of two or three, children begin to consider others as distinct physical entities with their own feelings, thoughts, and emotions. Due to their newfound rudimentary perspective-taking capabilities, they can now figure out ways to respond that are likely to alleviate the other's distress rather than their own.

Until they are between six and nine years of age, children's empathic and sympathetic responses are restricted to another's immediate, transitory, and situation-specific distress. With greater cognitive maturity and awareness of their own and other's continuing existence, children begin reacting to general conditions (including deprivation, oppression, illness, and incompetence), as well as to immediate distress. Thus, the adolescent is able to comprehend the plight not only of an individual but also of an entire group or class of people—such as the economically impoverished, politically oppressed, or mentally retarded (Hoffman, 1982).

Hoffman's theorizing provides a developmental framework for understanding how sociocognitive skills influence emotional responding in helping contexts, and how the development of empathy and sympathy influences both the quantity and quality of children's prosocial behaviors. Although the emphasis is on sociocognitive skills, Hoffman's theory also is compatible with the perspective that learning in a social context influences *the* development of empathy, sympathy, and altruism. For example, Hoffman has emphasized the importance of perspective-taking skills in empathy and especially sympathy (called sympathetic distress by Hoffman) and has pointed out that socializers' behaviors and practices affect the child's ability or willingness to take others' perspectives (Hoffman, 1970). In addition, learning is likely to affect whether the child who is able to empathize feels sympathy for another and attempts to help people who are distressed or needy. I return to the topic of the socialization of sympathy shortly.

### Empathy and Sympathy: Research Findings

As noted previously, a number of researchers and theorists have asserted that empathy and sympathetic concern are critical motivational factors in the performance of prosocial behavior, including altruistic behavior. Although, in the past, the empirical support for this assertion was equivocal (Underwood & Moore, 1982), research support for the association between sympathy or empathy and prosocial behavior, including altruism, is now substantial (Batson, 1987; Eisenberg & Miller, 1987).

The clearest findings with regard to the role of empathy in prosocial behavior have come from studies with adults. Particularly relevant are the studies conducted by Batson (1987).

Batson has made an important conceptual differentiation in his work—between empathy (i.e., sympathy in my terminology) and personal distress. *Personal distress* is an affective reaction to another's emotional state or condition that is experienced as a personally aversive emotion such as anxiety, discomfort, alarm, or worry. According to Batson, sympathy results in altruistic, other-oriented motives (e.g., the desire to reduce another's distress) whereas personal distress is associated with the egoistic motivation to reduce one's own distress.

Thus, people who experience personal distress will sometimes assist others, but primarily when helping is an easy way to relieve their own distress. For example, individuals experiencing personal distress are likely to help if helping is an easy way to terminate exposure to the aversive cues emanating from the needy other. However, if it is possible to easily escape from the aversive stimulus (e.g., the needy other), they will tend to do so rather than assist.

There is considerable support for Batson's hypotheses. In a number of studies, he and other researchers have found that people induced to experience sympathy for a needy other are more likely than persons experiencing personal distress to assist when it is easy to escape from dealing with the needy other (i.e., in situations in which they would not have to interact with the needy other). However, even people experiencing personal distress often help if they would have to continue dealing with the needy other and cues indicative of the other's need (see Batson, 1987, 1990, for reviews). Moreover, in a number of other types of studies—involving a variety of laboratory manipulations of empathy, self report of empathy/sympathy in simulated distress contexts, and/or questionnaire indices of sympathy/empathy—empathy and sympathy have been positively related to adults' sharing and helping or their willingness to assist others (see Eisenberg & Miller, 1987).

The research involving children has yielded somewhat less consistent findings than that involving adults, but nevertheless indicates that sympathy is positively related to prosocial behavior. Specifically, some measures of empathy are associated with children's prosocial behavior, whereas others are not (Eisenberg & Miller, 1987). Often empathy in children has been assessed with what have been called picture-story indices. With measures of this sort, children are exposed to stories and/or pictures containing information about another's affective state or situation (e.g., a child who lost his dog). Then they are asked to report, either verbally or by means of nonverbal responses (that is, pointing to pictures of facial expressions), what they themselves are feeling. Children are scored as empathizing if they report experiencing the emotion the story protagonist would be expected to feel. Picture-story indices of empathy have not been positively related to prosocial behavior (see Eisenberg & Miller, 1987). However, it is likely that these indices are not valid measures of emotional empathy. The stories used to evoke emotion may be too short to elicit an emotional response. In addition, children may try to give what they think is the expected or desired answer even if they themselves feel nothing when they hear the stories. Also, children may not be able to shift their emotions as quickly as they are shifted from story scenario to scenario, and they tend to score higher when tested by same-sex experimenters (Eisenberg & Lennon, 1983).

The pattern of relations between measures of empathy and prosocial behavior is quite different when their observed (i.e., facial and gestural reactions) emotional responses and physiological reactions are the measures of empathy. For example, in one study, one-year-olds who exhibited sadness on their faces in response to viewing a sad adult were more prosocial at home (according to parental report; Weston & Main, 1980). Moreover, young children who exhibit emotional responsiveness to another's distress frequently try to comfort the distressed person (Radke-Yarrow et al., 1983). Similarly, preschoolers and elementary-school children (especially boys) who exhibit concern or empathic sadness when viewing distressed or needy children are more likely than other children to help the distressed or needy person. In addition, children who exhibited a heart rate pattern associated with an other-orientation are particularly likely to assist. In contrast, we have obtained some evidence that children's personal distress reactions were negatively related to children's prosocial behaviors (Eisenberg, Fabes, et al., 1989, in 1990).

Findings such as these provide strong support for the assumption that people's emotional reactions in helping contexts influence whether or not they assist those in need. If people feel empathy and sympathy for others, they will be motivated to improve the other person's situation. However, if they experience personal distress when confronted with someone in need or distress, observers are likely to try to avoid helping the other person, unless helping is the easiest way to make themselves feel better (e.g., when it is difficult to leave the situation). The bottom part of the model in Figure 15-1 ("Motivational Sources: Predominantly Emotional") reflects the theory and findings just reviewed.

Of course, not all prosocial behavior is motivated by empathic or sympathetic reactions. As discussed previously, in many situations people assist others for non-altruistic motives, for example, to attain rewards or social approval, or because of their desire to adhere to internalized moral values (Bar-Tal, 1982; Eisenberg, 1986). Moreover, in some circumstances in which people could assist another, there is no reason to feel empathy or sympathy because the potential recipient of aid does not seem distressed or feel distressed, or there are no cues regarding the other person's emotional state. In such situations, people frequently may assist for egoistic reasons (Schoenrade, Batson, Brandt, & Loud, 1986); for example, people often assist friends even when they are not distressed because of their desire to maintain the friendship. Nonetheless, it appears that empathy and sympathy frequently motivate altruistic behavior.

### The Socialization of Empathy

In a previous section of this chapter, socialization practices that have been linked with perspective taking and prosocial behavior were reviewed. In our model, socialization experiences also play an important role in how and if individuals respond emotionally to others in evocative situations, including situations in which others are in distress or are in need. Consequently, socialization practices can have an indirect influence on children's prosocial behavior, especially altruistic behavior, by means of their effect on children's sympathetic and empathic tendencies.

Socialization influences on vicarious emotional reactions such as empathy, sympathy, and personal distress may be of several sorts. First, socialization may affect whether or not children tend to focus on others' needs or their own in situations involving vicarious emotion. For example, children who come from warm, supportive homes tend to be relatively empathic (Barnett, 1987), and children exposed to sympathetic rather than personally distressed models (mothers) are sympathetic themselves (Fabes, Eisenberg, & Miller, 1990). In addition, children with secure attachments to their parents seem to be prone to orient toward others and engage in prosocial behaviors when coping with others' emotions (Kestenbaum et al., 1989). Thus, children who are likely to feel loved and emotionally secure seem to have the resources to attend to and deal with others' problems.

Second, how socializers react to the expression of emotion in general, and if they themselves readily exhibit emotions, seem to affect the likelihood of offspring expressing emotion (Eisenberg, Fabes, Schaller, et al., 1991; Halberstadt, 1986) and whether the child feels sympathy or distress when confronted with others' emotional displays. Buck (1984) has suggested that if there are sanctions for emotional expressiveness in the home, children learn to hide their emotions and feel anxious when in emotionally evocative situations (due to prior association between punishment and emotional expressivity). Thus, parents who emphasize a relatively high degree of emotional control may raise children who are uncomfortable with their own empathic responses and prone to experience personal distress when confronted with others' distress. In addition, parents who model sympathetic responses may subtly teach their children that the expression of emotion is acceptable and that sympathetic concern is a valued behavior. Finally, socializers' willingness to discuss emotions with their children appears to be linked with children's subsequent references to emotions (Dunn, Bretherton, & Munn, 1987). Thus, it is plausible to expect parental willingness to discuss the causes of their own, their child's, and others' emotional reactions to be associated with children's awareness of, and responsivity to, others' emotional displays.

In the model in Figure 15-1, it is clear that socialization experiences are viewed as affecting children's sociocognitive capabilities and, as a consequence, children's vicarious emotional responses. Not as clear, but also implied in the figure, is a more direct effect of socialization practices on vicarious emotional responding (one not mediated by the child's sociocognitive abilities). Thus, socialization experiences are viewed as influencing sympathy, personal distress, and prosocial behavior in multiple ways.

### Guilt

Another emotional reaction that frequently may influence whether people assist others is guilt. As for empathy and sympathy, children's tendencies to experience guilt seem to change somewhat with age.

Indeed, there often may be a strong link between empathy and guilt. Hoffman (1982) has hypothesized that guilt over hurting others is based in part on the experience of empathizing with another's pain. In his theory, guilt is defined as the painful feeling of dissatisfaction with the self because of the harmful consequences of one's own actions. In Hoffman's view, children first experience guilt when they are both aware of being the cause of another's distress and experience empathy with the other person's distress.

In the first year of life, children may not have a clear conception of themselves as entities that are separate from others. Thus, Hoffman has argued that very young children may feel that they are at fault simply because their actions happen to occur at the same time as something negative happens to someone else. However, by about two years of age, children become more aware of the effects of their actions and begin to experience true interpersonal guilt when they cause others physical harm. Next, with further cognitive development and increased understanding of others' internal states, children become capable of feeling guilt for causing others emotional harm and for failing to act on another's behalf. Finally, in late childhood or early adolescence, children become aware that others have personal identities that extend beyond the immediate situation and are continuing in time. Then children may experience guilt over harmful actions or inaction that has effects beyond the immediate context (e.g., guilt over the plight of impoverished people; see Hoffman, 1982; Zahn-Waxler & Kochanska, 1990, for more discussion of theory concerning the development of guilt).

Although the specifics of Hoffman's theory have not been adequately tested, the ability to experience guilt, and the type and scope of an individual's guilt, undoubtedly change with the child's cognitive and sociocognitive development. In addition, there is mounting evidence that guilt often is associated with attempts to assist those who have been harmed, and that children prone to experience normal amounts of guilt tend to act prosocially (Chapman, Zahn-Waxler, Cooperman, & Iannotti, 1987; Zahn-Waxler & Kochanska, 1990). Thus, it is reasonable to assume that developmental changes in the experience of guilt during childhood affect, to some degree, whether or not children assist others who they have harmed or have failed to assist previously.

Individual differences in the tendency to experience guilt would fall into the box "Antecedent State and Trait Characteristics" in Figure 15-1; the actual experience of guilt in a given context is represented by the box entitled "Motivational Sources: Predominantly Emotional." As for sympathy and empathy, both levels of sociocognitive development and socialization are viewed as influencing dispositional and situationally produced guilt (see Zahn-Waxler & Kochanska, 1990, for a review of the relevant literature). Thus, empathy, sympathy, and guilt may separately, or in combination, motivate a potential benefactor to assist another person who is distressed or needy,

## Personal Factors as Sources of Motivation

As can be seen in Figure 15-3, personal factors that may motivate prosocial action in a helping context include the potential helper's self-identity with regard to helpfulness, self-esteem, and personal values, goals, and preferences. All of these may change somewhat with development during childhood. For example, as was mentioned previously, young children have difficulty understanding that aspects of one's personality, especially psychological components such as kindness, are stable over time and situations (Rholes & Ruble, 1984). Thus, they may not have a self-identity as a helpful or unhelpful person. It is not until the early elementary-school years that children seem to be able to use information relevant to their self-identity (e.g., information provided by means of their own prior behaviors or socializers' attributions; see prior section on socialization) to formulate a self-identity in regard to altruism (Eisenberg, Cialdini, McCreath, & Shell, 1987; Grusec & Redler, 1980). Thus, the role that an individual's altruism-related self-identity plays in prosocial action seems to change with age.

In addition, until children come to think of themselves in terms of lasting, psychological attributes, it is unlikely that children's evaluations of their own altruism and consideration for others will affect their self-esteem. Therefore, maintenance of one's own self-esteem is unlikely to motivate prosocial behavior until at least middle childhood. Consistent with this prediction, in studies of moral reasoning, very few children mention the implications of acting selfishly or prosocially for their own self-esteem until early adolescence or later (Eisenberg, 1986).

As was discussed earlier, children's personal values, goals, and preferences also seem to change somewhat with age. For example, children become somewhat less hedonistic in their orientations as they progress from the preschool years into school (Eisenberg, 1986). These age-related changes in values and goals would be expected to be reflected in the motives that are elicited in specific helping contexts. Stated differently, we have argued that the ordering of personal values, motives, and goals in the individual's hierarchy of personal goals in the specific helping situation likely changes with age.

In summary, in our model, developmental changes during childhood in personal characteristics, as well as changes in emotional reactions such as empathy, sympathy, and guilt, are viewed as influencing the motive to assist in specific helping contexts. In addition, the ways in which children cognitively evaluate aspects of the helping context may change with age and, therefore, influence their motivation to help. We now turn to cognitive sources of motivation.

## *Motivational Sources:*
## *Evaluative (Predominantly Cognitive)*

Due to the marked age-related changes in children's cognitive and sociocognitive abilities, one would expect changes in the ways children "size up" various helping contexts. For example, children's assessments of the costs and benefits of assisting in a given situation would be expected to reflect age-related changes in their values and goals. Thus, adolescents and adults would be expected to weigh the costs of violating internalized values and norms if they do not help more heavily than would children, whereas children might be expected to weigh material costs and adults' approval more heavily. In addition, individuals' abilities to assess whether or not the other person really wants to be helped probably change in childhood with the development of more sophisticated sociocognitive (e.g., perspective taking) skills (Barnett, Darcie, Holland, & Kobasigawa, 1982). Sometimes needy or distressed people do not want help because they feel belittled, incompetent, or inferior to the helper if they accept aid (Fisher, Nadler, & Whitcher-Alagna, 1982); older persons probably are better able to determine when this is the case.

These are just a few examples of how changes in children's understanding of the world might influence their motivation to assist someone else in a potential context. Undoubtedly, there are many other examples. Interactions among people involve complex cognitive evaluations of other people, their motives, the costs and benefits of various courses in actions, situational constraints, and many other variables. The ways in which changes in children's cognitive and sociocognitive abilities influence behavior, including prosocial behavior, have not been adequately delineated. Nonetheless, developmental changes in cognitive evaluative skills are an important element in models of prosocial development.

### Consequences for Prosocial Action

As alluded to previously, the consequences of enacting prosocial behaviors may differ somewhat with age. For example, for young children who do not readily use information about their own performances to predict their own future behavior (Ruble et al., 1976), behaving prosocially may have little impact on how the children view themselves. In contrast, enacting prosocial behaviors may reinforce or bolster older children's images of themselves as altruistic persons and result in subsequent prosocial behavior. Thus, it is not surprising that engaging in voluntary prosocial behaviors has been found to enhance the likelihood of further prosocial responding for older but not younger elementary school children (Eisenberg, Cialdini, McCreath, & Shell, 1987). In addition, due to changes in evaluative skills and morally relevant values, it is likely that older children evaluate their own helping behaviors differently than do younger children (e.g., are better at evaluating whether it was altruistically motivated; Eisenberg, 1986), which may influence children's self-perceptions and future behavior.

## Conclusion

In this chapter, I have tried to demonstrate some of the many ways in which developmental factors might influence prosocial responding. The diversity of ways in which development is relevant to prosocial behavior can only be understood, however, if one recognizes the multitude of factors that can affect any given prosocial behavior. If individual differences in personal characteristics, sociocognitive/cognitive abilities, and emotional predispositions all influence motivation and decision-making processes in regard to prosocial action, then developmental factors that influence all of these processes and characteristics must be considered. Similarly, all these factors and processes likely interact in a given context. Thus, we need to be sensitive to the role of developmental factors in determining the relative influence of various personal, sociocognitive and cognitive, emotional, and situational factors in particular contexts. In addition, it is important to attend to aspects of the social environment that help to shape characteristics of the individual and his or her emotional and cognitive functioning. These include socializers and cultural values (although, of course, characteristics of the child, including biologically based characteristics, often influence how others treat a child).

If we are interested in the development of altruistic tendencies, it also is important to attend to how children's understanding of altruistic and egoistic behavior changes with age, and how enduring altruistic values and sympathetic tendencies develop. This is difficult to do because it often is impossible to differentiate between altruistically and egoistically motivated behaviors. Nonetheless, by considering the situational factors used by children in their morally relevant decisions and by examining the decision-making process, we can further our understanding of the development of altruistic tendencies.

## Author's Note

The writing of this chapter and some of the research discussed in this chapter was supported by grants to Nancy Eisenberg from the National Science Foundation (DBN-9208375 and BNS-8807784), the National Institute of Child Health and Development (K04 HD00717), and the National Institute of Mental Health (K02 MH00903).

## References

Ajzen, I., & Fishbein, M. (1977). Attitude-behavior relations: A theoretical analysis and review of empirical research. *Psychological Bulletin, 84,* 888-918.

Bandura, A. (1986). *Social foundations of thought and action: A social cognitive theory.* Englewood Cliffs, NJ: Prentice-Hall, Inc.

Barnett, K., Darcie, G., Holland, C. J., & Kobasigawa, A. (1982). Children's cognitions about effective helping. *Developmental Psychology, 18,* 267-277.

Barnett, M. A. (1987). Empathy and related responses in children. In N. Eisenberg & J. Strayer (Eds.), *Empathy and its development* (pp. 46-162). Cambridge: Cambridge University Press.

Barrett, D. E., & Yarrow, M. R. (1977). Prosocial behavior, social inferential ability, and assertiveness in young children. *Child Development, 48,* 475-481.

Bar-Tal, D. (1982). Sequential development of helping behavior: A cognitive learning approach. *Developmental Review, 2,* 101-124.

Bar-Tal, D. (1984). American study of helping behavior: What? Why? and Where? In Staub, E., Bar-Tal, D., Karylowski, J., & Reykowski, J. (Eds.), *Developmental and maintenance of prosocial behavior: International perspectives on positive morality* (pp. 5-27). New York: Plenum.

Batson, C. D. (1987). Prosocial motivation: Is it ever truly altruistic? In L. Berkowitz (Ed.), *Advances in experimental social psychology* (Vol. 20, pp. 65-122). New York: Academic Press.

Batson, C. D. (1990). How social an animal? The human capacity for caring. *American Psychologist, 45,* 336-346.

Beaman, A. L., Cole, C., Preston, M., Klentz, B., & Steblay, N. M. (1983). Fifteen years of foot-in-the-door research. *Personality and Social Psychology Bulletin, 9,* 181-196

Blum, L. A. (1980). *Friendship, altruism and morality.* London, England: Routledge and Kegan Paul.

Buck, R. (1984). *The communication of emotion.* New York: Guilford Press.

Chapman, M., Zahn-Waxler, C., Cooperman, G., & Iannotti, R. (1987). Empathy and responsibility in the motivation of children's helping. *Developmental Psychology, 23,* 140-145.

Dovidio, J. F. (1984). Helping behavior and altruism: An empirical and conceptual overview. In L. Berkowitz (Ed.), *Advances in experimental social psychology* (Vol. 17, pp. 361-427). New York: Academic Press.

Dunn, J., Bretherton, I., & Munn, P. (1987). Conversations about feeling states between mothers and their young children. *Developmental Psychology, 23,* 132-139.

Eisenberg, N. (1986). *Altruistic emotion, cognition and behavior.* Hillsdale, NJ: Erlbaum and Associates.

Eisenberg, N., Cialdini, R. B., McCreath, H., & Shell, R. (1987). Consistency-based compliance: When and why do children become vulnerable? *Journal of Personality and Social Psychology, 52,* 1174-1181.

Eisenberg, N., Fabes, R. A., Miller, P. A., Fultz, J., Mathy, R. M., Shell, R., & Reno, R. R. (1989). The relations of sympathy and personal distress to prosocial behavior: A multimethod study. *Journal of Personality and Social Psychology, 57,* 55-66.

Eisenberg, N., Fabes, R. A., Schaller, M, Miller, P. A., Carlo, G., Poulin, R., Shea, C., & Shell, R. (1991). Personality and socialization correlates of vicarious emotional responding. *Journal of Personality and Social Psychology, 61,* 459-471.

Eisenberg, N., Fabes, R. A., Miller, P. A., Shell, C., Shea, R., May-Plumlee, T. (1990). The relation of preschoolers' vicarious emotional responding to situational and dispositional prosocial behavior. *Merrill Palmer Quarterly, 36,* 507-529.

Eisenberg, N., & Lennon, R. (1983). Sex differences in empathy and related capacities. *Psychological Bulletin, 94,* 100-131.

Eisenberg, N., & Miller, P. A. (1987). The relation of empathy to prosocial and related behavior. *Psychological Bulletin, 101,* 91-119.

Eisenberg, N., Miller, P. A. Shell, R., McNalley, S., & Shea, C. (1991). Prosocial development in adolescence: A longitudinal study. *Developmental Psychology, 27,* 849-857.

Eisenberg, N., Shell, R., Pasternack, J., Lennon, R., Beller, R., & Mathy, R. M. (1987). Prosocial development in middle childhood: A longitudinal study. *Developmental Psychology, 23,* 712-718.

Eisenberg, N., & Strayer, J. (1987). Critical issues in the study of empathy. In N. Eisenberg & J. Strayer (Eds.), *Empathy and its development* (pp. 3-13). Cambridge, England: Cambridge University Press.

Fabes, R.A., Eisenberg, N., & Miller, P. A. (1990). Maternal correlates of children's vicarious emotional responsiveness. *Developmental Psychology, 26,* 639-648.

Feshbach, N. D. (1978). Studies of empathic behavior in children. In B. A. Maher (Ed.), *Progress in experimental personality research* (Vol. 8, pp. 147). New York: Academic Press.

Festinger, L. (1957). *A theory of cognitive dissonance.* Stanford, CA: Stanford University Press.

Fisher, J. D., Nadler, A., & Whitcher-Alagna, S. (1982). Recipient reactions to aid. *Psychological Bulletin, 91,* 27-54.

Grusec , J . E ., Kuczynski , L., Rushton, J . P ., & Simutis, Z. M. (1978). Modeling, direction instruction, and attributions: Effects on altruism. *Developmental Psychology, 14,* 51- 57 .

Grusec, J. E., & Redler, E. (1980). Attribution,

reinforcement, and altruism: A developmental analysis. *Developmental Psychology, 16,* 525-534.

Halberstadt, A. G. (1986). Family socialization of emotional expression and nonverbal communication styles and skills. *Journal of Personality and Social Psychology, 51,* 827-836.

Hoffman, M. L. (1970). Moral development. In P. H. Mussen (Ed.), *Carmichael's manual of child development, 2* (pp. 261-359). New York: Wiley.

Hoffman, M. L. (1982). Development of prosocial motivation: Empathy and guilt. In N. Eisenberg (Ed.), *The development of prosocial behavior* (pp. 218-231). New York: Academic Press.

Hoffman, M. L. (1984). Interaction of affect and cognition in empathy. In C. E. Izard, J. Kagan, & R. B. Zajonc (Eds.), *Emotions, cognitions, and behavior* (pp. 103-131). Cambridge, MA: Cambridge University Press.

Kant, I. (1964). *The doctrine of virtue.* New York: Harper & Row. (Originally published, 1797.)

Kestenbaum, R., Farber, E. A., & Sroufe, L. A. (1989). In N. Eisenberg (Ed.), *New Directions for Child Development: Vol. 44. Empathy and related emotional responses* (pp. 51-64). San Francisco: Jossey-Bass.

Kohlberg, L. (1984). *Essays on moral development. Vol. II. The psychology of moral development.* San Francisco, CA: Harper and Row.

Latane, B., & Darley, J. (1970). *The unresponsive bystander: Why doesn't he help?* New York: Appleton.

Lepper, M. R. (1983). Social-control processes and the internalization of social values: An attributional perspective. In E. T. Higgins, D. N. Ruble, & W. W. Hartup (Eds.), *Social cognition and social development: A sociocultural perspective* (pp. 294-330). Cambridge, UK: Cambridge University Press.

Light, P. (1979). *The development of social sensitivity: A study of social aspects of role-taking in children.* Cambridge, UK: Cambridge University Press.

Moore, B. S., & Eisenberg, N. (1984). The development of altruism. In G. Whitehurst (Ed.), *Annals of Child Development* (pp. 107-174). Greenwich, CT: JAI Press.

Pearl, R. (1985). Children's understanding of others' need for help: Effects of problem explicitness and type. *Child Development, 56,* 735-745.

Peterson, L. (1983). Influence of age, task competence, and responsibility focus on children's altruism. *Developmental Psychology, 19,* 141-148.

Piliavin, J. A., Dovidio, J. F., Gaertner, S. L., & Clark, R. D. III (1981). *Emergency intervention.* New York: Academic Press.

Pomazal, R. J., & Jaccard, J. J. (1976). An information approach to altruistic behavior. *Journal of Personality and Social Psychology, 33,* 317-326.

Radke-Yarrow, M., Zahn-Waxler, C., & Chapman, M. (1983). Prosocial dispositions and behavior. In P. Mussen (Ed.), *Manual of child psychology: Vol. 4. Socialization, personality, and social development* (E. M. Hetherington, Ed.) (pp. 469-545). New York: John Wiley & Sons.

Rholes, W. S., & Ruble, D. N. (1984). Children's understanding of dispositional characteristics of others. *Child Development, 55,* 550-560.

Ruble, D. N., Parsons, J. E., & Ross, J. (1976). Self-evaluation responses of children in an achievement setting. *Child Development, 47,* 990-997.

Schoenrade, R. A., Batson, C. D., Brandt, J. R., & Loud, R. E., Jr. (1986). Attachment, accountability, and motivation to benefit another not in distress. *Journal of Personality and Social Psychology, 51,* 557-563.

Schwartz, S. H., & Howard, J. A. (1984). Internalized values as motivators of altruism. In E. Staub, D. Bar-Tal, J. Karylowski, & J. Reykowski (Eds.), *International perspectives on positive development* (pp. 229-255). New York: Plenum Press.

Selman, R. L. (1980). *The growth of interpersonal understanding: Developmental and clinical analysis.* New York: Academic Press.

Shantz, C. V. (1975). The development of social cognition. In E. M. Hetherington (Ed.), *Review of child development research* (Vol. 5 ;

pp. 257-323). Chicago, IL: University of Chicago Press.

Shantz, C. V. (1983). Social cognition. In P. H. Mussen (Ed.), *Handbook of child psychology: Cognitive development* (Vol. 3, pp. 495-555). New York: Wiley & Sons.

Shure, M. B. (1982). Interpersonal problem solving: A cog in the wheel of social cognition. In F. C. Serafica (Ed.), *Social-cognitive development in context* (pp. 133-166). New York: The Guilford Press.

Staub, E. (1978). *Positive social behavior and morality: Social and personal influences.* New York: Academic Press.

Staub, E. (1979). *Positive social behavior and morality: Vol 2: Socialization and development.* New York: Academic Press.

Underwood, B., & Moore, B. (1982). Perspective-taking and altruism. *Psychological Bulletin, 91,* 143-173.

Weston, D. R., & Main, M. (1980, April). *Infant responses to the crying of an adult actor in the laboratory: Stability and correlates of "concerned attention."* Paper presented at the Second International Conference on Infant Studies, New Haven, CT.

Wispe, L. (1986). The distinction between sympathy and empathy: To call forth a concept, a word is needed. *Journal of Personality and Social Psychology, 50,* 314-321.

Zahn-Waxler, C., Kochanska, G. (1990). The origins of guilt. In R. Thompson (Ed.), *The 36th annual Nebraska symposium on motivation: Socioemotional development* (pp. 183-258). Lincoln, NE: University of Nebraska Press.

# Chapter 16

# The Roots of Prosocial and Antisocial Behavior in Persons and Groups: Environmental Influence, Personality, Culture, and Socialization

*ERVIN STAUB*
*University of Massachusetts at Amherst*

## Abstract

This chapter describes personal (social) goal theory, a theory of motivation and action, intended to account for the role of environmental, personality, culture, and socialization in influencing both prosocial and antisocial behavior. The chapter discusses the roots of prosocial and antisocial behavior in persons and groups. Research on both prosocial and antisocial behavior has focused on social-situational influences. But social-environmental conditions exert their influence by affecting people, by creating the psychological states and motivations that lead people to help or harm others. Their effects differ greatly depending on the characteristics of the people involved. This chapter describes a theory of action, which specifies how situations and personal characteristics join in giving rise to the psychological processes and motives that are the immediate influences on behavior. In addition to the characteristics of individuals, this chapter

*(continued)*

**Abstract** *(continued)*

also focuses on how the nature of societies, the characteristics of their culture and social institutions, affect prosocial and antisocial behavior. The personal (social) goal theory described in this chapter is a general framework for understanding social behavior, moral conduct, and specifically altruism and aggression. This chapter describes some of the influences that lead people to help or harm others, or to remain passive bystanders to others' suffering or to conditions that threaten or harm the social good. Understanding the origins of helping and harmdoing can help develop conceptions and practices for the creation of nonaggressive and caring persons and societies, and involved, responsible individuals.

In the history of research on both prosocial and antisocial behavior, a great deal of attention has focused on social-situational influences. How do environmental conditions and the influence of other people lead to helping or harmdoing? Attention has also focused on the psychological processes—thoughts, feelings, and motivations—that lead people to help or harm others, like feelings of empathy, or frustration and anger. But relatively little research and theorizing has been done about what personal characteristics of individuals make helping or harmdoing probable, and how they exert their influence.

But social-environmental conditions exert their influence by affecting people, by creating the psychological states and motivations that lead people to help or harm others. And we know that their effects differ greatly depending on the characteristics of the people involved, like their self-concepts, values, or competencies. While it has become a truism that personality and situations jointly affect behavior, we need to specify what characteristics of persons and what aspects of situations are important in influencing prosocial and antisocial behavior. We also need a theory of action, which specifies how situations and personal characteristics join in giving rise to the psychological processes and motives that are the immediate influences on behavior.

In addition to the characteristics of individuals, another neglected area of study has been how the nature of societies, the characteristics of their cultural and social institutions, affect prosocial and antisocial behavior. These characteristics shape individuals, form their personalities, and also represent an ongoing environmental influence on their behavior. In this chapter I will briefly review social-situational influences and then explore the influence of personality on people helping and harming others. I will also consider how cultural-societal characteristics affect behavior, especially individual and group violence. I will briefly describe personal (social) goal theory, a theory of motivation and action, to help us understand how various influences join in leading to prosocial and antisocial behavior. Then I will briefly discuss what socializing practices and what experiences of children (and adults) contribute to a disposition to help and not harm others.

## Social-Situational Influences on Helping and Harmdoing

Starting in the late 1960s, with the pioneering work of Latane and Darley (1970), a large body of research explored the conditions that influence helping behavior (for reviews see Staub, 1978; Piliavin et al., 1981; Rushton, 1980; Staub et al., 1984; Eisenberg, 1986; Krebs and Miller, 1985).

Darley and Latane (1970) addressed the puzzle of Kitty Genovese's murder, that 38 people had heard her cries for help when she was attacked in the middle of the night in Queens, but none of them attempted to help. Only one of these witnesses called the police, when it was too late, after he called his lawyer to reassure himself that this won't cause him problems.

Latane and Darley created lifelike experimental situations and found that as the number of people who witness an emergency increases, the likelihood that any one person will help declines. This is true both when the witnesses to the emergency are together in the same room, and when a witness has information about the number of people in the surrounding area who presumably can also hear the distress sounds that indicate a need for help. It is true with a wide range of emergencies: when a person appears to have an asthma attack, or falls off a ladder or gets hurt in some other way, or smoke begins to fill the room, or a thief steals liquor from a liquor store.

Latane and Darley proposed several explanations for their findings. First, with an increase in the number of witnesses, there is diffusion of responsibility. Each witness feels less responsibility to help. There is also a diffusion of blame, each witness feeling less blameworthy for not helping. Second, when witnesses are together, a condition of pluralistic ignorance exists. In public places, in the presence of others, people tend to hide their emotional response to events. As everyone appears poker-faced in the face of an emergency, each person decides that the others are unconcerned, and that there is no reason to act. That is, pluralistic ignorance leads to a definition of the situation as not an emergency. Third, people are afraid of appearing foolish in front of others, and by their inaction avoid negative evaluation of their actions, for example, judgments by people that their actions are inappropriate or incompetent.

Many replications have confirmed and extended Latane and Darley's original findings, and supported their explanation that the definition of the meaning of events and feelings of responsibility are central determinants of helping or not helping. There have been a couple "deviant" findings, which further clarify the phenomenon of bystander response to emergencies. First, I found (Staub, 1970) that pairs of young children, from kindergarten to second grade, help more in response to sounds of distress from another room than children who are alone. Upon hearing the distress sounds, the children in pairs began to talk to each other about them. Sharing rather than hiding their concern led them to help.

Second, Wilson (1976) and Schwartz and Clausen (1970) both reported that people with certain characteristics are not inhibited by conditions that normally inhibit helping. Wilson found that the presence of two passive bystanders (who were confederates), which normally decreases helping, did not do so with "esteem-oriented" persons. As measured by a sentence completion test, these people had a strong sense of personal adequacy, and strove for competence and efficacy in interpersonal relations.

Schwartz and Clausen found that helping by women who ascribe responsibility to themselves for the welfare of others did not decline with an increase in the number of bystanders. As I have suggested (Staub, 1978), certain environmental conditions (e.g. being alone), certain roles they occupy (special competence to help, e.g. a medical doctor or a leadership position, see Baumeister et al., 1988), and their own characteristics can all focus responsibility on people to help. Stable roles that have requirements and embody expectations are in between situational and personality influence. They represent stable, ongoing expectations, that can become part of the personality of individuals who long held these roles.

Many situational influences other than the number of bystanders affect helping behavior. Ambiguity of the need for help reduces helping. Great need for help, whether due to greater severity of distress or greater necessity for help in order to complete a task or fulfill a goal, increases helping. As the cost of helping increases, its likelihood decreases. As I already noted, conditions that focus responsibility on a person increase helping. For example, when I was thrown by a wave while body surfing in Hawaii, and was lying on the sand unable to move, people continued to pass me by until I directed my call for help to a specific person.

Defining the meaning of a situation as one in which someone is in need and defining helping as the appropriate response are crucial if helping is to occur. Inactive bystanders communicate that there is no need, or that helping is not necessary or appropriate, or both. When, by what they said, confederates of the experimenter acting as bystanders defined sounds of distress as serious and as showing a need for help, and helping as the appropriate response, helping behavior increased. When they defined the distress sounds as not serious and helping as unnecessary, helping decreased (Staub, 1974; see also Bickman, 1972). The influence of models on helping and sharing behavior, which is substantial, is probably partly definitional, and partly due to invoking or activating values and standards that prescribe helping.

Some people seem to defend themselves against engagement with a situation that might place demands on them. If they can avoid even interpreting the meaning of it, they can probably avoid the demands of helping as well as feelings of responsibility and guilt for not helping. Staub and Baer (1974) found that some individuals, who were walking down one side of the street when a person (a confederate) collapsed on the other side, looked away after a single glance and never looked back. Some of them turned at the next corner and moved away from the scene. Other people, after a single glance, ran across the street to the person who collapsed.

Real life examples of the influence of bystanders, or models, on others' helping behavior also abound. In LaChambon, a Huguenot village in France, the inhabitants, led by their Pastor Andre Trocme, took in over 2000 refugees who were escaping from Nazi persecution, many of them Jewish children. They hid the refugees and helped many of them escape to safety in Switzerland and elsewhere. The behavior of the villagers influenced members of the Vichy police. Telephone calls to the Presbyterie began to warn them of impending raids. This enabled them to hide the refugees in the nearby forest. The deeds of the village doctor who was executed and his words at his trial influenced a German major, who in turn persuaded a higher officer not to move against the village (Hallie, 1979).

Like helping, aggression is both instigated and modified by social-situational influences. While the stimulus for help is usually someone's need, the stimuli or instigators of aggression are: frustration (of one's goal-directed behavior and hence of the fulfillment of one's goals, or the feeling of frustration); attack on one's self (physical attack as well as verbal attack, like insult); or threat to oneself. The nature of instigation, its intensity, and conditions surrounding it, affect the response. For example, they determine whether the frustrated, attacked, or threatened person truly feels endangered. When conditions (or personality) lead people to believe that their frustrator or attacker intended to harm them (Pastore, 1952) and represents a continuing danger to them, an aggressive response is more likely. Information that makes the intentions of the harmdoer appear less harmful decreases aggression (Mallick & McCandless, 1966).

Certain general environmental conditions make aggression more likely, either because they themselves are instigators, or because they intensify the effects of frustration, attack, or threat. They include aversive conditions like unpleasant heat, noise, or crowding. These conditions are most likely to increase aggression if they occur following some instigation for aggression, like an experience of frustration or threat (Baron, 1977). Conditions that create arousal, for example sexual arousal, can also increase aggression. The example of others' behavior can indicate that aggressive behavior is acceptable, at least in the setting where the model is observed.

## *Psychological Processes, Motivations, and Personality Leading to Prosocial and Antisocial Behavior*

### *Prosocial Behavior*

In response to environmental conditions (and sometimes without any external events, as a result of internal activation), psychological processes and motives arise in people with certain personal characteristics that can lead them to help or harm others. An examination of the literature suggests four major motivations for prosocial behavior. Two of them are *altruistic*, which means that the intention underlying the behavior, or its "ultimate aim," is not self-gain but to benefit someone.

First, there is a desire to help based on *empathy*, the vicarious experience of the feelings of person(s) in need. There have been different definitions of empathy: my own inclination is to accept a broad definition, according to which any vicarious feeling that is *congruent* with the feelings of another person qualifies as empathy (Batson & Shaw, in press). Frequently, *parallel empathy,* a feeling identical to that of another person, for example, feeling sad when the other feels sad, is less likely to lead to helping than *reactive empathy,* a sympathetic feeling in response to the other's feelings like caring for the other or anger at the people or conditions that create the sadness (Staub & Feinberg, 1980).

There is a type of empathic emotion that is self-oriented rather than other-oriented in nature. Empathic distress, a feeling of distress upon witnessing another's need, can be differentiated from what might be called empathic caring. Empathic distress, as measured by the adjectives alarmed, grieved, troubled, distressed, upset, disturbed, worried, and perturbed, can lead people to help others. But when circumstances allow escape from the presence of the needy person, empathic distress can lead people to deal with their distress by escape rather than helping. In contrast empathic caring, as measured by the adjectives sympathetic, moved, compassionate, warm, softhearted and tender, is more likely to lead to helping even when escape is possible (Batson, 1990; Batson & Shaw, 1991).

Empathic emotion must arise as a result of certain characteristics of people who witness another's emotions. These characteristics "house" the inclination or disposition to respond with empathy. What might they be? Empathic emotion can be automatic—a conditioned response to others' feelings; that is, the result of a history of association between others' good and bad feelings and one's own. It may be the result of parents treating a child well when they themselves feel good, and badly when they themselves feel bad.

Another approach to empathy focuses on understanding people. Hoffman (1975) suggested that primitive empathy exists in infants (as indicated by their crying in response to others' crying). He described how the increasing capacity to perceive and understand other people's internal states and their circumstances in life leads to the development of more advanced forms of empathy. This capacity might be one component of a *tendency* to consider others' internal states and experiences. An implicit requirement for empathic caring, I believe, is a positive evaluation of human beings (Staub, 1986a). Experiences that lead to fear and dislike of people make it unlikely that automatic, conditioned reactions, or perspective taking and understanding people would lead to empathic caring. Instead, fear and dislike of people make the *enjoyment* of their suffering more likely.

In addition to a desire to help people based on empathic feelings, there can be a *values-based desire to help* (or a desire that people be helped). Valuing other people and their welfare can lead to a desire to help those in need even without the current experience of empathy. In a number of studies my students and I found that the more people possessed a personal characteristic that I named *prosocial value orientation*, the more they helped other people who were either in physical or in psychological distress (Staub, Erkut, & Jaquette in Staub, 1974; Feinberg, 1978; Grodman, 1979; see also Staub, 1978, Chapter 2). The tests we used to assess prosocial orientation indicate that it has three components: a positive evaluation of human beings, a concern about their welfare, and a feeling of personal responsibility for others' welfare. Presumably the feeling of personal responsibility intensifies the desire to help that arises from valuing people.

In these studies we aimed at in-depth assessment of both prosocial value orientations and helping behavior. We used most of the same 7–8 measures of values and beliefs in all three studies. In each case factor analyses showed that the behaviors measured were related to each other in similar ways. When we tested helping behavior in response to physical distress, people heard sounds of distress from another room. We created a well-defined but very lifelike sequence of events, so that whether subjects responded to the sounds of distress or not they engaged in an extensive interaction with the person in need, and had a series of opportunities to help, each offering the possibility of different degrees of helping. In the studies of psychological distress as well, the subjects and the distressed person (confederate) engaged in an extended interaction in the course of which subjects had repeated opportunities to respond in more or less helpful ways.

A third motivation to help I regard as *moral* rather than altruistic. It is really a class of motives that I have called *moral rule orientations* (Staub, 1980; 1986a). It is a commitment to and the desire to fulfill moral rules, standards, and principles which people have adopted as their own, and which require or prescribe that one help others in need. Some of these rules are specific norms and standards, applicable to specific situations, others are broad and general like the principle of justice. For example, Schwarz and his associates (Schwartz, 1977; Schwartz & Howard, 1984) proposed, and showed in their research, that a belief in prosocial personal norms tends to lead people to help others. People who showed higher stage "principled" moral reasoning using Kohlberg's measure, have been found to help more when they witness an emergency (Staub, 1974; Erkut, Jaquette, & Staub, 1981). While in values-based helping the motivation is to help the person in need, to improve his or her welfare, in moral rule orientation it is to fulfill the moral rule or principle.

A number of writers have distinguished between a rule-based morality, and the morality of caring (which I believe is expressed in prosocial value orientation). They include Durkheim (1961), who distinguished between duty or obligation on the one hand and the good on the other hand as the objects of morality, Hoffman (1970b) who differentiated between humanistic and conventional morality, and Gilligan (1982) who contrasted a morality of rules and logic and a morality of care and responsibility.

I developed a questionnaire to measure a range of other-oriented values including prosocial value orientation, empathy, and rule orientation (a commitment to rules that prescribe helping others). This questionnaire, which also included a self-report measure of 12 kinds of helping behavior, was published in *Psychology Today* (Staub, 1989c). More than 7000 questionnaires were returned; I used 2000 for data analyses (Staub, 1991b).

The sum of other-oriented values was very strongly related to the average of "effortful helping," and significantly but less strongly to the average of "less effortful helping," like giving people directions on the street, or giving someone one's seat on a train or bus. It is reassuring to know that other-oriented values find expression primarily in more effortful and significant kinds of helping, like consoling someone in distress, helping a person in an emergency, donating blood, helping others as a volunteer, engaging in social action, and others.

The relationship of prosocial value orientation to helping was much more substantial than of rule orientation or empathy, although each relationship was significant. Possibly rules themselves, and adhering to rules can become so important to people, that the underlying spirit of concern for human welfare becomes secondary. And feeling empathy with a person in need may not be translated into action for one of two reasons: first, because the type of emotion is primarily empathic distress, and second, because a feeling of personal responsibility for others' welfare, which is not inherent in empathy may often be crucial for translating caring into action.[1] Not surprisingly, our findings also showed that a feeling of competence to help was strongly related to helping. The combination of prosocial orientation and competence resulted in the strongest association with helping behavior of varied kinds (Staub, 1991b).

A fourth kind of motivation to help, again a class of motives, is *self-interest*. This can take many forms. Frequently occurring forms probably include helping in order to reduce one's own empathic distress; helping to avoid blame, criticism, or punishment for not having acted when social norms required one to help (as an extreme case, imagine someone not helping a young child who is drowning in shallow water) and to gain praise or other rewards; and helping in the hope of inducing reciprocity from someone who has the power to benefit us.

These motives often arise in response to environmental conditions, but it is the characteristics of the person that determine what impact the environment will have. Sometimes the force of environment is so great, that most people will act; at other times it is so weak that only people with the most well-developed potential for helping will do so.

At times the conditions in the environment activate motives that promote or inhibit helping. At other times, their influence is more indirect. For example, certain experiences, like another person's kindness, or success and failure on a task, or some accidental good fortune, increase helping immediately afterwards. Thinking about enjoyable, positive experiences one had in the past has the same effect (Rosenhan et al., 1981). Apparently, experiences that create positive mood increase helping. These experiences probably lessen self-focus and self-concern and thereby make people more open to seeing and responding to others' need. They probably also make people feel "richer," possessors of greater resources, including time, energy, and competence. This makes giving and helping easier. Negative moods, or experiences that give rise to them, have more complex effects: they sometimes increase and at other times decrease helping. The latter seems to happen when negative experiences lead to self-focus.

These orientations and feelings can be temporarily created by certain thoughts or experiences. Positive self-esteem is a more stable source of such feelings. The evidence, although limited, does show that positive self-esteem is associated with helping behavior (Yarymovitz, 1977; Karylowski, 1976; Loban, 1953).

## Antisocial Behavior

What are the motives that result from frustration, attack, or threat? Especially when they are intense, and when the harm they cause is perceived as intentional, they can give rise to intense feelings of anger, hostility, and the *desire to hurt* and to retaliate. This is the most basic motive, the motive most directly linked to aggression. Retaliation can also create a balance of power in a relationship that has become unbalanced as a result of the original acts of harmdoing (Bercheid, Boye, & Walster, 1968).

A variety of other motives can also be the source of aggression. A frequent source is self-defense, the defense either of the physical self or of the psychological self—one's self-concept, values, and ways of life. While attack or fear of attack can give rise to other behaviors, for example, escape, or self-blame and intra-punitive reactions, aggression is frequently the most direct way to deal with them. Laboratory research on the relationship between personality and aggression is limited. But the important role of personality is demonstrated in studies showing that people who have committed criminally aggressive acts often have low self-esteem, problems of identity, or certain kinds of self-concepts. Toch (1969) found that the aggression of individuals incarcerated for violent crimes often was a response to what they perceived as an insult or challenge. Their poor self-esteem made many of them highly sensitive and resulted in the perception of insult when there may not have been any, and aggressive response. Others committed violent crimes in the course of proving their toughness and masculinity. Toch called the former self-esteem defenders, the latter self-esteem enhancers. Other research has also shown a relationship between poor-self esteem and criminality or violence (Copeland, 1974; Gillooly & Bond, 1976; Theiss, 1985).

Dodge (1980) has found a tendency in aggressive boys to attribute hostile intentions to others, to perceive behavior directed at them that is ambiguous in nature as hostile and aggressive (for example, while playing soccer someone who is kicking at the ball ending up kicking them). Interestingly, this is not a perception of general hostility, but primarily of aggression directed at themselves, since such boys do not judge ambiguous acts in relation to other people as more hostile than do nonaggressive boys (but see also Dodge, 1993). Dodge and Frame (1982) have also shown that aggressive boys shape others' reactions to themselves, that by initiating aggression they create aggression directed at themselves.

I have proposed that one dimension of variation in the self-concept is defensive versus secure (Staub, 1993), corresponding to some of the differences in self-concept and self esteem that I have described so far. People with defensive selves would be less inclined to altruistic behavior, the unselfish helping of other people, and more inclined to aggressive "self-defense," while people with secure selves would show the opposite pattern.

Further motivations for aggression include efficacy, or *power*, when a person feels powerless and engages in aggression to gain a sense of efficacy (Becker, 1975; Staub, 1989b), and *instrumental aggression*, a person fulfilling nonaggressive goals (for example, the desire for material goods) by engaging in aggressive behavior. Obedience to (malevolent) authority frequently gives rise to aggression (Milgram, 1974; Staub, 1989b). These motivations are not intrinsically tied to aggression; their fulfillment does not inherently require aggression, but they often do lead to aggression.

Traditionally, children have been taught that aggression is wrong, that it is bad to be aggressive. Aggression anxiety as a personal characteristic decreases aggression in response to instigating conditions (Baron, 1977). Severe aggression anxiety can be a source of problems, for example, it can interfere with self-assertion and necessary self-defense. Some individuals find it extremely difficult to respond to others' harmful actions. Overly controlled aggressors usually remain passive in response to threat, or insult, or harm done to them, but finally burst forth with intense aggressiveness, at times, to mild provocation (Baron, 1977; Toch, 1969). Such a pattern is likely to be not only the outcome of aggression anxiety, but also of a negative self-concept that results in a feeling that one has no legitimate rights, and therefore it is wrong to impose one's needs and desires on other people, that is, to assert oneself.

In our contemporary world, experience in their families teaches many children that aggression is a normal, acceptable mode of behavior, and even that it is the appropriate mode of conflict resolution. They learn this from the physical punishment and abuse directed at them, or from the abuse and aggression they see among the members of their families or in their neighborhoods (Patterson, 1982; Straus, Gelles & Steinmetz, 1980). As a result of watching aggressive television programs, which is associated with (and probably made more likely by) the experience of physical punishment or abuse or neglect (Huesmann, Eron, et al., 1984; Huesmann, Lagerspetz, & Eron, 1984), aggression becomes even more part of certain children's cognitive system, their schemas or representations of appropriate behavior (Heussman & Eron, 1984; Dodge, 1993). In addition, there is a "socialization void" (Friedrich & Stein, 1973; Staub, 1979) in that their experience does not teach such children prosocial behaviors as a means of pursuing their goals.

But people develop not only cognitive representations and behavioral skills but also emotional orientations to people that makes aggression probable. Children and adults who experience rejection and abuse, whether physical or emotional, can learn to fear, dislike, and devalue people. This makes the desire to benefit them unlikely, the desire to harm them easier to arouse. I have suggested that in extreme cases individuals can develop an *antisocial value orientation*, a negative evaluation of and the desire to harm people (Staub, 1989b).

Helpful and aggressive behaviors seem like the opposite poles of a continuum. While the research evidence is limited, it seems that the motivations, and the characteristics that create the potentials for them, that make helping more likely make aggression less likely, and vice versa. Beyond a very young age, empathy in children reduces aggression and increases prosocial behavior toward peers (Feschbach & Feschbach, 1969). A prosocial value orientation is likely to reduce aggressive behavior. The most advanced levels of Kohlberg's stages of moral reasoning are associated with helping behavior, at least under certain conditions (Staub, 1974; Erkut et al., 1981), as well as with less obedience to an authority that requires aggression in Milgram's (1974) experiments (Kohlberg & Candee, 1984). A stable or temporary positive self-esteem is associated with helping, while a negative self-esteem is associated with aggression. A devaluation of certain people makes aggression against them easier and more intense (Bandura et al., 1975), and helping them less likely.

A further dimension of identity is also relevant to aggression and altruism. A number of writers have differentiated between autonomous or self-contained identities and selves-in-relation, or have focused on one or the other type of self-concept (Sampson, 1988; Surrey, 1985; Weiss et al., 1984). The latter may be more naturally empathic and caring, the former less so, their empathy and caring, when present, extensions of but not inherent to their identity.

I have extended the dimension of relatedness between self and others, suggesting in addition to autonomous and connected selves (a form of self-in-relation) the existence of embedded and disconnected selves (Staub, 1993). People with embedded selves are deeply connected to others or to a group, but their connection partly arises from dependency, lack of differentiation, and difficulty with independence. Such individuals might be helpful to others when helping seems the appropriate behavior, but not when it requires deviation from group beliefs and standards. Moreover, they would have difficulty separating themselves from and opposing their group when it embarks on a destructive or violent course (see below). In contrast, disconnected people would not possess a disposition for empathy or prosocial orientation. Their route to helping others, if any, would either be self-interest or conformity to learned moral rules that prescribe helping (Staub, 1993).

## Personal Goal Theory, Social Behavior, and Moral Conduct

I have proposed personal goal theory, a theory of motivation and action, as a general framework for understanding social behavior, moral conduct, and specifically altruism and aggression (Staub, 1978; 1980; 1986a; 1989b). The theory identifies different kinds of motives, all of which, in their particular manifestations, are characteristics of individuals: biologically based needs like hunger and sex that press for satisfaction; social rules, norms and standards that we have adopted as our own, which guide our behavior, their influence becoming especially evident when another motive makes us want to deviate from them; unconscious motives, desires that have become unacceptable to us so that we have become unaware of them, which nonetheless continue to exert influence; and personal goals which are purposive, future-oriented, and the motivation they embody incentive-like.

Personal goals are desires for classes of outcomes, with associated networks of thought that identify the meaning and value of the desired outcomes. They are the most advanced motives; but all human motives can potentially become goal-like in nature. Goals have ranges of applicability, that is, ranges of environmental conditions to which the goals apply and in which the goals can be satisfied. For example, an achievement goal, the desire to do well in comparison to standards of excellence, is for some people relevant to the domain of sports, for others to intellectual activity, for others to arts, for others to social situations where they like to shine. For some people the achievement goal can be applicable to all situations.

Other-oriented or moral values are goal-like in nature, with classes of desired outcomes and related networks of cognitions. I have differentiated between self-related goals, and other-related goals which are values like prosocial and rule orientation. Other-oriented values also have ranges of applicability, and circumstances or people can be excluded from their range. Moral exclusion (Opawa, 1990; Staub, 1978; 1989b; l990; in press), which makes moral values *inoperative* in relation to certain groups of people or certain individuals, removes the inhibitions against harming and even killing people that most human beings acquire (Staub, 1989b; 1990).

Personal goals are potentials possessed by persons. They become active either as a result of the activating potential of the environment for them, or by internal activation, a person's thoughts activating the goal. A primary activating potential for a prosocial goal is others' distress or their need for help. One purpose of the theory is to explain, given that human beings possess many motives, many potential aims for action, how particular aims become active and come to guide behavior. Another purpose is to identify important influences on behavior and specify how they join in determining action. But the theory also suggests the basis of the tendency to help (or harm) others: certain goals high in a person's hierarchy of goals, the person possessing competence and other "supporting" characteristics to fulfill these goals, and/or certain habitual modes of fulfilling these goals.

All motives, and personal goals in particular, can be arranged in a hierarchy according to their importance. It is the importance or strength of a particular goal, and the intensity of the activation potential of the environment for it (or of internal activation) that jointly determine whether a goal becomes active and dominant over other goals.

A further important concept in the theory is that of "supporting characteristics," such as competencies or role-taking capacity, which affect the likelihood that an active goal will be expressed in behavior and even that a goal becomes active. Another is the concept of integration, the development of a system of motives and goals that are coherent and mutually supportive. Goal or motive integration is itself a motivating force. The consideration of goal or motivational conflicts, and how they might be reduced is also an important aspect of the theory. I will give an example below of "moral equilibration" as a method of the resolution of conflict between a self-related and an other-related or moral motive.

## Group Violence: The Psychology of Perpetrators, Bystanders, and Heroic Helpers

The preceding parts of this chapter prepare us for a brief examination of the roots of group violence, which in turn can also increase our understanding of prejudice and discrimination against groups of people. The passivity of bystanders is important in allowing group violence or making it more probable. Coming to understand the psychology of passive bystanders can also help us learn about ourselves as bystanders—to homelessness, the abuse of children or sexual abuse, the torture and killing of people in many parts of the world, the continued existence of nuclear arms and their proliferation, and environmental destruction.

What instigates group violence, what characteristics of society and individuals contribute to it, how does the motivation for it arise and evolve, and how do inhibitions against killing people decline? The primary basis of the analysis that follows is my book, *The roots of evil: The origins of genocide and other group violence* (Staub, 1989b).

Usually difficult conditions in a society are the immediate instigating conditions for group violence. They include economic problems, political conflict and political violence, war, or intense social change. These conditions create frustration, represent threat to and attack on people, and give rise to profound needs: the need for defense of the physical self, that is, of one's safety and the satisfaction of one's material needs; the need for defense of the psychological self, one's self-concept, values, and ways of life; the need for a renewed comprehension of reality, in place of one's old world view that stopped providing useful guidance for understanding life and one's place in the world; the need for connection to other people and support from them, at a time when competition for scarce resources leads to self-focus; and a need for renewed faith in the benevolence of the world and hope in the future.

Certain characteristics of the group affect the nature and intensity of the needs that arise in response to difficult life conditions and the attempted avenues for their fulfillment; that is, for coping with at least the psychological effects of these life conditions. Unfortunately, most societies possess these characteristics to some degree; when most of them are present to a substantial degree, they represent a strong predisposition for group violence. A past history of devaluation of a subgroup of society (like antisemitism in Germany that contributed to the Holocaust) or substantial rifts and conflicts between subgroups (as between peasants in the countryside and government officials, professionals, and educated people in cities that contributed to the "autogenocide" in Cambodia) preselect certain groups as potential scapegoats and ideological enemies.

A strong respect for authority makes it difficult for people to stand on their own in the face of severe life problems. It leads them to turn to authorities and leaders for guidance and support. It makes opposition by them to leaders who turn the group against another group or a subgroup of society unlikely. A monolithic, in contrast to pluralistic, society with a limited number of predominant values and limited freedom of expression will also reduce the likelihood that initial acts of hostility against another group give rise to counter-reactions that inhibit an evolution towards intense group violence.

Certain cultural self-concepts contribute to the potential for group violence. A self-concept of superiority can intensify the need for self-defense in the face of severe life problems. Difficult life conditions can also activate feelings of vulnerability and weakness. At times, there is a combination of the two, a feeling of superiority and an underlying feeling of vulnerability. This combination has characterized Germany (Craig, 1982; Staub, 1989b), contributing to the Holocaust, and Argentina, contributing to the "disappearances," the killing of at least 9000 people in the late 1970s. A history of aggressive conflict resolution is another component of the cultural predisposition for group violence.

Difficult life conditions along with such a pattern of societal characteristics makes it probable that a group will turn against another group. Individuals and the group as a whole are likely to elevate themselves by further devaluing an already devalued subgroup of society (or at times an external enemy). They are likely to scapegoat this other group, to blame it for the difficulties of life, and thereby diminish their own feelings of responsibility. Scapegoating also creates a feeling of comprehension of the reasons for life problems and belief in the possibility of controlling events—by turning against the scapegoat. Adopting an ideology that offers a conception of a better way of life and better future helps people gain both a comprehension of reality and hope. But usually such ideologies identify groups of people as enemies who stand in the way of the ideology's fulfillment. Joining a movement to fulfill the ideology offers renewed connection to other people and a sense of significance.

Turning against a scapegoat or an ideological enemy does not immediately lead to intense violence against it. Usually there is an evolution, what I called "steps along a continuum of destruction." There is substantial evidence that as people help others, under at least somewhat supportive conditions, they become more helpful (Staub, 1979, Chapter 6). As they harm others without negative consequences to themselves, they become capable of increasing degrees of harmdoing or violence (Buss, 1966; Goldstein et al., 1975; Staub, 1989b).

Individuals, and whole groups, change as a result of their own actions. As a group begins to discriminate against and increasingly harm victims, members of the group are resocialized, group norms change, and institutions are created that serve the harmdoing. In the end, intense violence, such as mass killing, and even genocide, the extermination of the whole victim group, become possible.

There is a process of both self-selection and selection by authorities of people with certain characteristics for the role of perpetrators, or for roles like prison guards or SS members in which they are prepared to become perpetrators. As they harm their victims a number of psychological processes bring about change in the perpetrators. They are likely to engage in just world thinking (Lerner, 1980), that is, to believe that the world is just and that people who suffer must deserve it, which leads them to further devalue their own victims. They may overcome conflicts between the goals of harming or killing people and moral values that prohibit such conduct by moral exclusion. They may engage in moral equilibration, the replacement of moral values that inhibit harming and killing people with less stringent values, which are usually not moral values but are treated as such. In Nazi Germany one such "replacement value" was loyalty to the group and its leaders, especially Hitler.

Bystanders frequently remain passive observers to the mistreatment of the victim group. Internal bystanders, members of the same group, share a *societal tilt* with perpetrators: they are members of the same culture, experience the same life problems, experience similar needs, and probably share an inclination to fulfill them in the same way. They often also face a repressive system and the possibility of retaliation for opposition. But fear seems an insufficient explanation for the passivity of bystanders. In Germany, when people learned about the euthanasia program, the killing of mentally retarded, mentally ill, physically handicapped Germans, they protested. Protests by the population, by some Church leaders, and by professional groups brought the program to an end (Lifton, 1986). A societal tilt, and the values it implies, including the devaluation of victims and obedience to authority, is frequently one primary reason for bystanders' passivity; people's preoccupation with themselves in difficult times is another; fear of a repressive system is a third.

Unfortunately, as bystanders remain passive, they change. They also engage in just world thinking. To lessen the pain that would result from empathy with the victims' continued suffering, they distance themselves from the victims. This makes action on their behalf progressively less likely. Over time many bystanders engage with the systems that the perpetrators created, and some join the perpetrators (Staub, 1989a; 1989b).

External bystanders, other nations and external groups, also frequently remain passive. At times they start from having already devalued the victims. In the case of the Holocaust this was due to Christian antisemitism and its transformation in many places into cultural antisemitism; in other cases to a devaluation of Asian or Black people. In addition, the propaganda of the perpetrators affects bystanders and contributes to devaluation, as in the case of Nazi propaganda against Jews. As the victims are increasingly mistreated, just world thinking can contribute to their devaluation. Respect for the "internal affairs" of other countries and nations traditionally not regarding themselves as moral agents contribute to passivity. So does a belief that antagonizing the perpetrators is contrary to one's own interests, for example, financial interests. And progressively, external bystanders are affected by their own passivity and change as a result of it.

As I noted earlier, the behavior of bystanders can greatly influence other bystanders, and even perpetrators. In addition to the village of La Chambon, at other places like Denmark and Bulgaria attempts by the population to help Jewish victims influenced perpetrators and resulted in the survival of many Jews (Fein, 1979). Being abandoned by their neighbors and compatriots creates feelings of helplessness and despair and makes it difficult for victims to act in their own behalf. In contrast, attempts to help them greatly increased their resistance and their own attempts to help themselves (Fein, 1979; Staub, 1989b).

## The Influence of Culture and Society on Individual Aggression

Cultural-societal characteristics also have a role in creating and maintaining forms of individual violence that are widespread in a society, for example, in our society, the sexual abuse of women and incestuous relations with children. Sanday (1981) contrasted characteristics of "rape-prone" and "rape-free" societies. In the former, rape is accepted and can even be a ceremonial part of the life of the society, for example, signaling a girl's readiness for marriage. In the latter, rape is essentially absent. Rape-prone societies are characterized by aggressiveness in interpersonal relations, frequent warfare, a separation of the sexes and an adversarial interpersonal approach to sexual relations, and an ideology of male toughness. In contrast, in rape-free societies interpersonal violence is limited and women are accorded respect and prestige for their reproductive and productive roles. In Sanday's analysis, the evolution of cultural characteristics that create rape-prone societies begins with certain types of what I have called *difficult life conditions.*

In our society, there are many cultural-societal characteristics that contribute to the abuse of women and children, to their sexual abuse, and to incest. While a detailed exploration of this is not possible here (see Staub, 1991a), they include the devaluation of women and discrimination against them; relatively adversarial roles in sexual relations that stress men's authority, rights, and initiative; and a strong value placed on male strength and power and the resulting difficulty for many men to accept their vulnerability, powerlessness, and need for others, and limited skills to fulfill their needs for dependency and intimacy. There are also cultural attitudes towards children that make it more likely that they will be victimized, including the still widespread belief in physical punishment as appropriate and necessary in raising children (Straus, Gelles, & Steinmetz, 1980).

To have a full understanding of a certain type of individual aggression that characterizes a group it is necessary to: (a) identify the cultural/societal characteristics that represent a predisposition for them (Staub, 1995, in press); (b) identify the characteristics, including needs or motives, that make certain individuals especially inclined towards such aggressiveness; (c) identify general societal conditions that are activating conditions for the motives that give rise to such behavior, for example, in the United States, moderately difficult life conditions in the last two to three decades (Staub, 1989b); and (d) identify immediate or proximate environmental conditions that exert influence, for example, in the case of incest the nature of the family as a system, the characteristics and actions of family members in activating motives that lead to incest, and the role of family members as well as other people as bystanders (see Staub, 1991a).

Society can exert a negative influence in the moral realm not only by the existence of predisposing characteristics, but also by lack of support for families and individuals. Certain conditions make it difficult to fulfill basic needs for food, shelter, and health care and to lead ordered and reasonably structured lives. Disorganization and lack of structure within families is conceptually comparable to but perhaps has even greater impact than the disorganization and upheaval in the whole society that results from difficult conditions of life. Under such conditions parents are unlikely to raise children in ways that contribute to the development of an empathic disposition, a prosocial value orientation, and positive moral rules.

## Optimal Socialization: The Roots of Caring and Positive Self-Esteem

Human beings have a genetic potential for both altruism and aggression. Whether we become prosocial or antisocial depends on our experience. As I had noted earlier, parents who are rejecting, hostile, harsh, or punitive are likely to have children who are hostile and aggressive (Dodge, 1993; Eron, 1982; Huesman, Eron, et al., 1984; Huesmann, Lagerspetz, et al., 1984b; Staub, 1993).

What are the positive socialization practices that seem to contribute to caring and positive self-esteem in children? They include parental warmth and affection, which over time can lead the child to come to like and value both himself or herself, and other people (Coopersmith, 1967; Eisenberg, 1992; Staub, 1979, 1992a). Important aspects of warmth and affection include sensitivity and responsiveness, first to the infants' needs, which contributes to the development of a secure attachment (Sroufe, 1979), and soon to the child's feelings as well (Staub, 1979).

Reasoning with children, explaining to them the purpose or reason for rules, helps them develop a sense of a meaningful and trustworthy world. An important form of reasoning is *induction* (Hoffman, 1970a; 1975; Staub, 1971; 1979), explaining to the child the consequences of his or her actions for other people. This can help develop an awareness of others' inner world, the capacity for role taking and empathy, and a feeling of responsibility for others' welfare.

Firm control (Baumrind, 1975) is also important, the parents insisting that the child behave according to important values and fulfill important rules. Parents can allow a great deal of autonomy, an increasing amount as the child gets older. But if they do not succeed in getting the child to act on important values, separate verbal and behavioral systems can develop, the child learning to talk a language of caring, but not to act according to it. While control is important, it is also important that it not be forceful. Control that relies predominantly on the parents' greater power, and especially physically punitive control, contributes to aggression in children (Parke & Slaby, 1983). It counteracts the effects of nurturance and other positive practices.

As I noted, an important mode of learning to be caring and helpful is learning by doing, which can be created by guiding children to engage in prosocial behavior under supportive conditions. For example, children who made toys for poor hospitalized children, or taught younger children, were later more helpful (Staub, 1975; 1979). Engagement in helpful behavior can lead to a more positive evaluation of the beneficiaries of one's behavior and of human beings in general, and to a more caring attitude about their welfare. It can also lead to a perception of oneself as a more helpful or caring person (Eisenberg & Cialdini, 1984; Grusec, 1981; Grusec at al., 1978; Staub, 1979; 1981; 1989b; 1991, 1992).

There are other important influences as well, for example, the parents' example of helpful and generous behavior. And all these influences are also important in the child's life at school: the teachers' mode of relating to children (Battistich et al., 1991; Staub, 1979, 1992a); opportunities for learning by doing within the school and guidance by teachers that leads children to help others outside the school; and so on. Cooperative learning practices can lead children in heterogeneous groups to work together under conditions of equality, which can enhance their self-esteem and contribute to caring across group lines (Johnson et al., 1981; Staub, 1989b).

The experience cooperative learning provides is one of many ways that children can learn about their shared humanity with others. Another way is to include instruction in their various courses both about the great differences in the ways of life, beliefs, and modes of thinking of human beings, and about underlying communalities in needs and aspirations.

## Conclusion

Altruism and aggression are the result of stimulating or instigating conditions and the characteristics of persons and groups. External conditions are frequent initiators of people helping or harming others and have seemingly great power. This is due to shared characteristics among members of groups, and certain frequently existing but not inevitable human dispositions. Ultimately, it is the characteristics of the person (or group) that determine the response to external conditions. And often enough people will engage in prosocial or antisocial behavior that is internally instigated or initiated, a person's own thoughts or images giving rise to the psychological processes and motives that are the direct influences on their actions.

I described some of the influences that lead people to help or harm others, or to remain passive bystanders to others' suffering or to conditions that threaten or harm the social good. Understanding the origins of helping and harmdoing can help us develop conceptions and practices for the creation of nonaggressive and caring persons and societies, and involved, responsible individuals. This is an essential task for the future (Deutsch, 1973; Staub, 1988; 1989b, especially chapters 17 and 18; 1991, 1992a; 1991b).

## Endnote

1. Batson et al. (1986) conducted a study to examine whether there is an *altruistic personality*, "a disposition that leads people who have more of it to be more compassionate and caring toward others in distress?" They included a couple of the personality measures that my associates and I used in our early research to determine individuals' prosocial value orientation (Staub, 1974), and a few others measuring empathy and self-esteem. They found that several of these measures were related to helping behavior in the difficult escape condition but not in the easy escape condition, and concluded that this shows that the motivation for helping inherent in these personal dispositions is not altruistic.

There are problems with this study that make such a conclusion questionable. First, the basic findings that Batson and his associates (see, for example, Batson, 1990) reported in previous research about relationships between *situational empathy*, the self-report of feelings by subjects that indicate empathic caring rather than empathic distress, and helping were reversed in this study. This makes conclusions drawn about any related findings questionable.

Second, while Batson et al. indicate that their study is not a replication of the Staub (1974) study, a comparison is implied. However, the examination of the personality-behavior relation is not comparable in the two studies (and with the other studies on prosocial value orientation). First, only two of the seven measures used by Staub (1974) were used. Second, the measures were used separately rather than combined into a single whole by the use of factor analysis, which provides a meaningful composite score and as Staub (1974) found carries quite a different meaning from the individual scores. Moreover, in the Staub study helping behavior was measured in much greater depth, by a series of actions which subjects could perform, and by sum scores of all helping.

## References

Bandura, A., Underwood, B., Fromson, M. E. (1975). Disinhibition of aggression through diffusion of responsibility and dehumanization of victims. *Journal of Research in Personality, 9,* 253-269.

Baron, R. A. (1977). *Human Aggression.* New York: Plenum Press.

Batson, D. (1990). How social an animal? The human capacity for caring. *American Psychologist, 45,* 336-347.

Batson, D. C., Bolen, M. H., Cross, J. H., & Neuringer-Benefiel, H. E. (1986). Where is altruism in the altruistic personality. *Journal of Personality and Social Psychology, 50,* 212-220.

Batson, D. C., & Shaw, L. L. (1991). Evidence for altruism: Toward a pluralism of prosocial values. *Psychological Inquiry, 2,* 107-123.

Battistich, V., Watson, M., Solomon, D., Schaps, E., & Solomon, J. (1991). The child development project: A comprehensive program for the development of prosocial character. In W. M. Kurtines & J. L. Gewirtz (Eds.), *Handbook of moral behavior and development* (Vol. 3). Hillsdale, NJ: Lawrence Erlbaum Associates.

Baumrind, D. (1975). *Early socialization and the discipline controversy.* Morristown, NJ: General Learning Press.

Becker, E. (1975). *Escape from Evil.* New York: The Free Press.

Berscheid, E., Boye, D., & Walster, E. (1968). Retaliation as a means of restoring equity. *Journal of Personality and Social Psychology, 10,* 370-376.

Bickman, L. (1972). Social influence and diffusion of responsibility in an emergency. *Journal of Experimental and Social Psychology, 8,* 438-445 .

Buss, A. H. (1966). The effect of harm on subsequent aggression. *Journal of Experimental Research in Personality, 1,* 249-255.

Coopersmith, S. (1967). *Antecedents of self-esteem.* San Francisco: Fremont & Company.

Copeland, A. (1974). Violent Black gangs: Psycho- and sociodynamics. *Adolescent Psychiatry, 3,* 340-353.

Craig, G. A. (1982). *The Germans.* New York: The New American Library.

Deutsch, M. (1973). *The resolution of conflict: Constructive and destructive processes.* New Haven, CT: Yale University Press.

Dodge, K. A. (1980). Social cognition and children's aggressive behavior. *Child Development, 51,* 162-170.

Dodge, K. A., & Frame, C. L. (1982). Social cognitive biases and deficits in aggressive boys. *Child Development, 53,* 620-635.

Durkheim, E. (1961). *Moral Education.* New York: The Free Press.

Eisenberg, N. (1986). *Altruistic emotion, cognition and behavior.* Hillsdale, NJ: Lawrence Erlbaum Associates.

Eisenberg, N. (1992). *The caring child.* Cambridge: Harvard University Press.

Eisenberg, N. & Cialdini, R. B. (1984). The role of consistency pressures in behavior: A developmental perspective. *Academic Psychology Bulletin, 6,* 115-126.

Erkut, S., Jaquette, D., & Staub, E. (1981). Moral judgment-situation interaction as a basis for predicting social behavior. *Journal of Personality, 49,* 1-44.

Eron, L. D. (1982). Parent-child interaction, television violence, and aggression of children. *American Psychologist, 37,* 197-211.

Fein, H. (1979). *Accounting for Genocide: Victims and survivors of the Holocaust.* New York: Free Press.

Feinberg, J. K. (1978). *Anatomy of a helping situation: Some personality and situational determinants of helping in a conflict situation involving another's psychological distress.* Unpublished doctoral dissertation, University of Massachusetts, Amherst.

Feshbach, N. D., & Feshbach, S. (1969). The relationship between empathy and aggression in two age groups. *Developmental Psychology, 1,* 102-107.

Friedrich, L. K., & Stein, A. H. (1973). Aggressive and prosocial television programs and the natural behavior of preschool children. *Monographs of the Society for Research in Child Development, 38,* (4, Serial No. 151).

Gilligan, C. (1982). *In a different voice: Psychological theory and women's development.* Cambridge: Harvard University Press.

Gillooly, D., & Bond, T. (1976). Assaults with explosive devices on superiors. *Military Medicine, 141,* 10, 700-702.

Goldstein, J. H., Davis, R. W., and Herman, D. (1975). Escalation of aggression: Experimental studies. *Journal of Personality and Social Psychology, 31,* 162-170.

Grodman, S. M. (1979). *The role of personality and situational variables in responding to and helping an individual in psychological distress.*

Unpublished doctoral dissertation, University of Massachusetts, Amherst.

Grusec, J. E. (1981). Socialization processes and the development of altruism. In J. P. Rushton & R. M. Sorrentino (Eds.), *Altruism and helping behavior*. Hillsdale, NJ: Lawarence Erlbaum Associates.

Grusec, J. E., Kuczynski, L., Rushton, J. P., & Simutis, Z. M. (1978). Modeling, direct instruction, and attributions: Effects on altruism. *Developmental Psychology, 14*, 51-57.

Hallie, P. P. (1979). *Lest innocent blood be shed. The story of the village of Le Chambon, and how goodness happened there*. New York: Harper and Row.

Hoffman, M. L. (1970a). Moral development. In P. H. Mussen (Ed.), *Carmichael's manual of child development*. New York: Wiley.

Hoffman, M. L. (1970b). Conscience, personality, and socialization technique. *Human Development, 13*, 90-126.

Hoffman, M. L. (1975). Developmental synthesis of affect and cognition and its implications for altruistic motivation. *Developmental Psychology, 11*, 607-622.

Huesmann, L. R., & Eron, L. D. (1984). Cognitive processes and the persistence of aggressive behavior. *Aggressive Behavior, 10*, 243-251.

Huesmann, L. R., Eron, L. D., Lefkowitz, M. M., & Walder, L. O. (1984). Stability of aggression over time and generations. *Developmental Psychology, 20*, 6, 1120-1134.

Huesmann, L. R., Lagerspetz, K., & Eron, L. D. (1984). Intervening variables in the television violence-aggression relation: Evidence from two countries. *Developmental Psychology, 20*, 746-775.

Johnson, D. W., Maruyama, G., Johnson, R., Nelson, D., & Skon, L. (1981). The effects of cooperative, competitive and individualistic goal structures on achievement: A meta analysis. *Psychological Bulletin, 89*, 47-62.

Karylowski, J. (1976). Self-esteem, similarity, liking and helping. *Personality and Social Psychology Bulletin, 32*, 964-970.

Kohlberg, L., & Candee, L. (1984). The relationship of moral judgment to moral action. In

W. M. Kurtines, & J. L. Gewirtz (Eds.), *Morality, Moral Behavior, and Moral Development* (pp. 52-73). New York: Wiley-Interscience.

Krebs, D. L., & Miller, D. T., (1985). Altruism and aggression. In G. Lindzey, & E. Aronson (Eds.), *Handbook of Social Psychology*, 3rd ed. Random House.

Latane, B., & Darley, J. (1970). *The unresponsive bystander: Why doesn't he help?* New York: Appleton-Crofts.

Lerner, M. (1980). *The belief in a just world: A fundamental delusion*. New York: Plenum Press.

Lifton, R. J. (1986). *The Nazi doctors: Medical killing and the psychology of genocide*. New York: Basic Books.

Loban, W. (1953). A study of social sensitivity (sympathy) among adolescents. *Journal of Educational Psychology, 44*, 102-112.

Mallick, S. K., & McCandless, B. R. (1966). A study of catharsis of aggression. *Journal of Personality and Social Psychology, 4*, 591-596.

Milgram, S. (1974). *Obedience to authority: An experimental view*. New York: Harper and Row.

Opawa, S. (Ed.) (1990). The scope of justice. *Journal of Social Issues*. Vol. 45.

Parke, R. D., & Slaby, R. G. (1983). The development of aggression. In P. Mussen (Ed.), *Manual of Child Psychology* (Vol. 4). New York: Wiley.

Pastore, N. (1952). The role of arbitrariness in the frustration aggression hypothesis. *Journal of Abnormal and Social Psychology, 47*, 728-731.

Patterson, G. R. (1982). *Coercive family processes*. Eugene, OR: Castilia Press.

Piliavin, J. A., Dividio, J. F., Goertner, S. L., & Clark, R. D. (1981). *Emergency Intervention*. New York: Academic Press.

Rosenhan, D. L., Salovey, P., Karylowski, J., & Hargis, K. Emotion and altruism. In J. P. Rushton & R. M. Sorrentino (Eds.), *Altruism and helping behavior*. Hillsdale, NJ: Lawrence Erlbaum.

Rushton, J. P. (1980). *Altruism, socialization and society*. Englewood Cliffs, NJ: Prentice-Hall.

Sampson, E. E. (1988). The debate on individualism. Indigenous psychologies of the individual and their role in personal and societal functioning. *American Psychologist, 47*, 15-22.

Sanday, P. R. (1981). The socio-cultural context of rape: A crosscultural study. *Journal of Social Issues, 37*, 5-27.

Schwartz, S. H. (1977). Normative influences on altruism. In L. Berkowitz (Ed.), *Advances in experimental social psychology*, Volume 10. New York: Academic Press.

Schwartz, S. H., & Clausen, G. T. (1970). Responsibility norms and helping in an emergency. *Journal of Personality and Social Psychology, 16*, 299-310.

Schwartz, S. H., & Howard, J. (1984). Internalized values as motivators of altruism. In E. Staub, D. Bar-Tal, J. Karylowski, & J. Reykowski (Eds.), *The development and maintenance of prosocial behavior*. New York: Plenum Press.

Sroufe, E. (1979). The coherence of individual development: Early care, attachment, and subsequent developmental issues. *American Psychologist, 34*, 834-842.

Staub, E. (1970). A child in distress: The effects of focusing responsibility on children on their attempts to help. *Developmental Psychology, 2*, 152-154.

Staub, E. (1971). The learning and unlearning of aggression: The role of anxiety, empathy, efficacy and prosocial values. In J. Singer (Ed.), *The control of aggression and violence: Cognitive and physiological factors*. New York: Academic Press.

Staub, E. (1974). Helping a distressed person: Social, personality and stimulus determinants. In L. Berkowitz (Ed.), *Advances in experimental social psychology, 7*. New York: Academic Press.

Staub, E. (1975). To rear a prosocial child: Reasoning, learning by doing, and learning by teaching others. In D. DePalma, & J. Folley (Eds.), *Moral development: Current theory and research*. Hillsdale, NJ: Lawrence Erlbaum Associates.

Staub, E. (1978). *Positive social behavior and morality: Social and personal influences*. Vol. 1.

New York: Academic Press.

Staub, E. (1979). *Positive social behavior and morality: Socialization and development*. Vol. 2. New York: Academic Press.

Staub, E. (1980). Social and prosocial behavior: Personal and situational influences and their interactions. In. E. Staub (Ed.), *Personality: Basic aspects and current research*. Englewood Cliffs, NJ: Prentice-Hall.

Staub, E. (1981). Promoting positive behavior in schools, in other educational settings, and in the home. In J. P. Rushton, & R. M. Sorrentino (Eds.), *Altruism and helping behavior*. Hillsdale, NJ: Lawrence Erlbaum Associates.

Staub, E. (1986a). A conception of the determinants and development of altruism and aggression: Motives, the self, the environment. In C. Zahn-Waxler (Ed.), *Altruism and aggression: Social and biological origins*. Cambridge, MA: Cambridge University Press.

Staub, E. (1986b). The ideology of antagonism, societal self concept, and other cultural preconditions of war. Paper presented at the Symposium, "The social causes and effects of the nuclear arms race," Budapest, Hungary.

Staub, E. (1989a). Steps along the continuum of destruction: The evolution of bystanders: German psychoanalysts and lessons for today. *Political Psychology, 10*, 39-53.

Staub, E. (1989b). *The roots of evil. The origins of genocide and other group violence*. New York: Cambridge University Press.

Staub, E. (1989c). What are your values and goals? *Psychology Today*, 46-49.

Staub, E. (1990). The psychology and culture of torture and torturers. In P. Suedfeld (Ed.), *Psychology and torture*. New York: Hemisphere Publishing Group.

Staub, E. (1990). Moral exclusion, personal goal theory, and extreme destructiveness. In S. Opawa (Ed.), The scope of justice. *Journal of Social Issues, 46*, 47-65.

Staub, E. (1991a). Psychological and cultural origins of extreme destructiveness and extreme altruism. In W. Kurtines & J. Gewirtz (Eds.), *The handbook of moral behav-*

*ior and development.* Hillsdale, NJ: Lawrence Erlbaum Associates.

Staub, E. (1991b). Values and helping. Unpublished manuscript. University of Massachusetts, Amherst.

Staub, E. (1992a). The origins of caring, helping, and nonaggression. Parental socialization, the family system, schools, and cultural influence. In S. Oliner & P. Oliner and others (Eds.), *Embracing the other: Philosophical, psychological and historical perspectives on altruism.* New York: New York University Press.

Staub, E. (1992b). Transforming the bystander: Altruism, caring, and social responsibility. In H. Fein (Ed.), *Genocide watch.* New Haven: Yale University Press.

Staub, E. (1993b). Societal-cultural, familial, and psychological origins of youth violence. Paper presented at the 101st Annual Convention of the American Psychological Association, Toronto, Canada.

Staub, E. (1995, in press). The cultural-societal roots of violence: The examples of genocide and of contemporary youth violence in the U.S. In Feldman, R. (Ed.), *The Psychology of adversity.* Amherst: University of Massachusetts Press.

Staub, E., & Baer, R. S. Jr. (1974). Stimulus characteristics of a sufferer and difficulty of escape as determinants of helping. *Journal of Personality and Social Psychology, 30,* 279-285.

Staub, E., & Feinberg, H. (1980). Regularities in peer interaction, empathy, and sensitivity to others. Presented at the symposium: Development of prosocial behavior and cognitions. American Psychological Association Meetings, Montreal.

Staub, E. (1993). Motivation, individual and group self concepts, and morality. In W. Edelstein et al., *Morality and the self.* Cambridge: MIT Press.

Straus, M. S., Gelles, R. J., & Steinmetz, S. K. (1980). *Behind closed doors: Violence in the American family.* New York: Anchor Books.

Surrey, J. (1985). *Self-in-relation: A theory of women's development.* Wellesley, MA: The Stone Center, Wellesley College.

Theiss, A. (1985). Self-esteem and attitudes towards violence: A theory about violent individuals. Unpublished dissertation, University of Massachusetts, Amherst.

Toch, H. (1969). *Violent Men.* Chicago, IL: Aldine.

Weiss, J. R., Rothbaum, F. M., & Blackburn, T. C. (1984). Standing out and standing in. The psychology of control in America and Japan. *American Psychologist, 39,* 955-969.

Wilson, J. P. (1976). Motivation, modeling and altruism: A person x situation analysis. *Journal of Personality and Social Psychology, 34,* 1078-1086.

Yarymovitz, M. (1977). Modification of self-worth and increment of prosocial sensitivity. *Polish Psychological Bulletin, 8,* 45-53.

# Chapter 17

# Social Domain Theory

*MARTA LAUPA*
*University of Nevada, Las Vegas*

*ELLIOT TURIEL*
*University of California, Berkeley*

**Abstract**

A theoretical approach is presented, based on the proposition that children's social and moral judgments develop within distinct domains. The focus is upon the domains of morality (concerns with welfare, justice, and rights), social convention (uniformities that are part of social organization), and personal jurisdiction (individual prerogatives). After contrasting this developmental perspective with cultural construction and transmission theories, we consider research on the sources of development within domains, on the ways children make judgments within each domain, and on reasoning about various types of domain mixtures. A large body of evidence has demonstrated that from an early age children make judgments about moral issues using criteria that differ from the criteria applied to conventional or personal issues. Moral issues are judged as universal, non-contingent, and impersonal, whereas social conventional issues are judged as context-specific, contingent, and within authority jurisdiction. The research also shows that there are age-related changes in the justifications supporting judgments within each domain. We also consider how this approach can inform an understanding of moral development and cultural contexts.

In this chapter we present a theoretical approach based on the idea that moral and social judgments develop within distinct conceptual domains. We focus on research that has uncovered the existence, starting in early childhood, of reasoning about three social domains. These are (1) the *moral*, which pertains mainly to concerns with welfare, justice, and rights, (2) the *social-conventional*, which pertains to understanding of social uniformities and regularities that are part of the smooth and efficient functioning of social organizations, and (3) the *personal*, which pertains to those individual prerogatives and entitlements considered to be exempt from social regulation.

The proposition that children develop these distinct ways of thinking about social relationships is in contrast with contemporary views in which the impact of a particular culture's moral system is regarded as primary in the formation of the moral judgments of children growing up in that culture. Within that view, morality is a "social construction" specific to the make-up of each culture. Whereas morality is constructed through the traditions of a society by virtue of its history, individuals incorporate (not construct) morality by virtue of their socialization in the cultural setting. Our domain-specific view, in contrast, is partially based on the idea of development as formulated by Jean Piaget and others. A developmental perspective is premised on the proposition that children generate or construct moral and social understandings of the world around them, not solely because of what is transmitted to them by adults, but also through their inference about events and social relationships that they experience directly. Accordingly, moral judgments are not solely reflections of ready-made cultural codes and can entail solutions to problems that may exist across societal boundaries.

It should be noted that these current debates are not entirely new. Philosophers and social scientists have long debated issues revolving around the definition, nature, and development of morality. A central issue of debate has been to what extent and in what ways culture influences and/or determines individuals' moral judgments and choices. Can an individual's moral standards be self-generated or does the individual invariably adopt the mores and values culturally transmitted to him or her? In this chapter we first briefly consider some of the issues central to the contemporary debates in order to set the stage for the presentation of the propositions and research findings of the domain-specific perspective.

## Theory

### Background

In saying that individuals develop distinctly different domains of social reasoning, we are claiming that they maintain a diverse set of social judgments about diverse components of the social world. Individuals are concerned with welfare, justice, and rights, as well as with the "efficient" operation of society, as well as personal goals. We use the term "heterogeneity" to refer to the diversity of social reasoning within individuals. This is in contrast with the proposition that there are "homogeneous" social orientations determined by the make-up of the culture. The homogeneous view is that cultures usually have organizing features that constitute all-encompassing moral perspectives on social relationships. These organizing features may differ from one culture to another. Moreover, each represents a coherent orientation particular to a culture, such that one cannot be compared with another.

We can make this more concrete by considering frequently found characterizations of the culture in North America as individualistic. It has been maintained (e.g. Hogan, 1975; Kessen, 1979; Sampson, 1977; Shweder, 1986) that our culture is mainly oriented toward self-contained individualism which contrasts with cultures oriented toward tradition, authority, duty, or collectivism. In an individualistic culture, according to these accounts, the morality of its members stresses self-sufficiency, personal goals, autonomy, and detachment from others. In such a culture, moral judgments focus on maintaining equality, protecting individual rights, and insuring that persons have freedoms and liberties. Other nonWestern cultures, such as in India or China, are said to have a morality fundamentally different from individualism in that they focus on maintaining traditions and social hierarchies (non-equality) and upholding duties prescribed by the social order. In those societies, individual rights and freedom are unimportant since persons are subordinate to the larger system (e.g., religion, society). The concepts of rights and freedoms, and even the whole idea of the "individual" are unique cultural constructions to which Americans pay much attention.

Are these accurate characterizations of different homogeneous cultural orientations or are they one-dimensional stereotypes imposed upon complex and heterogeneous social orientations in each culture? From our domain-specific perspective they are, by and large, stereotypes of societies and of persons in these societies. They are stereotypes in that cultures are portrayed as only of one type or another. They are stereotypes because cultures are not only of one kind; instead, they include a coexistence of orientations.

Consider the characterization of Western culture as individualistic, with its morality of rights and freedoms. There is much evidence that this is a limited and one-sided view of the moral concerns of persons in this society. Some of the evidence comes from a series of survey studies conducted by sociologists and political scientists over the past fifty years on Americans' attitudes toward civil liberties and rights. Over and over again the reaction to the results of the survey studies has been one of surprise. This is because of the findings that Americans endorse civil liberties and rights to a much lesser extent than would be expected from the idea that this culture is highly individualistic. An example is a comprehensive survey conducted in the 1970s with large samples of adults (McClosky and Brill, 1983). Subjects were asked to respond to a large number of survey items (about 300) dealing with issues that would normally be regarded to be at the heart of individualism: rights and liberties (freedom of speech, press, assembly, and religion, as well as academic freedom and the right to dissent, the right to have privacy and to choose one's own lifestyle). The subjects were presented with questions in general, abstract terms, (e.g., "I believe in free speech for all, no matter what their views might be."), and questions posed with regard to particular situations (e.g., "A community should allow the American Nazi party to use its town hall to hold a public meeting.").

The results were clear cut in their diversity: Members of this society sometimes uphold personal rights and liberties and sometimes they do not. In the abstract, rights and freedoms are supported (89 percent supported the first statement). They are also supported when they are not in strong conflict with other moral goals (such as preventing harm) or concerns with cultural traditions and maintaining the social order. But, the same respondents who endorsed rights and freedoms in some contexts failed to do so in other contexts. In many contexts, freedom of speech, religion, privacy, and assembly, to cite a few examples, were not upheld (only 18 percent agreed with the second statement). These findings do not portray Americans as individualistic. Rather, Americans have a complex and differentiated understanding of their social world which includes both individualistic and collectivistic orientations. An adequate theory of social development needs to account for this diversity.

It is also interesting that this culture is not always characterized as individualistic. For instance, as recently as 20 or 30 years ago it was common to characterize this society in terms opposite to individualism. It was then commonplace to portray U.S. culture as populated by dependent, conformist persons primarily oriented to fitting into the group or society. Popular social scientific treatises had titles like *Organization Man* (William Whyte), *White Collar* (C. Wright Mills), and *The Lonely Crowd* (David Reisman). They wrote about other-directed people as interchangeable links in social organizations, whose lives revolved around the corporation. The society was seen as deifying collectivism and as dominated by those who "take the vows of organization life" and are "the mind and soul of our great, self-perpetuating institutions."

Also, there are now social scientists who characterize the society as homogeneous—but with characteristics opposite to individualism. A prominent example comes from proponents of "character education" (Bennett and Delattre, 1978; Wynne, 1986), who claim that the morality of this society is represented by its traditions, with concerns for virtuous acts, conformity to duties, and upholding the social order. It turns out, therefore, that one group of scholars from this society maintains that individualism, liberalism, and concerns with rights do capture this society's morality, which is different from the nonsecular, traditional, duty-bound morality of other cultures. But we have another group of scholars from this society who maintains that individualistic and secular notions of morality fail to adequately characterize this society. This situation, with its set of contradictory claims, comes about, we believe, because there is a great deal of stereotyping through global homogeneous cultural categories.

### Social Domains Defined

Heterogeneity in social orientations stems from the different domain-specific types of social judgments children make. As noted earlier, we consider judgments in the moral, conventional, and personal domains. Research into children's reasoning in these domains has been guided by philosophical definitions of these realms, with an attempt to translate the philosophical criteria into research methods that would yield information about how children form and apply judgmental criteria to different social issues. Moral philosophers have long been concerned with a distinction between morality and convention, a concern evident in contemporary philosophical treatises (e.g., Dworkin, 1978; Gewirth, 1978; Rawls, 1971). They have stressed the analytic distinction between moral imperatives and the standards, conventions, or practices of social organizations and institutions.

Distinctions of this sort go as far back as Aristotle, who discussed natural justice and conventional justice:

> There are two forms of justice, the natural and the conventional. It is natural when it has the same validity everywhere and is unaffected by any view we may take of the justice of it. It is conventional when there is no original reason why it should take one form rather than another and the rule it imposes is reached by agreement after which it holds good. . . . Some philosophers are of opinion that justice is conventional in all its branches, arguing that a law of nature admits variation and operates in exactly the same way everywhere—thus fire burns here and in Persia while rules of justice keep changing before our eyes. It is not obvious what rules of justice are natural and what are legal and conventional, in cases where variation is possible. Yet it remains true that there is such a thing as natural, as well as conventional justice. (Aristotle, *Nicomachean Ethics,* as cited in Winch, 1972)

In a similar vein, but without using the concepts of natural justice, contemporary philosophers have drawn such distinctions. The philosopher Alan Gewirth (1978) has written, "Judgments of moral obligation are categorical in that what persons morally ought to do sets requirements for them that they cannot rightly evade by consulting their own self-interested desires or variable opinions, ideals or institutional practices" (p. 24).

On the basis of this type of distinction, social conventions are defined as behavioral uniformities which coordinate interactions of individuals within social systems. Conventions involve coordinations at the level of social organization; they are uniformities that coordinate the stable interactions of individuals functioning within a social system and their ends are social organizational. Conventions are relative to the societal context, and may be altered by consensus or general usage within a social system.

Unlike conventional prescriptions, moral prescriptions are not perceived to be alterable by consensus. This is not to say that morality is fixed and unalterable. We know, for instance, that historical changes have occurred with regard to such matters as slavery. However, the bases for those changes are not perceived as shifts in the general consensus or in social organization, but on the intrinsic merits, from the moral point of view, of one type of action over another. The individual's moral prescriptions (e.g., regarding killing and the value of life) are determined by factors inherent to social relationships. An individual's perception of an act such as the taking of a life as a transgression is not contingent on the presence of a rule, but rather stems from factors intrinsic to the event (e.g., from the perception of the consequences to the victim). This means that moral issues are not perceived as relative to the societal context. The moral theories formed by individuals are based on concepts regarding the welfare of persons, the rights of persons, and justice in the sense of comparative treatment of individuals.

In contrast to both moral and conventional prescriptions, actions in the personal domain are those actions which are considered to be outside the jurisdiction of moral concern or social regulation (Nucci, 1981). These actions are judged by individuals to be of a personal nature, and to be regulated by the personal preference of the actor, and not by moral concerns or the demands of social custom or convention. Whereas the classification of actions as pertaining to the moral domain is considered objective and universal, actions pertaining to the social conventional and personal domains are culturally variable. Different cultures may choose to regulate different actions for purposes of behavioral uniformity, and leave others to personal choice. Further, individuals within a culture may vary as to their interpretations of a given event as justifiably regulated by convention or left to personal preference.

## *The Sources of Development*

Proposing that there are domains of social judgments implies that individuals make discriminations in their understandings and evaluations of the social environment. Correspondingly, social experiences are not all of one kind. If social development were mainly the learning of cultural codes, then children would be experiencing the one kind of social input given to them by others. We propose, however, that children attempt to make sense of qualitatively different types of social events. For instance, moral judgments might be formed out of experiences in which persons inflict harm on one another. Children's judgments of the rightness and wrongness of these sorts of acts need not be pointed out to them by adults, as the effects of the act are apparent to the victim and observers. Moral rules are constructed by inference from acts which cause harm to persons or entail unfairness. The resulting moral rules are non-arbitrary and not dependent upon the particular social system in which they occur.

In contrast, knowledge of social conventions develops out of situations in which there are implicit or explicit statements given as to what is considered conventional behavior in a social group. Social conventional transgressions do not have intrinsic consequences to the acts involved; they are arbitrary in content. Conventional rules are constructed by children through interactions in which other members of the social group react to the transgression. They are meaningful only to the extent that they serve the function of organizing behavior in social groups.

The following events serve to illustrate the difference between moral and conventional transgressions (Turiel, 1983). The first is an example of a moral transgression.

> A number of nursery school children are playing outdoors. There are some swings in the yard, all of which are being used. One of the children decides that he now wants to use a swing. Seeing that they are all occupied, he goes to one of the swings, where he pushes the other child off, at the same time hitting him. The child who has been pushed is hurt and begins to cry.

Children judge actions like these, in which there is clear harm to the victim, as morally unacceptable. In these cases, knowledge of morality is constructed by considering the consequences of the act and not whether or not it is regulated by rules or authority.

In contrast, below is an example of the violation of a conventional rule.

> Children are greeting a teacher who has just come into the nursery school. A number of children go up to her and say "Good morning, Mrs. Jones." One of the children says, "Good morning, Mary."

In this event there are no intrinsic consequences to calling the teacher by her first name. Children must infer the unacceptability of this sort of behavior from the actions of other children and adults when the custom is violated. If no statements are made as to the unacceptability of this behavior, the child will not come to the conclusion that it is a conventional violation.

Research has demonstrated that both children and adults respond differently to conventional and moral transgressions, such as those in the above examples (Much and Shweder, 1978; Nucci and Nucci, 1982a, 1982b; Nucci and Turiel, 1978; Smetana, 1981). As an example, one study (Nucci and Turiel, 1978) focused on social interactions occurring among children in a preschool setting. Two interrelated measures of systems of social interaction were obtained. One was a measure of social transgressions. Descriptions were recorded of naturally occurring events that exemplified transgressions in the moral domain (e.g., inflicting harm, taking the possessions of another) and in the conventional domain (e.g., behavior inconsistent with uniformities in dress or modes of eating). The second measure obtained was of the types of social interactions generated by each type of transgression. The reactions and interactions that resulted from the transgressions (among the children and teachers) were recorded.

In this study, different types of responses were elicited by the two types of events. Almost all responses to conventional transgressions were initiated by teachers (92 percent of conventional transgressions had a teacher as the sole respondent). Teachers responded to conventional transgressions by invoking school rules, sanctions, and prohibitions regarding norm-violating behavior. In contrast, children and teachers responded with equal frequency to the moral transgressions (38 percent of the moral transgressions had an adult as the sole respondent, 46 percent had a child as the sole respondent and 16 percent had both adults and children as respondents). Children responded to moral transgressions with physical reactions and expressions of emotional states. They also responded by pointing out the consequences of the transgression, such as the pain experienced or loss incurred. Teachers responded to moral transgressions by pointing out to the transgressor the effects of his or her actions upon the victim, or by providing children with reasons for objections to their behaviors.

These results suggest that judgments about moral and conventional rules are constructed by children out of qualitatively different categories of experience. For children to judge that a moral transgression, such as the one in the first example above, is wrong, they need not be told by an authority that the act is prohibited. In contrast, transgressions like the one in the second example above, since they have no intrinsic consequences, will not be interpreted by children as transgressions unless the existing rules or social expectations are pointed out to them. Observational studies, such as the one described here, have shown that adults in this society do take on the task of making children aware of when they have transgressed existing social conventions. However, children themselves respond to moral transgressions as frequently as adults, and in such a way as to demonstrate that they are aware of the effects of the transgressions and judge them unacceptable.

## Research

### Children's Social Reasoning

A large body of research has shown that these domains are distinguished by children starting as young as three years of age (Nucci, 1981; Nucci, Turiel, and Encarnacion-Gawrych, 1981; Nucci and Turiel, 1978; Smetana, 1981; Turiel, 1983; Weston and Turiel, 1980). Consistent with the proposed distinction between the moral and conventional as qualitatively distinct domains of knowledge, children of varying ages have been shown to discriminate between events pertaining to different domains and reason about them differently depending on the specific domain to which they pertain.

In investigating children's abilities to discriminate between different domains, studies have employed assessments of two types, corresponding to two dimensions of children's thought. First, there is the ability to discriminate between events pertaining to different domains, on the basis of judgments about criteria which define each domain. Assessments are made of the *criterion judgments* used by children in evaluating the rightness and wrongness of different acts. The criterion judgments are judgments of the generalizability, universality, rule-contingency, and alterability of the prohibition regarding an act. For example, in the study described above (Nucci and Turiel, 1978), after the occurrence of an event, children were taken aside by the observer and asked whether the act they had observed "would be right to do if there were no rule in the school about it," (Is the act contingent on the existence of a rule?). It has been found that children reliably classify events as moral on the basis of their evaluation of the event as generalizable, universal, non-rule contingent, and non-alterable. Social conventions, on the other hand, are judged by children to be local, relative, contingent on rules, and alterable by authority and/or consensus.

The second aspect of children's thought which has been assessed are their reasons or justifications for judging an event to pertain to one or the other domains. Assessments are made of the *justifications* used by children in accordance with their criterion judgments. It has been shown that children use different justifications when reasoning about acts from different domains. When reasoning in the moral domain, children refer to issues of harm, welfare, and fairness. When reasoning about social conventional acts, children use justifications referring to manners, rules, and customary practice. Events in the personal domain are reasoned about as matters of personal choice and jurisdiction, which do not affect others.

Most studies of children's ability to discriminate between acts pertaining to different domains have focused on the distinction between the moral and conventional domains. A brief description of one study which investigated reasoning in all three domains (Nucci, 1981) can serve to illustrate some of the methods used and findings obtained on variations in children's judgments by domain.

Subjects (ranging in age from 7 to 19 years) were presented with a list of descriptions of social transgressions to sort according to the criteria of rule contingency (evaluation of the act based on the existence of a social rule) and personal jurisdiction (judgment of the act as being within the purview of personal choice). The transgressions presented to subjects were of three kinds, as determined by definitional criteria: moral (hitting and stealing), conventional (e.g., forms of address and table manners), and personal (events which in this culture are likely to be considered outside the realm of societal regulation, e.g., choices of friendships or recreation groups).

A two-step categorization procedure was used. Subjects were presented with the complete list of event descriptions and first instructed to group together all the acts considered "wrong even in the absence of a rule" pertaining to the act (rule contingency). With very few exceptions, subjects at all ages classified only the moral transgressions as wrong even in the absence of a rule. After sorting the acts on the basis of rule contingency, subjects were presented with the complete list of events and instructed to group together those that "should be the person's own business" (personal jurisdiction). Again, with very few exceptions, subjects classified only the personal acts as ones that should be the person's own business. Therefore, the moral acts were judged to be impersonal and their status as transgressions was independent of the existence of societal rules. The conventional acts were considered to be out of the realm of personal choice insofar as there is a relevant societal rule, and some acts were regarded as legitimately determined by personal choice.

As in many other studies using a variety of acts as stimuli, subjects in the Nucci study displayed different kinds of judgments. The observation of these judgments in the same group of subjects indicates that individuals have differentiated understandings of social interactions and cultural systems and that their social judgments do not correspond to a unitary category. Consequently, what might appear as opposing or contradictory orientations are all part of the individual's reasoning. These orientations are applied in non-contradictory ways insofar as they stem from conceptualizations of different types of social interactions within a cultural or social system. The meaning and functions of moral prescriptions are different from the meaning and functions of conventions in systems of social organization.

The claim is, then, that children's ability to differentiate between events pertaining to different domains, as assessed by their criterion judgments, begins at least as young as three years. This ability does not undergo developmental change. Rather, conceptual development is found in children's reasoning about events within domains as assessed by the justifications for their criterion judgments.

However, although no age differences have been found in the basic ability of children to distinguish among domains, there is indication that for younger children the criteria are not as consistently applied (Davidson, Turiel, and Black, 1983). In this study, 6-, 8-, and 10-year-old subjects were interviewed about moral and conventional transgressions that had been assessed as familiar or unfamiliar to them (familiar moral, unfamiliar moral, familiar conventional, and unfamiliar conventional). Assessments were made of subjects' criterion judgments of acceptance of authority, punishment orientation, and acceptance of rule change, as well as their justifications for these judgments. For familiar transgressions all age groups showed a differentiated understanding of moral and conventional issues, both in criterion judgments and in justifications. Younger subjects showed less differentiation than older subjects when the transgressions were unfamiliar. These findings indicate that the familiarity of the event has an effect on the ability of young children to consistently distinguish between the moral and social-conventional domains.

In addition to the basic domain distinctions, researchers have investigated the development of children's reasoning (justifications) within domains. Studies have demonstrated development in each domain. Research on the social-conventional domain (Turiel, 1978) has described children's understanding of conventions as progressing through levels of affirmation and negation of conventions. Each level of affirmation is negated at a subsequent level as it is restructured into a more adequate understanding of social-conventions and their place in social organizations. At Level 1 and its negation, Level 2 (6-9 years), convention is descriptive of social uniformity and not conceived as part of the structure or function of social interaction. At Levels 3 and 4 (10-13 years), convention is seen as a system of rules and the conception of a social system is concrete. At Levels 5 and 6 (14-18 years), convention is mediated by a social system with fixed roles and static hierarchical organization. Finally, at Level 7 (19-22 years), convention is seen as coordinating social interactions and facilitating operations of a social system.

Researchers have investigated development in the moral domain as well (Damon, 1977; Davidson, Turiel, and Black, 1983). Findings suggest that young children reason about moral transgressions in terms of welfare and harm to others. As they get older, children continue to reason about welfare and harm, but, in addition, refer to reasons of justice, fairness, and obligation when justifying their judgments of the wrongness of moral transgressions. Development has also been found in reasoning about the personal domain (Broughton, 1978; Nucci, 1981).

## Social Reasoning about Domain Mixtures

The research findings we have considered thus far indicate that children develop fundamental categories of social judgment. In the types of studies conducted in order to illuminate judgments within domains, researchers have deliberately chosen issues that are characteristic of one or another of the domains of interest. Therefore, children have been presented with issues that primarily bear upon considerations from within a domain. For example, the issues used to study moral judgments are ones that mainly entail considerations of welfare or justice or rights (an example is intentional and unprovoked infliction of physical harm). Whereas this research strategy has provided a good means for ascertaining how children reason about each of the domains, it does not deal with those social situations entailing components from more than one domain. Thus far, the domain analyses have been extended to address three types of social issues that are not clearly within domains. These have been referred to as *second-order phenomena*, *domain mixtures*, and *ambiguous issues*.

First consider the possibility that some conventional issues are primarily judged as conventional, but that, in certain circumstances, they could take on moral connotations because of the reactions of some people to the acts. For instance, there are actions that individuals consider to have no intrinsic harmful consequences, but are seen as having the potential to harm others through others' interpretation of them as offensive or repugnant. An example in some cultures is that it is not socially acceptable to wear a bathing suit to a funeral. It is not that the wearing of a bathing suit in this case is intrinsically wrong; however, individuals at the funeral may take offense at what they consider to be disrespectful behavior.

A study by Turiel (1983) investigated adolescents' and adults' reasoning about such an action, that of sunbathing nude on a public beach. Although the act was considered wrong by some subjects, it was not reasoned about as a moral issue. Subjects in this study did not view nude sunbathing as intrinsically wrong; they considered the social prohibition against it as arbitrary. However, they reasoned that the act could have moral implications to the extent that others viewing it might take offense. The results show that an act which is unconventional can take on secondary, second-order moral implications. There are also social events which simply include components from more than one domain, with the components sometimes coming into conflict with each other (domain-mixtures). Recently researchers have looked at the way in which children and adults reason about events that do involve issues from more than one domain (Duncan, 1984; Killen, 1990; Turiel, 1983). One such study by Killen (1990) investigated children's reasoning about events in which either personal or conventional considerations conflicted with moral considerations. Children from the ages of 6 to 12 years were presented with hypothetical scenarios in which a child is faced with a choice between two courses of action which entail a conflict of concerns of the moral and conventional domains or the moral and personal domains. For example, in one story a child has the opportunity to prevent another child from being harmed (moral component), but the child has to decide to help either a child whom he does not know, or his own sibling (personal component). Subjects were asked to determine which course of action the child in the story should engage in. There were three types of reasoning found in children's responses: (1) some children viewed the dilemma as entailing only one domain, in this example, either the moral or the personal; (2) some viewed the dilemma as combining both moral and personal elements, and were unable to relate or coordinate these elements so that they wavered back and forth in their reasoning; and (3) still other children viewed the dilemma as combining both moral and personal elements and coordinated the elements by subordinating one to the other with explicit reasons. As might be expected, there were age differences, such that the ability to recognize two considerations and coordinate them increased between 6 and 12 years of age.

These findings indicate that in addition to distinguishing between domains, children are also able to identify the domain considerations involved in a given event and that there is development in the ability to identify and coordinate these considerations. The issue of domain mixtures, and the coordination of different domain considerations in individuals' reasoning, is an important one for the study of the relationship between moral judgments and actions (Turiel, 1983; Turiel and Smetana, 1984). This is because in many real-life situations persons must choose between moral concerns and concerns from other domains. There is not a simple relation between moral and social judgments and actions. Rather, choices are often made between compelling moral alternatives and compelling actions from another domain. For instance, a desire to avoid harming another sometimes conflicts with social-organizational rules and authority dictates to inflict harm. The famous studies by Stanley Milgram (1974) on obedience to authority involved just this kind of conflict. Subjects were highly conflicted by the choice forced upon them between avoiding harming another person (subjects were instructed to administer electric shocks in a purported experiment on learning and memory) and adhering to the regulations and authority dictates, as well as promoting a scientific enterprise. Often, subjects chose one alternative over the other, but with a great deal of conflict. Insofar as real life behavioral decisions entail such conflict, it is important to know how individuals coordinate and choose between their different domain judgments in deciding to act.

The types of social situations we have referred to as entailing second-order phenomena and mixed domains are ones in which separate moral, conventional, or personal components are brought together. Insofar as individuals recognize the different components, their task is to then integrate them or resolve conflicts between them. There is another group of issues that entail components from more than one domain in a different way from mixed domain issues. We are referring to social issues that many persons do not conceive, for one reason or another, as unambiguously in one social domain. There are several such issues that have been researched, including abortion, pornography, and homosexuality, which we label as potentially ambiguous with regard to the domain demarcations.

It should be noted that these particular issues are very controversial, in this society, at least. Recent political events and judicial decisions have amply shown that abortion, pornography, and homosexuality are highly contested issues. For instance, recent decisions on these issues by the U.S. Supreme Court have evoked a great deal of public controversy. There are disagreements over whether the practices are acceptable, whether they are moral issues, and whether they should be under personal or legal jurisdiction. As an example, public opinion surveys (e.g., McClosky and Brill, 1983) show that people are divided as to whether abortion is acceptable, with some treating it as a moral issue and others not. In addition, many who evaluate abortion as wrong nevertheless believe it should not be illegal.

Research conducted with adolescents and young adults was aimed at determining how people reason about these controversial issues and how their reasoning about these issues compares with their reasoning about moral issues. In one study (Turiel, Hildebrandt, and Wainryb, 1990), subjects' criterion judgments and justifications were assessed about ambiguous issues (abortion, pornography, homosexuality) and straightforward moral issues (i.e., killing, rape). The ways in which subjects evaluated the ambiguous issues readily constituted two groups: those evaluating the issues as unacceptable and those evaluating the issues as acceptable. This division in evaluations of the ambiguous issues clearly contrasted with the ways the moral issues were evaluated. Just about all subjects evaluated killing and rape (acts in the moral domain) as wrong.

Furthermore, the patterns of criterion judgments differed for the two types of issues. Subjects were generally consistent in the ways the moral acts were judged. The acts were judged as wrong and it was thought that the acts should be prohibited by law. Subjects also judged that the moral acts would be wrong even if they were not prohibited by law (rule contingency). In contrast, many of the subjects who evaluated the ambiguous issues as wrong also judged that they should not be illegal or that the acts would not be wrong in another culture if they were accepted in that culture. There was a tendency for those subjects to, on the one hand, evaluate the acts as wrong and, on the other hand, to state that decisions should be up to individual choice. The justifications given for each type also differed. Whereas judgments about the moral acts were justified or reasoned about consistently in terms of welfare, justice, and rights, the ambiguous issues were justified in terms of their deviation from what is natural, religious, or given by society.

A central source of the ambiguity stems from assumptions that people hold about certain matters related to evaluations of the issues. These assumptions include beliefs about natural, biological functioning, such as the start of life, as in the case of abortion and natural sexual functioning, as in the case of homosexuality. We can illustrate this with reference to assumptions held that are relevant to decisions about abortion. The central assumption here is whether the fetus is considered to be a life (a person). Those evaluating abortion as wrong also usually assumed that the fetus is a life at conception. Those evaluating abortion as acceptable usually assumed that life does not begin until late in the pregnancy or at birth. For those assuming that life does not begin at conception, abortion is considered the woman's decision since it does not entail the taking of the life of a person. For many people, however, these types of assumptions are held in an ambiguous way. That is, there is a great deal of uncertainly about the start of life. This uncertainly results in inconsistencies in the ways evaluations and judgments about abortion are made.

## Rules and Authority

A social-constructionist view, as discussed earlier, proposes that children acquire moral knowledge through transmission of cultural rules and mores from persons in authority. In contrast, the domain-specific perspective regards children as actively constructing their knowledge of morality, as well as knowledge of rules and authority, through their experience of their social world. Within this perspective, rules and authority play a different role in children's development. Rather than being the process by which the values of the culture are transmitted to the child, rules and authority are an integral part of the social groups and organizations which the child experiences throughout his or her development, and constructs knowledge about. Just as children's judgments about a heterogeneous social environment are heterogeneous, their judgments about rules and authority are heterogeneous as well. Neither rules nor authority comprise a domain of knowledge in themselves. Thus, children do not have a unitary orientation toward them, but make different judgments based on whether the rules or authority in a given case pertain to moral, conventional, or personal matters.

Recent research has demonstrated the way in which children reason about rules and authority across domains. As an example, we will discuss recent research regarding children's reasoning about authority. First, studies have demonstrated that children's concepts of authority are differentiated with respect to the content of the command given (Damon, 1977; Laupa and Turiel, 1986; Smetana, 1988, 1989; Tisak, 1986). This means that children will not accept all commands from legitimate authorities if the command is found to be morally unacceptable. Damon (1977) asked children aged 4-10 years about a mother issuing various commands to a child, such as to clean his room, to stay inside rather than going out to play, or to steal something from another child. He found that children of all ages rejected the authority of the mother to command her child to steal. Laupa and Turiel (1986) presented children aged 6 to 12 years with hypothetical scenarios in which a teacher at school instructed children that they were allowed to fight if they wanted to. All the children rejected the authority of a teacher to allow children to fight. Subjects justified their responses on the grounds that fighting can cause harm. Weston and Turiel (1980) found that children did not accept the legitimacy of school authorities to adopt a policy that allowed hitting at school, while they did accept their legitimacy to adopt a policy allowing nudity. Subjects in this study also justified their judgments on the grounds that hitting can cause harm. These results demonstrate that children make judgments about actions and rules in their social world and whether they are morally acceptable without reference to authority dictates, and that they do not judge any act as acceptable simply because it is endorsed or commanded by authority.

Second, studies have shown that when reasoning about authority commands which they consider acceptable, children make differentiated judgments about authorities, showing that they are not overwhelmingly oriented toward the superior size and power of adults (Laupa and Turiel, 1986, 1993; Laupa, 1991, 1994). Children in these studies were presented with hypothetical situations in which different individuals issued commands to children at school. Individuals varied with respect to whether they possessed the attributes of adult status, knowledge, and social position. For example, individuals presented included a teacher (who possesses adult status, knowledge, and social position), a peer authority (who possesses knowledge and social position, but not adult status), and a former teacher (who possesses knowledge and adult status, but no social position). Results show that adult status is not the most important attribute upon which children base their judgments of authorities' legitimacy. Children give greater weight to both knowledge and social position in certain cases, depending on the social context.

Overall, it can be seen that authority is not simply an institution by which a culture's value system is transmitted to its children. Instead, authority is a social relation in which children take part throughout their development and about which they form judgments. Rather than making moral judgments based on authority dictates, children make different judgments about authority based on their reasoning about the moral acceptability of the commands authorities give. Further, children are not solely oriented toward obedience to adults as authorities, but make differentiated judgments about the legitimacy of authority based on a consideration of the authority's various attributes and the social context.

## Conclusion

The social environment which children experience while growing up is complex and heterogeneous. Children reflect on the social interactions and events which they experience, thus this heterogeneity is found in their judgments about their social world. The social-domain perspective and the research done from this perspective call into question the usefulness of stereotypes of different cultures and societies, or their members, in homogeneous terms. We have reviewed a body of research that demonstrates that children, as well as adults, reason about different social acts in different ways; moral rules are judged to be universal and unalterable, while conventions are judged to be contextual and based on consensus. While it is true that diversity of social judgments exists among persons within and across cultures, this diversity, rather than resulting from differences in cultural training, results in large part from the differing assumptions individuals hold about factual matters which underlie their social judgments.

As discussed above, differences in individuals' underlying assumptions have been shown to relate to their different evaluations of the acceptability of abortion. Further evidence of the relation of underlying assumptions to moral judgments is found in a recent study (Wainryb, 1991, 1993) which investigated the importance of underlying factual assumptions in children's judgments about various social events. In this study, subjects aged 11-21 years were presented with hypothetical stories containing standard moral transgressions, for example, a father spanking his child out of frustration. Then subjects were presented with stories in which the same act is performed under different circumstances which could allow for an interpretation of the act as morally acceptable, for example, a father spanks his child for repeatedly misbehaving. Subjects were asked to evaluate the act under these different circumstances.

It was found that while all subjects evaluated the act as wrong when it was presented as a moral transgression, only half the subjects evaluated the act as wrong when it is performed under different circumstance which might justify it. More important, there was a positive correlation between the subjects' underlying assumptions about an event and their moral judgments of that event. For example, subjects who judged it morally acceptable to spank a child who misbehaved reasoned that spanking is an efficient way to teach a child to behave. Subjects who thought it morally wrong to spank a child for misbehaving reasoned that it was not efficient, or were uncertain about its efficiency.

Further, this study demonstrated that subjects' judgments about an act, based on underlying factual assumptions, will change when they accept hypothetically that the opposite fact is true. For example, subjects who judge spanking wrong because it is not an efficient teaching method will judge spanking as acceptable in the hypothetical case that it is shown to be efficient. Overall, these findings demonstrate that the assumptions that individuals make concerning the underlying facts involved in a social issue are implicated in their moral judgments about that issue.

Findings such as these are important in the consideration of cross-cultural research on moral development. The relevance of underlying factual assumptions, beliefs, and information about the natural order in the forming of moral judgments has been considered before (Asch, 1952; Duncker, 1939; Hatch, 1983). These studies indicate that in assessing the moral judgments and actions of individuals in different cultures, it is essential to take into account the underlying beliefs that bear on the judgments being made.

Cross-cultural differences found in social judgments cannot be accounted for through broad cultural stereotypes of individuals as having unitary social orientations. Different social orientations coexist in the reasoning of members of a culture. The cross-cultural differences found in social judgments are due to a number of factors, including differences in social organizations and institutions, and differences in assumptions and beliefs about the natural order. To effectively study the development of children's social reasoning and behavior, both within and across cultures, it is necessary to take into account the distinctions children make among basic domains of social knowledge.

## Recommended Readings

Damon, W. (1977). *The social world of the child.* San Francisco: Jossey-Bass.

Kohlberg, L. (1969). Stage and sequence: The cognitive-developmental approach to socialization. In D. A. Goslin (Ed.), *Handbook of socialization theory and research.* Chicago: Rand-McNally.

Piaget, J. (1965). *The moral judgment of the child.* New York: Free Press. (Originally published in 1932.)

Shweder, R., Mahapatra, M., & Miller, J. G. (1989). Culture and moral development. In J. Kagan and S. Lamb (Eds.), *The emergence of morality in young children.* Chicago: University of Chicago Press.

Turiel, E. (1983). *The development of social knowledge: Morality and convention.* Cambridge, England: Cambridge University Press.

Turiel, E., Killen, M., & Helwig, C. (1989). Morality: Its structure, functions, and vagaries. In Kagan, J. and Lamb, S. (Eds.), *The emergence of morality in young children.* Chicago: University of Chicago Press.

## References

Asch, S. E. (1952). *Social Psychology.* Englewood Cliffs, N.J.: Prentice-Hall.

Bennett, W. J. & Delattre, E. J. (1978). Moral education in the schools. *The Public Interest, 50,* 81-98.

Broughton, J. M. (1978). Development of concepts of self, mind, reality, and knowledge. In W. Damon (Ed.), *New directions for child development. Vol. 1: Social cognition.* San Francisco: Jossey-Bass.

Damon, W. (1977). *The Social World of the Child.* San Francisco: Jossey-Bass.

Davidson, P., Turiel, E., & Black, A. (1983). The effect of stimulus familiarity on the use of criteria and justifications in children's social reasoning. *British Journal of Developmental Psychology, 1,* 49-65.

Duncan, B. (1984). *The coordination of moral and social-conventional knowledge: A developmental analysis of children's understandings of multi-faceted social stories.* Unpublished doctoral dissertation, University of

California, Berkeley.

Duncker, K. (1939). Ethical relativity? (An inquiry into the psychology of ethics). *Mind, 48*, 39-53.

Dworkin, R. (1978). *Taking rights seriously.* Cambridge, Mass.: Harvard University Press.

Gewirth, A. (1978). *Reason and morality.* Chicago: University of Chicago Press.

Hatch, E. (1983). *Culture and morality: The Relativity of values in anthropology.* New York: Columbia University Press.

Hogan, R. (1975). Theoretical egocentrism and the problem of compliance. *American Psychologist, 30*, 533-539.

Kessen, W. (1979). The American child and other cultural inventions. *American Psychologist, 34*, 815-820.

Killen, M. (1990). Children's evaluations of morality in the context of peer, teacher-child, and familial relations. *Journal of Genetic Psychology, 151*, 395-410.

Laupa, M. (1991). Children's reasoning about three authority attributes: Adult status, knowledge, and social position. *Developmental Psychology, 27*, 321-329.

Laupa, M. (1994). "Who's in charge?" Preschool children's concepts of authority. *Early Childhood Research Quarterly, 9*, 1-17.

Laupa, M. and Turiel, E. (1986). Children's conceptions of peer and adult authority. *Child Development, 57*, 405-412.

Laupa, M. & Turiel, E. (1993). Children's concepts of authority and social contexts. *Journal of Educational Psychology, 85*, 191-197.

McClosky, H. & Brill, A. (1983). *Dimensions of tolerance: What Americans believe about civil liberties.* New York: Russell Sage Foundation.

Milgram. S. (1974). *Obedience to authority.* New York: Harper & Row.

Mills, C. W. (1956). *White collar: The American middle class.* New York: Oxford University Press.

Much, N. C. & Shweder, R. A. (1978). Speaking of rules: The analysis of culture in the breach. In W. Damon (Ed.), *New directions for child development: Moral development.* San Francisco: Jossey-Bass.

Nucci, L. (1981). The development of personal concepts: A domain distinct from moral or societal concepts. *Child Development, 52*, 114-121.

Nucci, L. & Nucci, M. (1982a). Children's social interactions in the context of moral and conventional transgressions. *Child Development, 53*, 403-412.

Nucci, L. & Nucci, M. (1982b). Children's responses to moral and social conventional transgressions in free-play settings. *Child Development, 53*, 1337-1342.

Nucci, L. & Turiel, E. (1978). Social interactions and the development of social concepts in preschool children. *Child Development, 49*, 400-407.

Nucci, L., Turiel, E. & Encarnacion-Gawrych, G. E. (1983). Children's social interactions and social concepts: Analyses of morality and convention in the Virgin Islands. *Journal of Cross-Cultural Psychology, 14*, 469-487.

Rawls, J. (1971). *A theory of justice.* Cambridge, Mass.: Harvard University Press.

Reisman, D., Glazer, N. & Denney, R. (1953). *The lonely crowd: A study of the changing American character.* New York: Doubleday & Co.

Sampson, E. E. (1977). Psychology and the American ideal. *Journal of Personality and Social Psychology, 35*, 767-782.

Shweder, R. (1986). Divergent rationalities. In D. W. Fiske and R. A. Shweder (Eds.), *Metatheory in social science: Pluralisms and subjectivities* (pp. 163-196). Chicago: University of Chicago Press.

Smetana, J. (1981). Preschool children's conceptions of moral and social rules. *Child Development, 52*, 1333-1336.

Smetana, J. (1988). Adolescents' and parents' conceptions of parental authority. *Child Development, 59*, 321-335.

Smetana, J. (1989). Adolescents' and parents' reasoning about actual family conflict. *Child Development, 60*, 5, 1052-1067.

Tisak, M. S. (1986). Children's conceptions of parental authority. *Child Development, 57*, 166-176.

Turiel, E. (1978). The development of concepts of social structure: Social convention. In J.

Glick and A. Clarke-Stewart (Eds.), *The development of social understanding.* New York: Gardner Press.

Turiel, E. (1983). *The development of social knowledge: Morality and convention.* Cambridge, England: Cambridge University Press.

Turiel, E., Hildebrandt, C. & Wainryb, C. (1990). *Inconsistency and consistency in reasoning about social issues.* Unpublished manuscript, University of California, Berkeley.

Turiel, E. & Smetana, J. (1984). Social knowledge and action: The coordination of domains. In W. M. Kurtines and J. L. Gewirtz (Eds.), *Morality, moral behavior, and moral development: Basic issues in theory and research.* New York: Wiley.

Wainryb, C. (1991). Understanding differences in moral judgments: The role of informational assumptions. *Child Development, 62,* 840-851.

Wainryb, C. (1993). The application of moral judgments to other cultures: Relativism and universality. *Child Development, 64,* 924-933.

Weston, D. & Turiel, E. (1980). Act-rule relations: Children's concepts of social rules. *Developmental Psychology, 16,* 417-424.

Whyte, W. H. (1956). *The organization man.* New York: Simon and Schuster.

Winch, P. (1972). *Ethics and action.* London: Routledge, Kegan Paul.

Wynne, E. A. (1986). The great tradition in education: Transmitting moral values. *Educational Leadership, 43,* 4-9.

*C h a p t e r* **18**

# Moral Balance:
# A Model for Moral Choice

*MORDECAI NISAN*
*The Hebrew University of Jerusalem*

## Abstract

This chapter presents a model of moral choice, as distinguished from moral judgment. This model is based on the theses of limited morality, moral balance, and balanced identity. The thesis of limited morality contends that people allow themselves some deviation from what they judge to be proper behavior. Such deviation does not stem from weakness of will or imply a departure from the moral community. The thesis of moral balance argues that people calculate a sort of moral balance for themselves on the basis of all their morally relevant actions within a given time span. When considering a deviation from proper behavior, they compare their current moral balance to a personal standard below which they do not allow themselves to descend. Finally, the thesis of balanced identity claims that, in choosing between conflicting value considerations, people select the option that enables them to maintain a satisfactory balance between all the components of their identity. Thus, on the basis of their current balance of identity components, people may allow a personal consideration to override a moral one.

## Moral Judgment and Moral Choice

*Moral judgment* refers to what is perceived as the right way to behave in a given situation. For instance, Kohlberg's (1984) famous "Heinz dilemma" considers whether or not it is permissible (or even obligatory) for a man to steal medication that can save his wife's life when he has no way to obtain the money needed to buy it. What would be morally right—to steal the medication and save her life, or to refrain from stealing regardless of the consequences? One's response to that question constitutes one's moral judgment.

It is commonly assumed that once someone has arrived at a moral judgment, he or she will decide to behave accordingly. After all, this is the nature of moral judgments; they obligate a person and override all other considerations. So, if, in your judgment, cheating on an examination is morally unacceptable, this is expected to lead to a decision not to cheat when actually taking an exam. Yet, all of us are surely aware of many instances where people make behavioral decisions that run contrary to their moral judgments. Judging an act as morally right does not guarantee that you will make the moral choice to behave accordingly.

Consider the following situation:

> Yossi is taking an exam which will determine whether or not he can continue his studies in his desired field, something which he deems very important for his future. There is an important question on the exam that Yossi cannot answer, but he clearly recalls that the key to the answer appears on the notes which he prepared while studying for the exam. These notes are in his pocket and he could easily take a peek without arousing the slightest suspicion. He would thereby be able to answer the question correctly.

Might not someone who believes it is morally wrong to cheat nevertheless find it permissible to do so under the circumstances described?

### When Moral Choice Diverges from Moral Judgment

In a study that examined the possibility of a discrepancy between moral judgment and moral choice, the above scenario was presented to third-year university students. They were subsequently asked what they thought would be the right thing to do (i.e., their moral judgment), whether or not they felt it would be all right for Yossi to cheat, and whether they themselves would decide to cheat if faced by the same situation (their moral choice). While 80 percent maintained that it would be wrong to cheat, a full 50 percent stated that they would choose to cheat nevertheless.

This apparent contradiction implies that judgment of proper behavior and the decision of how to behave are two distinct components in the moral decision-making process. In fact, they correspond to the second and third components in Rest's (1984; Chapter 14, this vol.) scheme, namely, moral judgment and moral choice. In contrast to the discrepancy between judgment and behavior, which has been widely investigated, that between moral judgment and moral choice has received little attention. The following section presents several commonly accepted explanations for the gap between judgment and behavior and examines their applicability to the revealed discrepancy between judgment and choice.

## Explanations for Behavior That Diverges from Morality

Over the centuries, scholars have sometimes ascribed immoral behavior to improper judgment. In ancient Greece, Socrates attributed it to mistaken or insufficient knowledge. Thousands of years later, Kohlberg, too, tended to explain it as the result of an incorrect judgment, in which the individual chooses a "quasi-obligation" (one which is only ostensibly valid) over the true obligation (Kohlberg & Candee, 1984). In the same vein, Sykes and Matza (1957) pointed out that people often "neutralize" the transgression, justifying the improper act in some manner (e.g., when they view tax evasion as merely a matter of keeping what belongs to them). All of the above explanations, however, are inappropriate in the case cited above (and many other real-life situations, as well). In our example, the person making the judgment knew and acknowledged that cheating is wrong. Nevertheless, the decision to cheat was made.

Another common explanation of immoral behavior is in terms of weakness of will. According to this argument, the individual's actions are directed by an uncontrollable urge, against his or her will. Such an explanation does not hold for the cases we are dealing with. Our subjects made considered decisions to act in opposition to their moral judgment; their responses can hardly be ascribed to an irresistible passion.

Other cases of immoral behavior are attributed to a weak conscience, signifying that the transgressor does not mind excluding himself or herself from the moral community. Yet, again, this explanation does not apply to our example. People who do not care whether or not they are moral are *always* willing to transgress in the absence of fear of punishment, and they do not feel guilty about such action. Our subjects, in contrast, expressed feelings of discomfort that accompanied their decision to cheat. Further, they maintained that they would not be willing to cheat, or to otherwise deviate, under all circumstances, even if there was no chance of being detected. All of this suggests that their moral standing is important to them. Indeed, day-to-day observations, biographies, and classical literature abound with cases of individuals who knowingly deviate from what is morally considered correct without feeling that their actions cause them to be branded as "immoral." They continue to see themselves as moral people and wish to maintain their moral status.

Our example thus suggests a type of moral deviation that cannot be attributed to lack of knowledge, mistaken judgment, weakness of will, or abandonment of morality. Reference is to transgressions made deliberately and voluntarily without any indication that the individual has withdrawn from the moral community. Included in this category are many common everyday deviations, especially in the sphere of "small sins." I have used the concept of "limited morality" to describe and explain this type of transgression.

## Limited Morality

### Deviation from a Recognized Moral Imperative

Based on everyday observations and on the findings of empirical studies, I have suggested (Nisan, 1985) that people (although probably not all people and not in all cultures) who accept the validity and force of moral imperatives do not *always* demand proper moral action of themselves. At certain times and under certain circumstances, they allow themselves to deviate to a certain degree. Moral perfection is generally not required, either of oneself or of others. Yet, a moral line is usually drawn beyond which one does not allow oneself to descend. This line, which is personal and rather flexible, allows the individual to view himself or herself as a moral person, and it serves as a barrier against unlimited transgressions.

This description of limited morality underscores its inherent contradiction: If we acknowledge the moral imperative and consider ourselves members of the moral community, how can we allow ourselves to deviate? Moral judgments are considered unconditionally obligatory and overriding all other types of considerations. These characteristics of morality (Frankena, 1973) have not been invented by philosophers; they are actual psychological phenomena. Even young children distinguish between moral demands, perceived as unconditionally obligatory; weaker or contingent types of obligations (values and social conventions, respectively) (Nisan, 1988; Turiel, 1979); and still other types of behavior, which do not involve any obligation, but rather are open to personal preference (Nucci, 1981). In light of this, how can we understand a conscious decision to act against one's own moral judgment without relinquishing one's standing in the moral community? A brief look at the question of moral motivation may be of help in this respect. We will see that the very factor which explains why people behave in accordance with their moral judgment can also explain why they sometimes allow themselves to deviate from that judgment.

### Moral Identity

When a person makes a moral judgment, he or she is guided by a desire to arrive at the truth, at the single right judgment that any reflective individual would make with respect to the dilemma at hand. To borrow a well-known expression of Piaget's (1965), moral judgment reflects the "logic of action." Therefore, it is not expected to be affected by personal interests and conditions. This, however, raises the question of why anyone would choose to behave according to this "objective" judgment if it disregards his or her personal considerations and interest.

Essentially, this is the major question posed by moral psychology. To rephrase it: What motivates an individual to act in opposition to such basic principles of behavior as maximization of pleasure or utility? Varied answers have been offered to that question by different psychological approaches to morality. One, on which the concept of limited morality is based, refers to maintenance of one's moral identity (Blasi, 1984). According to this approach, one of the major reasons that people choose to behave in accordance with their moral judgment is that they find it imperative to perceive themselves as moral people, i.e., to maintain their moral identity.

The consideration of maintaining one's moral identity does not generally arise in response to a direct question, such as "Why don't you cheat?" A typical answer would be "because it is bad," implying "I don't want to be bad." This consideration does emerge, however, from the explanations given by our subjects for deciding to cheat, even though they thought cheating was wrong (with respect to the dilemma presented above). Such responses as: "I thought I could afford to do this" and "This doesn't make me so bad" suggest that an important consideration in making the choice was the need to maintain a perception of the self as a "good" person. At the same time, statements of this sort imply that, while we do not allow ourselves just any deviation, there is a degree of latitude in choice based on our evaluation of our moral status. Thus, beyond a judgment of the act as improper, we consider whether or not we can allow ourselves, under the present circumstances (which are everchanging), to perform the act. Accordingly, the principle underlying moral choice can be said to revolve around the following question: Will the intended "improper" behavior hurt my self-image as a moral person to an unacceptable degree, or does it constitute a "tolerable" blow that my moral identity can withstand? Or, to put it more simply: If I were to perform this act, would I still be a good enough person? Would I remain the type of person I want to be?

From this perspective, an individual's identity encompasses several components or characteristics that he or she perceives to constitute his or her very being. These may be innate, such as gender, or acquired, such as a love of classical music; they may be beyond one's control, such as being born into a particular family, or a matter of choice, such as acting morally or otherwise. We perceive the components of our identity as essential to our wholeness as a person. In their absence, we would not be the same person; we would not be ourselves. Of these components, morality is central; we perceive our morality as a necessary and significant aspect of who we are. This perception is reflected in the findings of a study in which we asked adults the extent to which they felt similar to or different from someone who resembles them in every aspect, with one exception—with regard to morality, gender, external appearance, ideology, or nationality. Responses indicated that subjects felt most different from their imaginary counterpart when he or she was described as immoral.

Several psychological theories (e.g., Maslow, 1968; Stryker, 1987) suggest that individuals strive to maintain, preserve, and give expression to their identity components. It is my contention that this tendency is associated with a "sense of the desirable," which brings on a perception of what one ought to do. One feels that it is desirable and, therefore, a sort of duty, to be true to oneself and to express what one considers essential to the self (Nisan, 1993). This tendency constitutes an important (if not the sole) motivational factor for moral behavior. Moral behavior preserves and affirms, while immoral behavior denies and betrays one's personal identity.

Judgments made from the perspective of moral identity generate evaluations which differ significantly from the impersonal moral judgment. As mentioned earlier, a moral judgment relates to an act, and although the seriousness of moral transgressions may vary, in the final analysis, they are judged as either "right" or "wrong." In contrast, evaluation of a considered behavior in terms of its effect on one's moral identity is made along a continuum, ranging from very good behavior (which confirms and strengthens one's moral identity) to very bad behavior (which challenges and may even seriously damage that identity). Whereas a dichotomous evaluation forces the individual to take a clear stand, evaluation along a continuum allows for flexibility. An ideal is aspired towards, but it is not necessarily obligatory; people are more concerned with not falling too short of the ideal than they are with actually attaining it. They allow themselves a certain moral deviation, provided that their moral identity remains "satisfactory." This returns us to the thesis of "limited morality."

## Limited Morality, Supererogation, and Bounded Rationally

The thesis of limited morality may be regarded as an extension of the concept of supererogation into the sphere of transgression. Supererogation refers to good deeds which are beyond the call of duty; these are perceived as commendable but non-obligatory. People who perform such acts are considered "good," but those who do not are not necessarily "bad." They may tell themselves: "I know that it is morally desirable to perform these acts, but I am not and do not aspire to be righteous." In the context of supererogation, this is an acceptable statement, for no clear boundary exists, for example, between helping others and self-sacrifice, and people are not actually expected to do the latter. The examples we have cited above suggest that similar considerations apply in the case of non-performance of clearly defined obligations as well as commission of prohibited acts. Here, too, people allow themselves to deviate from the absolute ideal; indeed, they may perceive behavior that is in keeping with moral ideals as analogous to self-sacrifice.

The concept of limited morality also corresponds in certain respects with that of Simon's (1957) "bounded rationality." Simon posited that our limited capacity for information processing may lead us to adopt a principle of "satisficing," in lieu of the "rational" principle of maximizing utility. In such cases, people prefer an "acceptable" alternative, which satisfies their minimal requirement, to a search for the best option.

However, there is an important difference between *bounded rationality* and *limited morality*: in the former case, the concession is anchored in cognitive shortcomings, whereas in the latter, it is anchored in motivational reasons. The right to deviate from ideal behavior seems to be associated with a widely accepted view of human nature, at least in Western society. (In the field of psychology, this view is most prominently represented by the Freudian approach.) According to this perspective, the human being is the arena of a struggle between flesh and spirit, instinct and reason, egoistic and moral inclinations. As the opposing forces are an inherent part of human nature, the struggle is inevitable and perpetual. It therefore follows that it is impossible for people to be morally perfect; everyone surrenders to weaknesses, from time to time. A good person, therefore, is not necessarily perfect (in fact such a person may be suspect), but rather one who preserves a reasonable "moral balance." Such a conception is implicitly accepted by society as normative: certain transgressions which would be morally rejected are thus occasionally forgiven.

This view is not considered contradictory, nor is there any indication that the norms are judged as invalid. Even if we are willing to forgive certain transgressions and sins, we are not prepared to do so if they are committed continuously. Religious precepts, literary works and popular proverbs acknowledge the inevitability of occasional concessions, and distinguish between major and minor transgressions. Courts of justice also consider the seriousness of violations; some may be forgiven or only lightly punished, even if they are deliberate. This suggests that the idea of "acceptable" concessions, implicit in the concept of limited morality, is transferred through direct socialization. Parents may instill in their children the conviction that they must behave morally but do not have to be absolutely virtuous—that it is commendable to be "saintly," but quite acceptable to be "human."

## Moral Balance

In the previous section, I suggested that moral choice is guided by the will to maintain an acceptable level of moral identity. We feel obligated to behave properly, yet allow ourselves room for deviations that do not seriously damage our moral identity. This thesis raises several interrelated questions that I shall presently address: What constitutes "serious damage"? How do we calculate our moral standing? What determines the limits beyond which we do not allow ourselves to deviate?

## *The Severity of the Violation*

Notwithstanding the dichotomous nature of moral judgment, there is also a quantitative dimension according to which we evaluate the extent of an act's "badness" or "goodness." At one end of this continuum lies behavior that is perceived to be so serious as to be outside the range of actions that we permit ourselves within the framework of limited morality. Actions that cause immediate and irrevocable damage to others (such as murder) fall in this category, as do behaviors that arouse tremendous emotion (such as betrayal of a dear friend). These transgressions are considered unthinkable; the damage they would cause to our moral identities is so great that we consider them solely in dichotomous terms, as bad and prohibited, rather than good and permitted. At the other end of the continuum lie behaviors which, though judged as wrong, are perceived as causing little damage to our moral identity (such as telling a white lie). It is easy to commit such transgressions, especially when considerable personal interest is involved.

Children and adults alike find it quite natural to judge transgressions by their severity, and there is considerable consensus as to the criteria of evaluation. Some of these criteria are "objective"; they measure such dimensions of the act as the extent of damage caused, or the degree of deviation from the law or from justice. Subjects, who were asked to describe transgressions they committed intentionally and explain why they allowed themselves to do so, mentioned such "light" misbehaviors as "sneaking into a show without taking anybody's seat" (little damage) or "smuggling a taxable item which is not worth much more than what one is allowed to bring in" (a minor deviation from the rules, as they perceived it).

In addition, there are "subjective" factors which influence how serious we perceive the transgression to be. These relate to the nature and intensity of the affect aroused by the act; this affect is a result of socialization regarding the act's seriousness. A particularly interesting subjective factor is the degree of temptation aroused by the situation and the effort required to resist it. Children and adolescents have been found to evaluate a transgression resulting from a strong temptation as less serious than one committed when the temptation was not very strong (Nisan, 1979). Thus, when we are faced with a strong temptation, we tend to believe that succumbing to it is less serious than performing the very same act when the temptation is weaker. According to the theory of limited morality, this makes it easier to commit the transgression. Another factor worth mentioning is the perceived prevalence of a prohibited act. The more prevalent a transgression, the less serious it is perceived to be. High prevalence is sometimes viewed as a sign of strong temptation. Moreover, it raises a question regarding the justice of the demand to refrain from the transgression: If others allow themselves to cheat on an exam, then I, too, am justified in doing so *occasionally*; otherwise, I will be at a disadvantage.

## A Personal History of Past Actions

While the severity of a violation seems to be an important factor determining the boundaries of limited morality, it is only a partial answer. It does not sufficiently explain the inconsistency of moral choice with regard to the very same acts in different situations (apparently with the same degree of severity). For instance, subjects indicated that they restricted themselves regarding the frequency of certain allowable transgressions (such as private phone calls at work, at the company's expense). As one subject, who recalled copying someone else's homework, said: "You can do it once, maybe twice in a row, but if you do it more than that, then you are a cheat." These statements imply that moral choice is determined in the context of a chain of events (past behavior and, in a certain sense, future behavior as well), rather than in terms of an isolated incident. When deciding whether or not to transgress, we assess the damage to our moral identity not only in terms of the severity of the deed, but also with respect to the entire history of our actions up to the present, as well as future acts to which we have committed ourselves.

It is therefore my contention that individuals calculate a sort of moral balance for themselves, quantitatively weighing their morally relevant commissions and omissions within a given time span. According to this Moral Balance model (Nisan, 1990), we compare our moral balance to our personal "level of acceptable morality"—a level below which we will not allow ourselves to descend. This level is usually lower than the ideal moral judgment, according to which we judge the rightness or wrongness of actions. We calculate our moral balance on the basis of our recent moral behavior: "good" deeds raise the balance and "bad" actions lower it. The number and weight of deeds are also taken into consideration. In an effort to preserve our moral identity, we attempt to maintain our moral balance and even aspire to a higher one.

## Applying the Model to Daily Experience

The Moral Balance model is clearly applicable to everyday situations. It can explain, for example, the commission or omission of acts of voluntary helping. Though well aware of the praiseworthiness of helping behavior, we do not spend all our free time helping others. Rather, feelings of obligation to aid someone in a specific situation appear to be a function of our own perceptions, be they clear or vague, of the extent of help we have already offered (the time span involved is not clear). Each of us can be said to employ a sort of "helping balance sheet," so as to maintain our identity as a considerate, helpful person. This thesis seems to be applicable not only to helping behavior, but also to the domain of duties. Thus, when deciding whether or not to allow ourselves to cheat on an exam, we examine our past behavior and weigh the consequences of the action in terms of its cumulative effect on our identity as an honest person.

An interesting question is whether there is one general moral balance, across positive and negative behaviors and across different domains (e.g., honesty in business, helping others, fidelity to a friend), or whether there are compartmentalized moral balances for each. Findings in our research tend to support the former argument, although they have not discounted the latter.

## Empirical Support for the Model

### Qualitative Data

The claims raised by the Moral Balance model have been supported by studies of people of various ages, by means of personal interviews and anonymous questionnaires comprising open-ended and structured items (Nisan, 1991). Subjects were asked about transgressions they had committed or about hypothetical dilemmas and transgressions, their evaluations of these transgressions, and their feelings afterwards. In addition, a number of specific questions were posed with respect to antecedents and consequences of the transgressions.

The results corroborated the model's claims. They suggested, for instance, that there is an ideal moral judgment which we perceive as impersonal and obligating, and that we permit ourselves to commit limited moral deviations as a form of compromise with our personal interests, recognizing that they are "wrong." The findings also supported the argument that we strive to keep our moral balance, maintaining a level of acceptable morality below which we do not wish to descend. They suggested that a considerable reduction in that balance leads to an uncomfortable feeling, one which is connected with an evaluation of our present, *temporary* state, rather than with the more stable aspect of self-evaluation. That is, after committing a transgression, we do not define ourselves as evil, but rather perceive ourselves as being in a "bad" situation—of having a low moral balance.

### Quantitative Data

Several controlled studies were conducted to complement the qualitative data; these, too, tended to support the claims raised by the Moral Balance model. Two of these studies (Nisan & Horenzcys, 1989) investigated one of the model's major arguments—that perceived moral balance will affect moral choice, allowing or disallowing deviation from behavior perceived as "right." The more "positive" that balance, the more willing we will be to allow ourselves to deviate, as the danger to our moral identity will be small. Similarly, the more "positive" another's moral balance is perceived to be, the more we are willing to allow that person to deviate.

While this hypothesis seems reasonable with respect to normative judgments, in the sense of the extent to which we are willing to allow (and forgive) a certain deviation, it appears to be implausible regarding descriptive judgments (which predict behavior). People tend to attribute the behavior of others to stable traits (Ross, 1977), and therefore tend to believe that a person will continue to behave as he or she has been behaving all along.

In these controlled studies, subjects were presented with descriptions of people with obviously divergent moral balances, expressed in one of two ways: (1) by characterizing the modal behavior of the protagonist (good, ordinary or bad), assuming that the better that behavior, the higher his or her moral balance is perceived to be; or (2) by describing a moral or immoral act recently committed by the protagonist, assuming that, being the sole information given, it would affect the perceived level of the protagonist's moral balance. We measured the subject's willingness to allow deviation from the proper course of action in several different manners. In the first study, subjects were asked which of two protagonists they would be more willing to allow to transgress, and who *ought* to feel more guilty following the action. We also requested reasons for their answers. In the second study, we asked for evaluations of the seriousness of given deviations. In both studies, subjects were also asked to make descriptive judgments, i.e., to predict how protagonists would act.

The findings revealed that predictions of the behavior of others (descriptive judgments) followed the trait model, whereas all normative judgments, as well as descriptive judgments of one's own behavior, were in keeping with the Moral Balance model. On the whole, subjects predicted that the "bad" person would be more likely to transgress and that the "good" person would feel guiltier, in keeping with the trait model. Guilt feelings are apparently perceived as a part of the actor's stable traits; someone who is accustomed to evil behavior lacks guilt, while someone who usually does not transgress is perceived as feeling guilty after committing a bad action. In contrast to these descriptive judgments, subjects made normative judgments that tended to follow the Moral Balance model. They were more inclined to allow transgressions to a "good" person, who is not accustomed to doing bad deeds and generally helps others, than to an "ordinary" or "bad" person. Similarly, they thought the "bad" person *should* feel guiltier and the "good" person less guilty than the "ordinary" person. These results held both with respect to not helping and with respect to stealing, although the effect was stronger in the former case. The model thus seems more suited to supererogatory behavior than it does to avoidance of transgressions, yet it applies to—and predicts—the latter type of behavior as well. The findings of this study were corroborated by those of the second study: transgressions were judged as less serious when committed by a protagonist who had recently acted morally than when committed by one who had recently behaved badly, regardless of whether the protagonist was the self or another person.

The reasons that subjects gave for their responses provided added support for the model. The large majority of reasons for allowing the good person (rather than the bad or ordinary ones) to commit the transgression reflected considerations of the actor's moral balance (e.g., "As David is a good person . . . in this particular case you can allow him . . ."; "Yaacov helps only a little and has to start helping"). As for the relatively few respondents who allowed the bad person (rather than the good one) to misbehave, the reason most frequently given was "so as not to corrupt the good person." This response points to the perceived importance of maintaining a person's virtue, even if this contradicts considerations of fairness.

In short, the above studies directly support the Moral Balance model. They suggest that, in making moral choices and evaluations, we take into account previous morally relevant behaviors. We consider the actor's level of moral balance, which is presumably higher after doing a good deed than after transgressing. Note that the effect of past behaviors was not to "neutralize" the improper actions, as Sykes and Matza (1957) have suggested; rather, the transgressions were clearly seen as "wrong." Nonetheless, they were allowed, presumably because they did not cause the actor to feel that he or she was falling below his or her accepted level of morality.

### Testing the Model in Behavioral Terms

The research outlined above deals with moral evaluations; its implications for moral behavior are unclear (Blasi, 1980). Indeed, the Moral Balance model itself deals with moral decision-making, rather than actual behavior. Nevertheless, we expect considerations of moral balance to affect behavior; in fact, this is what gives the model its value. Hence, there is a need for behavioral examination of the model. While existing empirical research gives it partial support, showing that transgression leads to altruistic behavior (Rosenhan et al., 1981), other aspects of the model still require investigation; e.g., that people are less willing to transgress following immoral behavior and more willing following positive moral behavior.

## Extending the Model: The Resolution of Conflict between Identity Components

### The Right to Prefer the Non-moral

Employing the concepts of limited morality and moral balance, I have attempted to explain pre-planned limited deviations from the moral ideal in favor of personal interest. These deviations were described as concessions reflecting an acknowledgment of human imperfection. In this section, I introduce another type of concession, which stems from perception of a "right" to choose the non-moral (i.e., the personal consideration) over the moral (in a narrow sense, referring to interpersonal rights and obligations). This type of concession, which stems from reasoned deliberation, may seem less disturbing than relinquishment of the moral owing to acknowledgement of human imperfection. Yet, the very reasoning underlying the concession makes it more disturbing; one wonders if, in the framework of our understanding of morality, it is possible to justify subordination of the moral to the personal. What type of personal consideration could be perceived so worthy as to be preferred to the moral one?

This problem has received attention in recent philosophical literature. Williams (1981) raised it with respect to the Gauguin Dilemma, which, to facilitate our discussion, may be outlined as follows: How are we to view the decision made by the artist, Gauguin, to abandon his wife and children in order to actualize his creative talent in Tahiti? Or, to rephrase the question: How do we judge Gauguin's decision to place his personal consideration of self-actualization above his moral obligation to his family?

Moral conflicts are frequently conflicts between identity components or identity values, in the sense discussed above. For instance, the Gauguin Dilemma may be described as a conflict between two of his identity components, the moral and the creative. For the sake of argument, let us assume that the moral value was a central part of Gauguin's personal identity and, therefore, abandonment of his family (which he perceived as immoral behavior) would constitute denial of an essential component of his being. Yet, artistic creation was also a central aspect of his identity, one that was stifled by remaining with his family. In this respect, discussing the personal consideration exemplified by the Gauguin Dilemma, I shall borrow the concept of "personal project" introduced by Williams (1981). The reference is to a unique type of personal consideration, one which is so important to the individual that it can be considered part of his or her identity. The conflict he faced was whether to preserve the moral value to the detriment of the creativity value, or to relinquish the former in favor of the latter. Another example is that of a scientist who must decide between taking advantage of a highly anticipated opportunity to test his theory during a sabbatical at a distant institution, or remaining with his aged and ill parents, fulfilling his filial duties as an only child. Here, too, the conflict entails a choice between two values which are central components of one's identity.

## *The Principle of Balanced Identity*

The accepted approach to such dilemmas is that values are arranged according to a hierarchy which serves as a basis for the individual's choice (e.g., Rokeach, 1973). Whenever a moral consideration is involved in a conflict, it is expected (according to accepted philosophical assumptions) to override any non-moral ones. While this indeed seems to be true of decontextualized moral judgment, it is not necessarily true of moral choice, which is guided by a different principle. Instead, I propose (Nisan, 1993) that the conflict between two or more identity values is decided on the basis of the "balanced identity" principle. That is, we are apt to choose the alternative that leads to an optimal state of balance between all our identity components.

When two values relating to what ought to be done conflict with one another, preference of one consideration is tantamount to denial of the other. That aspect of one's identity which is connected with the rejected consideration is consequently harmed. In the above case of the scientist, a decision to take his sabbatical will violate the moral consideration of honoring one's parents, an important component of his identity. On the other hand, a decision to stay with his parents denies the value consideration of actualizing his personal project, which is also an important aspect of his identity. It is my contention that he will choose the alternative which he perceives as least harming the general balance of his current personal identity. That is, the choice is not made by evaluating and comparing the alternative actions (which is supposed to take place at the stage of judgment); rather, it is arrived at on the basis of the current implications of those alternatives with respect to the individual's personal identity.

This argument assumes that there is a difference between the behavior's significance to the identity of the actor and its objective evaluation. The former is related to the unique structure of the individual's identity (what he or she considers more and less important), as well as to the current "balances" of that identity (the extent to which components have been given expression or denied in a given time span). This leads to the hypothesis that someone who has recently given expression to a certain identity component will be more likely to focus on another component that has not yet been emphasized. It also suggests that an identity component which carries more weight or meaning for the individual will be preferred to one which has less personal significance (even if the former is a non-moral consideration and the latter is a moral one).

## Testing the Hypotheses

Several studies were conducted in order to test the above hypotheses. In one, university students were presented with three dilemmas, each of which involved a conflict between two values. The first was between a moral consideration and a consideration of self-actualization (the scientist's dilemma outlined above). The second dilemma was between a national consideration (working in research of importance to the country) and a consideration of self-actualization (acceptance of an offer to work at a prestigious university). The third dilemma was between a moral and a national consideration (along lines similar to the above). These situations were presented in two versions; in each, a different one of the two conflicting values had been given expression recently. For example, one version stated: "Up to now, Dr. Barnea had devoted a lot of time to taking care of his parents at the expense of his scientific work." The other one stated: "Up to now, Dr. Barnea had devoted a lot of time to his scientific work at the expense of his parents' care."

A large number of responses indicated a clear inclination to choose according to the balanced identity principle. That is to say, if the scientist had focused on Value "X" up to a given point in time, there was a tendency to advise him to choose Value "Y." Some of the explanations offered by respondents were explicitly based on this principle: "Up to this point, [the scientist] has mainly fulfilled obligations towards his parents. Now he deserves to fulfill an obligation to himself." Along these lines, the balanced identity principle appears to explain cases in which people choose nonmoral over moral considerations—where they believe that selecting the moral alternative would have harmed their overall identity to a greater extent.

## Conclusions

This chapter has presented a model of moral choice—the choice of whether or not to commit an act that one has already judged as morally improper. In this context, I have introduced the principles of limited morality and moral balance, which contend that people may intentionally deviate from what they judge to be proper behavior, as long as they maintain what they perceive to be an "acceptable" level of morality. Several aspects of this conceptual framework are likely to arouse criticism from various quarters—I shall address two possible criticisms.

Some might argue that the "right" to deviate without considering ourselves bad is a contradiction in terms. Indeed, the concept of limited morality, whereby moral considerations are perceived as categorically valid in an ideal sense, yet not in a practical one, seems to conflict with an intuitive interpretation of the moral imperative. Furthermore, the application of an economic model of "balance" to behavior in the moral domain seems difficult to accept. Nonetheless, everyday life is full of instances in which moral deviations are executed intentionally—deviations that are not committed out of weakness, nor do they exclude the actor from the moral community. While people aspire to maintain their moral identity, they do not require themselves to be perfect saints. The right to deviate, though posing a real conceptual dilemma, seems to be one of the paradoxes that we learn to live with and come to view as an expression of human imperfection and an inability to completely avoid contradiction. Further, no matter how inappropriate the economic concept of balance might first appear with regard to the moral domain, it nevertheless seems to be inherent in Western perceptions of morality. How else could one explain the idea of extreme versus insignificant deviations, of lofty good deeds versus lesser ones, of heavy guilt versus slight uneasiness, of a more and a less moral person, of weighing the good and bad on Judgment Day?

The model of moral choice presented here is also challenged by the Slippery Slope thesis, which contends that small moral deviations open the way for more and greater deviations. The Moral Balance model suggests the very opposite—that committing a transgression may actually lead the individual to avoid a future deviation in order to maintain his or her moral balance. Notwithstanding the empirical basis for the Slippery Slope approach under certain circumstances, my own empirical studies, qualitative and controlled experimental research alike, suggest that it is the Moral Balance model that helps us to better understand the overall process of moral decision-making, to formulate hypotheses, and to predict moral choice and behavior. Indeed, the Slippery Slope thesis seems to be refuted by daily observations of transgressions that do not lead to unlimited slippage.

This is not to suggest that the principle of moral balance explains every aspect of moral choice. Our findings clearly indicated that moral choice is affected by several factors, some of which work in the opposite direction of that predicted by moral balance. Central among these is the tendency to strive to raise one's moral balance, not merely maintain it. This tendency impels the individual to raise his or her "level of accepted morality" and thus his or her moral balance ("If I can keep myself from cheating this one time, I'll continue to do so in the future and will therefore preserve my high personal standards"). Another factor is the apprehension that a small deviation will inevitably lead to greater ones (the Slippery Slope thesis). This feeling of apprehension may lead an individual to refrain from taking advantage of his or her allowance to deviate ("I would have cheated, but I'm afraid that if I cheat once, I will lose all restraint").

I believe that the effect of these tendencies is limited, and the question to be addressed is when their effect is likely to override that of moral balance. One possibility is that there are consistent individual differences in terms of the extent to which one follows the Moral Balance model, so that some people tend to act more in accordance with it, while others are apt to act more in accordance with the other tendencies. My empirical research, however, failed to reveal consistent individual differences in that regard. Therefore, it would seem advantageous to investigate the conditions under which the Moral Balance model becomes more dominant than others.

Without purporting to offer an inclusive answer to this question, I would like to introduce two conditions suggested by my studies. The first relates to the nature of the intended act; the second, to the nature of the actor's personal consideration. Certain acts seem to lend themselves to the balance model more than others—i.e., those which are not very serious and those which are perceived as part of a behavioral sequence, so that deviation can be compensated for later on. This, indeed, is how many of my subjects appear to have considered the dilemmas of copying part of a university paper, arguing that they would allow themselves the deviation once, but not twice. This is also how one of my subjects perceived his recalled misbehavior (infidelity to his girlfriend), which he explained as "a rare exception" in his model "honest friendship." Of course, the question of what causes a given act to be perceived as part of a behavioral sequence remains open.

The second condition relates to the nature of the competing personal consideration. The findings of my studies suggest that individuals are more likely to follow the Moral Balance model when they perceive the personal consideration to be highly meaningful to themselves. Thus, subjects were more willing to allow cheating in order to join an astronomy club when it was motivated by a real interest in astronomy than when motivated by the desire to join friends in the club. Along these lines, I contend that considerations of high personal significance are those related to one's identity—interests which the individual perceives as essential and necessary to his or her perception of self. Such interests may include personal projects comprising "lofty" considerations, such as self-actualization (the Gauguin Dilemma), which make a person unique and constitute an essential identity component. With due caution, I further posit that they may also include "lower" and temporary considerations, such as those related to immediate gratification, when these are of great importance to the individual (e.g., when he or she views the issue as expressing or denying his or her personal autonomy). Indeed, it is only because of the central importance of such considerations that we begin to consider the possibility of "giving in" to them. In contrast, we are not inclined to allow ourselves deviations that lack primary personal importance, even though they entail less severe transgressions.

This leads to what I have termed the principle of "balanced identity," according to which the desire to maintain one's moral balance is part of a more general need to preserve one's personal identity. While the moral component of that identity plays a central role, it may be challenged by other identity components. Hence, when a moral choice involves a conflict between essential identity components—e.g., between the personal value of self-actualization and the moral value of duty to one's parents—people consider their current identity balance. In an attempt to maintain a balanced identity, personal considerations may outweigh moral ones.

## Recommended Readings

Blasi, A. (1984). Moral identity: Its role in moral functioning. In W. M. Kurtines & J. L. Gewirtz (Eds.), *Morality, moral behavior and moral development* (pp. 128-139). New York: Wiley.

Frankfurt, H. (1982). What we care about. *Synthese, 53,* 257-272.

March, J. G. (1978). Bounded rationality, ambiguity and the engineering of choice. *The Bell Journal of Economics, 9,* 587-608.

Nisan, M. (1985). Limited morality: A concept and its educational implications. In M. W. Berkowitz and F. Oser (Eds.), *Moral education: Theory and application.* Hillsdale, NJ: Lawrence Erlbaum.

Nisan, M. (1990). Moral balance: A model of how people arrive at moral decisions. In T. Wren (Ed.), *The moral domain.* Cambridge, Mass.: M. I. T. Press.

Williams, B. (1981). Moral luck. In *Moral luck* (pp. 20-39). New York: Cambridge University Press.

## References

Blasi, A. (1980). Bridging moral cognition and moral action: A critical review of the literature. *Psychological Bulletin, 88,* 1-45.

Blasi, A. (1984). Moral identity: Its role in moral functioning. In W. M. Kurtines & J. L. Gewirtz (Eds.), *Morality, moral behavior and moral development* (pp. 128-139). New York: Wiley.

Frankena, W. A (1973). *Ethics*. Englewood, N.J.: Prentice-Hall.

Kohlberg, L., & Candee, D. (1984). The relationship of moral judgment to moral action. In L. Kohlberg (Ed.), *The psychology of moral development*, New York: Harper & Row.

Maslow, A. (1968). *Toward a psychology of being*, 2nd edition. New York: Van Nostrand.

Nisan, M. (1979). Judgments of seriousness of transgressions. Unpublished manuscript, School of Education, The Hebrew University of Jerusalem.

Nisan, M. (1985). Limited morality: A concept and its educational implications. In M. W. Berkowitz and F. Oser (Eds.), *Moral education: Theory and application* (pp. 403-420). Hillsdale, NJ: Lawrence Erlbaum Associates.

Nisan, M. (1988). The child as a philosopher of values: Development of a distinct perception of values in childhood. *Journal of Moral Education, 17,* 8-18.

Nisan, M. (1990). Moral balance: A model of how people arrive at moral decisions. In T. Wren (Ed.), *The moral domain*. Cambridge, Mass.: M.I.T. Press.

Nisan, M. (1991). The moral balance model: Theory and research extending our understanding of moral choice and deviation. In W. M. Kurtines and J. L. Gewirtz (Eds.), *Handbook of moral behavior and development. Vol. 3: Application* (pp. 213-249). Hillsdale, NJ: Lawrence Erlbaum Associates.

Nisan, M. (1993). Balanced identity: Morality and other identity values. In G. G. Noam and T. E. Wren (Eds.), *The moral self* (pp. 239-266). Cambridge, MA: M.I.T. Press.

Nisan, M. & Horenczvk, G. (1989). Moral balance: The effect of prior behavior on decision in moral conflict. *British Journal of Social Psychology, 29,* 29-42.

Nucci, L. (1981). Conceptions of personal issues: A domain distinct from moral or social concepts. *Child Development, 52,* 114-121.

Piaget, J. (1965). *Moral judgment of the child* (M. Gabain, Trans.). New York: Free Press. (Original work published 1932).

Rest, J. (1984). The major components of morality. In W. M. Kurtines & J. L. Gewirtz (Eds.), *Morality, moral behavior, and moral development* (pp. 24-38). New York: Wiley.

Rokeach, M. (1973). *The nature of human values*. New York: The Free Press.

Rosenhan, D. L., Salovev, P., Karvlowski, J., & Hargi, K. (1981). Emotion and altruism. In J. P. Rushton & R. M. Sorrentino (Eds.), *Altruism and helping behavior* (pp. 233-248). Hillsdale, NJ: Lawrence Erlbaum.

Ross, L. (1977). The intuitive psychologist and his shortcomings: Distortions in the attribution process. In L. Berkowitz (Ed.), *Advances in experimental social psychology*, (Vol. 10, pp. 173-220). New York: Academic Press.

Simon, H. (1957). *Models of man*. New York: Wiley.

Stryker, S. (1987). Identity theory: Developments and extensions. In K. Yardley and T. Honess (Eds.), *Self and identity: Psychosocial perspectives* (pp. 89-103). Chichester: Wiley.

Sykes, G.M. & Matza F. (1957). Techniques of neutralization: A theory of delinquency. *American Sociological Review, 22,* 664-670.

Turiel, E. (1979). Distinct conceptual and developmental domains: Social conventions and morality. In H.E. Howe & C.B. Keasey (Eds.), *Nebraska Symposium on Motivation, 1977: Social cognitive development, 25,* pp. 77-116. Lincoln, NE: University of Nebraska.

Williams, B. (1981). *Moral luck*. Cambridge: Cambridge University Press.

# *Part* VI

# *New Directions in Research on Moral Development*

## *Prologue*

The phenomenal growth that has taken place over the past several decades in the moral development field has been fueled not only by the emergence of integrative perspectives, but also by the emergence of new programs of research, which help to push forward the leading edge of knowledge in the field and point to new directions for growth and evolution. The chapters in the final part of this book do not exhaust the range of new perspectives that have begun to emerge, but they do illustrate the creativity, drive, energy, and excitement that is associated with the emergence of new perspectives and programs of research. The two chapters in this part describe "new" programs of research that represent efforts to expand our understanding of the process of moral development by identifying new areas of theoretical and practical significance. More specifically, Chapter 19 moves into an area that has been relatively overlooked, very early moral development, and explores the earliest signs of moral awareness and sentiment in infants. Chapter 20 seeks to move beyond the development of our understanding of personal conduct, and explores the process by which children and adolescents construct different conceptions of fair social practices.

### *Overview of Chapters in Part VI*

Chapter 19, by *Sharon Lamb* and *Norah C. Feeny*, examines current research which looks at young children's growing ability to differentiate good from bad and to pick up on the culture's associations with each, as well as young children's tendencies towards acting in ways that our culture would define as good and bad. One important focus of work with young children has been research on socialization for compliance and the implications that socialization practices have for the early development of a moral sense. Much of the research relating moral development to early childhood examines how parents begin to control their children's impulses, teach them to inhibit on command, and also to appreciate their parents' prohibitions. For over two decades psychologists have investigated maternal control techniques and have shown that differences in technique have an effect on preschool children's socialization as well as that mothers differ in the techniques they use with their young children depending on the gender of their child and the mother's degree of education. Other studies have focused on changes within the child, his or her increasing ability to inhibit actions and comply with parental desires, to, in effect, be open to socialization efforts. This research on parental socialization for compliance suggests that children do not merely learn to do "what is right" through their parents' behavioral shaping of their children's behavior. The child, developing new competencies and capacities, contributes to the development.

The most important achievement of the second year that contributes to a moral sense, whether a product of developmental maturation or parental socialization efforts, is the child's awareness of standards. We see this awareness when the child shows distress at a crack in a table, a torn piece of clothing, or failure to meet a standard of performance, or when the child attempts to make reparations or "tattles" on him or herself. The capacity to form and use symbols emerges around the middle of the second year. That is, it is at this time that toddlers begin to use symbols to refer to absent objects. In pretend play, they begin to symbolize the interactions between two people. The development of symbolization may be necessary for the categorization of acts as right and wrong. The capacity for making inferences has also been implicated as a contributor to awareness of standards. The child who shows distress at a flawed object makes an inference that another person (e.g., another child) did something that violates a parental standard.

Perhaps the most striking event of the second year of life suggestive of a beginning moral sense is the tendency of the toddler to occasionally attempt to comfort another in distress. For many years observers have remarked about what seem to be empathic affect of the one- to two-year-old, calling these signs "gentle feelings," "sympathy," and "tenderness" for others. Only a handful of studies document the emergence of empathy in the second year of life but the observational data on related behaviors are compelling evidence for the assumption that these children feel empathically towards others in distress.

While the incidence of impulsivity and aggression in the pre-school child is often used to demonstrate their amoral nature, the incidence of kindness and helpfulness is not concomitantly used to demonstrate moral leanings. Aggression is frequently viewed as an expression of natural childhood impulses, vestiges of the animal within us. Loving attention, sharing, and protecting is often attributed to imitation of loving parental role models. Yet both capacities are truly essential to human nature. They receive their moral labels from the culture—at this age, parents. Because of this early labeling of these behaviors they must be viewed within the realm of moral development.

Sharing, helping, protecting, and nurturing are among the most frequently noted prosocial behaviors in early childhood. While most studies have examined caregiving unidirectionally, mother to child, mothers often perceive their children as extremely nurturant. Research suggests, in fact, that all children nurture their dolls and animals. They bed, caress, feed, groom, and talk to them.

By overemphasizing the socialization component of morally related behaviors in the second year of life, many have previously underestimated the interests, if not the capacities, of the very young with regard to moral development. While it is unlikely that eighteen-month-olds can "know the good" and "choose the good" consistently, they show concern for knowing about, doing, and not doing "good." They begin to evaluate the world around them and to respond affectively to harm, wrongdoing, and pleasing or not pleasing others. Perhaps if adults could consistently respond affectively to harm and wrongdoing, and then act on these affects, we would be in far better shape in this world.

Chapter 20, by *Theresa A. Thorkildsen*, describes research on the development of knowledge about the fairness of societal practices—the justice of the ways schools, courts, churches and other social institutions operate. The specific focus of this work has been on childrens' conceptions of fair educational practices. This research has found that when evaluating the justice of societal practices, children take into account the goal or definition of the situation. In U.S. schools, for example, the two goals of (1) helping all students learn (regardless of their current abilities and family backgrounds) and (2) finding out what each student knows are considered essential operations. Practices, such as peer tutoring, that are fair for helping students learn are not usually seen as fair for testing situations. These two types of situations have different goals. Peer tutoring can help achieve a learning goal but not a testing goal.

Because children recognize (at some level) that different issues are at stake in learning and testing, their understanding of fair practices will develop differently for the two types of situations. Therefore, the research described in this chapter sought to determine the development of concepts of fair practices separately for each situation.

Students' concepts of fair learning practices parallel, in form and age of appearance, their concepts of the long-term acquisition of intelligence. Determining what is a fair way to help everyone learn, in other words, depends on how you define intelligence or the rate at which one can learn. Adultlike conceptions of intelligence and of fair learning practices appear only after about age 18.

Students' concepts of fair testing practices, however, parallel the development of their conceptions of ability and effort as factors limiting immediate performance. After about age 12, most students realize that one's current ability will put limits on the extent to which our effort will pay off. Younger children have difficulty understanding this fact. Hence, it seems likely that those who have this concept of ability as capacity will hold different conceptions of fair testing practices than those who do not hold this concept ability.

Children's understanding of the situation places constraints on their reasoning about the fairness of particular practices. They are not always aware of the many competing issues that must be considered when judging fair practices. Nor do they necessarily have a complete understanding of the problems associated with any one particular issue. Structured interviews were used to examine children's concepts of fair learning practices. At every grade, students thought peer tutoring was the most fair practice. When students were asked to compare practices and judge which is more fair, however, age-trends were evident in their views. Older adolescents judged enrichment and acceleration more fair and peer tutoring less fair than did younger children. When students' choices of fair practices and their justifications for those choices were considered jointly, five conceptions of fair learning practices were evident.

In testing situations, the purpose is to assess current abilities rather than to promote learning or intellectual development. Children's understanding of the psychology of testing situations differ from their understanding of the psychology of learning situations. Furthermore, their understanding of fairness differs for testing and learning situations. It should not be surprising, therefore, to find that conceptions of fair testing practices develop differently from conceptions of fair learning practices. In fact, adultlike conceptions of fair testing practices emerge in early adolescence (after about age 11) whereas adultlike conceptions of fair learning practices emerge in late adolescence (after about age 18).

In its application, these findings would appear to suggest that discourse about the intellectual side of education is important. Students should discuss the ethics of selecting the types of information to be learned, helping students acquire new skills, and assessing student progress. Reasoning about the moral dimensions of education (and other institutional practices) cannot be ignored if we are to foster the development of a just society.

# Chapter 19

# Early Moral Sense and Socialization

SHARON LAMB
Bryn Mawr College

*SHARON LAMB*
*Bryn Mawr College*

*NORAH C. FEENY*
*Bryn Mawr College*

**Abstract**

This chapter explores the earliest signs of moral awareness and sentiment. It presents a review of the research on child compliance, maternal socialization practices, prosocial behavior, empathy, and awareness of stan-dards. Maturational and socialization explanations for the emergence of these signs of moral development in the second year of life are explored.

In the not so distant past, the investigation of moral development was primarily applied to those subjects who could rationally choose right from wrong, that is, to children over the age of 5 and to adults. Freudians, cognitive develop-mentalists, and even those who studied morality cross-culturally, looked to the thinking and reasoning child to understand the cultural transmission of morals or the beginning of a person's ethical judgments. If moral behavior was studied at all, it was studied in relation to moral judgments, or in more narrowly defined areas such as cheating behaviors of elementary school children, as in the old studies by Hartshorne and May (1928).

But over the past two decades, as developmental psychology improved its methodology regarding observation, and turned to more naturalistic settings as a source of observational data, the field of moral psychology blossomed in several different directions. Moral behaviors began to be noticed, described, and reexamined, and when researchers depended less on what subjects "said" or "judged," they were able to look at so-called "moral" behaviors exhibited by children even as young as ten months. The babe who orients towards another in distress, or the toddler who shows distress at a torn piece of clothing were as likely to be subjects of moral investigations as the adolescent who was asked to explain why Heinz should steal the drug that his wife needed to get well.

The change in methodology is not the only reason why these behaviors began to be described and examined: the expansion of the field of developmental psychology allowed for new conceptualizations under more specific topic areas of behaviors that had been studied in earlier decades. Early moral behavior and understanding was one such field. For example, while compliance with parental prohibitions has been a topic of research interest for quite some time, it was examined earlier in order to understand the influence of parenting behaviors, and only recently has the focus changed to the child so that we may understand the development of compliance. With the development of areas of research that examined topics like early empathy, children's kind and caring responses (sometimes called "prosocial behavior"), the beginning of an awareness of standards and other such areas, it was now possible to think of the young child as having a nascent "moral" sense and to bring together these various studies in a way that would enable us to talk about early "moral" sense and socialization.

In this chapter, we will review three areas of research that taken together show the possibilities for an early moral sense and for the workings of moral socialization. Luckily enough at this moment in the history of developmental psychology, the nature-nurture debate has become boring; most developmental psychologists would argue that there is always an interaction between the two, between sense and socialization. In the three areas we will examine, compliance, sensitivity to standard violations, and empathy and prosocial behavior, it will be clear that for each there is some part that is dependent on the child's developmental "preparedness" and a good deal dependent on socialization.

## Compliance

The earliest way adults in our society decide whether to label a child as "good" or "bad," as in "what a good little girl!," is through making a judgment about how frequently and how readily a child complies with adult demands. Much of the earlier research relating moral development to early childhood took the parents' point of view and examined how successfully parents control their child's impulses, teach them to inhibit on command, and help them to appreciate parental prohibitions. As unfortunate as this may seem to those of us who prize assertiveness and individuality, it is true that the child who complies pleases others. Indeed, early noncompliance has been seen as indicative of some disturbance in the child (Crockenberg & Litman, 1990; Kuczinsky & Kochanska, 1990).

When we look at what we know about children's compliance, we find that young children have been known to comply with up to 80 percent of the demands made on them by their parents (Forehand, 1977; Power & Chapieski, 1986). The ability to comply with parental demands does increase during the second and third years of life (Kopp, 1982; Vaughn, Kopp, & Krakow, 1984); but measurement of compliance can be tricky. One study, for example, shows eighteen-month-olds restraining themselves only fleetingly in experimental tasks (Vaughn et al., 1984).

If we look at the other side of compliance, one study shows twenty-seven-month-old children making approximately nine violations per hour, most having to do with the destruction of household objects, and maternal restrictions occurring about once every 6-8 minutes (Minton, Kagan, & Levine, 1971). In another study of mothers and their toddlers, toddlers made 5.5 transgressions an hour, almost all occurring during play (Smetana, 1989).

Kochanska (1991) has remarked that early compliance has been viewed as a marker for early internalization of standards, but it needn't be. The methods by which such compliance is obtained may have more importance. For example, she found that mothers who de-emphasized power strategies when trying to get their toddlers to comply, had children who, when studied six years later, had a more internalized sense of conscience, particularly those who temperamentally seemed prone to be fearful.

Other psychologists who have investigated maternal control techniques have also shown that differences in technique have an effect on preschool children's socialization for morality. One study found that mothers using strategies of direct control were associated with children using strategies of direct defiance; whereas mothers using negotiations had children more likely to use negotiations (Kuczynski, Kochanska, Radke-Yarrow, and Gurnius-Brown, 1987). Yet another study showed that a mother's flexibility and ability to adjust her helping strategy when her child was on task, was associated with the child's compliance (Westerman, 1990). Minton et al. (1971) observed that mothers generally spoke in a mild tone to their children unless the children did not comply, and the forcefulness of the mother's intervention depended on the most recent interaction between mother and child. Physically punishing mothers have toddlers who are least likely to comply with maternal restrictions. Their children are also most likely to manipulate breakable objects in the household (Power & Chapieski, 1986). Research also shows that mothers aiming for short-term compliance tend to explain less and are less nurturant in their interaction than mothers who are looking for long-term compliance (Kuczinsky, 1984). Overall, it has been found that children's compliance is positively associated with mothers' enjoyment of the parental role and negatively associated with mothers' negative affect during socializing interactions (Kochanska, Kuczinsky, & Radke-Yarrow, 1989).

Researchers have also found that mothers differ in the techniques they use with their one-to-two-year-olds depending on the gender and age of their child. In a study comparing 15-month-olds to 24-month-olds, mothers tended to repeat themselves more frequently with older children, but also used the strategy of repetition quite often independent of age, 65 percent of the time with the younger group and 75 percent of the time with the older group (Schaffer & Crook, 1980). Parents use instruction and direction at much greater rates with 18-month-olds than 12-month-olds (Fagot & Kavanaugh, 1993) because 18-month-olds require more management. Mothers use more physical strategies with younger children and more verbal strategies with older ones (Kuczinsky, et al., 1987).

A strong argument for socialization of early morality is presented by Smetana (1984; 1989) who asserts that the categories of moral transgressions (harm to others and rights violations) and conventional transgressions (not following a system's rules, for example) are responded to differently by mothers and caregivers and thus contribute to the way the very young child constructs these two categories. In her two studies, both mothers and caregivers responded more often to moral than to conventional transgressions of preschoolers. The second year of life may be a central time for such socialization, for caregivers of one- to two-year-olds responded more often to moral transgressions than caregivers of two- to three-year-olds (Smetana, 1984).

Results from a longitudinal study of four toddlers over the second year (Lamb, 1993) suggests that socializing interactions about prohibitions between toddlers and their mothers qualitatively change between 15 and 19 months. The middle of the second year was observed to be a time when children experimented with standards and noncompliance; they were questioning, playful, and even willful. The children smiled when they disobeyed and teased their mothers. When they confronted their mothers, it appeared as if they were testing her; there was little negative affect and few full-blown confrontations. Sometimes after an act was prohibited the children would stand in front of their mothers and almost repeat it, poising in mid-act, smiling, waiting for a response. Sometimes they would transgress in front of her and wait expectantly for a response. They were mostly happy to challenge their mothers and rarely distressed.

After about 19 months there was another change in mother child interactions around compliance and transgressions. The children, who began to understand their mothers' wishes and desires with regard to standards earlier, now also began to show a desire to do what their mothers want them to do. They made reparations for transgressions; they "tattled" on themselves and asked for praise then they showed restraint; they hid wrongdoings from their mothers; and they even showed signs of inner conflict when their mothers' wishes conflicted with their own. Emotionally they showed concern, distress, devilish glee, pleased to be doing what their mothers wanted and anguished when they were torn between what they wanted to do and what their mothers wanted them to do. No longer nonchalant though sometimes willful about transgressions, they would now even get distressed about the violation of a standard.

Such observations along with the research on parental socialization for compliance suggest that children do not merely learn to do "what is right" through their parents' behavioral shaping of their children's behavior. The child, developing new competencies and capacities, contributes to the development.

## *Awareness of Standards: The Capacity for Making Moral Evaluations*

The most important achievement of the second year that contributes to a moral sense, whether a product of developmental maturation or parental socialization efforts, is the child's awareness of standards. We see this awareness when the child shows distress at a crack in a table, a torn piece of clothing, or failure to meet a standard of performance, or when the child attempts to make reparations or "tattles" on him or herself.

In her longitudinal studies of British toddlers and their mothers over the toddlers' second and third year of life, Dunn (1987; 1988) saw signs of an awareness of standards. Teasing behavior increased over the second year and was increasingly sophisticated showing that toddlers were able to infer and understand what might bother their siblings and mothers. They also showed the capacity to infer or anticipate their mothers' reactions to acts of aggression or teasing. They made appeals to their mothers after a sibling aggressed on or teased them but not after they teased or aggressed on their siblings.

As language development increased, the children in Dunn's study began to refer to the responsibility of their siblings when discussing conflicts and to make references to social rules. In pretend play they would even negotiate rules with their older siblings.

Dunn's toddlers drew attention to a previously forbidden act as they were committing the transgression. They also, on occasion, laughed when doing something their mothers had previously forbidden them to do. Dunn notes that most theorists have studied the negative emotions that accompany transgressing—shame, guilt, anxiety, fear. In contrast, she observed children's amusement, pleasure, and joking about rule violations as well.

In the longitudinal study of four toddlers discussed earlier (Lamb, 1991), children were observed to express an awareness of standards in various ways around the middle of the second year. One child expressed his awareness primarily through interactions around transgressions and "uh oh's" over accidents, another through "uh oh's" about accidents and distress and/or delight at not meeting or meeting a standard of achievement. A third child expressed awareness through her reactions to transgressions (reparations, willful defiance, experimentation) and in her interest in and distress at flawed objects. The fourth child began to label incidents and objects as "good," "bad," "yukky," or "dirty" as well as express an awareness of standards of achievement.

Each child expressed his or her awareness of standards in different ways; however, when behavioral and verbal expressions of awareness in the six categories were aggregated to obtain total incident scores for each session, the number of morally related incidents peaked at the same age, between seventeen and eighteen months, for all four children. While other researchers have observed different behaviors relating to moral development steadily increase over the second year, the aggregation of these specific behaviors shows an increase and then a decrease around the middle of the second year.

Mothers' socializing comments relating to the six areas of interest were counted to determine to what extent they may be promoting this interest in the second year. (See Lamb, 1993, for a fuller description of the methodology.) While mothers made socializing comments in most areas throughout the second year, these comments did not increase or peak before the children's peaks in awareness of standards. In fact, the mothers' comments seemed more to follow the children's interest rather than lead it, supporting the children's attempts to understand, explore, and/or respond to morally related events in their lives. In that morally related events have special salience for children in the middle of the second year somewhat independent of mothers' socializing comments, there may be maturational factors mediating the peaking of such interest at precisely this time.

Smetana (1984) notes toddlers' responses to and differentiation of transgressions that seem to emanate from the children themselves in the second year. In her daycare study, one- to two-year-olds responded more to moral transgressions than the two- to three-year-olds, and children in both groups did not respond to conventional transgressions. Other research suggests that while children in late toddlerhood can differentiate between parental standards and other kinds of standards, in early toddlerhood they do not make this distinction (Stipek, Gralinski, & Kopp, 1990).

Kagan (1981) points to the middle of the second year as a time that is crucial in the emergence of a moral sense. He notes that children's speech first refers to standards after nineteen months. And children first use moral language, words such as "good," "bad," "naughty," and "nice" (Bloom et al., 1975; Kagan, 1981) at this time. He also suggests that a sensitivity to right and wrong can not appear until children are able to consciously infer possible causes and feeling states in others.

Lamb (1988) designed a task to examine inference of wrongdoing in the second year. The child was shown two objects (two dolls, shoes, or cups); one was broken and soiled; the other was fine. The child was then asked to hand the examiner the "bad" one. Three of the children began to pass this task consistently before the peak in awareness of standards around 17 to 18 months which suggests that the task may be tapping an inferential capacity in an area that would soon become a major interest.

Kagan (1981) investigated children's awareness of standards by presenting them with flawed objects and noting their reactions. His research involved presenting one- to two-year-olds with an object that violated a standard adults regard as normative. Over one-half of the nineteen-month-olds in his sample showed distress over a broken toy or a torn piece of clothing while no fourteen-month-old did. Children in the latter half of the second year also expressed distress after an examiner modeled an act that was too difficult for the child to imitate. Kagan suggests that these children were aware of a standard of performance and were upset because they could not meet it. Largo and Howard's (1979) work supports this assumption of Kagan's and demonstrates children over fifteen months judging whether a task is "too easy" for them. When completing a difficult task, children in the second year will sometimes smile whether or not an adult is watching them (Kagan, 1981; Stipek and McClintic, 1989) thus suggesting an understanding that they have met a standard of performance.

Dunn (1987) also kept track of children's responses to flawed objects in their households. Measuring their interest solely by their communications about such objects, she found their interest to steadily increase over the second year. While it is possible her measure confounds increasing language ability with increasing interest, it is still important that the children continue to use their increasing language to draw attention to flawed objects. In other words, their language directed towards flawed objects reflects, if not an *increasing* interest, still a strong one.

Unlike Kagan (1981) but like Dunn, Lamb (1993) found that the four children observed longitudinally expressed enormous interest in flawed objects and little actual distress. It was interesting that the mothers in the study did not even once express interest in a flawed object or discrepant event. This was an interest that appeared to be entirely child motivated; however, one-quarter of the mothers' prohibitions they directed to their children were about destruction of property. While they may not be drawing attention to this area, they are certainly making it known that destruction of property is wrong. This may mean that the children's interest in flawed objects may derive from their inference that somebody had transgressed by destroying property, rather than discomfort at a standard of form being violated.

Recently, Barrett and colleagues (Cole, Barrett, & Zahn-Waxler, 1992; Barrett, Zahn-Waxler, & Cole, in press) have conducted experiments with toddlers in which a child is led to believe that she or he broke a doll or spilled juice on a new shirt. These one- to two-year-olds show distress and try to make reparations, and, in fact, the expression of sadness correlated, in their studies, with attempts to make reparations. Emde and Buschbaum (1990) also report that toddlers who merely were tempted to transgress at times will spontaneously confess their imagined transgressions.

Kochanska (in press) extended Barrett et al.'s research on toddler mishaps to three-year-olds and found that they were interested in flawed objects regardless of whether or not they were the ones who produced the flaw, that is, regardless of culpability. Moreover, by age two-and-a-half, these toddlers showed a distinct preference for whole as opposed to flawed objects.

Researchers such as Barrett and Kochanska have brought to light the emotional underpinnings of early awareness of standards. For example, Kochanska has also shown that toddlers who according to maternal report are more arousable and fearful, are also those toddlers who maternal report suggests are more reactive and reparative when they have transgressed (Kochanska, DeVet, Goldman, Murray, and Putnam, 1994). This distress and concern that toddlers can show when they have transgressed is a relatively new area of study, but those who have worked in the area of empathy have long been aware of the "moral" feelings.

## Empathy and Response to Distress

Perhaps the most striking event of the second year of life suggestive of a beginning moral sense is the tendency of the toddler to, on occasion, attempt to comfort another in distress. For many years observers have remarked about what seem to be empathic affect of the one- to two-year-old calling these signs "gentle feelings," "sympathy," and "tenderness" for others (Murchison & Langer, 1927; Murphy, 1942; Valentine, 1938). In the late 18th century, Tiedemann wrote of his young son who was fourteen-and-a-half months and wept when someone refused his hand which he had offered as a sign of affection. Later, at almost seventeen months, he "wept with his sister when she cried" and soon after "objected against having either (his dog or sister) suffer certain harm" (Murchison and Langer, 1927). Gesell and colleagues described children this young as essentially "self-interested" yet also documented the emergence of "symptoms" of pity, sympathy, modesty, shame, and guilt around the second year. By age two, they claimed, the child has "great complexity, depth, and sensitiveness" (Gesell, et al., 1940).

The discussion of empathy as an emotional experience raises interesting questions. Some researchers have looked to evolutionary theory for an explanation of empathy as an instinctual and/or involuntary response (Campbell, 1965; Church, 1959 in Rushton & Sorrentino, 1981; McDougall, 1923; Sullivan, 1953). Hoffman (1982) supports this view, noting that empathy is overdetermined, self-reinforcing, largely involuntary, requiring little cognitive processing, and thus of survival value in human evolution.

A number of studies have documented behaviors suggesting that toddlers feel empathically towards others in distress. Between twelve and twenty months children will respond to distress by orienting to another (Eisenberg-Berg, 1982). They will make tentative approaches to victims, sometimes attempt to comfort people in distress (Hoffman, 1982), and even try to make upset siblings laugh (Dunn and Kendrick, 1979).

The most extensive work on toddlers' responses to people in distress has been done at the National Institute of Mental Health by Zahn-Waxler and associates. They have shown that during the second year, children become sensitive to the distress of other family members (Zahn-Waxler, Yarrow, & King, 1979) and that prosocial acts and imitation of the victim's distress increased with age while self-distress decreased with age (Zahn-Waxler and Radke-Yarrow, 1982). In this latter study, mothers as well as "visitors" served as recorders of the child's behaviors and found that after eighteen months, toddlers responded with prosocial behavior to about one-third of all distresses they witnessed. They also found that the greatest increase of prosocial behavior to distress situations was between sixteen and twenty-four months.

A similar, more recent study suggests that prosocial behaviors as well as "looks of concern" increase over the second year. These researchers found that by the end of the second year toddlers responded prosocially to almost half of all distress incidents and showed empathic "concern" for a quarter of these. Mothers were better elicitors than unfamiliar persons but no comparison was made with concern for peers. These findings may be particular to the home or lab, or even more particular to adults, for in a daycare setting Howes and Farver (1987) found responding to the cries of peers to be around 22 percent, while Lamb and Zakhireh (1993) found that while toddlers paid attention to the distress of peers, there were practically no prosocial responses.

Gender has been examined in relation to frequency of responding to distress and in two studies, girls score higher on observational measures of empathy as well as maternal reports (Zahn-Waxler, Radke-Yarrow, Wagner, & Chapman, 1992a; Zahn-Waxler, Robinson, & Emde, 1992b). However, Howes and Farver found that in their daycare setting, boys responded more than girls by consoling.

Researchers have wondered why toddlers might respond to another in distress. It may, as suggested earlier, be related to emotional development. There is a peak in the imitation of affect in the second year which also indicates a focus on others' feelings (Kuczynski, et al., 1987). Kagan (1988) discusses research on young monkeys' brains which suggest that synaptic density in human limbic structures, structures that regulate the experiencing of emotion, may reach a peak during the second year. This may heighten a child's emotional responsivity to distress cues emitted by victims. If empathy is a state of "unpleasant affect," as Hoffman (1975) and Kagan (1984) suggest, it may motivate a child to respond to another in distress in order to be more personally comfortable.

Self-distress has been studied along with empathy. In an older sample, Caplan & Hay (1989) found that self-distress was negatively correlated with orienting to distress. This jibes with research by Eisenberg et al., 1987, that shows that personal distress causes one to turn inwards. In the more recent study by Zahn-Waxler and associates (1992a), toddlers showed less personal distress as they developed more organized response patterns.

Of considerable interest is the role that genetics plays in the development of empathy. Are some children "programmed" to be more responsive to others' distress? Research investigating the development of empathy in twins has shown that mothers' verbal reports of children's empathic concern contain evidence of heritability at 14 and 20 months (Zahn-Waxler et al., 1992b).

## Conclusions

While the incidence of impulsivity and aggression in preschool children is often used to demonstrate their amoral nature, the incidence of kindness, empathy, and the urge to please is not concomitantly used to demonstrate moral leanings. Aggression is frequently viewed as an expression of natural childhood impulses, vestiges of the animal within us. Loving attention, sharing, and protecting is often attributed to the imitation of loving parental role models. And yet both capacities are truly essential to human nature.

Children learn to evaluate on the basis of their own experience with the world around them and their own capacities for construction (Turiel, 1983), and also from the culture at large, transmitted particularly during the toddler years through their parents. While there has always been disagreement about the content of good and bad, and about whether the categories of good and bad are defined naturally, religiously, and/or culturally, these categories exist.

Research in early childhood has examined independent aspects of the emergence of morality in the second year without yet integrating these various aspects into a unified theory of moral development. Studies on very young children sharing, helping, nurturing, and comforting others in distress contribute to our understanding of empathic responding. Studies that examine the developing child's ability to restrain herself when a limitation is imposed from without, the child's emerging pride when meeting a parental standard of performance, and the child's interest in flawed objects and discrepant events are relevant to awareness of standards.

According to some theorists (Emde, Kligman, Reich, & Wade, 1978; Malatesta, 1982), the second year is a time of great emotional development and lability. Infants appear adaptively to be insensitive to aversive information (La Barbera, Izard, Vietz, & Parisi, 1976) which suggests that as canalized behavior decreases, the child may be confronted or "flooded" with aversive emotional experience (Izard, 1978). This flooding may help explain infants' increased attention to emotional states suggested by their acquisition of emotion words. This new focus on affects and the capacity to take in more affective information could also heighten the toddler's awareness of parental prohibitions.

Kagan (1984) claims that all moral standards are based on fundamental affective states, three of which are anxiety in response to social disapproval, a feeling of uncertainty that accompanies encounters with discrepant events, and discomfort in hearing or seeing someone in distress. These emotions, salient as they are for the child in the second year, may form the basis of morality (Kagan, 1981; 1984).

By overemphasizing the socialization component of morally related behaviors in the second year of life, many have previously underestimated the interests, if not the capacities, of the very young with regard to moral development. While it is unlikely that eighteen-month-olds can "know the good" and "choose the good" consistently, they show concern for knowing about, doing, and not doing "good." They begin to evaluate the world around them and to respond affectively to harm, wrongdoing, and pleasing or not pleasing others. Perhaps if adults could consistently respond affectively to harm and wrongdoing, and then act on these affects, we would be in far better shape in this world.

## References

Barrett, K. C., Zahn-Waxler, C., & Cole, P.M. (In press). Avoiders vs. amenders: Implications for the investigation of guilt and shame during toddlerhood? *Cognition and Emotion.*

Bloom, L., Lightbown, P., & Hood, L. (1975). Structure and variation in child language. *Monographs of the Society for Research in Child Development, 40.*

Campbell, D. T. (1967). Ethnocentric and other altruistic motives. In D. Levine (Ed.), *Nebraska Symposium on Motivation, 13.* Lincoln: University of Nebraska Press.

Caplan, M. Z., & Hay, D. (1989). Preschoolers' response to peers' distress and beliefs about bystander intervention. *Journal of Child Psychology & Psychiatry, 30,* 231-242.

Cole, P. M., Barrett, K. C., & Zahn-Waxler, C. (1992). Emotion displays in two-year-olds during mishaps. *Child Development, 63,* 314-324

Crockenberg, S. & Litman, C. (1990). Autonomy as competence for two-year-olds: Maternal correlates of child defiance, compliance, and self assertion. *Developmental Psychology, 26,* 961-971.

Dunn, J. (1987). The beginnings of moral understanding: Development in the second year. In J. Kagan & S. Lamb (Eds.), *The emergence of morality in young children.* Chicago: University of Chicago Press.

Dunn, J. (1988). *The Beginnings of Social Understanding* Cambridge, MA: Harvard University Press.

Dunn, J., & Kendrick, C. (1979). Interaction between young siblings in the context of family relationships. In M. Lewis & L. A. Rosenblum (Eds.), *The child and its family.* New York: Plenum Press.

Eisenberg-Berg, N. (1982). *The development of*

*prosocial behavior*. New York: Academic Press.

Eisenberg, N., Fabes, R., Bustmante, D. & Mathy, R. (1987). Physiological indices of empathy. In N. Eisenberg & J. Strayer (Eds.), *Empathy and its development*. New York: Cambridge University Press.

Emde, R. N., & Buschbaum, H. K. (1990). "Didn't you hear my mommy?" Autonomy with connectedness in moral self emergence. In D. Cicchetti & M. Beeghly (Eds.), *Development of the self through the transition* (pp. 35-60). Chicago: University of Chicago Press.

Emde, R. N., Kligman, D. H., Reich, J. H., & Wade, T. D. (1978). Emotional expression in infancy: I. Initial studies of social signaling and an emergent model. In M. Lewis & L. A. Rosenblum (Eds.), *The development of affect*. New York: Plenum Press.

Fagot, B. I. & Kavanagh, K. (1993). Parenting during the second year: Effects of children's age, sex, and attachment classification. *Child Development, 64*, 258-271.

Forehand, R. (1977). Child noncompliance to parental requests: Behavioral analysis and treatment. In M. Hersen, R. M. Eisler, & P. M. Miller (Eds.), *Progress in behavior modification* (Vol. 5). New York: Academic Press.

Gesell, A., Halverson, H., Ilg, F. L., Thompson, H., Castner, B. M., Ames, L. B., & Amatruda, C. S. (1940). *The first five years of life: The pre-school years*. New York: Harper.

Hartshorne, H. & May, M. S. (1928). Studies in the nature of *character*. New York: Macmillan.

Hoffman, M. (1975). Developmental synthesis of affect and cognition and its implications for altruistic motivation. *Developmental Psychology, 11*, 607-622.

Hoffman, M. (1982). The development of prosocial motivation: Empathy and guilt. In N. Eisenberg-Berg (Ed.), *The development of prosocial behavior*. New York: Academic Press.

Howes, C., & Farver, J. (1987). Toddlers' response to the distress of their peers. *Journal of Applied Developmental Psychology, 8*, 441-452 .

Izard, C. (1978). On the ontogenesis of emotion and emotion-cognition relationships in infancy. In M. Lewis & L. A. Rosenblum, (Eds.), *The development of affect*. New York: Plenum Press.

Kagan, J. (1981). *The second year: The emergence of self awareness*. Cambridge, MA: Harvard University Press.

Kagan, J. (1984). *The nature of the child*. New York: Basic Books.

Kagan, J. (1987). Introduction. In J. Kagan & S. Lamb (Eds.), *The emergence of morality in young children*. Chicago: University of Chicago Press.

Kochanska, G. (in press). Sensitivity to standard violations in toddlers. *Child Development.*

Kochanska, G. (1991). Socialization and temperament in the development of guilt and conscience. *Child Development, 62*, 1379-1392.

Kochanska, G., DeVet, K., Goldman, K. M., Murray, K., & Putnam, S. (1994). Maternal reports of conscience development and temperament in young children. *Child Development, 65*, 852-868.

Kochanska, G., Kuczynski, L., & Radke-Yarrow, M. (1989). Correspondence between mother's self-reported and observed child-rearing practices. *Child Development, 60*, 56-63.

Kopp, C. B. (1982). Antecedents of self-regulation: A developmental perspective. *Developmental Psychology, 18*, 199-214.

Kuczynski, L. (1984). Socialization goals and mother-child interaction: Strategies for long-term and short-term compliance. *Developmental Psychology, 20*, 1061-1073.

Kuczynski, L., & Kochanska, G. (1990). Children's noncompliance from toddlerhood to age five. *Developmental Psychology, 26*, 398-408.

Kuczynski, L., Kochanska, G., Radke-Yarrow, M., Girnius-Brown, O. (1987a). A developmental interpretation of young children's noncompliance. *Developmental Psychology, 23*, 799-806.

Kuczynski, L., Zahn-Waxler, C., & Radke-Yarrow, M. (1987b). Development and content of imitation in the second and third years of life: A socialization perspective. *Developmental Psychology, 23,* 276-282.

La Barbera, J. D., Izard, C. E., Vietz, P., & Parisi, S. A. (1976). Four- and six-month-old infants' visual responses to joy, anger and neutral expressions. *Child Development, 47,* 535-538.

Lamb, S. (1988). *The Emergence of Morality in the Second Year of Life.* Unpublished doctoral dissertation. Harvard Graduate School of Education.

Lamb. S. (1991). First moral sense: Aspects of and contributors to a beginning morality in the second year of life. In W. M. Kurtines and J. L. Gewirtz (Eds.), *Handbook of moral behavior and development*: Vol. 2 *Research* (pp. 171-189). Hillsdale, NJ: Erlbaum.

Lamb S. (1993). First moral sense: An examination of the appearance of morally related behaviors in the second year of life. *Journal of Moral Education, 22,* 97-109.

Lamb, S. & Zakhireh, B. (1993). Toddler's attention to distress of peers in a daycare setting. Presentation at the biennial meeting of the Society for Research in Child Development. March, New Orleans, Louisiana.

Largo, R. H., & Howard, J. A. (1979). Developmental progression in play behavior of children between nine and thirty months. *Developmental Medicine and Child Neurology, 1-2,* 299-310.

Malatesta, C. Z. (1982). The expression and regulation of emotion: A lifespan perspective. In T. Field and A. Fogel (Eds.), *Emotional and early interaction.* Hillsdale, NJ: Erlbaum.

McDougall, W. (1908). *An introduction to social psychology.* London: Methuen.

Minton, C., Kagan, J., & Levine, J. A. (1971). Maternal control and obedience in the two-year-old. *Child Development, 42,* 1873-1894.

Murchison, C., & Langer, S. (1927). Tiedemann's observations on the development of the mental faculties of children. *Pedagogical Seminary and Journal of Genetic Psychology, 34,* 204-230.

Murphy, L. B. (1937). *Social behavior and child personality.* New York: Columbia University Press.

Power, T. G., & Chapieski, M. L. (1986). Childrearing and impulse control in toddlers: A naturalistic investigation. *Developmental Psychology, 22,* 271-275.

Schaffer, R. H., & Crook, C. K. (1980). Child compliance and maternal control techniques. *Developmental Psychology, 16,* 54-61.

Smetana, J. (1984). Toddlers' social interactions regarding moral and conventional transgressions. *Child Development, 55,* 1767-1776.

Smetana, J. (1989). Toddlers' social interactions in the context of moral and conventional transgressions in the home. *Developmental Psychology, 25,* 499-508.

Stipek, D., Gralinski, S., & Kopp, C. B. (1990). Self-evaluation in young children. *Monographs of the Society for Research in Child Development, 57,* (1, serial #226).

Stipek, D., & McClintic, S. (1989, April). *Factors affecting toddlers' reactions to completing tasks.* Paper presented at the Society for Research in Child Development Conference, Kansas City, Missouri.

Sullivan, H. S. (1940). *The interpersonal theory of psychiatry.* New York: W.W. Norton.

Turiel, E. (1983). *The development of social knowledge: Morality and convention.* New York: Cambridge University Press.

Valentine, C. W. (1938). A study of the beginnings and significance of play in infancy. *British Journal of Educational Psychology, 8,* 285-306.

Vaughn, B. E., Kopp, C. E., & Krakow, J. B. (1984). The emergence and consolidation of self-control from eighteen to thirty months of age. *Child Development, 55,* 990-1004.

Westerman, M. (1990). Coordination of maternal directives with preschoolers' behavior in compliance-problem and health dyads. *Developmental Psychology, 26,* 621-630.

Zahn-Waxler, C. Z., Yarrow, M. R., & King, R. A. (1979). Child rearing and children's prosocial initiations towards victims of distress. *Child Development, 50,* 319-330.

Zahn-Waxler, C., & Radke-Yarrow, M. (1982). The development of altruism: Alternative research strategies. In N. Eisenberg-Berg

(Ed.), *The development of prosocial behavior.* New York: Academic Press.

Zahn-Waxler, C., Radke-Yarrow, M., Wagner, E., & Chapman, M. (1992). Development of concern for others. *Developmental Psychol-ogy, 28,* 126-136.

Zahn-Waxler, Robinson, J. L., & Emde, R.N. (1992). The development of empathy in twins. *Developmental Psychology, 28,* (5), 1038-1047.

*Chapter* **20**

# Conceptions of Social Justice

*THERESA A. THORKILDSEN*
*University of Illinois at Chicago*

### Abstract

Conceptions of fair educational practices develop differently for learning and testing situations. Peer tutoring is judged the fairest way to help students learn until at least age 17. Yet, after about age 8, children say that peer tutoring is an unfair practice during a test. (Most 6- to 8-year olds say peer tutoring is a fair way to have a test.) When justifying their choices, students discuss different issues for testing and learning. When their choices and justifications are considered jointly, five levels of conceptions of fair learning practices are evident. Adultlike conceptions of fair learning practices emerge at about age 18. For testing, however, four levels of conceptions of fair practices are evident and adultlike conceptions emerge at about age 11, well before adultlike conceptions of fair learning practices. These findings support the conclusion that children construct different conceptions of fair social practices as they come to understand the different types of situations they face.

Most research on moral development concerns the norms and values that regulate personal conduct. Researchers have asked, for example, how children construe moral actions and how schools and parents can produce moral children (Damon, 1988). It would be foolish for a society to ignore such important issues. Nevertheless, the development of knowledge about the justice of societal practices—the fairness of the ways schools, courts, churches, and other social institutions operate—is also important in democratic societies. Conceptions of fair social practices are, therefore, the focus of this chapter.

Children recognize the importance of studying the fairness of societal practices. This is suggested by a story told to me by a 9-year-old girl as she was about to be interviewed about fair school practices. She arrived at her scheduled interview eager to tell me that she was initially reluctant to participate because she hated school and her teacher—she would only say bad things. Her 10-year-old brother, who had been interviewed a few days earlier, convinced her she "had to do it." She said, "He kept at me for days. I'd tell him I hate school, my teacher is mean, and to leave me alone. He kept telling me that the questions weren't about liking school, but about what we think *should* happen. I'd tell him I wouldn't have anything nice to say and there is no way I'd do it. But, he'd keep nagging me. He'd follow me around the house. He'd say, 'If we never tell anyone what we think, schools would never get better.' and 'If nobody helped [researchers] out, how could anyone know how we feel.' So, here I am! And you have my brother to thank for it."

Raymond clearly recognized that my interview was about the fairness of the way schools work; not about the personal conduct of particular teachers and students. He also hoped, and eventually convinced his sister, that the way schools operate might be improved by considering children's perspectives on the fairness of educational practices.

Educational practices designed to help students learn and to find out how much they know involve the rights and welfare of everyone who spends time in schools. Decisions about which practices to implement hold moral implications. Therefore, I began considering the development of conceptions of social justice by focusing on fairness in school learning and testing situations.

# Theory

## The Emphasis on Conduct: Examples from the Past

General theories of moral development typically confound reasoning about moral conduct and social justice. Kohlberg, for example, derived general stages of justice reasoning from interviews about a series of standard dilemmas. The types of situations and the issues at stake (referred to as content by Kohlberg) are not considered essential to understanding moral development. (see Higgins, Chapter 3, this vol.) Based on these interviews, Kohlberg and his colleagues suggested that many individuals do not understand the contractual basis for moral rules until after about 20 years of age (Colby & Kohlberg, 1987). Elementary- and high-school students, in other words, would have difficulty evaluating the fairness of school practices.

Yet, this conclusion is suspect. The questions used in Kohlberg's moral judgment interviews focus primarily on the conduct of the actors in the dilemmas rather than on the justice of societal practices. Heinz, for example, must decide whether to steal a drug that could save the life of his ailing wife because he could not obtain it by legal means. Those who were interviewed about Heinz's dilemma were asked to decide what Heinz should do, if it would be right or wrong for him to steal the drug, the extent of his obligations to various individuals, and whether people should obey the law. They were not asked to evaluate the fairness of the institutional practices that defined Heinz's dilemma. Nor were they asked to consider alternative practices that might lead to a more fair health care system. In other words, Kohlberg's interviews are not designed to clarify conceptions of fair social practices.

Similarly, those who have examined children's understanding of moral and conventional rules have not focused on the justice of societal practices. They have examined questions such as whether changing a rule would affect the legitimacy of a person's conduct, whether it would be legitimate to change existing rules governing conduct, and the relative importance of different types of rules that regulate individuals' conduct (e.g., Shweder, Mahapatra, & Miller, 1987; Smetana, 1981; Tisak & Turiel, 1988; Turiel, 1983).

This point is best illustrated by looking at the types of questions these researchers asked. In one study, for example, high-school and college-age Catholics considered the violation of specific church rules (sinful acts) (Nucci, 1985). These students were asked to rate the seriousness of different kinds of transgressions. Conduct such as stealing and murder which involves direct harm to others was seen as more problematic than conduct involving church norms like ordaining women and using birth control. Students were also asked to decide if it would be wrong for the Pope and Cardinals to drop rules prohibiting each act and whether it would be all right for someone from another religion to engage in the acts. Conduct that involved inflicting harm was seen as wrong even if rules prohibiting such behavior were dropped and if the transgressor was not Catholic. Ordaining women and using birth control, however, were seen as legitimate for those of other faiths and as something a papal edict could make legitimate.

As you can see, the focus of these questions remain on the legitimacy of personal conduct. Students were asked to consider what constitutes a good Catholic and whether the rules defining this could be changed—not what constitutes fair religious practices. Asking whether rules can legitimately be changed is not the same as asking whether the existing church practices are fair. If someone says the Pope could permit women to be priests, we do not know if they think this would be more fair than the present practice. Students were not asked to decide if a church that prohibits women from becoming priests or prohibits the use of birth control could be just. Nor were they asked to define the goals of the church and evaluate the fairness of alternative practices for achieving these goals. It would be difficult, therefore, to use this type of work to draw conclusions about children's knowledge of fair practices.

## Conceptions of Social Justice: An Example from Education

A theme of this chapter is that when evaluating the justice of societal practices, children take into account the goal or definition of the situation. In U.S. schools, for example, the two goals of: (a) helping all students learn (regardless of their current abilities and family backgrounds) and (b) finding out what each student knows are considered essential operations. Practices, such as peer tutoring, that are fair for helping students learn are not usually seen as fair for testing situations. These two types of situations have different goals. Peer tutoring can help achieve a learning goal but not a testing goal.

Because children recognize (at some level) that different issues are at stake in learning and testing, their understanding of fair practices will develop differently for the two types of situations. Therefore, we must determine the development of concepts of fair practices separately for each situation. As you will see, the development of conceptions of fair learning and testing practices follow very different courses.

Students' concepts of fair learning practices parallel, in form and age of appearance, their concepts of the long-term acquisition of intelligence. Determining what is a fair way to help everyone learn, in other words, depends on how you define intelligence or the rate at which one can learn. Adultlike conceptions of intelligence and of fair learning practices appear only after about age 18. Only then do students commonly incorporate an understanding of individual differences in learning speed into their judgments.

Students' concepts of fair testing practices, however, parallel the development of their conceptions of ability and effort as factors limiting immediate performance. After about age 12, most students realize that one's current ability will put limits on the extent to which our effort will pay off. That is, most of us know that we have limits on what we can achieve at a particular point in time—this ability might change in the future, but right now there are things we can and cannot do no matter how hard we try. Younger children have difficulty understanding this fact. Hence, it seems likely that those who have the more complex concept of ability as capacity will hold different conceptions of fair testing practices than those who do not hold this concept of ability. The remainder of this chapter will provide evidence to support these assertions and conclude with suggestions for fostering social justice reasoning among those involved in schools.

## Research

### *Pluralistic Conceptions of Fairness*

The purpose of this first study was to determine if children are able to distinguish between different goals or definitions of educational and sporting situations, and judge the fairness of specific practices accordingly (Thorkildsen, 1989a). Put more concretely, practices that were seen as fair in learning situations were expected to be seen as unfair in test and contest situations.

To test this, first, third, and fifth graders were asked to consider common educational situations involving the goals of: (1) fostering learning or mastery (learning to read), (2) determining who is the most able (spelling bee), and (3) testing to discern each child's capabilities (reading test). For each of these situations, children evaluated the practices of: (1) peer tutoring, (2) racing, and (3) solitary performance.

### *What's Fair Isn't Always Fair*

In these interviews, children clearly considered the goal of the situation when evaluating the fairness of a particular practice. Practices were not universally judged fair or unfair. The practice of peer tutoring, for example, was seen as fair in learning or mastery situations, but unfair in test and contest situations. Racing to see who is best was seen as fair only in contest situations. Solitary work was seen as fairest in testing situations.

Even though these children thought about their current definitions of learning, contest, and test situations when making fairness decisions, they also realized that there might be other definitions of such situations and valid positions regarding the fairness of these practices. To them, all practices could become fair in another country, in the future, and over time—even those practices they said were unfair. (These questions about universality and changeability are similar to those asked when distinguishing moral and conventional rules of conduct. See Turiel, 1983.)

In summary, although children consider the situational goal when judging the fairness of social practices, they do not argue that "anything goes." Practices are decisively evaluated as fair or unfair in light of current assumptions about the nature of the situation. In this sense, children are not relativists. But, children recognize that if the nature of the situation changes, the justice of practices will have to be re-evaluated. They are what Walzer (1983) would call particularists. They recognize that the fairness of a specific practice depends on what is defined as important. This should become more evident when, later in the chapter, conceptions of fair learning and testing practices are considered in greater detail.

### *Distinctions between Fair Practices and Personal Harm*

Moral issues are often defined as those involving the welfare and rights of individuals (e.g., Rawls, 1971; Turiel, 1983). Like these theorists, children usually held that unfair practices were harmful. Nevertheless, this was not always the case. Some practices were seen as fair, but harmful ways to achieve a particular goal (e.g., competition during a spelling bee).

This finding appears, at first glance, to be inconsistent with the above definition of moral issues. One might expect harmful practices to be judged unfair. On the other hand, the potential for harm might be an accepted part of the definition of the situation—it might be the risk one knowingly takes when deciding to participate in a particular activity. Tackling someone during a football game, for example, is likely to hurt the person being tackled, but the sport of football is presumably seen as fair by those who participate in it. As children seem to understand, it would be problematic to argue that all practices which cause harm are, therefore, unjust. Children, in other words, consider the purpose of the practice or the goal of the situation when judging fairness.

### Fairness and Effectiveness

Overall, judgments of fairness and effectiveness varied across situations in a similar way. Practices children saw as fair for attaining a particular goal were generally seen as effective for attaining that goal. Peer tutoring, for example, was seen as an effective and fair way to help students learn to read. In addition, practices that would not work in a particular situation were generally seen as unfair. For example, children thought that racing, a practice judged unfair for a learning situation, would not help students learn to read. These findings suggest that, to children, practices must at least be effective before they can be fair.

Nevertheless, practices were not judged fair simply because they were effective for attaining a particular goal. Practices were sometimes seen as unfair, but effective ways of attaining situational goals. Children held, for example, that racing was an effective, but unfair way to find out what students know. In other words, they clearly distinguish fairness and effectiveness.

### Confirming Evidence

Similar findings were also evident when a second group of children considered sporting activities (Thorkildsen, 1989a). When considering a roller skating contest, children said interpersonal competition was the most fair and effective practice. For a gymnastics skills test, independent performance was seen as the most effective and fair. Having more able athletes help the less able athletes was seen as unfair and ineffective for both the skating contest and skills test. However, when hiking through the woods (a mastery situation), children said helping less able hikers was both effective and fair. These similarities in the results for sport and school indicate the robustness of the finding that from first grade on, children can distinguish testing, learning, and contest situations.

## Conceptions of Fair Learning Practices

Children's understanding of the situation places constraints on their reasoning about the fairness of particular practices. They are not always aware of the many competing issues that must be considered when judging fair practices. Nor do they necessarily have a complete understanding of the problems associated with any one particular issue. To examine children's conceptions of fair practices, therefore, requires a method that would enable us to discern their definition of the situation and the relevant issues at stake as well as their fairness evaluations. We must, in other words, be able to assess the criteria children use when making their fairness decisions. The structured interview method seems ideal for this purpose because by presenting students with dilemmas to resolve we are able to test the limits of children's reasoning and at the same time allow the child to assert a point of view we might not predict. (See Damon, 1977; Piaget, 1951; and Turiel, 1983 for descriptions of this methodology.)

Structured interviews, therefore, were used to examine children's concepts of fair learning practices (Thorkildsen, 1989b). Children and adolescents (first grade to college) were asked to think about how teachers might help high ability students (fast workers who always get the answers right) and low ability students (slow workers who usually make a lot of mistakes) learn. They evaluated the fairness of five practices:

1. *Peer tutoring:* high ability students help the low ability.
2. *Enrichment:* extra reading and computer time for the high ability students while the low ability students finish.
3. *Acceleration:* high ability students do more advanced work, leaving low ability students behind.
4. *High ability sit and wait:* high ability students sit quietly and wait for low ability students to finish assignments.
5. *Low ability never finish:* low ability students are never allowed enough time to finish assignments, high ability students set the pace.

At every grade, students thought peer tutoring was the most fair practice (97 percent said this was fair). Having faster learners participate in enrichment activities usually ranked second (66 percent said this was fair). The remaining three practices were usually seen as unfair. (The percent of students saying practices 3, 4, and 5 were fair are 39, 27, and 4, respectively.) When students were asked to compare practices and judge which is more fair, however, age trends were evident in their views. Older adolescents judged enrichment and acceleration more fair and peer tutoring less fair than did younger children.

When students' choices of fair practices and their justifications for those choices were considered jointly, five conceptions of fair learning practices were evident (Table 20-1). At Level 5, the most advanced level observed, students emphasized a meritocratic or equity-based distribution of learning. Acceleration for high ability students was always described as fair and generally selected as more fair than other practices. As one 21-year-old put it, acceleration is fair because "These [faster] students are able to do the work and they shouldn't be held back with these [slower] students. And, these [slower] students

**TABLE 20-1  Conceptions of Fair Learning Practices and the Long-Term Acquisition of Intelligence**

| Level and Approx. Ages When It Is Common | Fair Learning Practices (Thorkildsen, 1989) | Intelligence (Nicholls, Patashnick, & Mettetal, 1986) |
|---|---|---|
| Level 1 (6-7 years) | *Equality of rewards:* Doing schoolwork to gain rewards is more important than ensuring that slower workers finish the work. Finishing schoolwork or getting rewards is not associated with understanding or learning. | Intellectual skills are evaluated in terms of their subjective difficulty. Intrinsic properties of different skills are not referred to. |
| Level 2 (8-10 years) | *Equality in the amount of schoolwork completed:* Practices that allow everyone to have equal piles of work finished are judged fair. Completing an assignment is not yet associated with learning. | |
| Level 3 (11-16 years) | *Equality of learning:* Learning is the most important social good to be considered. Everyone should learn the same material equally well. Practices that allow this are judged fair. | Intelligence involves effortful learning or acquisition of information—a "Trivial Pursuit" conception. Abstract reasoning is seen as easier because it involves little use of memory or effort. |
| Level 4 (16-18 years) | *Equity and equality of learning are partially differentiated:* Students vacillate between endorsing practices that promote simple equality of learning (as in Level 3) and equity of learning (as in Level 5), wherein more able students learn more. | |
| Level 5 (18+ years) | *Equity of learning:* Meritocratic systems (wherein those capable of doing so learn more) are judged most fair. | Acquisition of information is distinguished from problem solving. Verbal reasoning reflects memory whereas abstract reasoning reflects problem solving. |

shouldn't have to be pushed to go farther because these are their abilities." She said faster learners would think acceleration is fair because "That's what they're able to do. They should be able to go on." And, she thought slower learners would also think it is fair because "I wouldn't want someone who is quicker than I am to hold back because of me. If I honestly couldn't handle it, I would want to complete it, but it would have to be in my own time."

This individual clearly has a sense that students differ in the rate at which they learn and that this difference will lead to unequal attainment. Therefore, practices that result in unequal amounts of learning for fast and slow learners are judged fair. Nevertheless, equal attainment is not judged unfair. This student, for example, also says that peer tutoring is a fair practice because "Maybe by helping [slow learners], they might understand it better—if they weren't understanding it. And, it might help [the fast learners], too—in explaining it. It might help [the slow learners] understand it better or it might help them by [having the fast learners] teaching." Fast learners, she says, might agree that peer tutoring is fair because "If I work faster than somebody else I would think it's all right to help. If I understand it and they have problems with it . . . I would go ahead and explain it to them." And, slower learners were also expected to think it is fair because "they would be getting done quicker and they would be having help if they didn't understand it."

Nevertheless, when Level 5 students are asked to decide whether acceleration or peer tutoring is more fair, acceleration is typically chosen. The above college student said acceleration is more fair than peer tutoring "because the faster kids do get to advance and go on to where they should be." She expected most faster learners to agree that acceleration is more fair "because little kids would feel good if they could pass others up." Slower learners, on the other hand, were expected to think peer tutoring is more fair "so that they could get finished faster."

Occasionally at Level 5, the practices of peer tutoring and enrichment were favored over acceleration. But, this is because these practices were seen to provide opportunities for high ability students to keep learning. For example, when asked whether peer tutoring or acceleration is more fair, two 21-year-olds said peer tutoring is more fair because "Fast workers will still be learning if they help the slow workers." and "If the fast workers get a chance to help the slow workers it might enable the fast workers to understand the slow workers a little bit better." The dominant theme at Level 5 still involves the recognition that unequal levels of attainment is fair because students differ in the rate at which they can learn.

Level 4 is best seen as transitional between Levels 3 and 5. Students at Level 5 clearly recognize that not everyone can learn at the same rate, but at Level 4 this is only partially recognized. Level 4 students (usually ages 16 to 20) sometimes reject acceleration in favor of practices that have everyone finishing the same work. This, and their supporting justifications (e.g., "Everyone should learn the same things.") indicate an emphasis on equality in the amount of material learned by each student. However, Level 4 students also contradict themselves by sometimes selecting acceleration as a fair practice and justifying this with statements like "Everyone should be able to learn at their own rate." This suggests that a meritocratic or equity-based distribution of learning is seen as fair. Consider the following responses from a 17-year-old:

WOULD IT BE FAIR FOR THE FAST WORKERS TO DO MORE AD-VANCED WORK THAN THE SLOW WORKERS?

That's pretty hard! Yes. Probably, because if the people that are working faster have to wait for the other ones, they won't learn as fast as they might. They have to wait for the others instead of working to their ability.

WOULD THE FAST WORKERS THINK IT WAS FAIR?

Yes, because they're getting more attention, probably.

WOULD THE SLOW WORKERS THINK IT WAS FAIR?

Probably not! Well because the teacher might teach the ones that are ahead of them, more.

WOULD IT BE FAIR IF THE FAST WORKERS HELPED THE SLOW WORKERS?

Yes. Maybe the ones that are a little slower will learn it quicker that way.

WOULD THE FAST WORKERS THINK IT WAS FAIR?

No. Maybe not. They wouldn't get to work on other things that way.

WOULD THE SLOW WORKERS THINK IT WAS FAIR?

Yes. They get their work done, probably.

WHICH WOULD BE MORE FAIR, HAVING THE FAST WORKERS WORK AHEAD OF THE SLOW WORKERS OR HAVE THEM HELP THE SLOW WORKERS?

Have them help. Then everybody would be getting all the same work done.

WHICH WOULD THE FAST WORKERS THINK IS MORE FAIR?

(Acceleration). They'll be able to go at their own pace and not have to wait for the slower people.

WHICH WOULD THE SLOW WORKERS THINK IS MORE FAIR?

(Peer tutoring). They'll be able to keep up with the faster people and (the faster workers) will be able to help them.

Notice that when this student discussed acceleration, he said that it would be fair to let faster learners do advanced work so they could "work to their ability." But later, when comparing acceleration and peer tutoring, he emphasized "getting the same work done" and "keeping up with the faster people" as being more fair.

Students at Level 3 (usually ages 10 to 17) emphasize simple equality of learning or attainment and consistently reject acceleration as unfair. Peer tutoring is consistently judged the most fair practice because it enables slower learners to compensate for their limited background knowledge and "catch up" with faster learners. This 12-year-old's responses are typical of Level 3:

> WOULD IT BE FAIR IF THE FAST WORKERS WORK AHEAD OF THE SLOW WORKERS?
>
> No. If (faster workers) get some ahead of the other ones then slow workers won't learn as much. If you get (the faster workers) learning more, then they get crammed with stuff.
>
> WOULD THE FAST WORKERS THINK IT WAS FAIR?
>
> Yes. They could keep learning and the slow workers could do their stuff.
>
> WOULD THE SLOW WORKERS THINK IT WAS FAIR?
>
> No. Slow workers would feel left out because fast workers would brag and make the slow workers not feel as smart as them.
>
> WOULD IT BE FAIR IF THE FAST WORKERS HELP THE SLOW WORKERS?
>
> Yes. Sometimes teachers don't explain it enough. They're grown-ups and kids are afraid to ask questions—afraid of the teacher. But fast workers could explain it better.
>
> WOULD THE FAST WORKERS THINK IT WAS FAIR?
>
> Yes. They might have a little fun while they're doing it.
>
> WOULD THE SLOW WORKERS THINK IT WAS FAIR?
>
> Yes. They need the help.
>
> WHICH IS MORE FAIR, HAVING THE FAST WORKERS HELP THE SLOW WORKERS OR HAVING THEM DO MORE ADVANCED WORK?
>
> Having them help. If you don't keep (everyone) at the same level, some parents might get mad. If fast workers are ahead, they might start bragging and make the slow workers feel dumb.

Both faster and slower learners are also seen as judging peer tutoring more fair for reasons similar to those given above. Notice that this student talks about learning as getting "crammed with stuff." This conception of learning is quite telling. It suggests that to this student learning involves simply memorizing bits of information. Other students show evidence of this by inferring that less able students are lazy, in spite of the fact that they are explicitly told that everyone always works as hard as they can.

At Levels 3 to 5, students indicate that schoolwork should help students learn and use terms like "know," "learn," and "understand" to justify their choices. Their justifications and choices of fair practices indicate that learning, not merely the amount of work or reward received, was a significant consideration. As you can see, these levels are distinguishable from one another by the distributions of learning seen as fair.

At Levels 1 and 2, however, references to learning are conspicuously absent from children's discussion of fair practices. Level 1 students (usually ages 6 to 8) were unique because they accepted the practice of having the slower workers never finish assignments as more fair than at least one of the other practices (all of which allow slower workers to finish the work). Such choices and supportive justifications (e.g., "They can all go out for recess.") indicate that mastering the lesson or completing assignments is of lower priority than attainment of reward as such (not reward contingent on the amount of work finished). Consider the following responses from a Level 1, 7-year-old:

WOULD IT BE FAIR IF EVERYONE WENT ON WHEN THE FAST WORKERS WERE FINISHED—SO, THE SLOW WORKERS NEVER FINISHED ANY OF THESE PAPERS?

Yes, because the slow workers work slow, maybe too slow and the fast workers get their work done.

WOULD THE FAST WORKERS THINK IT WAS FAIR?

Not if they like the other people in the class.

HOW ABOUT MOST FAST WORKERS, WOULD THEY THINK IT WAS FAIR?

Yes, because if that wasn't their friend, they'd just start bragging. They'd brag that they got their pages done and (the slower workers) didn't.

WOULD THE SLOW WORKERS THINK IT WAS FAIR?

They'd think it was unfair, because they don't get their work done— Well, mostly they think about recess and so they might not work too fast.

WHICH WOULD BE MORE FAIR, HAVING THE FAST WORKERS READ BOOKS AND WORK ON THE COMPUTER OR HAVING THE SLOW WORKERS NEVER FINISH ANY OF THE WORK?

(Have the slower workers never finish.) Because those guys were playing on the computer! (This is seen as very unfair.) Those (faster workers using the computer) would have all their papers done and those (slower workers) would have some papers left.

WHICH WOULD THE FAST WORKERS THINK IS MORE FAIR?

Keep going with their work (so slower workers never finish assignments). They would think it's really fun doing that.

WHICH WOULD THE SLOW WORKERS THINK IS MORE FAIR?

Let those guys just keep going on those papers.

EVEN IF THE SLOW WORKERS DON'T FINISH?

Yes.

Level 2 students (usually ages 7 to 10) consistently rejected the practice of not giving the slower workers time to finish assignments. Statements like "Everyone should have the same pile of work done" were used to justify this stance, indicating a greater concern with equal amounts of work than with equal amounts of reward. In other respects, Levels 1 and 2 are the same. Students (like those at Level 3) consistently reject acceleration and judge peer tutoring as the fairest practice for helping students learn. Their justifications, however, indicated that they thought schoolwork should be completed to keep busy and gain rewards, not because it would promote learning.

At Levels 1-4, enrichment is seen as a reward for completing schoolwork. It is not viewed, like many teachers intend, as an opportunity to learn new things. Enrichment is frequently chosen over acceleration for such reasons as "(The faster workers) can just mess around while slow workers finish and they all start the next page together." and "They can keep the kids at the same work level and still let the slow workers catch up."

## Conceptions of Intelligence and Fair Learning Practices

It appears that students consider individual differences in intelligence to be an important issue when determining the fairness of learning practices. There are obvious parallels between the development of conceptions of fair learning practices and conceptions of intellectual development (Table 20-1). In late adolescence (about age 18), for example, students distinguish the amount of information one has acquired (analogous to crystallized intelligence) from one's ability to "reason" or "think" (Nicholls, Patashnick, & Mettetal, 1986). With this distinction clear, they can recognize that differences in reasoning ability means that individuals have limits on the rate at which they can learn. Students at this age also begin to judge as fair those learning practices that allow more able students to learn at a faster rate. They appear to see that practices promoting equality of learning might unfairly limit the development of those with greater fluid intelligence.

For students of about 10 to 18 years, intellectual skills are believed to be acquired through effort and memorization (Nicholls et. al, 1986) and intelligence is a "moral" matter of working hard (Leahy & Hunt, 1983). They appear to have a "Trivial Pursuit" conception of learning: Knowledge is acquired by diligently memorizing specific facts and those who learn slow are simply not working hard enough and haven't had the right teaching experiences. When judging fair learning practices, students at this age also focus primarily on the amount of learning that takes place. For them, the prospect of everyone learning the same things seems possible and practices that promote this are judged most fair.

Finally, children of about 6 to 10 years construe intelligence in terms of the subjective difficulty of different tasks—what is hard for them to improve at is hard for everyone (Nicholls et al., 1986). In other situations, children at this age argue for compliance with established social arrangements on the grounds of personal gain (material rewards and personal comforts) or to avoid punishment (e.g., Kohlberg, Levine, & Hewer, 1983; Piaget, 1932/1965). Likewise, when considering fair learning practice, children of about 6 to 10 years do not focus on the amount of learning promoted by different practices. They focus, instead, on more observable consequences of completing assignments, such as opportunities to play. Practices that enable high and low ability students to gain the same rewards are judged fair, even if the amount of learning is unequal (e.g., when low ability students do not finish assignments).

## Alternative Conceptions of Fair Learning Practices

When judging fair learning practices, most students focused on enhancing or preventing individual differences in intelligence. Yet, there might be other dimensions or ways of defining learning situations that are more important. To some, for example, fostering a desire to engage in life-long learning activities and become productive members of society (equality of motivation), might be more important than enhancing or preventing individual differences in intelligence. This construct is explored more fully in Nicholls (1989). Hints of this belief are evident in the responses of one 21-year-old. Although he judged acceleration unfair, he did not argue that everyone should learn the same things. Instead, he argued:

WOULD IT BE FAIR IF THE FAST WORKERS WORKED AHEAD OF THE SLOW WORKERS?

No. I think it should be up to the people who are better at this kind of work. I think maybe the teacher should give them interesting projects to keep them busy . . . but, (acceleration) is an easy way out for the teacher.

WOULD THE FAST WORKERS THINK IT WAS FAIR?

No, because of all the extra work they are doing.

WOULD THE SLOW WORKERS THINK IT WAS FAIR?

They'd think it was pretty fair because they know that (the faster workers) have an advantage anyway. The slow workers are working to their best capabilities. So they probably figure that the fast workers should do twice as much work—because for the slow workers, work is harder.

Implied in this response, is the belief that fair learning practices must foster interest in school learning for both high and low ability students. Another hint of this is evident in this student's choice of acceleration as more fair than enrichment: "So that if you do teach computer work, you should teach it to the whole class." He appears to recognize that one's potential to learn is not entirely controllable—that the luck of genetics and one's fluid intelligence plays a substantial role in how quickly one learns new things. Awarding extra opportunities to faster learners creates an unfair advantage for those lucky enough to have high ability while undermining the motivation of those less fortunate. The "moral lesson" he refers to below, concerns helping students to learn this by taking perspectives beyond that of self-interest.

> WHICH IS MORE FAIR, HAVING THE FAST WORKERS WORK AHEAD OR HELP THE SLOW WORKERS?
>
> Helping. The slow workers are at a disadvantage already. And the fast workers, they already do their work quicker so they probably already understand it better. Well . . . enough so that they wouldn't benefit all that much from accelerated work. So, I think it would be more of a learning experience for both of them because they're interacting with each other and maybe it's more of a moral lesson.

## Conceptions of Fair Testing Practices

In testing situations, the purpose is to assess current abilities rather than to promote learning or intellectual development. Children's understanding of the psychology of testing situations differs from their understanding of the psychology of learning situations. Furthermore, their understanding of fairness differs for testing and learning situations (Thorkildsen, 1989a). It should not be surprising, therefore, to find that conceptions of fair testing practices develop differently from conceptions of fair learning practices. In fact, adultlike conceptions of fair testing practices (Table 20-2) emerge in early adolescence (after about age 11) whereas adultlike conceptions of fair learning practices (Table 20-1) emerge in late adolescence (after about age 18).

In the study on conceptions of fair testing, children (grades 1 to 6) compared the fairness of peer tutoring and solitary work during tests (Thorkildsen, 1991). They considered the fairness of these two practices in light of three possible test score outcomes: (1) everyone gets all the answers right, (2) faster learners get all the answers right and slower learners get half of them right, (3) everyone gets half the answers right and half wrong. Examination of children's views on the fairness of peer tutoring and solitary work makes it possible to compare the development of conceptions of fairness in learning and testing situations. Furthermore, it helps us understand their views on one of the

**TABLE 20-2   Conceptions of Fair Testing Practices and Conceptions of Ability and Effort as Factors Limiting Performance**

| Level and Approx. Ages When It Is Common | Fair Testing Practices (Thorkildsen, 1991) | Ability and Effort (Nicholls, 1978; 1989) |
|---|---|---|
| Level 1 (6-7 years) | *Fair practices produce equal test scores.* Peer tutoring is more fair than solitary work because it enables everyone to finish and get the same perfect score. Equal test scores tautologically mean equal ability and effort. | *Effort or outcome is ability.* Accomplishment with higher effort means higher ability. Effort, ability and outcome are not differentiated as cause and effect. |
| Level 2 (8-9 years) | *Fair practices produce equal effort and test scores.* Solitary work is seen as the most fair way to achieve this because it would indicate, more clearly than peer tutoring, how much each person knows. Yet, peer tutoring is seen as fair to avoid unequal scores by helping slower learners work harder. Equal test scores mean equal attainment regardless of how they are obtained. | *Effort is the cause of outcomes.* Equal effort by different students is expected to lead to equal outcomes. If attainment is equal but effort varies, this is due to compensatory or misapplied effort. |
| Level 3 (10-11 years) | *Fair practices produce equal effort and unequal test scores are possible.* Helping on tests is unfair because students are harmed if they do not learn to think for themselves and remedy their own mistakes. But, peer tutoring still enables students to know the work equally well. | *Ability is partially differentiated from effort.* It is recognized that people who work hard and achieve an equal score may be brighter. Yet, children assert that students would achieve equally if they applied equal effort. |
| Level 4 (12-13 years) | *Fair practices produce equal representation of abilities.* Fair testing requires solitary work. Peer tutoring is cheating. Different scores for fast and slow learners are seen as fair and possible even if everyone works hard. Helping will not make everyone equal in ability. | *Ability is conceived as a capacity that limits the effect of effort on immediate performance.* One's ability may limit the effect of effort on performance. Conversely, when achievement is equal, low effort implies higher ability. |

important questions they have to face in school—when is collaboration cheating and when is it a legitimate method of promoting learning?

Children of all ages considered solitary work on tests a fair practice, but only first and second graders thought peer tutoring was the most fair way to have a test. This age trend provides a hint of the considerable developmental variation in conceptions of fair testing which was revealed in the structural analysis of children's decisions and justifications (Table 20-2).

Children at Level 4, like most adults, argued that fair testing practices produce the most complete possible presentation of all students' abilities. They judged peer tutoring as unfair, regardless of the resulting distribution of test scores, because it would mask actual differences in students' abilities. Solitary work was always seen as a fair practice because students must think for themselves if they are to reveal their individual abilities and only then can teachers find out what each child knows. Consider the following views of an 11-year-old:

WOULD IT BE FAIR TO HAVE EACH PERSON DO THE TEST BY THEMSELVES?

Yes. Well, it would be cheating if they looked at somebody and said "Hey, how did you do this problem?"

IF EVERYONE DOES THE TEST BY THEMSELVES, WOULD THE TEACHER FIND OUT HOW MUCH EACH PERSON KNOWS?

Yes.

WOULD IT BE FAIR TO HAVE THE FAST WORKERS HELP THE SLOW WORKERS?

No, cause (the teacher) can't figure out the meaning—cause the fast workers can tell (the slow workers) the answers and stuff. I mean it would be fair if the slow workers were just learning something and it wasn't a test, like it was an assigned thing. On a test it really wouldn't be fair.

IF THE FAST WORKERS HELP THE SLOW WORKERS COULD THE TEACHER FIND OUT HOW MUCH EACH PERSON KNOWS?

No.

Students at Level 4 consistently argued that peer tutoring is unfair even when they are shown different score arrangements and they justify their decisions in much the same way as is evident above. Furthermore, they consistently say that if peer tutoring is allowed, teachers will not be able to find out how much each person knows. These children, unlike those at earlier levels, also realize that if they are able to help, faster learners must know the work better. In addition, only children at Level 4 clearly understand that, even if peer tutoring increased the scores of slower learners, their ability would not thereby be equivalent to that of faster learners. In essence they know that if peer tutoring is permitted, test scores would not reflect students' abilities and they see this as unfair. This is evident in an 11-year-old's responses to the following question:

IF THE FAST WORKERS HELP THE SLOW WORKERS AND EVERYONE GETS HALF THE ANSWERS RIGHT, WHO WOULD BE SMARTER AT DOING THIS WORK?

> The fast workers would be (smarter) because they just go right through their work. They know what they're doing and the slow workers have to think about it, so it takes them longer.

Another 11-year-old responds to the same question by saying: "If they get the same score they could be the same. But in a way the fast workers probably told all the answers to the slow workers so they'd probably be [smarter]." The second part of his response suggests that he understands that faster learners would have to know the work better in order to help, but his first statement shows signs of reasoning common at Level 3.

To children at Level 3, fair practices mean that everyone tries their best, even if test scores are unequal. Like children at Level 4, these children realize that test scores may be unequal even if effort is optimal and this is seen as fair. Solitary work is judged to be the fairest testing practice because, unlike peer tutoring, it enables teachers to figure out differences in students' abilities. Peer tutoring is consistently judged unfair because it is believed to lead to unequal effort on the test (with slower learners getting more help and more opportunity to work on their own test than faster learners). Peer tutoring is also seen as unjust because students might be harmed if they do not learn to think for themselves and remedy their own mistakes. However, these children do not consistently exhibit the apparent adultlike logic of this position. Unlike those at Level 4, these children say that everyone would be equally smart (or know the work equally well) when peer tutoring is used and equal test scores result. This is evident in the following 11-year-old's apparently contradictory views:

WOULD HELPING BE FAIR IF EVERYONE GETS HALF THE ANSWERS RIGHT AND HALF WRONG?

> No, cause that wouldn't tell the teacher how much (the faster workers) know separately and how much the slow workers know.

WHO WOULD BE SMARTER AT DOING THIS WORK?

> They'd be the same because the scores came out the same.

At Level 3, testing practices that produce unequal scores can be fair, but at Level 2 this is not the case. Children at Level 2 see both optimal effort and equal test scores for all students as essential for fair practices. These children, like those at Levels 3 & 4, judge solitary work as the most fair way to run a test and indicate some awareness that solitary work is important for finding out how much each child knows. But, they also say that peer tutoring is a fair way to help slower learners work harder and perform as well as faster learners. Furthermore, they say solitary work and peer tutoring are fair if test scores are equal, but judge both practices unfair when test scores are unequal. These children do not see that when peer tutoring is allowed and everyone gets the same score, the teacher would not find out how much each person knows or how competent they really are. So, peer tutoring is judged fair when test scores are equal for reasons like:

Age 9:  Because they'd both be working together. They'd both be like giving each other hints and stuff.

Age 8:  It would be fair because the (slower workers) probably couldn't get the work done on time and (the faster workers) can help them get it.

Age 7:  They could all be the same in the fall (of the next school year).

Children at Level 2, like those at Levels 1 and 3, accept equal outcomes as reflecting equal ability, even when one student helps another. To them, equal test scores reflect equal ability for reasons like: "They're working together and they all got the same scores, so they'd be alike—the same!"

Level 1 is the only one wherein peer tutoring is said to be more fair than solitary work. These children consistently say that peer tutoring is a fair practice (no matter what the outcome) and judge it more fair than solitary work. When asked if teachers could find out how much each person knows if peer tutoring was allowed, they answer "Yes". When asked how the teacher might know this, these children say:

Age 7:  She'd go around and look at the papers and stuff. That's what our teacher does.

Age 8:  See . . . if the slow workers got done! See? They'd get everyone right. They would get the same amount of grades.

Age 7:  She'd see how much they got done during the time they have.

Notice that for these children, working hard to get answers written down constitutes knowing how to do the work: If students finish the work, their answers will be right. Children at Level 1 assume that fair testing practices will produce equal test scores. They tautologically assume that if equal scores result, this will indicate equal ability. It is difficult for them to understand how test scores could be unequal if peer tutoring is used. When faced with this possibility, they assume, for example, that faster learners must be nasty and misinform slower learners about how to do the work. If they are then told to "suppose the faster workers in this class are not mean," they become quite perplexed. One 7-year-old, for example, became indignant when asked if peer tutoring would be fair, if it led to faster workers scoring higher than slower workers, saying "NO!

I can make it look fair. . . ." He then proceeded to adjust the magnetic chart on which scores were depicted to indicate that all students would have equal test scores. More often children looked puzzled, said things like "I don't see how that can be!" or otherwise indicated that they did not understand the question. When asked to decide who is smarter in such situations, they say everyone would be equally smart and give reasons like, "They're both in first grade and they do the same things." and "I think they'd all be smart if they just tried hard!"

As might be expected, there were variations across levels in the extent to which children defined peer tutoring as cheating. When cheating was discussed at Level 1, it was done so only in relation to solitary work—not peer tutoring. For Level 2, references to cheating were made for both situations, but not nearly as often for peer tutoring as for solitary work. But, for Levels 3 and 4, such references were almost as likely to be made for peer tutoring as for solitary work.

Children, ages 6 to 8, usually showed reasoning at Levels 1 and 2, with most 8-year-olds reasoning at Level 2 (and sometimes Level 3). Nine-year-olds were found at all the different levels. But, by about age 10, reasoning was usually at Levels 3 or 4, and the number of children exhibiting reasoning at Levels 1 and 2 sharply dropped off. Level 4 is common at about age 12.

## Conceptions of Effort, Ability, and Fair Testing Practices

Conceptions of fair testing practices parallel, in form and age of appearance, conceptions of effort and ability as these effect immediate performance (Table 20-2). Students with the adultlike understanding of ability as capacity realize that when achievement is equal (and no one is cheating), lower effort implies higher ability. They also see that if one's ability is lower, greater effort will have to be put forth to accomplish a task—equalizing effort will not lead to equal performance on tests. When considering fair testing practices, such students argue that fair testing practices should facilitate maximum performance. They emphasize independent thinking and judge solitary work to be most fair. They do not argue that fair testing practices should facilitate equal outcomes because they understand that helping could not make everyone equal in ability, even if test scores are equal.

Younger children have great difficulty comprehending how equal effort on a task would not lead to equal performance. To them, ability and effort are not clearly distinguished. For the youngest children, effort, ability, and performance are indistinguishable, and for slightly older children effort is understood as the cause of ability. At about the same ages, students define fair testing practices as those that result in equal test scores if everyone works hard. They also see equal test scores as indicative of equal ability even if peer tutoring is allowed. So, although most elementary school students see telling answers as wrong during a test, they do not have an adult understanding of why it is wrong.

As was found for conceptions of fair testing practices, most 6- to 8-year-olds usually held conceptions of effort and ability that were at Levels 1 and 2. Eight-year-olds held conceptions of effort and ability that were at Levels 1, 2, and 3. Nine-year-olds were found at all the different levels. But, most 10-year-olds were reasoning at Levels 3 and 4. And, the Level 4 conception of ability as a capacity that limits the effect of effort on immediate performance was not common until about age 12.

## Application

Evidence that conceptions of fair testing and learning practices follow different developmental patterns supports the work of philosopher Michael Walzer (1983). He asserts that to understand social justice we must begin by examining how individuals define the goals of particular types of situations. In other words, we must examine the ways people define the social goods that are at stake—we must understand what individuals see as important in particular contexts.

To hold adultlike conceptions of fair practices, children must have an adultlike understanding of the goals and characteristics of the relevant situation. Yet, it does not follow that understanding the situational goals and relevant social goods occurs prior to conceptions of fairness. Confronting different situations and reflecting on why adults find them important might lead children to simultaneously understand both the definition of the situation and what makes a fair practice. Conceptions of intelligence, for example, may not develop prior to conceptions of fair learning practices. Confronting school learning and thinking about why it is important may lead children to differentiate conceptions of intelligence in the process of coming to understand what constitutes a fair learning practice. Therefore, it seems possible that for children in cultures where the learning process takes a different form, the development of conceptions of intelligence and fair learning practices may also take a different form.

In the past, when developmental psychologists have identified levels or stages of development, practitioners devoted much energy toward helping children to quickly "pass through" these stages and to acquire the most differentiated conceptions asserted by researchers. If we are to learn from the wisdom of the many children I interviewed, application of my work toward these ends should be seen an unethical. Children described a fair classroom as one in which all students are helped to develop their individual talents and acquire basic skills. They advocated unequal distributions of educational resources when the focus is on personal interests (e.g., for enrichment practices) and equal distributions when the focus is on material all students need to learn. Children of different ages emphasized different educational goods or issues when asserting this vision of schooling. Nevertheless, they did not see adults' preoccupation with academic competition as a relevant criteria when evaluating the fairness of learning and testing practices.

To take seriously students' visions of a fair classroom, adults would do well to converse with children and adolescents about the personal and collective agendas behind particular practices. Take, for example, the insight gained by Susan Hazzard when she asked her students: "Is it fair to copy?" Responses such as: "Not when you're grown up."; "The only way babies learn to talk is from copying."; "The only way four-year-olds learn to write words is to copy."; "My little brother copies."; and "Like if you're from a different country, you have to copy to learn words." came forth as children eagerly struggled with this issue. Some children began by arguing that it is always wrong to copy while others argued that it is sometimes all right. Sue later asked, "What if you get the wrong answers by copying?" The children said, "You don't learn from copying. If you did that for a long time, you wouldn't learn anything." and "It's like lying. It's a hard thing to get out of." After a lengthy discussion in which children openly changed their minds, Sue summarized the children's conclusions and checked their newfound understanding of the definitions of testing and learning situations by saying, "I think I hear two things coming out here. Is this what I'm hearing? First of all, you can copy to learn. (A chorus of "Yes!" is her answer.) But when you have to show what you have learned, you should not copy." [Again, all agree.] (Abstracted from Nicholls and Hazzard, 1993, pp. 46-47.)

Sue learned, first hand, about the confusion among her students over when copying is legitimate and when it is a form of cheating. She did not need to conduct cleverly constructed interviews to discover the nature of children's confusions: My interviews served only to help her anticipate the need for this conversation. What Sue did was respect the wisdom of her students and take time to carefully listen to their concerns. She questioned the common assumption that children always understand the goals of educational situations and the purposes of specific practices. She remembered that simply telling children how to behave is not the same as helping them understand why practices are organized as they are. Sue learned that her students made progress in understanding the agendas behind particular classroom practices only after repeated opportunities to think, experience, and talk about them. The most powerful lesson from this work, then, might be to think again about religious testaments asserting the importance of respecting the wisdom of children.

## Recommended Readings

Damon, W. (1988). *The moral child: Nurturing children's moral growth.* New York: The Free Press.

Jackson, P. W., Boostrom, R. E., & Hansen, D. T. (1993). *The moral life of schools.* San Francisco: Jossey Bass Publishers.

Nicholls, J. G., & Thorkildsen, T. A. (1995). *Reasons for learning: Expanding the conversation on student-teacher collaboration.* New York: Teachers College Press.

Power, F. C., Higgins, A., & Kohlberg, L. (1989). *Lawrence Kohlberg's approach to moral education.* New York: Columbia University Press.

## References

Colby, A., & Kohlberg, L. (1987). *The measurement of moral judgment (Vol. 1).* New York: Cambridge University Press.

Damon, W. (1977). *The social world of the child.* San Francisco, CA: Jossey-Bass, Inc.

Damon, W. (1988). *The moral child: Nurturing children's natural moral growth.* New York: The Free Press.

Kohlberg, L., Levine, C. & Hewer, A. (1983). *Moral stages: A current formulation and a response to critics.* Basel, Switzerland: Karger.

Leahy, R. L. & Hunt, T. M. (1983). A cognitive-developmental approach to the development of conceptions of intelligence. In R. L. Leahy (Ed.), The child's construction of social inequality, (pp. 135-160). New York: Academic Press.

Nicholls, J. G. (1978). The development of the concepts of effort and ability, perception of own attainment, and the understanding that difficult tasks require more ability. *Child Development, 49,* 800-814.

Nicholls, J. G. (1989). *The competitive ethos and democratic education.* Cambridge, MA: Harvard University Press.

Nicholls, J. G. & Hazzard, S. (1993). *Lessons from the second grade.* New York: Teachers College Press.

Nicholls, J. G., Patashnick, M., & Mettetal, G. (1986). Conceptions of ability and intelligence. *Child Development, 57,* 636-645.

Nucci, L. P. (1985). Children's conceptions of morality, societal convention, and religious prescription. In C. G. Harding (Ed.), *Moral dilemmas: Philosophical and psychological issues in the development of moral reasoning,* (pp. 137-174). Chicago, IL: Precedent Publishing.

Piaget, J. (1951). *The child's conception of the world.* Savage, MD: Rowman & Littlefield.

Piaget, J. (1965). *The moral judgment of the child.* New York: Free Press. (Original work published in 1932.)

Rawls, J. (1971). *A theory of justice.* Cambridge, MA: Harvard University Press.

Shweder, R. A., Mahapatra, M. & Miller, J. G. (1987). Culture and moral development. In J. Kagan & S. Lamb (Eds.), *The emergence of morality in young children,* (pp. 1-83), Chicago, IL: University of Chicago Press.

Smetana, J. (1981). Preschool children's conceptions of moral and social rules. *Child Development 52,* 1333-1336.

Thorkildsen, T. A. (1989a). Pluralism in children's reasoning about social justice. *Child Development, 60,* 965-972.

Thorkildsen, T. A. (1989b). Justice in the classroom: The student's view. *Child Development, 60,* 323-334.

Thorkildsen, T. A. (1991). Defining social goods and distributing them fairly: The development of conceptions of fair testing practices. *Child Development, 62,* 852-862.

Tisak, M. S. & Turiel, E. (1988). Variation in seriousness of transgressions and children's moral and conventional concepts. *Developmental Psychology, 24,* 352-357.

Turiel, E. (1983). *The development of social knowledge: Morality and convention.* Cambridge, England: Cambridge University Press.

Walzer, M. (1983). *Spheres of justice: A defense of pluralism and equality.* New York: Basic Books.

# Name Index

*Note:* Page numbers followed by *n.* indicate material in Endnotes.

# Subject Index

52 - P & memo proquem 1 Kohl
53 - moral at machine age; cannot reduce to the types definby
54 - Good m mostly - definition!
55 - Women
178 - good behavior & context.